I0815466

Praise for the Reformation Commentary on Scripture

"Protestant reformers were fundamentally exegetes as much as theologians, yet (except for figures like Luther and Calvin) their commentaries and sermons have been neglected because these writings are not available in modern editions or languages. That makes this new series of Reformation Commentary on Scripture most welcome as a way to provide access to some of the wealth of biblical exposition of the sixteenth and seventeenth centuries. The editor's introduction explains the nature of the sources and the selection process; the intended audience of modern pastors and students of the Bible has led to a focus on theological and practical comments. Although it will be of use to students of the Reformation, this series is far from being an esoteric study of largely forgotten voices; this collection of reforming comments, comprehending every verse and provided with topical headings, will serve contemporary pastors and preachers very well."

Elsie Anne McKee, *Retired Archibald Alexander Professor of Reformation Studies and the History of Worship, Princeton Theological Seminary*

"This series provides an excellent introduction to the history of biblical exegesis in the Reformation period. The introductions are accurate, clear and informative, and the passages intelligently chosen to give the reader a good idea of methods deployed and issues at stake. It puts precritical exegesis in its context and so presents it in its correct light. Highly recommended as reference book, course book and general reading for students and all interested lay and clerical readers."

Irena Backus, *Professeure Ordinaire, Institut d'histoire de la Réformation, Université de Genève*†

"The Reformation Commentary on Scripture is a major publishing event—for those with historical interest in the founding convictions of Protestantism, but even more for those who care about understanding the Bible. As with IVP Academic's earlier Ancient Christian Commentary on Scripture, this effort brings flesh and blood to 'the communion of saints' by letting believers of our day look over the shoulders of giants from the past. By connecting the past with the present, and by doing so with the Bible at the center, the editors of this series perform a great service for the church. The series deserves the widest possible support."

Mark A. Noll, *Professor Emeritus, University of Notre Dame*

"For those who preach and teach Scripture in the church, the Reformation Commentary on Scripture is a significant publishing event. Pastors and other church leaders will find delightful surprises, challenging enigmas and edifying insights in this series, as many Reformational voices are newly translated into English. The lively conversation in these pages can ignite today's pastoral imagination for fresh and faithful expositions of Scripture."

J. Todd Billings, *Gordon H. Girod Research Professor of Reformed Theology, Western Theological Seminary*

"The reformers discerned rightly what the church desperately needed in the sixteenth century—the bold proclamation of the Word based on careful study of the sacred Scriptures. We need not only to hear that same call again for our own day but also to learn from the Reformation how to do it. This commentary series is a godsend!"

Richard J. Mouw, *President Emeritus and Senior Professor of Faith and Public Life, Fuller Theological Seminary*

"Like the Ancient Christian Commentary on Scripture, the Reformation Commentary on Scripture does a masterful job of offering excellent selections from well-known and not-so-well-known exegetes. The editor's introductory survey is, by itself, worth the price of the book. It is easy to forget that there were more hands, hearts and minds involved in the Reformation than Luther and Calvin. Furthermore, encounters even with these figures are often limited to familiar quotes on familiar topics. However, the Reformation Commentary helps us to recognize the breadth and depth of exegetical interests and skill that fueled and continue to fuel faithful meditation on God's Word. I heartily recommend this series as a tremendous resource not only for ministry but for personal edification."

Michael S. Horton, *J. Gresham Machen Professor of Systematic Theology and Apologetics, Westminster Seminary, California*

"The Reformation was ignited by a fresh reading of Scripture. In this series of commentaries, we contemporary interpreters are allowed to feel some of the excitement, surprise and wonder of our spiritual forebears. Luther, Calvin and their fellow revolutionaries were masterful interpreters of the Word. Now, in this remarkable series, some of our very best Reformation scholars open up the riches of the Reformation's reading of the Scripture."

William H. Willimon, *Professor of the Practice of Christian Ministry, Duke Divinity School*

"The Reformation Scripture principle set the entirety of Christian life and thought under the governance of the divine Word, and pressed the church to renew its exegetical labors. This series promises to place before the contemporary church the fruit of those labors, and so to exemplify life under the Word."

John Webster, *Professor of Divinity, University of St. Andrews*†

"Since Gerhard Ebeling's pioneering work on Luther's exegesis seventy years ago, the history of biblical interpretation has occupied many Reformation scholars and become a vital part of study of the period. The Reformation Commentary on Scripture provides fresh materials for students of Reformation-era biblical interpretation and for twenty-first-century preachers to mine the rich stores of insights from leading reformers of the sixteenth century into both the text of Scripture itself and its application in sixteenth-century contexts. This series will strengthen our understanding of the period of the Reformation and enable us to apply its insights to our own days and its challenges to the church."

Robert Kolb, *Professor Emeritus, Concordia Theological Seminary*

"The multivolume Ancient Christian Commentary on Scripture is a valuable resource for those who wish to know how the Fathers interpreted a passage of Scripture but who lack the time or the opportunity to search through the many individual works. This new Reformation Commentary on Scripture will do the same for the reformers and is to be warmly welcomed. It will provide much easier access to the exegetical treasures of the Reformation and will hopefully encourage readers to go back to some of the original works themselves."

Anthony N. S. Lane, *Professor of Historical Doctrine, Lecturer in Doctrine, London School of Theology*

"This volume of the RCS project is an invaluable source for pastors and the historically/biblically interested that provides unparalleled access not only to commentaries of the leading Protestant reformers but also to a host of nowadays unknown commentaters on Galatians and Ephesians. The RCS is sure to enhance and enliven contemporary exegesis. With its wide scope, the collection will enrich our understanding of the variety of Reformation thought and biblical exegesis."

Sigrun Haude, *Associate Professor of Reformation and Early Modern European History, University of Cincinnati*

"This grand project sets before scholars, pastors, teachers, students and growing Christians an experience that can only be likened to stumbling into a group Bible study only to discover that your fellow participants include some of the most significant Christians of the Reformation and post-Reformation (for that matter, of any) era. Here the Word of God is explained in a variety of accents: German, Swiss, French, Dutch, English, Scottish and more. Each one vibrates with a thrilling sense of the living nature of God's Word and its power to transform individuals, churches and even whole communities. Here is a series to anticipate, enjoy and treasure."

Sinclair Ferguson, *Professor of Systematic Theology, Reformed Theological Seminary*

"I strongly endorse the Reformation Commentary on Scripture. Introducing how the Bible was interpreted during the age of the Reformation, these volumes will not only renew contemporary preaching, but they will also help us understand more fully how reading and meditating on Scripture can, in fact, change our lives!"

Lois Malcolm, *Professor and Olin and Amanda Fjelstad Registad Chair for Systematic Theology, Luther Seminary*

"Discerning the true significance of movements in theology requires acquaintance with their biblical exegesis. This is supremely so with the Reformation, which was essentially a biblical revival. The Reformation Commentary on Scripture will fill a yawning gap, just as the Ancient Christian Commentary did before it, and the first volume gets the series off to a fine start, whetting the appetite for more. Most heartily do I welcome and commend this long overdue project."

J. I. Packer, *Board of Governors' Professor of Theology, Regent College*†

"There is no telling the benefits to emerge from the publication of this magnificent Reformation Commentary on Scripture series! Now exegetical and theological treasures from Reformation era commentators will be at our fingertips, providing new insights from old sources to give light for the present and future. This series is a gift to scholars and to the church; a wonderful resource to enhance our study of the written Word of God for generations to come!"

Donald K. McKim, *Executive Editor of Theology and Reference, Westminster John Knox Press*

"Why was this not done before? The publication of the Reformation Commentary on Scripture should be greeted with enthusiasm by every believing Christian—but especially by those who will preach and teach the Word of God. This commentary series brings the very best of the Reformation heritage to the task of exegesis and exposition, and each volume in this series represents a veritable feast that takes us back to the sixteenth century to enrich the preaching and teaching of God's Word in our own time."

R. Albert Mohler Jr., *President, The Southern Baptist Theological Seminary*

"Today more than ever, the Christian past is the church's future. InterVarsity Press has already brought the voice of the ancients to our ears. Now, in the Reformation Commentary on Scripture, we hear a timely word from the first Protestants as well."

Bryan Litfin, *Moody Publishers*

"I am delighted to see the Reformation Commentary on Scripture. The editors of this series have done us all a service by gleaning from these rich fields of biblical reflection. May God use this new life for these old words to give him glory and to build his church."

Mark Dever, *Senior Pastor, Capitol Hill Baptist Church, and President of 9Marks Ministries*

"Monumental and magisterial, the Reformation Commentary on Scripture, edited by Timothy George, is a remarkably bold and visionary undertaking. Bringing together a wealth of resources, these volumes will provide historians, theologians, biblical scholars, pastors and students with a fresh look at the exegetical insights of those who shaped and influenced the sixteenth-century Reformation. With this marvelous publication, InterVarsity Press has reached yet another plateau of excellence. We pray that this superb series will be used of God to strengthen both church and academy."

David S. Dockery, *President of the International Alliance for Christian Education*

"Detached from her roots, the church cannot reach the world as God intends. While every generation must steward the scriptural insights God grants it, only arrogance or ignorance causes leaders to ignore the contributions of those faithful leaders before us. The Reformation Commentary on Scripture roots our thought in great insights of faithful leaders of the Reformation to further biblical preaching and teaching in this generation."

Bryan Chapell, *President Emeritus, Covenant Theological Seminary*

"After reading several volumes of the Reformation Commentary on Scripture, I exclaimed, 'Hey, this is just what the doctor ordered—I mean Doctor Martinus Lutherus!' The church of today bearing his name needs a strong dose of the medicine this doctor prescribed for the ailing church of the sixteenth century. The reforming fire of Christ-centered preaching that Luther ignited is the only hope to reclaim the impact of the gospel to keep the Reformation going, not for its own sake but to further the renewal of the worldwide church of Christ today. This series of commentaries will equip preachers to step into their pulpits with confidence in the same living Word that inspired the witness of Luther and Calvin and many other lesser-known reformers."

Carl E. Braaten, *Cofounder of the Center for Catholic and Evangelical Theology*

"As a pastor, how does one cultivate a knowledge of the history of interpretation? That's where IVP's Reformation Commentary on Scripture and its forerunner, the Ancient Christian Commentary on Scripture, come in. They do an excellent job in helping pastors become more aware of the history of exegesis for the benefit of their congregations. Every pastor should have access to a set of each."

Carl R. Trueman, *Professor of Biblical and Religious Studies, Grove City College*

Reformation Commentary on Scripture

New Testament

XV

Revelation

Edited by
Rodney Petersen
and Gerald L. Bray

General Editor
Timothy George

Associate General Editor
Scott M. Manetsch

An imprint of InterVarsity Press
Downers Grove, Illinois

InterVarsity Press
P.O. Box 1400 | Downers Grove, IL 60515-1426
ivpress.com | email@ivpress.com

InterVarsity Press® is the publishing division of InterVarsity Christian Fellowship/USA®. For more information, visit intervarsity.org.

Cover design: Kate Lillard
Interior design: Daniel van Loon

ISBN 978-0-8308-2978-1 (print) | ISBN 978-0-8308-4254-4 (digital)

Printed in the United States of America ♾

Library of Congress Cataloging-in-Publication Data
A catalog record for this book is available from the Library of Congress.

32 31 30 29 28 27 26 25 | 13 12 11 10 9 8 7 6 5 4 3 2 1

Reformation Commentary on Scripture
Project Staff

Project and Associate Managing Editor
Zachary Gordon

Executive Editor
Elissa Schauer

Copyeditor
Claire VanderVelde Brubaker

Assistant Project Editor
Travis Ables

Editorial and Research Assistants
David J. Hooper
Alberto I. Bonilla-Giovanetti

Assistants to the General Editors
Evan Musgraves
Bryan Just
Christopher Gow

Design
Cindy Kiple

Proofreader
Michael LeFebvre

InterVarsity Press

President and Publisher
Terumi Echols

Divisional Vice President, Editorial
Cindy Bunch

Associate Publisher and Academic Editorial Director
Jon Boyd

Divisional Vice President, Operations, and Chief of Staff
Benjamin M. McCoy

CONTENTS

ACKNOWLEDGMENTS

From Rodney

With thanks to friends and colleagues at the Boston Theological Institute and for encouragement from family and my wife, Rebecca. Thanks to the Duke University Divinity School and to its Center for Reconciliation for welcoming me as a visiting scholar, without which I would still be at work on the Apocalypse.

ABBREVIATIONS

ACCS	Ancient Christian Commentary on Scripture. 29 vols. Edited by T. C. Oden. Downers Grove, IL: InterVarsity Press, 1998–2009.
CO	*Ioannis Calvini Opera Quae Supersunt Omnia.* 59 vols. Corpus Reformatorum 29–88. Edited by G. Baum, E. Cunitz, and E. Reuss. Berlin: C. A. Schwetschke, 1863–1900. Digital copy online at archive-ourverte.unige.ch/Calvin.
CR	*Corpus Reformatorum.* Edited by C. G. Bretsjchneider. Halle, 1834–1860.
CRR	Classics of the Radical Reformation. 12 vols. Scottdale, PA: Herald Press, 1973–.
CTS	Calvin Translation Society edition of Calvin's commentaries. 46 vols. Edinburgh, 1843–1855.
LCL	Loeb Classical Library. Cambridge, MA: Harvard University Press, 1911–. Digital copy online at www.loebclassics.com.
LW	Luther's Works [American edition]. 82 vols. planned. St. Louis: Concordia; Philadelphia: Fortress, 1955–1986, 2009–.
MO	*Philippi Melanthonis Opera Quae Supersunt Omnia.* 28 vols. Corpus Reformatorum 1–28. Edited by C. G. Bretschneider. 1834–1860. Digital copy online at books.google.com and archive.org.
NPNF	*A Select Library of the Nicene and Post-Nicene Fathers of the Christian Church.* 28 vols. in two series. Edited by Philip Schaff et al. Buffalo, NY: Christian Literature, 1887–1894. Available online at www.ccel.org.
PG	*Patrologiae cursus completus.* Series Graeca. 166 vols. Edited by J.-P. Migne. Paris: Migne, 1857–1886.
PL	*Patrologiae cursus completus.* Series Latina. 221 vols. Edited by J.-P. Migne. Paris: Migne, 1844–1864.
r, v	Some early books are numbered not by page but by folio (leaf). Front and back sides (pages) of a numbered folio are indicated by *recto* (r) and *verso* (v) respectively.
WA	*D. Martin Luthers Werke: Kritische Gesamtausgabe.* 73 vols. Weimar: Hermann Böhlaus Nachfolger, 1883–2009. Digital copies online at archive.org.
ZSW	*Huldreich Zwinglis Sämtliche Werke.* 14 vols. Corpus Reformatorum vols. 88–101. Edited by E. Egli et al. 1905–1959; reprint ed., Zürich: Theologischer Verlag Zürich, 1983.

A GUIDE TO USING THIS COMMENTARY

Several features have been incorporated into the design of this commentary. The following comments are intended to assist readers in making full use of this volume.

Pericopes of Scripture

The scriptural text has been divided into pericopes, or passages, usually several verses in length. Each of these pericopes is given a heading, which appears at the beginning of the pericope. For example, the first section in this commentary is Revelation 1:1-3, "The Title." This heading is followed by the Scripture passage quoted in the English Standard Version (ESV). The Scripture passage is provided for the convenience of readers, but it is also in keeping with Reformation-era commentaries, which often followed the patristic and medieval commentary tradition, in which the citations of the reformers were arranged according to the text of Scripture.

Overviews

Following each pericope of text is an overview of the Reformation authors' comments on that pericope. The format of this overview varies among the volumes of this series, depending on the requirements of the specific book(s) of Scripture. The function of the overview is to identify succinctly the key exegetical, theological, and pastoral concerns of the Reformation writers arising from the pericope, providing the reader with an orientation to Reformation-era approaches and emphases. It tracks a reasonably cohesive thread of argument among reformers' comments, even though they are derived from diverse sources and generations. Thus, the summaries do not proceed chronologically or by verse sequence. Rather, they seek to rehearse the overall course of the reformers' comments on that pericope.

We do not assume that the commentators themselves anticipated or expressed a formally received cohesive argument but rather that the various arguments tend to flow in a plausible, recognizable pattern. Modern readers can thus glimpse aspects of continuity in the flow of diverse exegetical traditions representing various generations and geographical locations.

Topical Headings

An abundance of varied Reformation-era comment is available for each pericope. For this reason we have broken the pericopes into two levels. First is the verse with its topical heading.

The reformers' comments are then focused on aspects of each verse, with topical headings summarizing the essence of the individual comment by evoking a key phrase, metaphor, or idea. This feature provides a bridge by which modern readers can enter into the heart of the Reformation-era comment.

Identifying the Reformation Authors, Texts, and Events

Following the topical heading of each section of comment, the name of the Reformation commentator is given. An English translation (where needed) of the reformer's comment is then provided. This is immediately followed by the title of the original work rendered in English.

Readers who wish to pursue a deeper investigation of the reformers' works cited in this commentary will find full bibliographic detail for each Reformation title provided in the bibliography at the back of the volume. Information on English translations (where available) and standard original-language editions and critical editions of the works cited is found in the bibliography. The Biographical Sketches section provides brief overviews of the life and work of each commentator, and each confession or collaborative work, appearing in the present volume (as well as in any previous volumes). Finally, a Timeline of the Reformation offers broader context for people, places, and events relevant to the commentators and their works.

Footnotes and Back Matter

To aid the reader in exploring the background and texts in further detail, this commentary utilizes footnotes. The use and content of footnotes may vary among the volumes in this series. Where footnotes appear, a footnote number directs the reader to a note at the bottom of the page, where one will find annotations (clarifications or biblical cross references), information on English translations (where available) or standard original-language editions of the work cited.

Where original-language texts have remained untranslated into English, we provide new translations. Where there is any serious ambiguity or textual problem in the selection, we have tried to reflect the best available textual tradition. Wherever current English translations are already well rendered, they are utilized, but where necessary they are stylistically updated. A single asterisk (*) indicates that a previous English translation has been updated to modern English or amended for easier reading. We have standardized spellings and made grammatical variables uniform so that our English references will not reflect the linguistic oddities of the older English translations. For ease of reading we have in some cases removed superfluous conjunctions.

GENERAL INTRODUCTION

The Reformation Commentary on Scripture (RCS) is a twenty-eight-volume series of exegetical comment covering the entire Bible and gathered from the writings of sixteenth-century preachers, scholars and reformers. The RCS is intended as a sequel to the highly acclaimed Ancient Christian Commentary on Scripture (ACCS), and as such its overall concept, method, format, and audience are similar to the earlier series. Both series are committed to the renewal of the church through careful study and meditative reflection on the Old and New Testaments, the charter documents of Christianity, read in the context of the worshiping, believing community of faith across the centuries. However, the patristic and Reformation eras are separated by nearly a millennium, and the challenges of reading Scripture with the reformers require special attention to their context, resources and assumptions. The purpose of this general introduction is to present an overview of the context and process of biblical interpretation in the age of the Reformation.

Goals

The Reformation Commentary on Scripture seeks to introduce its readers to the depth and richness of exegetical ferment that defined the Reformation era. The RCS has four goals: the enrichment of contemporary biblical interpretation through exposure to Reformation-era biblical exegesis; the renewal of contemporary preaching through exposure to the biblical insights of the Reformation writers; a deeper understanding of the Reformation itself and the breadth of perspectives represented within it; and a recovery of the profound integration of the life of faith and the life of the mind that should characterize Christian scholarship. Each of these goals requires a brief comment.

Renewing contemporary biblical interpretation. During the past half-century, biblical hermeneutics has become a major growth industry in the academic world. One of the consequences of the historical-critical hegemony of biblical studies has been the privileging of contemporary philosophies and ideologies at the expense of a commitment to the Christian church as the primary reading community within which and for which biblical exegesis is done. Reading Scripture with the church fathers and the reformers is a corrective to all such imperialism of the present. One of the greatest skills required for a fruitful interpretation of the Bible is the ability to listen. We rightly emphasize the importance of listening to the voices of contextual theologies today, but in doing so we often marginalize or ignore another crucial context—the community of believing Christians through the centuries. The serious study of Scripture requires more than the latest

Bible translation in one hand and the latest commentary (or niche study Bible) in the other. John L. Thompson has called on Christians today to practice the art of "reading the Bible with the dead."[1] The RCS presents carefully selected comments from the extant commentaries of the Reformation as an encouragement to more in-depth study of this important epoch in the history of biblical interpretation.

Strengthening contemporary preaching. The Protestant reformers identified the public preaching of the Word of God as an indispensable means of grace and a sure sign of the true church. Through the words of the preacher, the living voice of the gospel (*viva vox evangelii*) is heard. Luther famously said that the church is not a "pen house" but a "mouth house."[2] The Reformation in Switzerland began when Huldrych Zwingli entered the pulpit of the Grossmünster in Zurich on January 1, 1519, and began to preach a series of expositional sermons chapter by chapter from the Gospel of Matthew. In the following years he extended this homiletical approach to other books of the Old and New Testaments. Calvin followed a similar pattern in Geneva. Many of the commentaries represented in this series were either originally presented as sermons or were written to support the regular preaching ministry of local church pastors. Luther said that the preacher should be a *bonus textualis*—a good one with a text—well-versed in the Scriptures. Preachers in the Reformation traditions preached not only about the Bible but also from it, and this required more than a passing acquaintance with its contents. Those who have been charged with the office of preaching in the church today can find wisdom and insight—and fresh perspectives—in the sermons of the Reformation and the biblical commentaries read and studied by preachers of the sixteenth century.

Deepening understanding of the Reformation. Some scholars of the sixteenth century prefer to speak of the period they study in the plural, the European Reformations, to indicate that many-diverse impulses for reform were at work in this turbulent age of transition from medieval to modern times.[3] While this point is well taken, the RCS follows the time-honored tradition of using *Reformation* in the singular form to indicate not only a major moment in the history of Christianity in the West but also, as Hans J. Hillerbrand has put it, "an essential cohesiveness in the heterogeneous pursuits of religious reform in the sixteenth century."[4] At the same time, in developing guidelines to assist the volume editors in making judicious selections from the vast amount of commentary material available in this period, we have stressed the multifaceted character of the Reformation across many confessions, theological orientations, and political settings.

Advancing Christian scholarship. By assembling and disseminating numerous voices from such a signal period as the Reformation, the RCS aims to make a significant contribution to the ever-growing stream of Christian scholarship. The post-Enlightenment split between the study of the Bible as an academic discipline and the reading of the Bible as spiritual nurture was foreign

[1]John L. Thompson, *Reading the Bible with the Dead* (Grand Rapids: Eerdmans, 2007).

[2]WA 10,2:48.

[3]See Carter Lindberg, *The European Reformations*, 2nd ed. (Malden, MA: Wiley-Blackwell, 2010).

[4]Hans J. Hillerbrand, *The Division of Christendom* (Louisville, KY: Westminster John Knox, 2007), x. Hillerbrand has also edited the standard reference work in Reformation studies, *OER*. See also Diarmaid MacCulloch, *The Reformation* (New York: Viking, 2003), and Patrick Collinson, *The Reformation: A History* (New York: Random House, 2004).

to the reformers. For them the study of the Bible was transformative at the most basic level of the human person: *coram deo.*

The reformers all repudiated the idea that the Bible could be studied and understood with dispassionate objectivity, as a cold artifact from antiquity. Luther's famous Reformation breakthrough triggered by his laborious study of the Psalms and Paul's letter to the Romans is well known, but the experience of Cambridge scholar Thomas Bilney was perhaps more typical. When Erasmus's critical edition of the Greek New Testament was published in 1516, it was accompanied by a new translation in elegant Latin. Attracted by the classical beauty of Erasmus's Latin, Bilney came across this statement in 1 Timothy 1:15: "Christ Jesus came into the world to save sinners." In the Greek this sentence is described as *pistos ho logos,* which the Vulgate had rendered *fidelis sermo,* "a faithful saying." Erasmus chose a different word for the Greek *pistos—certus,* "sure, certain." When Bilney grasped the meaning of this word applied to the announcement of salvation in Christ, he tells us that "immediately, I felt a marvellous comfort and quietness, insomuch as 'my bruised bones leaped for joy.'"[5]

Luther described the way the Bible was meant to function in the minds and hearts of believers when he reproached himself and others for studying the nativity narrative with such cool unconcern:

> I hate myself because when I see Christ laid in the manger or in the lap of his mother and hear the angels sing, my heart does not leap into flame. With what good reason should we all despise ourselves that we remain so cold when this word is spoken to us, over which everyone should dance and leap and burn for joy! We act as though it were a frigid historical fact that does not smite our hearts, as if someone were merely relating that the sultan has a crown of gold.[6]

It was a core conviction of the Reformation that the careful study and meditative listening to the Scriptures, what the monks called *lectio divina,* could yield transformative results for *all* of life. The value of such a rich commentary, therefore, lies not only in the impressive volume of Reformation-era voices that are presented throughout the course of the series but in the many particular fields for which their respective lives and ministries are relevant. The Reformation is consequential for historical studies, both church as well as secular history. Biblical and theological studies, to say nothing of pastoral and spiritual studies, also stand to benefit and progress immensely from renewed engagement today, as mediated through the RCS, with the reformers of yesteryear.

Perspectives

In setting forth the perspectives and parameters of the RCS, the following considerations have proved helpful.

Chronology. When did the Reformation begin, and how long did it last? In some traditional accounts, the answer was clear: the Reformation began with the posting of Luther's Ninety-five

[5]John Foxe, *The Acts and Monuments of John Foxe: A New and Complete Edition,* 8 vols., ed. Stephen Reed Cattley (London: R. B. Seeley & W. Burnside, 1837), 4:635; quoting Ps 51:8; cited in A. G. Dickens, *The English Reformation,* 2nd ed. (University Park, PA: The Pennsylvania State University Press, 1991), 102.

[6]WA 49:176-77, quoted in Roland Bainton, "The Bible in the Reformation," in *CHB,* 3:23.

Theses at Wittenberg in 1517 and ended with the death of Calvin in Geneva in 1564. Apart from reducing the Reformation to a largely German event with a side trip to Switzerland, this perspective fails to do justice to the important events that led up to Luther's break with Rome and its many reverberations throughout Europe and beyond. In choosing commentary selections for the RCS, we have adopted the concept of the long sixteenth century, say, from the late 1400s to the mid-seventeenth century. Thus we have included commentary selections from early or pre-Reformation writers such as John Colet and Jacques Lefèvre d'Étaples to seventeenth-century figures such as Henry Ainsworth and Johann Gerhard.

Confession. The RCS concentrates primarily, though not exclusively, on the exegetical writings of the Protestant reformers. While the ACCS provided a compendium of key consensual exegetes of the early Christian centuries, the Catholic/Protestant confessional divide in the sixteenth century tested the very idea of consensus, especially with reference to ecclesiology and soteriology. While many able and worthy exegetes faithful to the Roman Catholic Church were active during this period, this project has chosen to include primarily those figures that represent perspectives within the Protestant Reformation. For this reason we have not included comments on the apocryphal or deuterocanonical writings.

We recognize that "Protestant" and "Catholic" as contradistinctive labels are anachronistic terms for the early decades of the sixteenth century before the hardening of confessional identities surrounding the Council of Trent (1545–1563). Protestant figures such as Philipp Melanchthon, Johannes Oecolampadius and John Calvin were all products of the revival of sacred letters known as biblical humanism. They shared an approach to biblical interpretation that owed much to Desiderius Erasmus and other scholars who remained loyal to the Church of Rome. Careful comparative studies of Protestant and Catholic exegesis in the sixteenth century have shown surprising areas of agreement when the focus was the study of a particular biblical text rather than the standard confessional debates.

At the same time, exegetical differences among the various Protestant groups could become strident and church-dividing. The most famous example of this is the interpretive impasse between Luther and Zwingli over the meaning of "This is my body" (Mt 26:26) in the words of institution. Their disagreement at the Colloquy of Marburg in 1529 had important christological and pastoral implications, as well as social and political consequences. Luther refused fellowship with Zwingli and his party at the end of the colloquy; in no small measure this bitter division led to the separate trajectories pursued by Lutheran and Reformed Protestantism to this day. In Elizabethan England, Puritans and Anglicans agreed that "Holy Scripture containeth all things necessary to salvation: so that whatsoever is not read therein, nor may be proved thereby, is not to be required of any man" (article 6 of the Thirty-Nine Articles of Religion), yet on the basis of their differing interpretations of the Bible they fought bitterly over the structures of the church, the clothing of the clergy and the ways of worship. On the matter of infant baptism, Catholics and Protestants alike agreed on its propriety, though there were various theories as to how a practice not mentioned in the Bible could be justified biblically. The Anabaptists were outliers on this subject. They rejected infant baptism altogether. They appealed to the example of the baptism of Jesus and to his final words as recorded in the Gospel of Matthew (Mt 28:19-20): "Go therefore, and make disciples of all nations, baptizing them in the name of the Father, and of the Son, and of the Holy Spirit, teaching them to observe all that I have commanded you." New Testament Christians, they argued, are to follow not only the commands of Jesus in the Great Commission, but also the exact order in which they were given: evangelize, baptize, catechize.

These and many other differences of interpretation among the various Protestant groups are reflected in their many sermons, commentaries and public disputations. In the RCS, the volume editors' introduction to each volume is intended to help the reader understand the nature and significance of doctrinal conversations and disputes that resulted in particular, and frequently clashing, interpretations. Footnotes throughout the text will be provided to explain obscure references, unusual expressions and other matters that require special comment. Volume editors have chosen comments on the Bible across a wide range of sixteenth-century confessions and schools of interpretation: biblical humanists, Lutheran, Reformed, Anglican, Puritan, and Anabaptist. We have not pursued passages from post-Tridentine Catholic authors or from radical spiritualists and antitrinitarian writers, though sufficient material is available from these sources to justify another series.

Format. The design of the RCS is intended to offer reader-friendly access to these classic texts. The availability of digital resources has given access to a huge residual database of sixteenth-century exegetical comment hitherto available only in major research universities and rare book collections. The RCS has benefited greatly from online databases such as Alexander Street Press's Digital Library of Classical Protestant Texts (DLCPT) and Early English Books Online as well as freely accessible databases like the Post-Reformation Digital Library (prdl.org). Through the help of RCS editorial advisor Herman Selderhuis, we have also had access to the special Reformation collections of the Johannes a Lasco Bibliothek in Emden, Germany. In addition, modern critical editions and translations of Reformation sources have been published over the past generation. Original translations of Reformation sources are given unless an acceptable translation already exists.

Each volume in the RCS will include an introduction by the volume editor placing that portion of the canon within the historical context of the Protestant Reformation and presenting a summary of the theological themes, interpretive issues and reception of the particular book(s). The commentary itself consists of particular pericopes identified by a pericope heading; the biblical text in the English Standard Version (ESV), with significant textual variants registered in the footnotes; an overview of the pericope in which principal exegetical and theological concerns of the Reformation writers are succinctly noted; and excerpts from the Reformation writers identified by name according to the conventions of the *Oxford Encyclopedia of the Reformation*. Each volume will also include a bibliography of sources cited, as well as an appendix of authors and source works.

The Reformation era was a time of verbal as well as physical violence, and this fact has presented a challenge for this project. Without unduly sanitizing the texts, where they contain anti-Semitic, sexist or inordinately polemical rhetoric, we have not felt obliged to parade such comments either. We have noted the abridgement of texts with ellipses and an explanatory footnote.

While this procedure would not be valid in the critical edition of such a text, we have deemed it appropriate in a series whose primary purpose is pastoral and devotional. When translating *homo* or similar terms that refer to the human race as a whole or to individual persons without reference to gender, we have used alternative English expressions to the word *man* (or derivative constructions that formerly were used generically to signify humanity at large), whenever such substitutions can be made without producing an awkward or artificial construction.

As is true in the ACCS, we have made a special effort where possible to include the voices of women, though we acknowledge the difficulty of doing so for the early modern period when for a variety of social and cultural reasons few theological and biblical works were published by women. However, recent scholarship has focused on a number of female leaders whose literary remains show us how they understood and interpreted the Bible. Women who made significant contributions to the Reformation include Marguerite d'Angoulême, sister of King Francis I, who supported French reformist evangelicals including Calvin and who published a religious poem influenced by Luther's theology, *The Mirror of the Sinful Soul*; Argula von Grumbach, a Bavarian noblewoman who defended the teachings of Luther and Melanchthon before the theologians of the University of Ingolstadt; Katharina Schütz Zell, the wife of a former priest, Matthias Zell, and a remarkable reformer in her own right—she conducted funerals, compiled hymnbooks, defended the downtrodden, and published a defense of clerical marriage as well as composing works of consolation on divine comfort and pleas for the toleration of Anabaptists and Catholics alike; and Anne Askew, a Protestant martyr put to death in 1546 after demonstrating remarkable biblical prowess in her examinations by church officials. Other echoes of faithful women in the age of the Reformation are found in their letters, translations, poems, hymns, court depositions, and martyr records.

Lay culture, learned culture. In recent decades, much attention has been given to what is called "reforming from below," that is, the expressions of religious beliefs and churchly life that characterized the popular culture of the majority of the population in the era of the Reformation. Social historians have taught us to examine the diverse pieties of townspeople and city folk, of rural religion and village life, the emergence of lay theologies, and the experiences of women in the religious tumults of Reformation Europe.[7] Formal commentaries by their nature are artifacts of learned culture. Almost all of them were written in Latin, the lingua franca of learned discourse well past the age of the Reformation. Biblical commentaries were certainly not the primary means by which the Protestant Reformation spread so rapidly across wide sectors of sixteenth-century society. Small pamphlets and broadsheets, later called *Flugschriften* ("flying writings"), with their graphic woodcuts and cartoon-like depictions of Reformation personalities and events, became the means of choice for mass communication in the early age of printing. Sermons and works of devotion were also printed with appealing visual aids. Luther's early writings were often accompanied by drawings and sketches from Lucas Cranach and other artists. This was done "above all for the sake of children and simple folk," as Luther

[7]See Peter Matheson, ed., *Reformation Christianity* (Minneapolis: Fortress, 2007).

put it, "who are more easily moved by pictures and images to recall divine history than through mere words or doctrines."[8]

We should be cautious, however, in drawing too sharp a distinction between learned and lay culture in this period. The phenomenon of preaching was a kind of verbal bridge between scholars at their desks and the thousands of illiterate or semiliterate listeners whose views were shaped by the results of Reformation exegesis. According to contemporary witness, more than one thousand people were crowding into Geneva to hear Calvin expound the Scriptures every day.[9] An example of how learned theological works by Reformation scholars were received across divisions of class and social status comes from Lazare Drilhon, an apothecary of Toulon. He was accused of heresy in May 1545 when a cache of prohibited books was found hidden in his garden shed. In addition to devotional works, the French New Testament and a copy of Calvin's Genevan liturgy, there was found a series of biblical commentaries, translated from the Latin into French: Martin Bucer's on Matthew, François Lambert's on the Apocalypse and one by Oecolampadius on 1 John.[10] Biblical exegesis in the sixteenth century was not limited to the kind of full-length commentaries found in Drilhon's shed. Citations from the Bible and expositions of its meaning permeate the extant literature of sermons, letters, court depositions, doctrinal treatises, records of public disputations and even last wills and testaments. While most of the selections in the RCS will be drawn from formal commentary literature, other sources of biblical reflection will also be considered.

Historical Context

The medieval legacy. On October 18, 1512, the degree *Doctor in Biblia* was conferred on Martin Luther, and he began his career as a professor in the University of Wittenberg. As is well known, Luther was also a monk who had taken solemn vows in the Augustinian Order of Hermits at Erfurt. These two settings—the university and the monastery—both deeply rooted in the Middle Ages, form the background not only for Luther's personal vocation as a reformer but also for the history of the biblical commentary in the age of the Reformation. Since the time of the Venerable Bede (d. 735), sometimes called "the last of the Fathers," serious study of the Bible had taken place primarily in the context of cloistered monasteries. The Rule of St. Benedict brought together *lectio* and *meditatio*, the knowledge of letters and the life of prayer. The liturgy was the medium through which the daily reading of the Bible, especially the Psalms, and the sayings of the church fathers came together in the spiritual formation of the monks.[11] Essential to this understanding was a belief in the unity of the people of God throughout time as well as space, and an awareness that life in this world was a preparation for the beatific vision in the next.

[8]Martin Luther, "Personal Prayer Book," LW 43:42-43* (WA 10,2:458); quoted in R. W. Scribner, *For the Sake of Simple Folk: Popular Propaganda for the German Reformation* (Cambridge: Cambridge University Press, 1981), xi.

[9]Letter of De Beaulieu to Guillaume Farel (1561) in *Theodor Beza nach handschriftlichen und anderen gleichzeitigen Quellen*, ed. J. W. Baum (Leipzig: Weidmann, 1851), 2:92.

[10]Francis Higman, "A Heretic's Library: The Drilhon Inventory" (1545), in Francis Higman, *Lire et Découvrire: la circulation des idées au temps de la Réforme* (Geneva: Droz, 1998), 65-85.

[11]See the classic study by Jean Leclercq, *The Love of Learning and the Desire for God* (New York: Fordham University Press, 1961).

The source of theology was the study of the sacred page *(sacra pagina)*; its object was the accumulation of knowledge not for its own sake but for the obtaining of eternal life. For these monks, the Bible had God for its author, salvation for its end and unadulterated truth for its matter, though they would not have expressed it in such an Aristotelian way. The medieval method of interpreting the Bible owed much to Augustine's *On Christian Doctrine*. In addition to setting forth a series of rules (drawn from an earlier work by Tyconius), Augustine stressed the importance of distinguishing the literal and spiritual or allegorical senses of Scripture. While the literal sense was not disparaged, the allegorical was valued because it enabled the believer to obtain spiritual benefit from the obscure places in the Bible, especially in the Old Testament. For Augustine, as for the monks who followed him, the goal of scriptural exegesis was freighted with eschatological meaning; its purpose was to induce faith, hope, and love and so to advance in one's pilgrimage toward that city with foundations (see Heb 11:10).

Building on the work of Augustine and other church fathers going back to Origen, medieval exegetes came to understand Scripture as possessed of four possible meanings, the famous *quadriga*. The literal meaning was retained, of course, but the spiritual meaning was now subdivided into three senses: the allegorical, the moral, and the anagogical. Medieval exegetes often referred to the four meanings of Scripture in a popular rhyme:

> The letter shows us what God and our fathers did;
> The allegory shows us where our faith is hid;
> The moral meaning gives us rules of daily life;
> The anagogy shows us where we end our strife.[12]

In this schema, the three spiritual meanings of the text correspond to the three theological virtues: faith (allegory), hope (anagogy), and love (the moral meaning). It should be noted that this way of approaching the Bible assumed a high doctrine of scriptural inspiration: the multiple meanings inherent in the text had been placed there by the Holy Spirit for the benefit of the people of God. The biblical justification for this method went back to the apostle Paul, who had used the words *allegory* and *type* when applying Old Testament events to believers in Christ (Gal 4:21-31; 1 Cor 10:1-11). The problem with this approach was knowing how to relate each of the four senses to one another and how to prevent Scripture from becoming a nose of wax turned this way and that by various interpreters. As G. R. Evans explains, "Any interpretation which could be put upon the text and was in keeping with the faith and edifying, had the warrant of God himself, for no human reader had the ingenuity to find more than God had put there."[13]

With the rise of the universities in the eleventh century, theology and the study of Scripture moved from the cloister into the classroom. Scripture and the Fathers were still important, but they came to function more as footnotes to the theological questions debated in the schools and brought together in an impressive systematic way in works such as Peter Lombard's *Books of Sentences* (the standard theology textbook of the Middle Ages) and the great scholastic *summae* of the thirteenth

[12]Robert M. Grant, *A Short History of the Interpretation of the Bible* (New York: Macmillan, 1963), 119. A translation of the well-known Latin quatrain: *Littera gesta docet/Quid credas allegoria/Moralis quid agas/Quo tendas anagogia.*

[13]G. R. Evans, *The Language and Logic of the Bible: The Road to Reformation* (Cambridge: Cambridge University Press, 1985), 42.

century. Indispensable to the study of the Bible in the later Middle Ages was the *Glossa ordinaria*, a collection of exegetical opinions by the church fathers and other commentators. Heiko Oberman summarized the transition from devotion to dialectic this way: "When, due to the scientific revolution of the twelfth century, Scripture became the *object* of study rather than the *subject* through which God speaks to the student, the difference between the two modes of speaking was investigated in terms of the texts themselves rather than in their relation to the recipients."[14] It was possible, of course, to be both a scholastic theologian and a master of the spiritual life. Meister Eckhart, for example, wrote commentaries on the Old Testament in Latin and works of mystical theology in German, reflecting what had come to be seen as a division of labor between the two.

An increasing focus on the text of Scripture led to a revival of interest in its literal sense. The two key figures in this development were Thomas Aquinas (d. 1274) and Nicholas of Lyra (d. 1340). Thomas is best remembered for his *Summa Theologiae*, but he was also a prolific commentator on the Bible. Thomas did not abandon the multiple senses of Scripture but declared that all the senses were founded on one—the literal—and this sense eclipsed allegory as the basis of sacred doctrine. Nicholas of Lyra was a Franciscan scholar who made use of the Hebrew text of the Old Testament and quoted liberally from works of Jewish scholars, especially the learned French rabbi Salomon Rashi (d. 1105). After Aquinas, Lyra was the strongest defender of the literal, historical meaning of Scripture as the primary basis of theological disputation. His *Postilla*, as his notes were called—the abbreviated form of *post illa verba textus*, meaning "after these words from Scripture"—were widely circulated in the late Middle Ages and became the first biblical commentary to be printed in the fifteenth century. More than any other commentator from the period of high scholasticism, Lyra and his work were greatly valued by the early reformers. According to an old Latin pun, *Nisi Lyra lyrasset, Lutherus non saltasset*, "If Lyra had not played his lyre, Luther would not have danced."[15] While Luther was never an uncritical disciple of any teacher, he did praise Lyra as a good Hebraist and quoted him more than one hundred times in his lectures on Genesis, where he declared, "I prefer him to almost all other interpreters of Scripture."[16]

Sacred philology. The sixteenth century has been called a golden age of biblical interpretation, and it is a fact that the age of the Reformation witnessed an explosion of commentary writing unparalleled in the history of the Christian church. Kenneth Hagen has cataloged forty-five commentaries on Hebrews between 1516 (Erasmus) and 1598 (Beza).[17] During the sixteenth century, more than seventy new commentaries on Romans were published, five of them by Melanchthon alone, and nearly one hundred commentaries on the Bible's prayer book, the Psalms.[18] There were two developments in the fifteenth century that presaged this development and without which it

[14]Heiko Oberman, *Forerunners of the Reformation* (Philadelphia: Fortress, 1966), 284.

[15]Nicholas of Lyra, *The Postilla of Nicolas of Lyra on the Song of Songs*, trans. and ed. James George Kiecker (Milwaukee: Marquette University Press, 1998), 19.

[16]LW 2:164 (WA 42:377).

[17]Kenneth Hagen, *Hebrews Commenting from Erasmus to Bèze, 1516–1598* (Tübingen: Mohr, 1981).

[18]R. Gerald Hobbs, "Biblical Commentaries," *OER* 1:167-71. See in general David C. Steinmetz, ed., *The Bible in the Sixteenth Century* (Durham: Duke University Press, 1990).

could not have taken place: the invention of printing and the rediscovery of a vast store of ancient learning hitherto unknown or unavailable to scholars in the West.

It is now commonplace to say that what the computer has become in our generation, the printing press was to the world of Erasmus, Luther, and other leaders of the Reformation. Johannes Gutenberg, a goldsmith by trade, developed a metal alloy suitable for type and a machine that would allow printed characters to be cast with relative ease, placed in even lines of composition and then manipulated again and again, making possible the mass production of an unbelievable number of texts. In 1455, the Gutenberg Bible, the masterpiece of the typographical revolution, was published at Mainz in double columns in gothic type. Forty-seven copies of the beautiful Gutenberg Bible are still extant, each consisting of more than one thousand colorfully illuminated and impeccably printed pages. What began at Gutenberg's print shop in Mainz on the Rhine River soon spread, like McDonald's or Starbucks in our day, into every nook and cranny of the known world. Printing presses sprang up in Rome (1464), Venice (1469), Paris (1470), the Netherlands (1471), Switzerland (1472), Spain (1474), England (1476), Sweden (1483), and Constantinople (1490). By 1500, these and other presses across Europe had published some twenty-seven thousand titles, most of them in Latin. Erasmus once compared himself with an obscure preacher whose sermons were heard by only a few people in one or two churches while his books were read in every country in the world. Erasmus was not known for his humility, but in this case he was simply telling the truth.[19]

The Italian humanist Lorenzo Valla (d. 1457) died in the early dawn of the age of printing, but his critical and philological studies would be taken up by others who believed that genuine reform in church and society could come about only by returning to the wellsprings of ancient learning and wisdom—*ad fontes*, "back to the sources!" Valla is best remembered for undermining a major claim made by defenders of the papacy when he proved by philological research that the so-called Donation of Constantine, which had bolstered papal assertions of temporal sovereignty, was a forgery. But it was Valla's *Collatio Novi Testamenti* of 1444 that would have such a great effect on the renewal of biblical studies in the next century. Erasmus discovered the manuscript of this work while rummaging through an old library in Belgium and published it at Paris in 1505. In the preface to his edition of Valla, Erasmus gave the rationale that would guide his own labors in textual criticism. Just as Jerome had translated the Latin Vulgate from older versions and copies of the Scriptures in his day, so now Jerome's own text must be subjected to careful scrutiny and correction. Erasmus would be *Hieronymus redivivus*, a new Jerome come back to life to advance the cause of sacred philology. The restoration of the Scriptures and the writings of the church fathers would usher in what Erasmus believed would be a golden age of peace and learning. In 1516, the Basel publisher Froben brought out Erasmus's *Novum Instrumentum*, the first published edition of the Greek New Testament. Erasmus's Greek New Testament would go through five editions in his lifetime, each one with new emendations to the text and a growing section of annotations that expanded to include not only technical notes about the text but also theological comment. The influence of Erasmus's Greek New

[19]E. Harris Harbison, *The Christian Scholar in the Age of the Reformation* (New York: Charles Scribner's Sons, 1956), 80.

Testament was enormous. It formed the basis for Robert Estienne's *Novum Testamentum Graece* of 1550, which in turn was used to establish the Greek *Textus Receptus* for a number of late Reformation translations including the King James Version of 1611.

For all his expertise in Greek, Erasmus was a poor student of Hebrew and only published commentaries on several of the psalms. However, the renaissance of Hebrew letters was part of the wider program of biblical humanism as reflected in the establishment of trilingual colleges devoted to the study of Hebrew, Greek and Latin (the three languages written on the *titulus* of Jesus' cross [Jn 19:20]) at Alcalá in Spain, Wittenberg in Germany, Louvain in Belgium, and Paris in France. While it is true that some medieval commentators, especially Nicholas of Lyra, had been informed by the study of Hebrew and rabbinics in their biblical work, it was the publication of Johannes Reuchlin's *De rudimentis hebraicis* (1506), a combined grammar and dictionary, that led to the recovery of *veritas Hebraica*, as Jerome had referred to the true voice of the Hebrew Scriptures. The pursuit of Hebrew studies was carried forward in the Reformation by two great scholars, Konrad Pellikan and Sebastian Münster. Pellikan was a former Franciscan friar who embraced the Protestant cause and played a major role in the Zurich reformation. He had published a Hebrew grammar even prior to Reuchlin and produced a commentary on nearly the entire Bible that appeared in seven volumes between 1532 and 1539. Münster was Pellikan's student and taught Hebrew at the University of Heidelberg before taking up a similar position in Basel. Like his mentor, Münster was a great collector of Hebraica and published a series of excellent grammars, dictionaries and rabbinic texts. Münster did for the Hebrew Old Testament what Erasmus had done for the Greek New Testament. His *Hebraica Biblia* offered a fresh Latin translation of the Old Testament with annotations from medieval rabbinic exegesis.

Luther first learned Hebrew with Reuchlin's grammar in hand but took advantage of other published resources, such as the four-volume Hebrew Bible published at Venice by Daniel Bomberg in 1516 to 1517. He also gathered his own circle of Hebrew experts, his *sanhedrin* he called it, who helped him with his German translation of the Old Testament. We do not know where William Tyndale learned Hebrew, though perhaps it was in Worms, where there was a thriving rabbinical school during his stay there. In any event, he had sufficiently mastered the language to bring out a freshly translated Pentateuch that was published at Antwerp in 1530. By the time the English separatist scholar Henry Ainsworth published his prolix commentaries on the Pentateuch in 1616, the knowledge of Hebrew, as well as Greek, was taken for granted by every serious scholar of the Bible. In the preface to his commentary on Genesis, Ainsworth explained that "the literal sense of Moses's Hebrew (which is the tongue wherein he wrote the law), is the ground of all interpretation, and that language hath figures and properties of speech, different from ours: These therefore in the first place are to be opened that the natural meaning of the Scripture, being known, the mysteries of godliness therein implied, may be better discerned."[20]

The restoration of the biblical text in the original languages made possible the revival of scriptural exposition reflected in the floodtide of sermon literature and commentary work. Of even

[20]Henry Ainsworth, *Annotations upon the First Book of Moses Called Genesis* (Amsterdam, 1616), preface (unpaginated).

more far-reaching import was the steady stream of vernacular Bibles in the sixteenth century. In the introduction to his 1516 edition of the New Testament, Erasmus had expressed his desire that the Scriptures be translated into all languages so that "the lowliest women" could read the Gospels and the Pauline epistles and "the farmer sing some portion of them at the plow, the weaver hum some parts of them to the movement of his shuttle, the traveler lighten the weariness of the journey with stories of this kind."[21] Like Erasmus, Tyndale wanted the Bible to be available in the language of the common people. He once said to a learned divine that if God spared his life he would cause the boy who drives the plow to know more of the Scriptures than he did![22] The project of allowing the Bible to speak in the language of the mother in the house, the children in the street and the cheesemonger in the marketplace was met with stiff opposition by certain Catholic polemists such as Johann Eck, Luther's antagonist at the Leipzig Debate of 1519. In his *Enchiridion* (1525), Eck derided the "inky theologians" whose translations paraded the Bible before "the untutored crowd" and subjected it to the judgment of "laymen and crazy old women."[23] In fact, some fourteen German Bibles had already been published prior to Luther's September Testament of 1522, which he translated from Erasmus's Greek New Testament in less than three months' time while sequestered in the Wartburg. Luther's German New Testament became the first bestseller in the world, appearing in forty-three distinct editions between 1522 and 1525 with upward of one hundred thousand copies issued in these three years. It is estimated that 5 percent of the German population may have been literate at this time, but this rate increased as the century wore on due in no small part to the unmitigated success of vernacular Bibles.[24]

Luther's German Bible (inclusive of the Old Testament from 1534) was the most successful venture of its kind, but it was not alone in the field. Hans Denck and Ludwig Hätzer, leaders in the early Anabaptist movement, translated the prophetic books of the Old Testament from Hebrew into German in 1527. This work influenced the Swiss-German Bible of 1531 published by Leo Jud and other pastors in Zurich. Tyndale's influence on the English language rivaled that of Luther on German. At a time when English was regarded as "that obscure and remote dialect of German spoken in an off-shore island," Tyndale, with his remarkable linguistic ability (he was fluent in eight languages), "made a language for England," as his modern editor David Daniell has put it.[25] Tyndale was imprisoned and executed near Brussels in 1536, but the influence of his biblical work among the common people of England was already being felt. There is no reason to doubt the authenticity of John Foxe's recollection of how Tyndale's New Testament was received in England during the 1520s and 1530s:

[21]John C. Olin, *Christian Humanism and the Reformation* (New York: Fordham University Press, 1987), 101.

[22]This famous statement of Tyndale was quoted by John Foxe in his *Acts and Monuments of Matters Happening in the Church* (London, 1563). See Henry Wansbrough, "Tyndale," in *The Bible in the Renaissance*, ed. Richard Griffith (Aldershot, UK: Ashgate, 2001), 124.

[23]John Eck, *Enchiridion of Commonplaces*, trans. Ford Lewis Battles (Grand Rapids: Baker, 1979), 47-49.

[24]The effect of printing on the spread of the Reformation has been much debated. See the classic study by Elizabeth L. Eisenstein, *The Printing Press as an Agent of Change* (Cambridge: Cambridge University Press, 1979). More recent studies include Mark U. Edwards Jr., *Printing, Propaganda and Martin Luther* (Minneapolis: Fortress, 1994), and Andrew Pettegree and Matthew Hall, "The Reformation and the Book: A Reconsideration," *Historical Journal* 47 (2004): 1-24.

[25]David Daniell, *William Tyndale: A Biography* (New Haven: Yale University Press, 1994), 3.

> The fervent zeal of those Christian days seemed much superior to these our days and times; as manifestly may appear by their sitting up all night in reading and hearing; also by their expenses and charges in buying of books in English, of whom some gave five marks, some more, some less, for a book: some gave a load of hay for a few chapters of St. James, or of St. Paul in English.[26]

Calvin helped to revise and contributed three prefaces to the French Bible translated by his cousin Pierre Robert Olivétan and originally published at Neuchâtel in 1535. Clément Marot and Beza provided a fresh translation of the Psalms with each psalm rendered in poetic form and accompanied by monophonic musical settings for congregational singing. The Bay Psalter, the first book printed in America, was an English adaptation of this work. Geneva also provided the provenance of the most influential Italian Bible published by Giovanni Diodati in 1607. The flowering of biblical humanism in vernacular Bibles resulted in new translations in all of the major language groups of Europe: Spanish (1569), Portuguese (1681), Dutch (New Testament, 1523; Old Testament, 1527), Danish (1550), Czech (1579–1593/94), Hungarian (New Testament, 1541; complete Bible, 1590), Polish (1563), Swedish (1541), and even Arabic (1591).[27]

Patterns of Reformation

Once the text of the Bible had been placed in the hands of the people, in cheap and easily available editions, what further need was there of published expositions such as commentaries? Given the Protestant doctrine of the priesthood of all believers, was there any longer a need for learned clergy and their bookish religion? Some radical reformers thought not. Sebastian Franck searched for the true church of the Spirit "scattered among the heathen and the weeds" but could not find it in any of the institutional structures of his time. *Veritas non potest scribi, aut exprimi,* he said, "truth can neither be spoken nor written."[28] Kaspar von Schwenckfeld so emphasized religious inwardness that he suspended external observance of the Lord's Supper and downplayed the readable, audible Scriptures in favor of the Word within. This trajectory would lead to the rise of the Quakers in the next century, but it was pursued neither by the mainline reformers nor by most of the Anabaptists. Article 7 of the Augsburg Confession (1530) declared the one holy Christian church to be "the assembly of all believers among whom the Gospel is purely preached and the holy sacraments are administered according to the Gospel."[29]

Historians of the nineteenth century referred to the material and formal principles of the Reformation. In this construal, the matter at stake was the meaning of the Christian gospel: the liberating insight that helpless sinners are graciously justified by the gift of faith alone, apart from any works or merits of their own, entirely on the basis of Christ's atoning work on the cross. For Luther especially, justification by faith alone became the criterion by which all other doctrines and

[26]Foxe, *Acts and Monuments*, 4:218.

[27]On vernacular translations of the Bible, see *CHB* 3:94-140 and Jaroslav Pelikan, *The Reformation of the Bible/The Bible of the Reformation* (New Haven: Yale University Press, 1996), 41-62.

[28]Sebastian Franck, *280 Paradoxes or Wondrous Sayings*, trans. E. J. Furcha (Lewiston, NY: Edwin Mellen Press, 1986), 10, 212.

[29]BoC 42 (BSLK 61).

practices of the church were to be judged. The cross proves everything, he said at the Heidelberg disputation in 1518. The distinction between law and gospel thus became the primary hermeneutical key that unlocked the true meaning of Scripture.

The formal principle of the Reformation, *sola Scriptura*, was closely bound up with proper distinctions between Scripture and tradition. "Scripture alone," said Luther, "is the true lord and master of all writings and doctrine on earth. If that is not granted, what is Scripture good for? The more we reject it, the more we become satisfied with human books and human teachers."[30] On the basis of this principle, the reformers challenged the structures and institutions of the medieval Catholic Church. Even a simple layperson, they asserted, armed with Scripture should be believed above a pope or a council without it. But, however boldly asserted, the doctrine of the primacy of Scripture did not absolve the reformers from dealing with a host of hermeneutical issues that became matters of contention both between Rome and the Reformation and within each of these two communities: the extent of the biblical canon, the validity of critical study of the Bible, the perspicuity of Scripture and its relation to preaching, and the retention of devotional and liturgical practices such as holy days, incense, the burning of candles, the sprinkling of holy water, church art, and musical instruments. Zwingli, the Puritans, and the radicals dismissed such things as a rubbish heap of ceremonials that amounted to nothing but tomfoolery, while Lutherans and Anglicans retained most of them as consonant with Scripture and valuable aids to worship.

It is important to note that while the mainline reformers differed among themselves on many matters, overwhelmingly they saw themselves as part of the ongoing Catholic tradition, indeed as the legitimate bearers of it. This was seen in numerous ways including their sense of continuity with the church of the preceding centuries; their embrace of the ecumenical orthodoxy of the early church; and their desire to read the Bible in dialogue with the exegetical tradition of the church.

In their biblical commentaries, the reformers of the sixteenth century revealed a close familiarity with the preceding exegetical tradition, and they used it respectfully as well as critically in their own expositions of the sacred text. For them, *sola Scriptura* was not *nuda Scriptura*. Rather, the Scriptures were seen as the book given to the church, gathered and guided by the Holy Spirit. In his restatement of the Vincentian canon, Calvin defined the church as "a society of all the saints, a society which, spread over the whole world, and existing in all ages, and bound together by the one doctrine and the one spirit of Christ, cultivates and observes unity of faith and brotherly concord. With this church we deny that we have any disagreement. Nay, rather, as we revere her as our mother, so we desire to remain in her bosom." Defined thus, the church has a real, albeit relative and circumscribed, authority since, as Calvin admits, "We cannot fly without wings."[31] While the reformers could not agree with the Council of Trent (though some recent Catholic theologians have challenged this interpretation) that Scripture and tradition were two separate and equal sources of divine revelation, they did

[30]LW 32:11-12* (WA 7:317).
[31]John C. Olin, ed., *John Calvin and Jacopo Sadoleto: A Reformation Debate* (New York: Harper Torchbooks, 1966), 61-62, 77.

believe in the coinherence of Scripture and tradition. This conviction shaped the way they read and interpreted the Bible.[32]

Schools of Exegesis

The reformers were passionate about biblical exegesis, but they showed little concern for hermeneutics as a separate field of inquiry. Niels Hemmingsen, a Lutheran theologian in Denmark, did write a treatise, *De methodis* (1555), in which he offered a philosophical and theological framework for the interpretation of Scripture. This was followed by the *Clavis Scripturae Sacrae* (1567) of Matthias Flacius Illyricus, which contains some fifty rules for studying the Bible drawn from Scripture itself.[33] However, hermeneutics as we know it came of age only in the Enlightenment and should not be backloaded into the Reformation. It is also true that the word *commentary* did not mean in the sixteenth century what it means for us today. Erasmus provided both annotations and paraphrases on the New Testament, the former a series of critical notes on the text but also containing points of doctrinal substance, the latter a theological overview and brief exposition. Most of Calvin's commentaries began as sermons or lectures presented in the course of his pastoral ministry. In the dedication to his 1519 study of Galatians, Luther declared that his work was "not so much a commentary as a testimony of my faith in Christ."[34] The exegetical work of the reformers was embodied in a wide variety of forms and genres, and the RCS has worked with this broader concept in setting the guidelines for this compendium.

The Protestant reformers shared in common a number of key interpretive principles such as the priority of the grammatical-historical sense of Scripture and the christological centeredness of the entire Bible, but they also developed a number of distinct approaches and schools of exegesis.[35] For the purposes of the RCS, we note the following key figures and families of interpretation in this period.

Biblical humanism. The key figure is Erasmus, whose importance is hard to exaggerate for Catholic and Protestant exegetes alike. His annotated Greek New Testament and fresh Latin translation challenged the hegemony of the Vulgate tradition and was doubtless a factor in the decision of the Council of Trent to establish the Vulgate edition as authentic and normative. Erasmus believed that the wide distribution of the Scriptures would contribute to personal spiritual renewal and the reform of society. In 1547, the English translation of Erasmus's *Paraphrases* was ordered to be placed in every parish church in England. John Colet first encouraged Erasmus

[32]See Timothy George, "An Evangelical Reflection on Scripture and Tradition," *Pro Ecclesia* 9 (2000): 184-207.

[33]See Kenneth G. Hagen, "'*De Exegetica Methodo*': Niels Hemmingsen's *De Methodis* (1555)," in *The Bible in the Sixteenth Century*, ed. David C. Steinmetz (Durham: Duke University Press, 1990), 181-96.

[34]LW 27:159 (WA 2:449). See Kenneth Hagen, "What Did the Term *Commentarius* Mean to Sixteenth-Century Theologians?" in *Théorie et pratique de l'exégèse*, eds. Irena Backus and Francis M. Higman (Geneva: Droz, 1990), 13-38.

[35]I follow here the sketch of Irena Backus, "Biblical Hermeneutics and Exegesis," *OER* 1:152-58. In this work, Backus confines herself to Continental developments, whereas we have noted the exegetical contribution of the English Reformation as well. For more comprehensive listings of sixteenth-century commentators, see Gerald Bray, *Biblical Interpretation* (Downers Grove, IL: InterVarsity Press, 1996), 165-212; and Richard A. Muller, "Biblical Interpretation in the Sixteenth and Seventeenth Centuries," *DMBI* 22-44.

to learn Greek, though he never took up the language himself. Colet's lectures on Paul's epistles at Oxford are reflected in his commentaries on Romans and 1 Corinthians.

Jacques Lefèvre d'Étaples has been called the "French Erasmus" because of his great learning and support for early reform movements in his native land. He published a major edition of the Psalter, as well as commentaries on the Pauline Epistles (1512), the Gospels (1522), and the General Epistles (1527). Guillaume Farel, the early reformer of Geneva, was a disciple of Lefèvre, and the young Calvin also came within his sphere of influence.

Among pre-Tridentine Catholic reformers, special attention should be given to Thomas de Vio, better known as Cajetan. He is best remembered for confronting Martin Luther on behalf of the pope in 1518, but his biblical commentaries (on nearly every book of the Bible) are virtually free of polemic. Like Erasmus, he dared to criticize the Vulgate on linguistic grounds. His commentary on Romans supported the doctrine of justification by grace applied by faith based on the "alien righteousness" of God in Christ. Jared Wicks sums up Cajetan's significance in this way: "Cajetan's combination of passion for pristine biblical meaning with his fully developed theological horizon of understanding indicates, in an intriguing manner, something of the breadth of possibilities open to Roman Catholics before a more restrictive settlement came to exercise its hold on many Catholic interpreters in the wake of the Council of Trent."[36] Girolamo Seripando, like Cajetan, was a cardinal in the Catholic Church, though he belonged to the Augustinian rather than the Dominican order. He was an outstanding classical scholar and published commentaries on Romans and Galatians. Also important is Jacopo Sadoleto, another cardinal, best known for his 1539 letter to the people of Geneva beseeching them to return to the Church of Rome, to which Calvin replied with a manifesto of his own. Sadoleto published a commentary on Romans in 1535. Bucer once commended Sadoleto's teaching on justification as approximating that of the reformers, while others saw him tilting away from the Augustinian tradition toward Pelagianism.[37]

Luther and the Wittenberg School. It was in the name of the Word of God, and specifically as a doctor of Scripture, that Luther challenged the church of his day and inaugurated the Reformation. Though Luther renounced his monastic vows, he never lost that sense of intimacy with *sacra pagina* he first acquired as a young monk. Luther provided three rules for reading the Bible: prayer, meditation, and struggle *(tentatio)*. His exegetical output was enormous. In the American edition of Luther's works, thirty out of the fifty-five volumes are devoted to his biblical studies, and additional translations are planned. Many of his commentaries originated as sermons or lecture notes presented to his students at the university and to his parishioners at Wittenberg's parish church of St. Mary. Luther referred to Galatians as his bride: "The Epistle to the Galatians is my dear epistle. I have betrothed myself to it. It is my Käthe von Bora."[38] He considered his 1535 commentary on Galatians his greatest exegetical work, although his massive commentary on Genesis

[36]Jared Wicks, "Tommaso de Vio Cajetan (1469-1534)," *DMBI* 283-87, here 286.

[37]See the discussion by Bernard Roussel, "Martin Bucer et Jacques Sadolet: la concorde possible," *Bulletin de la Société de l'histoire de protestantisme français* (1976): 525-50, and T. H. L. Parker, *Commentaries on the Epistle to the Romans, 1532–1542* (Edinburgh: T&T Clark, 1986), 25-34.

[38]WATR 1:69 no. 146; cf. LW 54:20 no. 146. I have followed Rörer's variant on Dietrich's notes.

(eight volumes in LW), which he worked on for ten years (1535–1545), must be considered his crowning work. Luther's principles of biblical interpretation are found in his *Open Letter on Translating* and in the prefaces he wrote to all the books of the Bible.

Philipp Melanchthon was brought to Wittenberg to teach Greek in 1518 and proved to be an able associate to Luther in the reform of the church. A set of his lecture notes on Romans was published without his knowledge in 1522. This was revised and expanded many times until his large commentary of 1556. Melanchthon also commented on other New Testament books including Matthew, John, Galatians, and the Petrine epistles, as well as Proverbs, Daniel, and Ecclesiastes. Though he was well trained in the humanist disciplines, Melanchthon devoted little attention to critical and textual matters in his commentaries. Rather, he followed the primary argument of the biblical writer and gathered from this exposition a series of doctrinal topics for special consideration. This method lay behind Melanchthon's *Loci communes* (1521), the first Protestant theology textbook to be published. Another Wittenberger was Johannes Bugenhagen of Pomerania, a prolific commentator on both the Old and New Testaments. His commentary on the Psalms (1524), translated into German by Bucer, applied Luther's teaching on justification to the Psalter. He also wrote a commentary on Job and annotations on many of the books in the Bible. The Lutheran exegetical tradition was shaped by many other scholar-reformers including Andreas Osiander, Johannes Brenz, Caspar Cruciger, Erasmus Sarcerius, Georg Maior, Jacob Andreae, Nikolaus Selnecker, and Johann Gerhard.

The Strasbourg-Basel tradition. Bucer, the son of a shoemaker in Alsace, became the leader of the Reformation in Strasbourg. A former Dominican, he was early on influenced by Erasmus and continued to share his passion for Christian unity. Bucer was the most ecumenical of the Protestant reformers seeking rapprochement with Catholics on justification and an armistice between Luther and Zwingli in their strife over the Lord's Supper. Bucer also had a decisive influence on Calvin, though the latter characterized his biblical commentaries as longwinded and repetitious.[39] In his exegetical work, Bucer made ample use of patristic and medieval sources, though he criticized the abuse and overuse of allegory as "the most blatant insult to the Holy Spirit."[40] He declared that the purpose of his commentaries was "to help inexperienced brethren [perhaps like the apothecary Drilhon, who owned a French translation of Bucer's *Commentary on Matthew*] to understand each of the words and actions of Christ, and in their proper order as far as possible, and to retain an explanation of them in their natural meaning, so that they will not distort God's Word through age-old aberrations or by inept interpretation, but rather with a faithful comprehension of everything as written by the Spirit of God, they may expound to all the churches in their firm upbuilding in faith and love."[41] In addition to writing commentaries on all four Gospels, Bucer published commentaries on Judges, the Psalms, Zephaniah, Romans, and Ephesians. In the early years of the Reformation, there was a great deal of back and forth between Strasbourg and Basel, and both

[39]CNTC 8:3 (CO 10:404).

[40]*DMBI* 249; P. Scherding and F. Wendel, eds., "Un Traité d'exégèse pratique de Bucer," *Revue d'histoire et de philosophie religieuses* 26 (1946): 32-75, here 56.

[41]Martin Bucer, *Enarrationes perpetuae in sacra quatuor evangelia*, 2nd ed. (Strasbourg: Georg Ulrich Andlanus, 1530), 10r; quoted in D. F. Wright, "Martin Bucer," *DMBI* 290.

were centers of a lively publishing trade. Wolfgang Capito, Bucer's associate at Strasbourg, was a notable Hebraist and composed commentaries on Hosea (1529) and Habakkuk (1527).

At Basel, the great Sebastian Münster defended the use of Jewish sources in the Christian study of the Old Testament and published, in addition to his famous Hebrew grammar, an annotated version of the Gospel of Matthew translated from Greek into Hebrew. Oecolampadius, Basel's chief reformer, had been a proofreader in Froben's publishing house and worked with Erasmus on his Greek New Testament and his critical edition of Jerome. From 1523 he was both a preacher and professor of Holy Scripture at Basel. He defended Zwingli's eucharistic theology at the Colloquy of Marburg and published commentaries on 1 John (1524), Romans (1525), and Haggai–Malachi (1525). Oecolampadius was succeeded by Simon Grynaeus, a classical scholar who taught Greek and supported Bucer's efforts to bring Lutherans and Zwinglians together. More in line with Erasmus was Sebastian Castellio, who came to Basel after his expulsion from Geneva in 1545. He is best remembered for questioning the canonicity of the Song of Songs and for his annotations and French translation of the Bible.

The Zurich group. Biblical exegesis in Zurich was centered on the distinctive institution of the *Prophezei*, which began on June 19, 1525. On five days a week, at seven o'clock in the morning, all of the ministers and theological students in Zurich gathered into the choir of the Grossmünster to engage in a period of intense exegesis and interpretation of Scripture. After Zwingli had opened the meeting with prayer, the text of the day was read in Latin, Greek, and Hebrew, followed by appropriate textual or exegetical comments. One of the ministers then delivered a sermon on the passage in German that was heard by many of Zurich's citizens who stopped by the cathedral on their way to work. This institute for advanced biblical studies had an enormous influence as a model for Reformed academies and seminaries throughout Europe. It was also the seedbed for sermon series in Zurich's churches and the extensive exegetical publications of Zwingli, Leo Jud, Konrad Pellikan, Heinrich Bullinger, Oswald Myconius, and Rudolf Gwalther. Zwingli had memorized in Greek all of the Pauline epistles, and this bore fruit in his powerful expository preaching and biblical exegesis. He took seriously the role of grammar, rhetoric, and historical research in explaining the biblical text. For example, he disagreed with Bucer on the value of the Septuagint, regarding it as a trustworthy witness to a proto-Hebrew version earlier than the Masoretic text.

Zwingli's work was carried forward by his successor Bullinger, one of the most formidable scholars and networkers among the reformers. He composed commentaries on Daniel (1565), the Gospels (1542–1546), the Epistles (1537), Acts (1533), and Revelation (1557). He collaborated with Calvin to produce the *Consensus Tigurinus* (1549), a Reformed accord on the nature of the Lord's Supper, and produced a series of fifty sermons on Christian doctrine, known as *Decades*, which became required reading in Elizabethan England. As the *Antistes* ("overseer") of the Zurich church for forty-four years, Bullinger faced opposition from nascent Anabaptism on the one hand and resurgent Catholicism on the other. The need for a well-trained clergy and scholarly resources, including Scripture commentaries, arose from the fact that the Bible was "difficult or obscure to the unlearned, unskillful, unexercised, and malicious or corrupted wills." While forswearing papal claims to infallibility, Bullinger and other leaders of the magisterial Reformation saw the need for a kind of Protestant magisterium as a check against the tendency to read the Bible in "such sense as everyone shall be persuaded in himself to be most convenient."[42]

Two other commentators can be treated in connection with the Zurich group, though each of them had a wide-ranging ministry across the Reformation fronts. A former Benedictine monk, Wolfgang Musculus, embraced the Reformation in the 1520s and served briefly as the secretary to Bucer in Strasbourg. He shared Bucer's desire for Protestant unity and served for seventeen years (1531–1548) as a pastor and reformer in Augsburg. After a brief time in Zurich, where he came under the influence of Bullinger, Musculus was called to Bern, where he taught the Scriptures and published commentaries on the Psalms, the Decalogue, Genesis, Romans, Isaiah, 1 and 2 Corinthians, Galatians and Ephesians, Philippians, Colossians, 1 and 2 Thessalonians, and 1 Timothy. Drawing on his exegetical writings, Musculus also produced a compendium of Protestant theology that was translated into English in 1563 as *Commonplaces of Christian Religion*.

Peter Martyr Vermigli was a Florentine-born scholar and Augustinian friar who embraced the Reformation and fled to Switzerland in 1542. Over the next twenty years, he would gain an international reputation as a prolific scholar and leading theologian within the Reformed community. He lectured on the Old Testament at Strasbourg, was made regius professor at Oxford, corresponded with the Italian refugee church in Geneva and spent the last years of his life as professor of Hebrew at Zurich. Vermigli published commentaries on 1 Corinthians, Romans, and Judges during his lifetime. His biblical lectures on Genesis, Lamentations, 1 and 2 Samuel, and 1 and 2 Kings were published posthumously. The most influential of his writings was the *Loci communes (Commonplaces)*, a theological compendium drawn from his exegetical writings.

The Genevan reformers. What Zwingli and Bullinger were to Zurich, Calvin and Beza were to Geneva. Calvin has been called "the father of modern biblical scholarship," and his exegetical work is without parallel in the Reformation. Because of the success of his *Institutes of the Christian Religion* Calvin has sometimes been thought of as a man of one book, but he always intended the *Institutes*, which went through eight editions in Latin and five in French during his lifetime, to serve as a guide to the study of the Bible, to show the reader "what he ought especially to seek in Scripture and to what end he ought to relate its contents." Jacob Arminius, who modified several principles of Calvin's theology, recommended his commentaries next to the Bible, for, as he said, Calvin "is incomparable in the interpretation of Scripture."[43] Drawing on his superb knowledge of Greek and Hebrew and his thorough training in humanist rhetoric, Calvin produced commentaries on all of the New Testament books except 2 and 3 John and Revelation. Calvin's Old Testament commentaries originated as sermon and lecture series and include Genesis, Psalms, Hosea, Isaiah, minor prophets, Daniel, Jeremiah and Lamentations, a harmony of the last four books of Moses,

[42]Euan Cameron, *The European Reformation* (Oxford: Oxford University Press, 1991), 120.

[43]Letter to Sebastian Egbert (May 3, 1607), in *Praestantium ac eruditorum virorum epistolae ecclesiasticae et theologicae varii argumenti*, ed. Christiaan Hartsoeker (Amsterdam: Henricus Dendrinus, 1660), 236-37. Quoted in A. M. Hunter, *The Teaching of Calvin* (London: James Clarke, 1950), 20.

Ezekiel 1–20, and Joshua. Calvin sought for brevity and clarity in all of his exegetical work. He emphasized the illumination of the Holy Spirit as essential to a proper understanding of the text. Calvin underscored the continuity between the two Testaments (one covenant in two dispensations) and sought to apply the plain or natural sense of the text to the church of his day. In the preface to his own influential commentary on Romans, Karl Barth described how Calvin worked to recover the mind of Paul and make the apostle's message relevant to his day:

> How energetically Calvin goes to work, first scientifically establishing the text ("what stands there?"), then following along the footsteps of its thought; that is to say, he conducts a discussion with it until the wall between the first and the sixteenth centuries becomes transparent, and until there in the first century Paul speaks and here the man of the sixteenth century hears, until indeed the conversation between document and reader becomes concentrated upon the substance (which must be the same now as then).[44]

Beza was elected moderator of Geneva's Company of Pastors after Calvin's death in 1564 and guided the Genevan Reformation over the next four decades. His annotated Latin translation of the Greek New Testament (1556) and his further revisions of the Greek text established his reputation as the leading textual critic of the sixteenth century after Erasmus. Beza completed the translation of Marot's metrical Psalter, which became a centerpiece of Huguenot piety and Reformed church life. Though known for his polemical writings on grace, free will, and predestination, Beza's work is marked by a strong pastoral orientation and concern for a Scripture-based spirituality.

Robert Estienne (Stephanus) was a printer-scholar who had served the royal household in Paris. After his conversion to Protestantism, in 1550 he moved to Geneva, where he published a series of notable editions and translations of the Bible. He also produced sermons and commentaries on Job, Ecclesiastes, the Song of Songs, Romans and Hebrews, as well as dictionaries, concordances, and a thesaurus of biblical terms. He also published the first editions of the Bible with chapters divided into verses, an innovation that quickly became universally accepted.

The British Reformation. Commentary writing in England and Scotland lagged behind the continental Reformation for several reasons. In 1500, there were only three publishing houses in England compared with more than two hundred on the Continent. A 1408 statute against publishing or reading the Bible in English, stemming from the days of Lollardy, stifled the free flow of ideas, as was seen in the fate of Tyndale. Moreover, the nature of the English Reformation from Henry through Elizabeth provided little stability for the flourishing of biblical scholarship. In the sixteenth century, many "hot-gospel" Protestants in England were edified by the English translations of commentaries and theological writings by the Continental reformers. The influence of Calvin and Beza was felt especially in the Geneva Bible with its "Protestant glosses" of theological notes and references.

During the later Elizabethan and Stuart church, however, the indigenous English commentary came into its own. Both Anglicans and Puritans contributed to this outpouring of biblical studies.

[44]Karl Barth, *Die Römerbrief* (Zurich: TVZ, 1940), 11, translated by T. H. L. Parker as the epigraph to *Calvin's New Testament Commentaries*, 2nd ed. (Louisville, KY: Westminster John Knox, 1993).

The sermons of Lancelot Andrewes and John Donne are replete with exegetical insights based on a close study of the Greek and Hebrew texts. Among the Reformed authors in England, none was more influential than William Perkins, the greatest of the early Puritan theologians, who published commentaries on Galatians, Jude, Revelation, and the Sermon on the Mount (Mt 5–7). John Cotton, one of his students, wrote commentaries on the Song of Songs, Ecclesiastes, and Revelation before departing for New England in 1633. The separatist pastor Henry Ainsworth was an outstanding scholar of Hebrew and wrote major commentaries on the Pentateuch, the Psalms, and the Song of Songs. In Scotland, Robert Rollock, the first principal of Edinburgh University (1585), wrote numerous commentaries including those on the Psalms, Ephesians, Daniel, Romans, 1 and 2 Thessalonians, John, Colossians, and Hebrews. Joseph Mede and Thomas Brightman were leading authorities on Revelation and contributed to the apocalyptic thought of the seventeenth century. Mention should also be made of Archbishop James Ussher, whose *Annals of the Old Testament* was published in 1650. Ussher developed a keen interest in biblical chronology and calculated that the creation of the world had taken place on October 26, 4004 B.C. As late as 1945, the Scofield Reference Bible still retained this date next to Genesis 1:1, but later editions omitted it because of the lack of evidence on which to fix such dates.[45]

Anabaptism. Irena Backus has noted that there was no school of "dissident" exegesis during the Reformation, and the reasons are not hard to find. The radical Reformation was an ill-defined movement that existed on the margins of official church life in the sixteenth century. The denial of infant baptism and the refusal to swear an oath marked radicals as a seditious element in society, and they were persecuted by Protestants and Catholics alike. However, in the RCS we have made an attempt to include some voices of the radical Reformation, especially among the Anabaptists. While the Anabaptists published few commentaries in the sixteenth century, they were avid readers and quoters of the Bible. Numerous exegetical gems can be found in their letters, treatises, martyr acts (especially *The Martyrs' Mirror*), hymns, and histories. They placed a strong emphasis on the memorizing of Scripture and quoted liberally from vernacular translations of the Bible. George H. Williams has noted that "many an Anabaptist theological tract was really a beautiful mosaic of Scripture texts."[46] In general, most Anabaptists accepted the apocryphal books as canonical, contrasted outer word and inner spirit with relative degrees of strictness and saw the New Testament as normative for church life and social ethics (witness their pacifism, nonswearing, emphasis on believers' baptism and congregational discipline).

We have noted the Old Testament translation of Ludwig Hätzer, who became an antitrinitarian, and Hans Denck that they published at Worms in 1527. Denck also wrote a notable commentary on Micah. Conrad Grebel belonged to a Greek reading circle in Zurich and came to his Anabaptist convictions while poring over the text of Erasmus's New Testament. The only Anabaptist leader with university credentials was Balthasar Hubmaier, who was made a doctor of theology (Ingolstadt, 1512) in the same year as Luther. His reflections on the Bible are found in his numerous

[45]*The New Scofield Reference Bible* (New York: Oxford University Press, 1967), vi.
[46]George H. Williams, *The Radical Reformation*, 3rd ed. (Kirksville, MO: Sixteenth Century Journal Publishers, 1992), 1247.

writings, which include the first catechism of the Reformation (1526), a two-part treatise on the freedom of the will and a major work *(On the Sword)* setting forth positive attitudes toward the role of government and the Christian's place in society. Melchior Hoffman was an apocalyptic seer who wrote commentaries on Romans, Revelation, and Daniel 12. He predicted that Christ would return in 1533. More temperate was Pilgram Marpeck, a mining engineer who embraced Anabaptism and traveled widely throughout Switzerland and south Germany, from Strasbourg to Augsburg. His "Admonition of 1542" is the longest published defense of Anabaptist views on baptism and the Lord's Supper. He also wrote many letters that functioned as theological tracts for the congregations he had founded dealing with topics such as the fruits of repentance, the lowliness of Christ, and the unity of the church. Menno Simons, a former Catholic priest, became the most outstanding leader of the Dutch Anabaptist movement. His masterpiece was the *Foundation of Christian Doctrine* published in 1540. His other writings include *Meditation on the Twenty-fifth Psalm* (1537); *A Personal Exegesis of Psalm Twenty-five* modeled on the style of Augustine's *Confessions; Confession of the Triune God* (1550), directed against Adam Pastor, a former disciple of Menno who came to doubt the divinity of Christ; *Meditations and Prayers for Mealtime* (1557); and the *Cross of the Saints* (1554), an exhortation to faithfulness in the face of persecution. Like many other Anabaptists, Menno emphasized the centrality of discipleship *(Nachfolge)* as a deliberate repudiation of the old life and a radical commitment to follow Jesus as Lord.

Reading Scripture with the Reformers

In 1947, Gerhard Ebeling set forth his thesis that the history of the Christian church is the history of the interpretation of Scripture. Since that time, the place of the Bible in the story of the church has been investigated from many angles. A better understanding of the history of exegesis has been aided by new critical editions and scholarly discussions of the primary sources. The *Cambridge History of the Bible*, published in three volumes (1963–1970), remains a standard reference work in the field. The ACCS built on, and itself contributed to, the recovery of patristic biblical wisdom of both East and West. Beryl Smalley's *The Study of the Bible in the Middle Ages* (1940) and Henri de Lubac's *Medieval Exegesis: The Four Senses of Scripture* (1959) are essential reading for understanding the monastic and scholastic settings of commentary work between Augustine and Luther. The Reformation took place during what has been called "le grand siècle de la Bible."[47] Aided by the tools of Renaissance humanism and the dynamic impetus of Reformation theology (including permutations and reactions against it), the sixteenth century produced an unprecedented number of commentaries on every book in the Bible. Drawing from this vast storehouse of exegetical treasures, the RCS allows us to read Scripture along with the reformers. In doing so, it serves as a practical homiletic and devotional guide to some of the greatest masters of biblical interpretation in the history of the church.

The RCS gladly acknowledges its affinity with and dependence on recent scholarly investigations of Reformation-era exegesis. Between 1976 and 1990, three international colloquia on the

[47]J-R. Aarmogathe, ed., *Bible de tous les temps*, 8 vols.; vol. 6, *Le grand siècle de la Bible* (Paris: Beauchesne, 1989).

history of biblical exegesis in the sixteenth century took place in Geneva and in Durham, North Carolina.[48] Among those participating in these three gatherings were a number of scholars who have produced groundbreaking works in the study of biblical interpretation in the Reformation. These include Elsie McKee, Irena Backus, Kenneth Hagen, Scott H. Hendrix, Richard A. Muller, Guy Bedouelle, Gerald Hobbs, John B. Payne, Bernard Roussel, Pierre Fraenkel, and David C. Steinmetz (1936–2015). Among other scholars whose works are indispensable for the study of this field are Heinrich Bornkamm, Jaroslav Pelikan, Heiko A. Oberman, James S. Preus, T. H. L. Parker, David F. Wright, Tony Lane, John L. Thompson, Frank A. James, and Timothy J. Wengert.[49] Among these scholars no one has had a greater influence on the study of Reformation exegesis than David C. Steinmetz. A student of Oberman, he emphasized the importance of understanding the Reformation in medieval perspective. In addition to important studies on Luther and Staupitz, he pioneered the method of comparative exegesis showing both continuity and discontinuity between major Reformation figures and the preceding exegetical traditions (see his *Luther in Context* and *Calvin in Context*). From his base at Duke University, he spawned what might be called a Steinmetz school, a cadre of students and scholars whose work on the Bible in the Reformation era continues to shape the field. Steinmetz served on the RCS Board of Editorial Advisors, and a number of our volume editors pursued doctoral studies under his supervision.

In 1980, Steinmetz published "The Superiority of Pre-critical Exegesis," a seminal essay that not only placed Reformation exegesis in the context of the preceding fifteen centuries of the church's study of the Bible but also challenged certain assumptions underlying the hegemony of historical-critical exegesis of the post-Enlightenment academy.[50] Steinmetz helps us to approach the reformers and other precritical interpreters of the Bible on their own terms as faithful witnesses to the church's apostolic tradition. For them, a specific book or pericope had to be understood within the scope of the consensus of the canon. Thus the reformers, no less than the Fathers and the schoolmen, interpreted the hymn of the Johannine prologue about the preexistent Christ in consonance with the creation narrative of Genesis 1. In the same way, Psalm 22, Isaiah 53, and Daniel 7 are seen as part of an overarching storyline that finds ultimate fulfillment in Jesus Christ. Reading the Bible with the resources of the new learning, the reformers challenged the exegetical conclusions of their medieval predecessors at many points. However, unlike Alexander Campbell in the nineteenth century, their aim was not to "open the New Testament as if mortal man had never seen it before."[51]

[48]Olivier Fatio and Pierre Fraenkel, eds., *Histoire de l'exégèse au XVIe siècle: texts du colloque international tenu à Genève en 1976* (Geneva: Droz, 1978); David C. Steinmetz, ed., *The Bible in the Sixteenth Century* [Second International Colloquy on the History of Biblical Exegesis in the Sixteenth Century] (Durham: Duke University Press, 1990); Irena Backus and Francis M. Higman, eds., *Théorie et pratique de l'exégèse. Actes du troisième colloque international sur l'histoire de l'exégèse biblique au XVIe siècle, Genève, 31 août–2 septembre 1988* (Geneva: Droz, 1990); see also Guy Bedouelle and Bernard Roussel, eds., *Bible de tous les temps*, 8 vols.; vol. 5, *Le temps des Réformes et la Bible* (Paris: Beauchesne, 1989).

[49]For bibliographical references and evaluation of these and other contributors to the scholarly study of Reformation-era exegesis, see Richard A. Muller, "Biblical Interpretation in the Era of the Reformation: The View From the Middle Ages," in *Biblical Interpretation in the Era of the Reformation: Essays Presented to David C. Steinmetz in Honor of His Sixtieth Birthday*, ed. Richard A. Muller and John L. Thompson (Grand Rapids: Eerdmans, 1996), 3-22.

[50]David C. Steinmetz, "The Superiority of Pre-Critical Exegesis," *Theology Today* 37 (1980): 27-38.

[51]Alexander Campbell, *Memoirs of Alexander Campbell*, ed. Robert Richardson (Cincinnati: Standard Publishing Company, 1872), 97.

Rather, they wanted to do their biblical work as part of an interpretive conversation within the family of the people of God. In the reformers' emphatic turn to the literal sense, which prompted their many blasts against the unrestrained use of allegory, their work was an extension of a similar impulse made by Thomas Aquinas and Nicholas of Lyra.

This is not to discount the radically new insights gained by the reformers in their dynamic engagement with the text of Scripture; nor should we dismiss in a reactionary way the light shed on the meaning of the Bible by the scholarly accomplishments of the past two centuries. However, it is to acknowledge that the church's exegetical tradition is an indispensable aid for the proper interpretation of Scripture. And this means, as Richard Muller has said, that "while it is often appropriate to recognize that traditionary readings of the text are erroneous on the grounds offered by the historical-critical method, we ought also to recognize that the conclusions offered by historical-critical exegesis may themselves be quite erroneous on the grounds provided by the exegesis of the patristic, medieval, and reformation periods."[52] The RCS wishes to commend the exegetical work of the Reformation era as a program of retrieval for the sake of renewal—spiritual réssourcement for believers committed to the life of faith today.

George Herbert was an English pastor and poet who reaped the benefits of the renewal of biblical studies in the age of the Reformation. He referred to the Scriptures as a book of infinite sweetness, "a mass of strange delights," a book with secrets to make the life of anyone good. In describing the various means pastors require to be fully furnished in the work of their calling, Herbert provided a rationale for the history of exegesis and for the Reformation Commentary on Scripture:

> The fourth means are commenters and Fathers, who have handled the places controverted, which the parson by no means refuseth. As he doth not so study others as to neglect the grace of God in himself and what the Holy Spirit teacheth him, so doth he assure himself that God in all ages hath had his servants to whom he hath revealed his Truth, as well as to him; and that as one country doth not bear all things that there may be a commerce, so neither hath God opened or will open all to one, that there may be a traffic in knowledge between the servants of God for the planting both of love and humility. Wherefore he hath one comment[ary] at least upon every book of Scripture, and ploughing with this, and his own meditations, he enters into the secrets of God treasured in the holy Scripture.[53]

Timothy George
General Editor

[52]Richard A. Muller and John L. Thompson, "The Significance of Precritical Exegesis: Retrospect and Prospect," in *Biblical Interpretation in the Era of the Reformation: Essays Presented to David C. Steinmetz in Honor of His Sixtieth Birthday*, ed. Richard A. Muller and John L. Thompson (Grand Rapids: Eerdmans, 1996), 342.
[53]George Herbert, *The Complete English Poems* (London: Penguin, 1991), 205.

INTRODUCTION TO REVELATION

He will wipe away all tears from their eyes; there will be no more death, and no more mourning or sadness. . . . "Now I am making the whole of creation new. . . . It is already done. I am the Alpha and the Omega, the Beginning and the End."
Revelation 21:4-6, Jerusalem Bible

Authorship and Canonicity

Literature on the authorship and canonicity of Revelation has grown in recent years along with recognition of the diversity and significance of apocalyptic literature.[1] This section offers a brief summary of work on the authorship and canonicity of Revelation with its textual exegesis and interpretation insofar as it relates to sixteenth-century commentaries.[2]

Among the apocalyptic literature available to early Christian communities, Revelation is the only work to have been accepted as a part of the biblical canon. Despite the existence of Jewish and Christian apocalyptic literature, exegetes in the sixteenth century were aware that elements from Daniel, Ezekiel, Zechariah, and other books of the Hebrew canon had been imported into the text of John's Revelation. Daniel is generally regarded as marking the beginning of the genre of apocalyptic literature, dated as having been written during the persecution of Antiochus Epiphanes (175–164 BC).[3] Important Jewish apocalyptic writings outside the Old Testament exist, such as Enoch, the Apocalypse of Baruch, the Assumption of Moses, and the Ascension of Isaiah. Apocalyptic literature was associated with the destruction of the Jewish temple in AD 70, prior to or contemporary with the reign of the Roman Emperor Domitian (AD 81–96).[4] This history served as a foundation to later speculation on the meaning of the text.

According to historian Irena Backus, "The chief characteristic of apocalyptic literature is its recourse to one or several visions of the past, the present, and the future," visions normally granted by

[1]See William C. Weinrich, introduction to *Revelation*, ACCS New Testament 12 (Downers Grove, IL: InterVarsity Press, 2005); Adela Yarbro Collins, *Crisis and Catharsis: The Power of the Apocalypse* (Philadelphia Westminster, 1984). On apocalyptic literature generally, see *The Encyclopedia of Apocalypticism*, vol. 1, *The Origins of Apocalypticism in Judaism and Christianity*, ed. John J. Collins; vol. 2, *Apocalypticism in Western History and Culture*, ed. Bernard McGinn; vol. 3, *Apocalypticism in the Modern Period and the Contemporary Age*, ed. Stephen J. Stein (New York: Continuum, 2000–2003).

[2]On apocalyptic literature affecting the exegesis and interpretation of Revelation during the Reformation, see Irena Backus, *Reformation Readings of the Apocalypse: Geneva, Zurich, and Wittenberg* (Oxford: Oxford University Press, 2000), xi-xx, 3-36.

[3]Paul Hanson, *The Dawn of Apocalyptic: The Historical and Sociological Roots of Jewish Apocalyptic Eschatology* (Minneapolis: Augsburg, 1979); John J. Collins, *The Apocalyptic Imagination: An Introduction to Jewish Apocalyptic Literature*, 3rd ed. (Grand Rapids, MI: Eerdmans, 2016).

[4]Elaine Pagels, *Revelations: Visions, Prophecy, and Politics in the Book of Revelation* (New York: Penguin Books, 2013).

God but "mediated by one or several angels. This enables the author to transmit new prophecies without fearing accusations of excessive self-importance."[5] Differently from Jewish apocalyptic works, Revelation is written in the author's own name (Rev 1:9)—whichever John it was, he wanted his name known to the communities he was addressing. How one reads a piece of apocalyptic literature shapes interpretation: as happening in the time of its authorship (preterist), in the future (futurist), throughout the events in the history of the church (historicist), or as symbolic of those events (spiritualist).

Revelation was held in high regard by the millenarian ante-Nicene Fathers, including Justin Martyr and Irenaeus, who took it to be the work of John the Evangelist. However, as Backus writes,

> as millenarianism began to lose hold in the Eastern, and particularly the Alexandrian, church, the respectability of the Apocalypse was challenged. Dionysius of Alexandria questioned its apostolic authorship, ca. A.D. 250, on grounds of difference in style and content from the Fourth Gospel. Eusebius of Caesarea admitted its place in the canon with some reluctance. Some subsequent Eastern writers and councils (Cyril of Jerusalem, Council of Laodicea, John Chrysostom) did not include it in the canon.[6]

This negative perspective on Revelation eventually reached Western Europe, when Erasmus and others discovered the Greek fathers, but it was not characteristic of the Latin Middle Ages. In the churches of the West the attribution of Revelation to John the Evangelist was maintained in the Muratorian fragment or canon (c. 170) and by Tertullian (c. 155–c. 240) and Hippolytus (d. 235). Here the perspective on Revelation was more positive.

Commentaries and the Interpretation of Revelation

Five periods of interpretation of Revelation contributed to how the text was understood in the sixteenth century.

1. Patristic and early Greek commentaries: Spiritual interpretation. The thrust of an early and literal exegetical tradition was shaped by the work of such later commentators as Origen (185–254); Victorinus of Petovium (d. 304), a disciple of Origen; and Tyconius (d. c. 380). In particular, Victorinus, Tyconius, and their predecessors shaped the exegesis of Revelation in the West around a method of textual recapitulation, in Victorinus, and symbolic interpretation, in Tyconius, in late antiquity and the early Middle Ages.

A Platonist, Origen was author of the *Hexapla*, a critical edition of the Hebrew Bible in six versions. It was central to knowledge of the LXX and imperative for a knowledge of the true text of Scripture. This monumental analysis of the Old Testament, written in response to Jewish and Gnostic critics, heightened Origen's influence among sixteenth-century radicals, magisterial Reformers, and humanists on such issues as the nature of the soul, universalism, free will, and pacifism.

Victorinus, referred to as the first exegete of the Western church, suffered martyrdom under Diocletian. His commentary on Revelation is cited by later critics both for his comprehensiveness

[5] Backus, *Reformation Readings*, xii.
[6] Backus, *Reformation Readings*, xii.

and for his contribution to a theory of recapitulation, according to which similar spiritual truths are embedded in different but logically parallel symbols.[7] As an example, the vision of the angel with the seal of the living God (Rev 7:2) is understood to be Elijah. Victorinus gives this figure a threefold task: (1) to anticipate the time of antichrist, (2) to preach penance, and (3) to convert to faith many from Israel as well as from the Gentile nations. This image comes together with the warning cry of the eagle who flies across the heavens (Rev 8:13), which Victorinus views as the Holy Spirit speaking, as it were, through the mouths of the prophets (Rev 11:3). Victorinus reads Revelation not as a prophecy but as an unveiling by Christ of the true sense of Scripture. Through recapitulation, Revelation relates the same events in different ways, for example, the bowls of wrath (Rev 16:1-17) do no more than elaborate on the persecutions already revealed by the trumpets (Rev 8:6–11:15). At issue is not chronology but an understanding of the text.[8] Victorinus's way of reading the text was handed down to the medieval church under the authoritative name of Jerome (c. 342–420), who, however, was uncomfortable with Victorinus's millenarian viewpoint and therefore revised the ending of Victorinus's commentary, bringing the heavenly Jerusalem down and to the realm of prophecy.[9]

The spiritual or symbolic interpretation of the text was taken up by Tyconius and given structure by his *Book of Rules*. No longer extant, the contents of this work have been reconstructed from later commentaries that cite it, for example, Primasius (d. c. 560), Bede the Venerable (c. 673–735), and Beatus of Liebana (730–785). Contemporary scholarship on Tyconius circled around the question of whether this lost commentary could be recovered and reconstructed from such later sources as those cited. Work by Kenneth Steinhauser (1987) and Roger Gryson (2011) led to Gryson's publication of a reconstructed Latin edition of Tyconius's *Exposition of the Apocalypse*.[10]

Tyconius's comments on Revelation were guided by the hermeneutical orientation set forth in his *Book of Rules*. He begins the *Book of Rules* with this prologue:

> Before anything else that seemed good to me, I considered it necessary to write a little guidebook and to fabricate, as it were, keys and windows to the secrets of the law. For there are certain mystic rules which maintain the inner recesses of the entire law and make the treasures of truth invisible to some people. If the logic of the rules is accepted without ill will, as we communicate it, then whatever is closed will be opened and whatever is obscure will be elucidated, so that anyone who walks in the vast forest of prophecy guided by these rules as, in a way, by pathways of light, may be kept from error. Now, these are the rules: (1) on the Lord and his body, (2) on the bipartite body of the Lord, (3) on the promises and the law, (4) on the particular and the general, (5) on times, (6) on recapitulation, and (7) on the devil and his body.[11]

[7]Wilhelm Bousset, *Die Offenbarung Johannis* (Göttingen Vandenhoeck & Ruprecht, 1906), 54; R. H. Charles, *Studies in the Apocalypse* (Edinburgh: T&T Clark, 1913), 10-11.

[8]On Victorinus, see Claudio Moreschini and Enrico Norelli, *Early Christian Greek and Latin Literature*, vol. 1 (Grand Rapids, MI: Baker Academic, 2005).

[9]See Martine Dulaey, "Jerome 'editeur' du Commentaire sur l'Apocalypse de Victorinus Poetovio," *Revue des Etudes Augustiniennes* 37 (1991): 199-236; Victorinus of Poetovio, *Sur l'Apocalypse et autres ecrits*, ed. Martine Dulaey, SC 423 (Paris: Cerf, 1997).

[10]Tyconius, *Exposition of the Apocalypse*, trans. Francis X. Gumerlock (Washington, DC: Catholic University of America Press, 2017).

[11]Tyconius, *Exposition of the Apocalypse*, 7.

Tyconius's *Exposition* was written after a period of persecution of Donatists, of which Tyconius had been one. Rather than finding in Revelation the time of the antichrist and the end of the world, Tyconius interpreted John's visions as figurative of the struggles facing the church in the period between the incarnation and the second coming of Christ.[12] The satanic forces of the text represented worldly and decadent ecclesiastical powers. The two witnesses of Revelation 11 were not seen as persons from the past or present but as symbolic of the church holding the two Testaments. Similarly, a corporate identity was granted the antichrist, not as a specific person but as a body, the *corpus diaboli*, omnipresent evil and false Christians.

Tyconius "completely neutralized the millenarianism of the Apocalypse by referring the thousand years of the chaining up of Satan to the incarnation."[13] Backus continues,

> However, while doing away with the messianic interregnum [Rev 20:1-3], the Donatist did not minimize the importance of the Apocalypse as the text of the latter days, seeing himself as living at the end of time. Taking the cosmic week as the basic scheme of the duration of the world, he thought that Christ was born halfway through the sixth day, the seventh day being already situated after the Last Judgment. The three and half years of Apc 12 thus stood for 350 years, the period of the church's testimony. By the time Tyconius was writing, 850 years of the "sixth day" had passed, which meant that around 150 years were left until the Last Judgment.[14]

Augustine of Hippo (354–430) also influenced the Reformers' thinking on Revelation. Three points are important for the use of Augustine's theology by sixteenth-century commentators. First, with respect to the millennium, in *De civitate Dei* 20.7-20 he adopts Tyconius's interpretation of one thousand years, beginning with the chaining of Satan at the incarnation. He writes that the millennium (Rev 20:2) runs from the incarnation to the second coming of Christ as associated with the last judgment. In his *Sermon* 259, he adopts a millenarian position and envisages a period of earthly peace for the righteous before the final resurrection. Second, while believing he was in the last days, what interests Augustine most is not the days left to the millennium but rather, as Backus writes, "the identity of 'the devil' and the relative nature of both his captivity and his release. For Augustine as for Tyconius, 'the devil' represents all the wicked and the enemies of the Christian church, whose power is contained by Christ."[15]

A third point of interest relates to a spiritual resurrection. The first resurrection for Augustine is that life of true believers during the time of the chaining of Satan, a sort of spiritual millennium. As Backus says, "The spiritual school of the exegesis of the Apocalypse which was to dominate the Western interpretations of the book for several centuries was thus born."[16] In the medieval period, this was especially visible in Primasius and Bede, both of them making use of Tyconius while adopting his work to ecclesiastical use.

[12]Tyconius, *Exposition of the Apocalypse*, 177.

[13]Backus, *Reformation Readings*, xiii; see Tyconius, *Exposition of the Apocalypse*, 130. The same period of time is designated by 1,260 days, forty-two months, and three and a half days (see Tyconius's comments on Rev 11:3, 9; 12:6).

[14]Backus, *Reformation Readings*, xiii-xiv; see Tyconius, *Exposition of the Apocalypse*, 176-77.

[15]Backus, *Reformation Readings*, xiv.

[16]Backus, *Reformation Readings*, xiv.

The oldest Greek commentary on Revelation is said to be that of Oecumenius (early sixth century), probably a contemporary and supporter of Severus, monophysite patriarch of Antioch (c. 465–538).[17] While there remains debate as to the identity of Oecumenius, he appears to be, like Origen, interested in the spiritual or intellectual meaning of the text rather than a literal meaning. This alignment is indicative of a strong mystical interpretation. Oecumenius draws out the layered symbolism of the text by turning to the Hebrew prophets, particularly Zechariah.[18]

Also of importance is Primasius (d. c. 560), who was bishop of Hadrumetum and primate of Byzacena, in North Africa.[19] His commentary on Revelation makes use of the commentary of Tyconius. A Latin contemporary of Oecumenius, Primasius was also drawn to a spiritual interpretation of the text and wrote in the tradition of Tyconius.[20] His allegorical commentary can be seen to represent a symbolic interpretation through the tenth century.[21]

Turning to the West, it is important to mention Caesarius of Arles (468/470–542), a Gallic bishop, administrator, preacher, and theologian. Caesarius foresaw the institutional shape of medieval Christendom and also focused on the idea of the millennium. This focus is given graphic orientation in the *Commentary on the Apocalypse*, a book written in the eighth century by Spanish monk and theologian Beatus of Liebana (730–785) and copied and illustrated in manuscript in works called "Beati" during the tenth and eleventh centuries. "Beati" also refers to any manuscript copy of this work, especially the twenty-seven extant illuminated copies.

The influence of these Greek and patristic commentaries on exegetes in the sixteenth century primarily concerned a hermeneutical orientation that affirmed recapitulation. While some tension existed in the church of the second and third centuries around an earlier literal interpretation, Tyconius's orientation and affirmation of the figurative and corporate identity of the church as Christ's body, granting also a corporate body to the devil, was carried forward to the Carolingian period. This contributed to the idea that European Christianity was favored by God.

2. Early Western Latin exegetical tradition. A lively exegetical tradition of the interpretation of Revelation took place in the Latin churches in the West.[22] Interpretation of apocalyptic literature in Eastern Orthodoxy tended not to advance beyond early Greek and patristic literature, except in Kievan Russia of the thirteenth century. However, an awakened interest in the Apocalypse can be discerned in the Carolingian age with Bede "the Venerable" (c. 673–735), whose commentary on Revelation evinces historical movement under apocalyptic symbolism. Together with Ambrosius Autpertus (d. 778/781), Bede moved interpretation forward to the sharpened historical and

[17]The text was rediscovered by Franz Diekamp. See Oecumenius, *The Complete Commentary of Oecumenius on the Apocalypse, ed.* H. C. Hoskier (Ann Arbor: University of Michigan Press, 1928), 1-25.

[18]Oecumenius, *Commentary on the Apocalypse*, trans. John N. Suggit (Washington, DC: Catholic University of America Press, 2006), 4.

[19]M. L. W. Laistner, *Thought and Letters in Western Europe: A.D. 500 to 900*, 2nd ed. (Ithaca, NY: Cornell University Press, 1957), 114.

[20]*Primasius, Comentariorius super Apocalypsim* (PL 68.793-936). Others who follow Tyconius are summarized by Bousset, *Die Offenbarung Johannis*, pp. 65-72.

[21]Bousset finds Primasius's adoption of Tyconius's exegetical method of recapitulation important for later exegetes who will follow Primasius (see *Die Offenbarung Johannis*).

[22]Matthew Gabriele and John T. Palmer, eds., *Apocalypse and Reform from Late Antiquity to the Middle Ages* (New York: Routledge, 2018); K. Emmerson and Bernard McGinn, *The Apocalypse in the Middle Ages* (Ithaca, NY: Cornell University Press, 1993).

polemical exegesis associated with apocalyptic thought in the twelfth and thirteenth centuries.[23] In the introduction to his commentary Bede acknowledges dependence on Tyconius and lists Tyconius's seven exegetical rules.[24] The thrust of his work is typological rather than allegorical.[25] It is more attuned to historical models in a fixed biblical pattern than to symbolic truth. Bede shows a greater interest in history than either Tyconius or Primasius. It is still the case, Bede argues, that the world has entered its sixth and last age.[26] Into this thinking drawn from Augustine (*De civitate Dei* 22.30; see also 22.77), Bede finds an integral sense of development, a process like that which he observed within each day of creation: initial creative activity, development, and decline.[27]

Bede's intent was to divide Revelation into seven sections or summaries, which became the seven visions, the standard division of the text.[28] This would be of importance to sixteenth-century commentators on the text. Backus describes Bede's seven divisions:

> The first section comprises the address to the seven churches which represent the church universal and the promise of the return of the Son (Apc 1–3). The second section describes the opening of the seven seals of the book in which the Lamb will read the conflicts and triumphs that the church has been confronting since the Incarnation. The order of opening is maintained until the sixth seal; the contents of the six seals are then recapitulated in a narrative section, before the narrator moves on to the seventh seal (Apc 4–8.5). The third section follows the same pattern, depicting the same events in the form of seven trumpets (Apc 8.6–11.19). The fourth section (Apc 12–14) describes the joys and tribulations of the church, while the fifth "afflicts the earth with seven plagues" (Apc 15–16). The sixth section describes the judgment on the great whore, Babylon (Apc 17–20), and the seventh (Apc 21–22) describes the heavenly Jerusalem and the eternal peace after the Last Judgment.[29]

Bede used the seals of Revelation to picture a similar division in the sixth age, as in every other, in distinction from Augustine, who had left the last period undifferentiated.[30] The opening of the first seal was symbolic of the primitive church's triumph. The next three seals reveal forms of

[23]*Bede, Explanatio Apocalypsis* (PL 93.129-206). Wilhelm Kamlah maintains that the door from the patristic to the medieval age is Bede and Ambrosius Autpertus. See Kamlah, *Apokalypse und Geschichtstheologie: Die mittelalterliche Auslegung der Apokalypse vor Joachin von Fiore* (Berlin: Emil Ebering, 1935), 12-13. The awakened interest in apocalyptic speculation in the Carolingian age is illustrated by C. Heitz as a part of his general thesis, followed here, that "every profound change in society has been triggered by a notable vogue for apocalyptic thought." ("Chaque profond changement de societe a ete procede par une vogue notable de la pensée apocalyptique.") See Heitz, "Retentissement de l'Apocalypse dans l'art de l'epoque carolingienne," in *L'Apocalypse*, ed. Yves Christe (Geneva: Droz, 1979), 217.

[24]Bede, *Explanatio Apocalypsis* (PL 93.131-33). Backus writes, "The Apocalypse was thus stabilized in the spiritual and ecclesiological realm. However, changing social conditions soon dictated a different way of reading the text" (*Reformation Readings*, xv).

[25]Gerald Bonner argues for the dominance of typological thinking in Bede's works in *Saint Bede in the Tradition of Western Apocalyptic Commentary* (Newcastle upon Tyne: J. and P. Bealls, 1966), 5-31.

[26]Richard K. Emmerson gives a tabular presentation of these ages in *Antichrist in the Middle Ages: A Study of Medieval Apocalypticism, Art, and Literature* (Seattle: University of Washington Press, 1981), 18.

[27]R. W. Southern writes, "Each age acquired a distinct momentum . . . an act of restoration, succeeded by a period of divergent development, leading to a general disaster which set the scene for the new act of restoration." See Southern, "Presidential Address: Aspects of the European Tradition of Historical Writing. Vol. 2: Hugh of St. Victor and the Idea of Historical Development," *Transactions of the Royal Historical Society* 21 (1971): 162.

[28]Rodney L. Petersen, *Preaching in the Last Days: The Theme of "Two Witnesses" in the Sixteenth and Seventeenth Centuries* (Oxford: Oxford University Press, 1993), 28-30.

[29]Backus, *Reformation Readings*, xiv-xv.

[30]Bede divides his commentary into three books, which conflate apocalyptic imagery in the manner prescribed by Tyconius's sixth rule.

warfare against the church: the attack of tyrants, consequent martyrdom, false brethren, and heretics. The fifth seal, not a part of the historical sequence, reveals the glory of deceased martyrs. The sixth seal represents the time of antichrist's persecution. The seventh seal marks the beginning of eternal rest. "As well as 'conveniently' dividing the text into easily distinguishable sections, it had the advantage of concealing any millenarian tendencies of the text and of focusing the reader's attention on the trials and tribulations of the church since the Incarnation. In other words, it provided an ecclesiological as well as a spiritual framework."[31]

A strong moral thrust is added to the temporal tendencies found in Bede's work by the commentary on Revelation by Ambrosius Autpertus. Intent on discovering the mystical or spiritual sense of the text, he not only follows Bede but also draws on the allegorical and recapitulative exegesis of Tyconius and Primasius. Autpertus's moral interests are developed in relation to Jerome and Gregory the Great. Israel's prophets are held up as examples for moral modeling.

In the commentary attributed to Alcuin (c. 735–804), the Carolingian "schoolmaster," a work that evinces the influence of Bede and Autpertus, Bede's division of history and Tyconius's exegetical rules are first cited as guiding principles. Alcuin notes the work of Victorinus and Tyconius and then discusses the spiritual value to be gained by studying Revelation. When Alcuin addresses the question of the identity of the witnesses of Revelation 11, he notes the interpretation of Victorinus but believes it is better to understand them literally and not as the revivified Enoch and Elijah. Yet, following Tyconius's fourth exegetical rule, he concludes that one may find in their persons a figurative description of the church. This church is based on two Testaments, two peoples (Jew and Gentile), and two love commandments. Alcuin adds an additional dyad, two kinds of martyrdom, physical and monastic, and concludes that the time of their ministry is the entire age of the church.

The witnesses and their foe, antichrist, are perceived symbolically in Haimo of Halberstadt (d. 853). The prophets of Revelation 11 preach repentance and work in their humility for restitution. The whole church is understood in their persons and preaching, both in the present as well as at the end of history. He adds, pointedly, that at the time of their appearance prior to the reign of antichrist, there will be a spirit of deception and persecution, but this will not destroy the work of the church.[32]

This recapitulative, allegorical, and at times typological interpretation that emerged in medieval interpretation of Revelation is continued in several other commentators of interest to sixteenth-century exegetes of the Apocalypse. They include Walafrid Strabo (c. 808–849), Berengaudus (ninth century), Anselm of Laon (d. 1117), and Bruno of Segni (d. 1123). Both Strabo and Berengaudus added historical concerns in their understanding of apocalyptic symbolism. Strabo carefully correlates periods of history since the inception of the church with the seven seals. Berengaudus connects a long systematic outline of history with the seals and their apocalyptic symbolism. God's saints, the witnesses of Revelation 11, are tested in seven days of world history, as

[31]Backus, *Reformation Readings*, xv.
[32]Petersen, *Preaching in the Last Days*, 29.

was the faith of Israel in its seven-day journey around Jericho. The angel of Revelation 10 is Christ at his incarnation. The book given to John (Rev 10:9) is the Scriptures, to be preached by John, by all apostles, and by Christian teachers. This history continues in Revelation 11, which pictures the church from the expulsion of the Jews (Rev 11:1-2) to their return. They will be called back to true worship by Enoch and Elijah, the two who will fulfill the prophecy of Revelation 11 in a specific way and fight antichrist. They will precede the second coming of the Lord as John the Baptist preceded the first.

The question of the identity of the witnesses of Revelation 11 raises the question of the identity of the antichrist. The rules for interpretation laid down by Tyconius allowed for a corporate identity as well as individual identity. The play *Antichrist* (c. 1160), dependent on the work of Adso Dervensis (d. 992), presents one of the more complete apocalyptic plots found in medieval literature. It introduces the growing use of apocalyptic themes, particularly their politicization in the papal-imperial conflicts that characterize the period ahead. With the Carolingian Renaissance in the rearview mirror, the play *Antichrist* leads into a period in which the witnesses will be called on as symbolic representations of good versus evil among competing claims of social legitimacy.

Antichrist suggests insight into sixteenth-century conflict. The play offers implicit criticism of the medieval church, which under Pope Gregory VII had sought to reorganize itself independent of the political imperium. Antichrist is at first defeated by the Germanic king, then converts the king by his miracles. Next, *Synagoga* and the Jews are converted by antichrist, but Enoch and Elijah draw them to Christ. These prophets preach for three and a half years and "unmask" antichrist but are finally killed by him. He, in turn, is destroyed by Christ. The appearances and work of the witnesses help to mark the last stage of history as time hastens to the last judgment.

Whether in drama or apocalyptic commentary, symbolic representatives of ethical dualism emerged for reformist purposes in an envisioned development of history. By the eleventh century new questions were being raised about the church's place in society. These pertained not only to issues of political order, such as how church and civil ideals were to relate, whether canon law was definitive in civil court, and who was to govern the church. Such questions inevitably opened the debate about the nature of history and of historical periodization, which had been worked on by authorities such as Augustine and Bede. In different ways commentators and social theorists of the day sought a deeper understanding of patterns of political and religious legitimacy through society's heritage of biblical narrative. Augustine's (and Tyconius's) sixth age, contemporary history for medieval Europe, had been defined through recourse to such narratives and in particular to apocalyptic symbolism.

3. Medieval Latin church and reform movements. Such a symbolic understanding of history was developed by Rupert of Deutz (1070–1129/1135?) in support of monastic reform with attendant social implications. Known for his historico-prophetic method of interpretation, which according to Wilhelm Kamlah by the sixteenth century became integrated into a spiritual hermeneutic, prophecy was united to politics.[33] The two characteristic representatives of this exegetical approach are Rupert of Deutz and Nicholas of Lyra (see further below on Lyra's interpretive approach). According to Backus, "The basic feature of the historical approach was to divide the Apocalypse into six rather than seven parts and to read it as a history of salvation from Adam until a certain date in the present or proximate future. Depending on the *terminus ad quem* chosen by the exegete, John thus became either a historian or simultaneously a historian and a prophet." She goes on to contend, "For Rupert of Deutz, John was basically a historian and the Apocalypse a history of salvation from Adam until the Council of Nicaea, although the commentary also contains numerous references to Rupert's own time and to the life of the church in general."[34]

History was becoming a mode of prophecy. History was viewed as the unfolding or historical working out of the trinitarian Godhead (Father, Son, and Holy Spirit), divided into periods reflective of the personalities and work of each of the members of the Trinity: a historical age before the law (i.e., before God had begun to reveal God's nature [*ante legem*]), an age characterized by the revelation of his law for humankind (*sub lege*), an age revealing God's graciousness (*sub gratia*), and eventually a unifying age of the Spirit. Each age was further divided into periods characterized by particular virtues that were at the same time proper for the whole church through all history. These virtues marked a growth in grace through history and provided a set of spiritual symbols and examples available for polemical purpose.

Rupert's eschatological mysticism is reflected in his treatment of antichrist, the beast of Revelation (Rev 13:1-18; 16:13; 19:20) but a term not found in Revelation (see 1 Jn 2:18; 2 Jn 7), and the two witnesses. In Rupert's elaborate historical scheme, antichrist is not denied a final appearance but may be seen spiritually as internal decay and hypocrisy.[35]

Honorius of Autun (early twelfth century) continued the interest in historical periodization noted with Rupert of Deutz. Honorius marked history by a continuous line of ten *ordines* or states of the church (five before and five after Christ), each indicating a specific conflict between God and Satan. Similar tendencies are found in Otto of Freising (c. 1110–1158) and Hildegard of Bingen (1098–1179).

In the more optimistic historical understanding of Anselm of Havelberg (1100–1158), the new monastic orders in the church, pointedly the friars, Dominicans and Franciscans, are given deepened spiritual significance. Anselm's use of apocalyptic symbolism to understand reform adds significance. Successive states of the church, natural changes or mutation, are foreshadowed in the seven apocalyptic seals. The present church is located under the fourth of seven periods, a time of conflict between true and false disciples. The end of history is still distant.

---

[33]Kamlah, *Apokalypse und Geschichtstheologie*, 12-13.

[34]Backus, *Reformation Readings*, xvi.

[35]See Backus, *Reformation Readings*, xvi: "The sea of glass evokes to Rupert the crossing of the Red Sea in the Old Testament, and baptism in the New Testament. Both denote liberation. The Christocentric nature of his commentary coupled with his interest in the Old Testament and his interest in the history of the early church in general was probably what made Rupert's commentary popular with reformers like Sebastian Meyer."

More immediate conflict characterizes the work of Gerhoh of Reichersberg (1093–1169), as he put the periodization of church history in the service of reform, thus shaping its prophetic thrust. Despite Gerhoh's commitment to holiness and social purity, a certain ambiguity in his work exists as he first wrote in defense of the papacy (viewing Emperor Henry IV as antichrist). Following Jerome's reflection on the two witnesses of Revelation 11, Gerhoh found in these symbols a spiritual work of the Law and Prophets in the church, without denying a possible literal interpretation, arguing that before the end new spiritual men (possibly the friars) living in a state of apostolic purity would reform the church. Later, Gerhoh grew disillusioned with the church's leadership and charted a less obvious path of reform: the black night of history is periodically broken by the night watches of those who name evil and deception for what they are.

4. Joachim of Fiore and his successors. The optimistic historical perspective just referenced came as the result of the exegetical work of Joachim of Fiore (c. 1132–1202), whose work ensured the greater visibility of spiritual renewal and established an apocalyptic tradition from which Protestants and others drew in the years ahead.[36] Joachim wrote his commentary around 1195, but it was not published until 1527. This was due to the papal condemnation of the Franciscan Gerard of Borgo San Donnino in 1254 for his proclamation of the Eternal Gospel, excerpts of which were drawn from Joachim's work. This was a Gospel that was intended to supersede the Old and New Testaments. Joachim's own doctrine was condemned in 1215 by the Lateran Council and by the Council of Arles in 1263.[37]

Joachim's ideas underlay some of the commentaries of the sixteenth century. Backus writes,

> Two features of Joachim's hermeneutic would have been of interest to the Protestant commentators of the Apocalypse—first, his idea that after a series of struggles there would emerge an age in which the faithful would be in some sense "closer to God" than hitherto, and, second, his idea that the Antichrist was an unspecified individual (emanating from Rome) who would combine all the heresies. The latter idea in fact captured the imagination of the spiritual Franciscans long before the Reformation.[38]

Joachim divided Revelation into eight parts. Unlike Bede, Joachim begins part seven with Revelation 20 (not Rev 21) and ends part seven at Revelation 20:10. For Joachim, part eight begins with Revelation 20:11, the vision of the last judgment, and carries on to the end of the book, Revelation 22, which defines a state of eternal rest.

Revelation encapsulates the latter two *status* in history, according to Joachim the Age of the Son and the Age of the Holy Spirit. The first six parts of the commentary depict the Age of the Son (forty-two generations, each about thirty years). Part one, which comprises Revelation 1–3,

[36]I follow Backus, *Reformation Readings*, xvii-xviii.

[37]Riedl Matthias, *A Companion to Joachim of Fiore* (Leiden: Brill, 2017); Marjorie Reeves, *Joachim of Fiore and the Prophetic Future* (New York: Sutton, 1999); Kevin Madigan, *Medieval Christianity: A New History* (New Haven, CT: Yale University Press, 2015); Julia Eva Wannenmacher, *Joachim of Fiore and the Influence of Inspiration* (New York: Routledge, 2016); Bernard McGinn, *Apocalyptic Spirituality, Classics of Western Spirituality* (Mahwah, NJ: Paulist Press, 1979).

[38]Backus, *Reformation Readings*, xviii.

contains seven generations and represents the struggle of the apostles against the synagogue, or the Jews. Part two, which comprises Revelation 4:1–8:1, illustrates the struggle of martyrs with pagan persecutions. Part three, which comprises Revelation 8:2–11:18, depicts the doctors of the church against heretics up until the Constantinian settlement. Part four, which comprises Revelation 11:19–14:20, illustrates the struggle of new monastic orders, or more precisely with friars, against Islam. Part five, which comprises Revelation 15:1–16:17, shows the conflict between the Church of Rome and the Holy Empire. Part six, which comprises Revelation 16:18–19:21, shows the struggle of spiritual men (represented in two new religious orders, Franciscans and Dominicans) against the dragon and the two beasts, understood to be "Saladin and the 'maximus Antichristus,' a person who combines the heresy of Islam and all the Western heresies."[39] The Age of the Son would come to an end around 1260.

Part seven begins the Age of the Holy Spirit, which comprises Revelation 20:1-10. Under these verses Satan is chained and the church freed from persecution. Following a final conflict, the contemplative order takes control of the church and promotes spiritual renewal. There is spiritual progress in this part, but Joachim is not a hard and fast millenarian. Revelation 20 distinguishes between the chaining of Satan, which does not begin until the defeat of the beast and the false prophet, and the one thousand years, symbolic in nature, which begins with the resurrection of Christ. Part eight, which comprises Revelation 20:11 to the end of Revelation 22, describes the last judgment and heavenly new Jerusalem.[40]

That Joachim of Fiore was influential, even within his own generation, is without debate.[41] Who his heirs were is another question: whether the free-thinking sects of the later Middle Ages or the Franciscans and others within the church.[42] When the orders of Dominic and Francis appeared in the thirteenth century, they seemed to express concretely the aspirations embodied in Joachim's prophecies.[43] Within the Franciscan Order itself there developed a strong attachment to the Joachite prophecies, particularly among the spirituals with their strict adherence to Francis's Rule.[44] Having caught the imagination of his age, Francis of Assisi (1181–1226) embodied for many the dramatic sense of history defined by Joachim's figural imagery.[45]

[39]Backus, *Reformation Readings*, xvii. Saladin was a contemporary of Joachim.

[40]Backus, *Reformation Readings*, xviii.

[41]Morton Bloomfield and Marjorie Reeves, "The Penetration of Joachimism into Northern Europe," *Speculum* 29 (1954): 772-93; see also Marjorie Reeves, *The Influence of Prophecy in the Later Middle Ages: A Study in Joachimism* (Oxford: Clarendon, 1969), 37-44.

[42]Herbert Grundmann contends that Joachim's proper heirs were the free-thinking sects attempting to break with religious authoritarianism. Grundmann later modified this view, offering them a measure of orthodoxy. See Grundmann, *Studien uber Joachim* (Leipzig: Teubner, 1927), 182. Ernst Benz held that the spiritual Franciscans were the heirs of Joachim but that their "reformation" was rejected by ecclesiastical authority. See Benz, *Ecclesial Spiritualis: Kirchenidee und Geschichtstheologie der Franziskanischen Reformation* (Stuttgart: W. Kollhammer, 1934).

[43]Reeves cites the joint encyclical issued in 1255 by the generals of the two orders, Humbert de Romanis and John of Parma, describing the two orders in Joachim's parallel twos (*Influence of Prophecy*, 146-47).

[44]Reeves, *Influence of Prophecy*, 45-58; cf. Ruth Kestenberg-Gladstein, "The Third Reich: A Fifteenth Century Polemic Against Joachimism, and Its Background," *Journal of the Warburg and Courtald Institute* 18 (1955): 245-95. She holds that Joachim's followers generally held three ideas: (1) an imminent future will soon overtake an imperfect present, (2) the present is evolving into that future perfected state, and (3) a heightened sense of anticipation is present among the believers.

[45]Reeves writes about the Franciscans, "Thus they transformed Joachim's system into a drama shaped by the clues he had given and leading towards a final act which would embody his expectation. . . . For those who were too impatient to wait for divine

From the middle of the thirteenth century, pseudo-Joachite works such as the *Commentary on Jeremiah* and the works of Salimbene of Parma and Gerard of Borgo San Donnino portrayed an impending sense of the end of history that appealed to new orders in the church as well as to Apostolic Brethren, flagellants, and other late-thirteenth century movements. Even in the work of Bonaventure (1221–1274), author of the official biography of Francis, the *Legenda Maior* (1263), Francis was more than just another saint. He is said to have come in the spirit and power of Elijah. He is identified as the second angel of Revelation (Rev 7:2).[46]

For Peter John Olivi (c. 1248–1298) and Ubertino da Casale (c. 1259–1330), the coming of the person of Francis signaled the beginning of Joachim's Age of the Spirit. Ubertino wrote *The Tree of the Crucified Life of Jesus* (1305), drawing relationships between his order and the ministry of Jesus and commenting on them in connection to Revelation. In this classic expression of apocalyptic mysticism, the two beasts (Rev 13:1, 11) have arisen, Boniface VIII and Benedict XI, but are countered by the renovation of the evangelical life in Francis, the second (spiritual) of three comings of Christ.[47] As Backus writes, "Slowly, the idea of the Roman Antichrist took shape and was ready for use by the reformers. However, at the same time, the Franciscan exploitation of the Apocalypse certainly did not improve the reputation of the book."[48]

Spiritual apocalyptic speculation continued in such persons as Jacopone da Todi (c. 1230–1306) and Angelo of Clareno (c. 1255–1337).[49] Thomas Aquinas (1225–1274) emerged as the chief critic of their theology of history.[50] The Joachite view of history tended to find more of a role for outstanding prophets. Francis was a new man in spiritualist exegesis, effecting a new covenant with a Spirit-filled band of prophets.[51] Aquinas's theology of history ran differently. His two eras of old and new law (Old Testament, New Testament) appear to leave little room for fresh prophetic insight and even pump the brakes on religious enthusiasm. The state of the new law (the gospel) is imperfect, but no state of present life can be better than that embodied in and brought by Christ.

Thomas argued pointedly: (1) perfection can only be achieved in heaven, not in some further age on earth; and (2) the church's theology of the Spirit has emphasized that the Spirit was given when Christ was glorified—not separately or at a different time. Thomas emphasizes immanence over economy with respect to the Trinity and history. The gospel of Christ is the only gospel of

intervention to reshape the authority of the Church the revolutionary implications of Joachimism offered an opportunity to cast themselves in the key roles in the final age" (*Influence of Prophecy*, 62-63, 67).

[46]Bonaventure, *Legenda Maior S Francisci*, preface.2; 13.10; Marion A. Habig, ed., *St. Francis of Assisi: Writings and Early Biographies: English Omnibus of the Sources for the Life of St. Francis* (Chicago: Franciscan Herald, 1973), 632, 736. See Bernard McGinn, "The Significance of Bonaventure's Theology of History," *Journal of Religion* 58 supplement (1978): 565-81.

[47]Gordon Leff, *Heresy in the Later Middle Ages: The Relation of Heterodoxy to Dissent c. 1250–c. 1450* (New York: Barnes and Noble, 1967), 1:152-53.

[48]Backus, *Reformation Readings*, xviii.

[49]Bernard McGinn, *Visions of the End: Apocalyptic Traditions in the Middle Ages (New York: Columbia University Press, 1979)*, 205-7.

[50]Bernard McGinn, "The Abbot and the Doctors: Scholastic Reactions to the Radical Eschatology of Joachim of Fiore," *Church History* 40 (1971): 30-47; cf. Y. D. Gelnas, "La critique de Thomas d'Aquin sur l'exegese de Joachim de Fiore," in *Tommaso d'Aquino nel suo settino centenaria* (Rome, 1974), 1:368-75; Peter Meinhold, "Thomas von Aquin und Joachim von Fiore Deutung der Geschichte," *Speculum* 27 (1976): 66-76.

[51]Olivi's sermon on Francis as filled with the Spirit so as to become another man follows 1 Sam 10:6. See Ernst Benz, "Die Kategorian des eschatologischen Zeitbewusstseins," *Deutsche Vierteljahrsschrift für Literaturwissenschaft und Geistesgeschichte* 11 (1933): 203-5, 215.

the kingdom. It is to be publicly proclaimed throughout the world. When the church has been established among all peoples, then the end will come (ST 1a2ae, 106, 4).

Aquinas's criticism of Joachite history was pointedly refuted by Arnold of Villanova (c. 1240–1312), for whom Thomas was prefigured in the star that fell from heaven (Rev 9:1).[52] Disappointed with the papacies of Boniface VIII and Clement V, Arnold promoted an apocalyptic piety of great lay appeal with hopes focused on Frederick II, Aragonese king of Sicily (1296–1337).[53] But it was another Franciscan, Peter Aureoli, and his fellow Franciscan Nicholas of Lyra who carried interpretation forward. Both viewed Revelation as a "prophetic compendium" of church between the two advents.[54] Aureoli drew on the work of Joachim and Olivi. He marked out seven epochs of church history, the seventh falling after judgment. Many of the favorite spiritualist images were turned to support the church. For example, Gregory VII, not Francis, is seen to be the sixth trumpeting angel. Still, appearing in the sixth epoch are the two witnesses of Revelation 11, the Franciscan and Dominican Orders. The first resurrection (Rev 20:5) is the renewal of piety through their efforts.[55]

Nicholas of Lyra (1270–1340), regent master at Paris, is a figure often cited by sixteenth-century exegetes.[56] Lyra drew widely on the work of Jewish scholars, particularly the commentator Rashi (1040–1105), in his effort to combat allegory in favor of a more literal sense of the text. In his discussion of Revelation (1329), he identified the two witnesses of Revelation 11 as Pope Silverius (c. 536) and Patriarch Menas of Constantinople (522).[57] The significance of this identification lies not so much in these individuals as in the precedent that was set for a specific identification of the prophetic vision with historical events.[58] Such focus was of determinative influence through the balance of the later Middle Ages and into the sixteenth century.

5. Revelation and the dawn of the Reformation. The history of patristic and medieval commentaries and their use in Carolingian and Gregorian reforms, together with the heightened spiritual interests of Joachite interpretation, created an incendiary atmosphere for the historical interpretation of efforts at church and social reform by the fifteenth and sixteenth centuries. The path to the commentaries written on Revelation in the sixteenth century must go by way of the late medieval Hussite revolt in central Europe. The unity offered to European identity in a postclassical Roman world, seen many years earlier in the work of Caesarius of Arles as found in the visionary text of

[52]Arnold can be seen as the second of three types of Franciscans: radical followers of Peter John Olivi, exponents of a spiritual lay movement, and (with Peter Aureoli) those faithful to the church. See Ernst Benz, "Die Geschichtstheologie der Franziskaner-spiritualen des 13 und 14 Jahrhunderts nach neuen Quellen." *Zeitschrift fur Kirchengeschichte* 52 (1933): 92.

[53]Benz, "Die Geschichtstheologie der Franziskaner-spiritualen," 99-111.

[54]The term is Charles's, from *Studies in the Apocalypse*, 27-30.

[55]Benz, "Die Geschichtstheologie der Franziskaner-spiritualen," 113-19.

[56]Philip D. W. Krey and Lesley Smith, eds., *Nicholas of Lyra: The Senses of Scripture*, Studies in the History of Christian Thought (Leiden: Brill, 2000).

[57]*Nicholas of Lyra, Postlla super Apostolorum, Epistolas canonicales, et Apocalypsim* (Mantua: Paulus de Butzbach, 1480). The pages are unnumbered, but the text is divided into chapter headings.

[58]The seals describe the events in history through Domitian; the seven trumpets, history from Arius through Patriarch Anthemus. Revelation 12 pictures the conflict between Chosroes of Persia and the Byzantine general and emperor Heraclius. The first beast is the son of Chosroes, while the second is Muhammad. Revelation 14 describes Charlemagne, the seven vials the history of the Crusades, and Rev 20 the conflict between Pope Calixtus and Henry V.

Revelation, was now about to face its greatest challenge. What happened would determine the extent to which a common European culture would continue intact.

It is helpful to begin a survey of the influences drawn on by sixteenth-century commentators to assess their historical context with Matthew of Janov (c. 1355–1394), in whom is found a polemical periodization of history. The Hussite reform movement had its origin in the imperial desire of the king, Emperor Charles IV (1347–1378), and in a succession of preachers beginning with Conrad of Waldhausen, called to preach in Prague. Critical of privileged wealth and clerical simony, Conrad anticipated many of the themes of interest to sixteenth-century commentators, particularly the visible purity of the church, Christ's body. This theme runs throughout the movement from Milic of Kromeriz (d. 1374), often referred to as the father of the Bohemian reform, into the split between Utraquists and Taborites to the later Bohemian Brethren. In his brief work *Libellus de Antichristo*, Milic reminds his readers of the close connection of the proclamation of the gospel, the coming of antichrist, and the Lord's return to rule. On the basis of detailed calculations, he was convinced that antichrist was already at large. Placing his confidence in the promise of a new Jerusalem, he worked to establish a foretaste of this hope by founding a school for preachers and a house for repentant prostitutes in Prague. Frequent reception of the Eucharist in bread and wine became the eschatological symbol of one's new spiritual identity in Christ.

Matthew of Janov was the chief biblical theorist for the Czech reform. His primary work, *Regulae veteris et novi testimenti* (begun in 1388), had as its aim the recovery of the apostolic life. Critical of papal or curial institutionalism and moral hypocrisy, it distinguished true from false Christians against an eschatological horizon. Reform was to be carried out by a holy people within the existing church. With the triumph of ecclesial hypocrisy (c. 1200), antichrist had been slowly growing in power. Rather than being some figure reserved for the future (Jew, pagan, or Saracen), antichrist was best understood as a hypocritical Christian, conceived corporately and spiritually, both singly and a body with many members.[59] At the height of antichrist's power, inspired prophets, preaching with the zeal, innocence, and humility of Enoch and Elijah, would begin to slay antichrist. This was the work of the preachers and teachers in the Bohemian reform, specifically that of Conrad of Waldhausen and Milic.[60]

Bohemian students were increasingly attracted to Oxford for study as the Western Schism (1378–1417) continued. This had the effect of adding the influence of John Wycliffe to the Bohemian reform. Jan Hus (d. 1415) employed much of Wycliffe's theology, particularly the idea of the indestructibility and purity of Christ's church, his mystical body and pure bride. This church was grounded in the grace of predestination, not in the habitual grace of the visible church. Adherence to the wrong church could mean complicity with an antichurch, even antichrist, an issue already implied by Janov. Schism could only come to the body of antichrist, not Christ's true body. The

[59]R. R. Betts, "The Regulae Veteris et Novi Testamenti of Matej z Janova," *Journal of Theological Studies* 32 (1931): 344-51. On the edition by V. Kybal, see Kestenberg-Gladstein, "Third Reich," 288n112, who sees stronger resemblances to Olivi than to Joachim. Leff finds Janov's ideas distinctly individual and dissimilar from either (*Heresy in the Later Middle Ages*, 615).

[60]Petersen, *Preaching in the Last Days*, 40-43; cf. Amadeo Molnar, "Le movement préhussite et la fin des temps," *Communio Viatorum* 1 (1958): 30.

current ecclesial turmoil raised the historical question of when antichrist had entered the institutional church. Wycliffe argued that after the church's first one thousand years Satan has been loosed in the world. The visible church declined markedly from that date despite the efforts of Francis and Dominic.[61]

In the Lollard commentary on Revelation, written by a student of Wycliffe, the two witnesses of Revelation 11 are identified with true doctrine and emerge triumphant over antichrist, the papacy. The eschatology of followers of Hus and Wycliffe was sharpened in its historical dimensions when Hus came under attack by the papacy. Called before the Council of Constance (1414), Hus was martyred on July 6, 1415. From 1415 on, Hus's martyrdom along with that of his fellow preacher, Jerome of Prague (c. 1370–1416), became for some the image and fulfillment of the death of the witnesses of Revelation 11.

The Hussite movement divided into Utraquists, who were moderates (emphasizing the laity's right to Communion of both bread and wine), and Taborists, those who were more radical and separatist (see Mount Tabor in Josh 19:22, in the New Testament identified with the Mount of Transfiguration). The militant Taborites read the political events of the times through an apocalyptic lens.[62] Tabor soon became a theological and political center filled with refugees, while Prague was identified with Babylon (Rev 18:4). Ensuing civil conflict and subsequent defeat led to the absorption of Taborites into another Hussite-influenced group, the Unity of the Brethren, known today as the Moravians (see John Amos Comenius, 1592–1670).

A prophetic, even apocalyptic horizon characterized the years leading up to the sixteenth century. The church drew on the rich exegetical heritage reaching back to its foundation and embedded in the christological assumptions separating synagogue Judaism from Messianic Judaism associated with Jesus.[63] There was literal interpretation of apocalyptic imagery, but a symbolic representation was added by Tyconius and furthered by Augustine. Tyconius's exegetical rules gave strength to the recapitulative methodology pioneered by Victorinus. In this the temporal or apocalyptic horizon was not completely lost, but it was muted. The Carolingian period grounded apocalyptic symbolism in historical movement. Drawn into the reformist impetus following the Gregorian reforms, interest in the imagery of an antichrist grew and became associated with Revelation. Interest in a spiritual age on earth, for which there would be spiritual prophets as forerunners, became envisioned in new orders and in Joachite exegesis. This history of exegetical understanding was placed within a framework of temporal periodization related to the septenary imagery of the text. Late medieval exegetes such as Nicholas of Lyra set the drama into a firm historical mold, matching prophetic vision with historical event. In the Hussite-Taborite movement the entire history of interpretation was drawn into contemporary politics.

[61]H. B. Workman, *John Wyclif: A Study of the English Medieval Church*, 2 vols. (Oxford: Oxford University Press, 1926). Workman discusses the prevalence of Joachite ideas at Oxford and Wycliffe's early attraction to the Franciscan spirituals, whom he later rejected (2:97-108).

[62]Leff, *Heresy in the Later Middle Ages*, 1-46. References to final witnesses and antichrist are found in the Taborite, *De Anatomia Antichristi* (1421).

[63]Paula Fredriksen, *When Christians Were Jews: The First Generation* (New Haven, CT: Yale University Press, 2018).

There was not a uniform way in which Protestants appropriated this tradition of the complex history of interpretation. Some rejected it outright; others followed it only at points and then cautiously. Some, more inclined to Joachite interests, to a spirituality and spiritual age on earth, adopted it wholly. Interpretation of Revelation affected Protestant-Roman Catholic polemics.[64] Generally, Protestant exegetes adopted a corporate or Tyconian reading of the text together with varying degrees of historical periodization, influenced in various revival movements, in particular by Joachite interpretation. As Backus argues,

> Lutherans saw the Reformation as an upheaval ushering in the Last Judgment just as John had predicted. The Zürich reformers saw it mainly as a movement affecting social ethics in the daily lives and behavior of states and individuals, which accounts for the practical tone of their exegesis. Neither they nor the Calvinists saw themselves as fulfilling John's prophecy to the letter in the sense that the Lutherans did.[65]

This is not to say that Catholic commentators in the sixteenth and seventeenth centuries did not use these texts.[66] Indeed, Protestant historicist appropriation helped to stimulate Jesuit preterist and futurist explanation of apocalyptic drama even as the book was interpreted in deeper literal, spiritualist, and proto-rationalist ways. This is delineated by George H. Williams in his study of the "radicals"—evangelical rationalists, spiritualists, and Anabaptists—of the Reformation.[67]

If the Reformation proper is viewed as two centuries of conflict extending from the Franco-Habsburg wars in Italy in the 1490s through to the onset of the Thirty Years' War of 1618–1648, then in the roughly one hundred years between Luther's two prefaces to Revelation in his translation of the Bible (1522, 1530) and the *Commentary on the Apocalypse* by David Pareus (1618) commentaries on Revelation gave vision to the violence of the times as well as to its deepest hopes for social order and moral renewal.

The work of Erasmus of Rotterdam set the stage for the early interpretation of Revelation in the sixteenth century. Luther quickly built on this scaffolding but was himself caught up in the early sixteenth-century apocalyptic fervor that was characteristic of radical Reformers such as Thomas Müntzer, Hans Hut, and Melchior Hoffman.[68] In their different approaches to interpretation—Erasmus emphasizing style and philology while Luther focused more on theology—they marked in broad strokes the exegetical positions taken by subsequent commentators.[69]

[64]The break with catholic universalism and developing use of history was clearly seen early on in the use of history for verification of ecclesial authenticity by Mathias Flacius Illyricus (Lutheran) and Robert Bellarmine (Roman Catholic). The inception of national churches across Europe replicated this process in different national settings. See, e.g., Felicity Heal, *Reformation in Britain and Ireland* (Oxford: Clarendon, 2003).

[65]Backus, *Reformation Readings*, 137-38.

[66]Ludovici ab Alcasar, *Vestigatio Arcani Sensus in Apocalpsi* (Antwerp: Heredes Martini Nutii, 1614, 1619), as a period of time in the first century (preterist); or, as argued by Francisco Ribera, *Commentarius in Apocalypsim* (Salamanca, Spain: Excudebat Petrus Lassus, 1585, 1591), as in the future (futurist). Protestant futurist views would be championed by the Plymouth Brethren leader John Nelson Darby (see Petersen, *Preaching in the Last Days*, 244-46).

[67]George H. Williams, *The Radical Reformation* (Philadelphia: Westminster, 1962).

[68]Peter Way, "A 'Lutheryan' Copy of St. Augustine," *Humanae Literae* 8 (2003): 69-116; *Lutheran Quarterly* 14, no. 4 (Winter 2000): 373-408; Petersen, *Preaching in the Last Days*, 59-119.

[69]Michael Massing, *Fatal Discord: Erasmus, Luther, and the Fight for the Western Mind* (New York: Harper One, 2018).

Most of the earlier influential commentaries on Revelation that affected sixteenth-century commentaries are from the churches of the West. Irena Backus summarizes the problems of canonicity for the churches of the early Reformation.[70] She argues that Erasmus's textual objections to the book and Luther's theological reticence with reference to it gradually gave way through the sixteenth century to the acceptance of Revelation as a book of New Testament prophecy that could answer the question of the meaning of history since the incarnation and the significance of the historical present. By tracing the history of the exegesis of the text of Revelation, this volume illustrates her contention.

Sixteenth-Century Commentaries

These sixteenth-century commentaries on Revelation and related literature in the Christian Bible provided a means to measure the church's fidelity to the gospel message. They offered pastoral encouragement for Christians confronted with opposition and persecution. Through their rich symbolism, they also offered a warning to those tempted to find profit or partnership with seductive worldly systems.

But commentaries on Revelation offered even more. They also gave vision to the search for reform and moral order in church and society. They provided cover to such ensuing conflict as the violence of the Peasants' Wars in German lands (1524–1525) and the Lutheran-inspired Schmalkaldic Wars from 1547, which was succeeded by the Reformed-inspired wars of religion between the 1560s and 1590s. This civil unrest was followed by the Thirty Years' War (1618–1648), with a continuing impact on English reforms and civil wars (1642–1651) and their shaping of colonial settlements.[71] In a word, it was a period of uncertainty.

The theological intentions in these sixteenth-century commentaries have sent continuing eddies of historical interpretation into twenty-first-century commentaries and schools of thought even as they pick up on themes developed in the early Western and medieval churches and schools.[72] Commentaries on Revelation serve as a distillation of medieval worldviews in Europe. They chart lines of direction in the modern world insofar as the latter remains connected to the biblical narrative for social interpretation.

The social upheaval in these hundred years, marked by the wars of reform and resettlement that were a part of the Reformation, exacerbated the biggest population movement in European history between the years that dismantled the western Roman Empire and the twentieth century's First and Second World Wars. This movement of European peoples involved a transplanting of population into previously largely uncharted lands by Europeans, later identified as colonialism.

[70]Backus, *Reformation Readings*, 3-36.

[71]Diarmaid MacCulloch, *The Reformation: A History* (New York: Viking, 2003); see also Mark Greengrass, *Christendom Destroyed: Europe 1517–1648* (New York: Viking, 2014). See also Carter Lindberg, *The European Reformations, 2nd ed.* (Malden, MA: Wiley-Blackwell, 2011), who sheds light on both the sixteenth century and our own.

[72]Examples of different schools of interpretation include Reformed, as with Kenneth Gentry, *Before Jerusalem Fell: Dating the Book of Revelation* (Tyler, TX: Institute for Christian Economics, 1998); dispensational, as with Clarence Larkin, *The Book of Revelation* (N.p.: CreateSpace, 2017); spiritual, as with Bruce Metzger, *Breaking the Code: Understanding the Book of Revelation*, rev. ed., updated by David A. deSilva (Nashville: Abingdon, 2019).

The divisions in apocalyptic thinking shaped theology from New England south along the Atlantic Seaboard and wherever the currents carried European settlement.

These hundred years were marked not only by the trauma of shifting patterns of conflict and population settlement but also by the kind of technological change we have only seen in contemporary times. Then it was Johannes Gutenberg and the invention of the movable-type printing press; today it is Bill Gates and a digital world. Commentaries on Revelation were a means to make sense of social change and order.

A new heaven and a new earth were being born as the Peace of Westphalia opened up a new historical era after 1648, referred to in philosophy as the Enlightenment. In his *Eicasmi* (Greek for "speculations," 1596), English reformer and commentator John Foxe used the exodus analogy for the faithful remnant in the Middle Ages now coming into its own, as did Continental theologian David Pareus in 1618. English New Testament scholar and exegete Thomas Brightman heralded God's work in the world through outpourings of the Spirit together with new learning led by England's new Constantine, Elizabeth I. A new era was being birthed in the following four areas, and Revelation served as midwife.[73]

1. Historical context
2. Theological themes
3. Interpretive issues
4. Historical reception of Revelation by radicals of the Reformation, Lutherans, the Reformed, and English Reformers

1. Historical context. The social and political context for this volume is framed by the appearance of Martin Luther's 1522 *Commentary on the New Testament* and the English translation of David Pareus's *Commentary on the Apocalypse* in 1644, the latter published at the onset of the Thirty Years' War.[74] Andrew Cunningham and Ole Peter Grell present these years as an entire age subject to the underlying cause for apocalyptic anxiety—the human and the natural disasters of the sixteenth and seventeenth centuries.[75] This period was already foreshadowed in Albrecht Dürer's famous 1498 woodcut *The Four Horsemen of the Apocalypse*. It raised questions about the relation of an apocalyptic mentality and the confessionalization of Christianity, differences in the intensity and character of end-time outlooks in a time of social change. While three of the horses depicted war, famine, and death, the white horse was symbolic of the second coming of Christ.

A spirit of confessionalism tinged with apocalyptic fervor followed the Imperial Diet of Augsburg (1530), called by Holy Roman Emperor Charles V to deal with the defense of the empire against the Turkish threat, with disagreements about Christian doctrine and practice subsequent to Lutheran unrest, and with issues related to policy and public well-being in the empire. The diet, or conference, confirmed the resolutions embodied in the Edict of Worms (1521), causing the

[73]Brightman, *Revelation*, 123.
[74]Peter H. Wilson, *The Thirty Years War: Europe's Tragedy* (Cambridge, MA: Belknap, 2009), 25-40.
[75]Andrew Cunningham and Ole Peter Grell, *The Four Horsemen of the Apocalypse: Religion, War, Famine and Death in Reformation Europe* (New York: Cambridge University Press, 2001).

Protestant princes to come together in a defensive posture in the Schmalkaldic League (1531). At the diet, as the leading representative of the Reformation, Philipp Melanchthon prepared the Augsburg Confession (1530), which prompted division and other credal statements of protest. These included Huldrych Zwingli's *Fidei Ratio* (1530), an appeal to the sympathies of Venice and Francis I of France, partly in view of their political hostility to the empire.

Lutheranism had begun as an attempt to reform the church through a public debate around Luther's Ninety-Five Theses. With roots in late medieval reform and humanist learning, Lutheranism drew on religious movements in the late medieval period such as the Hussites, Waldensians, and followers of Girolamo Savonarola. The conditions created by the Renaissance allowed thinkers such as Erasmus to bring humanist learning to question the role and nature of the church. Lutheranism quickly allied itself with the office of the magistrate after an initial radical social phase. The period drew on prophetic scenarios, astrology, Neoplatonic philosophy and other extrabiblical materials. Concerning Lutheranism's focus on the end of all things, Robin Barnes writes,

> Martin Luther would have been disappointed to know that his five hundredth birthday would be celebrated on earth. He believed in the imminence of the end of the world and the Last Judgment; this belief was widely shared among his colleagues and followers. Much more than Catholics or Calvinists, Lutherans kept alive the tense hopes and fears for the future that had characterized the late Middle Ages.[76]

Those hopes and fears pervaded the Diet of Speyer, which nevertheless saw a growing separation of magisterial from radical Reformers and subjected those who envisioned a more radical reform to the penalty of death with the concurrence of Catholics and Lutherans. One of the first Anabaptist leaders, Felix Manz, was drowned in Zurich in 1527, and persecution eliminated other Anabaptist leaders. Thomas Müntzer typified the radicals and began drawing out Anabaptist apocalyptic expectancy. Such expectation characterized the political Münster uprising of 1535.

Politics also pervaded the reform movement as it became defined by magisterial leadership in the Swiss cantons and cities. In 1519, Zwingli became the people's priest of the Grossmünster in Zurich. There he began to preach on reform of the church. This included expository preaching through the entire New Testament, quite different from the Catholic Mass.

In 1529, a war within the Swiss Confederation was staved off at the last moment between those who preferred to remain Catholic and those supportive of reform. At the same time, Martin Luther and others became aware of Zwingli's ideas. They held the Marburg Colloquy (1529) and concurred in many areas of doctrine but could not come to agreement on the doctrine of the real presence of Christ in the Eucharist. Heinrich Bullinger followed Zwingli, serving as a pastor to the pastors, but leadership among the Reformation defined as "Reformed" fell to John Calvin, Reformer of Geneva.

[76]Robin Barnes, *Prophecy and Gnosis: Apocalypticism in the Wake of the Lutheran Reformation* (Stanford, CA: Stanford University Press, 1988), 216.

The evolution of the science of history emerged by the 1550s, when Lutheran Matthias Flacius Illyricus (1520–1575) organized a collaborative century-by-century history (ending in 1298) of where Luther's doctrine of grace could be found, called *Magdeburg Centuries*.[77] This confessional project never reached completion and was criticized by his coreligionists and Roman Catholics, especially Cesar Baronius (1538–1607). However, the project provided a model for how history might be written. This conflict between Flacius and Baronius provides a background for stepping in the direction of a secular history seen in Pareus, Brightman, and Johann Heinrich Alsted, hastened by the Thirty Years' War.

The reading and interpretation of Revelation became an important source for establishing Protestantism in the sixteenth century as the movement emanated out of Wittenberg, Zurich, Geneva, and the Rhineland as well as elsewhere.[78] Defined in an age of increasing conflict, by midcentury the example of the flight of over 800 refugees (and 288 burned at the stake) from England of English Queen Mary's exiles, which took place less than two decades after the radical millenarian uprising at Münster, offered a lens to communities that by the end of the century "became the laboratories of a new ideology which inject an exegetical shock into conventional Augustinian amillennialism."[79] This laboratory largely took place under Reformed rather than Lutheran direction, but millenarianism continued suspect in the Protestant communities.

British historian Katherine Firth writes, "No six years were more important [in England] than those from 1553–1559" in the development of the native apocalyptic tradition.[80] The Geneva Bible, with its apocalyptic annotations from the commentary of Francis Junius and further development by commentators such as Pareus and Brightman, set the agenda for interpretation and conflict in the seventeenth century. Western European history was redefined as significantly as it had been since Augustine's *De civitate Dei* (*City of God*) up until the current era.[81] Crawford Gribben writes, "History would be rewritten as a polemical exposition of Revelation. And the imminent climax of the ages would be postponed to allow for an increasingly optimistic eschatology involving massive numbers of conversions of Jews and of unbelieving Gentiles into the Christian church."[82]

2. Theological themes. Paul Tillich's phrase "ultimate things" can function as a contemporary organizing principle to compare the eschatology of each Reformer of the sixteenth century and hence catch a bit of what made their movements so divergent while they agreed on so much.[83] One might do this with Luther and Calvin, as both stood out with such theological prominence.

[77]Lutheran theologian Werner Elert argues that the *Magdeburg Centuries* became the basis of modern church history. See Elert, *The Structure of Lutheranism: The Theology and Philosophy of Life Especially in the Sixteenth and Seventeenth Centuries* (St. Louis: Concordia, 1962), 485.

[78]David C. Steinmetz, ed., *The Bible in the Sixteenth Century* (Durham, NC: Duke University Press, 1990).

[79]Crawford Gribben, "Deconstructing the Geneva Bible: The Search for a Puritan Poetic," *Literature and Theology* 14, no. 1 (March 2000): 2.

[80]Katherine Firth, *The Apocalyptic Tradition in Reformation Britain, 1530–1645* (Oxford: Oxford University Press, 1979), 69; also Jane Dawson, "The Apocalyptic Thinking of the Marian Exiles," in *Prophecy and Eschatology: Studies in Church History, ed.* Michael Wilks, *Subsidia* 10 (Oxford: Blackwell, 1994), 77.

[81]Francis Fukuyama, *The End of History and the Last Man* (New York: Free Press, 2006).

[82]Gribben, "Deconstructing the Geneva Bible," 2.

[83]Paul Tillich's treatment of this theme is found in his *Systematic Theology*, vol. 1 (Chicago: University of Chicago Press, 1951).

What is one to make of a relationship, that between Luther and Calvin, that was so close and yet so distant? R. Ward Holder raises this question in the introduction to his edited collection *Calvin and Luther: The Continuing Relationship*.[84] They represent two sides of the magisterial Reformation, that is, ongoing confessional antipathy. In speaking of Karl Barth, Holder writes, "Reformed and Lutheran faiths were foundationally and irreconcilably divergent."[85] The course of this volume will reveal lines of controversy opened up by a study of the eschatology of leading Reformation theologians.

Eschatology concerns what indeed is said or believed to happen in the last days, that is, what the universal cosmic narrative is and how it relates to a narrative of documented history. How is this tied to the afterlife, that is, what happens or is believed to happen to an individual after death? To what extent is this proclaimed personal expectation caught up in the larger picture of what happens to the church and the world, and to what extent is it individualized? All of this is often caught up in the concept of a church militant, a church expectant, and a church triumphant. What verses in Scripture might reflect these concerns? How do they appear in Luther, and how do any of his viewpoints appear in Calvin's work? How do they appear in the work of other leading commentators such as Bullinger, Junius, Pareus, and Brightman?[86] There are other eternal issues, such as eternal personal issues in an individual's life (sin, of course, but also growth, love, learning, and the shaping/narrative path of a lifetime) held up along the tensile continuum between the here-and-now and the eternal.

Luther's reform gave way to the rise of confessionalism throughout Europe and prompted similar confessionalisms among those adopting the term *reformed* as well as among the various groups identified as the "radicals of the Reformation" and then in the colonial diaspora of the regional European reform movements.[87] The biblical narrative discerned in Revelation provided the dominant lens for making sense of the times, and in this canon, recourse was frequently made to apocalyptic texts (Revelation, Daniel, 2 Thessalonians, the Johannine Epistles—and then, too, extracanonical material such as the medieval Joachite and other prophecies that characterized the early Greek and Latin traditions).

Event and interpretation come together in theology. Revelation was increasingly discerned as bearing theological foci for Christian doctrine. Theologically suspect at first, Revelation was increasingly understood to present a high Christology in opposition to antichrist. This Christology is seen in the Son of Man (Rev 1:9-18), the Lamb who opens the scroll (Rev 5:1-14), the child sequestered in the desert (Rev 12:5-7), the victorious Lamb (Rev 14:1-5), the wedding supper of the Lamb (Rev 19:9), the victorious rider on the white horse (Rev 19:11-16), the light of the heavenly

[84]R. Ward Holder, "Calvin and Luther: The Relationship That Still Echoes," in *Calvin and Luther: The Continuing Relationship*, ed. R. Ward Holder (Göttingen: Vandenhoeck & Ruprecht, 2013), 7-12.

[85]Holder, "Calvin and Luther," 8.

[86]Carter Lindberg, *The Reformation Theologians: An Introduction to Theology in the Early Modern Period* (Malden, MA: Wiley-Blackwell, 2017).

[87]George H. Williams, *The Radical Reformation* (Kirksville, MO: Truman State University Press, 1993); Carter Lindberg, *The European Reformations*, 2nd ed. (West Sussex, UK: Wiley-Blackwell, 2004).

temple (Rev 21:22), and the root and offspring of David and bright morning star (Rev 22:16). Revelation was increasingly seen to be all about Christ.[88]

Having largely settled the issue of canonicity by midcentury, a host of issues become identified in the history of exegesis. These included characters and events associated with Christ's role in the midst of the churches, the seven seals, the identity of the Lamb, the martyrs under the throne, the antichrist, the dragon and the devil, the false prophet, the seven trumpets, the book to be eaten by John, the two witnesses, the woman clothed with the sun, the two beasts, the Lamb and the everlasting gospel, the destruction of Babylon, the seven bowls of wrath, the whore on the seven-headed beast, the fall of Babylon, the chaining and loosing of the serpent, the millennium, the new Jerusalem, the new heaven and the new earth, the first and second resurrection, rule of Christ, and the last judgment.

The nature of the millennium, the thousand-year rule of Christ and the church along with the binding of Satan, arose as a consuming theological theme driving politics. Subject to early Reformed debate, this theme became the focus of radical debate with Münster's Anabaptists, millenarians who insisted that Revelation described a utopian millenarian period that could be anticipated by revolutionary ferment (1534–1535). The writings of Antoine du Pinet are seen to represent the thought of Calvin's doctrine on the millennium (see Calvin's *Psychopannychia*, 1534) and context for the first edition (1536) of his seminal work, *The Institutes of the Christian Religion* (1559).[89] Lutheran development took place around the three "solas" against an eschatology outlined by Flacius.[90]

The theological themes for Anglicanism at first were shaped by the Henrican and Elizabethan reforms and came to a head in the formation of an evolving Puritanism and its dissemination of the 1560 edition of the Geneva Bible project. Beginning in 1557 and carried into the seventeenth century, this project was intended to guard against an illicit reading of Revelation. In its definitive edition it carried the annotations of Francis Junius.[91] It taught a theme

> that was not explicated from *Revelation* 20, as in later postmillennialism and in the Münster theology, but found its roots in the annotations on *Romans* 11. These notes suggested that the elect Gentiles were to be called into the church for the duration of the time when the Jews had been blinded by God to the truths of Christianity, but that when the "fulnes of the Gentiles" had entered the church, grace would again be extended to the Jews and that their conversion *en masse* to Christian faith would encourage yet greater revival amongst the Gentiles. "The Jewes now remaine, as it were, in death for lacke of the Gospel: but when they & the Gentiles shal embrace Christ, ye world shalbe restored to a newe life" [Geneva Bible 1560, note on Rom 11:15]. Once adopted by [William] Perkins, this

[88]Frederick J. Murphy, *Fallen Is Babylon: The Revelation to John* (Harrisburg, PA: Trinity Press International, 1998).

[89]John T. McNeill, *The History and Character of Calvinism* (Oxford: Oxford University Press, 1967), 312.

[90]Elert, *Structure of Lutheranism*.

[91]Huguenot scholar Franciscus Junius, highly interested in apocalyptic thought, in 1589 published *Notae in Apocalypsim*, followed three years later with the longer *Exposition de l'Apocalypse* (1592). Both texts were translated into English, and the shorter work, now titled *Apocalypsis, a Brief and Learned Commentarie upon the Revelation of St. John* (1592), was adapted to become the marginal annotations on Revelation in the 1599 edition of the Geneva Bible, a fourth Genevan *Revelation*. This edition accounted for over half the Genevan Bibles printed, combining Thomson's New Testament with the new annotations on Revelation taken from the work of Junius.

teaching would go on to influence the major puritan expositors throughout the evolution of the movement and remain a staple of mainstream protestant eschatology for ensuing centuries.[92]

A final theological theme to be raised at this point is that related to church and state, or national identity, a direct outgrowth over the struggle for the Geneva Bible and its acceptance.[93] Gribben calls the Geneva Bible the "flagship" of English reform. It was designed, he argues, "to counter one and a half thousand years of established commentary and argue that the Protestant exegesis was history's best" interpretative structure for understanding Revelation.[94] This becomes abundantly clear in the commentaries of Swiss Bullinger, French Reformed Junius, German Pareus, and English Brightman.

> It was vital for the Reformation project that this argument was enforced. . . . Within this overarching aim, Junius was forced into re-reading the Reformation's central document without drawing attention to his hermeneutical manoeuvring. Yes, Protestant readings were the best, but his Protestant reading was the best of all. It was highly ironic that Junius' ending was the fourth attempt to close the Geneva Bible.[95]

Although each of these four commentators demonstrates it differently, this view of the superiority of Protestant exegesis is clear once the Lamb breaks open the first seal (Rev 5:6) held by the one on the throne. Gribben writes,

> The first thing a reader would notice as he turned to Revelation [in the Geneva Bible] was a table of dates and historical events, describing itself as "The order of time whereunto the contents of this booke are to be referred." This table summarised the annotator's notes, and indicated Junius' attempt to provide a comprehensive explication of the text which was sensitive to Revelation's authorial context. It was an attempt at justification by history alone which would lead to a confusion of genres, investing futuristic speculation with the weight of proven fact. The similarity with [John] Foxe's method is immediately apparent, but despite their common historical project, the notes of the Geneva Bible offered a far more sophisticated and extensive reading of Revelation than did Foxe's *Acts and Monuments*. They also extended into the future in a way that Foxe never imagined.[96]

Gribben continues concerning the interpretation of Revelation in the Geneva Bible:

> Perhaps the most obvious difference between Foxe and Junius was their dating of the millennium. Both writers agreed that it was to be applied to the past, but while Foxe situated it as a period of initial glory which began with the accession of the archetypal "Christian emperor" Constantine in AD 324, Junius placed the binding of Satan as a period of martyrdom which began with the Roman sacking of Jerusalem in AD 70. This alternative explication was bound up with the competing political ideologies of the Genevan texts. Reflecting Puritan frustration at the continuation of the

[92]Crawford Gribben, *The Puritan Millennium: Literature and Theology, 1550–1682*, rev. ed. (Eugene, OR: Wipf & Stock, 2008), 74, italics original. See Avihu Zakai, "From Judgment to Salvation: The Image of the Jews in the English Renaissance," *Westminster Theological Journal* 59 (1997): 213-30.

[93]Lewis Lupton, *History of the Geneva Bible* (London: Fauconberg, 1966), 157-83.

[94]Gribben, "Deconstructing the Geneva Bible," 6-7.

[95]Gribben, "Deconstructing the Geneva Bible," 7.

[96]Gribben, "Deconstructing the Geneva Bible," 7.

> via media ecclesiologies throughout the three kingdoms, Junius was much less interested than Foxe in the theology of a "godly prince" who would promote reform.[97]

The theological theme of church and nation becomes clear as one moves into and through the seventeenth century.[98] In the case of Britain, it was played out in the English Civil War (1642–1651). So also on the Continent in the Dutch and Spanish wars, in conflict in France, and in the German principalities and Habsburg Empire. Nation and church remained contentious on both sides of the Atlantic.[99]

*3. **Interpretive issues.*** The content of Revelation is of great interest today. Such was also the case in the sixteenth century. In her *Reformation Readings of the Apocalypse*, Backus goes to the roots of the conflict over interpretation as she examines selected commentaries in Geneva, Zurich, and Wittenberg, three centers of Continental Protestantism.[100] She focuses on these select commentaries written between the 1520s and 1580s, with two main goals: (1) to consider various views of Revelation's status via commentators' differing methods of interpretation to illustrate the place of the text "in the religious and cultural context of the Reformation"; and (2) "to examine whether there was a single Protestant approach to the Apocalypse or whether varying social, linguistic and political conditions determined the way different writers read the text."[101]

In Backus's detailed analysis, she reflects on three distinct confessional orientations in the interpretation of Revelation in the first half of the century. First, there are the Genevan commentators, particularly Antoine du Pinet, Augustan Marlorat, and Nicholas Colladon.[102] These "combined a restrained and traditional form of exegesis with strong polemics against the papal Antichrist. The main concern reflected in their commentaries was . . . the battle for converts in France."[103]

Second, there are the Zurich commentators, scholar-prophets such as Leo Jud, Theodore Bibliander, and Bullinger.[104] These "took a far more historical, less spiritualized approach to the book.

---

[97]Gribben, "Deconstructing the Geneva Bible," 8.

[98]Christopher Hill, *The Century of Revolution: 1603–1714 (London: Routledge, 1961)*; Hill, *The World Turned Upside Down: Radical Ideas During the English Revolution* (repr., New York: Penguin, 2020); Hill, *Antichrist in Seventeenth-Century England* (London: Oxford University Press, 1971), 3-4.

[99]Lindberg, *European Reformations*.

[100]Backus, *Reformation Readings*.

[101]Backus, *Reformation Readings*, xix.

[102]On Antoine du Pinet, see Backus, *Reformation Readings*, 37-59 and throughout. Du Pinet was considered Calvin's mouthpiece on the Revelation. Backus allows for du Pinet's use of François Lambert and Sebastian Meyer. Of Marlorat she writes, "Marlorat was not the first Protestant theologian to see that the object of the Apocalypse was to provide an answer to the problem of how to cope with the present in view of Christ's first (past) and (future) Second Coming and his intervening presence 'elsewhere.' He was, however, the first Protestant theologian to formulate the problem succinctly and to see that the Apocalypse of John provided a better solution to it than any other biblical book" (29).

[103]Robin B. Barnes, "Review: *Varieties of Apocalyptic Experience in Reformation Europe*," *Journal of Interdisciplinary History* 33, no. 2 (Autumn 2002): 266.

[104]Backus writes of Jud, "In 1542, Leo Jud published his German translation of Erasmus' *Paraphrases* on the New Testament. As Erasmus had left out the Apocalypse, Jud simply added his own Paraphrases of it in German" (*Reformation Readings*, 29-30). Of Bibliander she says, "Although Bibliander was the only one of the Zürich commentators to undertake a systematic defense of the book's canonicity, all three [Jud, Bibliander, and Bullinger] assumed that the text was a revelation divinely conferred on the apostle John and as such automatically part of the canon" (30). On Bullinger, see Herman Selderhuis, "Kirche unter dem Kreuz: die Ekklesiologie Heinrich Bullinger," in *Heinrich Bullinger (1504–1575): Leben, Denken, Wirkung. Internationaler Bullingerkongress 2004*, ed. Emidio Campi and Peter Opitz (Zurich: Theologische Verlag Zurich, 2007), 513-36.

Their orientation was not fundamentally eschatological. Rather, they tended to stress the use of Revelation for daily ethical and pastoral purposes."[105] Preeminently, this applied to Bullinger's commentary, which consisted of 101 sermons on Revelation preached in the German vernacular as well as in Latin, widely translated and publicized across all of Europe.[106] None of the Geneva or Zurich commentators interpreted Revelation in such a way as to find it unique to their day, except for what it revealed about the Roman (papal) antichrist.[107]

Third are the Lutherans, commentators such as David Chytraeus and Nicholas Selnecker. For them Revelation was

> a prophetic mirror for their own times, the last times of the world. Following Luther, they saw the Reformation itself as a final burst of the gospel truth preceding the Last Judgment, but they shared none of the early Luther's reservations about the clarity or value of the Apocalypse. They were heirs of the later Luther, who had come to see the book as a summary of God's plan for the world.[108]

They saw this history as played out in history in the *Magdeburg Centuries*. "The Lutherans brought a more strongly apocalyptic orientation to their readings of Revelation than did other mainline Protestants."[109] These latter kept social radicalism, seen among select groups of Anabaptists, spiritualists, and evangelical rationalists, tethered to the political control of the magistrate. But for Lutherans—including Selnecker, who viewed Luther as a final Elijah—and their more radical brethren, the present age was a time of transcendent crisis.[110] From the last third of the sixteenth century and into the seventeenth century, the hesitancy about the canonicity of Revelation diminished. The issues that animated the intellectual struggle embedded in Revelation shifted from the study of Scripture to the study of history.[111]

Special note must be made in this volume of four interpreters of Revelation, each with his own unique contribution: Bullinger, Junius, Pareus, and Brightman.

1. Scholars and pastors drew on Bullinger's work throughout the sixteenth and seventeenth centuries. I have already noted his academic, pastoral, and civic contributions.

2. Junius produced a commentary on Revelation in 1592. His apocalyptic annotations were used in the notes of the Geneva Bible.

3. Pareus was aware that the intellectual struggle against the papacy had shifted from the study of Scripture to the study of history. History drew attention to questions such as why so many millions had consented to papal leadership. Pareus produced 237 theses for the *Reformationsjubileum*, which attempted to answer these questions. The historical problems presented by the

[105]Barnes, "Review: *Varieties of Apocalyptic Experience*," 266.

[106]See the preface to Bullinger's *Hundred Sermons*; also J. Wayne Baker, *Heinrich Bullinger and the Covenant: The Other Reformed Tradition* (Athens: Ohio University Press, 1980), xi-xxvi.

[107]Backus, *Reformation Readings*, 137.

[108]Barnes, "Review: *Varieties of Apocalyptic Experience*," 266-67.

[109]Barnes, "Review: *Varieties of Apocalyptic Experience*," 267.

[110]Robert Kolb, Irene Dingel, and L'ubomir Batka, eds., *The Oxford Handbook of Martin Luther's Theology* (Oxford: Oxford University Press, 2014). Selnecker states that Melanchthon referred to Luther as father, preceptor, and the Elijah of the last times (530).

[111]Daniel John Toft, "Shadows of Kings: The Political Thought of David Pareus, 1548–1622" (PhD diss., University of Wisconsin, 1970), 96.

papacy increasingly occupied Pareus's mind. History could not stand alone in the explanation of these problems, of course, but "history in the light of Scripture and experience" would exonerate and justify the Reformation.[112] In turning to history in the light of Scripture, Pareus made use of Old Testament prophecy, but above all his attention turned to Revelation. In 1618 his commentary on Revelation appeared, an astonishing document that linked the right of political resistance to papal depredations and intervention into the political sphere, an intervention that had taken place in Carolingian times and continued to the present to the corruption of the world.

This recourse to history for legitimation of the Reformation raised not only the question of the lineage or precursors to Luther's doctrine of grace, seen in Flacius's efforts, but also the question of where Protestantism was headed. Pareus put forward the idea of an ecumenical and perpetual reform envisioned in the millennium first expressed by Augustine. This amillennial vision had been suggested by Augustine in opposition to early church premillennialism, but these historical projects were now challenged at the end of the sixteenth century by the emergence of postmillennialism, seen in the work of Brightman and Alsted.[113]

4. Brightman was a leading commentator on Revelation.[114] His commentary was published posthumously and proved to be an important revision of the interpretation of eschatology set down by John Foxe. His work weakened the imperial associations to the Emperor Constantine I, condemning the Church of England as "Laodicean" (lukewarm), and helped to move English Puritanism in favor of the urgency of church reform as perceived in Revelation.[115]

In the sixteenth century, issues of interpretation of Revelation were overlapping but generally moved from the question of canonicity to issues of confessionalism, then historical legitimacy, and on to the direction of historical progression or the political embodiment of the new heavens and new earth. If we were to reach into the seventeenth century and the English civil wars, the issue of postmillennialism would be embodied in such questions as how King Jesus rules, raising issues such as "the First Resurrection (whether spiritual, corporeal, or political); the nature of the millennium (whether inchoate or perfect); Christ's appearance (whether invisible or corporeal); and the nature of Satan's binding (partial, spiritual, or literal)—in short, whether the millennium is part of the Church Militant or of the Church Triumphant," or merely that of the church expectant.[116]

[112]Daniel John Toft, "Shadows of Kings: The Political Thought of David Pareus, 1548–1622" (PhD diss., University of Wisconsin, 1970), 96.

[113]Reiner Smolinski, "Caveat Emptor: Pre- and Postmillennialism in the Late Reformation Period," in *Millenarianism and Messianism in Early Modern European Culture: The Millenarian Turn*, ed. J. E. Force and R. H. Popkin (Dordrecht: Kluwer Academic, 2001), 145-69; see also Howard Hotson, *Paradise Postponed: Johann Heinrich Alsted and the Birth of Calvinist Millenarianism* (Dordrecht: Kluwer Academic, 2000).

[114]A. Crome, "Appendix: A Comparison of Editions of Brightman's Revelation of the Revelation," in *The Restoration of the Jews: Early Modern Hermeneutics, Eschatology, and National Identity in the Works of Thomas Brightman* (Dordrecht: Springer International, 2014), 213.

[115]Avihu Zakai, "Thomas Brightman and English Apocalyptic Tradition," in *Menasseh ben Israel and His World, ed.* Yosef Kaplan, Henry Méchoulan, and Richard H. Popkin (Leiden: Brill Academic, 1989), 31-44. See also William Lamont, *Godly Rule, Politics and Religion 1603–1660* (London: Palgrave Macmillan, 1969).

[116]Smolinski, "Caveat Emptor," 146.

4. Historical reception of Revelation by radicals of the Reformation, Lutherans, the Reformed, and English Reformers. In the first and second generations of the Reformers, most either condemned Revelation (Zwingli, Luther) or ignored it (Melanchthon, Bucer, Calvin). Among Anabaptists it was seen to be of immediate value. For those who were considered magisterial Reformers, "only Bullinger attempted to make it suitable reading for the faithful, no doubt due partly to his encounter with the English refugees whose enthusiasm for the book is well known."[117] By the latter third of the century, it was widely accepted for the light it shed on political revolutions on the Continent and in Britain.

Concerning the Lutheran and Reformed reception of Revelation, Luther was at first more uneasy with Revelation than with other apocalyptic or prophetic texts of the Christian Bible. Only later did he come to accept it as apostolic, despite the apparent congruence of prophetic and doctrinal arguments based on it. Daniel's prophecies had the seer's own interpretation; the description of antichrist in 2 Thessalonians 2:3-4—which suggested to Luther certain medieval church developments—was Pauline.[118] But Luther, reading other writings on Revelation and other works critical of the papacy, gradually grew more confident in his use of the apocalyptic text.[119] With the growth of the Turkish threat, heresies, sects, and contemporary unbelief, Revelation's images clearly signaled the end of the age. Luther thus left a trail of his developing perspective on the apocalyptic vision from the crucial early years of his work to the end of his life. He subdivided known history into three periods, each with a witness and a mission, and he came to believe he was living at the end of the time of the third witness. For him, Enoch affirmed hope for the righteous of the first historic era. Elijah witnessed to the rewards intended for those who kept the Mosaic law in the second period.[120] And, with Christ as its witness, current history appeared to participate in the third and final world, with the gospel as a last word and promise that the life lost in paradise would be restored.

Special prophetic missions were not alone in Luther's thinking. Early in his work Luther had adopted a prevailing interpretation of the four world kingdoms envisioned by Daniel. In this view the fall of the last kingdom, Rome, would coincide with the end of the world.[121] In Luther's mind Revelation came to prefigure the chief eras of church history.[122] He concluded that the seals

[117]Backus, *Reformation Readings*, 35.

[118]Luther was easily drawn to the book of Daniel in the development of his historical perspective. "Vorrede vber den Propheten Daniel," in WA, DB 11:2.13.

[119]On works critical of the papacy, see, e.g., a document describing the vision of Nicolaus von der Fluhe and a collection of prophecies by astrologer Johann Lichtenberger in G. F. Hall, "Luther's Eschatology," *Augustana Quarterly* 25 (1944): 13-21. Concerning Revelation specifically, Luther read the commentary by John Purvey (ca. 1390), published under the title *Commentarius in Apocalypsin ante centum annos editus* 1528 (cf. WA 26:123).

[120]His thinking about the name of Elijah begins at least with the completion of his treatise to the German nobility. See: WA, Br 2:167.7-8; a similar reference is found in a letter from Wartburg, dated May 26, 1521, in which Luther writes that he is only an Elijah in comparison with Melanchthon, his Elisha (WA, Br 2:348.49-50).

[121]The little horn arising on the head of the fourth beast is usually identified by Luther with the Turk, God's scourge on Christendom for its sin, which will in its own time be judged and fall (Ezek 39). See John M. Headley, *Luther's View of Church History (New Haven, CT: Yale University Press, 1963)*, 228.

[122]There is a somewhat fuller sense of identification between prophecy and event in the later preface of 1546 compared with the earlier one of 1530 (WA, DB, 7:407, 409, 411, 413, 415, 417, 419, 421); see Headley, *Luther's View of Church History*, 106-56.

represented physical or political evils; the trumpets suggested the spiritual evils the church suffered from the early Christian era to the present. The first four trumpeting angels represented works-righteousness (Tatian), enthusiasm (Marcion), philosophy (Origen), and the quest for unwarranted purity (Novatian).[123] The three woes that beset the church were the teachings of Arius (Rev 9:1-12), the political threat of the Turks (Rev 9:13–11:14), and the papacy (Rev 11:15-19), particularly as the latter's secular hegemony grew.[124] This pattern in declension in the era of Christ's first advent paralleled that of previous historical eras, which had ended with the flood and the advent of Christ. History ended with acts of God's judgment, which was merciful even in its severity.[125]

Like Luther, the Reformed worked from an Augustinian paradigm of history. History was seen to be reflected in the duality of Augustine's *De civitate Dei*. But Calvin's reforming work was shaped differently from that of Luther. Written to explain the evangelical faith and defend the reform movement from charges of social sedition and religious radicalism after the debacle of Münster (1535–1536), the *Institutes* set forth Calvin's own ideas about church order, scriptural exegesis, and how to bring humanity into God's own realm.[126] His emphasis on sanctification and bringing all under the rule of Christ included a strong sense of history, which he perceived as a process in which God's purposes were progressively realized.

Like Luther, Calvin openly criticized Thomas Müntzer, Melchior Hoffman, and Nicholas Storch, who inspired dissent in the French Protestant congregation of refugees at Strasbourg, which he pastored during his exile from Geneva (1539–1541).[127] These individuals enthusiastically anticipated Christ's imminent second coming and stirred up hope for such among others. Calvin clearly distinguished between God's old and new dispensations of faith but strongly denied chiliasm.[128] He sought no new revelations or prophecies; willing even to see in Luther's work a parallel to Elijah, Calvin was yet unwilling to refer to Luther as "the Last Elijah."[129] He did not hope to rehabilitate an office of prophecy in any charismatic sense of the word. Word and Spirit were bonded together for Calvin: both pointed to Christ, and both were best understood by seeing Christ as the final prophet (Deut 18:18; Mk 6:15; Jn 6:14) while emphasizing personal sanctification and social justice.[130]

---

[123]WA, DB, 7:410.18-412.2; 411.26–413.2.

[124]WA, DB, 7:412.10-35, 413.10–415.2. See Friedrich Myconius to Martin Luther, December 2, 1529, WA, Br 5:191.29-37.

[125]Elert, *Structure of Lutheranism*, 485.

[126]I follow Willem Balke, *Calvin and the Anabaptist Radicals*, trans. William Heynen (Grand Rapids, MI: Eerdmans, 1981): 39-71; see also Walter Kohler, "Das Taufertum in Calvins *Institutio* von 1536," *Mennonitische Geschichtsblatter* 2 (1936): 1-4.

[127]CO 9:96. Calvin refers to these three self-proclaimed prophets as Thomas Monetarius, Melchior Pellionius, and Nicholas Pelagius, phrases written in defense of the Reformed position against Joachim Westphal's charges that the Reformed were one with the radicals (see Balke, *Calvin and the Anabaptist Radicals*, 297). On Hoffman, see Klaus Deppermann, *Melchior Hoffman: Sociale Unruhen und apokalyptische Visionen im Zeitalter der Reformation* (Göttingen: Vandenhoeck & Ruprecht, 1979), 331-32.

[128]*Institutes* 1.9.1. Most of the 1539 edition was carried into the 1559 edition (see Balke, *Calvin and the Anabaptist Radicals*, 98-115, 299). On Calvin's sense of eschatology and history, see Heinrich Berger, *Calvins Geschictsauffassung* (Zürich: Zwingli, 1955), 153-54; David E. Holwerda, "Eschatology and History: A Look at Calvin's Eschatological Vision," in *Exploring the Heritage of John Calvin: Essays in Honor of John Bratt*, ed. D. E. Holwerda (Grand Rapids, MI: Baker Books, 1976), 111-13, 125-27.

[129]CO 9:238. I owe this reference to Brian A. Gerrish, *The Old Protestantism and the New* (Chicago: University of Chicago Press, 1982), 45, 289.

[130]*Institutes* 4.1.5-6, sections on education in the church and the meaning and limits of ministry.

Like Luther, then, Calvin saw the radicals as theologically and pastorally problematic. His interactions with them and their followers may even have led to what Heinrich Quistorp calls his "aversion to the Apocalypse."[131] Also like Luther, Revelation stayed in Calvin's canon. He occasionally cited it, saying in the *Institutes*, "Those for whom prophetic doctrine is tasteless ought to be thought of as lacking taste buds."[132] But Calvin also tended toward a typological approach to his exegetical work, especially seeking images and symbols in the Hebrew Scriptures by which to understand the prophetic passages in Revelation. Luther's approach was more Christocentric and literalistic. For example, rather than finding prophetic figures such as Enoch and Elijah, whose return was to be expected at the end of history, Calvin understands them to be models of the meaning and limits of the ministry of the church. Writing of a second Elijah, Calvin notes, "The task of the second Elijah was, according to Malachi, to enlighten the minds and 'to turn the hearts of the fathers to the children, and the unbelievers to the wisdom of the just.'"[133] After this remark he continues to discuss the work of the minister and the nature of the church, issues that were vital to him in the fight against the spirit of antichrist in Rome and the excesses of the Anabaptists.[134] Arguing, as Thomas Aquinas had done in the thirteenth century, against the Joachites, Calvin posited no new age of the Spirit. Rather than looking for new prophets who were to come heralding new eras and prophesying future events, Calvin writes, "But for my part, as doctrine is the present subject, I would rather explain it [prophecy], as in I Cor. 14, to mean outstanding interpreters of prophecies, who, by a unique gift of revelation, applied them to the subjects on hand; but I do not exclude the gift of foretelling, so far as it was connected with teaching."[135]

Teaching became the accepted form of prophecy at the Academy of Geneva and in weekly meetings of pastors and laity for prayer and Scripture study.[136] Charismatic foretelling was rare, generally seen as having been limited to the apostolic age. The church in Calvin's time had Christ; its prophets were forth-tellers of this highest gift. Special prophets and latter-day prophecies were not needed.[137]

Without denying God's direction in final temporal events, Calvin's references to last things emphasized God's judgments in time. But in reading prophetic texts Calvin developed an

[131] Heinrich Quistorp, *Die letzten Dinge im Zeugnis Calvins* (Güttersloh: Bertelsmann, 1941), 116. In addition to an Erasmian doubt, Calvin's aversion to Revelation was occasioned by what he felt was its misuse by the radicals of the Reformation. See Otto Weber, "Calvins Lehre von der Kirche," in *Die Treue Gottes in der Geschichte der Kirche*, vol. 2, *Gesammelte Aufsätze* (Neukirchen: Neukirchen Verlag des Erziehungsvereigns, 1968), 103.

[132] *Institutes* 1.7.2 (Battles-McNeill ed., 83).

[133] *Institutes* 4.6.1 (Battles-McNeill ed., 35).

[134] *Institutes* 4.2.12.–4.3.1; see T. H. L. Parker, *John Calvin: A Biography* (Philadelphia: Westminster, 1975), 35.

[135] Calvin's discussion of the development of the spirit of antichrist is located in *Institutes* 4.7.4-25.

[136] Denis notes that, for the sake of purity and agreement in doctrine, Calvin organized weekly "Conferences de l'Ecriture" (also called *Congrégation*) as part of his *Ecclesiastical Ordinances*. Through such meetings, it was hoped that all the prophets of the city would speak with one voice in order to expose error and seek agreement around the proper interpretation of Scripture (Philippe Denis, "La Prophétie dans las églises de la Réforme au XVIe siècle," RHE, 72 [1977]: 289-316 [299]).

[137] Peter Martyr Vermigli, a Florentine reformer at Zurich, Basel, and then Strasbourg, cited in evidence the growing numbers of books and numerous teachers of his time. He noted that there was no need for special prophets since books and teachers were by then so numerous (*Loci communes* 1.19). See Elizabeth L. Eisenstein, *The Printing Press as an Agent of Change: Communication and Cultural Transformations in Early-Modern Europe* (Cambridge: Cambridge University Press, 1979).

exegetical methodology relating biblical promises to patterns of fulfillment. In Calvin's technical interpretation, the Hebrew Scriptures' promises found fulfillment in the Christian New Testament and the establishment of Christ's dominion, beginning with the first advent. Since then a tension intensified in God's dominion between promise and fulfillment. Richard Müller, using the term *kerygmatic analogy*, illustrates the way in which Calvin developed the idea of an extended meaning of the text, permitting its literal reading while finding—often through preaching—a contemporary application or meaning of the text. The logic or dynamism of the text might thus carry the gathered assembly into an unanticipated future meaning.[138]

By applying the logic of this exegetical method with what many view as optimism about the prospects for human betterment or analogy with the growth of Christ's kingdom, many see Calvin as contributing to the idea of progress in human history, a kind of historical meliorism wherever the gospel is heard and appropriated.[139] This exegetical integrity gave an inner logic to the idea of the kingdom of God in Martin Bucer's theology, an idea that impressed Calvin during his sojourn in Strasbourg.[140] Calvin's meliorism contributed to an enduring, if less apocalyptic, interest in the nature of Christ's kingdom among the Reformed. A proleptic sharing in Christ's resurrection and session in glory might be seen to work its way backwards to present times insofar as one believed that the present times stood in the shadow of the end of history.

Like Calvin, other later Reformed theologians located special prophets and prophecy in Christ alone as the last prophet. His ministers were to herald Christ's name against the antichrist. Thus, the vexed question between those who believed the gift of the charismata for prophecy was given to the whole congregation of believers (1 Cor 14:26-32) or alone to those duly trained and approved (1 Tim 2:2) was demonstrably one of Christ-centered piety and not Spirit-led ecstasy. As the apocalyptic texts were reading this context, a number of implications became clear that ensured their longevity and contributed to a new form of chiliasm that looked not to a new age following the second advent of Christ but rather to an age of increasing spiritual—and, often derivatively, material—improvement prior to Christ's return for his bride, the church, which has made itself ready for his return (Rev 19:7).

[138]Jaroslav Pelikan notes a parenetical and polemical use of Revelation in Luther and Calvin. In terms of the former, he sketches the importance of Rev 14:13. For views on the death and afterlife of the individual believer and on Rev 1:6 on the social life of the Christian, see Pelikan, "Some Uses of Apocalypse in the Magisterial Reformers," in *The Apocalypse in English Renaissance Thought and Literature*, ed. C. A. Patrides and Joseph Wittreich (Ithaca, NY: Cornell University Press, 1984), 74-92.

[139]Richard A. Müller, "The Hermeneutic of Promise and Fulfillment in Calvin's Exegesis of the Old Testament Prophecies of the Kingdom," in *The Bible in the Sixteenth Century*, ed. David Steinmetz (Durham, NC: Duke University Press, 1990), 68-82, esp. 71-76.

[140]Quistorp, *Die letzten Dinge*, 113.

COMMENTARY ON REVELATION

1:1-3 THE TITLE

1 The revelation of Jesus Christ, which God gave him
to show to his servants[a] *the things that must soon*
take place. He made it known by sending his angel to
his servant John, 2 *who bore witness to the word of God*
and to the testimony of Jesus Christ, even to all that he
saw. 3 *Blessed is the one who reads aloud the words of*
this prophecy, and blessed are those who hear, and
who keep what is written in it, for the time is near.

a For the contextual rendering of the Greek word *doulos*, see Preface; likewise for *servant* later in this verse

---

Overview: Reading the book of Revelation in the sixteenth century begins with awareness of two matters. First is what Renaissance historian Paul Oskar Kristeller refers to as "sacred philology," a common effort on the part of the Renaissance and Reformation to find the scholarly renovation or grounding for "the Reformation of the Bible," which reveals "the Bible of the Reformation."[1] Second is the text's proclamation of a clear Christology. This appears in the growing clarity on the part of the four primary parties to the Reformation—Lutherans, Reformed, radicals, and Anglicans (and reform-minded Catholics)—that the text of the Apocalypse was all about Jesus Christ. Particular ways of reading the Bible enabled the Reformers to draw out Christ from the text and gain an understanding of its overlapping visions.[2]

Revelation begins with the acknowledgment that it is a revelation God gave to Jesus Christ to be given by his angel by way of John to his servants. Christ is the author of the revelation given by God, while John is merely the recipient. Lack of clarity as to the identity of this John, whether he was also the author of the Gospel and Johannine Epistles, was one reason for hesitancy on the part of the early church to adopt Revelation into the canon. Certain doubts about the book's authenticity were shared by conservative Roman theologians. Textual issues, such as the nature of the Trinity or the identities of the key figures of the text, creating ambiguities requiring insight from the Old Testament, led Martin Luther to allow each to make up their own mind, while he himself chose to avoid the book.

The appeal of Revelation for the Reformers was the clarity it was thought to bring to the identity of the antichrist. While this was generally true among all Reformers, it was particularly the case among the French Reformed, such as Antoine Du Pinet, who ventured where John Calvin was reluctant to go. Yet, clear in their affirmation of the book's Christology, they were fearful of the radical social unrest it seemed to elicit.

[1] Paul Oskar Kristeller, *Renaissance Thought: The Classic, Scholastic, and Humanist Strains* (New York: Harper Torchbooks, 1961), 79; cited by Jaroslav Pelikan in *The Reformation of the Bible: The Bible of the Reformation* (New Haven, CT: Yale University Press, 1996), 3.
[2] Jean-Pierre Prévost, *How to Read the Apocalypse* (New York: Crossroad, 1993).

1:1 *The Revelation of Jesus Christ*

The Title of the Book. Giovanni Diodati: This book has the title *Apocalypse*, a Greek word that means "Revelation," because the whole subject of it is of prophetic revelations, by which to St. John, and by him to all the church, have been revealed the chief events after Christ's first coming in the flesh to his last coming to judgment. . . . Now, as among these prophecies there are some so clear by the event that one cannot be doubtful or ignorant of them except through a willful blindness, so there are others that are yet under God's secret seal, the explication of which is as uncertain as the undertaking to give it, that is, it is rash. Therefore, adoring what as yet lies hidden and meditating on what is manifest, the church has a great deal of instruction and comfort in this book, looking for the full accomplishing that shall bring to light all the obscurities. Pious Annotations upon the Holy Bible.[3]

Interpreting Prophecy. Martin Luther: So long as this kind of prophecy remains without explanation . . . since it is intended as a revelation of things that are to happen in the future, and especially of tribulations and disasters that were to come upon Christendom, we consider that the first and surest step toward finding its interpretation is to take from history the events and disasters that have come upon Christendom till now, and hold them up alongside one of these images, and so compare them very carefully. If, then, the two were perfectly coincided and squared with one another, we could build on that as a sure, or at least an unobjectionable, interpretation. Preface to the Revelation of Saint John.[4]

Which John? Desiderius Erasmus: But in these so mysterious conversations with the angels, as many places as I can inculcate, "I John" was not the title of John the Evangelist but of John's theology in the Greek manuscripts which I saw, so as not to mention a style that is not a little different from the one in the Gospel and the Epistle. For it is not of great business to refute the arguments concerning the places which some are falsely accused, as smelling of the dogmas of some heretics. These things, however, made me somewhat less inclined to believe that it was the evangelist of John unless the consent of the world would call me elsewhere, and the principal authority of the church, if, however, the church approves of this work with the intention that it may wish to be regarded as John the Evangelist and be of equal weight with other canonical books. Annotations on the New Testament.[5]

A Highly Necessary Book. John Bale: So highly necessary (good Christian reader) is the knowledge of St. John's Apocalypse or Revelation . . . to one who is a true member of Christ's church, as much as of any other book of the sacred Bible. For in none of them all are the faithful diligent hearers and readers more blessed or livelier . . . observing its contents than in this one book. Nowhere is it more clearly specified the Father, the Son, and the Holy Spirit to be one everlasting God, and Jesus Christ to be the eternal son of the Father (which are the first and chief grounds of our Christian faith), than here. Nowhere is the durable kingdom and priesthood of Jesus Christ more plenteously spread, more plainly proved and more largely uttered than in this holy oracle. Nowhere is the doctrine of health more purely taught, faith more thoroughly commended, nor yet righteousness more highly rewarded than here. Nowhere are heresies more earnestly condemned, blasphemous vices more vehemently rebuked, nor yet their just plagues more fiercely threatened than in this compendious work. The Image of Both Churches.[6]

Concerning the Order and Connection of the Visions. Joseph Mede: The Apocalypse

[3]Diodati, *Pious Annotations**, 98-99.
[4]LW 35:399-401.

[5]Erasmus, *Annotations*, 782.
[6]Bale, *Image** (1570), preface.

considered only according to the naked letter, as if it were a history and not prophecy, has marks and signs sufficient inserted by the Holy Spirit, whereby the order, synchronism, and sequel of all the visions in it contained may be found out and demonstrated without supposal of any interpretation whatsoever. This order and synchronism thus found and demonstrated (as it were) by *argumenta intrinseca* is the first thing to be done and laid down as a foundation, ground, and only safe rule of interpretation. Interpretation is not to be made the ground and rule of it. If the order, method, and connection of the visions are framed and grounded on supposed interpretation, then all proofs out of that book must be founded on begged principles and human conjectures. But, on the contrary, if the order is first fixed and settled out of the unquestioned characters of the letter of the text, and afterward the interpretation guided, framed, and directed by that order—then will the variety of expositions be drawn into a very narrow compass, and proofs taken from this book be evident, infallible, and able to convince the gainsayers. REMAINS ON SOME PASSAGES IN THE APOCALYPSE.[7]

ANGELS REFER TO BISHOPS. MARTIN LUTHER: Accordingly, we hold—as indeed the text says—that the first three chapters, which speak of the seven congregations in Asia and their angels, have no other purpose than simply to show how these congregations stood at the time, and how they are exhorted to be steadfast and increase or reform. From these chapters we learn in addition that the word "angel" is to be understood later, in other images or visions, to mean bishops and teachers in Christendom—some good, such as the holy fathers and bishops, some bad, such as the heretics and false bishops. And in this book, there are more of the bad than of the good. PREFACE TO THE REVELATION OF SAINT JOHN.[8]

SENT BY AN ANGEL. HEINRICH BULLINGER: Moreover, the manner of revealing is also touched on. For Christ revealed those things sending by his angel, or his angel sent forth, to whom he gave in commandment what he should say and do. As a result, this angel is after also called Christ because he represented the person of Christ. Therefore, not the angel in this book but Christ must always be considered the true Author of all these things. And indeed, the divinity of Christ is here commended unto us, . . . that Christ is the Lord of angels. HUNDRED SERMONS ON THE APOCALYPSE.[9]

1:2 *The Testimony of John*

FREE TO BELIEVE WHAT ONE WILLS. MARTIN LUTHER: About this book of the Revelation of John, I leave everyone free to hold his own opinions. I would not have anyone bound to my opinion or judgment. I say what I feel. I miss more than one thing in this book, and it makes me consider it to be neither apostolic nor prophetic. First and foremost, the apostles do not deal with visions, but prophesy in clear and plain words, as do Peter and Paul, and Christ in the gospel. For it befits the apostolic office to speak clearly of Christ and his deeds, without images and visions. Moreover, there is no prophet in the Old Testament, to say nothing of the New, who deals so exclusively with visions and images. . . . But to teach Christ, this is the thing which an apostle is bound above all else to do; as Christ says in Acts 1, "You shall be my witnesses." Therefore, I stick to the books which present Christ to me clearly and purely. PREFACE TO THE REVELATION OF SAINT JOHN.[10]

JOHN'S PURPOSE. ULRICH ZWINGLI: This John sought to paint the salvation of Christ, his teaching, which God opened for us through him, the calling of all Jews and heathen, the glory and honor of Christ, the joy of all the saints, several punishments and signs which God is about to send us, in

[7] Mede, *Works** (1672), 581.
[8] LW 35:401.

[9] Bullinger, *Hundred Sermons** (1561), 15-16.
[10] LW 35:398-99; citing Acts 1:8.

obscure words. Defense of the Reformed Faith.[11]

John's Name Renowned. Antoine Du Pinet: To which all the doctors are so conformable [to the name of John] that all of them with one mouth attribute to it . And even the consent of the church, both Greek and Latin, is there: given that certain lessons of this book were ordinary in the service of the church, under the name of Saint John. . . . Wherefore it seems that the Holy Spirit, in order to give authority to this prophethood, willed that the apostle should take care oftentimes to be named in it. Exposition on the Apocalypse of Saint John[12]

1:3 *The Time Is Near*

Christ Is the Fulfillment of Time. Pilgram Marpeck: In him virtue, such as the power of love, is completed and revealed before time, in the time of his flesh, as well as after this time to eternity. As this is declared and witnessed to in that manner before the Father, so the Father will fully glorify the Son in the fulfillment of time in all of Christ's elect, and they will be as he is and he as his own in God and God in them eternally. It is not as though he had just become love, but this shows he is from eternity. Thus, the incarnate Word is God and man, man and God, two natures, one God, and also two natures, one man, the beginning of time, the center, and end of all things, A and O. For his sake are all things. He is the breaking in of time out of eternity and into eternity. Concerning the Love of God in Christ.[13]

The Nearness of the End. Thomas Müntzer: Now is the time of antichrist, as Matthew 24 most clearly manifests. When the Lord says that the gospel must be proclaimed in the whole world, then the abomination of desolation will be seen. But the reprobate are not going to believe just as they clung to a straw in the days of Noah. All those who say that the pope is the superior antichrist err. Indeed, he is his true herald. But the fourth beast will rule the whole world and its reign will be greater than all. Indeed, the persecution of Christians is already in the public places, and I don't know why you think it is the favor of your princes, for if you do you will behold your own destruction. Letter to Nikolaus Hausmann.[14]

Last Times Are Shortly Come to Pass. David Pareus: This notes the subject of the book, which does not contain a history of things already past but things to come afterward, both to the church and its enemies. They must come to pass not by a fatal or absolute necessity but hypothetically or supposedly. According to the apostle, scandals and heresies must come. . . . But how shortly? Seeing as, after so many ages, they are not as yet come to pass and are for the most part to be fully accomplished near the very last times, which is distant from the time this was revealed, more than fifteen hundred years, some extend this to the whole time of the New Testament, which, though it were to continue more than one thousand years yet is called short, both in regard to the age of the world then already past as also in regard to eternity, in which shall be neither shortness nor length of time. A Commentary upon the Divine Revelation.[15]

A Prophecy About Calamities in the Church. David Chytraeus: Finally, the whole book of the Apocalypse is such a prophecy about the confusion and corruption of doctrine and other calamities that will follow in the church of Christ. This did not happen by accident, by chance, but by God the Father and the Lamb and our Redeemer

[11]Zwingli, *Defense of the Reformed Faith*, 1:166.
[12]Du Pinet, *Exposition* (1545), aiv.
[13]Marpeck, *Writings*, 535.
[14]Müntzer, *Schriften und Briefe*, 381, lines 22-24. See Ozment, *Mysticism and Dissent*, 71.
[15]Pareus, *Revelation**, 4.

and our Lord Jesus Christ. By a most wise counsel and just judgment, he had sat down to rule and govern all that happens in the church, good and bad. Explication of the Apocalypse of Saint John.[16]

Testament Means Covenant. Heinrich Bullinger: For *Testament,* which also is the title for all of Scripture, surely stands for the content of all Scripture. This is not to be wondered at as something recent and devoid of meaning. For by the word *Testament,* we understand the covenant and the agreement by which God agreed with the entire human race to be himself our God, our sufficiency, source of good, and horn of plenty. And this he would abundantly prove by the gift of the fertile earth and the incarnation of his son. People, however, ought to pursue integrity, that they may stand before God with a perfect and upright mind, that they may walk in his ways and commit themselves totally to him as to the highest God and most loving Father. The Prophetic Office.[17]

[16]Chytraeus, *Explicatio Apocalypsis Johannis apostoli**, B5r-v.

[17]Bullinger, *De prophetae officio**, Aivv-Avr03.

1:4-8 The Greeting

[4]*John to the seven churches that are in Asia:*

Grace to you and peace from him who is and who was and who is to come, and from the seven spirits who are before his throne, [5]and from Jesus Christ the faithful witness, the firstborn of the dead, and the ruler of kings on earth.

To him who loves us and has freed us from our sins by his blood [6]and made us a kingdom, priests to his God and Father, to him be glory and dominion forever and ever. Amen. [7]Behold, he is coming with the clouds, and every eye will see him, even those who pierced him, and all tribes of the earth will wail[a] on account of him. Even so. Amen.

[8]"I am the Alpha and the Omega," says the Lord God, "who is and who was and who is to come, the Almighty."

a Or *mourn*

Overview: In Antoine Du Pinet early in the Reformation, and later in David Pareus, the book's structure is given as a preface (Rev 1:1-8) followed by a series of seven visions (Rev 1:9—3:22; 4—7; 8—11; 12—14; 15—16; 17—19; 20:1—22:6) and a conclusion (Rev 22:7-21). The greeting, as part of the preface, offers the Reformers an opportunity to sketch the identity of the one offering and the one receiving the greeting. This greeting is from Jesus Christ, who is described as the faithful witness. He is the firstborn from the dead and ruler of the kings of the earth. He loves his followers and has freed them from their sins by his blood. God's people are told who they are, a kingdom of priests in service to God the Father. The heart of the greeting is the grace and peace, glory and power that are promised and were held dear by the likes of Puritan Westminster preacher John Downame.

1:4 *The Sender and the Recipient*

First Vision and First Book. Antoine Du Pinet: The Father as fountain and original, of whom the Son is engendered, is first described, for he is the one who is, was, and is to come. Those words John takes from Moses . . . and out of many testimonies of Isaiah. And he says nothing but that God the father is an eternal essence, which consisted by and of itself, and is and gives life to all, and in all preserves the same. . . . The Holy Spirit therefore is of the same glory, power, and majesty with God. Now he comes to Christ, whom by his properties he describes most abundantly. You know that Jesus is the proper name of Christ, which Matthew expounded, a Savior, Christ is the surname of his office and dignity, as you would say, anointed, that is, bishop and king.

1. First he calls Christ our Lord, a faithful witness. . . .
2. He is the first begotten of the dead.
3. Christ is prince over the kings of the earth, a monarch truly, and Lord of all rulers.
4. Christ has loved us with an incomparable love.
5. In the fifth place is shown the effect of our redemption, purifying.
6. In the sixth place, in the description of Christ he shows the glory and rule is due to God alone through Christ in the church for evermore.
7. Seventh, in the description follows the coming Christ to judgment and the manner of his coming. Exposition on the Apocalypse of Saint John[1]

The Divisions of the Book. David Pareus: The book ordinarily is variously divided. I shall not

[1]Du Pinet, *Familere et Brieve Exposition* (1539), 3. For Christ's seven titles, see Bullinger, *Hundred Sermons* (1561), 20-21 (Sermon 3).

much differ from the common partition but distribute the same into a preface; prophecy, or visions; and a conclusion.

1. The preface contains the title and dedication of the book, Revelation 1:1-9.

2. The prophesy I separate into seven visions, clearly enough and distinctly showed by Christ to John in the Spirit, in the Isle of Patmos, up until Revelation 22:6. But those who suppose and urge that the book consists of one continued vision do wholly stray from the scope and in vain weary the reader, as I shall show by and by.

The first vision is of Christ gloriously walking among the seven golden candlesticks and commanding John to write certain commandments, and also the following visions, to the seven churches of Asia for the perpetual doctrine, instruction, and consolation of the faithful (Rev 1:9–3:22). This vision is not prophetic of future things, as the six following, but wholly doctrinal, confirming John in the function of teaching and commending his apostolical authority to the seven churches of Asia. The second concerns God's majesty sitting in the throne and of the Lamb standing in the throne, and of the book sealed with seven seals, and of the opening of the seal and of the book by the Lamb, and diverse wonders proceeding from there (Rev 4–7).

The third is of the seven trumpets of the angels and wonderful apparitions following (Rev 8–11). The fourth is of the woman in travail of a man-child, and of the dragon persecuting the man-child and woman, of the woman's flight into the wilderness, and of the rage of the two beasts against the saints (Rev 12–14). The fifth is of the seven angels pouring forth the seven vials of the last plagues on the adversaries, and throne of the beast (Rev 15–16). The sixth is of the judgment of the great whore and ruin of Babylon, and of the casting of the beast and false prophet with all his followers into the lake of fire and brimstone (Rev 17–19).

The seventh and last is of the binding and loosing of the dragon at the end of a thousand years, and of the last judgment of the devil, death, hell, and all reprobates who were not written in the book of life, and of the figure and glorious state of the heavenly Jerusalem (Rev 20–22:6).

3. The conclusion of the book commends the profitableness of the prophecy and by an anathema established the divine authority of it (Rev 22:6-21). A Commentary upon the Divine Revelation.[2]

The Interpretive Rules of Tyconius. Sebastian Meyer: [We] should not lose sight of the rules of Tyconius[†] mentioned by Augustine in *De doctrina christiana* 3 and by Bede in his preface to this commentary. The first of those is that things that refer to the head, Christ, should often be referred to Christ's body, that is, the church, and, conversely, things that are referred to in the church should refer to Christ. The same applies to Satan and his body, that is, the church of evildoers. The second rule is that of the double body of Christ. One is the internal church, assembled in the Spirit, which is the church before God; it cannot be seen but only believed. The other is the mixed body because of the communion of the sacraments, as in the Song of Songs: "I am black but comely," and so on. . . . The third is that genus can be understood from the species and the other way around. The same goes for the whole and its parts with synecdoche. The fourth is how to understand recapitulation and anticipation. Augustine and Bede explain all those rules in greater detail. The Apocalypse of John.[3]

Four Rules—Recapitulation and Anticipation. Antoine Du Pinet: [We] should not lose sight of the four rules of Tyconius.[†] The first is that which belongs to Christ as head is often attributed to his body, which is the church, and vice versa. The same can be said of Satan and his body, which is the assembly of the wicked. The second

[2]Pareus, *Revelation**, 19.

[3]Meyer, *Apocalypsis**, a6r-a6v; citing Song 1:5. †Tyconius (d. c. 380) was a major theologian of fourth-century North African Latin Christianity. His *Book of Rules* is no longer extant, but the contents of this work have been reconstructed from later commentaries that cite it.

rule is that Christ's church should be taken in two ways, that is to say, veritably and spiritually. Spiritually, it is the church before God, and we do not see it but only believe in it. Carnally, it is the visible church in which the Word and the sacraments are administered. The third rule is that by the special the general is often understood, and vice versa; similarly, the whole is sometimes taken for a part, and a part for the whole. The fourth rule is that several things in this book are said by recapitulation and anticipation. Exposition on the Apocalypse of Saint John.[4]

John as the Author. David Pareus: That John (whose Gospel and three canonical epistles are extant) is the author can be proved by solid and undoubted reasons. . . . For John in the very first verse says, "The Revelation of Jesus Christ, which he signified by his angel unto his servant John," . . . and the church up to this point has always called this book the Revelation of John and not the Revelation of Jesus. A Commentary upon the Divine Revelation.[5]

1:4-8 *Grace and Peace, Glory and Power*

"I Am Alpha and Omega." Heinrich Bullinger: He concluded this place with these words: "I am Alpha and Omega." What followed ("the beginning and end") is omitted in some copies, as though that interpretation of "I am Alpha and Omega" crept in out of the margin. It is a proverb of St. John the apostle, "I am Alpha and Omega." Heretics, such as Basilides† and Valentinus‡ were wonderfully delighted in letters. But against those lettered heretics John spoke plainly by the mouth of Christ, "I am Alpha and Omega." If anything ought to be ascribed to letters, I am fully that everlasting virtue, essence, and eternity. For the sense is that God is the beginning and end, that is, eternal, unspeakable, best, and greatest. . . . There is added "almighty." For by this is declared the unity and majesty of God, of whom the Trinity was opened also before. By this also the authority of this book is confirmed, the author of which is showed to be God the eternal and almighty, to whom be glory. Hundred Sermons on the Apocalypse.[6]

Sacrifices of Praise. John Calvin: Even while the people of God as yet continued under the outward tutelage of the law, the prophets clearly enough announced that a truth, common to the Christian church and Jewish nation, underlay these carnal sacrifices. In this way David prayed that his prayer might ascend like incense into God's presence. . . . And Hosea called thanksgivings "the calves of lips." . . . David elsewhere called them "the sacrifices of praise." . . . The apostle, following him, also calls them sacrifices of praise and explains them as "the fruit of our lips confessing his name." . . . The Lord's Supper cannot be without a sacrifice of this kind, in which, while we proclaim his death . . . and give thanks, we do nothing but offer a sacrifice of praise. From this office of sacrificing, all Christians are called a royal priesthood . . . because through Christ we offer that sacrifice of praise to God of which the apostle speaks: "the fruit of our lips confessing his name. . . .

And we do not appear with our gifts before God without an intercessor. The mediator interceding for us is Christ, by whom we offer ourselves and what is ours to the Father. He is our pontiff, who has entered the heavenly sanctuary . . . and opens a way for us to enter. . . . He is the altar . . . upon which we lay our gifts, that whatever we venture to do, we may undertake in

[4]Du Pinet, *Familere et Brieve Exposition**, b2r-v. †Tyconius (d. c. 380) was a major theologian of fourth-century North African Latin Christianity. His *Book of Rules* is no longer extant, but the contents of this work have been reconstructed from later commentaries that cite it.

[5]Pareus, *Revelation**, 6-7.

[6]Bullinger, *Hundred Sermons** (1561), 25. †Basilides was a Gnostic (117–138) who negated both emanation and the eternity of matter, associating creation with a divine command rather than material processes. ‡Valentinus (c. 100–c. 180) taught that there were three kinds of people: the spiritual, psychical, and material. He also taught only those of a spiritual nature received the *gnosis* (knowledge) that allowed them to return to the divine Pleroma.

him. He it is, I say, that "has made us a kingdom and priests unto the Father." Institutes of the Christian Religion.[7]

Kings and Priests Saved by Grace. Joseph Mede: Though by ourselves we are in no way able to perform those works of obedience ordained by God before time in his law for us to walk in, yet now God has, as it were, newly created us in Christ, that we might perform them in him—namely, by way of acceptance, though they come short of that exactness the law requires. Thus to be saved is to be saved by grace and favor and not by the merit of works, because the foundation on which ourselves and services are approved in the eyes of God and have promise of reward is the mere favor of God in Jesus Christ and not anything in us or them. Agreeable to these Scriptures is the place in Revelation where glory is ascribed to Jesus Christ, who loved us, washed us from our sins in his own blood, and has made us kings and priests to God his Father: . . . kings, to subdue the world, the flesh, and the devil; priests, to offer sacrifices of prayer, thanksgiving, works of mercy, and other acceptable services to our heavenly Father. Discourses on Diverse Texts of Scripture.[8]

The Seven Spirits of God. John Downame: By "the seven spirits," I make no question that the Holy Spirit is meant and not the holy angels. First, because these seven spirits stand before the throne, inserted between the Father and the Son, the apostle wishes grace and peace from them; they are the horns and eyes of the Lamb, indeed, of his own very nature, being consubstantial and coessential things, not in the least degree pertaining to the angels. Further, let the text be marked: it is apparent that these seven spirits, the horns and eyes of the Lamb, are noted to be that strength and most absolute and perfect Wisdom, by whom this Lion of the tribe of Judah overcame to open the book and the seven seals of it, which none in heaven, or earth, or under the earth, that is, no creature, could do. And when all other angels and elders are said to fall down and adore God only, these seven spirits do not. Sum of Sacred Divinity.[9]

The Unchangeable God Is the Alpha and Omega. John Downame: The unchangeableness of his nature, remaining always one and the same without alteration, is set forth . . . when he says that with him is neither change nor shadow of turning, and, "I am Jehovah, and do not change." All this Isaiah does include, as much to say, "as I am, or I will be." When therefore the Lord says that he is or will be, he means that he is without change and so will continue ever. "For I am or I will be" shows that he is the cause of his own being and therefore without beginning. Alluding to this word, John in Revelation calls him "Alpha and Omega," that is, the first and the last, "he who is, and who was, and who is to come." Sum of Sacred Divinity.[10]

[7]Calvin, *Institutes* 4.18.17; citing Ps 141:2; Hos 14:3; Ps 50:23; 51:19; Heb 13:15 Vulg.; 1 Cor 11:26; 1 Pet 2:9; Heb 13:15 Vulg.; Heb 9:24; 10:20; 13:10; Rev 1:6.
[8]Mede, *Works** (1672), 113.
[9]Downame, *Sacred Divinity**, 56.
[10]Downame, *Sacred Divinity**, 23-24, citing Jas 1:17; Mal 3:6.

1:9-20 THE OPENING VISION

[9]I, John, your brother and partner in the tribulation
and the kingdom and the patient endurance that are
in Jesus, was on the island called Patmos on account
of the word of God and the testimony of Jesus. [10]I was
in the Spirit on the Lord's day, and I heard behind me
a loud voice like a trumpet [11]saying, "Write what you
see in a book and send it to the seven churches, to
Ephesus and to Smyrna and to Pergamum and to
Thyatira and to Sardis and to Philadelphia and
to Laodicea."
[12]Then I turned to see the voice that was speaking
to me, and on turning I saw seven golden lampstands,
[13]and in the midst of the lampstands one like a son of
man, clothed with a long robe and with a golden sash
around his chest. [14]The hairs of his head were white,
like white wool, like snow. His eyes were like a flame
of fire, [15]his feet were like burnished bronze, refined in
a furnace, and his voice was like the roar of many
waters. [16]In his right hand he held seven stars, from
his mouth came a sharp two-edged sword, and his
face was like the sun shining in full strength.
[17]When I saw him, I fell at his feet as though dead.
But he laid his right hand on me, saying, "Fear not, I
am the first and the last, [18]and the living one. I died,
and behold I am alive forevermore, and I have the
keys of Death and Hades. [19]Write therefore the things
that you have seen, those that are and those that are
to take place after this. [20]As for the mystery of the
seven stars that you saw in my right hand, and the
seven golden lampstands, the seven stars are the
angels of the seven churches, and the seven lamp-
stands are the seven churches.

Overview: The focus of this vision is on the voice and appearance of the one who is like a Son of Man, who appears to John. This vision sets the context for Reformation preaching in the sixteenth century. John is told to write what he sees on a scroll and to pass it on to the seven churches of Asia Minor. To the anxieties of the sixteenth century—political fears of internal social disintegration, Turkish advances into Europe, natural catastrophes, or even the existence of a corrupt clergy—Martin Luther's answer was to preach the effective graciousness of God. Preachers and prophets, conceived of as candlesticks, stars, and angels in this Apocalypse, carried God's last call to humanity to accept grace prior to judgment. Protestant culture galvanized around these preachers and the Lord's Day, the Christian Sabbath (Rev 1:10).

1:9-20 *The Voice*

John as a Brother of All Churches. Heinrich Bullinger: He added to his name certain teaching concerning the state of the apostle and certain profitable matters. First, he calls himself a brother, namely, of those seven churches and of all ours, as where I have admonished you that in the number seven are comprised all churches of all times throughout the whole world. We are all, so many believe, the children of one heavenly Father and therefore all spiritual siblings in Christ, co-inheritors with Christ, and heirs of God, which St. Paul taught after Christ. And seeing as our dignity is so great, let us once be ashamed of our misdeeds, lest our memory be put out of this most noble and celestial family. It is a shame the brother of Christ, of St. John and all the apostles, should degenerate and so on. But why have not they so instantly urged this brotherhood, as the monks have rehearsed in their forged fraternities the rosaries of the Virgin Mary and of saints? Because that was free and cost nothing, but the monks sell theirs dear. They are therefore deceivers and seducers. Hundred Sermons on the Apocalypse.[1]

The Sabbath. Martin Luther: The Sabbath . . . has been appointed for man's sake, that in it the knowledge of God may be exercised and increased. And although man by sin has lost the knowledge of God, yet it has been the will of God to let the command of keeping holy the Sabbath remain, and he has willed that men on the seventh day should train themselves in and pursue his word, and the service appointed by him, that we men first of all be reminded what is preeminently our calling and position, that our nature was created that we might know and praise God. Commentary on Genesis.[2]

The Regnant Christ on the Lord's Day. Heinrich Bullinger: Moreover, he notes the time also in which these mysteries began to be revealed to him, in that solemn day of the Lord, namely, the Sunday. For so have the ancient fathers called one of the Sabbaths, that is to say, the first day in the week, when Christ rose again from the dead. . . . And this day have the churches chosen to themselves instead of the Sabbath day as holy in the remembrance of the Lord's resurrection, when they might keep their sacred and solemn assemblies. That this day was solemnized and consecrated for assemblies in the congregation of Corinth appeared manifestly in 1 Corinthians 16, where the apostle commanded them to lay a part their collections in one of the Sabbaths. The same day also the faithful celebrated their service with St. Paul. . . .

Where Sozomen reported . . . that great Constantine made certain holy days, and even the Lord's Day for one, which is called by the heathen the Sunday, it is to be understood that he renewed the custom of the apostles and catholic church rather than newly instituted it. And freely of their own accord have the churches received that day, for we do not read that it was anywhere commanded. And the congregations saw how it was altogether necessary that there should be a certain time in which the saints should meet and come together. They chose therefore the day of the resurrection. They did not maliciously contend among themselves for these things, as history testifies was done in the churches afterward. And on this day, the superstitious holy days being abrogated, truly it is better to observe certain and moderate days and to keep peace and quietness in the church.

But this apostle knew that the faithful on Sunday served God in all assemblies, and where he could not be present in body, he was with them in spirit and contemplation. And as he was thus in the spirit and contemplation of matters divine and in holy prayers, he heard a voice, of which I will speak later. But here we are presently taught what the religion of the Sunday is and how it is proper to observe it.

Finally, worldly people are reproved, who pollute with profane works and affairs. David, when he suffered persecution by Saul, lamented chiefly that he might not come to the Lord's tabernacle. Our people count it a great felicity never to enter into the fellowship of saints so as to abuse Sunday in gaming, drinking, dancing, and worldly business. Hundred Sermons on the Apocalypse.[3]

Worship on the Sabbath. Philipp Melanchthon: Nor has the church dispensed with the Decalogue, but the authority of God has abrogated the ceremonies of the Mosaic law, and yet it is necessary that the people should know when they were to come together to the gospel and the ceremonies instituted by Christ. And the genus in the Decalogue that at certain times we should come together to these holy exercises remains. But the species, which was a ceremony, is free; therefore the apostles did not retain the seventh day but preferred to use the first, that they might remind

[1]Bullinger, *Hundred Sermons** (1561), 26-27.
[2]Luther, *Commentary on Genesis*, first part written 1536.
[3]Bullinger, *Hundred Sermons** (1561), 29-30; citing Mt 28; Mk 16; Acts 20; 8.

the pious both of their liberty and of the resurrection of Christ. The Augsburg Confession.[4]

Message to the Seven Churches. Heinrich Bullinger: These things on this wise declared, he comes at length to the revelation, setting forth the express commandment of God by which he was commanded both to write the things revealed and to send them to the seven churches of Asia. . . .

He heard a voice, a notable one, as the sound of a trumpet, for so we read it happened in the law given at Mount Sinai. Now is declared whose voice it was and who was the author of the revelation: truly the eternal God, who calls himself Alpha and Omega, that is, the beginning and the end—or, as it is said in Isaiah, first and last. Now follows the commandment, which has two parts. For first the Lord commanded St. John to write, and to write such things as he saw, that is, the Apocalypse. And he should write neither in the sand nor on the wall but in a book, truly for the edifying and profit of the church present and of all posterity. After he is also commanded to send those writings to seven congregations and to all the churches of the whole world in all times and ages. Therefore, all these things belong to the profit of congregations, all that are, have been, or will be. Hundred Sermons on the Apocalypse.[5]

1:12-16 *The Vision*

John Turns to See One like the Son of Man. Heinrich Bullinger: And turning to see him, he saw a figure of Christ our Savior. Therefore, when the Lord speaks, let us turn also with all our heart, that we may likewise deserve to see the mysteries of the kingdom of God, for he gladly revealed himself to those who turn and desire heavenly things. And all things of salvation are hidden from those who neglect the mysteries of the kingdom of God. Furthermore, St. John exhibited to us the image of Christ, our catholic king and high bishop sitting in glory, in which description is contained the chief matters of Christ. For a taste of Christ is given to us here such as in this world our weak flesh is able to perceive. But we shall see him . . . in the world to come as he is, in the fullness of his majesty, in which shall be joy and life everlasting. But in this corrupt world, this is yet granted to no one. Therefore to us who live in this world only as much is permitted to be seen as is profitable and as our infirmity may perceive. But this is not little or nothing but great and large and most full of spiritual pleasure, I mean, if we behold these mysteries of God with a faithful eye and mind desirous of godly matters.

And doubtless these are certain and true things that here are revealed to us. For they are revealed by the very Son of God. Let us not wish to see more or desire greater things than these but take pleasure in those that Christ has granted us. And let us know for certain that a wonderful benefit of God is given us in this vision. For who would not covet to see Christ in glory sitting at the right hand of the Father? Who does not desire to know what our Savior does in heaven—who, his home being in heaven, is nevertheless present with his church in earth? But this sacred and holy image instructed all the faithful of Christ in all these points most fully.

Nevertheless, this image of Christ is not to be set forth with colors, since colors cannot attain to the majesty of it, but with the ecclesiastical doctrine, which has the promise of the spirit of Christ and is therefore more evident and only suitable for the true expressing of it. Let us also print the same image not on any dead tablet with colors that will perish and fade but in our hearts through the lively spirit of God, who may also keep it in our minds, never to be wiped out. And such things as are spoken in Revelation 2–3 are derived of this description of Christ, that the majesty of the thing might invite us to a singular diligence. The matter is very plain. Hundred Sermons on the Apocalypse.[6]

[4]Melanchthon, *Augsburg Confession.*
[5]Bullinger, *Hundred Sermons** (1561), 30-31.
[6]Bullinger, *Hundred Sermons** (1561), 32-34.

The Sword from His Mouth. Martin Luther: The prophet Isaiah also foretold that the Messiah would bring with him a cudgel or cane, but this would be "the rod of his mouth." . . . And in the papacy we find paintings which portray Christ with a sword issuing from one side of his mouth and a lily twig from the other; the point of the sword is to be directed against man. But this is not a true image of Christ. He should have been portrayed with a sword, cudgel, rod, or whip issuing from his mouth, as in the book of Revelation the Evangelist beheld a man "from whose mouth issued a sharp, two-edged sword, and whose face was like the sun shining in full strength." . . . Christ's kingdom is not to be administered with physical power, with the sword or the rod. It is the province of the parents to wield the rod, and that of government and executioner to use the sword. No, his are an oral rod and an oral sword. . . . [Isaiah] calls the Word of God "the rod of his mouth." God uses "the rod of his mouth" when he judges and punishes the unbelieving world. The Gospel of Saint John.[7]

Figurative and Sacramental Phrases. David Pareus: Furthermore, we are to take notice of these figurative and sacramental phrases. The stars are angels, that is, they represent the angels; the candlesticks are the churches, that is, they represent the churches; and according to Genesis, the seven cows are seven years, that is, they represent seven years. "And the rock was Christ," for it represented Christ, as Augustine expounded it. For there is nothing more familiar in Scripture then to name signs by the things they signify, and this manner of speech is not dark but plain in regard to the analogy between the sign and the thing signified. Therefore it was not obscure but familiar to the Scripture that Christ called the bread that was broken at the institution of the Supper his body, which was crucified for us, seeing it was a sacrament or holy sign of the same. Hence Augustine, opening the etymology or signification of a sacrament, applies it to the Lord's Supper, saying that the Lord Jesus did not doubt to say "This is my body" when he gave the sign only of it. A Commentary upon the Divine Revelation.[8]

Light from the Candlesticks. Heinrich Bullinger: Now concerning the candlesticks, there were truly in the tabernacle of Moses seven candles set in seven sockets. In Solomon's temple there were ten candlesticks. The one represented a figure of Christ, and the seven there and the ten betokened the universality of churches, which are all lighted only of the light of Christ and have whatever light they have from this one. And the candlesticks are of gold. Aretas[†] expounds the mystery of this: they are all gold, he says, for the purity and preciousness of faith lying hidden in them. And indeed, the candlesticks of themselves give no light but are receptacles of light. So, from us arises no light but darkness. But in that light everlasting, set a light in the candlestick, the light shines: if Christ illumined the church with faith, and then faith showed forth itself in open confession and the pureness of life in conversation. And this the Lord inquires of his church . . . that in the middle of a . . . crooked nation, it would shine like lights in the world.

And until this point we have handled the consolation of Christ and the exposition of that great and celestial vision when we have learned the mysteries of the faith of Christ and of his church, to the end we should know that Christ is the Lord reigning in his church and applying all things to the salvation of his faithful, that he sends preachers, teaches by them, and keeps and defends them. To him be glory. Hundred Sermons on the Apocalypse.[9]

The Sword of the Spirit. Chronicle of the Hutterian Brethren: In the book of Revelation, Christ appeared to the holy apostle

[7]LW 22:221-22, citing Is 11:4.

[8]Pareus, *Apoc.*, 28-29. See 1 Cor 10:4 for "And the rock was Christ."
[9]Bullinger, *Hundred Sermons** (1561), 46, citing Mt 5:14; Phil 2:15.
†Arethas, archbishop of Caesarea (c. 850–d. c. 944), was possibly a pupil of the patriarch of Constantinople, Photius.

John with a two-edged sword in his mouth. From this, we who are his disciples and believe in him learn that the sword belongs not in our hand but in our mouth, namely, that we are to wield the sword of the Spirit and not the sword of blood. Chronicle of the Hutterian Brethren.[10]

Found in Likeness as a Man. David Pareus: Now let us consider the description. First John showed the garments and habit in which Christ appeared; second, the admirable form of his body and members, which plainly showed that the man Christ did not appear really but typically, and the whole serves to make known to the churches his dreadful majesty and power. . . .

Daniel saw one like the son of man come with the clouds of heaven. So says Paul in his epistles that Christ was found in likeness as a man. Made like humans, that he was in the likeness of sinful flesh, not that he had only the form of a true man, as the Marcionites[†] do gather from this place. But nothing is more like to humans than he who is a true man, and the apostle seems to give a reason of this manner of speech where he says that Christ himself likewise took part of the flesh and blood of the children. . . .

"And girt about the chest with a golden girdle": Though there is a mystery in all these things, we must not be too curious in searching after the meaning of everything in it; interpreters are diversly minded about it. For our part it is sufficient we know by what follows that it is to set forth the majesty of Christ. It was the manner of men in the Eastern countries to gird up their garments, being long, that they might not be hindered in their work or any other businesses. So Christ's binding up of his garment with a girdle notes his care and diligence to accomplish the work that his Father gave him to do. In that it was a golden girdle is showed his majesty, of which the prophet Isaiah speaks. . . . Now, in that Christ is girded about the chest, not according to the ordinary custom, is manifested the love of Christ toward the church, because the heart, which is the seat of love, is between the breasts.

So the hair of the Ancient of Days was like pure wool. . . . This reverend hoariness or whiteness of hairs denotes prudency and wisdom, for Christ is the wisdom of the Father. . . . Eyes do manifest the fiery, heroic, and terrible motions of the heart. Hence . . . Christ is coming to take vengeance in a terrible manner on the enemies; his eyes appear like flames of fire, because in his wrath he will consume the wicked, as fire does chaff. . . .

First he heard his voice like a trumpet, and now similar to many waters, which make a terrible noise violently running and throw rocks and stones. They cannot be stopped with any power or force, as may be seen as the swift fallings of the River Nile and the Rhine. . . .

By the seven stars the seven pastors of the churches are to be understood; they are compared to stars because they ought to shine like stars to their flocks by the light of their life and doctrine. . . .

Now John showed how he was affected with the vision by reason of the glorious brightness of Christ's majesty. . . . For such is the great weakness of the most holy men of God, that they are not able to behold the divine majesty. . . . As a hand touched Daniel (in whom there remained no strength when he saw that great vision) and set him upon his knees and upon the palms of his hands, even so does Christ lift up John, who was greatly amazed, first by laying his hand on him and afterward speaking comfortably to him. . . . He bids him not to fear, because fear disturbs the mind and unfits people for instruction, and therefore the admonition at this time was very seasonable. . . .

But some heretics object that Christ is called first, as being the first of the church under the New Testament. But I answer that all the adjuncts disprove this gloss. For Christ does absolutely call himself the first and the last, by which very words the prophets declare the eternity of Jehovah God. Indeed, Christ said that he was not only before the church of the New Testament but also before

[10]Hutterian Brethren, *Chronicle*, 284.

Abraham. A Commentary upon the Divine Revelation.[11]

1:17-20 *The Explanation*

Visions and Wonders. Ursula Jost: After my husband and spouse was released from custody and let go, he and I together prayed earnestly and diligently to God, the Almighty merciful Father, that he would let me also see the wonderous deeds of his hand. God's grace and kindness granted this to us, and these visions written down here all appeared to me. I saw all these visions and wonders in the glory of the Lord, which always unfolded itself before me. And in it I received knowledge of the meaning of these visions of divine wonders. After that it always came together again and went away and disappeared. The course of these revelations, visions, and stories began, as one counts after the birth of Christ Jesus, our Lord. Prophetic Visions and Revelations of the Workings of God in These Last Days.[12]

Divine Authority in the Visions. David Pareus: He shows how he saw this revelation, that is, not with mortal eyes, but his mind was carried beyond itself, being ravished in spirit. So we read that Peter and Paul, praying earnestly, fell into a trance and conversed with God. This again confirms the divine authority of this book. For the following visions and the mysteries of them were revealed to John not by the power of any human mind but by the Holy Spirit.

Here it may be asked whether John saw the whole revelation on one Lord's Day. Indeed, it may seem by the coherence of the matter to be so, but I think that Christ did not at one time burden the mind of his servant with so many different and large visions. Neither is this probable, because the distinctions of time similar to what other prophets had in their visions appear also to be in these visions of John. . . . After he had seen the first vision, he came to himself before he was again ravished and saw other visions, and in likelihood this was on another Lord's Day. . . . Often it is said "after these things," but I do not conceive all of them import a distance of time. . . . Besides, all things were not revealed to John in one place, but some things he saw in Patmos, some in the heavens, some on the seashore, and some things in the wilderness. But seeing as we cannot certainly determine the matter, I will therefore leave it to the reader's choice.

Alcasar† untruly affirms that this voice was altogether like unto the sound of a trumpet. But the text says it was the voice not of one founding but speaking. Again, by this voice is signified how we should be stirred up to encounter all our spiritual adversaries as soldiers by the sound of the trumpet are emboldened to the battle. In that he heard the voice behind him, it indicates that John added nothing to these visions but that they were altogether divine, for we do not see the things that are behind us. Or, otherwise, he heard a voice behind to denote how the things he heard were suddenly to come to pass even immediately upon John's departure.

In this great voice are contained three things. First, the eternity of Christ is testified; second, John's commission to write the vision; and last, a commandment is given him to send the same to the seven churches. And hence it is very clear that Christ is that Son of God who spoke in verse 8. For both there and here he takes the same things to himself. And there is no question to be made but that in this place he spoke himself and of himself. Eniedinus the Samosatenian‡ objects that these words are not in all copies, nor yet in the Latin version, and for this cites the Annotations of Beza.

The command of writing confirms the authority of this book. For John wrote this prophecy not of himself but by the commandment of Christ, for

[11]Pareus, *Revelation**, 23-26, citing Dan 7:13; Rom 8:3; Heb 2:14, 17; Is 11:5; Dan 7:9; 10:6; Rev 19:11; Rev 19:1; Dan 8:18; Jn 8:58. †Marcionites were followers of the theologian Marcion. He taught there were three kinds of people, the spiritual, psychical, and material. He said only those of a spiritual nature received the *gnosis* (knowledge) that allowed them to return to the divine Pleroma.
[12]Snyder and Hecht, *Profiles of Anabaptist Women*, 282-83.

though here the commandment is particular, to write this first vision, in verse 19 it is general, not only of the things that are but that will be hereafter.

"Write what you see": This served for the authority of the book, for the apostle is to write not the things he thought fit but what God gave him to see and send it to the seven churches in Asia.

By seven Rupertus understands all the churches, but it is to be taken restrictively of the seven greater churches of Asia the Less, because they are expressly named, and epistles are directed to every one of the bishops or pastors of it, yet so as that saying of Christ pertained to this place. A Commentary upon the Divine Revelation.[13]

The Angels Are Bishops. Giovanni Diodati: [The angels refer to] the bishops, or the chief ministers honored sometimes in Scripture with this title, because of the resemblance of their office to that of the angels concerning believers' salvation. . . . [The seven refer to] the particular churches, because the Lord has set in them the gift of his Spirit, which is instead of oil, and faith, which is instead of fire, to carry and hold up before all the lamp of truth and knowledge of God and make it to shine before the eyes of the world by works. Pious Annotations upon the Holy Bible.[14]

The Church Is Oppressed by Antichrist. David Pareus: The third "distance" was of . . . the church trodden upon and oppressed by antichrist, especially the Western, until the measuring of the temple, which began to be effected by the two witnesses Jan Hus and Jerome of Prague,[†] who were slain by the beast in the Council of Constance, in 1414, and thence until Luther, by whose ministry the measuring of the temple (broken off or hindered through the tyranny of the popes) began to be continued, in 1517. The fourth "distance" was of . . . the church reformed from popery and of the declining of the papacy, to endure until the end. For the beast goes into destruction, whatever the gates of hell attempt to the contrary and Bellarmine their prophet said truly. From that time that pope began by you to be antichrist, his empire has been so far from increasing as it has always more and more decreased. A Commentary upon the Divine Revelation.[15]

Explanation of the Voice and Vision. Heinrich Bullinger: First, you have seen, says the Lord, a vision where you were amazed, but fear not. For you have not seen any evil or fearful spirit, boding any misfortune, but my shape, which is your Redeemer and Lord. I am first and last. And this manner of speaking (as I said a little before) he took out of the prophecies of Isaiah. . . . And he signifies himself to be coequal and of the same substance with the Father in all things, very God, eternal and incomprehensible. For look, what things the Father attributes to himself, the same also does the Son take. But there is no order or time certain to be understood in first and last, but plainly everlastingness. Therefore, Christ here signifies that he is very God, equal and of the same essence with the Father from all eternity. The same is also much confirmed in John. . . .

The heretics, who at that time also as at this day, the Servetanes,[†] deny the eternal deity of Christ the Lord. And thus when the true God is of us acknowledged and believed, he may be for our salvation. If Christ is not very God, he is not our salvation. "For I am God," he says truly, "and besides me there is no God, no salvation." Second, he says, "I am living and was dead," by which he signifies that he took the true human nature. Many also at the same time denied this, like how there are some

[13]Pareus, *Revelation**, 19-22, citing Rev 4:1-2; 17:3; 21:1. †Luis de Alcasar (1554–1613) was a Spanish Jesuit theologian. ‡The heresy of Georgius Eniedinus, a Samosatenian or Socinianism, was a Christian belief system that developed during the Protestant Reformation and was characterized by its rejection of the Trinity and the divinity of Christ.

[14]Diodati, *Pious Annotations**, 100.

[15]Pareus, *Revelation**, 25. †Jan Hus (d. 1415) and Jerome of Prague (c. 1370–1416) were Reformers martyred for their theological views.

today who do plainly detract from the humanity of Christ. Against all such manner of heresies the Lord himself confesses that he was dead. By this it is now manifest that he is very man as he is also very God, of the same essence with his Father in deity as he is also of the same substance with us in humanity, like unto us in all things, sin excepted. For he did not take the nature of angels but the seed of Abraham.

And it was suitable indeed that the Son of Man should be incarnate, that both he might die and shed blood. For the Old Testament is finally ratified that there is no remission made without blood shedding. The Lord therefore dies and sheds blood with the intent that he might give full remission of sin and confirm the New Testament. Yet even he who was thought to be dead now lives and is living, he who, having vanquished death, the third day rose again from the dead, repaired life for all believers, and inspires into them his own very life. Finally, he adds, "And I have the keys of hell and of death." By the which words again he comforted exceedingly and expresses his power, and declares how great he is and what we have of him. Here must we speak by the way of the keep. Hundred Sermons on the Apocalypse.[16]

[16]Bullinger, *Hundred Sermons** (1561), 41-43; citing Is 41; 44–45; 48; Jn 1; 5; 10; 14; 17. †Servetanes, or Socinianism is a non-trinitarian Christian belief system developed and cofounded during the Protestant Reformation by the Italian Renaissance humanists and theologians Lelio Sozzini and Fausto Sozzini, uncle and nephew.

2:1-3:22 THE SEVEN MESSAGES

2 "To the angel of the church in Ephesus write: 'The
words of him who holds the seven stars in his
right hand, who walks among the seven golden
lampstands.
2"'I know your works, your toil and your patient
endurance, and how you cannot bear with those who
are evil, but have tested those who call themselves
apostles and are not, and found them to be false. 3I
know you are enduring patiently and bearing up for
my name's sake, and you have not grown weary. 4But
I have this against you, that you have abandoned the
love you had at first. 5Remember therefore from where
you have fallen; repent, and do the works you did at
first. If not, I will come to you and remove your
lampstand from its place, unless you repent. 6Yet this
you have: you hate the works of the Nicolaitans,
which I also hate. 7He who has an ear, let him hear
what the Spirit says to the churches. To the one who
conquers I will grant to eat of the tree of life, which is
in the paradise of God.'
8"And to the angel of the church in Smyrna write:
'The words of the first and the last, who died and
came to life.
9"'I know your tribulation and your poverty (but
you are rich) and the slander[a] of those who say that
they are Jews and are not, but are a synagogue of
Satan. 10Do not fear what you are about to suffer.
Behold, the devil is about to throw some of you into
prison, that you may be tested, and for ten days you
will have tribulation. Be faithful unto death, and I will
give you the crown of life. 11He who has an ear, let him
hear what the Spirit says to the churches. The one who
conquers will not be hurt by the second death.'
12"And to the angel of the church in Pergamum
write: 'The words of him who has the sharp two-
edged sword.
13"'I know where you dwell, where Satan's throne
is. Yet you hold fast my name, and you did not deny
my faith[b] even in the days of Antipas my faithful
witness, who was killed among you, where Satan
dwells. 14But I have a few things against you: you
have some there who hold the teaching of Balaam,
who taught Balak to put a stumbling block before the
sons of Israel, so that they might eat food sacrificed to
idols and practice sexual immorality. 15So also you
have some who hold the teaching of the Nicolaitans.
16Therefore repent. If not, I will come to you soon and
war against them with the sword of my mouth. 17He
who has an ear, let him hear what the Spirit says to
the churches. To the one who conquers I will give
some of the hidden manna, and I will give him a
white stone, with a new name written on the stone
that no one knows except the one who receives it.'
18"And to the angel of the church in Thyatira
write: 'The words of the Son of God, who has eyes
like a flame of fire, and whose feet are like
burnished bronze.
19"'I know your works, your love and faith and
service and patient endurance, and that your latter
works exceed the first. 20But I have this against you,
that you tolerate that woman Jezebel, who calls herself
a prophetess and is teaching and seducing my servants
to practice sexual immorality and to eat food
sacrificed to idols. 21I gave her time to repent, but she
refuses to repent of her sexual immorality. 22Behold, I
will throw her onto a sickbed, and those who commit
adultery with her I will throw into great tribulation,
unless they repent of her works, 23and I will strike her
children dead. And all the churches will know that I
am he who searches mind and heart, and I will give
to each of you according to your works. 24But to the
rest of you in Thyatira, who do not hold this teaching,
who have not learned what some call the deep things
of Satan, to you I say, I do not lay on you any other
burden. 25Only hold fast what you have until I come.
26The one who conquers and who keeps my works
until the end, to him I will give authority over the
nations, 27and he will rule[c] them with a rod of iron, as
when earthen pots are broken in pieces, even as I
myself have received authority from my Father. 28And

*I will give him the morning star. [29]He who has an ear,
let him hear what the Spirit says to the churches.'*

3 *"And to the angel of the church in Sardis write:
'The words of him who has the seven spirits of
God and the seven stars.*

*"'I know your works. You have the reputation of
being alive, but you are dead. [2]Wake up, and
strengthen what remains and is about to die, for I
have not found your works complete in the sight of my
God. [3]Remember, then, what you received and heard.
Keep it, and repent. If you will not wake up, I will
come like a thief, and you will not know at what hour
I will come against you. [4]Yet you have still a few
names in Sardis, people who have not soiled their
garments, and they will walk with me in white, for
they are worthy. [5]The one who conquers will be clothed
thus in white garments, and I will never blot his name
out of the book of life. I will confess his name before my
Father and before his angels. [6]He who has an ear, let
him hear what the Spirit says to the churches.'*

*[7]"And to the angel of the church in Philadelphia
write: 'The words of the holy one, the true one, who
has the key of David, who opens and no one will shut,
who shuts and no one opens.*

*[8]"'I know your works. Behold, I have set before
you an open door, which no one is able to shut. I
know that you have but little power, and yet you have
kept my word and have not denied my name.
[9]Behold, I will make those of the synagogue of Satan
who say that they are Jews and are not, but lie—behold, I will make them come and bow down before
your feet, and they will learn that I have loved you.
[10]Because you have kept my word about patient
endurance, I will keep you from the hour of trial that
is coming on the whole world, to try those who dwell
on the earth. [11]I am coming soon. Hold fast what you
have, so that no one may seize your crown. [12]The one
who conquers, I will make him a pillar in the temple
of my God. Never shall he go out of it, and I will
write on him the name of my God, and the name of
the city of my God, the new Jerusalem, which comes
down from my God out of heaven, and my own new
name. [13]He who has an ear, let him hear what the
Spirit says to the churches.'*

*[14]"And to the angel of the church in Laodicea
write: 'The words of the Amen, the faithful and true
witness, the beginning of God's creation.*

*[15]"'I know your works: you are neither cold nor
hot. Would that you were either cold or hot! [16]So,
because you are lukewarm, and neither hot nor cold, I
will spit you out of my mouth. [17]For you say, I am
rich, I have prospered, and I need nothing, not
realizing that you are wretched, pitiable, poor, blind,
and naked. [18]I counsel you to buy from me gold
refined by fire, so that you may be rich, and white
garments so that you may clothe yourself and the
shame of your nakedness may not be seen, and salve
to anoint your eyes, so that you may see. [19]Those
whom I love, I reprove and discipline, so be zealous
and repent. [20]Behold, I stand at the door and knock.
If anyone hears my voice and opens the door, I will
come in to him and eat with him, and he with me.
[21]The one who conquers, I will grant him to sit with
me on my throne, as I also conquered and sat down
with my Father on his throne. [22]He who has an ear,
let him hear what the Spirit says to the churches.'"*

a Greek *blasphemy* **b** Or *your faith in me* **c** Greek *shepherd*

OVERVIEW: The opening vision in the book of Revelation gives way to instructions for John to send seven messages to seven churches in Asia. The letters come from the throne of God and were understood to defend the Reformation through the use of history by offering praise or censure, and sixteenth-century commentators see them as just as pertinent as when they were first written. As the century progressed, they became for some a measure of the spiritual and political progression of the Reformation. This theme can be tracked in Heinrich Bullinger, David Pareus, Thomas Brightman, Matthias Flacius Illyricus, and others.

The seven letters are held together by inscription, narration, and a concluding condemnation or commendation. Sixteenth-century commentators equate Pergamum with the church of the high medieval period. The antitype of Sardis is the first reformed church begun by Martin Luther. The church of Philadelphia is seen in the church of the Helvetians and the Reformed centers of Europe. The seventh church, the lukewarm church of Laodicea, is often equated with the English church.

Epistles Seen from the Throne of God. Heinrich Bullinger: Great is the authority of these epistles. For they are received from the throne of God by the Son of God, spoken by an angel, who prescribes what is to be written in those epistles. St. John received and witnesses the same, through Christ's commandment, and sends them to the seven congregations, and truly they pertain no less to us than if now the bearer entering into the church should deliver these letters to us. Moreover, in these seven churches is represented to us the nature, manners, vices, medicines, rebukes, prayers, of all churches in all times, and anything that happens to be by chance about them. . . . And those whom our Lord evidently instructs, reproves, rebukes, blames, praises, corrects, moves, exhorts, comforts, the same also he threatens and promises them joyful things, and so on. This is no light nor common example, but of the Son of God, the high, most blessed bishop, teaching us how we should deal with all congregations after the capacity and disposition of everyone. Hundred Sermons on the Apocalypse.[1]

The Seven Epistles Are the Seven Ages of the Church. Joseph Mede: It does not much belong to our purpose to inquire whether those seven epistles concern historically and literally only the churches here named or whether they were intended for types of churches or ages of the church to come afterward. It shall be sufficient to say that if we consider their number, being seven (which is a number of revolution of times, and therefore in this book the seals, trumpets, and vials also are seven), . . . it will seem that these seven churches, besides their literal respect, were intended (and it may be chiefly) to be as patterns and types of the several ages of the catholic church from the beginning of it unto the end of the world, that so these seven churches should prophetically sample to us a sevenfold temper and constitution of the whole church according to the several ages of it, answering the pattern of the churches named here. For as in the course of a person's life, diversity of age has diverse manners and conditions, so was it to be with the church of Christ; indeed, and as some diseases are more common to some people and not to others, so is it with the church. All of these—with their praises, if good, and remedies, if evil—are portrayed in these seven epistles unto the seven churches. Discourses on Diverse Texts of Scripture.[2]

Encouragement to Obedience. Martin Luther: Sinners should not be upbraided in such a way that they are only wounded and driven to despair; but they should be cherished again, so that they are encouraged to be obedient. But this will happen if they are never reproved without mixing some praise of them. On the other hand, they should never be praised without being reproved to some extent. . . . Thus in Revelation 2–3 John praises and censures the seven angels of the churches. Lectures on Hebrews.[3]

The Pastor Has Authority Only from Christ. Giovanni Diodati: The one who holds is the sovereign Lord and master of all the pastors, who have no authority but from him, who alone establishes them and likewise can depose them according to their works. The one who walks is always present and working in his church in the power of his Spirit, to preserve the light of his power and the oil of his grace in it, as in ancient times the priest had the charge of the great candlestick, to make it clean and keep the lamps

[1]Bullinger, *Hundred Sermons** (1561), 47.

[2]Mede, *Works** (1672), 295-96.

[3]LW 29:184.

lighted in it all the night. Pious Annotations upon the Holy Bible.[4]

2:1-7 *The Message to Ephesus*

First and Second Faith. Martin Chemnitz: There is also a most clear passage which contains and explains this expression of Paul about the first faith . . . where John is commanded to write to the minister of the church at Ephesus. . . . This passage tells most clearly what Paul means by the first faith, so that there is no need of prolonged debate or of an explanation sought from elsewhere. For Scripture speaks this way also about the spiritual espousal of Christ and the church, which come about by faith, in order that after a fall they may return to the first covenant of spiritual marriage . . . so that it is said to be the first faith in view of that by which those who had lapsed were afterward again reconciled to God when they were converted. This secondary faith, as it were, is nevertheless nothing other than a return to the first faith, which was sealed by the mark of baptism. Examination of the Council of Trent.[5]

Inscription, Narration, and Conclusion. Thomas Brightman: In every one of [these letters], there is an inscription, narration, and conclusion. The three first are of the church falling into a worse estate, of Ephesus, Smyrna, and Pergamum. The other followers are of the same returning, and so as the three next are opposed to the three first and are answerable one to the other: the Thyatirian to the Ephesian, the Sardinian to the Smyrnaean, the Philadelphian to the Pergamian. Only Laodicea has no equal to which she may be compared. Revelation of St. John.[6]

The Message to Ephesus. Heinrich Bullinger: Ephesians further addresses the immoral decline of the church in Ephesus. Throughout the letter, the author repeatedly draws a stark contrast between the authentic life of a true believer and the false testimony of one who would profess Christ but live a life of greed, impurity, vile speech, hatred, and anger. This life, Ephesians makes clear, is not the life of a believer. Rather, it is the life of one who embraces evil and undermines the integrity of Christianity. The church at Ephesus is called to be strong in Christ amid the evil forces that dominate its culture at the time. Ephesians makes it clear—known for having labored hard and not fainted and separating themselves from the wicked; admonished for having lost their first love. . . . Ephesus was most famous, called in the old time the light of Asia. Hundred Sermons on the Apocalypse.[7]

The Teaching of the Nicolaitans. Martin Chemnitz: The shamelessness of this unclean spirit is so great that when he has first obtruded his lusts on blinded and hardened hearts, and then has tried to sell them as something indifferent, he is finally not afraid to go further and to seek from Scripture itself with which he can disguise his shame, as though it were not an evil thing but good and honorable. In Revelation 2:6 mention is made of the teaching and life of the Nicolaitans. Clement [of Alexandria] tells the story, . . . also Eusebius,[†] namely that Nicolaus, one of the first seven deacons, . . . since he had a beautiful wife and was accused by certain persons of being jealous of her, brought her forth into the midst and said that he wanted to make her common to all. However, both Clement and Eusebius add that Nicolaus did this from a certain simplicity, in order that he might in this way remove the suspicion of jealousy from himself and furnish an example that he was not addicted to the things of this world, but that he could renounce them, since it is written: "If anyone . . . does not hate his . . . wife . . . he cannot be My disciple"; . . . likewise: "No one can serve two masters." . . . From this the Nicolaitans took occasion for their foul doctrine of the promiscuous

[4]Diodati, *Pious Annotations**, 100.
[5]Chemnitz, *Examination*, 3:105.
[6]Brightman, *Revelation**, 32.
[7]Bullinger, *Hundred Sermons** (1561), 48-49.

mixture of lusts, concerning which they blasphemously argued that it was not only lawful but also good. . . . With what zeal for chastity the apostles fought against these vices, as Revelation 2:6 shows. EXAMINATION OF THE COUNCIL OF TRENT.[8]

THE NECESSITY OF REPENTANCE. HEINRICH BULLINGER: Again, where the Lord repeats, "Unless you repent," he plainly testifies that the bosom of God's mercy and clemency is ready to open if we do penance, however we have offended him before. In the meantime we learn here openly and most certainly that we can by no counselors or consultations, no armies or policies, prevail one whit over our perils unless we repent. Therefore, unless we want our churches to be subverted and given over to be seduced and destroyed by the devil and his seducers, let us repent in time and receive again our first love.

Again, he commanded the singular virtue in this congregation especially for those who have hated the doings of the Nicolaitans, which God himself also hates. Let us here mark every word. He says not, "You did eschew and contain" but "You have hated." The force of hatred is great, moving to persecute that you hate. Moreover, he says not that you have hated the Nicolaitans but the works of the Nicolaitans. For we ought to hate no one in their person but rather the vice in the person, so that when the person will forsake it, we should love the person with all our heart. And that must be a great evil that God himself confesses that he hates. Here all congregations shall understand that they ought also to hate by all means the heresy and abomination of the Nicolaitans. Though on this day the name was extinguished, yet the heresy and abomination of the Nicolaitans remained. HUNDRED SERMONS ON THE APOCALYPSE.[9]

2:8-11 *The Message to Smyrna*

CALAMITY IN SMYRNA. THOMAS BRIGHTMAN: Now he instructed them against the future evils, which were more grievous than those that were past. Those things with which the Jews did trouble them at the present, and also those false accusations of the bishops while Constantine lived, were light skirmishes of a sharper battle following later. Therefore he describes diligently all the manner of this combat, who should be the chief captain of it, with what kind of cruelty he should rage, to what end, and how long. The prince is the devil, whom later we shall learn denotes the heathen emperors, open enemies of the truth. . . . This includes also the heresies, Christians in name but truly wolves devouring the flock.

The punishment is prison, which, as history teaches, includes proscriptions, confiscation of goods, banishment, slaughters, fires, tortures. With all these things the devil should greatly torment to draw people from the truth. But this persecution should endure for ten days only. And a day in this book is taken for a year. The number ten also sometimes means ten but sometimes by synecdoche refers to some uncertain number; I think that both are used here, that certain number should be of the type and certain of the antitype. Therefore, concerning Smyrna itself, this persecution occurred in the times of Trajan. That devil, a professed enemy of the truth, did reign next after this writing, very fierce against Christians, delivering people into prison and death that he might force them to renounce the profession of Christ. REVELATION OF ST. JOHN.[10]

2:12-17 *The Message to Pergamum*

THE SYNAGOGUE OF SATAN PERSECUTES THE SAINTS. JOHN JEWEL: Prophets of all ages who stood up against the prophets of God, who resisted Isaiah, Jeremiah, Christ, and the apostles, at no time complained about anything so much as they did of the name of the church. And for no other

[8]Chemnitz, *Examination*, 3:20-21; citing Clement, *Stromata* 3; Eusebius, *Ecclesiastical History* 3.29; Acts 6:5; Lk 14:26; Mt 6:24. †Clement of Alexandria (150–211/215) tells the story, which is also recounted by Eusebius (339–c. 340), regarding the martyrdom of James the apostle, including details about the man who led James to his execution being moved by his testimony and converting to Christianity himself; both men were then beheaded together.

[9]Bullinger, *Hundred Sermons** (1561), 57-61.

[10]Brightman, *Revelation**, 52-54; citing Rev 12:9.

cause did they so fiercely vex them and call them runaways and apostates than because they forsook their fellowship and did not keep the ordinances of the elders. Therefore, if we were to follow the judgments of those men only, who then governed the church, and would respect nothing else, neither God nor his Word, it must be confessed that the apostles were rightly and justly condemned to death. This because they fell away from the bishops and priests, that is, you must think, from the Catholic Church, and because they made many new alterations in religion contrary to the bishops' and priests' wills, indeed, and for all their spurning so earnestly against it.

Therefore, as how it is written that Hercules in old time was forced in striving with Antaeus† that huge giant to take him up from the earth that was his [Antaeus's] mother so that he could conquer him, even so must our adversaries be heaved from their mother, that is, from this vain color and shadow of the church, by which they so disguise and defend themselves, otherwise they cannot be brought to yield to the Word of God. And therefore, says Jeremiah the prophet, do not make such great boast that the temple of the Lord is with you; this is but a vain confidence, for these are lies. The angel also says in the Apocalypse that they say they are Jews, but they are the synagogue of Satan. An Apology or Answer in Defense of the Church of England.[11]

Rome Is the Synagogue of Satan and Body of Antichrist. John Downame: The body [of antichrist] is their Romish Catholic, apostolic church, seduced by such false teachers and by those lying signs and miracles. How marvelously do these things accord with what we find recorded in Thessalonians and by John in Revelation?

They shall, says Christ here, work great signs and wonders, such that they should deceive, if it were possible, the very elect. So says Paul. . . .

Therefore, God shall send them effectual errors to believe lies. And in Revelation, he makes the earth and the its inhabitants worship the first beast, and works great signs to the extent that he makes fire come down from heaven to the earth before people and deceives the inhabitants of the earth by the signs that were given to him to do.

These are the signs and wonders of which the papists so brag and make one special mark of their church, as universality, that is, their universal apostasy here also mentioned, is another. . . .

Against the error and superstition of the times, placing all religion and Christianity in the wilderness among the hermits or in their monkish cells and cloisters, he armed us with a double argument: first the light, he says, of the gospel (by which he meant the coming of the Son of Man . . .) is as the lightning, which flashes from the east to the west and lighted all the world; so does the gospel, and not in the deserts and cloisters only but in every place where those who fear God and work righteousness are accepted by him. Again, as the eagles (or, with us, crows and ravens) flock to a carcass wherever it may be found, so do the faithful to Christ, wherever he by the preaching of the gospel is crucified before their eyes. Sum of Sacred Divinity.[12]

The Manna of the Kingdom. Giovanni Diodati: I will cause him to enjoy the everlasting goods of my heavenly kingdom—terms taken from the manna that was kept in the sanctuary. . . .

[A white stone is] the figure of the new heart purified and made sound by faith, which God bestowed on those who are his, and on which by his Spirit he engraves and seals the testimony of their adoption, by which they obtain the new name and right of the children of God. [To the church in Pergamum he gave] certain judgment and knowledge of what lay in the closet of the believer's conscience and is not manifested except by the effects. Pious Annotations upon the Holy Bible.[13]

[11]Jewel, *Apology**, 1.91. †Antaeus, known to the Berbers as Anti, was a figure in Berber and Greek mythology. He was famed for his defeat by Heracles as part of the Labors of Hercules.

[12]Downame, *Sacred Divinity**, 530-31; citing 2 Thess 2:9-10, 8; Acts 10:35.

[13]Diodati, *Pious Annotations**, 100; citing Ex 16:32-33; Ps 65:4; Jn 6:31, 35, 48, 51; 1:12; Rev 3:12; Rom 8:16.

2:18-29 *The Message to Thyatira*

Jezabel in Thyatira. Heinrich Bullinger: To the former errors and sins of Jezebel he adds another sin, nothing light, namely, the abuse and even the contempt of God's longsuffering. God does not before long and out of hand destroy those who are in error and also most grievous sins. But sinners tend for the most part to abuse that longsuffering of God by taking the occasion and pretense to sin more impudently, saying, "If God did so much abhor these offenses, he would have destroyed us before," or, "But now he has treated us kindly; therefore he does not so greatly dislike it." But this is an abuse of God's longsuffering. For the Lord says at this time, "I have given Jezebel a time to repent and to leave her fornication and turn to the Lord; nevertheless, she has not converted." The Lord takes this as most evil, that his grace should be truly despised and disregarded. . . . If, then, the Lord has not soddenly in our sins oppressed us, let us not take this as a liberty to sin, but let us rather amend. Hundred Sermons on the Apocalypse.[14]

The Deep Things of Satan. Martin Chemnitz: When the remaining apostle had died and John had been banished to Patmos, Ebio and Cerinthus† stirred up contentions concerning the divinity of Christ, concerning an earthly reign of his, concerning Levitical observances, etc., and sadly disturbed the churches. . . . Because it was still fresh in the memory of the church that the apostles had transmitted certain other things concerning the deeds and words of the Savior beside what was written in the accounts of the three evangelists, Cerinthus and others misused this as a pretext and set forth their false doctrines. . . . St. John is looking back on those battles when he says, . . . "You have tested those who call themselves apostles but are not"; also, "Jezebel, who calls herself a prophetess," etc. Therefore, they boast of both revelations and traditions for which they want to claim prophetic authority. John says in the epistle to Thyatira that they called these doctrines "the deep things," that is, not the commonly proclaimed dogmas of the apostles, which were known to all in the church also from the Scriptures, but deep, hidden, and secret mysteries, which the apostles had delivered from hand to hand, not to anyone and everyone, but privately and orally to their friends, as mysteries that were to be honored in silence. But John calls them deep things not of the apostles but of Satan. Examination of the Council of Trent.[15]

Around 1300 Arose a New Company of Teachers. Thomas Brightman: Now Christ makes himself known by his name, eyes, and feet, every one of which appears more clearly from the antitype of what sort they are. Concerning the name, . . . there was mention of the Son of Man, . . . but the whole vision did declare sufficiently that he was the Son of God. It seemed here to be used as though now he would return out of Egypt. He had been exiled now a good while, but in the renewing of the church he returned home, as it were. . . .

The fire eyes are those spoken of in the first chapter . . . , by whose clearness he showed to the Thyatirians that now the time flourished in which the light of the truth should dispel darkness of errors and falsehood, as it flies at the sight of the fire. This came to pass about 1300, when a new company of teachers arose, and by the judgment of all of them the pope was strangled and began to be spoiled of his estimation, which he had kept now a good while by fraud. For they did maintain earnestly that the Imperial Majesty ought to be preferred above other and that the pope had no power over it. Among these were Ockamus, Marsilius, Patavinus, Dante, John de Ganduno, and many others.†

[14]Bullinger, *Hundred Sermons** (1561), 85-92; citing Rom 2:4.

[15]Chemnitz, *Examination*, 1:192; citing Rev 2:2, 20. †In Cerinthus' interpretation, the Christ descended upon Jesus at baptism and guided him in ministry and the performing of miracles, but left him at the crucifixion. Similarly to the Ebionites, he maintained that Jesus was not born of a virgin, but was a mere man, the biological son of Mary and Joseph.

The feet like fine brass teach with what kind of torment the Roman Balaam should rage against the faithful feet of Christ; he should deliver them to be burned in the flame, endeavoring to quench one burning by another. This cruelty he has not exercised now the first time but has brought it to noble infamy by more frequent burnings than ever before. The fires shined throughout all Europe, and many martyrs burnt every day. But notable before others were Jan Hus and Jerome of Prague,‡ who as a noble pair of feet like fine brass did shine in the furnace of Constance in the eyes of all our world. But antichrist, who thought to have consumed those feet by fire, was deceived. For now at length he has had experience that these feet are not stubble but fine brass, which shines more in the fire and is not consumed.

The works that are rehearsed—charity, ministration, faith, and patience—pertain to private duty rather than public office, as though this church were hid in some secret members and was not famous in an excellent administration of things. Such was doubtless the state of the Thyatirian city; it is plainly the antitype. For although there were everywhere many excellent people who defended the truth by writings and lively voice, yet no public churches' companies were constituted or set in order. Or, if any were, as around the end of this period people began to meet somewhat boldly, they did not obtain a lawful reformation.

The chief praise was of their love one to another, but not that feigned, by which men promise largely but perform nothing, but that by which both by deed and by work they helped where there was need, so that immediately after charity he added ministration. Their mutual faith also was excellent, free from all fawning and treachery. For this faith seemed to be a fruit of that which is properly so called, namely, faithfulness, by which they regarded from the heart one another's goods. . . .

The reprehension is that the woman Jezebel was permitted to deceive the servants of God with her vain shows. Therefore either their negligence or faint heart or both are blamed, in accordance with which it came to pass that she did not with the wicked according to their deserts, but they were allowed to sleep securely in their sins. Who this Jezebel was in the Thyatirian city, the old history did not show. From this place we understand that in the same place there was a certain chief and famous woman, an idolatress, sorceress, and harlot, like the ancient Jezebel, who was the wife of Ahab; yet she was much more furnished to destroy because this showed her to be openly an enemy and adversary to the truth that would be accounted for a prophetess. From what follows, it appears that she was taught to the naughty people in the school of the Nicolaitans, of which she became a schoolmistress, teaching others the same rules. For the heretics abused the labor of women to spread abroad their poisons. REVELATION OF ST. JOHN.[16]

3:1-6 *The Message to Sardis*

TWO SORTS OF PEOPLE. HEINRICH BULLINGER: In one congregation of Sardis were two sorts of people, professing on either side the name of Christ. But some indeed answered but little to the holy profession, living more licentiously than became them, and the others in holiness of life set forth the doctrine of our Savior that they professed. The first sort the Lord Jesus accuses in this epistle by St. John and showed also a medicine for the disease. And the latter he exhorted to perseverance, commending their integrity. Therefore, this epistle is divided in two parts, very fit and profitable for our time.

The first part of the epistle contained those things we have now recited, and he proceeds here in the same order in which we have seen him proceed up to this point. For first he shows to whom it is dedicated and sent: namely, to the pastor of the congregation of Sardis, and therefore

[16]Brightman, *Revelation**, 64-67; citing Rev 1:14-15. †These are William of Ockham (1285–1347/9), Marsilius of Padua (1280–1343), Dante Alighieri (c. 1265–1321), and John of Gand (1270/80–1328). ‡Jan Hus (d. 1415) and Jerome of Prague (c. 1370–1416) were Reformers martyred for their theological views.

also to the whole church. The second part of this heavenly epistle is contained in these points, in which is praised and commanded the innocence, holiness, and integrity of the faithful in the congregation of Sardis in true religion. He exhorted them to perseverance by a strong promise. Last, he put forward again to them most ample rewards, even to the corrupt sort, in case they amend, and to the faithful, if they continue as they are. HUNDRED SERMONS ON THE APOCALYPSE.[17]

NAMES OF REFORMERS. THOMAS BRIGHTMAN: Because Sardis should find the same safeguard of Christ in defending her pastors that he had showed in Ephesus, [John] uses the same similitude not without cause when there is so great conjunction of things. But of Sardis the history speaks not a word, which in her antitype is most clear. For he who gives the Spirit plentifully, to whom and when he will, poured out in those times so great plenty of all gifts as nowhere else in these last times. Good learning had been already essentially buried, being driven away for many ages by the simplemindedness of the scholastics, until at length, after the wonderful art of printing was discovered (which cunning flowed from the same fountain of the Spirit), many excellent intellects were raised up to search out the truth.

Among them were John Picus, Mirandulanus, Angelus Politianus, Platina, Trapezuntius, Gaza, Hermolaus Barbarus, Marsilius Ficinus, Pyrbachius, Joannes de monte Regio, Aldus Manutius, Rodolphus Agricola, Ioannes Iovianus, Pontanus, Philippus Beroaldus, Ioannes Reuchlinus, and many other most learned men, whose chief labor was in setting forth the languages, arts, and other disciplines of the humanities. But how great an entrance was made from hence to find out the mysteries of salvation, the conjoined times have taught. For not long after came Martin Luther, Philipp Melanchthon, Erasmus of Rotterdam, Zwingli, Oecolampadius, Capito, Blaurerus, Bucer, Musculus, Calvin,† and many other most learned men, so many lights of the Christian world.

Helped by the studies of those earlier men, they brought forth the truth, covered with great filthiness and uncleanness, dissipated the Romish darkness, and utterly dispelled all the subtilities of the enemies like smoke in every direction. Does not Christ worthily take on himself this ensign of the seven spirits, enriching this time with such a great plenty of gifts? Neither was his power and grace less famous in preserving safety for the pastors. Who would not have thought that Luther—so greatly hated and envied of all men, for whom almost the whole world laid wait, even also the one under whose feet the emperors once were compelled to subject themselves—that Luther, I say, should have died a thousand deaths? But by chance, troubles being raised up, he did scarcely endure; indeed, for almost thirty years he remained in the battle safe even from privy assaults, with which the pope tends to do away those men whom he cannot conquer with open war and force. At length, lying sick in his bed and giving up his soul to him who gave it, he slept quietly in Christ.

What should I speak of Melanchthon, Peter Martyr, John Calvin, and the rest of the valiant heroes? Bucer, being buried a few years before, at length turned to dust, was dragged out of his grave, or rather another buried there later, that they might show their cruelty even in the burning of the ashes of one whom they could not and did not hurt while he lived. Who then has not seen the stars in the right hand of Christ, so wonderfully defending his servants against all force of adversaries? And ought not the fresh memory of these things give constancy and courage to all, reposing themselves in the same protection, that they may go boldly to the defense of the truth, everyone according to their calling? There is not indeed the same express promise of other times, yet there is always the same crown for those who fight lawfully. REVELATION OF ST. JOHN.[18]

[17]Bullinger, *Hundred Sermons** (1561), 106-7.

[18]Brightman, *Revelation**, 78-79. †Select names cited in order of appearance include Pico della Mirandola (1463–1494); Angelo or simply Poliziano, anglicized as Politian (1454–1494); George of Trebizond (1395–1486); Ermolao or Hermolao Barbaro, also

Seeds Planted by Luther. Thomas Brightman: In the antitype the thing is so clear that anyone may bewail it with tears rather than prosecute it in words. For how many excellent men has that monster of ubiquity cast headlong into death? Luther sowed the seeds of this in 1526 and 1528 in a dispute against Zwingli and Oecolampadius. But they ought to have been pulled out of his books, at least after the controversy was brought to sleep, lest lurking in the furrows, as it were, they should break forth at length into deadly poison. But Luther himself was careless about it, providing after the manner of men rather for his own estimation, then, as was proper, for the safety of the brethren.

Moreover, I find your faithfulness and diligence lacking, O Holy Philip, because you have not thrust through so foul an error according to his desert. Perhaps you thought it was to be handled more gently by you, partly in favor of your friend, partly because you supposed that it might be abolished by silence more easily than by sharp inveighing of words. But the errors that are not refuted seem to be allowed, and as much as they are dealt with gently they grow all the more, for they are gangrenes, which gentle remedies do not heal but make worse. While therefore neither of you watched or did his duty for many days, how many, I pray, and how great men? A huge number indeed of all degrees, of which the principal as standard bearers were Johannes Brenz, Jakob Andreae, Selnecker, Kirchner, Chemnitz, and others of that sort, who have increased this monster of ubiquity, of itself horrible, with so many and notable errors that there has been scarce in this time any other more foul and deadly.† Lamentable indeed is the fall of the famous men, whose labor was once courageous and no less profitable against the common enemies. And what a crown they would have received if they had continued in the same warfare and had not been as cruel elephants turned back by the enemies, wasting their own friends.

But my office is of an interpreter and not of a quarreler, and therefore I leave off these things. This death invaded not only some particular men but also many whole cities and provinces, as may appear by the Book of Concord published in 1580, which is not of so great force to establish the error with the consent of so many as to testify this miserable calamity of the brothers. And to this error concerning the Supper of the Lord and person of Christ were many other also added, namely, of original sin, of free will, of justification, of good works, of the law and gospel, of indifferent things, and of predestination. Therefore, death assailed with a manifold dart: how great must the slaughter be, seeing she cast to the ground, even with one, great troops of men?

"For I have not found your works perfect": the reason so many fell into death. The church of Sardis, as far as it seemed, did not admit the sincere truth of God but retained some ethnic superstition. The church of Germany did indeed cast away many popish errors, yet in the sacrament of the Supper, she stuck still, as it were, in the clay of bodily presence—not as Rome, dreaming of a changed substance of bread and wine into a true and real flesh and blood, but, no less contrary to and disagreeing from the truth, continuing the true flesh and blood together with the outward signs, affirming that he is present here on earth.

This leaven Luther never cast out but contended fiercely with Zwingli and Oecolampadius to defend and retain. Neither would God . . . have let go unpunished the neglect of amending this point. Of this punishment to come some proof was made when Luther was constrained for the defense of an unjust cause, to flee for assistance to ubiquity

Hermolaus Barbarus (1454–1493); Marsilio Ficino (1433–1499); Georg von Peuerbach (1423–1461); Johannes Müller von Königsberg (1436–1476), better known as Regiomontanus; Aldus Manutius (Aldus Pius Manutius, c. 1449/1452–1515); Rodolphus Agricola (Rudolphus Agricola Phrisius, 1443/4–1485); Giovanni Pontano (1426–1503), later known as Giovanni Gioviano; Johan Isaaksz Pontanus (1571–1639); Philippus Beroaldus Angelus Politianus; Johann Reuchlin (1455–1522); Martin Luther; Philipp Melanchthon; Erasmus of Rotterdam; Ulrich Zwingli; Johannes Oecolampadius; Wolfgang Fabricius Capito (1478–1541); Ambrosius Blaurerus (1509–1602); Martin Bucer; Wolfgang Musculus; and John Calvin.

and to confirm many other things concerning the manhood of Christ that are contrary to the truth. But for the heat of contention, he could not so well consider and mind that from those beginnings and flourishes, he should understand God to be angry. How did he not beware of that error that drew with it so great a multitude of wicked opinions? Why did he not fear what might have happened to others, having seen in himself what condition he was brought into by disputing? But his eyes were held that he could not foresee the time to come and turn away this so grievous punishment from his people. Therefore their works were not perfect, because a full reformation was not made but only one error changed into another no less grievous. REVELATION OF ST. JOHN.[19]

3:7-13 *The Message to Philadelphia*

THE VIRTUES OF CHRIST IN THE CHURCH OF PHILADELPHIA. HEINRICH BULLINGER: In this sixth epistle he commends the sincere faith and constancy of faith and admonishes to persevere, putting forward ample rewards. . . . And the Lord here follows the same order we see he has followed in others [letters]. For it is one and the same kind of doctrine with all churches and in all times. First, therefore, it is showed to whom the epistle is written or dedicated: to the pastor and whole congregation of Philadelphia. Philadelphia was a city of Lydia, neither very famous nor obscure. We read how it had been often shaken with earthquakes and repaired again. Strabo mentions this in his *Geography* 12, and so have other authors also. Yet it made itself famous by virtues. After this, the Lord Christ is signified to be Author of this epistle, who at other times also has told St. John what he should write.

And to Christ are attributed three things, or rather Christ attributes three things to himself, that he is holy, is true, and has the key of David. In this he has borrowed of the image of the first chapter. Christ is holy because he is pure and clean from all filthiness and from all unrighteousness, very God, a consuming fire, doing no one any wrong, having nothing at all that may be blamed. For to him the seraphim say rightly, "Holy, holy, holy, Lord God of Sabaoth." . . . Christ is also the Holy One of the saints, a sanctification that sanctifies all who are sanctified. He loves holiness in saints. Christ therefore is most truly called. Antichrist, the pope, has taken on himself this title, and so filthy sits on this beast. . . . Spit upon that vile and filthy beast, who suffers himself to be called the most holy father, and worship Christ the Holy One of all holy, unless you would rather understand by that holiness not every holiness but papal holiness, that is, stinking and swimming full of all abominations.

Christ is likewise called true, because he is eternal and faithful, evermore constant and incorrupt. He can neither deceive nor be deceived. He most constantly keeps his promises. All his words are undoubted and true. Although the flesh that can abide no delay starts many times to doubt, yet no single point or iota of them falls away. The truth of the Lord endures forever. You stand on a most sure foundation if you lean into Christ, who . . . also calls himself the truth.

Last he adds, "who has the key of David." . . . He alludes to . . . Isaiah, by which is signified the divine and almighty power of Christ, by which he brings us purified into the kingdom of heaven, a work that truly neither devils nor any power can stop. He casts down the unclean into hell. . . . He therefore says, aptly and expressly, that he has, not had or shall have, but he has now. For he alone has this power, which he shares with no one else. The pope of Rome who says that he has this power lies. The only Son of God excels in this prerogative. The apostles, as ministers and preachers, have received the keys of knowledge and of utterance, of learning, instruction, and introduction, by which also in threatening they exclude infidels from the kingdom of God, bind them in their sins, with Almighty

[19]Brightman, *Revelation**, 81-82; citing 1 Cor 11:30. †Lutheran standard-bearers cited here by Brightman include Johann (Johannes) Brenz, Jakob Andreae, Nikolaus Selnecker, Timothy Kirchner (1533–1587), and Martin Chemnitz.

God, who has the high power, ratifying the judgment of the minister, which he pronounced not of himself but of Christ's words. But these things agree well with those that follow of the opened door, which no one can shut. Hundred Sermons on the Apocalypse.[20]

3:14-22 *The Message to Laodicea*

Type and Antitype. Thomas Brightman: The antitype, I say, is the third reformed church, that is, ours of England. For all the purer churches are comprehended in this threefold difference, for either they persist and continue in those steps that Luther has traced out, such as the churches of Germany, especially of Saxony, and those next bordering of Sauerland† and Denmark; or they abhor that error of consubstantiation, as all the rest with one consent that yet do not agree in all things but follow a differing manner of governing and administering, the French and their companions one, our English another, a certain proper and peculiar one. . . .

There are three distinct [groups], to which the three types of Sardis, Philadelphia, and Laodicea—after that Jezebel was overthrown, that is, the yoke of the Romish tyranny shaken off—do answer. And to the last, Laodicea, the English do correspond, whose most recent origin takes her beginning at 1547, when Edward, the king of most famous memory, came to the rule and government of the commonwealth; but then at length she was confirmed and established when, eleven years after, our most peaceable Queen Elizabeth began the kingdom. Most mighty King Henry, her father, had expelled the pope but retained the popish superstition. And before he began to stir any amount, even against the pope, the churches of Germany and Helvetia were founded. The Scottish church is later in beginning then ours, yet by right it is numbered with those with which it agrees in ordinances, into whose time she is cast, and she is to be evaluated rather from the agreement of things than grouped by herself because of the difference of time. Therefore our English church alone constitutes the antitype answering to Laodicea. Revelation of St. John.[21]

The Effects of God's Afflictions. Joseph Mede: God chastises his children out of love and for their good. For all the actions of God toward those he loves must be out of love, and whatever he does out of love must be for the good of those he loves. Indeed, people who lack wisdom often do out of love that which hurts; as the proverb is, they kill with kindness. But with God it is otherwise; he does not lack skill to know what is best for his beloved, as people do, and therefore it is as certain that his chastisements shall end with our profit as we are sure they spring from our sins. The ignorance of this point causes many to err and, with the friends of Job, to judge amiss God's love and hate toward people. But we must know that God has two sorts of arrows, arrows of judgment and arrows of mercy: the first he shoots against those he hates, . . . the other he shoots at his own, even those whom he loves, and with them he wounds them that he may cure them. Such people may apply to themselves the words of the spouse in the Canticles, "I am wounded with love": God's love has wounded me, and the wound of God makes me love him; it begins in his love to me and aims at and ends in my love to him. For we must remember in this case what Austin well observes, that when the godly and the wicked suffer the very same things by outward appearance, there is a great difference in the sufferers, even in the appearance of suffering. The one are punished out of God's just displeasure and wrathful vengeance; the other are disciplined out of mercy, that God might fit them and keep them for himself because he loves them.

[20]Bullinger, *Hundred Sermons** (1561), 111-12; citing Is 7; Jn 14:1-31; Is 22.

[21]Brightman, *Revelation**, 103-4. †The Sauerland is a rural, hilly area spreading across most of the southeastern part of North Rhine-Westphalia, in parts heavily forested and, apart from the major valleys, sparsely inhabited.

And that we may understand this better, let us consider what effects afflictions work and what fruits they bring forth in those whom God loves.

1. Afflictions to those God loves are medicinal, and by this they recover their health by repentance from some spiritual disease they are sick of. For however the Lord gives the rein loose to the children of wrath and lets them enjoy their heart's desire, yet he will hedge with thorns the ways of those he loves and will awaken them by some sharp rod or other out of the sleep of security. So he taught Miriam by leprosy to leave her murmuring; he waked Jonah out of his sleep by casting him into the sea; Zachariah's unbelief was cured with dumbness; and blessed is the one whom the Lord chastens and corrects this way. . . .

2. Afflictions are preservatives to keep those God loves from sin. Thus, an angel of Satan must buffet Paul, lest he should be exalted above measure. . . . The earth that is not tilled and broken up bears nothing but thorns and briars. Vines wax wild in time unless we prune and cut them. Our hearts would be overgrown with evil affections and dispositions, as with so many harmful weeds, if God by his loving chastisements should not till and manure them: "My Father" (says Christ) . . . "is the Husbandman."

3. Afflictions make the fruitless bring forth fruit, beget many virtues, and make God's graces in us to bloom and bring forth works pleasing to our Heavenly Father. The prodigal son . . . never thought of returning to his father until he was brought low by affliction. Hagar was proud in the house of Abraham but humble in the wilderness. . . . Jonah slept in the ship but watches and prays in the whale's belly. *Sicut Aromata odorem non nisi cum accenduntur, expandunt*, says Gregory: as sweet spices do not send forth or spread abroad their sweet smell until they are burned or beaten, neither do the graces of God's children send forth so sweet, so rich, a fragrance as when they are exercised by afflictions.

4. Last, afflictions draw people nearer unto God. Manasseh, who lived in Jerusalem as a libertine, when he was bound with chains in Babylon, when he was in affliction, he besought the Lord and humbled himself greatly before the God of his fathers. . . . In the Gospel we read that corporal diseases brought many to Christ, whereas many who had their health neither regarded nor acknowledged him. Discourses on Diverse Texts of Scripture.[22]

A Warning About Hypocrisy. Dirk Philips: I have written here briefly concerning Jesus Christ, in part for the comfort and assurance of my brothers and sisters—to show that we stand in the true grace of God and walk in the right way so long as we follow Christ—and in part to warn the brothers and sisters of frivolous types who have appeared lately. They say much about the new creature and are themselves only hypocrites, self-inflated people and despisers of the word and commandments of Christ. . . . As is the way of lazy servants, they think they are being clever when they bury the Lord's talents in the ground. But when the Lord comes for an accounting, they will hear a terrible judgment and suffer an awful punishment, for they have hidden the Lord's talents, gaining nothing, rather than putting them to good use. They are like the church at Laodicea. . . .

They should take these words truly and earnestly to heart, these ones who are so rich in the Spirit that they think they need nothing—all the while not recognizing what poor and miserable creatures they really are. Let them hear the counsel of the Lord to buy the pure and refined gold of God's Word, the noble and precious pearls of gospel truth, that they might be rich in the faith. Let them put off the old Adam, the world and all that belongs to the world. Let them become conquerors in the faith so that the Lord might clothe them in white garments. Then, at the Lord's coming, they will not be ashamed. Let them salve their eyes well so that they might see clearly that the kingdom of God does not consist merely of words. It consists

[22]Mede, *Works** (1672), 296-97; citing Ps 7:13; 144:6; Song 2:5; Ps 94; 2 Cor 12:7; Jn 15:1; Lk 15; Gen 21; 2 Chron 33:11-12.

of power and deeds. Concerning the New Birth and the New Creature.[23]

The Battle Against Lukewarmness. Martin Luther: Tropologically the waters are the temptations of such men, inducements concerning peace and security. Today no battle is so necessary as the one against peace, security, boredom, and lukewarmness. And here it would be necessary for us to take a contrary stand with all our forces and weapons, for this is the most difficult of all, since it has nothing to compel to the good from the outside, as was formerly the case with persecution and heresy. Rather, it has an outside stimulus toward easing up and relaxing. For the devil realized that he could not succeed by attacking from the outside with violence and heresy. Therefore he has now begun to put aside such an attack in favor of resorting to a gentle allurement to cut them down in their smugness. Psalm 69.[24]

Protection from Punishment. Balthasar Hubmaier: Whoever recognizes that for him sin is a punishment, to him sin is not sin, but he will henceforth protect himself from the punishment so that the punishment does not again become sin for him and condemning.... For that is the grace and favor of God which he bears to us and with which he embraces us: that power which he offers us through his preached Word so that we—it lies now in our power—can become children of God and desire and complete his Father's will and please him. Freedom of the Will II.[25]

The Word and Faith. Heinrich Bullinger: The word of permission, and even Christ himself, is the object of faith, which is the very pureness itself. Therefore the Lord counseled that the congregation of Laodicea should buy refined gold; he counseled that they should hear God's word and believe it indeed. For the Lord uses the word *believing* for receiving, hearing, and obeying.

For no one should imagine that there is bargaining before God, as there is with people, as though the spiritual gifts of God might be bought for money. This is repugnant to the whole Scripture and especially against the determination of St. Peter pronounced against Simon Magus. But this is our exposition of the prophet Isaiah, . . . where he says, among other things, "Come, buy without money and without price or exchange." And not long after he says, "I am hearing, hear me, incline your care," and so on. Therefore, the Romish Canaanite has no hold of it, I mean the pope that great merchant, who sells all things in the church, even those things he does not have, the greatest deceiver in the world. To this is added, as it is in Isaiah plainly expressed, from whom such graces or gifts are to be bought, so Christ also here says expressly, "I counsel you to buy from me." Behold, he says, "from me": not from the pope, from monks, friars, from priests. For Christ alone has the things we may require. He alone does satisfy, he alone grants those gifts. And therefore he says in the Gospel of St. John, "Let the one who hungers or thirsts come to me: to me, I say, let him come." And St. Peter says, "Lord, to whom shall we go? You have the words of eternal life." It is as though he is saying, If we will live, we can go to none other but you. You are the life and fountain of all goodness.

Moreover, the use and profit of this pure gold, tried and most purified, by which I mean the word of God's truth and pure faith, is of three sorts. First, that you may be rich. Second, that you may buy yourself apparel. Third, that you may buy the eye ointment to heal the blindness of your eyes. For the word of God and faith in him is the foundation of true piety. Without the word and faith, nothing is sound. Hundred Sermons on the Apocalypse.[26]

[23]Liechty, *Early Anabaptist Spirituality*, 207-9.
[24]LW 10:351-53; citing Ps 69:1.
[25]Hubmaier, *Theologian of Anabaptism*, 467-68.
[26]Bullinger, *Hundred Sermons** (1561), 129-33; citing Is 55; Jn 7:37-38; 6:68-69.

4:1–5:14 THE THRONE SCENE IN HEAVEN

*4 After this I looked, and behold, a door standing
open in heaven! And the first voice, which I had
heard speaking to me like a trumpet, said, "Come up
here, and I will show you what must take place after
this." [2]At once I was in the Spirit, and behold, a
throne stood in heaven, with one seated on the throne.
[3]And he who sat there had the appearance of jasper
and carnelian, and around the throne was a rainbow
that had the appearance of an emerald. [4]Around the
throne were twenty-four thrones, and seated on the
thrones were twenty-four elders, clothed in white
garments, with golden crowns on their heads. [5]From
the throne came flashes of lightning, and rumblings[a]
and peals of thunder, and before the throne were
burning seven torches of fire, which are the seven
spirits of God, [6]and before the throne there was as it
were a sea of glass, like crystal.*

*And around the throne, on each side of the throne,
are four living creatures, full of eyes in front and
behind: [7]the first living creature like a lion, the second
living creature like an ox, the third living creature
with the face of a man, and the fourth living creature
like an eagle in flight. [8]And the four living creatures,
each of them with six wings, are full of eyes all
around and within, and day and night they never
cease to say,*

*"Holy, holy, holy, is the Lord God Almighty,
who was and is and is to come!"*

*[9]And whenever the living creatures give glory and
honor and thanks to him who is seated on the throne,
who lives forever and ever, [10]the twenty-four elders fall
down before him who is seated on the throne and
worship him who lives forever and ever. They cast
their crowns before the throne, saying,*

*[11]"Worthy are you, our Lord and God,
to receive glory and honor and power,
for you created all things,
and by your will they existed and were
created."*

*5 Then I saw in the right hand of him who was
seated on the throne a scroll written within and on
the back, sealed with seven seals. [2]And I saw a mighty
angel proclaiming with a loud voice, "Who is worthy
to open the scroll and break its seals?" [3]And no one in
heaven or on earth or under the earth was able to
open the scroll or to look into it, [4]and I began to weep
loudly because no one was found worthy to open the
scroll or to look into it. [5]And one of the elders said to
me, "Weep no more; behold, the Lion of the tribe of
Judah, the Root of David, has conquered, so that he
can open the scroll and its seven seals."*

*[6]And between the throne and the four living
creatures and among the elders I saw a Lamb
standing, as though it had been slain, with seven
horns and with seven eyes, which are the seven spirits
of God sent out into all the earth. [7]And he went and
took the scroll from the right hand of him who was
seated on the throne. [8]And when he had taken the
scroll, the four living creatures and the twenty-four
elders fell down before the Lamb, each holding a harp,
and golden bowls full of incense, which are the prayers
of the saints. [9]And they sang a new song, saying,*

*"Worthy are you to take the scroll
and to open its seals,
for you were slain, and by your blood you
ransomed people for God
from every tribe and language and people
and nation,
[10]and you have made them a kingdom and
priests to our God,
and they shall reign on the earth."*

*[11]Then I looked, and I heard around the throne
and the living creatures and the elders the voice of
many angels, numbering myriads of myriads and
thousands of thousands, [12]saying with a loud voice,*

*"Worthy is the Lamb who was slain,
to receive power and wealth and wisdom
and might
and honor and glory and blessing!"*

13 *And I heard every creature in heaven and on earth and under the earth and in the sea, and all that is in them, saying,*

"To him who sits on the throne and to the Lamb be blessing and honor and glory and might forever and ever!"

14 *And the four living creatures said, "Amen!" and the elders fell down and worshiped.*

a Or *voices*, or *sounds*

Overview: Having rehearsed the history of the seven churches, John is taken to the throne room in heaven. An angel with a voice like a trumpet calls John to come forward through an open door. Immediately he is caught up in the spirit and is told he will be shown what will now take place. The text enters at once into a movement from God's government in history and its depiction of the seven churches to an eschatological series of visions with which John will be preoccupied through the balance of Revelation (Rev 4:1–22:16).

For sixteenth-century commentators, seeing the Lamb in Revelation 5:6 implies seeing Christ and the mysteries of the kingdom of God. Readers come to understand the nature of the church, her ministry, and how faithful pastors are to work at repairing and preserving it. In the Lamb readers learn of the destiny of the church in the midst of adversity and of the way in which God governs history. Heinrich Bullinger also writes of the government and order of the Lamb in reference to the throne room visions. The nature of the Lamb's rule is filled out in the visions of seals, trumpets, and bowls of wrath.

4:1-11 *The Throne and Its Surroundings*

Christendom Will Endure. Martin Luther: In chapters 4 and 5, there is prefigured the whole of Christendom that is to suffer these coming tribulations and plagues. There are four and twenty elders before God (that is, all the bishops and teachers in unity); they are crowned with faith and praise Christ, the Lamb of God, with harps (that is, they preach); and they worship him with censers (that is, they exercise themselves in prayer). All this is for the comfort of Christians, that they may know that Christendom is to endure in spite of the plagues that are going to come. Preface to the Revelation of Saint John.[1]

Heavenly Archetypes of God's Counsels. Giovanni Diodati: That is to say, a second vision was presented to me, and at the first appearing of it I was ravished into a prophetic ecstasy. Now until the end of Revelation 11, these visions seem to represent the heavenly archetypes of God's counsels, concerning the state and chances of the Christian church, and from Revelation 12 forward, the execution of them on earth. Pious Annotations upon the Holy Bible.[2]

Explanation of the Four Living Creatures. Sebastian Meyer: "Holy, holy, holy is the Lord God Almighty." The Father is holy, the Son is holy, the Spirit, Paraclete, is also holy. There is one Lord and God Almighty, into whose name we are baptized and we believe, as Christ commands us at the end of Matthew. The Father sanctifies the Son, whom he sends into the world, that through his death, when the Spirit is imparted to us, by him also we may be made holy. . . . The one who sanctifies and those who are sanctified are all one. . . . So then, we wretched little men, for whose benefit divine mercy works all things whatsoever, had to carefully imitate those holy spirits. More than that, we had to imitate even the dumb and insensible creatures, all which constantly proclaim, each according to its capacity, God as their creator, just as we see in the Psalms

[1]LW 35:401.
[2]Diodati, *Pious Annotations**, 102.

and Isaiah. He says, "All the glory of the earth is his." But although I have explained these living creatures as cherubim, according to the opinion of certain persons, still I am aware that in Augustine and certain others of the Fathers, both here and in Ezekiel, the things that are said about the four living creatures are applied to the four Gospel writers. And likewise, certain other characteristics which are ascribed to angels they take as applying to leaders of the churches. But even in this there is some discrepancy, because Augustine takes the lion to mean Matthew, but the man to stand for Mark, while Pope Gregory and others hold that the lion is Mark, but the man is Matthew. But I am not at all comfortable agreeing with them, since they disagree on this point, for this reason: they think it means Christ is victor over the powers that oppose him, or that he rides through the earth in a triumphal chariot. But they should also grant us this point, that we ascribe these descriptions to the Gospel writers so as not to exclude angels from the interpretation. At the same time, there are some who take the four living creatures to mean the four principal mysteries of the Christian faith: the incarnation of the Word, which is the face of the man; his passion and death, which is the image of the ox; resurrection to eternal life, indicated by the lion; ascension into heaven, the eagle. THE APOCALYPSE OF JOHN.[3]

VISION OF THE THRONE IN SUPERCELESTIAL PLACES. HEINRICH BULLINGER: And here he declares with a godly voice what John should do and how he should behave himself. Christ bids John ascend into supercelestial places, not in body but in mind. Therefore, our mind must be lifted up into the contemplation of heavenly things and be purged as much as possible from earthly affections, such that we may behold heavenly things with a heavenly contemplation. . . . "I was in the spirit," that is, in a spiritual contemplation or ravished with the Spirit into the faithful consideration of those things that were shown to me.

Now also is compiled an argument of things that should be told: "I will show you what things must be done hereafter." For after the type of God, ordering or governing all things justly through Christ, immediately the destiny of the church is declared by seven seals and seven trumpets, in which most comfortable consolations, highly efficacious, are interlaced everywhere.

And first of all, before the seals and trumpets, is set forth a figure or type of God and his most righteous judgment and government in all things, and this runs throughout Revelation 4–5 wholly, that it might prepare us for the reading or hearing of those things that shall follow in Revelation 6–8. . . . In heaven itself appeared a seat or throne of majesty. He who sits there holds in his right hand a book, closed with seals. By him sits a Lamb, who takes the book and opens its seals. And out of this throne also proceeds a sevenfold Spirit, wonderfully uttering his virtues. Before the seat appears a glassy sea, bright and even like crystal. The throne itself rested like a wagon on four beasts full of eyes and wings, appearing beneath all around and running or encompassing the throne. A rainbow like an emerald goes all around the same. Around the throne by a circle appear twenty-four seats, and that many elders sitting in them, crowned and in white array. This is the order of this second vision. In their place shall be declared what the Lamb, what the beasts, what the elders and the other parties did. It suffices now to have touched on the chief points of the vision, shadowing some of the same.

Second, we must see what everything represents. For on this depends a great part of the whole mystery: concerning the manner of vision, St. John brings no new thing of the revelation of Christ. For we read that such manner of visions was given for the most part to the prophets. . . . And a throne represents an imperial majesty and judicial administration. And because the throne is not in earth but is seen in heaven, we shall think

[3]Sebastian Meyer, *In Apocalypsim Johannis Apostoli D, Sebastiani Meyer ecclesiastae Bernensis commentarius, nostro huic saeculo accommodus, natus et aeditus* (Tiguri, 1539), 16r-17; citing Jn 10; Heb 2.

the providence and administration of God's judgments to be celestial, sound, most holy and clean, void of all corruption. And upon this same throne is one sitting—sitting, I say, not lying or standing. For God the judge of all is of a quiet mind, and neither is he moved with any affections as people are. Here is no affection, injury, unrighteousness in the universal government of all things to be thought on. Elihu says, "Far from God be wickedness, and iniquity from the Almighty." Hundred Sermons on the Apocalypse.[4]

God's Glory as the End of All Our Actions. John Downame: The last thing required for this godly life is that we set forth God's glory as the main end of all our actions, not doing them for worldly respects or our own profit principally, either temporal or spiritual, but that God's will may be done in them; for he is the *summum bonum* and supreme end of all things, and for his glory we were elected, created, redeemed, justified, sanctified, and will be glorified. And when we have attained to heavenly happiness and have the possession and fruition of God's everlasting kingdom, the main end of all our glory will be to glorify God, who has thus advanced and glorified us. For the twenty-four elders . . . fell down before him who sat on the throne and worshiped him who lives forever and ever and cast their crowns before the throne, saying, "You are worthy, O Lord, to receive glory and honor and praise; for you have created all things, and for your pleasure they are and were created." We must imitate their practice in the kingdom of grace if we intend to ever reign with them in the kingdom of glory, laboring to do God's will on earth as it is done in heaven, with all alacrity and cheerfulness, speed and diligence, that his name may be hallowed and glorified and his kingdom advanced and magnified, as we beg in the Lord's Prayer. For as it is the secondary end of our election that we may be holy, so the main and supreme goal of this end is that our holiness and glorification may be to the praise of the glory of God's grace, who of his free mercy has sanctified and glorified us. And therefore, in all our actions we must set forth God's glory as their supreme end. A Guide to Godliness.[5]

We Must Be Willing to Cast Away Our Crowns. Chronicle of the Hutterian Brethren: The twenty-four elders who appeared at the throne of God cast their crowns before the throne. Where will those men find themselves who are unwilling to cast away their crowns here on earth but want to be crowned and honored by everyone, who tear each other apart over a crown? Their place will not be among the elders at the throne of God. They will find themselves at the throne of Lucifer. Chronicle of the Hutterian Brethren.[6]

The Elders Before God's Throne. Anna Jansz:

The twenty-four elders
Come before God's throne
And lay down their crowns,
Honoring the Lamb of God,
Together with all the heavenly hosts
Who live under the sun.

Another Martyr Song.[7]

The Four Beasts Are the Four Evangelists. John Napier: We say now further that they do represent the four Gospels for these reasons. First, *ab officio*, these four beasts here adorn the throne and never cease from praying to God day and night. And what on earth does more adorn God's true throne and Christian religion than these four Gospels and their true professions, who never cease from praising God continually? Second, they agree in number, for there are four beasts, so are there four Gospels.

---

[4]Bullinger, *Hundred Sermons** (1561), 139-41; citing Is 6; Ezek 1; 11; Dan 7; Job 34.

[5]Downame, *Guide**, 13.

[6]Hutterian Brethren, *Chronicle*, 284.

[7]Snyder and Hecht, *Profiles of Anabaptist Women*, 346.

Third, in their particular and distinct titles or faces they agree, considering the custom of the ancients, who used to title books according to the their beginning. . . . The faces of these beasts are compared to the titles or beginnings of these books because, as men or beasts are readily known and distinguished by their faces, so are books by their titles and beginnings. Particularly, like in Revelation, in Ezekiel their faces were one like a man, another like a lion, the third like a bullock, the fourth like an eagle. So, of these four Evangelists, Matthew begins his first face or leaf at the genealogy of Christ, as he is a man. And Mark begins his first face or leaf at the voice crying (like a roaring lion) in the wilderness, "Prepare the way of the Lord." And Luke begins his first face or leaf at Zachariah offering incense (as it were, a bullock) at the altar. And John begins his first face or leaf at the high and divine essence of Christ's Godhead, flying so high in his style that he is compared to an eagle.

Fourth, in their order of priority, according as they first wrote, they agree with Ezekiel's order, where the first was a man's face, that is, Matthew, who wrote first of all and did so in Hebrew. The second was a lion's face, and that is Mark, who was the second who wrote and did so in Greek. The third in Ezekiel is a bullock's face, and that is Luke, who was the third who wrote and did so in Greek. The fourth was the eagle's face, who is John, who wrote the Fourth Gospel and did so in Greek. And so the order of their first editions agrees precisely with Ezekiel's order.

Fifth, their order of translation or edition in Greek agrees with the order that here Saint John (who wrote both in Greek and to the Greek churches) sets them in, namely, the lion, Mark, wrote first of all in Greek. The bullock, Luke, wrote second in Greek. Then was the man's face, that is, Matthew's Gospel, translated in Greek, who now is the third and before was the first. Afterward, last of all, the eagle, John (as before), wrote the Fourth Gospel. And so correspondingly, as Ezekiel, the Hebrew prophet writing to the Hebrews, preferred Matthew's Hebrew Gospel, because it was first written. So, Saint John, a Greek prophet, writing to the Greeks, spoke of Matthew's Greek Gospel and sets it in the third order because it came after both Mark's and Luke's. A Plain Discovery of the Whole Revelation of Saint John.[8]

The Church Is a Queen. Martin Luther: If someone prefers allegorical interpretation, he could do it by calling people of very humble circumstances "queens having crowns on their heads," as the church is portrayed in Revelation . . . ; then each soul would be a daughter of the King, since faith in Jesus Christ is a crown. The harps in their hands . . . are preaching, by which Christ is proclaimed throughout the church, so that every preacher is a harpist of God. . . . And they have incense, that is, prayer. . . . For these two, preaching and prayer, are the principal affairs of the church. They are our sacrifice and service, which belong properly to God and by which we are made priests. Psalm 45.[9]

The Twenty-Four Elders Are the Books of the Old Testament. John Napier: These twenty-four elders, being proved earlier to be on earth, because that the glory of the whole throne (of which they are one coherent part) is on earth, we say now further that they represent the twenty-four books of the Old Testament for these reasons. First, *ab officio*, because these ancients are said in the text to glorify God day and night, and what thing on earth is God more glorified by than his Scriptures and holy writings? . . .

Second, because they agree in name, for these twenty-four are called the ancients, so are these twenty-four books called the Old Testament. Third, they agree in number, for these ancients are twenty-four, so there be twenty-four authentic books of the Old Testament nominated by Jerome in his prologue to the books of Kings. Fifth and finally, whatever is spoken in the Revelation in the name and on behalf of any of the twenty-four

[8]Napier, *Plain Discovery**, 27-29; citing Ezek 1.
[9]LW 12:258; citing Rev 4:4; 5:8; 14:2; 8:3-4.

elders, the same you will find specially written in one of these twenty-four books of the Old Testament, as particularly shall be noted in their due place of our principal discourse. As to the second part of this proposition, that under the name of these twenty-four books both the true writers and true professors of them are spoken of by metonymy, it is certain. Otherwise they could not say that Christ has redeemed them and that they reign on earth. A Plain Discovery of the Whole Revelation of Saint John.[10]

The Throne of God Is His True Religion. John Napier: Because it is said in the text that this throne is set in heaven, some think this to be a vision of God's glory in heaven, but that cannot be for these reasons. First, because heaven, for the most part prophetically, is taken to be God's heavenly elect or true church on earth. Second, because it was superfluous curiosity for us to know any further of God's heavenly estate and glory of his majesty than the simple points of our salvation. Third, because the Scripture testifies that no pen can describe, nor mind comprehend, the glory of God's majesty in heaven. Fourth, because of the four beasts and twenty-four elders, who here are coherent members of his throne, confess themselves to reign on earth and that Christ has redeemed them with his blood. Fifth, because it is said that among them, even among these four beasts, arose a famine and dearth of barley and wheat. Therefore, this throne cannot be God's throne in heaven but must be his throne on earth among his heavenly elect here, and consequently is either his church or true religion; but his church is not properly his throne and seat but rather are these over whom he sits. Therefore, this throne must be his truth and true religion, where he sits and abides and, making his residence, there is authorized and enthroned here on earth, among his heavenly elect servants. A Plain Discovery of the Whole Revelation of Saint John.[11]

The Preaching of the Word Is the Witness of Christ. Martin Luther: What is the star [of the magi]? It is none other than the new light, preaching and the gospel, the oral and public preaching. Christ has two witnesses to his birth and realm. The one is Scripture, the word comprehended in the letters of the alphabet. The other is the voice, or the words proclaimed by mouth. St. Paul and St. Peter call this same word a light and a lamp. . . . We cannot understand the Scripture unless the light shines. For by the gospel the prophets are illuminated, so that the star must first rise and be seen. In the New Testament, preaching must be done orally and publicly, with the living voice, to produce in speech and hearing what prior to this lay hidden in the letter and in secret vision. For the New Testament is nothing but an uncovering and a revelation of the Old Testament, as is shown in Revelation 5, where the Lamb of God opens the book with the seven seals.

We also see this in the preaching of the apostles. All their preaching was simply setting forth Scripture and building on it. That is why Christ did not write his doctrine himself, as Moses did his, but transmitted it orally, and commanded that it should be orally continued giving command that it should be written. Likewise, the apostles wrote little, except Peter, Paul, John, and Matthew. . . . Those who did write, do no more than point us to the old Scripture, just as the angel pointed the shepherds to the manger and the swaddling clothes, and the star pointed the wise men to Bethlehem. The Gospel for the Festival of the Epiphany.[12]

The Key of David, the Cross of Christ, Unlocks the Scriptures. Leonhard Schiemer: It is not my intention with this writing to unlock the Scriptures for the godless. For it is sealed to them with seven seals which only the Lamb who is slain may break. . . . Who does not have the key of David (that is, the cross of Christ), to him it

[10]Napier, *Plain Discovery**, 26-27.
[11]Napier, *Plain Discovery**, 62.
[12]LW 52:205-6; citing 2 Cor 4:4; 2 Pet 1:19.

remains sealed for eternity. THREE KINDS OF GRACE FOUND IN THE SCRIPTURES.[13]

5:1-14 *The Seven-Sealed Scroll and the Lamb*

CHRIST THE LION AND THE LAMB. GIOVANNI DIODATI: [The scroll is] a figure of God's everlasting and secret decrees concerning the state and condition of his church, which none knows except the Son, who has the full knowledge of them, as true God with his Father. And likewise, it belonged to no one to declare them but only to he who alone has charge from the Father to reveal them, as Mediator and great Prophet of the church....

"The Lion," namely, Jesus Christ, descended from Judah according to the flesh, and to him in spiritual truth belonged the title of Lion attributed to Judah ... because of his sovereign strength to overcome and destroy all his enemies. "Has conquered": ... that is to say, has obtained, as in a trial, more than any other, has overcome all difficulties and brought it to pass, or has obtained, in regard to his humanity, this dignity of knowing all the Father's secrets and to unfold them by the battles he has undergone....

[The Lamb] represents Christ, who by his death has gotten that foresaid glorious title, ... who bore in his glorious body the marks of his death and sacrifice.

"Seven horns": a token of sovereign power in Christ, as King, as the seven eyes are symbols of perfect knowledge in the quality of a prophet. PIOUS ANNOTATIONS UPON THE HOLY BIBLE.[14]

WORTHY IS THE LAMB WHO WAS SLAIN. JOHN DOWNAME: [Christ] satisfied our cursedness in the whole course of his life, as the Evangelist out of the prophet notes, "He healed all that were sick, that it might be fulfilled which was spoken by Isaiah the prophet, saying, He took our infirmities, and bore our sickness."

Second, he satisfied on the cross the infinite wrath of God his Father, for the Scripture ever calls us there, "who bore our sins upon the wood, that he might reconcile both in one body unto God, through the cross, killing enmity through it, blotting out the handwriting of ordinances that was against us, which was secretly contrary to us; he took it away, nailing it to the cross."

Third, death in the grave. There, being solemnly buried, to assure us his death was a true death and not counterfeit or feigned, he lay three days under the ignominious dominion of it.

The fourth and last thing is the end, which is also the use and fruit of his sufferings: forgiveness of sins, mortification or abolishing of our sinful lusts, and freeing us from death and condemnation, as shall appear later.

To come to the last of those four heads: our Savior's humbling of himself, so far as to be obedient unto death, the death of the cross, it pleased God to crown him with an infinite weight of bliss, as the apostle teaches ... agreeing with the prophet Isaiah, "Seeing as he gives himself an oblation for sin, he shall see a seed, and prolong his days." ... It is the voice of infinite thousands of holy angels applauded by all the creatures in heaven, and on the earth, and by the four living creatures and the twenty-four elders, "Worthy is the Lamb that was slain, to receive power, and riches, and wisdom, and strength, and honor, and glory, and praise." In these two things, the sufferings of Christ and the glories that did follow, the whole substance of the gospel stands, as he himself teaches his disciples....

But had he no glory at all before he had finished his sufferings? Indeed, during the time of his humiliation, which was all his life long, while he bore the infirmity of our natures and the punishment due to the same, the great happiness belonging to him was smothered in some way so that it did not so appear, and the time for the full

[13]Liechty, *Early Anabaptist Spirituality*, 85.
[14]Diodati, *Pious Annotations**, 102-3; citing Gen 49:9; Zech 12:10; Jn 20:27; Rev 1:7.

manifesting of it was yet to come. Sum of Sacred Divinity.[15]

The Glory of the Father and Son. Pilgram Marpeck: To this Christ has witnessed and in love declared himself, with the incarnate Word, deed, and power. This is the Lamb that was found worthy to open the sealed and closed book, that is the hiddenness of all virtue, power, and effulgence of love and himself to reveal before the Father the glory of love in himself, according to his holy manhood. He declares that the Father himself has glorified him with that glory which he had with the Father before the foundation of the world was laid. And he was glorified in love in and before the Father before the beginning of the world, so he also glorified himself before men and angels, and so the Father will glorify him again. Concerning the Love of God in Christ.[16]

Christ Is Our Only Access to God. Ulrich Zwingli: I have shown here and in the previous article that Christ is our only access to God and that the hope which we were taught to put in creatures is utter falsehood and idol worship. Thus, it is high time that Scripture, which they have so dishonorably abused, must be torn out of their hands. . . . They cite two passages from the book of Revelation. . . . At this point they say, "Do you hear that the saints offer up our prayers to God? Or, that they pray for us?" Answer: Have they been turned into angels after their time here? (It is the office of angels to transmit our prayers to God, as you say.) You are forced to say no. For the angels are sent to render service to humans, but the persons who have died are not given to do such service; of that we have no reference at all in Scripture, but there are plenty of references to angels. . . .

It follows then that the sacrifice of the twenty-four elders is not the transmission of our prayers, or else you would here have to translate *sanctos* by "good Christians," which is not your custom, however; for if you did that, many of your arguments concerning intercession should fall by the board. It remains to examine your claim that the twenty-four elders offered their prayers to God on our behalf. But this is not the meaning of Scripture at all, as I shall prove to you. . . . Among other hidden things, he pointed to the joy and the pure worship of the saints (that's what "twenty-four elders" means; their prayers were symbolized by crystal bowls full of odorific savors), stressing that they were so pleasing to God in their dwelling with him now, as they are to us here on earth a well pleasing odor.

Such worship of the saints which I cannot understand as anything other than the joyous contemplation of God's face in which they were totally absorbed, John illustrated shortly before this passage in the fourth chapter by yet other figure, as follows, "When the beasts had paid their respects to God, etc., the twenty-four elders bowed down before the one who sat upon the throne and eternally worshipped the one who is alive forever, casting down their crowns or wreaths before his throne, saying, 'Lord, you are worthy to receive honor, etc.'"

In these words you may note how John sought to express the joy and amity of the saints through the image of a royal court where such customs are used; not that the heavenly joy is poor, as we might gather, but rather that he might honor the smallness of our understanding in his own way. Thus the prayers of the saints here are nothing other than the adoration of the twenty-four elders which they make to the eternal God in all eternity, in that they rejoice forever in the rest, peace, and amity in the presence of God, being eternally thankful for such grace.

Now *orationes* is *proseuchai* in Greek, which according to Suidas,[†] simply means "reunion of God and humankind" or "dialogue of the soul with God"; in German, we would call it "a prayer"; but more of this later. That the term "the prayers of the saints" means "the grateful and joyous

[15] Downame, *Sacred Divinity**, 311-13; citing Mt 8:17; Eph 2:16; Col 2:14-15; Is 53:10; Phil 2:9; Lk 24:26.
[16] Marpeck, *Writings*, 535.

adoration of the saints" is shown by the subsequent words where he says in a concluding remark, "Which odors are the prayers of the saints who sing a new song, saying, 'You are worthy to take the book and to open its seal, for you have been slain and have bought us out of the world,' etc." Note how he expressly says what the prayers were, namely the praise of the saints which they offered to Christ, the Lamb. Defense of the Reformed Faith.[17]

The True Service of God. David Chytraeus: The true and chief service of God is not the ceremonies of Moses or the offerings and bodies of beasts, but the spiritual hosts or sacrifices of praise, that is to say, to preach the true doctrine concerning God, to call on God rightly, to give him thanks, to acknowledge him, to disprove false opinions, to employ one's goods for the maintenance of the ministry and of learning, and to direct all the purposes, practices, and deeds of our life to the praise of God, as it is counted to do all things to the glory of God.

These chief and highest services of God are shadowed in the very presents of the Arabians. For gold is a representation of true doctrine and pure faith, as it is said in the psalm: "The commandments of the Lord are more to be desired than gold and much precious stone." Frankincense is an image of true prayer and thanksgiving, which rises up to heaven and refreshes God with a most sweet and acceptable scent. . . . They had vials full of odors, which are the prayers of the saints. The altar of atonement is Christ our Mediator, by whom only is God pacified and are acceptable sacrifices offered to him. For there is no altar accepted of God but only his Son Christ. On this altar let the Gentiles offer not rams or other dead beasts but spiritual sacrifices, living, holy, and acceptable to God, which is their reasonable service. . . . And let them glorify and pray to God for his mercy performed to them. A Postil or Orderly Disposing of Certain Epistles.[18]

Souls in Heaven Pray for the Kingdom. William Perkins: The fourth degree of the declaration of God's love is glorification. . . . Glorification is the perfect transforming of the saints into the image of the Son of God. . . . The beginning of glorification is in death, but it is not accomplished and made perfect before the last day of judgment. The death of the elect is but a sleep in Christ, by which the body and soul are severed—the body, that after corruption it may rise to greater glory; the soul, that it may immediately after departure from the body be transported into the kingdom of heaven, being fully sanctified. . . .

The faithful need not fear death because Christ has taken away its sting. . . . Souls, being once in heaven, remain there till the last day of judgment, where they partly magnify the name of God and partly wait and pray for the consummation of the kingdom of glory and full felicity in body and soul. . . .

And when he had taken the book, the four beasts and the twenty-four elders fell down before the Lamb, every one having harps and golden vials full of incense, which are the prayers of the saints. . . . And they sang a new song, saying, "You are worthy to take the book and to open its seals: because you were killed and have redeemed us to God by the blood of every kindred and tongue and people and nation." . . . I heard the voice of harpers harping with their harps. . . . And they sang, as it were, a new song before the throne. . . . And they cried with a loud voice, saying, "How long, Lord, holy and true? Do you not judge and avenge our blood on those who dwell on the earth?" A Golden Chain.[19]

The Benefits of the Gospel Are Limited to the Covenant. John Downame: Thus it appears by plain testimonies that the redemption

[17]Zwingli, *Defense of the Reformed Faith*, 1:158, 166-67; citing Heb 1:14; Rev 4:9. †In this passage the "prayers of the saints" are symbolized as golden bowls of incense, held by twenty-four elders.

[18]Chytraeus, *Postil**, 51-52; citing Ps 19:10; Rom 12.

[19]Perkins, *Golden Chain**, ch. 48; citing Rom 8:30; Phil 3:21; Rev 5:8-9; 14:2-3; 6:10.

wrought by Christ belonged only to the faithful, who also, by virtue of Christ's death and bloodshed, have their sins and corruptions in some measure mortified; and not to the wicked, who live and die in their sins without repentance. Now I will also confirm this truth by strong reasons. First, those who were never known by Christ (that is, acknowledged as his) were never redeemed by his precious bloodshed. . . . Second, for whomever Christ has offered a sacrifice unto his Father, for them also he makes intercession and has become their advocate. It is not likely that Christ would die for those for whom he will not entreat and that he would offer the sacrifice of his body for those for whom he would not offer the sacrifice of his lips. . . .

Third, Christ has died for those alone in whom he has attained the end of his death; for whatever did not attain his end is done in vain, which would imply a lack of wisdom or power in the agent and efficient, neither of which without blasphemy can be ascribed to Christ, who is in both infinite. But the end of Christ's death (that is, the eternal salvation of those for whom he died) is attained only in the elect and faithful. . . .

Fourth, if all were redeemed by the death of Christ, then also should all be saved, for what should hinder those who are redeemed from salvation, seeing as they have received the pardon and remission of their sins. . . . Seeing also that Christ, who has redeemed us, is stronger than Satan and all the power of hell, and therefore all their spiritual enemies conjoined together cannot pluck those whom he has redeemed out of his hand violently and against his will, then we cannot with any probable show of reason imagine that he would willingly lose those whom he has redeemed with the inestimable price of himself. And it will not stand with the justice of God to impute to their condemnation the sins of any whom Christ has fully satisfied, or to exact again that debt that he has paid. Therefore, if Christ had died for all, God in his justice could not choose but to save all; and Christ might well say to his Father, To what purpose have I died if you destroy those whom I have saved? What profit is in my blood, if you condemn those whom I have redeemed?

Last, if he died and by his death redeemed all, then also he died for and redeemed the pagans, Turks, atheists, and Epicureans, who were out of the church and covenant of grace; and so justification, redemption, and salvation should be out of the church and be extended to those whom God never received into his covenant, which is quite contrary to the whole course of the Scriptures. . . .

But against this it is objected that in the Scriptures Christ is said to have died and to have given himself a ransom for all people. . . . He is said to have tasted death for all people, and . . . he is said to be a reconciliation for the sins of the whole world. To this I answer, first, that these speeches are not to be understood of all and singular people but of all the faithful who are gathered out of the whole world. For the drift of the apostles is to show that our Savior Christ died not only for the believing Jews but for the Gentiles also, of whatever country, nation, or condition they were. And so these general speeches are expounded . . . where our Savior Christ is said to have died not only for the Jewish nation but that also he might gather together in one the children of God who were scattered. So also he is said . . . to have redeemed us (that is, all the faithful) to God by his blood out of every one of Satan's temptations grounded on the doctrine of kindred, tongue, people, nation, and so on, and . . . that all are the sons of God by faith in Christ Jesus, . . . that there is neither Jew nor Greek, slave nor free, male nor female, but all are one in Christ Jesus.

So these places are not to be understood to refer to all and singular people but all believers, of whatever nation or condition they are. For all the promises and benefits promised in the gospel, which is the covenant of grace, are to be restrained to the condition of the covenant, never so general and universal; and this condition is sometimes expressed and sometimes understood but never excluded. The Christian Warfare.[20]

[20]Downame, *Warfare**, 281-84; citing 1 Tim 2:6; Heb 2:9; 1 Jn 2:2; Jn 11:52; Rev 5:9; Gal 3:26, 28.

The Prayer of the Saints in Heaven. Martin Chemnitz: One does not need to use divination to know what these prayers of the saints were. For John himself soon explains: "They sang a new song, saying: Thou are worthy to take the book and to open the seals thereof. Thou was slain and hast redeemed us to God by thy blood, out of every kindred and tongue and nation, and hast made us unto our God kings and priests; and we shall reign on earth." From this passage, therefore, the invocation of the saints is not only not proved, since it is certain that the blest in heaven are neither dead nor idle, and concludes from this that they pray, it is shown in this passage what manner of prayers those of the blest in heaven are. Examination of the Council of Trent.[21]

[21]Chemnitz, *Examination*, 3:433-34.

6:1–8:5 Opening the Seven Seals of God's Scroll

6 Now I watched when the Lamb opened one of the seven seals, and I heard one of the four living creatures say with a voice like thunder, "Come!" 2 And I looked, and behold, a white horse! And its rider had a bow, and a crown was given to him, and he came out conquering, and to conquer.

3 When he opened the second seal, I heard the second living creature say, "Come!" 4 And out came another horse, bright red. Its rider was permitted to take peace from the earth, so that people should slay one another, and he was given a great sword.

5 When he opened the third seal, I heard the third living creature say, "Come!" And I looked, and behold, a black horse! And its rider had a pair of scales in his hand. 6 And I heard what seemed to be a voice in the midst of the four living creatures, saying, "A quart[a] of wheat for a denarius,[b] and three quarts of barley for a denarius, and do not harm the oil and wine!"

7 When he opened the fourth seal, I heard the voice of the fourth living creature say, "Come!" 8 And I looked, and behold, a pale horse! And its rider's name was Death, and Hades followed him. And they were given authority over a fourth of the earth, to kill with sword and with famine and with pestilence and by wild beasts of the earth.

9 When he opened the fifth seal, I saw under the altar the souls of those who had been slain for the word of God and for the witness they had borne. 10 They cried out with a loud voice, "O Sovereign Lord, holy and true, how long before you will judge and avenge our blood on those who dwell on the earth?" 11 Then they were each given a white robe and told to rest a little longer, until the number of their fellow servants and their brothers[c] should be complete, who were to be killed as they themselves had been.

12 When he opened the sixth seal, I looked, and behold, there was a great earthquake, and the sun became black as sackcloth, the full moon became like blood, 13 and the stars of the sky fell to the earth as the fig tree sheds its winter fruit when shaken by a gale. 14 The sky vanished like a scroll that is being rolled up, and every mountain and island was removed from its place. 15 Then the kings of the earth and the great ones and the generals and the rich and the powerful, and everyone, slave[d] and free, hid themselves in the caves and among the rocks of the mountains, 16 calling to the mountains and rocks, "Fall on us and hide us from the face of him who is seated on the throne, and from the wrath of the Lamb, 17 for the great day of their wrath has come, and who can stand?"

7 After this I saw four angels standing at the four corners of the earth, holding back the four winds of the earth, that no wind might blow on earth or sea or against any tree. 2 Then I saw another angel ascending from the rising of the sun, with the seal of the living God, and he called with a loud voice to the four angels who had been given power to harm earth and sea, 3 saying, "Do not harm the earth or the sea or the trees, until we have sealed the servants of our God on their foreheads." 4 And I heard the number of the sealed, 144,000, sealed from every tribe of the sons of Israel:

5 12,000 from the tribe of Judah were sealed,
12,000 from the tribe of Reuben,
12,000 from the tribe of Gad,
6 12,000 from the tribe of Asher,
12,000 from the tribe of Naphtali,
12,000 from the tribe of Manasseh,
7 12,000 from the tribe of Simeon,
12,000 from the tribe of Levi,
12,000 from the tribe of Issachar,
8 12,000 from the tribe of Zebulun,
12,000 from the tribe of Joseph,
12,000 from the tribe of Benjamin were sealed.

9 After this I looked, and behold, a great multitude that no one could number, from every nation, from all tribes and peoples and languages, standing before the

throne and before the Lamb, clothed in white robes,
with palm branches in their hands, [10]*and crying out*
with a loud voice, "Salvation belongs to our God who
sits on the throne, and to the Lamb!" [11]*And all the*
angels were standing around the throne and around
the elders and the four living creatures, and they fell
on their faces before the throne and worshiped God,
[12]*saying, "Amen! Blessing and glory and wisdom and*
thanksgiving and honor and power and might be to
our God forever and ever! Amen."

[13]*Then one of the elders addressed me, saying,*
"Who are these, clothed in white robes, and from
where have they come?" [14]*I said to him, "Sir, you*
know." And he said to me, "These are the ones coming
out of the great tribulation. They have washed their
robes and made them white in the blood of the Lamb.

[15]*"Therefore they are before the throne of God,*
and serve him day and night in his temple;
and he who sits on the throne will shelter
them with his presence.
[16]*They shall hunger no more, neither thirst*
anymore;
the sun shall not strike them,
nor any scorching heat.
[17]*For the Lamb in the midst of the throne will*
be their shepherd,
and he will guide them to springs of living
water,
and God will wipe away every tear from
their eyes."

8 *When the Lamb opened the seventh seal, there*
was silence in heaven for about half an hour.
[2]*Then I saw the seven angels who stand before God,*
and seven trumpets were given to them. [3]*And another*
angel came and stood at the altar with a golden
censer, and he was given much incense to offer with
the prayers of all the saints on the golden altar before
the throne, [4]*and the smoke of the incense, with the*
prayers of the saints, rose before God from the hand of
the angel. [5]*Then the angel took the censer and filled it*
with fire from the altar and threw it on the earth, and
there were peals of thunder, rumblings,[e] *flashes of*
lightning, and an earthquake.

a Greek *choinix*, a dry measure equal to about a quart **b** A *denarius* was a day's wage for a laborer **c** Or *brothers and sisters*. In New Testament usage, depending on the context, the plural Greek word *adelphoi* (translated "brothers") may refer either to *brothers* or to *brothers and sisters* **d** For the contextual rendering of the Greek word *doulos*, see Preface **e** Or *voices*, or *sounds*

OVERVIEW: The way into the future is revealed by a sacrificial Lamb who is worthy of breaking the seals and opening the scroll (Rev 6:1). This marks the beginning of the revelatory seven seals (Rev 6:1–8:5), the blowing of seven trumpets (Rev 8:6–11:19), and the pouring out of seven bowls of wrath (Rev 16:1-21). Heinrich Bullinger reads the imagery of Revelation 6:1–16:21 as a serial interpretation of history, with the seals, trumpets, and bowls of wrath depicting an ongoing story, not a recapitulation of events. In this he set the framework for much of Protestantism.

Piety is not lost to politics. The rod for measuring ecclesial integrity is held by God's prophets, known by their spiritual qualities and prophetic gifts. This contributes to the strengthening of the church between the incarnation and consummation. According to Lambert (c. 1486–1530) this begins with the white horse at Pentecost. The second seal reflects the persecution of the church by Roman emperors; the third is reflected in the peace of Constantine; the fourth seal is seen in the growth of Turkish power. Both pope and Turk prelude the spirit of antichrist adumbrated under the sixth seal, the revival of the gospel and the growth of persecution illustrated in Rev. 11 and 13. Following the destruction of antichrist (the papacy, Islam, and the sects), a brief period of peace on earth follows. This period is correlated with the millennial age of Rev. 20, making Lambert an early Reformed chiliast. Bibliander was instrumental in fostering interest in the Apocalypse with Leo Jud and Bullinger, but in marked contrast to Meyer and Lambert (and then Bullinger); Bibliander held that the seals represent universal history.

Most commentators who hold to a literal view of the 144,000 are futurist in their approach to interpreting Revelation. The twelve tribes are viewed as Israel during the tribulation, after the church has been raptured out of the world. Division existed in the sixteenth century and exists into the present over the identity of the 144,000 who are sealed in Revelation 7, settling into two main categories. Some interpret this group as the restored national tribes of the literal descendants of Abraham, while others identify the tribal list of John as a symbolic representation of the church in the last days. This latter interpretation follows that of Spanish Jesuit Francisco Ribera (1537–1591), who identified with the futurist Christian eschatological view in contrast to preterism, which interprets some or all prophecies of the Bible as events that have already happened. David Pareus, in addition to other Reformation commentators, often cites Rivera's commentary on Revelation.

6:1-8 *The Opening of the First Four Seals*

The Four Horsemen Are the Tribulations of the Ungrateful. Martin Luther: In chapter 6, the future tribulations begin. First come the bodily tribulations, such as persecution by the temporal government, which is the rider with the bow upon the white horse. Then come war and bloodshed, which is the rider with the sword on the red horse. Then come scarcity and famine, which is the rider with the balance on the black horse. Then come pestilence and the plague, the rider in the guise of death on the pale horse. For these four tribulations always surely follow the ungrateful and the despisers of the word of God, together with other [tribulations] such as the overthrow and the changing of governments, all the way down to the last day, as is shown at the end of chapter 6. And the souls of the martyrs also speak of this in their crying aloud. Preface to the Revelation of Saint John.[1]

Preaching Rejected Leads to Conflict and War. Heinrich Bullinger: Up to this point the apostle prepared the listener to hear with a quiet mind the judgments of God and fatal destinies of the church and to patiently bear all adversity, that we should worship him in all things and give glory to his name. Consequently, he expounds in a most goodly order the judgments of God and destinies of the church, showing how the Son of God governs the ordinances of God and his eternal providence. And this is, as it were, a prognostication for all times and ages until the world's end. For we shall not think that here are rehearsed only the acts of one age or two but of all. And first all things are generally described by parts, afterward particularly when we come to the opening of the seventh seal. The sum is that the Lord sends forth the preaching of the truth into the world; when people refuse and despise this, they are destroyed with wars and other innumerable calamities. Hundred Sermons on the Apocalypse.[2]

The Christian Hope. David Chytraeus: Indeed, in death itself is the assured hope of the resurrection and of the blessed life and everlasting company we shall have with God, truly because we are thoroughly persuaded that we who embrace Christ's doctrine by faith are not created for the miseries of this troublesome and mortal life only. It is not that he means the soul, which was created of nothing, the thing that was once nothing, utterly perishes and decays as if it should utterly return to nothing again. Rather, our souls do indeed remain alive after death, and as soon as they are loosed from the bond of their bodies, they are out of hand with the Lord and enjoy the sight of God in quiet peace and joy.

Our bodies, which sleep in death, shall assuredly revive and become again the dwelling places of

[1]LW 35:401-2.

[2]Bullinger, *Hundred Sermons** (1561), 181-82.

our souls, just as we, having received the same bodies again (which shall be glorified and have a lively beauty) and the same flesh we now carry about us, shall live for evermore with the Lord. We will be utterly free from all sin, labor, and grief, enjoying the sight, wisdom, light, righteousness, and blissfulness of the whole Godhead, and shall glorify God again forever and ever.

Of this hope, which is peculiar to Christians and the very helmet of our salvation, holy Job says, "This hope is laid up in my bosom. I know that my redeemer lives, and I shall rise out of the earth on the last day and shall be encompassed again with my skin, and in my flesh shall I see God, whom I shall see and none other for me, and with these eyes shall I behold him and with none other." . . . The souls of the saints are before the throne of God and serve him day and night. And God shall wipe all tears from their eyes, and there shall be no death, nor mourning, nor crying, nor labor. . . . Blessed are the dead who die in the Lord from now on. A Postil or Orderly Disposing of Certain Epistles.[3]

The Mysteries of the Seals. Francis Lambert: What is left is for me to deal specifically with the mysteries of the opening of individual seals. So then, the Lamb opened one of the seven seals. There is no doubt that the first one belongs to the Jews, that they may take one seal in the first position, according to the manner of speaking that John used here. This opening of that seal began from the time of Christ's passion, but became more obvious after Pentecost, when God's Spirit was poured out abundantly on the apostles and the first disciples. They were sent throughout the whole earth to carry the Lord Jesus Christ, by tireless preaching and swift progress, to all peoples and nations. On that interpretation, when this seal was opened John saw a white horse. The one sitting upon it held a bow in his hand, as well as a crown, and he went forth conquering, to conquer. But previously he saw one creature, that is, the first one, and this doubtless was the lion, or one having the face of a lion. This means the believers that are faithful and true. They, as I mentioned in that passage, because they put on the Lord Jesus Christ, since he is the true lion, became lions themselves and are represented by a lion. But they shouted as though with the sound of thunder. This means, very loudly and forcefully. "Come and see." But whom did they speak to? It was to John. So then, John represents the type of those who have not yet understood this mystery, just as the lion is the type of those who have understood it. The latter, while they understand something of the mystery of the book of God, desire nothing more than that this mystery become clear to everyone else. For they understand how powerful a factor is the sincere knowledge of the truth for stimulating all manner of good and salvation. So they say to the one who does not know, "Come and see." The one who believes, comes; the one who understands, sees. Therefore, this is the meaning: believe and understand, or believe and you will understand. I am talking about the meaning of the mystery, not of the figure or the type. As regards the type, the meaning is clear: that one should come and see the horse, etc. Although as it pertains to the mystery, the meaning can fit very well. Come, that you may learn about this, that you may look into the mysteries God is revealing. Therefore, the white horse is the apostles and the early disciples, whom the Holy Spirit also calls horses in Zechariah 10. He says, "He has sent them forth like a horse of his glory in war." Moreover, they are called "white," because they are pure, clean, and righteous through Christ Jesus whom they bear, that is, whom they profess. To "carry Christ" means to profess him before others. Thus, Paul was a white horse and belonged to the glory of God because he carried Christ's name before the nations, the tribes, and the sons of Israel. Exegesis of Francis Lambert.[4]

[3]Chytraeus, *Postil**, 395-96; citing Rev 6; 21; 14.

[4]Francis Lambert, *Exegeseos Francisci Lamberti Auenionensis in sanctam Diui Ioannis Apocalypsim libri VII. In Academia Marpurgensi praelecti* (Marburg: Franz Rhode, 1528), 117r-118r.

Going Forth to Conquer. Heinrich Bullinger: And after St. John diligently marked what was done, he sees the Lamb, Christ, I mean our Redeemer, open one seal, that is to say, the first. And straightaway came forth a white horse, on which he who sat had a bow bent and an arrow in it. To him was given a crown, and he went forth conquering that he might overcome. This is the vision; the exposition of it is easy. For the Lord says that he will declare the destinies of the church. Hundred Sermons on the Apocalypse.[5]

The White Horse is the Primitive Church. David Pareus: Now to speak of the opening of the seals in general, Andreae justly rejects the exposition of those who refer all of them to the manner of Christ's incarnation—as the first seal to his birth, the second to his baptism, the third to the signs he wrought after his baptism, the fourth to his unjust accusation before Pilate, the fifth to his cross, the sixth to his burial, and the seventh to his descension into hell. He says that all this was already done, whereas John speaks either of things present or what should come to pass afterward.

I see no reason for the common opinion of interpreters not to be embraced here, namely that this white horse with his rider notes the purity and integrity of the Christian church at first (for in Revelation, purity is signified by whiteness) and the speedy course of the gospel throughout the whole earth. Nevertheless, I do not limit this to the first two hundred or three hundred years, in which (notwithstanding all the cruel oppression and persecutions yet) the gospel was spread with happy success far and near. But I rather extend it to the whole time in which Christ, by the successors of the apostles, namely, many sincere bishops and faithful teachers, victoriously set up his kingdom throughout the whole Roman Empire, notwithstanding the tyranny of persecutors and the wickedness of heretics and apostates, until little by little the church decayed in her purity, and I say this contains the space of almost six hundred years.

Therefore the white horse first coming out of the seals is the primitive church, white and bright in purity of doctrine and discipline. The apostles were like horses running strongly and with great speed, propagating the faith of Christ in the whole earth, as their Acts and Epistles testify. After them God raised up apostolic men, bishops, teachers, and fathers both Greek and Latin, who firmly maintained and propagated the purity of doctrine delivered to them against tyrants, apostates and hypocrites, until the time of Gregory I, although even before his days the whiteness of this horse was somewhat changed and black spots began to appear, that is, corruptions in doctrine, discipline, and worship. This is what Hegesippus in Eusebius[†] complained of in these words: soon after the death of the apostles and those who had received the word at their mouth, the church remained not long a pure and unspotted virgin. Notwithstanding, the godly held the foundation of faith and salvation entire, namely, Christ the head. A Commentary upon the Divine Revelation.[6]

The Second or Red Horse. David Pareus: As the white horse was the church shining in doctrine and innocence, so the red horse is the church made red by martyrdom. But who was the rider? I will relate the common opinion. Because there was given to this rider a great sword to take peace from the earth and to stir up men to kill each other, therefore Lyra applies this red horse to the cruel and bloody Roman Empire, whose rider was Nero, disturbing the city of Rome by his wicked government so that the citizens were instigated to murder one another. A Commentary upon the Divine Revelation.[7]

[5]Bullinger, *Hundred Sermons** (1561), 187.

[6]Pareus, *Revelation**, 107-8. †Hegesippus is commonly known as the father of church history, although most of his works, except a few fragments, have perished. Nothing positive is known of his birth or early circumstances. Eusebius infers he was a Hebrew due to his use of the Gospel according to the Hebrews, written in the Syro-Chaldaic language of Palestine, his insertion in his history of words in the Hebrew dialect, and his mention of unwritten traditions of the Jews (*H. E.* iv. 22).

[7]Pareus, *Revelation**, 110.

The Third or Black Horse. David Pareus: Therefore Bede, Tyconius,† and others understand more rightly by the black horse heretics; by the rider, the devil, stirring them up to make black or darken the doctrine of the church; and by the balance, the Word of God, which heretics pretend to be on their side and with which they labor to beautify, maintain, and commend their errors to the end that people may the more readily receive them. This exposition Ribera‡ also approves of, for as the apostles are the white horse because they preached the glad tidings of salvation, so the black horse notes heretics, maintainers of pernicious doctrines, preaching things corrupt and hurtful. A Commentary upon the Divine Revelation.[8]

The Fourth or Pale Horse. David Pareus: But from where did this deadly disease and paleness come to the church? I answer that it was by accident occasioned by Constantine, that good emperor, his excessive bounty to Christian bishops, by which indeed he enriched but no way bettered the church. For as with much indulgence parents spoil a child, so this liberal emperor was a means to draw bishops to pride, luxury, idleness, security, and other vices. For after he first had restored peace to the church and heaped up honor and wealth on bishops (but especially enlarged the jurisdiction of Rome), there presently followed such a declining and corruption in doctrine and discipline as infected the church with a deadly poison and brought upon her (I say) a spiritual sickness, insomuch as the pest of antichrist began now to enter into her very heart and bowels. And hence it is reported that a voice from heaven was heard, saying, "Today venom is poured forth into the church." A Commentary upon the Divine Revelation.[9]

6:9-11 *The Opening of the Fifth Seal*

God Will Subdue Our Enemies. Martin Luther: Even if it had not already been promised by God, he will not eradicate all his enemies at once; we ought to pray God not to do so, but joyously suffer all these enemies can do to us, having the comfort that there are many who will follow us and complete the total. Thus Revelation 6:10-11 is addressed to the souls lying under the altar, who had been slain for God's Word and who cry to God, "O sovereign Lord, holy and true, how long before thou wilt judge and avenge our blood on those who dwell upon the earth?" They were told to "rest a little longer, until the number of their fellow servants and their brethren should be complete, who were to be killed as they themselves had been." We must look, as he does, upon the total number, which is not yet complete, but is daily in the process of being completed, until we have all been brought together. Meanwhile we must comfort ourselves that we have this King seated as our Lord, who has already subdued many of these enemies under his feet and continues to overthrow one after another. Ultimately, he will destroy them all at once. And though we die, oppressed and trampled by them, as it appears, we have the comfort that he will not forget us but fetch us when his time comes, and seat us above, so that they must forever lie under our feet. Psalm 110.[10]

Christ Intercedes for the Souls of Believers. Giovanni Diodati: This representation serves to show that the souls of believers do not appear before God except by the intercession of Christ, represented by those ancient perfumes. . . . "How long": a prayer not for any particular vengeance but of zeal for God's justice and of desire for the full coming of his kingdom in the total ruin of the wicked and in the last and final judgment. "Were given": that is to say, they were admonished to content themselves with the first and most excellent part of God's justice, which is to reward those who have suffered for him with glory, which is signified by these robes . . . expecting until in his appointed time he does accomplish the other, which is to cause vengeance to come upon the

[8]Pareus, *Revelation**, 112. †Tyconius (d. c. 380) was a major theologian of fourth-century North African Latin Christianity. ‡Francisco Ribera (1537–1591) was a Spanish Jesuit theologian.
[9]Pareus, *Revelation**, 117-18.

[10]LW 13:260.

persecutors. Pious Annotations upon the Holy Bible.[11]

Christ Will Conquer Godless Princes. Thomas Müntzer: Princes hold no terror for the pious. But should that change, then the sword will be taken from them and will be given to the people who burn with zeal so that the godless can be defeated . . . ; and then the noble jewel, peace, will be in abeyance on the earth. . . . He who sits on the white horse wants to conquer, but it is not for him. O high-born, kindly elector, there is need for diligence here, so that on the day of his wrath our Savior, who sits at God's right hand, (when he himself will pasture the sheep and drive away the wild beasts from the flock) will graciously break the might of the kings. Letter to Frederick the Wise.[12]

Heresies Are Spiritual Tribulations. Martin Luther: In chapters 7 and 8 begins the revelation of the spiritual tribulations, which are the many different heresies. Again, this is preceded by a comforting image in which the angel seals the Christians and wards off the four evil angels in order that we may again be assured that, even under heretics, Christendom will have good angels and the pure Word—as the angel with the censer, that is, with the prayers, demonstrates. These good angels are the holy fathers. Preface to the Revelation of Saint John.[13]

6:12-17 *The Opening of the Sixth Seal*

The Seal of the Baptized. Eitelhans Langenmantel: The Apocalypse tells of the seven angels who are commanded by God to pour seven plagues on the world in the last days. The Lord tells the first angel, "Do not harm the earth until I have sealed our brethren (*mitbrueder*) on their foreheads." . . . The accused understands this to refer to all Christian men who have been and shall be baptized. On the History of the Anabaptists in Upper Swabia.[14]

Baptism Is the Seal on the Forehead. Anna Jansz:

All the pious children of God
Who received their baptism
Sealed upon their brow
Also came this way,
Following the Lamb wherever it went,
Serving the Lamb with desire.

Such people must enter this valley
And all drink from the bitter cup
Until the number is fulfilled.
Zion, the worthy bride of God
To whom the Lamb itself is betrothed,
Who has calmed the wrath of God.

Another Martyr Song.[15]

7:1-8 *The 144,000 of Israel Sealed*

Two Sorts of Coming: Physical and Spiritual. Heinrich Bullinger: The restoring of Israel, or of all the faithful, is truly either corporal or spiritual. The corporal may be called historical and was done by Cyrus, Zerubbabel, Jehoshua, Ezra, Nehemiah, and the Maccabees, and the spiritual is fulfilled or shall yet be accomplished by the coming of our wholesome Messiah, our Lord Jesus Christ. And the coming of the Lord is of two sorts: the first indeed is in the flesh, and in it we believe many things to have been fulfilled of Christ, the apostles bearing witness; in the latter he shall come again from heaven into judgment. In that coming he shall most fully accomplish such things as we have not yet seen performed. And doubtless all our hope is here referred and comforted by this coming. Those things that are spoken by the apostle . . . of the conversion of the Jews have been fulfilled partly,

[11]Diodati, *Pious Annotations**, 103; citing Rev 3:4-5.
[12]Müntzer, *Collected Works*, 69-70; citing Dan 7; Rev 6.
[13]LW 35:402.
[14]Roth, "Zur Geschichte der Wiedertäufer," 30.
[15]Snyder and Hecht, *Profiles of Anabaptist Women*, 346.

and partly are fulfilled daily and are yet to be fulfilled.

Now we return to the many of those who will be saved and are already saved from the midst of the kingdom of antichrist to be declared. St. John divided the universality of humankind into Jews and Gentiles. Of the Jews are accounted 144,000. And after our judgment, of a thousand Jews there seems scarcely one or two to be saved, but according to the testimony of our Savior himself, so great a number is saved. Truly there is left of this number an infinite multitude of this stiff-necked people to be gathered who will be saved. And they are not saved by the law, or by circumcision, or by their damnable obstinacy, but by the grace of God in Christ their Messiah, the only Redeemer, revealed to them by God mercifully and by them received faithfully. For if the thief on the cross might be saved, now leaving his life, what shall hinder innumerable Jews to be saved by the same means? Nevertheless, I will here determine no measure. Neither will I also by this means frustrate the ministry of the Word and sacraments. Be that as it may, I know the things that are spoken here to be true. The measure or manner is known to God, and there is nothing impossible with him. Hundred Sermons on the Apocalypse.[16]

144,000 Believing Jews or Gentiles. David Pareus: There are also some of our interpreters who expound this number 144,000 of the Gentiles. But leaving such men's opinions, I follow the exposition of my Anonymous:[†] of all the tribes of the children of Israel, that is, of all nations imitating the faith of Israel, because God has elected some to salvation out of every part of the world, Christ also shall have his sealed ones in all places where antichrist reigns. Besides, the believers of the Gentiles are often in the New Testament called by the name of Israel, as following Israel's and Abraham's faith. . . . For they are not all Israel who are of Israel. . . . Now these are compared to the twelve tribes of Israel, because they succeeded in their place, and therefore it is said they shall sit on twelve thrones to judge the twelve tribes of Israel, who were apostate from God and Christ.

Therefore the distribution of these sealed ones, according to their tribes, is not to be taken literally but by a certain resemblance, because God has substituted other special nations instead of those apostate tribes in which he has a certain number of sealed ones, that is, those who are ordained to life eternal. And the reason for this is apparent: because the twelve carnal tribes of Israel, before the manifestation of this Revelation, were lost by the destruction of Judea and Jerusalem, and much less do they remain to this day. For concerning the small remainder of the Jews now in their dispersion, it is altogether uncertain of what tribes they are.

Furthermore Andreae (whom my Anonymous follows) applies certain virtues to each tribe from the etymology or signification of their names, for example, the sealed of the tribe of Judah are confessors of Christ; the sealed of Reuben are the pure in heart, enjoying the heavenly vision. But I pass this by as being more subtle then solid. . . . Now twelve thousand are sealed of every tribe, for many are chosen by Christ out of all peoples and nations under antichrist. A Commentary upon the Divine Revelation.[17]

The Hinge of the Prophecy. Joseph Mede: The connection of the beginning of the times of the beast with the beginning of the seventh or trumpet seal, from then the sealing of the 144,000, . . . and the connection of the end of the times of the beast with the end of the sixth trumpet, from then the finishing of the 1,260 days of the contemporary prophecy of the witnesses, . . . these, I say, concern me closely and are the two hinges by which the book-prophecy is hung (as if it were a door) on

[16]Bullinger, *Hundred Sermons** (1561), 222-24; citing Rom 11.

[17]Pareus, *Revelation**, 143; citing Rom 4; 9:6; Gen 29–30; 35.
†Dispensational interpreters think the number refers to Jews who are saved during the final seven-year tribulation period. One may say it is simply more convincing to say the 144,000 symbolically represent all Christians throughout history, both Jews and Gentiles.

the prophecy of the seals, without which there would be no ground in the text to connect them. If these are therefore seized from me, the whole scheme is dissolved and broken, and (which is worse) cannot again be restored. . . .

The sealing of 144,000 . . . seems not to be *narratio de praeterito* but *cautio de futuro*—not a narration of what had passed under the six seals but a caution against a danger to come under the seventh. For the seventh seal coming then to be opened and being a seal of destructions—lest the servants of God might utterly be extinguished in those calamitous ruins and horrible mutations by the seven trumpets—they are in this manner secured by the seal of providence and protection. It is true, the servants of God were in being before this time, but they were not sealed with this seal of protection until those calamities fell on the world from which they were to be protected. . . . The faithful Israelites, there and then sealed and marked in their foreheads, were in Jerusalem before that time of their marking but were not sealed and marked then but rather when destruction and (as it is there called) the slaughter-weapon came upon the land, from which the sealing was to secure them. Remains on Some Passages in the Apocalypse.[18]

7:9-17 *A Great Multitude from Every Nation*

The Lord Will Raise Up Reapers. Michael Sattler: Pray that reapers may be driven out into the harvest, for the time of threshing has come near. The abomination of desolation is visible among you. The elect servants and maidservants of God will be marked on the forehead with the name of their Father. The world has risen against those who are redeemed from its error. The gospel is testified to before all the world for a testimony. According to this the day of the Lord must no longer tarry. Letter to the Church at Horb.[19]

[18]Mede, *Works** (1672), 583-84; citing Rev 11; Ezek 9.
[19]Sattler, "Letter to the Church at Horb," 61.

A Great Innumerable Multitude. David Pareus: This multitude is a figure of the new triumphant church, so that it consisted both of the souls John shortly before saw under the altar—namely, those who in this world had fought the good fight of faith, from the time of the apostles for the space of six hundred years—and the 144,000 sealed ones, preserved by Christ during the troubles and commotions of that man of sin from the six hundredth year to the end of the world. This multitude is great and innumerable, consisting of all the forenamed persons, that is, both martyrs under the altar and the 144,000 sealed ones with all the other faithful from the apostles' time to the last day. This number, although it is small in comparison to those who perish, and is certain and defined in respect to God (who knows who are his), yet in itself it is great and cannot be reckoned by any creature. However much, therefore, the greater part shall follow the devil and cleave to antichrist, the Lord will still have a great multitude, and by such he will be praised forever.

Thus also the church . . . sings unto the Lord. . . . Hence we see that the sealed of the twelve tribes of Israel belong to this multitude; otherwise they could not be of every tribe and nation. So here is represented the whole triumphant church of the New Testament.

"Standing before the throne": This shows that they were in heaven and not on earth, for this standing denotes their celestial happiness, which consisted in the perpetual vision of God and the Lamb. The queen of Sheba counted Solomon's servants happy in that they always stood before Solomon and heard his wisdom, but how much greater is the happiness of the saints in heaven, who continually behold the majesty and glory of God and Christ? Now that this standing of the saints is opposed to the dreadful cry of reprobates, who can stand?

Their heavenly purity, brightness, and glory is here set forth. For the just shall shine as the stars of heaven. Hence again it appears that the souls of the martyrs, to whom white robes were given . . . and to whom it was said that they should rest for a little season, are joined to this multitude, being commanded to come forth from under the altar and placed before the throne. Moreover, palms were given into their hands in a sign of victory. For, as Gregory observes, these palms the multitude held in their hands are nothing other than the reward of victory following the works of martyrs. Yet God forbid we should, with Ribera,† attribute this reward to any meritorious work, seeing a far other meritorious cause of it is noted to us. . . .

Now follows what this multitude did: they together with the angels, elders, and beasts, that is, with the whole assembly of the heavenly inhabitants, sing joyfully to God and the Lamb. This joy of the saints, as I even now said, is opposed to the howling of the ungodly under their plagues, "Mountains fall on us." Here therefore is signified the most certain change of things as now they are, joyful indeed and desirable to the godly, now under affliction; but doleful and cursed to the wicked, now lifting up their horns. For it is a righteous thing with God (says Paul) to recompence tribulation to those who trouble you, and to you who are troubled, rest with us, and so on. Accordingly, as Abraham said to the glutton crying in hell, "Son, remember that you in your lifetime received good things, and likewise Lazarus evil things, but now he is comforted, and you are tormented."

This acclamation is not a wishing salvation, as is the manner of subjects desiring prosperity to their prince to cry, "Let the king live," but a shouting for joy and a blessing of God and the Lamb for humanity's salvation or blessed immortality and happiness. It is (I say) no wish but an action of thanksgiving, attributing to God what is due to him, namely, the praise and glory of their salvation. And the scene is: we ascribe our salvation received not to our own power but to the grace of God and merits of the Lamb. Therefore Beza, to express this scene, has rendered the words thus: "Salvation from our God and from the Lamb, namely, is given unto us." And thus Austin in his eleventh sermon concerning the saints: "They sing with a loud voice salvation to God, those who acknowledge with much thanksgiving that they have overcome in battle all fiery trials, not by their own power but by his assistance," and so on. The joy therefore and blessedness of the saints in heaven shall be an eternal celebration of God and of Christ. A Commentary upon the Divine Revelation.[20]

The Sign of Tau on Their Foreheads. Menno Simons: These are those who died with Christ to sin and have truly risen; they are the newborn, to whom the power is given to become the sons of God; who were redeemed out of all nations; who have on the wedding garments of the marriage of the Lamb; who have received the sign TAU on their foreheads, by which the servants of God are designated; these are the spiritual bride of Christ, his holy church, his spiritual body, flesh of his flesh, and bone of his bone.

They have come to the heavenly Jerusalem, the city of the living God, which came down from heaven; they have come to an innumerable company of angels, to the general assembly of the church of the firstborn who are written in heaven, and to Jesus, the Mediator of the new covenant; they are fellow citizens in the household of God who have put off the corruptible garment and put on the incorruptible; who have acknowledged the name of God and kept his commandments, and the faith of Jesus; the true sheep of Christ, who hear his voice and follow no other; the firstfruits of his creatures, who have the Spirit and mind of Christ, therefore they know what the will of the Lord is; indeed, the chosen generation, the spiritual and royal priesthood, a holy nation, a peculiar people, who in times past were not a people but now the people of God, for God had compassion on them; these are the souls who were slain under the altar for the word of God.

In short, with them old things have passed away; behold, all things have become new. But this is all of God, who has reconciled us unto himself through Jesus Christ; these are those who stand before the throne of God, with palms in their

[20]Pareus, *Revelation**, 146-47; citing Lk 16:25. †Francisco Ribera (1537–1591) was a Spanish Jesuit theologian.

hands and clothed in white, saying, "Blessing, and glory, and wisdom, and thanksgiving, and honor, and power, and might be unto our God forever and ever. Amen." The Spiritual Resurrection.[21]

8:1-5 *The Seventh Seal and the Golden Censer*

The Meaning and Length of Silence. Thomas Brightman: The seventh seal followed, whose effect, which proceeded from the opening, is called silence, which sometimes is used for any resting, such as "Why are you silent in bringing home the king?" that is, why do you rest? . . . Sometimes it is opposed to tumult, from the still waves of the waters, . . . of which sort is this silence made in heaven, that is, in the church on earth, which oftentimes is called by Christ the kingdom of heaven. The space of this silence is about half an hour, surely very short, which should almost end as soon as it should begin. In this is taught that the church afterward shall enjoy happy rest for a short time; after that, the open enemies should be driven away and that comfortable angel Constantine the Great should arise from the East. For this silence is joined together with that subduing of the cruel enemies, with which Revelation 6 was concluded. For the common type, of which sort was Revelation 7, does not interrupt the order of things.

And indeed, such quiet days followed by and by after those trumpets. For Maxentius being overcome at Rome by Constantine, and Maxentius in the East by Licinius, how glad a day appeared to the church through the whole world? How great delectation, how great joy, how great triumph was there of all degrees? How pleasant was it that the prisons were opened, that men were called back from the mines, that their feet were loosed from bonds, that their necks were delivered from the axe? Not only were there these things but also an emperor of whom never did anyone before so much as dream, who endeavored exceedingly to adorn by all means that he could every one of the least who was named a Christian. Eusebius triumphed not without cause, singing the words of the psalmist, "Go and see you the works of Jehovah, how he makes desolations in the earth, causing wares to cease unto the end of the earth, how he breaks the bow, and cuts in pieces the spear, he burns the chariots with fire." . . .

Now both the Augustes, along with Licinius as Constantinus, with one mind did procure diligently not only the peace of the church but also the ornaments of peace, as it is apparent from the decrees published in the name of them both. . . . But this was a short peace and indeed of but half an hour continuance. For first the Augustes themselves were at peace scarce three years' space: afterward, when they were reconciled, Licinius openly assailed the Christians and attempted a general slaughter. There came, moreover, civil war, which waxed fierce among the rulers of the church, the bishops themselves. Being void of all fear of the common enemy, they fell one on another with the weapons of words, as if they had been weary of peace even as soon as they had tasted the sweetness of it with the top of their lips.† Revelation of St. John.[22]

The Seventh Seal Opened. Thomas Brightman: Such had been the silence, from which at length proceeded the second period, distinguished from the former, because the entrance into this began at the end of the seals. For shall the trumpets be answerable to the seals, which are brought to their last end before the trumpets are prepared to sound? . . .

The heralds of this period are the seven angel trumpeters. The words themselves do not show plainly whether these angels were good or not. They are said to stand before God, but this is a doubtful kind of speaking, insomuch as it may be attributed as to the evil as to the good angels, and therefore it is said that Satan presented himself together with the sons of God before the Lord. . . .

[21]Simons, *Complete Writings**, 51-62.

[22]Brightman, *Revelation**, 215-16; 2 Sam 10:11; Ps 107:29. †For these events in church history, see Eusebius, *Ecclesiastical History* 1; 10.5-9; Sextus Aurelius Victor (c. 320–c. 390), *De Caesaribus*, part 2.

But the proportion of the beasts in the seals, and of the seven angel ministers of the vials, every one of which was clothed with pure linen . . . , may cause us to esteem and judge these trumpeters in the same number of holy ones, especially seeing that the article, those *seven* angels, refers to nothing that was known before unless the finger be pointed at those seven spirits of God, sent forth into all the world. . . . We said that the four angels . . . are the four first trumpets, but we mean not the trumpeters themselves but the events that followed when they blew their trumpets.

Furthermore, this heaven is the holy church on earth; the altar is the more inward holy place of the same, the ministry of the high priest, which the angels properly so called never execute, but the truth of which belonged only to Christ, the type to people only, who have a nature fit for sacrifice. With this the office of the priest is chiefly occupied, and seeing as the angels are void of this nature, they cannot represent the priest. Neither are these duties attributed to them anywhere in the Scriptures. Furthermore, the ministry was done before the throne, where there is no place for the angels, but in the circle of the throne and of the elders and of the beasts; that is to say, they circle around the uttermost limit of the church, watching on every side for its safety, for whatever is within the circle is the highest throne, the Lamb, the beasts, the lamps, the crystal sea, the altar, and so on, of which things there is a necessary use in the congregation of the faithful. I do not doubt that this angel is the same one who in the former chapter was said to ascend from the rising of the sun, namely, Constantine the Great. For what there summarily kept the angels from hurting until they had sealed the elect, that seemed in this place to be declared point by point in what manner it was done. Nothing prevents the same man from being described in diverse ways, according to the diverse nature of the things that are to be done.

And he stood before the altar. . . . The church about this time had gone into the temple and had hidden herself in its private places; therefore . . . he is said to stand before the altar, seeing as he was the chief of those who, having escaped from the corruptions of the world, went apart from others into the concealed part of the temple. But he stood in this place not as one of the common sort of the faithful but in the ornament of the priest, having a golden censer, many fragrances given to him that he should offer with the prayers of the saints. How may these things, will you say, apply to Constantine? Surely as the type of the high priest to Jesus Christ, whose person to represent is not proper now to one certain kind of people but is common to all the faithful, all of whom Christ has made priests, and not of the second but of the highest sort. But why should he not above all have the image of the priest, in whom most of all did shine the likeness of his kingly dignity? He spoke well of himself in the assembly of the bishops. "And I," says he, "am here as one of you, for I will not deny myself to be your fellow servant, in which name I rejoice most of all." Revelation of St. John.[23]

[23]Brightman, *Revelation**, 216-19; citing Job 1:6; Rev 15:6; 5:6; 11:1.

8:6–11:19 THE SEVEN TRUMPETS

6Now the seven angels who had the seven trumpets prepared to blow them.

7The first angel blew his trumpet, and there followed hail and fire, mixed with blood, and these were thrown upon the earth. And a third of the earth was burned up, and a third of the trees were burned up, and all green grass was burned up.

8The second angel blew his trumpet, and something like a great mountain, burning with fire, was thrown into the sea, and a third of the sea became blood. 9A third of the living creatures in the sea died, and a third of the ships were destroyed.

10The third angel blew his trumpet, and a great star fell from heaven, blazing like a torch, and it fell on a third of the rivers and on the springs of water. 11The name of the star is Wormwood.[a] A third of the waters became wormwood, and many people died from the water, because it had been made bitter.

12The fourth angel blew his trumpet, and a third of the sun was struck, and a third of the moon, and a third of the stars, so that a third of their light might be darkened, and a third of the day might be kept from shining, and likewise a third of the night.

13Then I looked, and I heard an eagle crying with a loud voice as it flew directly overhead, "Woe, woe, woe to those who dwell on the earth, at the blasts of the other trumpets that the three angels are about to blow!"

9 And the fifth angel blew his trumpet, and I saw a star fallen from heaven to earth, and he was given the key to the shaft of the bottomless pit.[b] 2He opened the shaft of the bottomless pit, and from the shaft rose smoke like the smoke of a great furnace, and the sun and the air were darkened with the smoke from the shaft. 3Then from the smoke came locusts on the earth, and they were given power like the power of scorpions of the earth. 4They were told not to harm the grass of the earth or any green plant or any tree, but only those people who do not have the seal of God on their foreheads. 5They were allowed to torment them for five months, but not to kill them, and their torment was like the torment of a scorpion when it stings someone. 6And in those days people will seek death and will not find it. They will long to die, but death will flee from them.

7In appearance the locusts were like horses prepared for battle: on their heads were what looked like crowns of gold; their faces were like human faces, 8their hair like women's hair, and their teeth like lions' teeth; 9they had breastplates like breastplates of iron, and the noise of their wings was like the noise of many chariots with horses rushing into battle. 10They have tails and stings like scorpions, and their power to hurt people for five months is in their tails. 11They have as king over them the angel of the bottomless pit. His name in Hebrew is Abaddon, and in Greek he is called Apollyon.[c]

12The first woe has passed; behold, two woes are still to come.

13Then the sixth angel blew his trumpet, and I heard a voice from the four horns of the golden altar before God, 14saying to the sixth angel who had the trumpet, "Release the four angels who are bound at the great river Euphrates." 15So the four angels, who had been prepared for the hour, the day, the month, and the year, were released to kill a third of mankind. 16The number of mounted troops was twice ten thousand times ten thousand; I heard their number. 17And this is how I saw the horses in my vision and those who rode them: they wore breastplates the color of fire and of sapphire[d] and of sulfur, and the heads of the horses were like lions' heads, and fire and smoke and sulfur came out of their mouths. 18By these three plagues a third of mankind was killed, by the fire and smoke and sulfur coming out of their mouths. 19For the power of the horses is in their mouths and in their tails, for their tails are like serpents with heads, and by means of them they wound.

20The rest of mankind, who were not killed by these plagues, did not repent of the works of their hands nor give up worshiping demons and idols of gold and silver and bronze and stone and wood, which cannot see or hear or walk, 21nor did they repent of their murders or their sorceries or their sexual immorality or their thefts.

10 Then I saw another mighty angel coming down from heaven, wrapped in a cloud, with a rainbow over his head, and his face was like the sun, and his legs like pillars of fire. 2He had a little scroll open in his hand. And he set his right foot on the sea, and his left foot on the land, 3and called out with a loud voice, like a lion roaring. When he called out, the seven thunders sounded. 4And when the seven thunders had sounded, I was about to write, but I heard a voice from heaven saying, "Seal up what the seven thunders have said, and do not write it down." 5And the angel whom I saw standing on the sea and on the land raised his right hand to heaven 6and swore by him who lives forever and ever, who created heaven and what is in it, the earth and what is in it, and the sea and what is in it, that there would be no more delay, 7but that in the days of the trumpet call to be sounded by the seventh angel, the mystery of God would be fulfilled, just as he announced to his servants the prophets.

8Then the voice that I had heard from heaven spoke to me again, saying, "Go, take the scroll that is open in the hand of the angel who is standing on the sea and on the land." 9So I went to the angel and told him to give me the little scroll. And he said to me, "Take and eat it; it will make your stomach bitter, but in your mouth it will be sweet as honey." 10And I took the little scroll from the hand of the angel and ate it. It was sweet as honey in my mouth, but when I had eaten it my stomach was made bitter. 11And I was told, "You must again prophesy about many peoples and nations and languages and kings."

11 Then I was given a measuring rod like a staff, and I was told, "Rise and measure the temple of God and the altar and those who worship there, 2but do not measure the court outside the temple; leave that out, for it is given over to the nations, and they will trample the holy city for forty-two months. 3And I will grant authority to my two witnesses, and they will prophesy for 1,260 days, clothed in sackcloth."

4These are the two olive trees and the two lampstands that stand before the Lord of the earth. 5And if anyone would harm them, fire pours from their mouth and consumes their foes. If anyone would harm them, this is how he is doomed to be killed. 6They have the power to shut the sky, that no rain may fall during the days of their prophesying, and they have power over the waters to turn them into blood and to strike the earth with every kind of plague, as often as they desire. 7And when they have finished their testimony, the beast that rises from the bottomless pit[e] will make war on them and conquer them and kill them, 8and their dead bodies will lie in the street of the great city that symbolically[f] is called Sodom and Egypt, where their Lord was crucified. 9For three and a half days some from the peoples and tribes and languages and nations will gaze at their dead bodies and refuse to let them be placed in a tomb, 10and those who dwell on the earth will rejoice over them and make merry and exchange presents, because these two prophets had been a torment to those who dwell on the earth. 11But after the three and a half days a breath of life from God entered them, and they stood up on their feet, and great fear fell on those who saw them. 12Then they heard a loud voice from heaven saying to them, "Come up here!" And they went up to heaven in a cloud, and their enemies watched them. 13And at that hour there was a great earthquake, and a tenth of the city fell. Seven thousand people were killed in the earthquake, and the rest were terrified and gave glory to the God of heaven.

14The second woe has passed; behold, the third woe is soon to come.

15Then the seventh angel blew his trumpet, and there were loud voices in heaven, saying, "The kingdom of the world has become the kingdom of our Lord and of his Christ, and he shall reign forever and ever." 16And the twenty-four elders who sit on their thrones before God fell on their faces and worshiped God, 17saying,

"We give thanks to you, Lord God Almighty,
who is and who was,
for you have taken your great power
and begun to reign.

[18] *The nations raged,*
but your wrath came,
and the time for the dead to be judged,
and for rewarding your servants, the prophets
and saints,
and those who fear your name,
both small and great,
and for destroying the destroyers of the earth."

[19] *Then God's temple in heaven was opened, and the ark of his covenant was seen within his temple. There were flashes of lightning, rumblings,[g] peals of thunder, an earthquake, and heavy hail.*

a *Wormwood* is the name of a plant and of the bitter-tasting extract derived from it b Greek the *abyss;* also verses 2, 11 c *Abaddon* means *destruction; Apollyon* means *destroyer* d Greek *hyacinth* e Or *the abyss* f Greek *spiritually* g Or *voices*, or *sounds*

Overview: As with the seals, the trumpets fall into two groups, the first four trumpets and then the final three. Together they recall the plagues on Egypt. Heinrich Bullinger sees the blowing of the trumpets as a call to preaching.

The first woe, and fifth trumpet, envisions a star falling from the sky with the key to an abyss, from which arise smoke, scorpions, and locusts. They are told not to harm those with the seal of God on their foreheads. Many commentators view the locusts as monks and nuns. For some commentators this fifth trumpet sounded the appearance of the antichrist in the West when Boniface III obtained from Emperor Phocas, the Eastern Roman emperor, the universal bishopric (607). The second woe, the sixth trumpet, is frequently identified with the primacy of Muhammad in the East (570–632). Four angels who were bound at the River Euphrates are released, charged with killing a third of humanity. The end of Revelation 9 describes those who worship demons and idols, which Bullinger and Martin Luther interpret as vain philosophies. The seventh trumpet is interpreted by Reformation commentators as referring to the last judgment.

8:6–9:13 *The First Four Trumpets, the Fifth Trumpet, and the Opening of the Bottomless Pit*

Where Was the Church During the Judgments of the Trumpets? Thomas Brightman: If one will count back the forty-two months in which the church should be in the temple, they contain not only that hour, day, month, and year of the sixth trumpet, . . . but also the five months of the fifth trumpet in the same place . . . , those four times repeated, in addition to all of which nevertheless there remain nine months to be reckoned. Besides, to what other thing can they be referred than to those four first trumpets of Revelation 8? But perhaps, you will say, these forty-two months take their beginning at the end of that hour, month, and year of the four angels, . . . and both the times together may pertain to the sixth trumpet. But this cannot be by any means. For the whole sixth trumpet is troublesome to the wicked, in which respect it is called the second woe. . . . But if the times are assigned in this manner, there is little misery for those who, for the space of forty-two months, triumphed in all mirth . . . while the godly are afflicted. What great hurt should the sixth trumpet bring them if after that short trouble of one year, month, day, and hour they should have a threefold longer felicity and more?

It is most certain, therefore, that this prophecy reaches back even to the first beginning of the trumpets but that it is set here because the whole race of this time could not be perceived before it should be brought to an end. And now indeed God raised up learned men, Philippus Bergomensis, Franciscus Guicciardinnus, Martin Luther, Johann Carion, Philipp Melanchthon, Gasper Peucer, Heinrich Bullinger, John Sleidan,† John Functius, and others, who, linking together the histories of things that were done, represented this face of the church in their writings. This prophecy doubtless was to be added at length necessarily. For not without cause some might ask what was done with the true church when the hail, smoke, a third of the grass, the burning mountain turned the sea into blood, the locusts, and the other fiends tyrannized. In all these trumpets has been a wonderful silence concerning it. Revelation of St. John.[1]

The Fifth Trumpet Is the Turk and His Army. John Napier: The fifth vial is all one with the fifth trumpet. But in that vial (says the text), there arose such a plague against the seat of that antichristian beast that his kingdom was darkened and they did gnaw their tongues for sorrow. This cannot in any way be himself arising against himself but rather some other godless tyrant like him, whom we shall prove to be the apostate Muhammad and his locusts the Turks. First, by the name of their chieftains; second, by the length of their reign; third and last of all, by all the indications and circumstances contained in the text.

As to the first, they shall have (says the text) their king, whose name shall be in Hebrew Abaddon, and in Greek Apollyon, and in Latin (as St. Jerome translated it) Exterminans, and in English a destroyer or a waster. It is such that, trying from language to language the names of princes, you will find both their temporal and spiritual kings' names to signify the same that Abaddon in Hebrew and Apollyon in Greek do, for their temporal king is called Turca, which is as much to say as a waster or destroyer, as testifies Philipp Melanchthon. . . . And their spiritual king's name, Muhammad, signifies *delens*, a destroyer or waster, and beside that, it signifies also a messenger or angel, most agreeable with this text, where he is also called the messenger or angel of the depths. Therefore, these locusts by the name of their chieftain align certainly with the Turks.

Second, as to the range of their dominion, the Turkish dominators reigned 150 years, and so long lasted these locusts, namely, five months, which, being prophetically taken (because this is a prophecy), makes just 150 years, as is proved by the first proposition. . . . Third and last of all, the whole circumstances and indications of the text agree most conveniently with the Turk, as at length our paraphrastically and historical discourse shall prove. Therefore, the star that in the fifth trumpet fell down from heaven and his locusts that arose must be Muhammad, who fell from his former Christian profession and became an apostate, and out of the smoke of his heresy stirred up the Turks to be his army. A Plain Discovery of the Whole Revelation of Saint John.[2]

9:13-21 *The Sixth Trumpet and Second Woe*

The Real Misery Begins. Martin Luther: In chapters 9 and 10 the real misery begins. For these earlier bodily and spiritual tribulations are almost a jest when compared with the plagues that are to come, as the angel himself also announces. . . . Three woes are to come, and these woes are to be inflicted by the other three angels—the fifth, sixth, and seventh. And with that the world is to end. Here both kinds of persecution, the bodily and the spiritual, converge. And there are to be three such persecutions: the first is to be great, the second greater, and the third is to be the greatest of all. Now the first woe, the fifth angel, is the great heretic Arius† and his companions, who have plagued Christendom so terribly. . . . The second woe is the sixth angel, the shameful Muhammad with his companions, the Saracens,

[1]Brightman, *Revelation**, 289; citing Rev 9:15, 12; 11:15. †Jacobus Philippus Bergomensis (also known as Giacomo Philippi Foresti, 1434–1520) of Bergamo was an Augustinian monk, historian, and theologian. Francesco Guicciardini (1483–1540) was an Italian historian and statesman. A friend and critic of Niccolò Machiavelli, he is considered one of the major political writers of the Italian Renaissance. Johann Carion (1499–1537) was a German astrologer known also for historical writings. Caspar Peucer (1525–1602) was a German reformer, physician, and scholar of Sorbian origin. Johannes Sleidanus or Sleidan (1506–1556) was a Luxembourgeois historian and annalist of the Reformation.

[2]Napier, *Plain Discovery**, 3-5.

who inflicted great plagues on Christendom, with his doctrines and with the sword. Along with this angel, in order that this woe may be all the greater, comes the mighty angel with the rainbow and the bitter scroll, that is the holy papacy, with its appearance of great spirituality. PREFACE TO THE REVELATION OF ST. JOHN.[3]

DO NOT ADD TO OR TAKE AWAY FROM GOD'S WORD. MARTIN CHEMNITZ: In the Apocalypse of John this must be observed first of all, that John at various time received the command from the Son of God to write to the churches the things which he both saw and heard. And yet so great is the impudence of Eck,[†] of Pighius,[‡] and of my Andrada[§] that they are not afraid to say that the apostles received the command from the Son of God not that they should write but that they should only preach the gospel. And yet John at various times receives an express command from the Son of God himself to write to the churches. And concerning the remaining writings of the New Testament, Paul affirms that they are divinely inspired, that is (as Peter interprets it), the men of God spoke not by human will but impelled by the Spirit of God.

Also, this needs to be observed by us in the Apocalypse, that John was not allowed to write everything, but those things which were necessary and could be grasped. For . . . he says: "When the seven thunders had sounded, I was about to write, but I heard a voice from heaven saying: 'Seal up what the seven thunders have said, and do not write it down.'" At the end he threatens with plagues anyone who would either add to or take away from the words of this book. Therefore, what is said of the Scripture of the Old Testament pertains also and is rightly applied to the New Testament. You shall add nothing and take away nothing. Do not turn from it either to the right or to the left. Let not everyone do what seems right to him, but that which I command you, that only do. EXAMINATION OF THE COUNCIL OF TRENT.[4]

THE SEVEN TRUMPETS AND THE SEVEN VIALS ARE ONE. JOHN NAPIER: Both the seven vials and the seven trumpets are the seven last plagues—the seven vials in that by the text they are called the seven last plagues, these same being hereafter called the seven golden vials and the seven vials of the wrath of God. As to the seven trumpets, the last contains the day of judgment, as testifies the angels' oath, swearing . . . that there shall be no more time, but in the days of the seventh angel, when he shall blow the trumpet, the great mystery of God shall be finished. This mystery Paul . . . makes the latter day and resurrection, saying . . . , "Behold, I declare unto you a mystery." And again . . . , "In a moment, in the twinkling of an eye, at the last trumpet (for the trumpet shall blow) and the dead shall arise." And seeing then that the seven trumpets follow one another in order in Revelation 8–11, and the last contains the day of judgment and general resurrection, therefore the seven trumpets must be also the seven last plagues, and consequently they and the seven vials must be all one.

[3]LW 35:404-5; citing Rev 8:13. †Arius was a Cyrenaic presbyter and ascetic. He has been traditionally regarded as the founder of Arianism, which holds that Jesus Christ was not coeternal with the Father.

[4]Chemnitz, *Examination*, 1:146. †Johann Maier von Eck, often anglicized as John Eck, was a German Catholic theologian, scholastic, prelate, and a pioneer of the Counter-Reformation who was among Martin Luther's most important interlocutors and theological opponents. ‡Albert Pighius of Kampen in Holland, educated at Louvain and Cologne, and a pupil of Pope Adrian VI, whom he followed to Rome, was a learned and eloquent divine and was deputed on various missions by Clement VII and Paul III. He died as canon and archdeacon of Utrecht, December 26, 1542, a few months after the publication of his book against Calvin and the other Reformers. Beza calls him the first sophist of the age, who, by gaining a victory over Calvin, hoped to attain to a cardinal's hat. §Diego Andrada de Payva was a celebrated Portuguese theologian of the sixteenth century, born in Coimbra on July 26, 1528 (d. 1 December, 1575, in Lisbon). After finishing his course at the University of Coimbra, he received holy orders and remained as professor of theology. So great was his reputation that King Sebastian appointed him theologian at the Council of Trent (1561). Here he merited the special thanks of the pope by an able work in defense of the papal authority. While at the council he wrote his *Decem libri orthodoxarum explicationum* (Venice, 1564, 1594; Cologne, 1564, 1574) against the work of Chemnitz, *Theologiae Jesuitarum praecipua capita.*

Moreover, for confirmation of this, they agree in their principal terms: the second trumpet with the second vial, the third trumpet with the third vial, the fourth trumpet with the fourth vial, the sixth trumpet with the sixth vial, the seventh trumpet with the seventh vial. Thereby we may be sure and conclude both those trumpets with those vials and the rest of the trumpets with the rest of the vials—respective in purpose, meaning, time, and in all other circumstances—to be one and the same thing. A Plain Discovery of the Whole Revelation of Saint John.[5]

10:1-11 *The Angel and the Little Scroll*

Sweet in the Mouth but Bitter in Affliction. Hugh Broughton: Now comes a most lively description of Christ, opening himself . . . for the thunder of his power, which is past understanding and shall not be perceived by the pope until the next trumpeter or commonplace teacher sounds and ends the world. Now the angel bids John take from Christ the little book of the gospel and to eat it, which was sweet in his mouth, in preaching, but bitter in affliction and to the enemy as Ezekiel's book. Revelation of the Holy Apocalypse.[6]

Enoch and Elijah, Prophecy Restored. Thomas Brightman: Such excellent fortitude was in those learned men of that age spoken of before. It must be that they knew certainly what great trouble they would procure for themselves by avowing the truth, yet nevertheless they labored valiantly, setting more by the sweetness they received from the joy of the Spirit than by all the bitterness of peril. By their example all ministers of the Word must go on boldly; the office is not to be forsaken because of the troubles. It is no new thing for something to be found bitter by experience that being tasted a little at the tongue's end seems sweet. Therefore, let every true prophet meditate well on this lesson, lest perhaps, lighting on unexpected evils, he is overcome at length through infirmity.

. . . Now in a few words he shows to what end the former sign was used, that it may be understood that prophecy was to be restored again to the church in those times. The preparation of it was the receiving and eating up of the book, namely, a burning desire for learning, which gave hope of a more perfect light to appear daily. But those who will from these words expect John at the end of the world with Enoch and Elijah—their opinion is foolish. These things belong not to the last time but to the sixth trumpet, which we will declare manifestly hereafter to be past. And John is set forth only as a type, not described by any office, which in his own person he should bear in the last times. Revelation of St. John.[7]

11:1-19 *The Two Witnesses and the Seventh Trumpet*

The Paucity of True Preachers. Sebastian Meyer: The two witnesses, he said, signify the paucity of true preachers at the time of persecution by the antichrist, when faith is already failing and charity is growing cold. In the same way, he might also say to one or the other how formerly, in the days of Elijah and Micah, the number of false prophets was exceedingly great, but true prophets of the Lord numbered scarcely one or two who dared to stand opposed to the general impiety. So again today, we see in the great cities of Germany, where the pure gospel is taught, that it is done by one or two only, and they are totally despised; yet in these cities a great number of lazy Baalites, haughty in bearing and voluptuously fed, exercise control. The Apocalypse of John.[8]

Hus and Jerome of Prague. Sebastian Meyer: Of these things you have the example of Jan Hus and Jerome of Prague,† champions of the

[5]Napier, *Plain Discovery**, 2-3; citing 1 Cor 15:51-52.
[6]Broughton, *Revelation**, 32; citing Is 19; 54; Gen 9; Rev 4; Dan 10; Ex 14; Dan 12; Is 31; Job.

[7]Brightman, *Revelation**, 286.
[8]Meyer, *Apocalypsis**, 41r.

truth of the gospel, who were burned at the Council of Constance; and Girolamo Savonarola, of the Order of Preachers, whom Pope Alexander VI commanded to be burned in Florence of Tuscany and who urged strongly the reform of the church, preaching to the people from the Apocalypse. The Apocalypse of John.[9]

Airy Philosophy. John Calvin: It is better to pass over the subtle questions with which men harass themselves. They ask what became of these two men, Enoch and Elijah. In case they may seem to ask empty questions, they prophesy that they are kept for the final day of the church so as to be displayed to the world suddenly then. The Apocalypse of John is cited in support of this. Let us leave this airy philosophy to those with small intellects which cannot find a firm foundation. It should be enough for us that their rapture was a kind of extraordinary death. Epistle of Paul the Apostle to the Hebrews and the First and Second Epistles of St. Peter.[10]

Doctrine and Prophecy Compared. John Calvin: But for my part, as doctrine is the present subject, I would rather explain it [prophecy] . . . to mean outstanding interpreters of prophecies, who, by a unique gift of foretelling, so far as it was connected with teaching. Commentary on Ephesians.[11]

Comforting Pictures Revealed Between the First Two Woes. Martin Luther: In chapters 11 and 12, two comforting pictures are interspersed between these evil woes and plagues. One is that of the two preachers, the other that of the pregnant woman who bears a male child despite the dragon. They indicate that some pious teachers and Christians are nevertheless to remain, both under the first two woes, and under the third which is yet to come. And now the last two woes combine and make a last combined attack upon Christendom. Thus, at last, all hell is loose. Preface to the Revelation of Saint John.[12]

The Spirit of Elijah. Thomas Müntzer: If the holy church is to be rejuvenated by the bitter truth a servant of God must step forward, full of grace, and endowed with the spirit of Elijah. . . . He must get everything into full swing. Many of you really will have to be aroused to sweep the Christian people free of its godless rulers, with burning earnestness and utmost zeal. A Manifest Exposé of False Faith.[13]

The Faithful in Switzerland. Leonhard Schiemer: They [the faithful] will lie buried for three and one-half days, that is three and a half years after which they will arise from the dead with all who sleep in the Lord. At exactly that time they began to kill the brethren of the community at Solothurn in Switzerland. A Letter to the Church at Rattenberg.[14]

The Church to Be Built Anew. Hugh Broughton: John shows that the church shall be built, as Jerusalem freed from Babylon under Zerubbabel and Joshua, when Zechariah sees an angel with a reed measuring the length and breadth. So John has a reed to measure the temple and altar, that is, from the little book, to show the breadth and length and depth and height of the love of God in Christ. Christ himself is the temple. Therefore to check Thalmudiques,† who to this day looks for a third temple, as shows Rambam,‡ whom on Qoheleth (Solomon the orator) I have cited and translated, to check them he shows that the court of sacrificing is given to the heathen, and Ezekiel's goodly city is a city of affliction, as Christ was afflicted forty-two months; Zechariah's olive trees;

[9]Meyer, *Apocalypsis**, 42r. †Jan Hus (d. 1415) and Jerome of Prague (c. 1370–1416) were Reformers martyred for their theological views.

[10]CNTC 12:161-62. Compare Calvin's commentary on Gen 5:22-24.

[11]CNTC 11:179; citing 1 Cor 14.

[12]LW 35:405.

[13]Müntzer, *Collected Works*, 300; citing Mt 17; 1 Kings 18; Rev 11.

[14]Müller, "Letter to the Church at Rattenburg," 54-56.

Zerubbabel with Israel and Jesus with Levi; and candlestick of God's favor. . . .

Here is a new Elijah, a new Moses, to call fire from heaven and to slay all dew of grace and success, and to turn their waters of armies into blood, and to plague their enemies with all kind of plagues. The experience follows.

. . . When the martyrs begin to revive the gospel, the city that is called for spiritual uncleanness of religion—spiritually Sodom, for cruelty against Israel, Egypt—sets forth the king of locusts, who comes with his locusts' wings of chariots and warhorses and fights in all nations, with the two captains of martyrs, and kills them, and their case is plain how they are murdered: as if a crowner's quest went on the policy that crucified Christ after his preaching forty-two months, or 1,260 days, or three and a half years. REVELATION OF THE HOLY APOCALYPSE.[15]

ENGLAND EXHIBITS THE SPIRIT OF BABYLON. ELIZABETH AVERY: But here it may be objected that this glorious church and state of England has appeared to be a golden cup in the Lord's hand . . . in respect to the spiritual excellencies that have been seen in her, and therefore how can it be compared to the feet and toes of the great image, which is the least part of the body?

To this I answer, Though the feet and toes are the least part of the body, it will appear that there are more excellencies in them than the head of gold, for though the feet and toes are thus mixed—partly of potter's clay and partly of iron, which shows that the kingdom is partly weak and partly strong—though this part is not strong by reason of the mixture, yet I say there is more excellency in this mixture then in the head of gold, for it is said of this state that they did mix themselves with the seed of men, which is a great mystery. And so though Babylon may be in all manner of professions and all states who govern in an arbitrary way, yet I may boldly say that Babylon, concerning whose destruction the prophets of old and John in the Revelation speak, that spiritual Babylon is a state and church, and mystically Babylon in our gathered churches, and antichrist rendered in a mystery in the saints. All of this, without question, is to be accomplished in this island of Great Britain, which by the learned is made evidently to appear to be the tenth part of the great city, which is spiritually called Sodom and Egypt, where also our Lord was crucified . . . that falls first. Now if this can be proved, as very probably it can, that this state and national church of England be Babylon, then I pray take notice of that which the Lord speaks . . . that as Babylon caused the slain of Israel to fall, so at Babylon shall fall the slain of all the earth. SCRIPTURE PROPHECIES OPENED.[16]

POWER TO THE COMMON FOLK. THOMAS MÜNTZER: Now that God has moved the whole world in a miraculous way towards a recognition of the divine truth, and (the world) is proving this by its great and earnest zeal against the tyrants, as Daniel 7 says clearly: that power should be given to the common folk; Revelation 11 also points out that the kingdom of this world is to belong to Christ. This confutes completely the false gloss of those who defend the godless tyrants, who will be confounded by deeds, not words. LETTER TO THE PEOPLE OF EISENACH.[17]

THE CHURCH SHALL NOT BE FORSAKEN IN THOSE ANTICHRISTIAN AND TURKISH DIFFICULTIES. HEINRICH BULLINGER: These things pertain also to the consolation of the faithful. For the Lord promises that he will send prophets, that is, preachers, who shall maintain and defend the verity of the gospel and the glory of Christ, assail antichrist and destroy his kingdom,

[15]Broughton, *Revelation**, 33-34. †The thought and culture derivative of the Talmud, the central text of rabbinic Judaism and the primary source of Jewish religious law (*halakah*) and Jewish theology. ‡Moses ben Maimon (1138–1204), commonly known as Maimonides, also referred to by the Hebrew acronym Rambam, was a Sephardic rabbi and philosopher who became one of the most prolific and influential Torah scholars of the Middle Ages.

[16]Avery, *Scripture-Prophecies**, 3-4; citing Jer 51:7; 49.

[17]Müntzer, *Collected Works*, 150.

and advance the salvation of the faithful. In the former chapters . . . was described the fight of antichrist and heretics against God and his Christ and against his church, and now a few words is set against the same contrary fight, and the army of Christ is magnified.

And he brings forth two prophets, that is, preachers, not that there shall be two only, but that by this he will indicate that the power of Christ in the world should be and seem small to worldly people (as I shall tell you shortly). In the meantime he understands all faithful preachers and pastors of all times who offer themselves to resist antichrist and heretics. There are those who expound these things of Enoch and Elijah that shall come corporally before the judgment. Nevertheless, St. Jerome in the epistle to Marcella† refers that opinion to Jewish fables, signifying that these things must be spiritually expounded of those prophets, as are also most things of the book. And in this manner all expositors with great concord interpret all these things of these prophets spiritually and not corporally after the letter. I suppose that for two causes there are two prophets only here rehearsed. Hundred Sermons on the Apocalypse.[18]

Christ Jesus Will Overthrow Antichrist by the Spirit of his Mouth. Francis Junius: The authority of the intended revelation being declared, together with the necessity of that calling that was particularly imposed on John, hereafter followed the history of the estate of Christ, his church both conflicting or waging war and overcoming in Christ. For both the true church of Christ is said to set its sights against that which is falsely so called, over the which antichrist rules, Christ Jesus overthrowing antichrist by the spirit of his mouth; and Christ is said to overcome most gloriously until he shall slay antichrist by the appearance of his coming, as the apostle excellently teaches. . . .

So this history has two parts: one of the state of the church battling temptations, to Revelation 16; the other of the state of the same church obtaining victory, to Revelation 20. The first part has two members, most conveniently distributed into their times, and the first of it contains a history of the Christian church for 1,260 years, during which time the gospel of Christ was, as it were, taken up from among people into heaven. The second contains a history of the same church until the victory perfected. And these two members are briefly though distinctly set forth in this chapter. But both of them are spoken of more extensively later in due order. For we understand the state of the church at war out of Revelation 12–13, and of the same growing out of afflictions out of Revelation 14–16. And St. John was not unaware when he joined together the history of these two times in this chapter. Because here is spoken of prophecy, which all but one confess to be just and immutable in the church, and which Christ commanded to be continual. The history of the former time reaches to Revelation 11:14. The latter is set down in the rest of this chapter. In the former are shown these things: the calling of the servants of God, . . . the conflicts the faithful must godly undergo in their calling, for Christ and for his church, . . . and their resurrection and receiving up into heaven. . . .

In the calling of the servants of God are mentioned two things: the begetting and settling of the church in two verses, and the education of it in two other verses. The begetting of the church is here commended to St. John by sign and by speech: the sign is a measuring rod, and the speech a commandment to measure the temple of God, that is, to reduce the same to a new form, because the Gentiles are already entered into the temple of Jerusalem and shall shortly defile and overthrow it utterly. A Brief and Learned Commentary.[19]

The Torment of the Prophets. Thomas Brightman: When the prophets have finished their testimony, the beast from the abyss will attack

[18]Bullinger, *Hundred Sermons** (1561), 305. †Jerome, *Letter* 48 to Paula and Eustochium, written to Marcella (AD 386).

[19]Junius, *Apocalypsis**; citing 2 Thess 2:8.

them, overpower them, and kill them. They are slain and lie unburied in the streets of Sodom, Egypt, and Jerusalem as their enemies rejoice over their death. This third temporal reference is undetermined, but we are told that after the three and a half days the two prophets will rise again. In this they, like the church, are not delivered from martyrdom and death, but through martyrdom and death they will experience a glorious resurrection.

The political implications in the preaching of the witnesses are seen in their aggressor's power "for forty-two months," or three and a half years, or 1,260 days. This is a term often assigned to the oppressor derived from Daniel 9:27; 12:7, where the primary reference is to the time of the defilement of the temple by the "abomination that desolates" set up by Antiochus IV from 167–164 BC. In the sixteenth century this was seen in the power of the papacy adumbrated in the opening of the fifth seal. Two churches, one of Christ and a second of antichrist, are seen to be revealed in this measurement. REVELATION OF ST. JOHN.[20]

THE TIME AND PLACE OF PROPHECY. THOMAS BRIGHTMAN: It being now known for certain to what both time and place these months belong, namely, to flight, wilderness, places to hide not in the first beginning but after a long and most grievous battle with the dragon, . . . it must be that, seeing these things are attributed to the beast, . . . that it is also a living creature of some wilderness (and what other place is fit for wild beast's dens? From where she is soon afterward more clearly in the wilderness . . .), and that is not the first, that is, the Roman Empire, but the second enemy, that is, antichrist, who, inasmuch as he could, would make this place of refuge dangerous to the woman. From these things it is apparent how absurd it is to end these months in the death of Licinius,† that is, straightaway after their beginning. This may yet appear more clearly if we shall pay attention to this term of time being given them, that the whole sixth trumpet also is concluded almost with the same limit, for when these are finished, there remains very little of this. How, then, is the mystery of God finished, as is foretold, . . . if the seventh trumpet has sounded now so many ages, that is, these 3,300 years, more or less? We know that a thousand years are even as one day to God, . . . but it seems strange that when the seven seals and six trumpets are finished in one three hundred years, that now one of the same trumpets should not find an end in four times three hundred years and more. REVELATION OF ST. JOHN.[21]

THE COUNCIL OF TRENT. THOMAS BRIGHTMAN: This beast known and declared long since can be none other than the angel of the bottomless pit, of whom we heard in Revelation 9:11, namely, the bishop of Rome. For we read of no other coming out from the bottomless pit when he sent the locusts out of the pit being opened, but we should understand from the things that follow that he rose up long before. Therefore he shall not be a beast of only three and a half years' continuance. He has gained five months more at the least, during which he should reign with the locusts. Hence there is another argument also to confirm this prophecy as belonging to the former trumpets, because the beast with whom the prophets have to do in the last course of their time pertained to the fifth trumpet. Furthermore, that of Revelation 13 belonged to the same period of the trumpets. For this and that is the same beast, and both again is the same angel of the bottomless pit of Revelation 9.

[20]Brightman, *Revelation**, 119-20.

[21]Brightman, *Revelation**, 296-97; citing Rev 12:6; 13:5; 17:3; 10:7; 2 Pet 3:8. †Valerius Licinianus Licinius, a Roman emperor, was executed in AD 325 by his rival Constantine I after being defeated in the Battle of Chrysopolis. Licinius was emperor from 308 to 324, and was a colleague and rival of Constantine I for most of his reign. Licinius and Constantine I coauthored the Edict of Milan in 313, which granted official toleration to Christians in the Roman Empire. After Licinius's death, his memory was branded with infamy, his statues were thrown down, and all his laws and judicial proceedings were abolished. This official erasure from the public record is called *damnatio memoriae*.

. . . Shall the beast now first of all call to weapons? He shall attempt to do violence the whole 1,260 days. . . . But this battle he shall make when that time is finished deserves before others the name of war, both for the kind of preparation and hostile cruelty and for the notorious slaughter done to the prophets. And the thing itself proves that at this very time there was very little war. For as concerning the Scriptures, the Council of Trent—begun on February 7, 1546, namely, after those 1,260 days were ended on their third session, April 8—pierced and murdered them most pitifully.† For here the Hebrew and Greek fountains were refused and the Latin corrupt translation established as authentic. Here unwritten traditions were placed in equal dignity with the Holy Scriptures. Here the interpretation of the Scriptures was taken away from the Scriptures and made subject to people's pleasure but chiefly to the pope's. Revelation of St. John.[22]

[22]Brightman, *Revelation**, 304-6. †The first session of the Council of Trent took place on December 13, 1545. Brightman treated the second session, which was the first working one, as the opening session, which met on January 7, 1546 (not February). The session held on April 8, 1546, was therefore the fourth, though (as Brightman states) it was only the third working one. For the text of the decrees he mentions, see N. Tanner, ed., *Documents of the Ecumenical Councils* (Washington, DC: Georgetown University Press, 1990), 663-65.

Queen Elizabeth and the Seventh Trumpet. Thomas Brightman: In these last ages also, those renowned princes of Germany had restored this kingdom a while before this, to whom Gustavus the king of Sweden and Christianus the king of Denmark may be added, who in the year 1558 put down antichristian impiety and set up the gospel in the place of it, . . . that this kingdom of Christ that began from this time to be great and manifest should never be obscured so again as the former kingdoms were, which came to an utter ruin in process of time. For so it is said, "And he shall reign for evermore."

The first entrance therefore of this trumpet should be famous by this increase of a new kingdom, even as it came to pass in our kingdom of England, to which Christ sent our most gracious Elizabeth to be queen at the first blast of the seventh trumpet, in the year 1558; and she again gave herself and her kingdom to Christ by way of thankfulness, which she showed by rooting out the Romish superstitions, for the greater part of them, throughout all her dominions, and by restoring the sincere and saving truth to her people that we might worship the Lord our God according to his appointment. Revelation of St. John.[23]

[23]Brightman, *Revelation**, 123; citing Rev 16:1-17.

12:1-17 Two Great Signs and Their Interpretation

12 *And a great sign appeared in heaven: a woman clothed with the sun, with the moon under her feet, and on her head a crown of twelve stars. 2She was pregnant and was crying out in birth pains and the agony of giving birth. 3And another sign appeared in heaven: behold, a great red dragon, with seven heads and ten horns, and on his heads seven diadems. 4His tail swept down a third of the stars of heaven and cast them to the earth. And the dragon stood before the woman who was about to give birth, so that when she bore her child he might devour it. 5She gave birth to a male child, one who is to rule*[a] *all the nations with a rod of iron, but her child was caught up to God and to his throne, 6and the woman fled into the wilderness, where she has a place prepared by God, in which she is to be nourished for 1,260 days.*

7Now war arose in heaven, Michael and his angels fighting against the dragon. And the dragon and his angels fought back, 8but he was defeated, and there was no longer any place for them in heaven. 9And the great dragon was thrown down, that ancient serpent, who is called the devil and Satan, the deceiver of the whole world—he was thrown down to the earth, and his angels were thrown down with him. 10And I heard a loud voice in heaven, saying, "Now the salvation and the power and the kingdom of our God and the authority of his Christ have come, for the accuser of our brothers[b] *has been thrown down, who accuses them day and night before our God. 11And they have conquered him by the blood of the Lamb and by the word of their testimony, for they loved not their lives even unto death. 12Therefore, rejoice, O heavens and you who dwell in them! But woe to you, O earth and sea, for the devil has come down to you in great wrath, because he knows that his time is short!"*

13And when the dragon saw that he had been thrown down to the earth, he pursued the woman who had given birth to the male child. 14But the woman was given the two wings of the great eagle so that she might fly from the serpent into the wilderness, to the place where she is to be nourished for a time, and times, and half a time. 15The serpent poured water like a river out of his mouth after the woman, to sweep her away with a flood. 16But the earth came to the help of the woman, and the earth opened its mouth and swallowed the river that the dragon had poured from his mouth. 17Then the dragon became furious with the woman and went off to make war on the rest of her offspring, on those who keep the commandments of God and hold to the testimony of Jesus. And he stood[c] *on the sand of the sea.*

a Greek *shepherd* **b** Or *brothers and sisters* **c** Some manuscripts *And I stood,* connecting the sentence with 13:1

Overview: This chapter marks the beginning of a new section of the Apocalypse, comprising Revelation 12–14. Revelation 12 is prominent in this new section because of the actors and events found in it: the celestial woman, the dragon (Satan), and the messianic child. It offers a fresh start or new movement in the story, setting the stage for the rest of the Apocalypse. The centrality of Revelation 12 is an important reason to read what sixteenth-century commentators wrote. Revelation 12 interferes with the flow of an otherwise clean story that could end with Revelation 11:19.

According to Brightman, the seventh trumpet is now in the past. Now is the time to turn to the three characters and a remembrance of time past: Revelation 12, concerning the dragon and things partly done in heaven (Rev 12:1-13) and on earth (Rev 12:14-17); Revelation 13, with its focus on the identity and work of the two beasts, one from the sea and another from the earth; and Revelation 14, where the Lamb and 144,000 are introduced again.

12:1-6 *The Two Signs: The Woman and the Dragon*

Fitting the Pieces Together. Thomas Brightman: Concerning what we are told in a word in the analysis, that the three next chapters together pertain to a continual history of the past, perhaps it may seem strange to somebody why the Spirit should do what is already done and rehearse again the former history, set forth sufficiently, it seems, in those things that have been said before, especially in this place after the blowing of the seventh trumpet, when shortly there should be an end of all things, as we have learned from Revelation 10. There are most just causes of both, for no one beholding separated and dispersed parts here and there of a building scarce comprehended in mind any fashion of the whole frame, much less perceived the handsomeness, which parts of them would be joined together, every one set in its own place, and laid together in fit order. The former handling was a certain preparation of devised parts, but this continual narration properly joins all things together in one and sets before our eyes the whole frame, that we may see to what sum at length that singular building comes.

But it is reserved to this time because before the last trumpet there could not be a full comprehending of these things. The events came forth by piecemeal and distinctly, the knowledge of which the world received each part little by little, after the manner of a folded tapestry, but all things at length being ended, now there was time to behold the whole unfolded cloth and of appropriating together the universal building. But chiefly by this rehearsal we are taught that such a history of all those things under the last trumpet is to be made, as is instituted typically in these three chapters. This came to pass about the year 1560, certain learned and skillful men framing that excellent work of the centuries at Magdeburg. In this thirteen centuries, whatever from the birth of Christ unto 1300, found here and there among the ancient churches or political writers, is brought into one body and is placed to be seen at once, as in a built house all things are fitly joined together.

From this our countryman John Foxe and John Sleidan received a great light and continued the history to 1555, to that time when two or three years went by before the blowing of the seventh trumpet. For this reason, namely, by the force of the restored church, and of that commandment, . . . the former times are repeated under the last trumpet, because now at length all things should be declared most copiously by the studies of the learned that had come to pass never before. The like industry of learned men about the end of the sixth trumpet brought forth that continual narration of which we spoke in the former chapter, but that was more general and obscure in speaking of that time, but this most full and abundant, obtained by a greater knowledge of things than ever before this time. These things are to be observed concerning the order of the prophecy to the end that we may see more easily these things to be set not, as some suppose, in another place, but most wisely and fitly to be reserved unto the last trumpet, as to their natural and most proper place. Revelation of St. John.[1]

The Decrees in Heaven Executed on Earth. Giovanni Diodati: Here begins the second prophetic part of this book, which contains the things done on earth of those celestial decrees that were described before.

"A woman": many circumstances induce us to understand this vision to be of the Jewish nation and of what has befallen it since the birth of Christ. "Clothed": environed; that is to say, a nation honored with the glorious title of people of God, environed with his presence, light, and grace. "Under her feet": that is to say, whose sight in the world was very variable, in increases, prosperities, decreases, failings, appearing again, and so on, even

[1]Brightman, *Revelation**, 324-25; citing Rev 16:1-17; 10:10-11.

as the moon. "A crown": by this is clearly meant the twelve tribes. . . . "With child": that is to say, having the promises of the Messiah, whose coming she had long before conceived by faith, and the time of the accomplishment of it drew near. "Cried": this may be referred to the dolorous state into which the people of God were brought about the time of Christ's coming, being oppressed by the Roman Empire and sighing after their deliverance by the Messiah.

"A great": A figure of the prince of devils, working by the Roman Empire (described . . . with the same heads and horns) to suppress Christ at his birth, which, having been first attempted by Herod, made a king by the Romans, was afterwards continued by their magistrates, induced to it by the Jews, even to his death.† "His tail": A figurative description of the apostasy of one part of the angels, adhering to the head of it. "And did cast them": that is to say, which part he drew after him in the society of his rebellion, in respect to his human nature. . . .

"Was caught up": Though he died, he was not devoured by the devil but did rise again and was taken up into heaven in glory. "The woman": this seems to point at the dispersion of the Jewish nation without any form of commonwealth of its own or of any church, without any grace or blessing of God or food of the soul, in which miserable state it is notwithstanding preserved until the time of its last conversion. "A thousand": that is to say, a certain space of limited and prefixed time, as the three and a half years of Antiochus's persecution were. Pious Annotations upon the Holy Bible.[2]

The Woman Clad with the Sun Is the True Church of God. John Napier: This is proved, first, by the Song of Solomon, Solomon bearing the figure of Christ, who descended of him. His beloved woman and spouse throughout all that canticle bears the figure of Christ's church. Second, spiritual Jerusalem, which is Christ's church by diverse Scriptures, is also called Christ's spouse in the Revelation. Third, bodily marriage is by Saint Paul called a symbol and a sacrament of the union of Christ and his church, according to which the husband represents Christ, and the woman espoused represents the church. Fourth, in the whole Scriptures, as idolatry is called spiritual whoredom, necessarily the true worshiping of God is represented by a perfect spouse, and the true church that worships him is his spouse, and so the church of God is figured by a woman. Last of all, the whole tokens of this woman contained in the text so truly and perfectly agree with Christ's church (as is declared in the principal treatise) that necessarily we must conclude this woman to refer to the true church of God. A Plain Discovery of the Whole Revelation of Saint John.[3]

The Wilderness Is the Place of Safety for the Saints. Elizabeth Avery: Now I shall sum up in brief the particulars of the fall of Babylon, which began in some and shall be accomplished in all, even in this island of Great Britain.

In the first place, Babylon is fallen in a very small part of the saints, even in the least number, but in a spiritual sense it is fallen in the least number, so when Babylon was thus fallen in them, light did appear in that they had brought forth a man-child spoken of, . . . which is understood in the first place to be only the glorious manifestations of God in the flesh of that number of saints in whom he appears. Now when God does thus appear in anyone, then that dragon that of late has made war in heaven . . . , who did not prevail because Michael did withstand him—I say, when that dragon was cast to the earth, even that glorious state that is now come to confusion—and so he saw his power, he did presently begin to persecute that part of the church that did

[2]Diodati, *Pious Annotations**, 105; citing Is 9:6. †Herod the Great is described in the Christian Bible as the person responsible for the massacre of the innocents. The remainder of the biblical references to Herod are all ascribed to Herod Antipas (c. 20 BC–c. AD 39), Herod the Great's son.

[3]Napier, *Plain Discovery**, 33-34.

represent the woman who had brought forth a man-child. But the woman had fled into the wilderness, where she is kept, as is spoken of in the Scripture, which in a spiritual sense is only that place of safety in which the spiritual person does reside. This is God himself, who does manifest his presence most to his saints in their desolate and disconsolate condition, and the saints live more in God in want of all help and comfort from the creature than in the enjoyment of all. But though that part of the church is secured in that place, which is God, in respect to the spiritual person, yet as she is in the flesh, she is in Babylon, among her hateful enemies, who have procured the greatest evil to themselves in persecuting of the saints. In that the violences done to us, to our flesh, are on Babylon, the inhabitants of Zion shall say, "Not only in what God has done already in the fall of this glorious state and church, which shall never be rebuilt again, but also our blood be on the inhabitants of Caldea," shall Jerusalem say. Scripture Prophecies Opened.[4]

The Woman Clothed in the Sun Flees. Leonhard Schiemer: The Lord says: Sun and moon will be changed. Then all the generations on earth will wail and will see the Son of Man coming in the clouds of heaven. The wailing of the godless will continue for five months, but before that they will seize you. Those days of the greatest tribulation are shortened, as Daniel says. . . . The woman, that is, the church clad with Christ the sun, will flee from the dragon for twelve hundred days. She will be miraculously nourished by God in the desert, where he has prepared her a place. That is forty-two months. The judgment begins with the house and people of God. A Letter to the Church at Rattenberg.[5]

Infant Baptism Is No Baptism. Balthasar Hubmaier: The first error, O Christian reader, which you recognize here, is that hitherto all of us in all of Europe . . . have missed the path of truth most crude, in that we have baptized children, although it was no baptism, since they did not yet know what God, Christ, baptism, faith, or vow is. But so it is; the great, red, seven-headed, ten-horned dragon stands unceasingly before the pregnant woman, who is in travail of childbirth, waiting, when she gives birth, hastily to swallow up the infant. But if he is not able to succeed in this, then the serpent shoots a torrent of water from its mouth at the woman to devour her. A Form for Water Baptism.[6]

Their Native Land Is Not the Saints' Home. Elizabeth Avery: For the saints, the land of their nativity is not their own country, if in such a place they are in bondage, for how was the land of Egypt the own country of the children of Israel, though it was the land of their nativity? And so was Babylon to many of the people of God, but the land of Canaan was the place of their rest. And so God has prepared a wilderness for the saints to depart into, when he shall gather them from the land of their captivity—not a wilderness where there is want of all things but where there shall be abundance both of spiritual and temporal enjoyments, as can be proved by the Scriptures quoted before, which is an undoubted truth, in a literal sense as well as spiritual. I say, it may appear to be a wilderness for the present to the carnal sense, but it shall not be so long, for the Scripture prefixes a time, a time, and half a time—that is, three and a half years—and then, when that time is accomplished, . . . the solitary places and the wilderness shall rejoice for them, and the desert shall blossom like a rose. Scripture Prophecies Opened.[7]

12:7-17 *The Interpretation of the Signs: The War in Heaven*

Certainty of Hope for Heaven. Hugh Broughton: The state of the faithful here is

[4]Avery, *Scripture-Prophecies**, 5-6; citing Is 9; 66. See also Jer 51:24.
[5]Müller, "Letter to the Church at Rattenburg," 323.
[6]Hubmaier, *Theologian of Anabaptism*, 389-90.
[7]Avery, *Scripture-Prophecies**, 8-9; citing Is 31.

sweetly called heaven, to show our certainty of hope for the proper heaven, as the word of law and gospel is as sure to us as if we saw the third heaven above the air and above the stars, as St. Paul did, at his first calling, to a comfort against all his following afflictions. So the holy Daniel, who in one image made a bridge from the end of the Old Testament to the beginning of the New, called the state after the abrogation of Moses the kingdom of heaven. John Baptist begins with his tongue. The kingdom of heaven is come, and the eternal Word the essential Word, who spoke and all was made, he confirmed the same speech to show that Daniel's image was ended and that the God of heaven sets up a kingdom that cannot be corrupted. The observation of this speech had kept Daniel in a clear meaning: not brought by the West empire of Christians, nor the East Greeks, Ptolemaic dynasties, and the Athena Parthenos. Nor times after Christ, for stories teaching when he would come. The terms of the Bible be pearls and still beat on the open story or noblest matters. So Saint Paul . . . speaking of the Maccabean martyrs, famous in the Talmud and after his days, written down by Greek Jews, said from Daniel's last speeches of double resurrection that they would not be delivered because they looked for the better resurrection. So he shows that Antiochus's persecutions were the last mentioned in Daniel. The Romans did not hinder the Jews' holy religion until by the Pharisees they vexed our Lord himself, when he opened the kingdom of heaven, 1,260 days. Those would know the gospel who without knowledge of Daniel are as people who would go from one land to another parted by great waters without a ship. All who care for the kingdom of heaven will care for him. . . . But since Bargulus Ilyricus† would cast him into the lion's den if lions did not rend his bones, I will commend him to the God of Daniel and the fiery flames streaming from his throne for his fighting for the dragon against Michael and his angels. Revelation of the Holy Apocalypse.[8]

How Scripture Speaks of Angels. Martin Luther: In order to understand the text, one must know first of all that Scripture uses the word "angel" in two ways and speaks about two kinds of angels. The first are those that are called holy, heavenly spirit, without flesh and blood. They are entirely pure, without any sin or flaws. Among them there is no strife nor any division or quarrels. As long as the world has stood—for more than fifty-five hundred years—they have even the face of God in heaven without ceasing. . . . Second, Scripture also designates as "angels" those with flesh and blood, including Christ himself, God's Son, with whom [Scripture] is primarily concerned. And here, in particular, pertains the article we believe that Jesus Christ, our Lord, is both true God and man. This is the sole foundation of the entire Christian doctrine and our salvation. The Epistle for the Festival of the Holy Angels.[9]

Preachers Are Stars and Angels. John Bale: Consider how those preachers throughout all this book are compared to stars and angels, their congregations called the right spouse of Christ. The other are compared to most filthy locusts, breeding of the smoke of the bottomless pit, and to hateful birds, foul spirits, and devils, their church called the proud synagogue of Satan and the most execrable whore of Babylon. The Image of Both Churches.[10]

The Kingdom of Heaven and Christians. Martin Luther: Here, however, we still remain concealed under a veil, that is, in the kingdom of heaven of his Son, or in the kingdom of faith. It is about this kingdom of Christ on earth that this text, too, is speaking when it says, "There was a great battle in heaven." For the entire book of the Revelation of John speaks about Christ's kingdom on earth and about his servants. Therefore, what is said here about a battle in heaven must take place here on earth in the visible church, and this battle must be

[8]Broughton, *Revelation**, 152-53; citing Heb 11. †Bargulus Ilyricus was an ancient Illyrian chieftain.

[9]LW 58:173.

[10]Bale, *Image** (1570), second preface.

understood not as a battle of the spirits in heaven, but rather as the battle of Christians who belong to Christ's kingdom through faith. You should not and must not believe that the devil is in heaven among the blessed angels, for soon after the beginning of the world, he fell from there, after which the human race also fell from paradise. Therefore, in the invisible, heavenly realm there can be neither devil nor serpent nor battle. THE EPISTLE FOR THE FESTIVAL OF THE HOLY ANGELS.[11]

THE WEAPONS OF THE CHRISTIAN. MENNO SIMONS: He that is not blind will understand with what weapons the Christian is to fight, namely, with the Word of God; with this they should be well armored. For thus speaks the holy church: "Behold, his bed which is Solomon's; threescore valiant men are about it, of the valiant of Israel; they all hold swords, being expert in war; every man hath his sword upon his thigh because of fear in the night," . . . that is, each one is armed with the sword of the Spirit against all the wiles of the devil, against all false doctrine. Concerning Christ it is written, "Gird thy sword upon thy thigh, O most Mighty, with thy glory and thy majesty. And in thy majesty ride prosperously, because of truth and meekness, and righteousness; and thy right hand shall teach thee terrible things. Thine arrows are sharp in the heart of the king's enemies; whereby the people fall under thee." . . . Here the Scriptures say that Christ shall have a sword. What sword now shall Christ have? This he himself tells in the Revelation, in these words, "Repent; or else I will come unto thee quickly, and will fight against them with the sword of my mouth." . . .

If Christ fights his enemies with the sword of his mouth, if he smites the earth with the rod of his mouth, and slay the wicked with the breath of his lips; and if we are to be conformed unto his image, how can we, then, fight our enemies with any other sword? TESTIMONY AGAINST JOHN VAN LEYDEN.[12]

THE WAR IN HEAVEN IS THE WAR AGAINST HERESY. MARTIN LUTHER: Concerning this, let anyone who wants to, read in the histories: how there has been war going on since the beginning in the church against all kinds of heresy, and it has continued now in our time for more than twenty years against our own sects that slander baptism and the holy sacrament and cast aside the spoken Word—and especially against the great, powerful dragon and great angel of the devil, the pope. This is not our own war and battle, but rather Michael's. To him and to his entire kingdom, Satan, the old serpent, is a mortal enemy, and he strives to destroy them. Thus, Christ must take the field against Satan at all times with his small flock—sometimes more vigorously, sometimes less so.

Today there is sore conflict over the faith, baptism, sacrament, and gospel of Christ. Especially in these last days, the devil is astonishingly [active in] setting up new heresies and sects. . . . Now, how should we deal with him? We who bear God's Word should take heart, expecting no peace here, but rather remembering that we are soldiers who must be on the battlefield. . . . For this is the sole cause of this battle: that Christians hear, believe, and preach the Word of this Lord. The devil cannot and will not tolerate this in the world. THE EPISTLE FOR THE FESTIVAL OF THE HOLY ANGELS.[13]

THE WINGS OF AN EAGLE TO FLEE PERSECUTION. CHRONICLE OF THE HUTTERIAN BRETHREN: In these times [1569] many accusations were made and decrees issued by the emperor and the king at the imperial diets, as well as in the provincial diets, which were made up of various estates and faiths. . . . Many resolved not to lay their heads on a pillow until they had expelled and exterminated God's people, and they received power (but not from God) for this purpose. But the Lord destroyed them before they could begin. Many intended to inflict suffering on our people but only brought harm to themselves. . . . Even the

[11]LW 58:176-77, 184.
[12]Simons, *Complete Writings*; citing Song 3:7-8; Ps 45:3-5.
[13]LW 58:179-81.

unbelievers often had to acknowledge that God refused to let this people be driven away or annihilated. They lived in the land God had provided especially for them. They were given the wings of a great eagle and flew to the place God had prepared for them, and there were sustained there as long as it pleased them. Chronicle of the Hutterian Brethren.[14]

The Woman Is Given Wings. Elizabeth Avery: Now there is another wilderness condition in reference to the saints while they are in Babylon, which is of another nature, . . . where there is mention made of the woman's fleeing into the wilderness before she has wings given her, as is spoken, . . . to flee into the wilderness in respect to a local separation, which has been the condition of the saints ever since the defection from the faith, for the space of 1,260 days.

But now it is accomplished in the condition of the saints who have brought forth a man-child, who is caught up to heaven, to God and to his throne, which shows that the spiritual man in those who are enlightened with that light of God, in whose light we see light—I say, the spiritual man in such a one lives in God, though as we are in the flesh, we are in Babylon, among our hateful enemies. And so our being in God in this sense may be understood to be that wilderness into which the woman flees immediately after she has brought forth a man-child, where she is kept in respect to her spiritual subsistence. And this we may likewise observe: she has fled into this wilderness before she is persecuted by the dragon, and so have wings been given to her to flee away. And so I see that this wilderness in a spiritual sense may be said to be God himself, . . . when the Spirit shall be poured down from on high. Even that wilderness . . . that we were made in our spiritual desertion shall be a fruitful field, and the fruitful field a forest. Scripture Prophecies Opened.[15]

[14]Hutterian Brethren, *Chronicle*, 402-3.

[15]Avery, *Scripture-Prophecies**, 34; citing Is 33; Hos 2.

Michael Casts Out the Dragon. Melchior Hoffman: In order to understand more clearly the truth concerning these present last times, the angel Michael is more clearly portrayed in the Revelation of John chapter seven. There we read about the power of his office, how, when, and with whom he struggles, namely with the dragon and his angels. The Spirit says it is a red dragon, by which we must understand a kingdom of bloodshed. . . . This kingdom ruled over Christians during the time of the apostles. Similarly, this great red dragon will quaff the blood of Christians. The woman, which is Christendom, will be persecuted by the dragon, who will attempt to drown her with a stream of water. However, she will be protected three and a half times with two wings. . . .

When the prince of this world is cast out with his teachers and angels by the angel Michael and his angels, the terror begins. Heaven must be understood here to mean the elect of God, who in the Word of God are called heaven and a temple of God where God dwells. All people whom God has designated as his temple and his dwelling are heaven. It is as David said: the heavens declare your glory. . . . When the Word of God enters this heaven of man, Satan and his teaching has to be thrown out. This happened in the time of the apostles through the apostles; the devil had to leave God's heaven which he had occupied and make place for the Spirit of God to enter again into the hearts of the elect. Daniel XII.[16]

The Church of God Understood as a Woman. Heinrich Bullinger: First he describes the church of God of all times under the type or figure of the woman. This is not a strange or rare thing, since at the first beginnings of things the woman began to represent the type of Christ's spouse, the church. . . . I do not now need to recite that Isaiah has more than once under the type of a woman figured the church of God: "Rejoice, you barren," says he, "who bring forth no children," and so on. Finally, St. Paul to the Galatians . . . has set

[16]Hoffman, "Daniel XII," 326-38.

forth Sarah a figure of the church, which Solomon also in his Canticles discoursed at length in describing his spouse. The church, then, is that woman coupled with Christ her spouse in true faith and continual love.

After he applies certain things part by part to the Virgin Mary, to whom notwithstanding the things that go before and follow after do not altogether agree, which both Methodius[†] and Primasius[‡] show, and other expositors also with great accord. Second, this woman is clothed with the sun, the sun that is Christ the sun of righteousness, the light, life, and righteousness of the church, as called by Paul. . . .

Third, the moon is subject to alterations, is variable, and receives sundry colors; she increases and decreases, and although it shines yet it appears always full of spots and borrows her light of the sun. Therefore, all courses and alterations of times, and whatever is mutable and corruptible in this world, all affections also and infirmities, the church treads under her feet. All the light that she has, she has it from Christ; the light of her righteousness increases and decreases. Finally, she always gathers some spots of the nature of flesh, which she cannot leave except by death. Therefore, she shines indeed; nevertheless, the church feels some diminishment, as the Lord has said also; every branch bearing fruit he purges, that he may bring forth more fruit. And he who is washed is all clean and needs no more but to wash his feet. . . .

Furthermore, she bears a crown of honor on her head, which is the sign of a kingdom. Christ is the beauty, comeliness, and king of the church. In this crown there are no precious stones but rather stars. For in Christ are lighted the church, the patriarchs, prophets, and twelve apostles. By this, therefore, is signified the doctrine of the ministers, as in Revelation 1. Neither is the shining ministry the smallest portion among the most excellent things of the church.

Fifth, moreover, that woman has "in her belly," which by a certain figure of speech is as much to say that woman was with child and had not only a great belly (as we say) but, after the manner of women travailing, cried out and was laboring full of pain that she might be delivered. This properly pertained not to the Virgin Mary but to the church. For the primitive church of that first promise of the blessed seed conceived in her mind a hope most assured that at length the son of God should be born of a virgin, namely, the seed promised, which should break the serpent's head. Therefore did the church with an earnest desire and with most fervent prayers covet and wish that Christ might once be engendered in and by the excellent member of the same the holy virgin. Moreover, Christ is begotten in his faithful when through his virtue they are regenerated. For St. Paul, "My little children," says he, "whom I travail for again, until Christ be shaped in us."

The church therefore travails and brings forth after two sorts: bodily, while she earnestly covets without pain that Christ might be born of the virgin, and ghostly by faith and regeneration, while she desires to be conformed to Christ in her members. This therefore is the nature and disposition of this woman, that with a great desire embracing the incarnation of Christ and redemption, she would have it known to many and that many times she wishes to be regenerated and reformed after the image of Christ. HUNDRED SERMONS ON THE APOCALYPSE.[17]

[17]Bullinger, *Hundred Sermons** (1561), 350-51; citing Gen 2:18-25; Eph 5:22-23; Is 54:1; Gal 4:27. † "Methodius" probably refers to the Apocalypse of Pseudo-Methodius", written in Syriac in the late seventh century. This work shaped and influenced Christian eschatological thinking in the Middle Ages. Falsely attributed to Methodius of Olympus, a fourth-century church father, the work attempts to make sense of the Islamic conquest of the Near East. Revelation is noted for incorporating numerous preexisting aspects of Christian eschatology, such as the invasion of Gog and Magog, the rise of the antichrist, and the tribulations that precede the end of the world. The book, however, adds a new element to Christian eschatology: the rise of a messianic Roman emperor. This element remained in Christian apocalyptic literature until the end of the medieval period. ‡Primasius (d. c. AD 560) was bishop of Hadrumetum and primate of Byzacena, in Africa. He was one of the participants in the three chapters controversy, and his commentary on Revelation is of interest to modern scholars for its use of the lost commentary of Tyconius on Revelation. On Tyconius, see the introduction to this volume.

The Song of Triumph of the Saints. Thomas Brightman: "And I heard a great voice": The song of triumph of the saints, celebrating God for his great benefit, which first of all is declared by those things in which the benefit itself consisted in this verse, and afterward it is set forth by his causes . . . and by his effects. . . . The benefit itself in respect to people is safety, the tyrants being destroyed, those who labored to satisfy their hatred with the destruction of the Christians. In respect to God, it is the glory of his might, of the kingdom and power of Christ. For then his power does appear when he utterly destroyed and abolished his enemies. Also, his visible kingdom is seen after a sort when he placed godly princes in the government of the commonwealth. From then likewise the power of Christ was much declared, which before seemed weak, being so trodden underfoot by the enemies, not punishing them according to their deserts. But Christ now, by taking to himself the kingdom, declared sufficiently that the former want of punishment and sufferance came not from imbecility but only from patience.

In respect of the devil, this benefit was a just reward of his ungodliness, who continually accused the godly before God. . . . But this accusation is those taunts, reproaches, and railings with which the spiteful enemies overwhelmed the saints continually, subjecting them to the suppers of Oedipus,† incest, adultery, mutual lusts, murders, conspiracies against princes, pestilences, famine, burnings, and whatsoever public calamity there was. Of this and the like things the ancient history is full. Surely the children learned of their father the devil, that ancient false accuser, so that it is not to be wondered at if wicked men do excel in the same arts. Revelation of St. John.[18]

The Angels of Michael. Thomas Brightman: "But they overcame": Who? The angels of Michael, for now the strength of the soldiers is commended, the praise of the emperor being celebrated in the former verse. But as touching the causes of the victory, the principal is the blood of the Lamb: the instrumental is the sincerity of the faith and a very great constancy, even to death. The blood of the Lamb is the fountain of all the benefits the elect enjoy, either in this life or in the life to come. For his sake alone God both delivered his people from all the miseries of this life and at length will make them joyful with eternal felicity.

The integrity of faith is showed in the next words, "by the word of his testimony," that is, by the truth of the gospel, which they professed freely and boldly. Before it was always called the testimony of God or of Jesus; . . . here it is called the testimony of themselves, which kind of speaking nevertheless comes to the same end. For it does not respect the subject of it but in it. In the last place is their constancy, because they esteemed more the truth and faith in Jesus than their own life. . . . This is a notable constancy of the saints, that by no torments they could be removed from faith in Christ. For this reason at length God gave to them the reward of victory. Revelation of St. John.[19]

Michael Prince over the People. Hugh Broughton: Michael and Gabriel are the only holy spirits who have names in the law. . . . Michael is used thrice in Daniel. . . . "Behold, Michael, the principal or only of the chief princes, is come to aide me." Daniel saw a glorious vision of Christ, before which he fell as dead; then an angel in the form of a man, that is, Gabriel, speaks how Christ shows his assistance against Cambyses's† prohibiting of the temple building and gives him a word: "He who is in the form of God." . . . "The angel who has the name of God in him." . . . "In our Lord's words," . . . "The Father and I are one." . . . The matter is plain: in these words, there is no one strong for you in these affairs but Michael, your prince. Daniel acknowledged no creature of spirits, his prince: therefore Michael must be the Son of

[18]Brightman, *Revelation**, 333-35. †*Oedipus Rex* is a play by Sophocles that explores themes of fate, guilt, and the relationship between the individual and the state. The play tells the story of Oedipus, who is told by the Oracle of Delphi that he will kill his father and marry his mother. Oedipus tries to avoid this fate, but ultimately ends up fulfilling the prophecy.

[19]Brightman, *Revelation**, 335-37; citing Rev 1:2-9.

God. So he is called . . . in the same angel's speech Michael the great prince who stands up for his people. No created spirit dare challenge a princehood over people; so here, in the exposition of praise, Michael is expounded as Christ. Revelation of the Holy Apocalypse.[20]

The Tail of the Dragon Makes Martyrs. Hugh Broughton: The pope's power (when Satan was let loose to deceive, such that kings gave their strength to Pseudo-Peter) drives the church not to be seen for certain hundreds of years; before [Peter] Martyr,† Zwingli at Zürich, in the church Charles the Great built, showed that he was the tail of the great dragon, which drew the stars of heaven from their place. . . . But yet in Spain holy martyrs daily find the forty-two months like affliction, to be conformed to the sufferings of Christ, because they worship God only, that is, as all Jews expound the phrase "pray only unto him" and rest in the abundance of grace of the gift of justice to reign by Christ. What authority on earth makes this dragon, Revelation 13 will tell plainly, and Revelation 14 how the tail of the dragon makes martyrs for idolatry rejected. Revelation of the Holy Apocalypse.[21]

[20]Broughton, *Revelation**, 150; citing Dan 8–9; Lk 1; Dan 12; 10:13; Ex 23; Heb 1:3; Jn 10; Dan 11. †Cambyses was the son of Cyrus the Great.

[21]Broughton, *Revelation**, 159-60. †Also, St. Peter Martyr (1205?–1252) was an inquisitor, vigorous preacher, and religious founder who, for his militant reformation, was assassinated by a neo-Manichaean sect, the Cathari.

13:1-18 The Two Beasts and Their Deception

13 And I saw a beast rising out of the sea, with ten horns and seven heads, with ten diadems on its horns and blasphemous names on its heads. 2 And the beast that I saw was like a leopard; its feet were like a bear's, and its mouth was like a lion's mouth. And to it the dragon gave his power and his throne and great authority. 3 One of its heads seemed to have a mortal wound, but its mortal wound was healed, and the whole earth marveled as they followed the beast. 4 And they worshiped the dragon, for he had given his authority to the beast, and they worshiped the beast, saying, "Who is like the beast, and who can fight against it?"

5 And the beast was given a mouth uttering haughty and blasphemous words, and it was allowed to exercise authority for forty-two months. 6 It opened its mouth to utter blasphemies against God, blaspheming his name and his dwelling,[a] that is, those who dwell in heaven. 7 Also it was allowed to make war on the saints and to conquer them.[b] And authority was given it over every tribe and people and language and nation, 8 and all who dwell on earth will worship it, everyone whose name has not been written before the foundation of the world in the book of life of the Lamb who was slain. 9 If anyone has an ear, let him hear:

10 If anyone is to be taken captive,
to captivity he goes;
if anyone is to be slain with the sword,
with the sword must he be slain.

Here is a call for the endurance and faith of the saints.

11 Then I saw another beast rising out of the earth. It had two horns like a lamb and it spoke like a dragon. 12 It exercises all the authority of the first beast in its presence,[c] and makes the earth and its inhabitants worship the first beast, whose mortal wound was healed. 13 It performs great signs, even making fire come down from heaven to earth in front of people, 14 and by the signs that it is allowed to work in the presence of[d] the beast it deceives those who dwell on earth, telling them to make an image for the beast that was wounded by the sword and yet lived. 15 And it was allowed to give breath to the image of the beast, so that the image of the beast might even speak and might cause those who would not worship the image of the beast to be slain. 16 Also it causes all, both small and great, both rich and poor, both free and slave,[e] to be marked on the right hand or the forehead, 17 so that no one can buy or sell unless he has the mark, that is, the name of the beast or the number of its name. 18 This calls for wisdom: let the one who has understanding calculate the number of the beast, for it is the number of a man, and his number is 666.[f]

a Or *tabernacle* **b** Some manuscripts omit this sentence **c** Or *on its behalf* **d** Or *on behalf of* **e** For the contextual rendering of the Greek word *doulos*, see Preface **f** Some manuscripts *616*

Overview: Revelation now proceeds at a different speed as its focus is on personalities, like portraits in a picture gallery. This is the place for speculation on the nature and identity of the antichrist. While Martin Luther had largely focused on the moral and ethical errors of the pope and the Roman curia, as the sixteenth century wore on the problems were increasingly seen to include politics and political theory.[1]

This movement in interpretation is visible in David Pareus, who was a part of a developing political consensus that included Reformed

[1] See Daniel John Toft, "Shadows of Kings: The Political Thought of David Pareus, 1548–1622" (PhD diss., University of Wisconsin, 1970).

theorists such as Wolfgang Musculus and Zacharias Ursinus. Pareus's political thought is consistently devoted to exploring the relationship between church and state, which is central to Revelation 13. They are depicted in the two iconic beasts, one that arises from the sea and the other from the land. The beast from the sea is often interpreted as a political-military leader, and the one from the land associated with worship and spirituality. In his sermons on this chapter, Bullinger references the visions of Daniel, where he follows the church father Jerome in interpreting the antichrist to be the little horn that arises among the ten horns of Daniel's final beast (Dan 7:1-8). Antichrist, or new Rome, originated with the claims to dominion by Boniface III (607). The actual "fall" of the church is identified with the number "666" (Rev 13:18), a specific period from the date of John's vision (for Bullinger, AD 97) to the manifestation of open error in the church. Adding 666 to 97 yields 763, the time of the reign of Pepin the Short, who gave the former exarchate of Ravenna to Rome, creating the papal state by this donation.

Pareus's commentary lifted up these concerns about church and state at the onset of the Thirty Years' War (1618–1648). Among the questions Pareus raised were the following: (1) Why, if the pope was antichrist, had God allowed him to flourish? (2) Why had Rome remained the center and seat of Christendom? and (3) Why had the doctrines of Roman Catholicism become accepted and revered? By the end of the sixteenth century, the papacy was perceived to be the active agent of confusion, encroachment, and intervention in politics. In his commentary Pareus recounts the historical disruption and final destruction of the divine ordinances by the papacy.

The Papacy's Swords. Martin Luther: Then comes chapter 13 (following the trumpets of the last of the seven angels, who blows at the beginning of chapter 12), this seventh angel's work, the third woe, namely the papal empire and the imperial papacy. Here the papacy gets the temporal sword also into its power. It rules not only with the scroll of the second woe, but also with the sword of the third woe, for they boast that the pope has both the spiritual and the temporal sword in his power. Here, then, are the two beasts. The one is the empire. The other, with the two horns, is the papacy; it has now become also a temporal kingdom, yet with the appearance of the name of Christ. For the pope has restored the fallen Roman Empire and conveyed it from the Greeks [i.e., the Byzantines] to the Germans [i.e., the Holy Roman Empire], though it is an image of the Roman Empire rather than the body of the empire itself as it once was. Nevertheless, he puts breath and life into this image, so that it has estates, laws, members, and offices, and operates to some extent. This is the image that was wounded and healed again.

The abominations, woes, and injuries which this imperial papacy has wrought cannot now be recounted. For, in the first place, by means of his scroll the world has been filled with all kinds of idolatry—with monasteries, foundations, saints, pilgrimages, purgatory, indulgences, celibacy, and innumerable other articles of human doctrine and works, etc. In the second place who can tell how much bloodshed, slaughter, war, and misery the popes have wrought, both by themselves fighting and by stirring up the emperors, kings, and princes against one another?

Here, now, the devil's final wrath gets to work: there in the East is the second woe, Muhammad and the Saracens; here in the West are papacy and empire, with the third woe. To these is added for good measure the Turk, Gog and Magog, as will follow in chapter 20. Thus, Christendom is plagued most terribly and miserably, everywhere and on all sides, with false doctrines and with wars, with scroll and sword. That is the dregs, the final plague. After that comes almost exclusively images of comfort, telling of the end of all these woes and abominations. Preface to the Revelation of St. John (1530/1546).[2]

[2]LW 35:405-6.

13:1-10 *The First Beast Arises from the Sea*

Kingdoms and Empires Are of the Lord. Heinrich Bullinger: And first he shows the beginning of this empire. A beast comes out of the sea, on the sand of which stands the dragon, and in Revelation 17 it is said how the beast came out of the bottomless pit. Therefore, the beginning of this refers to Satan. Notwithstanding, we must here take diligent heed that we take away nothing from the Lord our God but what he assigns to himself. The Scripture in various places, chiefly by two most excellent witnesses, Daniel 3 and St. Paul, . . . has set forth that kingdoms and empires are of the Lord and that he sets up and deposes kings. There is no power, says the apostle, but of God. And until this time indeed, the apostles command to obey princes and magistrates.

How is it that we hear that the Roman Empire came out of the bottomless pit, since the apostle speaks of the same? Doubtless the Roman Empire is not absolutely of the devil. For God is the author of monarchies and preserves realms and policies, giving to them certain faithful servants. But Satan meddles with people's matters and corrupted both kings and kingdoms, and so long they are of the devil. The Christians in all political matters obeyed emperors, but commanding idolatry they did not obey them. It is certain that God did institute the kingdom of Israel or of ten tribes by the prophet Ahab, yet nevertheless the Lord cries out in another prophet, "They have reigned indeed, but not by me." For the Lord would have had those kings frame all things after his word and to reign in the fear of God, and where they did do not so but, following the instigation of Satan, ordered all things after their own lust, they are rightly said to reign not of God but of the devil. Therefore, the godly have obeyed kings, but they have not obeyed them commanding wicked things, although they took them for their kings.

God has instituted the order of priests, but nevertheless Christ calls the doings of the same priests the works of darkness. And St. Peter says we must rather obey God than people. So truly the Roman Empire, which was of God, came also out of the sea (as Daniel says also), out of the troublesome world, and even out of hell, being made great through slaughter, murder, sedition, and treason. For the people of Rome with the most part of emperors regarded the devil and the world and not God.

And what the empire of Rome is at this day, he depicts now also. It has seven heads and ten horns, and every horn had his crown, signifying truly that by horns are signified kingdoms. We do not here bring in any new or farfetched exposition. In Revelation 17 the angel says that by seven heads are signified seven mountains or hills and even kings also. In Rome are many hills, but there are seven notable. For there is Mount Palatine, Capitoline, Aventine, Coelius, Esquiline, Viminalle, and Quirinalle. Propertius, expounding the same in one verse that I have expressed in two, says, *Septem urbs alta iugis totu quae praesidet orbi.*† Hundred Sermons on the Apocalypse.[3]

The Ten-Horned Beast Is the Latin Empire. John Napier: The most notable indicators assigned by the text to this beast agree only with the Latin or Roman Empire. For first the text says that the woman who sat on this beast is the great city that sits over the kings of the earth. So the chief seat and city of the Latin or Roman Empire is that great city Rome, which ruled over all the kingdoms of the earth.

Second, says Daniel, four chief kingdoms shall arise on earth, under the figure of four beasts, of which (by plain interpretation he says) the fourth beast that had these ten horns is the fourth kingdom of the earth. And so it is that the first great kingdom or monarchy is of the Babylonians; the second, of the Medes and Persians; the third, of the Grecians; and the fourth and last is certainly the monarchy of the Latins or Romans. Therefore that fourth beast that has ten horns,

[3]Bullinger, *Hundred Sermons** (1561), 369-71; citing Dan 3:24-49; Rom 13:1-17. †See Sextus Propertius, *Elegies* 3, for "the city set high on the seven hills which preside over the whole world."

both there in Daniel and here in John's Revelation, must necessarily be the Roman or Latin empire.

Third, this beast on which the said whorish woman or Babylonian city sits has seven heads, which the text interpreted to be seven mountains. Even so Rome, the chief city or metropolitan seat of the Latin Empire, is set on seven hills, as named and proved in the third reason of the former proposition. Fourth, the text says, there are here seven kings, that is, seven sorts of royal governments, for a king is often taken for a whole race of governors of one sort, as in Daniel 7. So had Rome seven royal governments, namely, kings, consuls, dictators, triumvirs, tribunes, emperors, and popes. . . .

Fifth, the text says this beast that Saint John did see was and is not and shall rise of low estate and shall go into decay. "Was," he says, because the Roman Empire and government of emperors was before that time; "is not," he says, because at the time in which he wrote, the Emperor Domitian was dead and the empire waked, for the next emperor, Nerva Cocceius, was not yet chosen, as appears in Irenaeus,[†] who says that Saint John saw these visions in the end of the reign of Domitian. . . .

Sixth, the text says the beast that was and is not is the eighth and is one of the seven, and that meant that that royal government of the empire by emperors, which was immediately before St. John wrote, and waked when he wrote, by the decease of Domitian, that same government shall be the eighth government and was also one of the said seven governments. . . .

Seventh, the text says one of these seven heads received a deadly wound, and that deadly wound was healed. So, the chief of the seven governments of the Roman Empire, namely, the estate of emperors, was cut off and abolished by the Huns, Goths, and Vandals, and backed up from the days of Augustulus, in 475, until Charlemagne came. . . .

Eighth, this beast has ten crowned horns, that is, ten kings, the text says, which when Saint John wrote had not received their kingdoms but should receive their kingdom at a time after the beast. Then (he says) they shall give their power again to the beast and all at once shall make war with the Lamb, but at length (he says), these shall hate and destroy that harlot beast. Even so it came to pass of the Roman Empire that, long after St. John's days, when that old empire began to fall and the estate of emperors was abolished, (as is said) immediately thereafter ten Christian kings sprang from it, who again gave their power, assistance, and fortification to the next governors of the new Latin empire, which was the pope, authorizing him, as their supreme head, with whom they concurred, fighting against Christ, as hereafter shall be showed. But at length shall these ten Christian kings destroy that spiritual harlot and idolatrous empire, as (praised be God) England and Scotland, with some others, have already begun.

Ninth, that beast is the Latin empire, and the chief seat of it is Rome, because in the text both the plain name of the Latin empire is figuratively expressed and the figurative name of Rome is plainly expressed. . . . Finally, all the rest of the smaller circumstances of this ten-horned beast contained in the text do so properly and fitly agree with the Latin empire . . . that we must necessarily conclude that selfsame beast to mean and signify the whole Roman Empire. A PLAIN DISCOVERY OF THE WHOLE REVELATION OF SAINT JOHN.[4]

CIVIL AND ECCLESIASTICAL BEASTS. FRANCIS JUNIUS: The apostle, having declared the springing up of the Christian church and the state of that church from which ours takes her beginning,

[4]Napier, *Plain Discovery**, 36-40; citing Dan 7:1-28. †Marcus Cocceius Nerva was a Roman emperor from 96 to 98. Nerva became emperor when aged almost 66, after a lifetime of imperial service under Nero and the succeeding rulers of the Flavian dynasty. Under Nero, he was a member of the imperial entourage and played a vital part in exposing the Pisonian conspiracy of 65. Later, as a loyalist to the Flavians, he attained consulships in 71 and 90 during the reigns of Vespasian and Domitian, respectively. Domitian was assassinated in a palace conspiracy involving members of the Praetorian Guard and several of his freedmen. On the same day, Nerva was declared emperor by the Roman Senate. As the new ruler of the Roman Empire, he vowed to restore liberties which had been curtailed during the autocratic government of Domitian.

does now pass to the story of the progress of it, as I showed in the beginning of the previous chapter. And this history of the progress of the church and its battles is set down in this chapter, but distinctly in two parts; one is of the civil Roman Empire, to Revelation 13:10; the other of the ecclesiastical body, to the end of the chapter. In the former part are shown these things: first the state of that empire, in four verses; then the acts of it, in three verses; after, the effect, which is exceeding great glory; . . . and last of all is commended the use and the instruction of the godly against all the evils that shall come from the same. . . . The history of the state contains a most ample description of the beast. A Brief and Learned Commentary.[5]

The Pope the Wonder of the World. Francis Junius: The dragon had seven crowns, because the thief avouches himself to be the proper lord and prince of the world, but this beast is said to have ten crowns, set on several not heads but horns, because the beast is beholden for all to the dragon . . . and does not otherwise reign except by law of subjection given by him, namely, that he employ his horns against the church of God. . . . Contrary to that is what God of old commanded should be written in the headpiece of the high priest, that is, "Sanctity Jehovah," holiness unto the Lord. The name of blasphemy imposed by the dragon is (as I think) what Saint Paul says. . . . He sits as God and boasts himself to be God. For this name of blasphemy both the Roman emperors did then claim for themselves, as Suetonius and Dion report of Caligula and Domitian, and after them the popes of Rome did fully profess the same of themselves when they claimed for themselves sovereignty in holy things, of which kind of sayings the sixth book of the decretals, the Clementines, and the *extravagantes* are very full.[†]

For these men were not content with what Anglicus wrote in his *Poëtria*, the beginning of which is, *Papa stupor mundi. Nec Deus es, nec homo; sed neuter es inter utrumque*[‡] ("The pope is the wonder of the world. Thou art not God, nor art thou man, but neuter mixt of both."). . . . But they were bold to take to themselves the very name of God and to accept it given by others; accordingly, almost 120 years ago, there was made for Sixtus the Fourth a pageant of triumph,[§] when he should first enter Rome in his dignity papal, cunningly fixed on the gate of the city he should enter at, having written on it this blasphemous verse.

Oraclo vocis mundi moderaris habenas,
Et merito in terries crederis esse Deus.
By oracle of thine own voice the world thou govern all,
And worthily a God on earth, men think and do thee call.

A Brief and Learned Commentary.[6]

Temporal and Spiritual Power. David Pareus: Last, I conclude that this double-bodied and double-faced antichrist, living both on the land and sea, signified by both the beasts, is none other but the Romish pope, clothed with the spoils of the Roman monarchy and the key of Peter, that is, with both powers: the temporal, to set up and put down emperors and kings, and so on; the spiritual, to give laws to them in heaven, on earth, and under the earth. . . . While one is clothed in his pontificate, the other comes armed into the council with

[5]Junius, *Apocalypsis**, 69.

[6]Junius, *Apocalypsis**, 70; citing 2 Thess 2:4. †The decretals are letters of a pope that formulate decisions in ecclesiastical law of the Catholic Church. Boniface VIII (1294–1303) compiled this sixth book of the Decretalium in 1298 as a supplement to the five books of canon law issued by Gregory IX in 1234. Pope John XXII (1316–1334) officially published Clement V's (1305–1314) decretals (the Clementines) in 1317. The term *extravagantes* is applied to the canon law of the Roman Catholic Church to designate some papal decretals not contained in certain canonical collections that possess a special authority. More precisely, they are not found in Gratian's Decretum or the three official collections of the Corpus Juris Canonici (the Decretals of Gregory IX, the Sixth Book of the Decretals, and the Clementines). ‡"Poetria nova" was the name assigned to the hexameter poem commencing, "Papa stupor mundi," inscribed, about the year 1200, to the reigning Pope, Innocent III, by Galfridus de Vino Salvo. §Sixtus IV (1414–1484) was pope from 1471–1484. He effectively made the papacy an Italian principality.

imperial ensigns, saying, "I am Caesar." A Commentary upon the Divine Revelation.[7]

The Identity of the Antichrist. David Pareus: This is my opinion of antichrist, who is here so evidently represented by the seven-headed beast and feigned likeness to the Lamb, . . . by the seven-headed beast and woman riding on it. No man, unless he willingly shut his eyes against the light, cannot but perceive this. This light our method brings to all (who without it are in darkness) what henceforward we will labor to illustrate by our interpretation unto God's glory.

But you will say, Why then does not John expressly name the pope or antichrist? Because here he stands not in the place of a teacher but of a prophet. Teachers indeed are to express things plainly, but prophets foretelling things to come, especially of dangerous consequence, set them forth under dark and obscure types, hereby to stir people up to the more diligent searching out of the events and to shun unnecessary displeasure. John in his Epistles, where he only teaches and exhorts the church, often names antichrist and bids us avoid him. But here as a prophet he paints his person and kingdom under the type of a beast, and from that would have us to judge the mystery of it. So Paul, prophesying of antichrist, purposely abstains from naming him, yet sets him forth in such lively colors that whoever looks on the Romish prelacy may plainly see who and what manner of person is.

"And I saw a beast rising out of the sea." We have heard who this beast is. It follows now concerning his rising that he ascends out of the sea. Before . . . he ascends out of the bottomless pit; the sense is all one, for the sea also in Scripture is called abyss, because of its deepness. . . . The preposition *of* may as well note the place as the beginning from which the beast derived his origin and received his power.

Understanding it originally of the place, by "the sea" is meant the infernal bottomless pit of the throne and kingdom of Satan, from which also the locusts came forth, . . . for antichrist is the angel of the bottomless pit, whose coming is after the working of Satan, with all deceitfulness of unrighteousness, lying signs and wonders. A Commentary upon the Divine Revelation.[8]

13:11-18 *The Beast from the Earth*

The First Beast and the Second Beast. Heinrich Bullinger: Again he spoke about the power of the second beast, or antichrist, and of popery. He does or executes, he says, the power of the former beast, that is to say, exercises the same authority, that the old Roman Empire exercised. Where he adds "in his presence," Aretas[†] expounds, "in following immediately after, and even in imitating the same." But what power and authority they exercised, I declared before in his place about the beginning of this chapter. Therefore, as the Roman emperors supposed all kingdoms and provinces to be theirs and to pertain to them, so do the bishops of Rome make their boast that all realms are theirs. I give nothing here to affection or hatred.

There came forth lately a book printed at Lyons, of Augustinus Steuchus, keeper of the pope's library, in the which he recites out of the register of one Gregory (I suppose the seventh) all the kingdoms of Europe, Spain, England, France, Denmark, Hungary, and so on.[‡] The propriety of it pertained to that seat of Rome; the use to the princes, clients of the same see. For often have the popes tried to bring into subjection to them and to their see the kingdoms of the East also, and that under pretense of the holy war and recovering the Lord's sepulcher. And as the old Romans vexed with continual war the nations that did not acknowledge or obey the old Roman eagles, so the see of Rome in our time and in the memory of our forefathers has put to business and trouble those kingdoms, nations, and people that went about to revolt and would not acknowledge those double keys, that is to say, two horns.

[7]Pareus, *Revelation**, 287-88.

[8]Pareus, *Revelation**, 287-88; citing Rev 11:7; 17:8; 9:1, 13.

For who does not know with what cruel wars he vexed the land of Bohemia in times past? Who does not know what Germany and England has suffered in recent years? So truly the second beast exercises gallantly the tyranny of the old beast. The old beast set forth proclamations concerning religion and paying tributes and customs, and so in a manner impoverished all realms, their riches being brought to Rome. And what other thing does that seat do at this day? What has it done, not to mention at least these past five hundred years? Who therefore does not see that the second beast exercises most abundantly the power of the first beast? Certain manmade verses in Latin taunting the covetousness and disciples of Rome, and where Rome does magnify herself to be head of the world, which in Latin is *caput*, thus he says:

> If Caput come of Capio, which signifies "to take"
> Then may Rome well be called so, which he does nothing forsake.
> If you decline Capio Capis, and to the ground come
> Her nets are large and cannot miss, to catch both all and some.

He adds to this another thing that this second beast procures, that those who dwell on earth should worship the first beast. Doubtless we see this fulfilled in the papal kingdom in two ways. For first the papists have procured such authority and reverence for the Roman Empire, which they call both sacred and holy, that as many as live at this day, when they merely hear the name of the Roman Empire spoken of, do imagine a certain divine thing brought to them from heaven. I grant that there have been many noble princes, godly and all praiseworthy, in that same empire: as was Constantine, with some of his sons, Gratian, Valentinian, Theodore, and many others. I grant that under these and similar others the empire was holy and was indeed the empire of Christ. For Christ was acknowledged with a true faith; and yet we see how the Lord Jesus has nevertheless, as Daniel has done also, called that empire a beast, doubtless figuratively and for the tyrannies. Therefore we must wisely and justly attribute to everyone what is his and not without respect embrace and reverence that bloody empire for sacred and holy. And we have also declared before what sort of kingdoms are of God and how far the works of those who are in kingdoms are to be allowed. . . .

Second, the second beast causes men to worship the first . . . that papistry has brought again the heathenish manner, with only the names changed. For I told you before that the first beast was worshiped in that people merely received the Roman religion and still worshiped idols. The heathen did truly confess the high God Almighty, but they joined to him many gods, to whom they submitted elements, diseases, arts, countries, cities, the members and parts of people, and such other like things.

And as we have read it to be said before, "And all who dwell on earth worshiped him, those whose names are not written in the book of life of the Lamb," so he says also here plainly, and he causes the earth and the inhabitants of the earth—that is, those who seek and regard only earthly things—to worship the first beast. For not all are polluted with popish idolatry. For to this matter pertained the noble history of Leo the third emperor, and Gregory the second, and of other popes, through whose wickedness idolatry was again brought into the church, which I wrote of long ago in my work *De origine erroris*. Hundred Sermons on the Apocalypse.[9]

The Ecclesiastical Dominion. Francis Junius: The second member of the vision concerns the ecclesiastical dominion, which in Rome succeeded that which was political and is in the power of the corporation of false prophets and of the forgers of false doctrine. Therefore the same beast and the same body or corporation is called of St. John by the name of false prophet. . . . The form

[9]Bullinger, *Hundred Sermons** (1561), 392-96. †Arethas, archbishop of Caesarea (c. 850–d. c. 944), was possibly a pupil of the patriarch of Constantinople, Photius. ‡Agostino Steuco (1497/1498–1548), born at Gubbio in Umbria, was an Italian humanist, Old Testament scholar, Counter-Reformation polemicist, and antiquarian.

of this beast is first described in this verse, then his acts in the verses following, and the whole speech is concluded in the last verse. This beast is by his breed a son of the earth (as they say) obscurely born, little by little creeping up out of his abject estate. A BRIEF AND LEARNED COMMENTARY.[10]

THE ACTS OF THE ECCLESIASTICAL BEAST. FRANCIS JUNIUS: The history of the acts of this beast are contained in three things: hypocrisy, the witness of miracles, and tyranny. . . . His hypocrisy is most full of leasing, by which he abuses both the former beast and the whole world, in that he has by his cunning, as if it were by lime,[†] made of the former beast a most miserable skeleton or anatomy, usurped all his authority unto himself, and most impudently exercises the same in the sight and view of him. Yet he carries himself as if he honored him with most high honor and did truly cause him to be revered by all people.

For to this beast of Rome, which of a civil empire is made an ecclesiastical hierarchy, are given honors and divine authority, so far as he is believed to be above the Scriptures, which the gloss on the decretals declares: . . . "He changes the articles of faith and gives authority to general counsels." This is spoken of the papal power. So, the beast is by birth, foundation, seat, and finally substance one; only the pope has altered the front and manner thereof, being himself the head both of that tyrannical empire and of their false prophets, for he has taken the empire to himself and has added to that this cunning device. Now these words whose deadly wound was cured are put here for distinction's sake, as also sometime afterward, that even at that time the godly readers of this prophecy might be brought by this sign to see the thing as present, as if it were said that they might adore this very empire that is now, whose head we have seen in our own memory to have been cut off and to be cured again.

The second point of the things done by the beast is the credit of great wonders or miracles pertaining to the strengthening of this impiety, of which some signs were given from above, as it is said that fire was sent down from heaven by false sorcery in this verse. Others were showed here below in the sight of the beast, to establish idolatry and deceive souls, which St. John sets forth, beginning (as they say) with that which is last in this manner. First the effect is declared in these words: "He deceives the inhabitants of the earth." Second, the common manner of working, in two sorts: one of miracles, "For the signs which were given him to do in the presence of the beast"; the other of the words added to the signs and the teaching the idolatry confirmed by those signs, "Saying to the inhabitants of the earth that they should make an image unto that beast," and so on.

Third, a special manner is declared that it is given to him to put life into the image of the beast, with such a kind of enlivening that the beast both answers those who ask counsel of it and pronounces death against all those who do not obey or worship it. All these things, oftentimes by false miracles through the procurement and inspiration of the devil, have been affected and wrought in images. The histories of the papists are full of examples of such miracles, most of them feigned, many also done by the devil in images, as of old in the serpent. . . . By these examples is confirmed not the authority of the beast but of the truth of God and of these prophecies.

The third place is a wicked and most insolent tyranny, as was said before, usurped over the people in this verse and over their goods and actions in the next verse. For he is said both to bring on all people a tyrannous servitude, that they might serve the beast as bondslaves, and to exercise over all their goods and actions a peddler-like abuse of indulgences and dispensations (as they term them) among their friends. A BRIEF AND LEARNED COMMENTARY.[11]

---

[10]*Junius, *Apoc.*, 74-75.

[11]Junius, *Apocalypsis**, 74-75; citing Rev 16:13; 19:20; Gen 3:1. †To paint or cover (a surface) with a composition of ***lime*** and water; whitewash. The government buildings were freshly limed.

The Mark and Number of the Beast. Heinrich Bullinger: And he made all, both small and great, rich and poor, free and bond, to receive a mark on their right hands or on their foreheads, that no one might buy or sell except those who have the mark or the name of the beast, either the number or his name. Here is wisdom. Let the clever one count the number of the beast. For it is the number of a man, and his number is 666.

He adds the rest by which antichrist may be known and shunned. And truly he may chiefly be known by these things that follow.

And he speaks of the subjects of antichrist and of this new king and bishop. He will procure to himself, he says, an infinite multitude of all kinds of people, of all states and degrees. For his kingdom shall be ample and large. Therefore the Lord resists here certain kinds and states of people, and here understand whatever is of the same state in the whole world. The Romish antichrist brought under his subjection small and great, rich and poor, free—that is, nobles—and bound. For we see that emperors, kings, dukes, marquesses, earls and barons, realms, countries, cities, patriarchs, archbishops and bishops, prelates, doctors, clerks, and laymen obey him, also men of greatest power, riches, and wisdom, together with the poor people. There is no such kingdom so widely diverse in the world, no, not among the Muslims. And all these verily willingly are subject to the seat; indeed, they have persuaded themselves that they cannot well live, that they cannot be saved, unless they are subject to the see of Rome. Hundred Sermons on the Apocalypse.[12]

[12]Bullinger, *Hundred Sermons** (1561), 421.

Predestination Is to Be Written in the Book of Life. William Ames: The third act of election is the purpose or intention of preparing and directing those means by which elected people are certainly led through to salvation as to an end. But these means are properly redemption and application of redemption. . . . This third act in a special respect is called predestination, which is sometime in the Scriptures distinguished from election, even as it concerns the elect above. . . . "Those whom he foreknew, he also predestined." "As he has chosen us." "Who has predestined us." Otherwise by synecdoche[†] it is used in the same sense as election.

Hence predestination is sometimes said to be according to his purpose, . . . and his purpose according to election, . . . and election also according to purpose, the counsel and good pleasure of the will of God. . . .

There a certain knowledge particularly accompanies these acts of will in election in the mind of God, by which God most certainly knows the heirs of eternal life, in accordance with which also election itself is called *knowledge* or *foreknowledge*. . . . But because this knowledge of God with greatest firmness retains the distinct names of those who are to be saved and the good things appointed for them, as if all were written in God's book, therefore it is called the book of life. The Marrow of Sacred Divinity.[13]

[13]Ames, *Marrow**, 120; citing Jn 6:37; 2 Thess 2:13-14; Rom 8:29; Eph 1:4-5; Eph 1:11; Rom 9:11; Eph 1:5; Rom 8:29; Ps 69:29; Rev 3:5; 13:8. †The word *synecdoche* comes from the Greek word *synekdochē*, which means "simultaneous meaning." It's closely related to metonymy, another literary device that involves using a word that's associated with something to refer to it. For example, using the word *crown* to refer to a king or queen is a metonymy.

14:1-20 THE FIRSTFRUITS AND THE HARVEST

14 Then I looked, and behold, on Mount Zion stood the Lamb, and with him 144,000 who had his name and his Father's name written on their foreheads. [2]And I heard a voice from heaven like the roar of many waters and like the sound of loud thunder. The voice I heard was like the sound of harpists playing on their harps, [3]and they were singing a new song before the throne and before the four living creatures and before the elders. No one could learn that song except the 144,000 who had been redeemed from the earth. [4]It is these who have not defiled themselves with women, for they are virgins. It is these who follow the Lamb wherever he goes. These have been redeemed from mankind as firstfruits for God and the Lamb, [5]and in their mouth no lie was found, for they are blameless.

[6]Then I saw another angel flying directly overhead, with an eternal gospel to proclaim to those who dwell on earth, to every nation and tribe and language and people. [7]And he said with a loud voice, "Fear God and give him glory, because the hour of his judgment has come, and worship him who made heaven and earth, the sea and the springs of water."

[8]Another angel, a second, followed, saying, "Fallen, fallen is Babylon the great, she who made all nations drink the wine of the passion[a] of her sexual immorality."

[9]And another angel, a third, followed them, saying with a loud voice, "If anyone worships the beast and its image and receives a mark on his forehead or on his hand, [10]he also will drink the wine of God's wrath, poured full strength into the cup of his anger, and he will be tormented with fire and sulfur in the presence of the holy angels and in the presence of the Lamb. [11]And the smoke of their torment goes up forever and ever, and they have no rest, day or night, these worshipers of the beast and its image, and whoever receives the mark of its name."

[12]Here is a call for the endurance of the saints, those who keep the commandments of God and their faith in Jesus.[b]

[13]And I heard a voice from heaven saying, "Write this: Blessed are the dead who die in the Lord from now on." "Blessed indeed," says the Spirit, "that they may rest from their labors, for their deeds follow them!"

[14]Then I looked, and behold, a white cloud, and seated on the cloud one like a son of man, with a golden crown on his head, and a sharp sickle in his hand. [15]And another angel came out of the temple, calling with a loud voice to him who sat on the cloud, "Put in your sickle, and reap, for the hour to reap has come, for the harvest of the earth is fully ripe." [16]So he who sat on the cloud swung his sickle across the earth, and the earth was reaped.

[17]Then another angel came out of the temple in heaven, and he too had a sharp sickle. [18]And another angel came out from the altar, the angel who has authority over the fire, and he called with a loud voice to the one who had the sharp sickle, "Put in your sickle and gather the clusters from the vine of the earth, for its grapes are ripe." [19]So the angel swung his sickle across the earth and gathered the grape harvest of the earth and threw it into the great winepress of the wrath of God. [20]And the winepress was trodden outside the city, and blood flowed from the winepress, as high as a horse's bridle, for 1,600 stadia.[c]

a Or *wrath* b Greek *and the faith of Jesus* c About 184 miles; a *stadion* was about 607 feet or 185 meters

OVERVIEW: Revelation leaves the beast and his cult and consequences to stand bravely beside the Lamb atop Mount Zion. With them are the 144,000 who bore the name of the Lamb and that of the Father on their foreheads.

In Revelation 14:4 is mentioned those "who have not defiled themselves with women, for they are virgins." According to Reformer John Bale, uncorrupted believers are virgins. The 144,000 "virgins" are understood figuratively in most sixteenth-century commentaries. John appears to adopt imagery from the Old Testament in which any contact with pagan worship is called fornication or adultery; thereby one might take the 144,000 as those who have not defiled themselves in idolatrous cults.

The encounter with the Lamb is followed by the messages of three angels. Many Lutherans in the sixteenth century understood the first angel with the eternal gospel (Rev 14:6) to be Martin Luther.

A vision of one on a white cloud like the son of man follows. Then another angel comes out of the temple with a sickle and with a loud voice calls for a harvest of the earth. A second angel also with a sickle comes forward, and they trample the winepress outside the city, blood flowing out of the press. The text flashes forward to the last day and presents the harvest of the earth, a vision of "the Son of Man coming on the clouds of heaven" to gather the elect.

14:1-5 *The Redeemed of the Earth*

The Gospel Separates and Condemns. Martin Luther: In chapter 14, Christ first begins to slay his antichrist with "the breath of his mouth," as Paul says. . . . The angel with the gospel encounters the bitter book of the almighty angel. The saints and virgins stand again about the Lamb and preach the truth. Upon the gospel follows the second angel's voice, saying that the city of Babylon shall fall, the spiritual papacy be destroyed.

It follows further that the harvest shall come, and those who cling to the papacy against the gospel shall be cast outside the city of Christ, into the wine press of God's wrath. That is, by the gospel they are separated from Christendom and condemned to the wrath of God. They are many, and the wine press yields much blood. Or there may perhaps be some other punishment and judgment appropriate to our sins, which are beyond all measure and are overripe. Preface to the Revelation of Saint John.[1]

[1]LW 35:406-7; citing 2 Thess 2:8.

Christ Stands with His Church. Heinrich Bullinger: If the books of the Gospel and New Testament are to be esteemed for the manifold description of Christ, and of salvation obtained by him for the faithful, if they are to be esteemed for the comfort and preaching of the gospel, this is doubtless a book most gospel-like as that which by continually turning to perilous things brings consolation.

St. John therefore sees the Lamb standing on Mount Zion. Christ therefore does not sleep; he is not ignorant of the perils and conflicts of his church, but he stands as prepared to aid and assist those who are his. He stands as a king invincible, whom neither the dragon nor the old nor the new beast has overthrown. For I have told you more than once, especially in Revelation 5, that by the Lamb is understood Christ. For he is the lamb and price of our redemption until the judgment; but then, putting aside the office of an intercessor, he will be a most severe and also a most holy judge. And Christ stands not in the sand, as did the dragon, but on a mount, and that on Mount Zion. Mount Zion was a figure of Christ's kingdom. . . .

And the kingdom of Christ is the church, triumphant as well as militant. Therefore, in the fellowship of saints stands Christ, the joy and glory of those who are in heaven, and the life and helper of those who still fight on earth. Let us believe, therefore, that in the antichristian persecution Christ will never fail his faithful, as he is written to never have failed the old afflicted saints under the old Roman Empire. For this consolation serves chiefly for us who are afflicted by antichrist, and served for those also who suffered martyrdom under the old Roman Empire. There is no doubt that they confirmed themselves with this in the greatest persecutions.

But also most full of consolation is that the Lamb is not alone but has with him 144,000, that is to say, a most ample church. Therefore, however the beast rages and slays the confessors of Christ, there shall always be a church that will never be plucked up even on the earth. . . . The number of those who will be saved will seem small in comparison to those who shall worship the beasts and perish. Be that as it may, we understand that the number of the body of the church, under their head, Christ, shall nevertheless be the greatest even when the pope with all the features of antichrist shall have poured out all their fury. Hundred Sermons on the Apocalypse.[2]

The Gospel Goes to All Nations, Including the Jews. Mary Cary: In Revelation 14:1-5 we have a declaration of Jesus Christ, standing on Mount Zion, appearing to his own people, and his peoples being gathered to him, who are described as pure, undefiled, and redeemed ones to God and to the Lord Jesus. They are said to be the firstfruits and to follow the Lamb wherever he goes, implying that they are the first of those who were called to wait on the Lamb in the services that he has to do for them for the setting up of his kingdom. They were brought into him before the everlasting gospel was generally preached and before the fall of Babylon. They were the firstfruits.

Now, who are these firstfruits who now stand on Mount Zion with the Lamb and follow him wherever he goes? Doubtless those whom he has now called forth to follow him and those he will call out of the rest of the ten kingdoms. Well, what follows? In verses 6-8 . . . we see that before the fall of Babylon and yet after the firstfruits come to the Lamb, the gospel must be preached to all nations. Doubtless the proceedings of Jesus Christ in the world will be glorious and wonderful now that he has begun to take the kingdoms and dominions of it into his possession. He has done great things in some kingdoms already and he will do the like in others shortly. He will pour out his Spirit on all of them and so cause the light to appear unto them, as will effectively reveal to them the baseness, the viciousness, the filthiness, and the abominableness of the cursed doctrines of the beast and the whore, and cause them to loathe them and to publish and manifest their dislike and hatred of them to all the world. With much zeal and fervency of spirit, all those who are enlightened and qualified will preach and publish the clear truths of the gospel, in opposition to the false doctrines of antichrist, in all parts of the world and to all nations, revealing also to them the glad tidings of the gospel, the saving of their souls, and the turning of them from idols and vanities to serve the true and living God. . . .

By this means a way will be made for the bringing in of the Jews, who are at this day earnestly expecting and waiting for the coming of the Messiah, Christ the anointed, to be their King, their Savior, and their Prophet. But before the ten kings hate the whore and before they manifest to all the world a detestation of her, they cannot come in. But then the everlasting gospel will be preached to all nations, Jews and Gentiles, and a spirit of zeal, for Christ will then be upon the saints such that they will not be able to hold back from preaching the gospel more generally in all the world. The Little Horn's Doom and Downfall.[3]

The Father's Name Written on Anne Askew's Forehead. John Bale: In every matter concerning our Christian belief, the Scripture is reckoned insufficient for this wicked generation. God was not wise enough in setting the order of it, but they must add to it their swabber-swill, that he may abhor it in us as he did the Jews' ceremonies. . . . But this godly woman would corrupt her faith with no such beggary, lest she in so doing should admit them and their pope to sit in her conscience above the eternal God, which is their daily study. . . . She was a virgin on that behalf, redeemed from the earth and following the Lamb and having written on her forehead the Father's name. The First Examination of Anne Askew.[4]

A Peculiar People of God. Dirk Philips: All Christians are also a peculiar people of God,

[2]Bullinger, *Hundred Sermons** (1561), 339-41; citing Ps 2; Is 2.

[3]Cary, *Doom**, 107.

[4]Bale, *Examinations of Anne Askew**, 95-96; citing Is 1; Jer 7; Zech 7; Amos 5; Mic 6; 2 Thess 2.

gathered from among all human beings. They are bought with the precious blood of the Lamb, Jesus Christ, and sanctified by the Holy Spirit as a sweet-smelling and worthy offering to God. That is why they are called the first fruits of God's creation. . . . From this passage it is clear what the first fruits of the creation are. They are those who stand on Mount Zion with Christ Jesus the Lamb of God. They are the community of God, marked on their foreheads with the name of the heavenly Father. In true faith they confess to the one whose name they bear. They praise God without ceasing and sing to God a new song. For they speak with new tongues and have a new spirit. They are virgins and maidens, a pure bride of the Lamb come down from heaven, enlightened by the radiance of God. They are gathered from among all human beings to be particular and holy people. In short, they stand blameless before the throne of God, by pure grace alone, by the service of our Lord Jesus Christ. Concerning the New Birth and the New Creature.[5]

Chastity and the Sacredness of Marriage. Martin Chemnitz: If they want to interpret this statement associated with worship and spirituality in such a way that the contrast is that marriage is defilement with women, and that on account of conjugal intercourse a mark is branded upon pious spouses before the throne of God, it will be not only false but also an insult to an institution of God, as we have shown from Scripture above, when we treated about chastity and the sacredness of marriage. Neither can it be said that only celibate persons bear the seal of the heavenly Father on their foreheads. For the seal is common to all. . . . Therefore this saying of the Apocalypse must not be understood of celibacy alone, and against marriage, but of all believers against the unbelievers. . . . By way of contrast, idolatry, false doctrine, turning away from God is called fornication, adultery, defilement with harlots, not only the Old Testament but in the New. For Christ calls the Pharisees an adulterous generation; and in that very chapter in the book of Revelation defilement with women is explained in so many words as fornication with the Babylonian harlot.

Therefore it is certain and evident from the plain circumstances of the text and the constant way of Scripture's speaking, and from the analogy of faith, that this passage is not properly speaking about carnal celibacy but about spiritual virginity, which is common to all believers. Examination of the Council of Trent.[6]

The Virgins Are Uncorrupted Believers. John Bale: The virgins, or uncorrupted believers, follow the Lamb wherever he goes. They go after Christ, believing his word, fashion their lives unto it, like how those who follow antichrist fashion their works to his doctrine. They walk in his steps, forsake themselves with him, yet bear the cross of persecution with him or suffer death for the truth with him. And yet they do not seek themselves, lying here in all pomp, voluptuousness, and tyranny. From this place the blind papists fetch a great argument for their wifeless chastity, and yet none followed Christ except those in this group because they are unmarried. Neither may Abraham, Moses, David, Zachariah, Peter, or Philip walk in this number because they had wives. So perilous a thing it is to have a wife. It is great miracle they admit Mary, Christ's mother, to it because she had a husband. Oh, ignorant asses and very beastly ideas. I think you follow Judas, who had neither wife nor child, unless he had them unexpectedly, as many of you have yet on this same day.

What is virginity before God more than marriage is? No more than circumcision in comparison to uncircumcision. And it is nothing. No more makes one than the other a Christian life. The Lord requires of us only faith effectually working by love. He respected only the faith of Mary and not her virginity. Those who live in matrimony after the Word of God are accepted before him as virgins and so are named by St. Paul.

[5]Liechty, *Early Anabaptist Spirituality*, 203-4.

[6]Chemnitz, *Examination*, 3:63-64; citing Rev 8:3.

Another objection they have is that none who has offended in this way before can be of this number. But they do not consider what is spoken here before, that they were redeemed from the earth and that the Spirit of the Lord has purified their hearts through faith. Neither do they have grace to remember that Christ's innocence is reckoned for a whole and perfect righteousness to those who believe in him, but they must bring in such trifles as are their own beggarly merits. The Image of Both Churches.[7]

The Lamb on Mount Zion. Heinrich Bullinger: As he has up to this point mixed joyful things with sorrowful and added a consolation to most hard and cruel events, so now he adjoins also to the tyranny of the Roman Empire an exposition with both a consolation and an exhortation most grave and weighty. Undoubtedly by the description of the Roman tyranny and reign of antichrist it might have seemed that the church and the preaching of the gospel had been utterly lost and that ungodliness should have triumphed forever. He therefore declares by a most excellent vision how Christ shall reign notwithstanding in his chosen and shall overcome and shall have his church continually, and that famously.

He describes what the elect will be. He adds that the preaching of the gospel cannot be so oppressed but that it shall rather be preached with great constancy throughout all the world. And Rome also shall fall, and all the ungodly be punished. He therefore exhorts most earnestly that we have nothing to do with antichrist, lest also we be made partakers of his damnation. And with the intent there might be nothing lacking concerning full comfort, he added a thing that may chiefly confirm the minds of all the godly even in the greatest dangers, that they who die in Christ do fly straightaway from the corporal death to life everlasting. This finished, he turned to the description of the punishment to be given assuredly to the antichristian. Hundred Sermons on the Apocalypse.[8]

Free Submission to the Son. Pilgram Marpeck: This intention of God [subjection of the angels to the Son] was proclaimed in the midst of heaven by an angel and is eternally so proclaimed, that all creatures of God should, like the Son of the Father, submit freely and without compulsion to such service and lowliness. Any creature that has not thus voluntarily served man with and in Christ prior to the revelation of the mighty glory of the Son is cursed and eternally damned. The fall of the angels on account of man took place in immediate response to the intention of God in the eternal gospel, preached from eternity to eternity, through which the envy and hate of the serpent, the fallen angel, has come upon man. In this [same envy and hate] he also turned man away from service together with the Son, from the law and obedience of God. Even today he continues to turn men away from believing the eternal gospel and giving free obedience and fellow-service in and to all, with and in Christ. The Servants and Service of the Church.[9]

14:6-13 *The Angel with an Eternal Gospel*

The Perseverance of the Gospel. Heinrich Bullinger: Antichrist desires nothing so much to be oppressed as the preaching of the gospel. For even therefore he has instituted the inquisitors of heretical depravity for those who dare call the gospel heresy. Therefore, he burned the Gospel books and preachers of the gospel and everywhere restrained the reading of the Gospel and evangelical books. Therefore the simple suppose that it must be that the gospel with all its adherents should perish utterly. Now therefore in the Lord's consolation is brought in a vision of an angel (for he is still in the vision) flying in the middle of heaven, having the everlasting gospel and

[7]Bale, *Image** (1570), ch. 14.

[8]Bullinger, *Hundred Sermons** (1561), 439; citing Ps 2; Is 2.

[9]Marpeck, *Writings*, 551.

preaching to the world. By this is signified that the gospel shall be preached to all despite all the enemies of it. And he gathered some of the things that by the gospel are preached to the world. Those pertain also to the comfort of the church, which under the old beast suffered persecutions for the gospel. Hundred Sermons on the Apocalypse.[10]

The Everlasting Gospel. David Pareus: Thus far [I have spoken] of the everlasting gospel published by the first angel, or reformer of popery. The sum of this is in these three things.

1. That God is to be feared and the spirit of antichrist to be repented of.
2. That glory is to be ascribed to God by believing in his Son.
3. That God is to be worshiped by fleeing the image of the beast and performing obedience to God.

"And another angel followed": Because the former angel, although he cried with a great voice, did little profit to the inhabitants of the earth, who were drowned with the wine of Babylonish whoredom, for after Wycliffe, Hus, and Jerome of Prague† were burned, the papacy remained still in its vigor and fury. Therefore another angel followed, who weakened antichrist's kingdom in many provinces, more forcibly assailing him. And here again by an analogy, one angel is put for angels, for there shall be multiple succeeding each other in multiple places. But one shall excel and continue the ministry of the former angel who was a while ago interrupted.

Now this angel, if we look into histories, who can he be except Luther? He followed 130 years after Wycliffe, and 100 after Hus and Jerome; he first began in Saxony, by word and writing, to thunder against the pope's pardons publicly put to sale, soon after against the whole papacy, in 1517. To him was joined Philipp Melanchthon as a most faithful assistant, and soon after many other excellent men, who little by little restored the everlasting gospel in many parts of Germany and expelled popery. A Commentary upon the Divine Revelation.[11]

Babylon and Rome. Heinrich Bullinger: For there is a great deception, as it were, between Babylon the first monarchy and Rome the last. Babylon sorely afflicted the people of God; so does Rome grievously vex the church of God. Babylon burdened Israel with a grievous captivity; so Rome vexes the church, with more than a long captivity. Babylon overcame the people of God and, burning the city of Jerusalem and destroying the temple, led away Israel captive; so Rome also, having razed the city of Jerusalem and subverting the temple, triumphed over Israel. Babylon planted idolatry, superstition, and all abominations, and advanced, maintained, and set forth the same to all people, but when she would have least expected it, she was utterly subverted, the people of God being suddenly delivered. So is Rome also the mother, nurse, and revealer of all abominations in the church of the last time, in which she shall perish at the last, with all those who believe truly in Christ being delivered.

And especially it is called great. For how great and mighty the church of Rome is, all we see and by experience know at this day. Neither am I the first to understand Babylon as Rome. For many expositors reading 1 Peter at the end of the epistle do understand by Babylon Rome. Oecumenius says, "And here he calls Babylon Rome, for the excellence and brightness of the empire, which Rome obtained a long time since." But the more ancient writers expound this more plainly, as Tertullian† in his book against the Jews, which says, "So Babylon with Saint John bears the figure of the city of Rome, therefore also great, proud in her kingdom, and a murderer of the saints." The same words in a manner he repeated in the third book

[10]Bullinger, *Hundred Sermons** (1561), 445-46.

[11]Pareus, *Revelation**, 343. †Jan Hus (d. 1415) and Jerome of Prague (c. 1370–1416) were Reformers martyred for their theological views.

against Marcion. And no less plainly did Saint Jerome call Rome Babylon, and that same Babylon of which St. John speaks in the Apocalypse. Read the epistle of Paula and Eustochium written to Marcella, by the help of Saint Jerome.[‡] Read him in the eleventh question to Algasia; again, in the preface to the book of Didymus of the Holy Ghost, to Pauliniane;[§] also in the end of the second book against the Ionians.

The same in the life of St. Mark: Peter, he says, in the first epistle figuratively signifies Rome under the name of Babylon. But St. John will expound himself in Revelation 17. And we understand that the city of Rome shall fall chiefly, with all her ungodliness, and with the same also the Romish superstition and abomination throughout the world. And the angel indeed says she is fallen who is yet to fall, and that by the prophetic manner of speaking, by which what shall assuredly come to pass is uttered as though it were now done. Hundred Sermons on the Apocalypse.[12]

Angels Are Preachers of the Gospel. David Pareus: "And I saw another angel": Here follows the second part concerning the angel's preaching against antichrist's kingdom. Who these are and to what times the prophecy pertains is much questioned. All agree on this, that these angels represent the preachers of the gospel in the times of antichrist. But popish expositors refer the same to the last four years of the world, in which time they absurdly imagine that antichrist will rule. For how should all those things that are treated concerning the beast and the whore from Revelation 13 to almost the end of the whole book be accomplished in so short a space? A Commentary upon the Divine Revelation.[13]

Babylon the Great City and Seat of Antichrist. David Pareus: Babylon neither was, is, nor shall be the seat of antichrist. For though there is an ancient fable of antichrist's rising out of Babylon, the same makes not Babylon but Jerusalem to be his seat. Now the Babylon here threatened by the angel shall be the seat of antichrist by the consent of all interpreters.

Second, this Babylon is that great city that in John's time ruled over the kings of the earth. . . . But then the Chaldeans did not hold the monarchy but the Romans.

Besides, this Babylon defiles all nations of the earth with her fornication. But now, why the Chaldean Babylon should so do in these last times, no sound reason can be given for it.

Last, the people of God are bid to go out of this Babylon. . . . But God's people for these thousand years have not been nor shall be in the Eastern Babylon and so on. Therefore, this Babylon is not Babylon in Chaldea, although the Holy Spirit does apply the prophetic threatening of old against Babylon, to good purpose and fitly here. From the letter, therefore, we must necessarily come to the figure, which Ribera[†] also acknowledges. A Commentary upon the Divine Revelation.[14]

Persecutions Shall Be Finished. Heinrich Bullinger: For the comfort of the faithful flock of Christ is brought forth another angel, a type of all godly preachers, who preaches with great constancy that the kingdom of antichrist shall fall, however it promises to itself everlastingness. And for this the saints gather, that persecutions shall be finished for all, along with all other abominations throughout the world. For where there is the continual persecution of the wicked, all the saints cannot but be greatly saddened. They truly must receive from this no small joy and comfort, that they hear how they shall not always endure.

And here it is said that Babylon shall fall. And indeed, it would be foolishness to apply these

[12]Bullinger, *Hundred Sermons** (1561), 451-53. †In his book *Adversus Judaeos*, or *Against the Jews*, Tertullian, a prominent Christian theologian, argues that God has replaced the Jews with the Christians as the people of divine favor. ‡Jerome, *Letter* 48 to Paula and Eustochium, written to Marcella (AD 386). §Jerome wrote to a woman of Gaul named Algasia to answer eleven questions she had submitted to him (AD 406). Didymus (the Blind) was a student of Origen.
[13]Pareus, *Revelation**, 337-38.

[14]Pareus, *Revelation**, 343-44. †Francisco Ribera (1537–1591) was a Spanish Jesuit theologian.

things to the old Babylon in Asia, which fell long ago, and scarcely any sign of it is left. . . . We must understand it of Rome. Hundred Sermons on the Apocalypse.[15]

Blessed Are the Dead Who Hereafter Die in the Lord. Heinrich Bullinger: The Lord pronounces those who depart out of this world in true faith to be all blessed and fortunate.

. . . The Lord himself adjoined a notable declaration to this brief sentence. For he set forth the circumstances of the time and the manner of the blessedness. For it is desired to ask, At what time do salvation and felicity happen to the dead? Immediately, or after a time? That is, do our souls fly by-and-by immediately after the death of the body to the blessed seats? Or are they intercepted for a certain time so that they might be purged in purgatory before they enter into heaven? Or are they held with a sleep, looking for the resurrection of the bodies, so that they might then awake and, together with their bodies, enter into heaven?

To all these things the celestial oracle answers that at once, that is, soon, that same felicity comes to souls. In the Latin copies this place is written thus, "Blessed are the dead who die in the Lord." Immediately now, says the Spirit, they may rest from their labors. In like manner reads the Spanish or Complutensian copy.† But Aretas‡ and the Greek copies, and also the example of Paris, are pointed so as to indicate that this should be the end of the sentence, as Erasmus notes. *After* followed, which is "yet, truly, certainly," says the Spirit. The sense is therefore that the faithful, being dead, shall straightaways and immediately achieve salvation. *For* (the word St. John uses) signifies "from the very instant, from that hour immediately." This has no time between but expresses what we are likely to note by the Dutch phrase.

Being admonished therefore by a divine oracle and confirmed by a writ brought from heaven, let us all be assured that the souls of all faithful do fly from the bodily death into life everlasting. These things are confirmed and made plain also by other innumerable Scriptures. I will choose only a certain few, and those also the testimonies of our Savior, who is the light of the world and the word of life. St. John . . . says expressly that the faithful are thus delivered from death by his cross as in times past by the sight of the brazen serpent the Israelites were delivered from the deadly sting of venomous poison. And it is plain that they were delivered immediately and most fully. . . . The same says, "He has passed from death to life." Let this place be weighed diligently, and it shall appear by itself to satisfy in this matter. . . . John . . . sayeth openly, "And I will raise him in the last day." But he raised not the bodies only at the last judgment, but in every person's last day, that is, in the death of everyone, he preserves the souls, that they should not perish or be tormented and so on.

We have even the Gospel examples most clear: namely, Lazarus the beggar, who was after his death carried up by the angels into the bosom of Abraham; and the thief who heard from the Lord, "This day you shall be with me in paradise"; and Stephen saying, "Lord Jesus, receive my spirit"; but especially our Savior saying on the cross, "Father, into your hands I commend my spirit," and so on.

By these are quite overthrown whatever things the monkish and antichristian doctrine has built of purgatory . . . and of the miserable state of souls in another world. Of this they made a most shameful gain. They are also confused about the belief that souls are mortal, yet they sleep in another world, where they cannot so much as here in this infirmity sleep. Therefore, you will say it is madness to think that souls sleep, having been relieved of the burden of the body.

But concerning the manner of the blessedness of saints, they rest from their labors. Salvation, therefore, is a most joyful tranquility. Away go at once diseases, sicknesses, griefs, affections, sorrow, famine, thirst, cold, in short, all things that vex or trouble people. Rest and tranquility, joy and blessings come in place. And since the dead rest from their labors, who can believe that they be vexed with torments? But lest anyone should ever

[15]Bullinger, *Hundred Sermons** (1561), 450-52.

doubt of this even a little, he provides a confirmation . . . that the dead shall be quiet from all their griefs. Let no one therefore doubt. Hundred Sermons on the Apocalypse.[16]

The Sweet Rest of the Saints. John Bale: Blessed are the dead, or those who are already departed and yet also shall later depart in the Lord. This voice from heaven is the infallible Scriptures ascertaining the faith of John in the sweet rest of the saints in the hands of God. And their end is not without honor, as the vain sort suppose, but they are counted among the dear children of God. Therefore let those who suffer in this age be earnestly spirited and not fear the torments of the enemies in Christ's cause.

For from henceforth (the Spirit says) they rest from their labors. In a wonderful quietness they dwell, by the very sentence of the Holy Spirit, and shall never more feel of any woe. God has wiped away all tears from their eyes, all sorrows and pains from their bodies, the first dangers being last. Happy are they therefore, and most godly fortunate, who are slain for Christ, because they will not worship the beast and his image, nor corrupt their faith with their wicked laws, but in a pure Christian belief departed from hence to the Lord. Their portion is in the land of the living, and their lot among the holy ones.

For certainly their works follow them. The promised reward of God for constantly standing by your truth, for the fruits of their Christian patience, and for other exercise of their faith is evermore to their glory present with them. Not as they deserve but Christ, in whose faith they wrought here and for the promise's sake, that they should be God's heroes together with Christ. The lively word also they earnestly received here and so rooted in their faith will never suffer them to perish, nor to be hurt by the second death. The Image of Both Churches.[17]

14:14-20 *The Harvest of the Earth*

God's Judgment. Heinrich Bullinger: Now he goes to the description of God's judgment, especially against the antichristians and against all the ungodly. This part might be joined with the matter following and chapters following as of the same argument. And it pertained to the consolation and confirmation of the faithful, persecuted by antichrist. There are those who think there shall never be any judgment. Therefore, however they oppress their neighbors, they think never to feel any displeasure of that matter. Moreover, the faithful are tempted also while they see the wicked flourish and themselves wither daily. Therefore they think also that the Lord tarried overlong. Yet more they expostulate with the Lord, and say, "When shall there be an end of injuries? If Christ will come to judgment, why does he defer it so long and to such great harm of those who are his?"

The Lord therefore shows now that the judgment shall certainly be and shall be at the time when all things will be ripe, namely, when the iniquities of the Amorrheans† shall be complete and the measure of iniquity filled. When wicked men are therefore ripe, the Lord will come to judge. In the meantime, we must abide in constancy and patience, as husbandmen wait for harvest and vintage. If any revolt through impatience, they are not allowed by the Lord, as the apostle alleges out of the Prophet. . . . And though we may have a desire and a longing for harvest and vintage, so may we not expostulate with God because he waited longer than we wish. Likewise, we ought not to contend with him about why he comes so late to judgment. And as harvest and vintage are certainly looked for and come, so without all doubt God will punish the wicked and save the godly. And these are truly, as it were, tastes of all that follow

[16]Bullinger, *Hundred Sermons** (1561), 460-62; citing Jn 3; 5–6.
†The Complutensian Polyglot Bible is the name given to the first printed polyglot of the entire Bible. The edition was initiated and financed by Cardinal Francisco Jiménez de Cisneros (1436–1517) and published by Complutense University in Alcalá de Henares, Spain. ‡Arethas, archbishop of Caesarea (c. 850–c. 944), was possibly a pupil of the patriarch of Constantinople, Photius.

[17]Bale, *Image** (1570), ch. 14.

plentifully and are more expressly declared and are added to the former matters, for they pertain to the consolation of the godly.

And for the purpose that all things might be more manifest, all things are set forth to be seen before our eyes by parables brought in. And he uses indeed two parables borrowed from the prophets and doctrine of the Gospel. For the prophets often conceive of the judgment of God by harvest and vintage. . . . The Lord says, "I will sit in the vale of Josaphat to judge all nations. Thrust in the sickle, for the harvest is ripe," and so on. And it is also most known what is read concerning the same matter in the story of the Gospel. We must therefore write out these things more inwardly into our hearts, and fear God, and abide his redemption in patience. HUNDRED SERMONS ON THE APOCALYPSE.[18]

TWO PARABLES OF THE LAST JUDGMENT. DAVID PAREUS: "And I looked, and behold, a white cloud": To this point we have handled three acts of the fourth vision. The first (to briefly repeat them again) comprehends the condition of the church in its beginning and growth, with her many combats under the Roman emperors, both pagan and Christian, until antichrist's rising, in the first six hundred years. . . . The second, opposed to the former, contains the consolation of the godly under the foresaid conflicts, in the same chapter. The third, having two parts, represents (1) antichrist's persecutions, which from his first rising until now have continued more than a thousand years; . . . (2) the church's preservation under the same, and her future purging from the dredges of antichrist in the last times. . . . The fourth act follows here, describing the joyful catastrophe or change of all the church's afflictions in the day of judgment, the form of which is figured out in two parables, namely, of the harvest and vintage, in the rest of this chapter.

Furthermore, I see all interpreters (only a few excepted) unanimously agree that the last judgment is here treated, and I wonder that any should dissent in a matter so clear and evident. For by types and words much alike, the judgment to come is described, . . . concerning the Son of Man coming in the clouds of heaven to judgment, and . . . the harvest of the tares and wheat. They agree also in the scope, that these types serve to comfort the godly and terrify the wicked. For the godly groan under their afflictions and troubles, desiring to know what end at length shall be put to their evils. On the contrary, tyrants and antichrist tumultuously rage without hindrance or punishment, promising to themselves perpetual prosperity.

Lest, therefore, the faithful be discouraged, seeing the son of perdition thus to rage and themselves overwhelmed with many sorrows and calamities, here the last judgment is propounded to John, in which shall follow a wonderful change of things. For then the wheat shall be gathered into the heavenly barn, and the chaff burned with unquenchable fire. This, I say, is the scope and use of the remaining matter in the chapter. A COMMENTARY UPON THE DIVINE REVELATION.[19]

HARVEST IN GERMANY. THOMAS BRIGHTMAN: For a thousand years from Constantine, the church was together with Christ hidden in most secret places, but she did nothing of great fame in the world. These thousand years being ended, Wycliffe preached the gospel to the world. Jan Hus and Jerome of Prague† continued, who threatened the ruin of Rome. After those followed Martin Luther, who very eagerly set upon the Roman prelate. Afterward there was a harvest in Germany by Frederick the Saxon, the other Protestant princes, and free cities; and also a vintage in England by Thomas Cromwell and Thomas Cranmer. REVELATION OF ST. JOHN.[20]

[18]Bullinger, *Hundred Sermons** (1561), 464-65; citing Heb 10; Joel 3. †A blind fury pushed fathers to murder their infants, and to burn them to their gods instead of incense. These sacrifices were common in the time of Moses and were only a part of these horrible iniquities of the Amorrheans, by whom God committed vengeance on the Israelites.

[19]Pareus, *Revelation**, 358-59; citing Dan 7; Mt 3; 13.

[20]Brightman, *Revelation**, 402-7. †Jan Hus (d. 1415) and Jerome of Prague (c. 1370–1416) were Reformers martyred for their theological views.

The Lord Will Judge in Due Time. Heinrich Bullinger: First is treated the parable of harvest, then the parable of vintage. Both show that the Lord will be judge and that in his most due time, against all those who either think there shall be no judgment or object to the Lord that he comes so slowly and late. And first indeed is described the owner of the harvest, the Lord himself and judge Jesus Christ. He is said to be like the Son of Man—not that he is not now the true Son of Man, and that he shall not come unto judgment in true human nature, which he has once taken from us and never put it off (for he is truly the Son of Man, and remains on the right hand of the Father, and shall truly come in the human nature to judge the quick and the dead)—but he seems to have alluded to Daniel and to have used his figure of speech, saying, "I looked in the mighty vision, and lo, there came one on the clouds as he were the son of man," and so on. There we read also the description of the judgment against the beast.

And therefore he has here made mention also of a cloud: "And I saw a white cloud, and one sitting on the cloud," and so on. Moreover, the angels in Acts say, "So he shall come, as you have seen him go up into heaven. And they saw him taken up, and a cloud to receive him, and convey him out of their sight." Therefore he shall come again in a cloud unto judgment. We read oftentimes in the Psalms that God sits on a white cloud. In this way is therefore signified the deity of the judge. Therefore, this judge is very God and very man, the Savior of the faithful, the revenger and judge of the infidels. We are therefore sent by St. John to Daniel 7.

Then he wears a golden crown on his head, not that there is any corruptible gold in heaven, but for corruptible people he speaks so that they may understand their judge to be the high king and may gather by this that no one is able to resist the power of this king. For otherwise our Lord has no need of any corruptible gold. Finally, our Lord here has a sickle, very sharp. By this is signified his exceedingly straight judgment and destruction of the wicked. . . . He adds that the axe is laid at the root of the tree, by which he signified that certain judgment was at hand, or rather destruction. Hundred Sermons on the Apocalypse.[21]

[21]Bullinger, *Hundred Sermons** (1561), 468-69; citing Heb 10; Joel 3; Mt 3.

15:1–16:21 THE SEVEN LAST PLAGUES

15 Then I saw another sign in heaven, great and amazing, seven angels with seven plagues, which are the last, for with them the wrath of God is finished.

2 And I saw what appeared to be a sea of glass mingled with fire—and also those who had conquered the beast and its image and the number of its name, standing beside the sea of glass with harps of God in their hands. 3 And they sing the song of Moses, the servant of God, and the song of the Lamb, saying,

"Great and amazing are your deeds,
  O Lord God the Almighty!
Just and true are your ways,
  O King of the nations![a]
4 Who will not fear, O Lord,
  and glorify your name?
For you alone are holy.
  All nations will come
  and worship you,
for your righteous acts have been revealed."

5 After this I looked, and the sanctuary of the tent[b] of witness in heaven was opened, 6 and out of the sanctuary came the seven angels with the seven plagues, clothed in pure, bright linen, with golden sashes around their chests. 7 And one of the four living creatures gave to the seven angels seven golden bowls full of the wrath of God who lives forever and ever, 8 and the sanctuary was filled with smoke from the glory of God and from his power, and no one could enter the sanctuary until the seven plagues of the seven angels were finished.

16 Then I heard a loud voice from the temple telling the seven angels, "Go and pour out on the earth the seven bowls of the wrath of God."

2 So the first angel went and poured out his bowl on the earth, and harmful and painful sores came upon the people who bore the mark of the beast and worshiped its image.

3 The second angel poured out his bowl into the sea, and it became like the blood of a corpse, and every living thing died that was in the sea.

4 The third angel poured out his bowl into the rivers and the springs of water, and they became blood. 5 And I heard the angel in charge of the waters[c] say,

"Just are you, O Holy One, who is and who was,
  for you brought these judgments.
6 For they have shed the blood of saints and
    prophets,
  and you have given them blood to drink.
It is what they deserve!"

7 And I heard the altar saying,

"Yes, Lord God the Almighty,
  true and just are your judgments!"

8 The fourth angel poured out his bowl on the sun, and it was allowed to scorch people with fire. 9 They were scorched by the fierce heat, and they cursed[d] the name of God who had power over these plagues. They did not repent and give him glory.

10 The fifth angel poured out his bowl on the throne of the beast, and its kingdom was plunged into darkness. People gnawed their tongues in anguish 11 and cursed the God of heaven for their pain and sores. They did not repent of their deeds.

12 The sixth angel poured out his bowl on the great river Euphrates, and its water was dried up, to prepare the way for the kings from the east. 13 And I saw, coming out of the mouth of the dragon and out of the mouth of the beast and out of the mouth of the false prophet, three unclean spirits like frogs. 14 For they are demonic spirits, performing signs, who go abroad to the kings of the whole world, to assemble them for battle on the great day of God the Almighty. 15 ("Behold, I am coming like a thief! Blessed is the one who stays awake, keeping his garments on, that he may not go about naked and be seen exposed!") 16 And

they assembled them at the place that in Hebrew is called Armageddon.

[17]*The seventh angel poured out his bowl into the air, and a loud voice came out of the temple, from the throne, saying, "It is done!"* [18]*And there were flashes of lightning, rumblings,*[e] *peals of thunder, and a great earthquake such as there had never been since man was on the earth, so great was that earthquake.* [19]*The great city was split into three parts, and the cities of the nations fell, and God remembered Babylon the great, to make her drain the cup of the wine of the fury of his wrath.* [20]*And every island fled away, and no mountains were to be found.* [21]*And great hailstones, about one hundred pounds*[f] *each, fell from heaven on people; and they cursed God for the plague of the hail, because the plague was so severe.*

a Some manuscripts *the ages* **b** Or *tabernacle* **c** Greek *angel of the waters* **d** Greek *blasphemed;* also verses 11, 21 **e** Or *voices,* or *sounds* **f** Greek *a talent in weight*

Overview: Among the Zurich reformers (e.g., Leo Jud, Ulrich Zwingli. Heinrich Bullinger), linguist Theodore Bibliander (1506–1564) offers an early and focused critique of the papacy as the Antichrist. He understood his own era to be situated in that of the seventh seal, viewing the seven trumpets as corresponding to the seven seals. Bibliander writes with sensitivity to his unique structure of the Apocalypse, history running from creation to final judgment as well by his desire to use the text to condemn the papacy and identify it as antichrist.

John sees seven angels with seven plagues and before him a sea of glass mixed with fire. Standing by the sea are those victorious over the beast. John also sees the tabernacle of testimony opened, out of which come seven angels with seven plagues. One of the four living creatures gives to the seven angels seven golden bowls filled with the wrath of God. John hears a loud voice instructing the seven angels to pour out their bowls of wrath. The first bowl is poured out on the land, the second on the sea, the third on rivers and springs of water, the fourth on the sun, the fifth on the throne of the beast, the sixth on the Euphrates River, and the seventh into the air.

Many Reformation commentators understood their own era to be that of the seventh seal, viewing the seven trumpets as corresponding to the seven seals. The end of the seventh seal is an important time in the history of salvation, and the commentators become more polemical. They interpret a number of events spoken of in Revelation 15–16 as referring to things and people from their own time.

Croaking Against the Gospel. Martin Luther: In chapters 15 and 16 come the seven angels with the seven bowls. The gospel thereupon increases and attacks the papacy on all sides by means of many learned and devout preachers; and the throne of the beast—the pope's power—becomes dark and wretched and despised. But they grow angry and confidently defend themselves. For three frogs, three foul spirits, issue from the mouth of the beast and stir up kings and princes against the gospel. But this does not help; their battle takes place nonetheless at Armageddon. The frogs are the sophists, such as Faber, Eck, Emser, etc. They croak much against the gospel but accomplish nothing and remain frogs. Preface to the Revelation of Saint John.[1]

The Poison of False Doctrine. John Bale: Seven angels had in their hands the seven last plagues. Some expositors have taken these angels for the right ministers in the seven ages of the Christian church. Some have thought them to be the perverse preachers and ungodly ministers of all the said ages, suffered by God strongly to delude the unbelievers, that he who hurts should hurt still and that he who is in filthiness should still be filthy. To every age corresponding there is an angel to declare the nature of those deceitful healings and lying masters, and this makes them to understand the text. They are here expressly noted to be in heaven.

[1]LW 35:407-8.

Among the congregation of God are the false prophets and dissembling hypocrites evermore, as the chaff among the corn, the tares among the wheat, and the filthy dregs among the pure wine. For that kingdom is as a net thrown into the sea, gathering all manner of fishes both good and bad. In all ages has the wicked generation increased to impugn the truth and stiffly to stand up against God and his Christ. . . . For no poison is to the soul so pestilent, nor yet venom so full, as is false doctrine. No plague can be thought more deadly or violent than to deprive us of that faith, of that verity, and of that life that is in Christ Jesus, or to bring us out of the way he has appointed. And all this seemed in all likelihood to be the proper understanding of the text here. Yet Francis Lambert gives a far better judgment, calling them the set sentences or variable decrees of God, defining his judgments against the wicked in his latter age of the world, to be uttered at their appointed times. For all these things are jointly to be considered.

These angels came not only from heaven, which is the congregation (as they have mentioned), but also out of the celestial temple of the tabernacle of testimony, which is the omnipotent God and his Christ, as Revelation 21 declares.

They are also clothed with pure white linen, girded with golden girdles; they have golden vials delivered to them by one of the four beasts, and one of them speaks with John, declaring to him the judgment and fall of the great whore. These are not arguments that they are here to be taken for ill preachers, though they here minister the last seven plagues. Therefore we should judge them here to be God's appointed purposes or eternally decreed pleasures against the willfully obstinate and indurate rebellions to the end of the world. THE IMAGE OF BOTH CHURCHES.[2]

THE APOCALYPSE IS NOT HIDDEN. THEODORE BIBLIANDER: First I showed that the divine Apocalypse of Jesus Christ has not been so bound up with Gordian knots that no one can understand it. Rather, it possesses a clear, straightforward, and supreme authority—especially since the majority of it deals with the prophecies about the great antichrist which have already been fulfilled, the mystery of which for a time escaped the notice of some of the church fathers, according to divine Providence. This authority it has both on its own and from God. Then, it has also been shown by example that the divine Scriptures, in their own character and nature, are clear, perspicuous, and reliable, except that God for a time, by his own secret counsel, conceals certain elements. He is the one who gives to each a revelation of the Spirit, in keeping with what is profitable. He does it for this reason, that all faith may rest upon God, not on the decrees of men. So then, my remaining task is to show by the same method that the divine Scriptures contain complete instruction for living well and happily. And that they contain a perfect knowledge for judging correctly, both for the present and for the future, all matters relating to the church and the Christian commonwealth. I shall endeavor to handle this passage along these lines: I will make the same effort to disprove vacuous interpretations, and especially those which guarantee knowledge of things to come, just the same as whatever commandments of men conflict with God's Word. First of all, there is widespread agreement among all the better theologians that the Revelation of Jesus Christ contains a prophecy of Christ's interests and church, as well as the enemies of his church, extending from the very last days of the Emperor Domitian to the end of the world. This is because it is useful for the whole church, as well as individual believers, to know such matters. An account of the destiny of God's people, as well as God's enemies, even beyond the judgment day, is laid out both here and in Daniel, our multifaceted historian, with very clear doctrines on the resurrection of the dead, general judgment, and eternal life. This is in fact a universal, predictive symbol of the affairs of his kingdom and his priesthood, as well as what pertains to the enemies of God and his church. Although that is

[2]Bale, *Image** (1570), ch. 15.

true, the Lord Jesus in the theology of Revelation has so managed events by his divine and infinite wisdom that he has included nothing that is redundant, nor left out anything useful or necessary for us to think about. Instead, Christ goes through in the most perfect order what he decided was proper for him to reveal, and used that manner of speaking that was most effective to illustrate the content and set it before our eyes. For in this work, events are not described in plain words, they are not depicted by a silent and mute image. No, here persons speak and act, as though in some kind of dramatic work in a theater and on stage a divine spectacle is set before us for our consideration. Here we are allowed to gaze upon not only those things which good as well as evil men do and endure on earth but also the plans, impulses, and thoughts of their hearts. More than that, the Lord in his Revelation reveals the very thoughts of Satan, something Paul calls "marvellous wisdom." Moreover, the antichrist is so completely described by name, location, time, deeds, character, and nature, that no painter could better depict the face of a man with a very carefully painted image or detailed likeness. Here is set forth what we ought to look upon when the heavens are opened, what sort of men reside in the heavenly dwellings of the blessed. On the other hand, the gate of the hellish prison is shown, so one may see the wicked plainly, and the men whom God has condemned, as well as their eternal punishments. The Faithful Relationship.[3]

15:1-8 *The Third Great Sign in Heaven*

The Vials of God's Mercy and Justice. John Napier: The Spirit of God, intending to repeat the prophecy of the seven ages now under the terms of vials—which before were expressed by seven trumpets, to the effect that the one may be a commentary to decipher the other—first sets down this chapter as a preface to it, containing in it chiefly two godly instructions. One is of God's mercy, that these last plagues, being imminent and ready, will not fall until God has first established in security, amid the raging seas and consuming fire of worldly persecution, those who refuse the antichristian errors, rejoicing triumphantly in God. A Plain Discovery of the Whole Revelation of Saint John.[4]

Two Kinds of Servants. Chronicle of the Hutterian Brethren: If government comes from God and is his servant, why—one may ask—can there be no Christians in it? Here is the answer: If the name "servant of God" makes a ruler into a Christian, then the Roman emperors Claudius and Nero would have been Christians too, since Paul called them servants of God by virtue of their scepters. When the powers that be were called servants of God, did Paul mean that a Turk who is a servant of God in this sense is therefore a Christian? Obviously not. The Lord spoke even of King Nebuchadnezzar and King Cyrus as his servants, yet they were pagans. Just as the Scriptures speak of two kinds of angels, good and evil, and both are called angels, in the same way God has two kinds of servants on earth.

A Christian cannot be a ruler in this world; but a ruler may certainly become a Christian if, with Christ, he strips himself of his glory, humbles himself, lays down the sword, takes up the cross, and follows him. From time immemorial the power of the sword has been identified with the government of this world to make it clear that its functions cannot be reconciled with those of the Christian church. Chronicle of the Hutterian Brethren.[5]

God's Judgment and Wrath. Thomas Brightman: Until this time the first part of the seventh trumpet is of things past: (1) the preparation of things to come is the seven angels with their vials; (2) the reformed churches disagree between

[3]Bibliander, *Omnium*, 161-63.

[4]Napier, *Revelation**, 186.

[5]Hutterian Brethren, *Chronicle*, 284-85.

themselves, but all triumph for the overthrow of the pope of Rome; (5) the temple is opened, and knowledge increases, and the citizens of the church are made ministers of the last plagues, the end of which the new people of the Jews expected before they come to the faith.

Victors separated from the beast by a sea of glass, foreshadowed by the song of Moses—some of these judgments parallel the plagues God brought on Egypt through Moses. . . . For some the seven bowls represent God's final judgments during the latter three and a half years of the tribulation.

At the command of a loud voice from the temple, the seven angels of chapter 15 pour out . . . God's wrath in rapid succession on those who reject God. Revelation of St. John.[6]

Judgment for the Wicked and Joy for the Godly. Heinrich Bullinger: On the occasion of harvest and vintage expounded in the last part of the former vision is added the fifth part of this godly work, which represents to us the fourth vision of this work, which some make the fifth. The same is of the judgments of God. It has two parts and therefore it might also be divided into more visions, but we would rather use fewer. For first he discourses most extensively about the pains or torments prepared by God to be executed on antichrist, his members, and all the ungodly. Here is treated the judgment of the whore of Babylon, the destinies and ruin of Rome and the church of Rome, the rejoicing and song of saints, the coming of the judge to judgment, and the pain and everlasting destruction of all the wicked. And these are interrelated in Revelation 15–20.

Then also he reasons most excellently about the reward of saints and the everlasting felicity. Throughout the whole of Revelation 21 and a good part of Revelation 22, everywhere is set open hell itself and heaven itself, given in manner to look in this mortal flesh, even into hell itself and into the very palace of heaven. You shall not find anywhere in all the Scriptures a continual treatise that is so extensively a disputation of the judgments of God, of the torments of the wicked, and of the felicity and joys of the godly as is present here. Hundred Sermons on the Apocalypse.[7]

Both the Ungodly and the Godly Marvel. Henrich Bullinger: First he showed the origin of all things that follow to be not earthly but heavenly. For he sees another sign in heaven. He said "another," for . . . we heard that mention was made of another certain sign. And he called that a sign or indication, which represents another thing and therefore is not to be considered of itself but inasmuch as it brings into knowledge another thing, and that much greater than it showed at the first sight. He calls this sign—that is, namely, that same vision—great and marvelous. For the judgments of God are greatest and most wonderful. While they are executed, the ungodly marvel, who had thought such things should never have come to pass; the godly also marvel at the great power of God, his most just righteousness, and his ripeness and faithfulness in delivering and saving his people.

Then he declared what sign was shown to him in heaven and by that celestial vision. He saw seven angels, having plagues in seven cups. That is, he perceived God prepared and furnished with divine power, by which he both might and would send plagues and fitting punishments on antichrist himself as well as on his members and all the ungodly people on earth for their wickedness committed against God. And as we have many times warned you in this book, the number seven is the amount of fullness. Therefore God has plenty of ministers by whose service he may plague and destroy the ungodly. And therefore the seven plagues are all manner of plagues. Temporal plagues are abundantly recited. . . .

Rich is the Lord, and in everlasting plagues of most diverse kinds also. For the Scripture in certain

[6]Brightman, *Apocalypse* (1611), 411*; citing Ex 7–12, meaning the God of the Hebrews would have victory over the gods of Pharoah. Numbering original.

[7]Bullinger, *Hundred Sermons** (1561), 470-71.

places rehearsed a gnawing worm, a fire unquenchable, weeping and gnashing of teeth, outward darkness, and many others of like sort. But these seven plagues he called the last and immediately showed the reason, for in them the wrath of God is fulfilled. For on those last and most corrupt ages the Lord will pour out his plague, and they will be the plagues of his just wrath, and he shall pour them out most fully to the end and shall execute his full wrath against the ungodly for evermore.

Yet now he suspended for a while that narration begun of the angels who are masters of the plagues, and he placed or sent before the great joys of the blessed martyrs triumphs, songs of praise, rejoicing, and thanksgiving. And this joy is interlaced here in the treatise of punishments for the consolation of the faithful, that they should know that they are delivered from punishments. And if it happens while the wicked are punished that any displeasure touches them also (as it cannot be helped, because some discommodities must also arise to the faithful when the wicked are being plagued), they may understand yet that the dangers of the discommodities must be recompensed with the excellent abundance of joys. For hereby is signified how the godly rejoice while the Lord executes his justice. To be also the changeable course of things, those who have once wept in the world should now be glad and joyful, according to the saying of our Savior. . . . Moreover, it was proper by the testimony of all saints to be declared to the saints who dwell on earth that the judgments of God are righteous and true, and when this is understood, questions and various mutinies against God cease.

First, he sees those who overcame antichrist and have had nothing to do with him. . . . He saw, I say, in heaven the blessed souls stand on a glassy sea, mixed with fire. And in another place I have told you that the sea represents the world, by reason of the rage and unstableness of it. Certainly Daniel takes it so. . . . And it is called glassy because of the frailty and brittleness. For worldly things shine, but they are soon broken, as a result of which it is said that worldly things are as brittle as glass, which, while they shine, break. And not without cause is fire mixed with worldly things. For the saints, while they are conversant on earth, feel always in a manner the fire of affliction. Of this St. Peter spoke. . . . And they stand on a glassy sea mingled with fire. For conquerors tread on the world, and on all the torments and mockeries of the world, as triumphing over all worldly things.

The prophet . . . brings in the saints singing a joyful song to God and saying, among other things, "You have brought us into snares, you have laid tribulations on our backs, you have set men on our necks. We have passed through fire and water, and you have brought us out into a place of relief." Therefore follow alterations in another world. As a result of this, Aretas,† expounding this passage, says the glassy sea seemed to intimate nothing else than truly the multitude, and by the brightness of the glass is expressed the purity by fire of those who are worthy of that blessed life. And certainly the same words in diverse respects may signify diverse things and make the sense agreeable. HUNDRED SERMONS ON THE APOCALYPSE.[8]

PLAGUE SENT BY ANGELS. THEODORE BEZA: Let us now come to what they allege concerning second causes, which they deny being any certain placing of the stars or corruption of the air, and neither will the physicians have any plague or infection to grow of those causes. But if we grant this and imagine that all natural causes of the plague are rehearsed by them, they must tell me why they shut out all these at once with the result that they will have those who have little skill in Scriptures impute the plague (next after God) to these causes. Because, they say, the Holy Scriptures bear record that the plague is sent by angels . . . in the Revelation, where there is mention made of a most noisome ulcer; for, say they, what God sends by angels is not of natural causes. I grant that, so far as concerning the angels themselves, who I yield are not reckoned among natural instruments, but

[8]Bullinger, *Hundred Sermons**, 472-74; citing Rev 12; Lev 26:14-46; Deut 28:15-68; Jn 16:20; Dan 7:3; 1 Pet 4:12-19; Ps 66. †Arethas, archbishop of Caesarea (c. 850–d. c. 944), was possibly a pupil of the patriarch of Constantinople, Photius.

what hinders God from commanding the natural causes themselves to be stirred up by the angels? For surely it cannot be doubted that they, both the good and the bad, do stir up the minds of people after a certain sort, whatever kind of moving it is, when as Satan is said to have entered into the heart of Judas (unless we shall perhaps say that the good angels have somewhat less power than the bad), and that also is manifest by the story of Ahab and by the efficacy and power of the spirits of error.

And who can deny that the will of humanity is to be reckoned among the chief causes of human actions? But if people's will is not forbidden from the ministry of angels, why shall we think that other natural causes must by the same be taken away? Moses, stretching forth his rod, raised up lice and innumerable sorts of flies, brought out the sudden fearful hail, and struck the Egyptians with most dangerous boils and harms. And this ministry of Moses was doubtless altogether as extraordinary as the ministry of angels. But did not therefore the lice and life come of rottenness, the hail of vapors growing together on the sudden by restraint of the contrary, and the boils and harms also of corruptions of the humors?

Satan, receiving a grant from God, by a sudden raising of the wind and by throwing abroad the fire from heaven, overthrew and burned the house of Job, together with all his children. But does it therefore follow that this came to pass without any natural causes stepping in between? Or shall we not rather say that those princes of the air (as the apostle, not without cause, calls them) made in a moment those indeed natural impressions of the air? The devil sends the godly to prison. . . . The pale horse on whom Death the rider sits received power to kill with the sword, famine, and pestilence, and sending of wild beasts. Here, if we will by that rider understand an angel, why shall we not say that he used natural matter to cause the plague and famine as well as a sword and wild beasts, which themselves are also natural instruments?

And afterwards . . . the angels are commanded to stand in the four quarters of the earth and to keep back the winds, that they not hurt the sea and the land with blowing. Of this followed that at the commandment of God, the winds are in like manner sent forth by them; from this doubtless it is manifest that many infections of the air, and chiefly infections, do proceed. So natural causes, whether they are moved little by little of their own force planted in them by nature or otherwise beyond order, God so commanding, they are in a moment carried to their effects, they are natural, and so far forth are their effects also worthily judged natural, which no one of reason can deny. For if there are no natural causes in the plague, those whom the plague has touched, doubtless they cannot be at all eased, much less be healed by natural remedies. A LEARNED TREATISE OF THE PLAGUE.[9]

VICTORY OVER THE BEAST. THOMAS BRIGHTMAN: In like manner those who get victory over the beast are those who prevail against him, his image, mark, and number of his name. These all are set down point by point, so that the victory should be full and absolute, though the beast remains for a little while. For they should not only reject antichrist himself but indeed abhor also his mark and not suffer themselves to be called by the number of his name. We have showed that the number of his name, which is to be called a *Latin*, is the least bond of society with which people are tied to antichrist, which was proper to the Greeks, who by admitting this symbol obtained mutual traffic. But the inhabitants of the West, who long ago easily suffered themselves to be made his marked soldiers and to be called papists and of the pope's religion, do now detest the very name *Latin*, which the Greeks so hardly and lately received. This victory is therefore full, as is signified by this particular rehearsal of the image, mark, and number of name.

But you will say, when did this victory come? At the sound of the seventh trumpet, when the Protestant princes in Germany, who had been

[9]Beza, *Learned Treatise**, 6-11; citing Ps 88:1; 1 Chron 21; Ezek 9; Rev 2:10; 6:8; 9:1.

granted by Charles to have their profession of religion free, did soon after his death get it to be confirmed and established by the Emperor Ferdinand in the year 1558, at which time our gracious Queen Elizabeth, being also crowned, did manifest to the world that the beast was overcome in England.† A few years before, the beast had begun to reign afresh and was never before fully vanquished, but God reserved it for this time to honor the chariot and triumph of our good queen. The year next after, they trod down the beast in Scotland.‡ Before these times the truth fought, but in doubtful battle; now it did plainly beat down and overthrow the enemies. To these many others are to be added, as in France, Svealand, Denmark, Sweden,§ Prussia, all of which joined together make up this company that stands at the glassy sea. Revelation of St. John.[10]

16:1-7 *The First Three Bowls of Wrath*

Sacred and Holy Judgments of God. Heinrich Bullinger: But before the angels pour out the cups of plagues received, they are most gallantly and diligently described. And it is showed from where they came out, that is, what is the original of the judgments of God. They come out of the temple set open, and out of the temple of the tabernacle of witness, which is in heaven. For Moses saw a temple on the mount, and that also in heaven, after the resemblance of which he was commanded by God to make the tabernacle of witness. Therefore the tabernacle of witness was fashioned and built after the shape exhibited and seen in heaven, which the blessed apostle to the Hebrews called the very example or patron. For it was said to Moses, "See that you make everything according to the pattern that was showed to you on the mount," which thing Moses did accordingly. But such things as came forth of the tabernacle of witness made on earth seemed to the Israelites just and holy. There were aired the oracles and answers of God, which it was not lawful to speak against.

Therefore when we hear now that the very judgments of God against the wicked world's pains and punishments come out of the true temple itself, the pattern, I mean, and that celestial, who should hereafter doubt that all the judgments of God with which he plagued the ungodly are sacred and holy? And while the ungodly are plagued, we must think nothing else but that a sentence, as it were, an oracle, is come or pronounced from heaven, which it is unlawful to deny. To conclude, the divine judgments do proceed out of the very throne of God, and therefore they cannot but be most holy. Otherwise we shall hear in Revelation 21 that there is no temple in heaven. These are therefore types and figures, not matters truest and permanent but passing and fading away after they have signified that for which they were instituted.

This matter also pertained to the apparel of angels, that by this one may also esteem the judgments of God. They are said to be clothed in pure linen, or clean and white or bright, by which is signified that the judgments of God are unspotted and bright. For we have heard that these things St. John saw were signs. Therefore we may not imagine carnal things in heavenly matters but spiritually to expound such things that in the sign seem to be, as it were, corporal. The garment in this world is changed with the state of things. For they

[10]Brightman, *Revelation**, 414. †Charles V (1500–1558) was Holy Roman Emperor and archduke of Austria, 1519–1556. Ferdinand I (1503–1564) was Holy Roman emperor (1558–1564) and king of Bohemia and Hungary from 1526. With his Peace of Augsburg (1555), he concluded the era of religious strife in Germany following the rise of Lutheranism by recognizing the right of territorial princes to determine the religion of their subjects. Elizabeth I (1533–1603) was queen of England and Ireland from 1558–1603. One of her first actions as queen was the establishment of an English Protestant church, of which she became the supreme governor. This creation, later named the Elizabethan Religious Settlement, evolved into the Church of England. ‡The Scottish Reformation Parliament of 1560 approved a Protestant confession of faith, rejecting papal jurisdiction and the Mass. Knox spent time in Geneva, where he became a follower of Calvin and emerged as the most significant figure there. §Svealand was the original Sweden, to which it gave its name. During the Reformation, the territories ruled by the Danish-based House of Oldenburg converted from Catholicism to Lutheranism. The Reformation in Sweden is generally regarded as having begun in 1527 during the reign of King Gustav I of Sweden, but the process was slow and was not definitively decided until the Uppsala Synod of 1593.

use white garments in victories and triumphs, black at burials and mourning, red in battle.

Here is therefore signified that the judgments of God are most pure and that God overcomes and triumphed over the ungodly. At the resurrection and ascension of our Lord, angels appeared in white garments, shining bright, to signify the glory of Christ. Now is the very chest girded with a girdle, and that indeed with a golden girdle. Gold is a sign of pureness. In the chest is the seat of affections. The girdle binds, moreover, prepares for the journey. Therefore it indicated that the judgments of God are prepared and in a readiness. Hundred Sermons on the Apocalypse.[11]

Queen Elizabeth Pours Out the First Bowl. Thomas Brightman: The vials are poured: the first by our most gracious Queen Elizabeth and other Protestant princes, as a result of which the whole flock of papists is full of ulcerous envy. . . . The second vial by Martin Chemnitz against the Tridentine Council,† as a result of which the sea of the popish doctrine, by the Jesuits the masters of the controversies, was made, as it were, the corrupt and filthy blood of a wonder. . . . The third by William Cecil‡ against the Jesuits, which are the wellsprings of the popish doctrine; and so far are our times gone.

The rest of the vials are to come but shortly to be poured out: . . . the fourth on the sun, that is, on the Scriptures, by whose light people shall be tormented and shall boil in great anger and contentions; the fifth on the city of Rome, the throne of the beast; the sixth on Euphrates, as a result of which a way shall be prepared to the eastern Jews, that after they have embraced the faith of the gospel, they may return into their own country, when there shall be also a great preparation of war, both by the Turks against these new Christians in the East and in the West by the pope; the seventh on the air, as a result of which the mystery will be finished, the Turks and the popes' names being razed out, and then also the church will be settled in exceedingly great felicity, as on the earth may be expected. Revelation of St. John.[12]

Sores, Pestilences, Rivers of Blood. Heinrich Bullinger: But while this first angel, executor of God's judgment, pours out his plague on people, there fell a harmful sore on people. This plague corresponded to the sixth plague of Egypt. And that sore signifies a canker, a fistula, and swelling sores or boils, but chiefly the pockets of Jude, which others call the disease of Naples, some the French pox, and some the Spanish; truly, for that in the war of Naples (which was made by the French men and Spaniards in 1494), they came up first in the camp of prostitutes, which infected the army. On this Mainardus the physician discoursed at large.

But however so diverse and venomous sores do infect many grievously, yet does the French pox chiefly corrupt the abbeys of monks and nuns, and colleges of priests, above others? For they are giving themselves to most filthy fornication, those who abhor and detest in others holy matrimony, and therefore receive from this the reward of their iniquity. Therefore is it said here expressly that the antichristians should be with this disease vexed or rather punished. You will find some whose face is eaten with this disease. All those who visit prostitutes and adulterers for the most part are troubled with this plague. Job also the excellent servant of God was covered with sores and boils, but by the singular counsel of God, as I mentioned before. Therefore it is no marvel, though sometimes very good men free from the uncleanness of prostitution are also infected with this disease.

[11]Bullinger, *Hundred Sermons** (1561), 476-78.

[12]Brightman, *Revelation**, 414-16. †Council of Trent, the nineteenth ecumenical council of the Roman Catholic Church, held in three parts from 1545 to 1563. Prompted by the Reformation, the Council of Trent responded emphatically to the issues at hand and enacted the formal Roman Catholic reply to the doctrinal challenges of the Protestants. It thus represents the official adjudication of many questions about which there had been continuing ambiguity throughout the early church and the Middle Ages. ‡William Cecil (1520–1598), first Baron Burghley, KG, PC, was an English statesman, the chief adviser of Queen Elizabeth I for most of her reign, twice secretary of state, and Lord High Treasurer from 1572.

The second angel poured his vial on the sea, and therefore the blood of living things became altogether such as is in dead men, namely, corrupt and turned into matter. As a result all that lived in the sea died. The sea is evermore stirring and variable, and rightly therefore by this the world is signified, or inconstant people in the world. These, for their sins, are infected with the pestilence and die in great plenty. In the words is the figure synecdoche, as every living soul is said to die. This second plague corresponded to the fifth of Egypt. Under this plague are grouped all kinds of pestilences and plagues. Hezekiah also was taken with the plague, as many godly men also die of the pestilence, but by the singular counsel of God.

The third angel shed his vial on the rivers and fountains of waters, which were turned into blood. This corresponded to the first plague of Egypt. The Egyptians had drowned in the Nile the newborn bodies of infants and had oppressed the innocent Israelites. Therefore they were worthy to drink of the Nile. Hundred Sermons on the Apocalypse.[13]

Oriented Toward Flesh and Blood. Thomas Müntzer: You cannot distinguish between the elect and the reprobate; as a result, you totally reject the coming church in which the knowledge of the Lord will dawn in all its fullness. But this error of your [*sic*], my most beloved, arises wholly from an ignorance of the living Word. . . . The phial of the third angel has already been sprinkled on the fountains of the waters (I know this and tremble), and the outpouring of blood has been accomplished; but their mind is oriented towards flesh and blood. Some are chosen, but their minds cannot be opened. . . . Hence their works are the same as those of the reprobate, with the exception of the fear of God, which separates them from the latter. . . . For such are the works which I find in you as long as there are contentions among you about abolition of the mass.

That some hate the abomination of the papist sacrifice I applaud and commend; for they have acted under the leading of the Holy Spirit. . . . Those who preach should examine their auditors when they have finished preaching, and those who have displayed the fruits of understanding should be set before the people, and the bread and the drink should be given them, because it is endowed with the understanding of the testimonies of God, not from books of dead promises but of living promises, who are possessed by the Spirit. Letter to Phillip Melanchthon.[14]

16:8-9 *The Fourth Bowl*

Wrath and Plague on the See of Rome. Heinrich Bullinger: That saying in the Gospel is known: "In the chair of Moses sit the scribes and Pharisees," and so on. It is known that in ancient times there were seats of patriarchs, Jerusalem, Antioch, Rome, Alexandria, Constantinople, and others, and that these are called apostolic seats, for as much as the apostles have taught there. And so is the apostolic seat used for the apostolic doctrine itself. That seat erected and established at Rome by the apostles and apostolic men, the beast that is the pope has subverted and in the place of it erected the seat of pestilence, which he dares nevertheless to call the seat of Christ and the seat of St. Peter. Christ has no longer any seat on earth, save that he dwells in the hearts of the faithful church. Otherwise, the true seat of Christ is the right hand of the Father. The true seat of Peter is heaven itself.

Rome is no longer his seat, for the apostolic doctrine and patriarchal chair is destroyed and trodden underfoot, and instead of it is an earthly empire or kingdom set up by the pope. Indeed, he pursues the apostolic seats by force of arms. Now therefore, God, having compassion on his people, poured out his wrath and plague on the see of Rome, illuminating people with the light of the gospel to the end they might know and see the wickedness and abomination of the Roman see. This is a wonderful benefit to those who are lighted, and a great grief and torment to the

[13]Bullinger, *Hundred Sermons**, 483.

[14]Müntzer, *Collected Works*, 43-46.

Roman sort. For the effect of the plague follows: "And his kingdom was made dark." This plague corresponded to number nine of Egypt. For as thick darkness plagued the Egyptians and bright light rejoiced the Israelites, so were the papists tormented with shameful errors, and it will grieve them also to have their errors detected and their glory obscured, and the faithful shall rejoice in the light of Christ. For now begins and already has begun the majesty of the seat and of he who sits in it to be obscured.

What was once called a holy seat is now by the godly and learned called wicked Rome, the whore of Babylon, the mother of all fornications, the den of thieves, Sodom, Egypt, the red harlot by reason of the purple senate of cardinals, who wore red and purple. It is said commonly and truly, the nearer Rome, the further from Christ. They most rightly call the cardinals, bishops, and spiritual fathers, the family and boundaries of antichrist, men deceased and deceivers, with Symon[†] and filthy lust most corrupt. Therefore, the kingdom of the beast (so he expounded the seat) was made dark. There is added, furthermore, how the worshipers of the seat of the beast have and do behave themselves. First for pain and sorrow, indignation, wrath and envy, they gnaw or bite their tongues, which is the gesture of angry men, impotently angry, I mean, those who burn in furious rage. HUNDRED SERMONS ON THE APOCALYPSE.[15]

16:10-11 *The Fifth Bowl*

THE DARKENED THRONE. HUGH BROUGHTON: The fifth angel's trumpet could not prevent the star of heaven from seeking supremacy and badness, but by increase of locusts he would be a king or a beast coming out of the earth, and with his keys of the kingdom of darkness he could bring a smoke of heresies that darkened all sun and air. . . . The pope's states shall have his throne darkened openly in this world by valiant and holy people strengthened by angels. Darkness is usual for a distressed state in Job and David and Isaiah. Albion,[†] with Denmark, is wholly gone from him: half Switzerland, Netherlands, Germany, and the poor school of Geneva said well to him, though it agrees with him to slander the pure text of Scripture. Where Beza does say, *Deus non agit in malis*, he calls back those errors of his and Calvin's, by which they seemed to make God author of sin. The senate's religion, as they gave me leave to express it, I dare defend against Turk and Jew and pope while my hand can guide the wobbling pen. And where Bodin[‡] says that Calvin should say of the Apocalypse, *miror quid tam obscurus scriptor velit*, it is not credible that one of his judgment, to shake off all the pope's trash, would speak so of a book penned by the father of light. And Bodin himself should have told the praise of God for the light of salvation by this book. God told him that those who read and mark the things written here were happy. . . . As Daniel calls to him all stories heathen for six hundred years, so John for sixteen hundred. And as Daniel tells the same things seven times over to infinite delight, so does John repeat and as pleasantly. The pope's divines, seeing his throne fall and decay, chew their tongues in speech not fitted to matter. REVELATION OF THE HOLY APOCALYPSE.[16]

16:12-16 *The Sixth Bowl*

THE SIXTH AGE OF THE CHURCH AND WORLDLY LUSTS. JOHN BALE: In course now followed the sixth angel of God's appointment, under the sixth seal opening, pouring out his ireful

[15]Bullinger, *Hundred Sermons** (1561), 489-92. †The term *simony* comes from Simon Magus, a figure in the book of Acts. In Acts 8:9-24, Simon Magus offered to pay two of Jesus' disciples to give him the power to grant the Holy Spirit to others. Simony is the act of buying or selling something spiritual or connected to the spiritual, such as a church office.

[16]Broughton, *Revelation*, 243-44; citing Rev 1:3. †Albion is the earliest-known name for the island of Britain. ‡Jean Bodin (1530–1596) was a French jurist and political philosopher, member of the Parlement of Paris and professor of law in Toulouse. Bodin lived during the aftermath of the Protestant Reformation and wrote against the background of religious conflict in France.

vial on the great River Euphrates, a flood of the Assyrians or of Babylon, representing in mystery the pleasant possessions and wavering delights of the papistic clearly with such like.

To all filthy desires of carnal and worldly lusts the Lord gave their hearts over in the sixth age of the Christian church for their unbelief's sake to do those things that are uncomely and beastly. So all their study, travail, and labor sought no other end except only to abound in them. They were given wholly to this, and nothing to the glory of God in all their practiced observations.

Yet the waters of it in process of time were dried up. Their wealthy pomp, possessions, and pleasures (their false feats once known) are and shall be clearly taken away from them. For after Jesus Sirach, the plant of sin shall be rooted out in the proud synagogue of the wicked.

And all this shall be to prepare the way of the kings from the spring of the sun.

Never shall the governors walk in the way of the Lord, nor rule according to Christian doctrine, nor yet that doctrine be evident and open until the waters are dried up, not one drop remaining. So long as the priests dwell in wanton delights and vain pleasures, the princes are either childish or tyrannous, according as their deeds require.

Never are they kings from the spring of the sun, or according to Christ's rule, seeking God's honor with David and Josiah. In England by the gospel preaching have many of these waters been dried up in the suppression of monasteries, priories, convents, and friars' houses, yet all things are not brought to Christ's clear institution. A sincere Christian order cannot yet be seen there, and there is a great cause why. For all is not yet dried up there. The bishops reign still in as much vainglorious pomp and with as many heathen observations as ever they did. As cruelly hearted and as bloody-minded they yet are as ever they were before, no mischief unsought to hold in the waters. Note how Winchester, Durham, York, London, and Lincoln worked with such another as pleasantly disposed Euphrates. But be of good comfort and pray in the meantime. For the Holy Spirit promised here they shall wither away with all that the Heavenly Father has not planted. The Lord's breath will consume all that generation. Now is the axe laid to the root of the tree, to hew down the unfruitful branches, the withered reserved to unquenchable fire.

God grant the princes at that day to bestow the waters of Euphrates more Christianly than they have yet been bestowed—no provision made for the poor, nor yet order set for the gospel preaching. For great part of it is now turned to the upholding of dice playing, masking, and banking; indeed, I would not speak of bribing, whoring, and swearing, the towns, peoples, and households miserably decayed that will one day not be unplagued unless they repent. The Image of Both Churches.[17]

An Allegory and Allusion to Old Babylon. Heinrich Bullinger: The sixth angel pours out his vial on the great river of Euphrates. The point of this pouring is that the way might be opened for the kings of the East, that is, that Babylon might be taken. This plague chiefly pertained to Rome and the Romish church. The speech has an allegory, or a secret comparison, and allusion to old Babylon. We read in Daniel 5 . . . that Babylon was taken the same night, wherein Belshazzar king of it had prepared a sumptuous banquet and looked for nothing less than for destruction. Herodotus[†] and Xenophon[‡] report how the kings of the East Darius Priscus, who is also called Mede, and Cyrus of Persia besieged the city all around, but where there was no hope to win it, Cyrus let out the Euphrates by ditches, so that the army might wade over the river. So was the city laid open and taken on the same side where it was fenced with the river. Euphrates therefore fortified Babylon and brought to it many other commodities and pleasures.

Here therefore are meant by Euphrates, riches, munition, pleasures, commodities, tributes, and customs, which the Romish churches call sacred or of the holy church. These commodities and pleasures, I say, are diminished of the kings of the

[17]Bale, *Image** (1570), ch. 16.

East, of true Christians, whom the Scripture calls the kings and priests, and derived and put to another use. Therefore the power of the Roman church begins to decay, with the intent that at length it may be taken and abolished by the Lord Christ himself. Doubtless the true Christians understand, believe, and profess that Christ alone is the Savior and that there is salvation in no other. And that this is given freely, that they be made and commit simony and sacrilege, which in this case is practicing and making merchandise. Hundred Sermons on the Apocalypse.[18]

16:17-21 *The Seventh Bowl*

Sundry and Horrible Tempests. Heinrich Bullinger: The seventh and last cup poured out onto the air signified the perturbation and alteration of all elements, and the horrible but just judgment of God, and finally the end of all things and pains everlasting. The things are enclosed with figurative speeches, taken for the most part out of the prophets and by a private comparison brought out of the holy story. This is done that all things might be fuller of majesty and that everyone should more diligently search for the sense of an excellent matter, and they might keep and retain in perfect memory the found ones.

At what time the air is moved, sundry and horrible tempests arise in the air. And the Lord Jesus in the Gospel of Mathew testifies that about the last coming of Christ, the powers of heaven shall be moved. Hundred Sermons on the Apocalypse.[19]

Three Kinds of People in the Church. Heinrich Bullinger: Then that great city shall be cut asunder, the universality of people in the great church divided into three parts: that is to say, in the end there shall be three kinds of people found in the church. There will be true Christians, who attribute to Christ his true glory, that is, all things of true salvation, and cleave to him alone by sincere faith. There will be papists, who after the letter ascribe to Christ many things, but not as became them, for they ascribe those things to antichrist that belong to Christ alone, and in communicating with him such things as not to be communicated, they deny Christ. For if the pope is head of the church universal, if he is king and priest and so on, where is Christ preached to have those things alone?

There are, moreover, neuters,† who will not seem to deny Christ and yet attribute not a little to antichrist, whom yet nevertheless in many things they contemn and despise utterly. These have no certain religion but established and conceived at their pleasure, as it pleases them, to believe this or that. There is a great number of these people at this day, deriding and mocking whatever is not tuned after their most light. . . . You may find also in the Gospel a field sown with sundry seed, to bring forth most diverse fruit, indeed, even cockle and darnel, which at length at the end of the world shall be gathered. . . .

Moreover, he says the cities of the Gentiles shall fall, by which I understand the Jewish, Turkish, and strange religions, placed into various sects or heresies. But every one of these has their societies, rites, and laws, which they commend to be the best and such as shall endure forever, but they shall fall also. Only the religion or faith of Christ shall prevail and overcome. Aretas‡ expounds this passage in the same way: the cities of the heathen, says he, falling, are various opinions of faith about religion and so on. They (I say) are all fallen.

[18]Bullinger, *Hundred Sermons** (1561), 492-93; citing Dan 5:5. †Herodotus (484–425/413 BC) was a Greek historian and geographer from Halicarnassus. Herodotus is known for his *Histories*, a detailed account of the Greco-Persian Wars. His work is considered the first great narrative history of the ancient world. Herodotus's work is also the source of the modern meaning of the word *history*. ‡Xenophon (431–350 BC) was a Greek military leader, philosopher, and historian. Xenophon was a pioneer in several literary genres. His work includes *Anabasis*, a first-person military memoir, *Education of Cyrus*, a biographical novel, and *Hellenica*, a continued history. Xenophon's work was influenced by Herodotus and Thucydides, and is characterized by optimism and pessimism, sparse narration, and the idea that ethical factors are crucial to historical outcomes.

[19]Bullinger, *Hundred Sermons** (1561), 499-500; citing Mt 24:29-31.

But he affirmed and showed diligently that it was especially measured and requisite that the city and church of Rome should be destroyed and committed to perpetual torments. I declared sufficiently before that Babylon is Rome, which indeed is very great not in Italy only but throughout all France, Spain, Germany, and other realms. The city and church of Rome has seemed to many that it should be everlasting and triumphant forever. Thus the Epicures'[§] cry that God cares not for these inferior things, but every man lives here either happily or unhappily, according as he has discreetly and cleverly framed his life, who does not know of our pleasures and displeasures and our conversation.

But contrarily Saint John affirmed that the Lord has remembered Babylon, and so, having remembered her, he has determined to commit her to torments. This he uttered by a prophetic figure of speech that he might give to her the cup of wine of indignation or fierceness of his wrath, that is to say, he might punish her accordingly, as the great indignation and wrath of God requires. Therefore she shall have no small punishment, for the wrath of God is not light but most gruesome and hot. For he requires and recompensed the slackness of punishment with the extremity of pain and torment. Similar things you may read in Malachi 3, as God has books written, and concerning also the cup of the wine of God's fury, spoken of before out of the prophets.

Now also among other things by a figure of speech he showed that the ungodly have no refuge or way to escape. Otherwise, the richer sort in danger would hide themselves far off in islands, that they might be out of gunshot; many flee into the mountains that they may there lurk safely. But now he says how the very islands flee that therefore they cannot be overtaken. He adds that the mountains, that is to say, places of refuge or lurking, cannot be found. Therefore, all ungodly in general being taken, there remained nothing but that should be put to torments. Hundred Sermons on the Apocalypse.[20]

[20]Bullinger, *Hundred Sermons** (1561), 501-3; citing Mt 13:24-30; Mal 3:16. †Christ and antichrist represent two poles with neuter representing neither of the opposites. ‡Arethas, archbishop of Caesarea (c. 850–c. 944), was possibly a pupil of the patriarch of Constantinople, Photius. §Greek philosopher who believed that the world is a random combination of atoms and that pleasure is the highest good (341–270 BC).

17:1–19:10 BABYLON AND HER DESTINY

17 Then one of the seven angels who had the seven bowls came and said to me, "Come, I will show you the judgment of the great prostitute who is seated on many waters, [2]with whom the kings of the earth have committed sexual immorality, and with the wine of whose sexual immorality the dwellers on earth have become drunk." [3]And he carried me away in the Spirit into a wilderness, and I saw a woman sitting on a scarlet beast that was full of blasphemous names, and it had seven heads and ten horns. [4]The woman was arrayed in purple and scarlet, and adorned with gold and jewels and pearls, holding in her hand a golden cup full of abominations and the impurities of her sexual immorality. [5]And on her forehead was written a name of mystery: "Babylon the great, mother of prostitutes and of earth's abominations." [6]And I saw the woman, drunk with the blood of the saints, the blood of the martyrs of Jesus.[a]

When I saw her, I marveled greatly. [7]But the angel said to me, "Why do you marvel? I will tell you the mystery of the woman, and of the beast with seven heads and ten horns that carries her. [8]The beast that you saw was, and is not, and is about to rise from the bottomless pit[b] and go to destruction. And the dwellers on earth whose names have not been written in the book of life from the foundation of the world will marvel to see the beast, because it was and is not and is to come. [9]This calls for a mind with wisdom: the seven heads are seven mountains on which the woman is seated; [10]they are also seven kings, five of whom have fallen, one is, the other has not yet come, and when he does come he must remain only a little while. [11]As for the beast that was and is not, it is an eighth but it belongs to the seven, and it goes to destruction. [12]And the ten horns that you saw are ten kings who have not yet received royal power, but they are to receive authority as kings for one hour, together with the beast. [13]These are of one mind, and they hand over their power and authority to the beast. [14]They will make war on the Lamb, and the Lamb will conquer them, for he is Lord of lords and King of kings, and those with him are called and chosen and faithful."

[15]And the angel[c] said to me, "The waters that you saw, where the prostitute is seated, are peoples and multitudes and nations and languages. [16]And the ten horns that you saw, they and the beast will hate the prostitute. They will make her desolate and naked, and devour her flesh and burn her up with fire, [17]for God has put it into their hearts to carry out his purpose by being of one mind and handing over their royal power to the beast, until the words of God are fulfilled. [18]And the woman that you saw is the great city that has dominion over the kings of the earth."

18 After this I saw another angel coming down from heaven, having great authority, and the earth was made bright with his glory. [2]And he called out with a mighty voice,

"Fallen, fallen is Babylon the great!
  She has become a dwelling place for demons,
a haunt for every unclean spirit,
  a haunt for every unclean bird,
  a haunt for every unclean and detestable
    beast.
[3]For all nations have drunk[d]
  the wine of the passion of her sexual
    immorality,
and the kings of the earth have committed
    immorality with her,
  and the merchants of the earth have grown
    rich from the power of her luxurious
    living."

[4]Then I heard another voice from heaven saying,

"Come out of her, my people,
  lest you take part in her sins,
lest you share in her plagues;
[5]for her sins are heaped high as heaven,
  and God has remembered her iniquities.

[6]Pay her back as she herself has paid back others,
and repay her double for her deeds;
mix a double portion for her in the cup she mixed.
[7]As she glorified herself and lived in luxury,
so give her a like measure of torment and mourning,
since in her heart she says,
'I sit as a queen,
I am no widow,
and mourning I shall never see.'
[8]For this reason her plagues will come in a single day,
death and mourning and famine,
and she will be burned up with fire;
for mighty is the Lord God who has judged her."

[9]And the kings of the earth, who committed sexual
immorality and lived in luxury with her, will weep
and wail over her when they see the smoke of her
burning. [10]They will stand far off, in fear of her
torment, and say,

"Alas! Alas! You great city,
you mighty city, Babylon!
For in a single hour your judgment has come."

[11]And the merchants of the earth weep and mourn
for her, since no one buys their cargo anymore, [12]cargo
of gold, silver, jewels, pearls, fine linen, purple cloth,
silk, scarlet cloth, all kinds of scented wood, all kinds
of articles of ivory, all kinds of articles of costly wood,
bronze, iron and marble, [13]cinnamon, spice, incense,
myrrh, frankincense, wine, oil, fine flour, wheat, cattle
and sheep, horses and chariots, and slaves, that is,
human souls.[e]

[14]"The fruit for which your soul longed
has gone from you,
and all your delicacies and your splendors
are lost to you,
never to be found again!"

[15]The merchants of these wares, who gained wealth
from her, will stand far off, in fear of her torment,
weeping and mourning aloud,

[16]"Alas, alas, for the great city
that was clothed in fine linen,
in purple and scarlet,
adorned with gold,
with jewels, and with pearls!
[17]For in a single hour all this wealth has been laid waste."

And all shipmasters and seafaring men, sailors
and all whose trade is on the sea, stood far off [18]and
cried out as they saw the smoke of her burning,

"What city was like the great city?"

[19]And they threw dust on their heads as they wept
and mourned, crying out,

"Alas, alas, for the great city
where all who had ships at sea
grew rich by her wealth!
For in a single hour she has been laid waste.
[20]Rejoice over her, O heaven,
and you saints and apostles and prophets,
for God has given judgment for you against her!"

[21]Then a mighty angel took up a stone like a great
millstone and threw it into the sea, saying,

"So will Babylon the great city be thrown down with violence,
and will be found no more;
[22]and the sound of harpists and musicians, of flute players and trumpeters,
will be heard in you no more,
and a craftsman of any craft
will be found in you no more,
and the sound of the mill
will be heard in you no more,
[23]and the light of a lamp
will shine in you no more,
and the voice of bridegroom and bride
will be heard in you no more,
for your merchants were the great ones of the earth,
and all nations were deceived by your sorcery.
[24]And in her was found the blood of prophets and of saints,
and of all who have been slain on earth."

19 After this I heard what seemed to be the loud voice of a great multitude in heaven, crying out,

"Hallelujah!
Salvation and glory and power belong to our God,
[2]for his judgments are true and just;
for he has judged the great prostitute
who corrupted the earth with her immorality,
and has avenged on her the blood of his servants."

[3]Once more they cried out,

"Hallelujah!
The smoke from her goes up forever and ever."

[4]And the twenty-four elders and the four living creatures fell down and worshiped God who was seated on the throne, saying, "Amen. Hallelujah!"
[5]And from the throne came a voice saying,

"Praise our God,
all you his servants,
you who fear him,
small and great."

[6]Then I heard what seemed to be the voice of a great multitude, like the roar of many waters and like the sound of mighty peals of thunder, crying out,

"Hallelujah!
For the Lord our God
the Almighty reigns.
[7]Let us rejoice and exult
and give him the glory,
for the marriage of the Lamb has come,
and his Bride has made herself ready;
[8]it was granted her to clothe herself
with fine linen, bright and pure"—

for the fine linen is the righteous deeds of the saints.
[9]And the angel said[f] to me, "Write this: Blessed are those who are invited to the marriage supper of the Lamb." And he said to me, "These are the true words
of God." [10]Then I fell down at his feet to worship him, but he said to me, "You must not do that! I am a fellow servant with you and your brothers who hold to the testimony of Jesus. Worship God." For the testimony of Jesus is the spirit of prophecy.

a Greek *the witnesses to Jesus* **b** Greek *the abyss* **c** Greek *he* **d** Some manuscripts *fallen by* **e** Or *and slaves, and human lives* **f** Greek *he said*

Overview: Theodore Bibliander depicted seven bowls of God's wrath. These are now set in an eschatological future. They are defined by a prostitute astride a beast, the fall of Babylon, and the wedding supper of the Lamb. The great prostitute is punished, intoxicated by her adulterous relations with the kings of the earth. Carried away by the Spirit, she is next seen on a scarlet beast with seven heads and ten horns covered with blasphemous names. Those whose names are not in the book of life will marvel to see the beast. Its seven heads are the seven hills on which the woman is seated. The beast is an eighth king, but it belongs to the seven and goes to its destruction. The ten horns are ten kings who will make war on the Lamb, but the Lamb will conquer them. Those with him are called chosen and faithful.

The great city is Babylon, whose fall is depicted in Revelation 18. Bullinger describes the contents of this chapter: (1) the total destruction of the city, (2) advice for the saints on how to behave in the face of such a great danger, (3) the manner of the desolation, (4) a lamentation in which the princes and merchants mourn for Rome, and (5) the rejoicing of the apostles and prophets at the just judgment of God.

Revelation 19 begins with a great multitude shouting "Hallelujah," then proceeds in four parts: (1) the announced end of antichrist, (2) the confirmation of the saints, (3) instruction for worship, and (4) a declaration that Jesus alone is Judge. The nature of appropriate worship of God and the testimony of Jesus are at issue. These topics became increasingly the focus of Roman Catholic and Protestant hermeneutical warfare. Between chapters 17 and 18 Brightman places a lengthy discourse on antichrist, increasingly less a matter of medieval morality and more one of polemical politics.

The Imperial Papacy Destroyed. Martin Luther: In chapter 17, the imperial papacy and papal empire is comprehended from beginning to end in a single image. As in a résumé, it is shown to be nothing (for the ancient Roman Empire is long since gone) and to be (for some of its lands indeed still exist, and the city of Rome besides). This image is presented here as one presents a malefactor publicly before a court—so that he may be condemned—that men may know that this beast too is shortly to be condemned and, as St. Paul says, "destroyed by the appearance and coming of our Lord." As he says in the text, the very patrons of the papacy begin this, those who are now its protectors, so that the clergy will sit utterly naked. Preface to the Revelation of Saint John.[1]

17:1-7 *The Vision of the Woman and the Scarlet Beast*

The Deception of Jezebel. Menno Simons: Thus, all false teachers forget the covenant of God whereby they are bound to him, as is, alas, the case with many at present, who have forgotten all upon which they were baptized, namely, the cross, and would recommend and make use of the sword. May the Almighty God save all true Christians from this, and may he give them wisdom and intelligence to keep the covenant of God and to be always mindful of what kind of a spirit Christ wants his disciples to be. . . .

Grant that they may be aware of this strange woman; for her house is inclined to death and her ways to corruption. All those who enter in unto her will not come out again, nor do they get on the way of life. And this strange woman now reigns extensively, and as she deceives many, as did and yet does the prophetess Jezebel, and as the serpent deceived Eve; therefore we will, by the grace of God, discover some things, that those who are yet blind may become seeing, and that when they acknowledge antichrist to be an abomination standing in the holy place, they may see all deceit. Testimony Against John Van Leyden.[2]

Rome Is the Woman on the Beast. Mary Cary: Now, since it is clear in Scripture (and all histories do acknowledge it) that Rome was the great city that reigned over the kings of the earth, then it appears that Rome is that woman who is said to sit on the beast. Now, this being apparent, it does appear all the more clearly what the beast is. It was clear before that the beast was a wicked one in whom the devil reigned, who had received power, and a seat, and great authority from the devil; but it did not so clearly appear who that wicked one in particular is.

But here it appears that it is particularly he on whom the city of Rome sits, he who supports it. Now it is apparent that it is that wicked one the pope who is the support of the cursed city. It is he who bears her up in her pomp, and pride, and filthy, abominable, sodomitical practices. He is the beast on which that great whore sits. And the city of Rome has been and to this day is such a fountain of filthiness, whoredoms, and all cursed abominations, as this name appears so perspicuously in her forehead as he who runs may read it, "Mystery, Babylon the Great, the Mother of Harlots and Abominations of the Earth." And it is apparent that she is drunken with the blood of saints and the blood of the martyrs of Jesus. The Resurrection of the Witnesses.[3]

Antichrist Is a Kingdom. Thomas Brightman: If antichrist comes, and has fixed his seat at Rome, ever since the empire was taken away from the heathen emperors: then can it not be doubted, but antichrist, in a common name, is a secret adversary; an impious kingdom, and not one singular man; that the time of his coming is past, and not now to come. . . . Antichrist is not particular men, but a certain kingdom and succession, from which God may exempt according to his own

[1]LW 35:408; citing 2 Thess 2:8.

[2]Simons, *Complete Writings*; citing Lk 9:55.

[3]Cary, *Resurrection**, 52-53.

will; wherein he shows the riches of his immeasurable mercy. But all these things, we have more largely handled and unfolded in opening the words of the apostle: Now we would but gather them into a brief summary, that the things which were spoken dispersedly, being set under one view, might show more clearly how by the apostles few words, all popish and Jesuit subtleties, as touched with lightning from heaven, do fly on fire, and come to nothing. These, therefore, are the common arguments, and to be applied unto all the chapters of the disputation following, which we thought good to warn you, reader, that you may set them rather from here, unto every question, than that we should often repeat them. Things that properly belong to every place, we will relate, as the matter shall require. Now, therefore, let us encounter with Bellarmine hand to hand and not balk any of his demands, that he may see better how in vain he has tried his strength against the truth. . . .

This, Bellarmine, shall be the true trial, both of you and of us, before God and his holy angels. The things that you propound are ridiculous. You will have it, that we have made defection, because we have departed from the superstition of our predecessors, both in doctrine and rites full of idolatry, as though we were not bidden to go out of Babylon and to have no communion with her at all. We have made defection from the whore, defection from antichrist, namely, defection from your pope of Rome. But thanks be to God, we have made defection unto the one true God; who of his infinite mercy will crown our defection with eternal glory, and your constancy, if you speedily repent not, with eternal ignominy, among them which obey not the truth. Now, therefore, cast up your accounts and gather the sum; then see, forasmuch as antichrist is an impious and apostate kingdom, and the popes of Rome have been principal apostates, and many, whether antichrist is a singular person or not.

In expounding the words of the prophecy, we concluded by most firm arguments that Rome is the seat of antichrist; and that forthwith, after the empire is taken from the heathen emperors. For the heads of the beast abide fixed to Rome. Where are both those hills and kings that the angel spoke of? And where these heads abide fixed, there must the seat of antichrist be. Moreover, seeing antichrist then also showed himself, when Constantine began to reign, as before it proved at large: he has no other seat than Rome. For whereas he abode a few years at Avignon, he did that with the purpose to sojourn for a time, not with the mind to change his seat. The Revelation of Saint John.[4]

The Doctrine of the Antichrist. Thomas Brightman: The doctrine of antichrist, we together with the Holy Ghost, do teach from the Scriptures, to be full of hypocrisy, fraud, treachery, which may deceive even the most prudent, whom the Spirit enlightens not with his truth. For one had need of singular prudence to know this beast, which has two horns like the Lamb, and is a false prophet seducing the earth. On the contrary, the papists will have this same doctrine to be so openly impious and blasphemous, that none is so blockish, but he may perceive it forthwith, and detest it. . . . Seeing he is also a false prophet, he will not boast himself to be the only God but shall do more harm by lying, than by force; and not show himself to be such as in deed he is. These few things (to keep me within the limits of the Apocalypse) may teach you the true nature of antichrist, unless you supply willingly to be ignorant, that you may the more confidently serve him. . . . Endlessly it were to sail into the sea of all your lying signs; therefore had I supply to relate one or two both publicly testified, and fresh in memory; than many other almost forgot with age. Wherefore your pope does so lively express antichrist both in multitude and falsity of miracles, that none I believe is so sharp sighted, as that he can discern any even the least difference. . . . Such stuff as this, are all the things that your men

[4]Thomas Brightman, *A revelation of the Apocalyps, that is, the Apocalyps of S. John illustrated with an analysis & scolions where the sense is opened by the scripture, & the events of things foretold, shewed by histories* (Amsterdam: Judocus Honius and Hendrick Laurenss, 1611), 492, 494, 509, 570.

are either wont or able to bring, for to defend the pope, and to free him from this most grievous crime. Therefore you toil in vain: the thing is manifest, it cannot be hidden by any subtleties. Why do you go about to cast a mist before the sun? Why do you frame arguments against the Spirit of God? Purge rather with flames, those writings of yours, wherewith you have labored his defense, and flee out of his den, as speedily as you can.

Here ends the refutation of antichrist against Bellarmine. The Revelation of Saint John.[5]

Popery and Idolatry. David Pareus: "If any man receives priesthood at the hand of any layperson, let both the giver and receiver be accursed.

"If any communicate with a married priest, or if a priest, having a wife, does not put her away, let him be accursed." By this compendious way he exempted at once all bishops, clerks, churches, and all who belonged to them from the power of emperors and brought them under his own empire, taking to himself the right of all ecclesiastical goods. . . . Histories also testify that after those thousand years, the god of strengths foretold by Daniel . . . that is, the idol of transubstantiation and stage-like Mass, was chiefly erected and confirmed, in which the whole strength of the papacy up to this point consisted. With this grew up the innumerable fraternities and families of clergymen, sacrifices, monks, and religious sects who, all of them being exempted from civil jurisdiction, are subject only to the pope's scepter.

Then were invented the jubilees, the gainful traffic of popish indulgences, or pardons, and a thousand tricks to draw money from all provinces into Rome's treasury. The infinite ceremonies, superstitions, and idols were brought in and established, so that if now you compare popery with paganism, you shall scarcely see any difference but in names. Therefore, it is not said without cause that Satan, being loosed after the thousand years, should deceive the nations of the whole earth. A Commentary upon the Divine Revelation.[6]

The Identity of the Great Whore. Heinrich Bullinger: First, the author of this horrible vision is the Lord Christ himself, but he uses the ministry of six others to pour out plagues and vials. This is the head minister. And it was seemly that the judgment of Babylon should be uttered by an angel who had the rule over torments. The Lord Jesus himself will take punishment of the beast, for whom this triumph is reserved. And we understand that such things as are set forth and treated here have proceeded from the high bishop himself, Jesus Christ, and the manners of speaking are angelical, heavenly, and godly.

Who shall then blame us if we, using the words of angels and of Christ himself, shall say that the bishop of Rome and all popery is that purple and great and most common harlot? It appeared also to many who seem godly that moderation is neglected when these things that are plainly set forth to us by the express words of angels and of Christ are repeated by the preachers. It seems that they would shut and stop the mouth of Christ himself. Nevertheless, they attempt that in vain. For if the preachers hold their peace, the stones will cry. For it is proper that like the glory of Christ, so the shame of antichrist, should be known to the whole world. But those who, in the sermons made against antichrist, require I know not what modesty offend most grievously. . . . After in Revelation 18, we shall hear the Lord command, "Render to her, as she has rendered to you," and so on.

Second, he expresses in few words the sum of all and showed to where we should refer all things. "Come," says the angel to St. John, "and I will show you the judgment, condemnation, and punishment of the great whore." And where he says "of the great whore," he intimates what the crime or cause of

[5]Thomas Brightman, *A revelation of the Apocalyps, that is, the Apocalyps of S. John illustrated with an analysis & scolions where the sense is opened by the scripture, & the events of things foretold, shewed by histories* (Amsterdam: Judocus Honius and Hendrick Laurenss, 1611), 579, 584, 590, 597.

[6]Pareus, *Revelation**, 534; citing Dan 11:38.

punishment is, fornication, infidelity, or ungodliness. This vision also pertained to this that we might understand how Rome should be punished or destroyed, that is to say, the Roman Empire, or the kingdom of the pope or antichrist, and why or how it deserved to be destroyed. She is a whore, and a great and errant whore. And who does not know that a marriage is contracted between God and all and singular faithful? that God is the bridegroom and the church his spouse? She is bound then and coupled to her husband alone in faith and truth. If she breaks this faith and loves others, gives herself to them, calls on and honors them, she is a whore. Of this I have spoken many times both in this book and elsewhere. Hundred Sermons on the Apocalypse.[7]

Description of the Woman on the Beast. Heinrich Bullinger: Moreover, all old writers show that God is not worshiped by the Christians with gold and silver but with faith, charity, and righteousness. What will you say that Daniel . . . shows that antichrist shall worship God with gold, silver, and precious things? He condemned and rejected this thing.

And does it not appear here plainly that the Lord Jesus himself has set forth to us the pope or antichrist painted, as it were, in a table. For he appeared altogether such and in such similar apparel that he showed himself to be seen of all people, as the whore of Babylon is decked with at this present. And he assigns himself this apparel by a certain right. For the papists bring forth a false, failed donation of Constantine, among other things, pronouncing thus in Distinction 96: "We give and demise to blessed Silvester[†] and to all his successors the palace Lateran of our empire, and moreover the diadem, namely, the royal crown of our head (which the pope calls a kingdom and has made it triple) and also our purple robe and coat of crimson, and all our imperial array" and so on. . . .

This whore, moreover, drinks to all nations of the cup of Circes,[‡] which the Lord calls of gold. And it signifies doctrine. For to give drink is to teach. . . . Gold betokens sincerity and pureness of doctrine. Doubtless under pretense of sincerity and truly divine, Rome has easily persuaded all people to receive the doctrine of the Roman see. For the pope has named both himself and the church of Rome apostolic. And in the canons he has written, "Rightly so are all the laws of the see apostolic to be taken, as though they were confirmed by the godly mouth of St. Peter himself" (Distinction 19). Hundred Sermons on the Apocalypse.[8]

17:8-18 *The Angel's Interpretation*

The Profane Religion of the Seven Hills. Theodore Bibliander: The fourth section of the exposition follows, describing the destiny of good men as well as of the wicked. It also contains the rewards that are provided to Christ's righteous worshipers, and on the other hand, the punishments prepared for the devil and antichrist, along with his followers and all the wicked. And verse 17, the beast with two heads. Take the first as the ancient Roman Empire, and the second one is the papist monarchy. Each is described by its own marks and features. The guilty are brought forth in full view of the people, when the sentence of death is pronounced against them, and their final judgment must be levied. The Lord himself gives the interpretation of the seven heads as seven mountains,[9] on which each beast has its dwelling place. The meaning is not

[7]Bullinger, *Hundred Sermons** (1561), 505-9.

[8]Bullinger, *Hundred Sermons** (1561), 510-11; citing Dan 11; Ezek 34. †The Donation of Constantine is a forged document that claims that Emperor Constantine the Great gave Pope Sylvester I power over the Roman Empire and the church in the 4th century. The document was likely written in the 8th century and was used to support the papacy's political authority, especially in the 13th century. ‡In the story, Circe is a sorceress who offers Odysseus a cup containing a potion to turn him into a pig, as she has done to his crew. However, Odysseus has been given a special plant by Hermes, the messenger of the gods, to protect him from the potion's effects. When Circe tries to transform Odysseus, he threatens her with his sword, and she seduces him into sleeping with her in exchange for returning his sailors to human form.
[9]The Latin text wrongly has *mentes* for *montes*, the former making no sense in this context.

obscure, namely, Rome with her seven hills. She had on those hills temples for idols and profane worship. And she is no more righteous today, after shamefully abandoning the apostolic teaching of Paul and Peter especially. Daniel also predicted that the antichrist would set up his dwelling between the two seas, that is, between the upper and lower sea. The Lord interprets the heads also as the seven kings who, in succession, held Rome after Nero. It was at Nero's death that the Roman monarchy had received its fatal blow. But the wound lay concealed. The Faithful Relationship.[10]

The Roots of Sin. Theodore Bibliander: At the same time, Muhammad emerged as the root of sin and Satan's favorite. For practicing an antichristian tyranny outside the church, he stood opposed to the antichrist that raged in the heart of the church and of God's people. And so the Roman pontiff became more bold, that one time poor man and servant of servants. He claimed for himself two horns, exercising his authority not only over men's bodies and their worldly concerns, but also over their souls and spiritual interests. Now this happened of course so that there would be some new Caligula among God's people, who would practice his strife and wicked rivalry against Christ the King, and demand that he be worshiped as the great high priest, and king of all kings. The Faithful Relationship.[11]

True Citizen of the True Church. Thomas Brightman: The church is both commonly so called, and properly so. The first, has piety corrupted; the word adulterated; the sacraments depraved; is full of superstition, and human devices, retaining Christ's name only, and boasting in the title thereof; and also commonly so accounted, while any of the foundation is remaining. The other is chaste, pure, entire, clean, hearkening to Christ's voice in all things, and not departing from his prescribed rule at all, so far as mortal infirmity suffers; and this always is the only and true spouse of Christ. However, the whore also takes this name to herself. . . . Therefore, that is not rightly transferred to the common church, which pertains to it properly so called. One may be an alien from the church commonly so called, and yet be a true citizen of the true church. If you could show that the pope of Rome has his chair in this, which properly enjoins this name, you might rightly conclude us all to be fugitives and very miserable. But while you shuffle together things disjoined and contrary, and dally, as your manner is, with the plain equivocation, the absurdity which you thought to throw against us is lighted upon your own head. The Revelation of Saint John.[12]

The Meaning of the Ten Horns. John Napier: Now we have to try, what these ten horns do mean: First by Daniel 7:24 and Revelation 17:12 these are ten kings. Second, their kingdoms must be part of the Roman beast, and fourth monarchy, as both appear . . . as also, because that whole ten-horned beast, meaning the whole Roman Empire . . . What else can the parts of that beast signify, than parts of that empire, and consequently the ten crowned horns of the beast, ten kings and kingdoms out of the empire? Third, by verse 12, hereof, and note following, it appears that these ten kings arose when the Roman government by emperors decayed, and when the pope began to claim temporal dignities, which all occurred between the 300 and 450 years of Christ . . . and approved histories. Fourth, by Revelation 17:13, 15 it appears that these shall be of one religion, and shall therefore authorize and give their power and assistance to the beast, that next governed that Roman seat, even to the pope (the emperors then

[10]Bibliander, *Omnium*, 155-56.

[11]Bibliander, *Omnium*, 144.

[12]Thomas Brightman, *A revelation of the Apocalyps, that is, the Apocalyps of S. John illustrated with an analysis & scolions where the sense is opened by the scripture, & the events of things foretold, shewed by histories* (Amsterdam: Judocus Honius and Hendrick Laurenss, 1611), 571.

being decayed). Fifth, though (as is said) these ten horns came at once with that papistical beast and little antichristian horn, yet they rose first to their kingdoms before this papistical horn rose to his monarchy, and then he suppressed three of them, which testifies . . . , saying, *Another* (even that antichrist) *shall rise up after them* (to wit after these ten kings) *and he shall subdue three kings*, and so the antichrist that comes at one time with them, rises not to an established monarchy until after their rising, yea, until three of them were fallen: for the term in the original Hebrew or Chaldee does not mean there of his first coming or simply beginning to rise, but of his establishing or confirming of his rising: for the same term that here is put for this rising, is expressly put in . . . diverse other places, for establishing and confirming. So by these notes, these ten appear to be the kings of Spain, France, Lombardy, England, Scotland, Denmark, Sweden, the Hunnes or Hungarians in Pannonia now called Hungary, the Goths in Italy, and the Exarchate of Ravenna, all start up with the pope, between the 300th and 450th years of God. . . . And so apparently, remain only the said ten kingdoms to be chiefly the beast's ten horns, with which the pope's little horn and small kingdom coming at one time, was afterward confirmed and established by Pipin, Charlemagne, and Lodouicus Pius, and they arose it greatest of all. And by his craft, and means of his confederates, he suppressed the kingdoms of the Goths, Lombards, and Exarchate and brooks their lands within Italy to this day. But the other seven kings yet extant, with the people also of these three kingdoms, shall (God willing) one day repay that antichristian seat, with fire, sword, and utter destruction, as appears by Revelation 17:16 and other places of this book.

Here does the angel declare to us, by whom and after what manner the antichristian and idolatrous city of Rome shall be destroyed. The doers thereof shall be (says he) the same ten Christian kings, who before had maintained her. The manner of this destruction of Rome seems to be threefold. First (says the text) they shall hate her and leave her desolate: that is to say (as appears by Paul . . .). The truths of God's Word and holy gospel shall be first publicly preached, and by the majesty of the coming thereof, and two-edged sword of that holy Word, many of these ten Christian princes, their kindred, and people shall be converted from their antichristian and papistical superstitions, and shall hate the Roman seat, turn back from it, and leave it destitute of their assistance; and this is her first ruin. Second (says the text) *They shall eat her flesh*: that is, these ten Christian kings, who before had enriched her, and made her fat with great benefices, rents and daily casualities, now hating her, shall eat up these rents and rich benefices, and live on them themselves: and both these two ruins are already come, though not yet altogether perfected. Third and last (says the text) *they shall burn her with fire*: which appears not to be figuratively taken, but literally, as in the next chapter . . . by which it appears that, at length, princes shall make war against the very city of Rome, take it captive, spoil it, and finally, so burn it with fire, that it shall be waste forever. A Plain Discovery of the Whole Revelation of Saint John.[13]

The Adversaries of God. John Bale: These adversaries of God and his Word shall have much gladness in their wicked hearts, when they behold the beast thus coming up again that was of such magnificence, and now is nothing, that was esteemed above God, and now is proud damnation. So long is this beastly antichrist, as he works the mystery of iniquity in the reprobate vessels, and when he leaves that working then is he no longer. Mark in this process past the nature of God's eternal decree for this age of his church. First it shows and then it condemns the cursed synagogue of the devil. In signification whereof the true preachers of our time have manifestly opened their wickedness unto all the world, whereupon her utter

[13]Napier, *Reuelation*, 210-12, 215; citing Dan 7:7, 23-24; Rev 12:3; 13:1; 17:3-7; Dan 7:24; Job 22:8; 2 Chron 7:18; 2 Thess 2:8; Rev 14:6; 18:8-9, 16-18, 21.

destruction must shortly follow. Watch, good Christian reader, and pray earnestly. The Image of Both Churches.[14]

The Pope Comes in His Wicked Name. John Bale: And when this seventh king comes (says the text) he must continue a for a time, or abide a little season. He must have a time by the permission of God, strongly to delude the unbelievers, which will neither see nor hear, read nor yet thankfully receive, his word of salvation, so graciously offered them. So corrupt are the fleshly affects of men, that much more prone they are to lies and superstitions than to the truth of the Lord, which is to be lamented.

Christ came first in the name of his heavenly Father, but him will they not receive. The pope comes in his own wicked name and to him run they by heaps, whose continuance here has been but a time. For yet is it not a thousand years since the papacy first began under Phocas, which is but as a day before God, and that day will be shortened by his own promise for his elect's sake, which to remember is their great comfort. And a great cause is engaged. For soon after that, shall they be fully restored into the persight number of the children of God. The Image of Both Churches.[15]

The Marks of the True Church. John Downame: The papists make three notes of the visible church: antiquity, unity, universality, most fondly and ridiculously, when as all these are to be found in the malignant church, and in the most wicked assemblies and societies.

Errors have been ancient, as long as since the apostles' time: for even then the mystery of iniquity began to work, . . . and then there were many antichrists. . . .

These are as united among themselves, and so are the devils one with another, else their kingdom could not stand. . . . It is said that God put into their hearts, with one consent to give their kingdom to the beast.

As for universality, that is so far from being a certain badge of the true church, that contrariwise Paul tells us when antichrist shall be revealed, there must be a general apostasy and defection from the truth. . . . We read that all the world went wondering after the beast, and worshiping the beast and the dragon that gave him power. . . . That is how we say the church of God is catholic or universal, but in a far other sense than they mean by their universality which they intend of a general spreading of itself, without any great opposition to the contrary in beauty and much bravery, and multitudes of men glittering and shining in the world, whereas we say, the true church of Christ is catholic or universal, because it is not tied to any one particular place or country, as sometimes among the Jews it was, but in every nation God has those that fear him, and belong to his election. It is not always visible and to be seen with the eye, but members through faith of the true catholic and invisible church of Christ. Sum of Sacred Divinity.[16]

18:1-3 *The Bright Angel's Announcement*

Plundered by Its Own Protector. Martin Luther: In chapter 18 the destruction begins. The glorious and great splendor falls to the ground, and the courtiers—who rob endowments and steal livings—cease to be. For even Rome had to be plundered and stormed by its own protector at the outset of the final destruction. They keep trying; they encourage, arm, and defend themselves. Preface to the Revelation of Saint John.[17]

Rome Is the Seat of Antichrist. David Pareus: We now take in hand to expound the second act of the sixth vision, concerning the lamentable destruction of Babylon, the royal seat

[14]Bale, *Image**, ch. 17.
[15]Bale, *Image**, ch. 17.
[16]Downame, *Sacred Divinity**, 351; citing 2 Thess 2:7; 1 Jn 5:3; 2:13; Mt 12:25-26; Rev 17:17; 2 Thess 2:3; Rev 13:4.
[17]LW 35:408-9.

of antichrist, that is, of Rome. Of this (God is my witness) I speak not of human or evil affection against the pope of Rome, or as being led by a dark conjecture, but induced by this divine prophecy and the clear demonstration of the foregoing chapter.

The angel showed to John in the wilderness—instead of the woman, the chaste mother of the man-child, that is, the true church of Christ—a scarlet-colored woman, a whore drunken with the blood of the saints, sitting on the beast, that is, the adulterous antichristian church.

For Ribera† (though he denies it in Revelation 17) is forced in Revelation 19–20 (where the casting of the beast into the lake of fire is described) to confess that this beast denotes antichrist. Now the angel had plainly said before that the woman was the great city that in John's time had dominion over the kings of the earth, which could not be any other city but Rome. Of the same it was said that the ten kings sworn to the beast, who before had employed their power in defense of his kingdom (at length his abominations being discovered, and hating his fornication, God so governing their hearts), should detest the whore, forsake, uncover, eat her flesh, and burn her with fire. All of this considered, these things evidently follow.

First, that Rome is the seat of antichrist.

Second, that the pope of Rome is antichrist.

Third, that before the last judgment papal Rome shall be miserably burned and utterly overthrown.

The first: Where the purpled woman sits, there is antichrist's seat, because she sits on the beast, who is antichrist. The purple-colored woman sits at Rome, because she sits on the seven heads of the beast, which are the seven mountains of Rome. Rome therefore is the seat of antichrist. This deduction the adversaries can no longer deny, only they dally, as if Rome were not yet but should hereafter be the seat of antichrist, namely, when antichrist shall come, who, thrusting out the pope, shall possess Rome. This fiction has often before been refuted and overthrows itself. The fictions do not consist of that Rome should be the seat of antichrist, and that Rome before antichrist's coming should be burned by the ten kings, and that antichrist is to have his seat in the temple at Jerusalem.

The second: He who in the last times possesses Rome, the seat of antichrist, he is antichrist. The Romish pope now possesses Rome, antichrist's seat. Therefore, he is antichrist.

The third thus: Babylon the great city shall be destroyed before the last judgment, because after its desolation, there shall be godly and ungodly, rejoicing and lamenting at the destruction of it. Popish Rome is Babylon the great city. Therefore, popish Rome shall be destroyed before the last judgment. The Jesuits, seeing they cannot deny the assumption, would shift it off by their fiction that Rome as yet is not but will be Babylon hereafter; but in vain, as has appeared. Revelation 18 will illustrate this proposition, thus much of the coherence. A Commentary upon the Divine Revelation.[18]

The Fall of Rome. Heinrich Bullinger: He pursues throughout all of Revelation 18 the destruction of old and new Rome, also of heathenness and antichristianism, and that with a marvelously great amount and evidence of speech, even so that you would think that you saw all the thing presently. And he uses also a most godly order. For first the angel declares the destruction of Rome with most apt words. Second, counsel is given to the godly, how to behave themselves in so great dangers. Then is added the manner of the desolation, that as Rome has greedily and cruelly spoiled and destroyed other nations, even so it shall happen to her also. After this a lamentation is made, in which the princes and merchants mourn for the ruin of Rome, where they also recite the riches and pleasures of Rome. Finally, the apostles and prophets rejoice at the most just judgment of God. Again, the angel of the Lord casts a millstone into the bottom of the sea so that the most certain,

[18]Pareus, *Revelation**, 450-51. †Francisco Ribera (1537–1591) was a Spanish Jesuit theologian.

unrecoverable, and most weighty destruction of Rome might be represented. To this again are added the causes of so great evils, and the same finished with the praise and congratulation of all the heavenly dwellers.

And most luckily does he imitate the holy prophets of God. Two of them in a similar way describe the destruction of old Babylon. . . . For as the lot and end of all the ungodly is alike, so does the canonical Scripture in painting their destruction properly agree with itself. The apostles, moreover, although they spoke and wrote to the Gentiles in Greek, they did not alter anything of their natural phrase of speaking and even employed strange tongues to serve the holy and not the Hebrew to serve heathen languages. For, speaking Greek, they observed the natural phrase of the Hebrew speech as first, divine, and holy. And though they could speak all languages, they neither spoke nor wrote any foreign language but what in the same the Hebrew phrase might be perceived.

Let some therefore beware at this day that they not . . . follow the purity of the Latin speech so that in expressing the same, they fail in the meantime from the simplicity of the holy tongue and lose not a few ministries. Those who are not forward had rather go themselves to the holy language and learn the phrases of it than subdue the same against the ear to strange tongues and compel it to serve our delicate ears. Moreover, we have already stated oftentimes what is the end and use of this treatise concerning the judgments or punishments of God. For the truthfulness and justice of God is confirmed, the afflicted receive comfort, the wicked and all God's enemies are made afraid, and so on. Hundred Sermons on the Apocalypse.[19]

18:4-20 *The Voice from Heaven*

Strong Is the Lord God Who Shall Judge Her. Heinrich Bullinger: And he has meddled with the causes of subversion, cruelty, covetousness, extortions, slaughters, burnings with which Rome has made desolate the whole world. But he proceeded more expressly to recite other causes: namely, pride, glorying and boasting, security, riot, pleasures and voluptuousness. For it follows as much as she has glorified herself, lived wantonly, and so on. And again, for in her heart she says, "I sit as a queen," and so on. He has borrowed these things also out of Isaiah 47, where Babylon gloried thus also and with so many words. Rome in times past gloried herself to be lady of the world and that she should be everlasting. For they stamped in silver coins of Rome eternal. They had thought that the kingdoms should never have been plucked from her. She thought therefore that she should never have been a widow. And I do not doubt the Germans borrowed from the Romans that German word *Roman*, by which they mean "to boast or brag stoutly," which seem to have been particular and proper to the Romans. She was careless or insecure. She had not thought to have been subverted. She said, "I shall see no mourning, I will have no mourning cheer, I will always sing *Gaudeamus*."

The Romanists at this day also full bravely make their boast that no emperors, no kings, no people, no heretics and schismatics (for so they term the enemies of the Romish wickedness, godly and learned men) have yet luckily assailed Rome. The enemies of the church of Rome have always been oppressed, and she has always triumphed over her enemies these seven or eight hundred years and more. The ship of St. Peter may be greatly agitated, tossed, and overwhelmed with waves and billows but cannot be drowned, and therefore that the see of Rome shall be perpetual queen and lady of all realms and churches and so on.

But hear now the judgment of God: for as much as she is proud, vainglorious, careless, and wicked, in one day shall come her plagues. Aretas[†] notes that by "one day" is signified a sudden destruction and that she should then perish when she would have thought not. And her plagues he recites in order, death, mourning, famine, and fire. And stories testify that these things were by the Goths

[19]Bullinger, *Hundred Sermons** (1561), 533-34; citing Is 13–14; 21; Jer 50–51; Ezek 26–28.

fulfilled accordingly in old Rome, of which I have spoken before.

Therefore, we doubt nothing at all but that new Rome also shall, by people and by God's angels, be torn asunder and plucked up by the roots. And lest anyone should think this impossible (for great is the power and majesty of either Rome, inasmuch that one who had said in St. John's time that Rome shall fall would have seemed to have spoken a thing as impossible as if he had said the sky shall fall), he adds without restraint, "For strong is the Lord God who shall judge her." Therefore let us not doubt of the fall of papistry. For the Lord is true, just, and almighty. To him be glory for ever and ever. Amen. Hundred Sermons on the Apocalypse.[20]

The Lamentation of Rome. Heinrich Bullinger: In the fourth part of this chapter follows the weeping or wailing or lamentation of Rome, burned and destroyed. The copy is plentiful and marvelous, by an evident hypotyposis[†] setting all things before our eyes. And our Lord God has always a familiar manner when he will evidently show before and fix in the hearts of all people the overthrow or destruction of a nation, kingdom, or city: he will command his prophets to sing an elegy, or lamentable song. And in such kind of lamentations not only is shown the subversion but also the causes of destruction, and the manner of desolation is rehearsed; the end also or use is declared, lest others be made like that nation and become partakers of the destruction. We have manifest examples in the writings of the Prophets, especially the lamentations of Jeremiah, and—which aligns better with this passage—the doleful ditty of Tyrus, song of Ezekiel. . . . And truly it appeared that St. John has borrowed many things from there.

There is nothing here to busy ourselves much about. The sum of all is this. Rome shall fall and perish utterly, and there should be nothing left, either of the empire or of that see, much less of the riches and pleasures. This was partly fulfilled in old Rome and partly shall be fulfilled in the new at the day of judgment.

Nevertheless, neither Christ himself nor the apostle is brought in, bewailing the subversion of Babylon, but wicked persons are induced, who are first to be considered. For they are kings and princes of the earth, merchants, or governors of ships or mariners, who have all committed whoredom with this prostitute and by her company have been made rich. And truly old Rome was furnished with the amenities of kings, and again, the presidents sent of them to govern provinces seemed to everyone to be kings and princes. And for as much as the riches of Rome were great and all states were wonderfully set a riot, the merchants there gained exceedingly much. . . . But when Rome, being destroyed, lay ruinous and the empire was rent in pieces, those whose profits and pleasure was lost could not but lament. Hundred Sermons on the Apocalypse.[21]

18:21-24 *The Angel with the Millstone*

Exhortation to Rejoice in the Fall of Babylon. Heinrich Bullinger: The angel of the Lord exhorted all the saints of heaven to rejoice for the overthrow of Babylon. And this rejoicing of saints is set against the wailing of the wicked. For as they lament for the causes of pleasures taken from them, so the saints rejoice over ungodliness oppressed and the glory of God revenged. We are truly forbidden in the Proverbs of Solomon, and in the doctrine of Christ and his apostles, to be glad of the calamities of our enemies, and neither should we say or do evil to our enemies. This is perpetual and commanded to all, never to be altered by any dispensation, but we must observe in the meantime that people do rejoice diverse ways. People are glad many times of the destruction of their enemies, and that of hatred and malice, which

[20]Bullinger, *Hundred Sermons** (1561), 545-47. †Arethas, archbishop of Caesarea (c. 850–c. 944), was possibly a pupil of the patriarch of Constantinople, Photius.

[21]Bullinger, *Hundred Sermons** (1561), 548-51; citing Ezek 27–28. †Sketch, model.

is not done without sin. Others are glad again of the calamities and plagues of the ungodly, yet bearing no malice toward those who are in this misery, to whom they would doubtless have wished a better state if they had been persuaded to turn. Rather, they rejoice over justice revenged and the godly delivered from the tyranny of the wicked.

Of this we read that the prophet said . . . , "The righteous shall rejoice when he shall see vengeance, he shall wash his feet in the blood of the ungodly" (namely, he shall purge his affections and evil manners when he sees the blood of the ungodly spilled, which he believed to be done for an example, lest we follow our evil affections and that our blood should be shed also of the most just God by his ministers). And one will say that truly there is a reward for the righteous, truly God judges the earth. Therefore are the righteous glad and rejoice when they see vengeance. And it is not said that they covet or wish for vengeance. "Vengeance is mine, says the Lord, I will reward." When the Lord therefore rewarded, they are glad for the deliverance and for the truth established and confirmed, and rejoice not from hatred toward the oppressors, whom they have wished lost and destroyed.

The godly wishes evermore the wicked to be converted and to return to favor with God. But when they see them moved with no repentance but obstinately to proceed and fall into their own destruction, and that God does intercept them for the salvation of the faithful and deliverance of the godly, the godly rejoice at this deliverance and praise the justice of God. Notwithstanding that they had always preferred, if it might have been, that the lost had otherwise led their life, but now since it cannot be otherwise, through their own obstinate malice, they do not speak against the judgments of God but rather command the same. These things the saints on earth truly do.

And the saints in heaven, since they are purified now from all affections, their rejoicing is altogether most pure, so that it would be superfluous to be curious about it. But where the heavenly rejoice at the destruction of the wicked, we may easily judge how much those who trust to the help or prayers of saints err. By these they alter nothing at all of their wicked life. It shall be easy also to discuss the doubt and carefulness of those who fear lest they should be sorry also, seeing their brethren, sisters, friends and kinsfolk condemned. For the saints do plainly consent to the will of God and extol the judgments of God and rejoice in them and can be sorry no more. Hundred Sermons on the Apocalypse.[22]

19:1-8 *The Rejoicing of Heaven and Earth*

The Word of God Wins. Martin Luther: He says here in chapter 19, when they can do nothing more with the Scriptures and scrolls, and when the frogs have croaked themselves out, then they take hold in earnest, try to win by use of force, gathering kings and princes for the battle. But they stumble, for the one on the white horse, the one called the Word of God, wins; both beast and [false] prophet are captured and thrown into hell. Preface to the Revelation of Saint John.[23]

The Jubilee of Saints. Heinrich Bullinger: For as much as the apostle in this book most plentifully has described the oppression of saints and the cruel, mischievous, and proud assaults of the persecutors of the gospel—by which they both mock God and torment his saints, as a result of which we read that the complaints even of the godly rise evermore at all times, as though God through his longsuffering and great patience should seem to neglect the oppressed—he speaks most greatly now of the rejoicings and praises of saints, by which they extol the virtue and justice of God, never neglecting those who are his and most grievously punishing the ungodly persecutors. Nevertheless, they rejoice here chiefly and praise God for the taking away of antichrist and all ungodliness with him.

This truly is the first part of this chapter. The second confirmed all saints, lest they should doubt

[22]Bullinger, *Hundred Sermons** (1561), 553-54; citing Ps 58.
[23]LW 35:409.

anything of the salvation of the faithful, which he showed to be most certain. The third part recited the sin of blessed John and the faithful doctrine of the holy angel, that we should worship no creatures, be they ever so holy. In the last part is described the judge or revenger Jesus Christ coming to judgment. There is moreover described the perdition or punishment of all ungodly, which the just and holy Lord gives to them. This point is now at last finished, truly appearing in Revelation 11 and suspended, and up to this point repeated somewhat in Revelation.

And truly the jubilee of saints is diverse, plentiful, and manifold over the lost and condemned enemies of the godly. First he hears a voice, a great voice, of many people in heaven. He showed therefore in general that all those in heaven (the angels not excepted) sing praises to God in heaven. We understand this to be at the last judgment, with all ungodly trodden underfoot. And before these things are done they are rehearsed and described, that by this the godly may comfort themselves in dangers and torments and may abide steadfast in the true saying, believing that they also, though now oppressed, shall sing praises of thanks to God.

And truly he has here compiled the whole hymn said in the praise of God the revenger. He placed foremost "Alleluia"; after he added the praises, "Salutation and glory," and so on. And *Alleluia* means "praise the Lord." He uses a most common word and by all people best known in the primitive church. For certain psalms have this title, *Hallelujah*. For the chanter so exhorted and stirred up the people to praise God. Hundred Sermons on the Apocalypse.[24]

Blessed Are Those Invited to the Marriage of the Lamb. Heinrich Bullinger: The second part of this chapter is of the certainty of the salvation of the faithful, where it is signified when, how, and in what manner is the blessing of the faithful. For there is said enough already of the marriage of the Lamb, that is to say, of the glory and blessing of the chosen, but many things are suggested to people in this life that bring salvation in doubt and go about, as it were, to make it uncertain, and therefore wavering minds are here now confirmed. This doctrine is profitable for afflicted and troubled consciences, and overthrows and batters down the doctrine of sophists, affirming that people are never assured of their salvation, for in another place the wise man says, "Man knows not whether he is worthy of love or hatred." . . .

Therefore at this present it is shown that the salvation of the faithful is most certain. For first the angel commanded the Evangelist to write. This is taken of the manner of humanity, who put in writing their testaments, covenants, and bargains and then sealed them for the cause of credit and for a perpetual memorial of the thing. Hundred Sermons on the Apocalypse.[25]

19:9-10 *John and the Angel*

Worship God Alone. Heinrich Bullinger: Here is added the third part of this chapter, namely, the doings of the apostle St. John and the angel of God. St. John would have worshiped the angel, but he is prohibited by the angel, who bids him worship God. And before all this the act and enterprise of John seem chiefly to be considered. Angels are surely noble creatures and of great power, by whom the Lord executes greatest affairs. They take on for the most part the shape of humans and very often appear to people to serve, keep, and do good to them, accordingly as God used their ministries. For the apostle speaking of angels . . . "Are they not all," he says, "ministering spirits who are sent forth to serve for the sakes of those who shall be made heirs of salvation?"

And these things the Scripture makes plain by many examples. Three appeared to Abraham in man's likeness, who were angels instructing him; two delivered Lot himself out of the hands of the Sodomites and brought him out of the fire; whole

[24]Bullinger, *Hundred Sermons** (1561), 558-60.

[25]Bullinger, *Hundred Sermons** (1561), 566-67.

armies of angels protecting Jacob, defending him against the force and violence of his brother, Esau. The Lord sent his angel before Moses and the children of Israel to lead them through the wilderness into the land of promise. Fiery chariots circled around Elijah. An angel levied the siege of Jerusalem, slaying 185,000 of the Assyrians. Daniel has angels familiar with him, and likewise the fathers and other prophets. An angel delivered Joseph out of all care; the same delivered the wise men from the treason of Herod; after a while he commanded to convey Christ away into Egypt; angels minister to Christ; in white garments they testified that the Lord was risen and ascended into heaven. They bring the apostles out of prison, and one of them delivered Peter out of Herod's prison. An angel is sent to Cornelius, a Roman captain. Angels many times talk with Paul. Oftentimes they apply great benefits to people. They declare themselves through God to be of great power.

And as people observe those things, they would worship angels, as even at this present, where the apostle St. John understood that Christ himself by his angel did open to him so great mysteries for the profit of churches. While he marveled at his brightness and godly gifts, he would soon have worshiped this his angel the bringer of mysteries—not that he intended or purposed to revolt from God and coveted instead of God to worship an angel, for is it not lawful to imagine such a wickedness of so great an apostle. He would therefore have worshiped and honored the angel with *douleia*, as they term it (and as Thomas Aquinas expounded it), not with *latreia*, that is to say, to worship and honor God as God, but the angel somewhat less as an excellent messenger of God.

Nevertheless, in this he offended to the end that all people who worship and honor angels or excellent creatures with godly worship should understand that they sin, as all the worshipers of saints do at this day in papistry. They do not have any other way to color their error but that same distinction—that God is worshiped and honored with worship lateral, and saints and angels with worship dulcian, and the virgin Mary with honor *hyperdulia*—and I do not write what else, because I am both ashamed and loath to rehearse them. Hundred Sermons on the Apocalypse.[26]

[26]Bullinger, *Hundred Sermons** (1561), 569-73.

19:11-21 The Battle and the White Horse

*11 Then I saw heaven opened, and behold, a white
horse! The one sitting on it is called Faithful and
True, and in righteousness he judges and makes war.
12 His eyes are like a flame of fire, and on his head are
many diadems, and he has a name written that no
one knows but himself. 13 He is clothed in a robe
dipped in[a] blood, and the name by which he is called
is The Word of God. 14 And the armies of heaven,
arrayed in fine linen, white and pure, were following
him on white horses. 15 From his mouth comes a sharp
sword with which to strike down the nations, and he
will rule[b] them with a rod of iron. He will tread the
winepress of the fury of the wrath of God the
Almighty. 16 On his robe and on his thigh he has a
name written, King of kings and Lord of lords.*

*17 Then I saw an angel standing in the sun, and
with a loud voice he called to all the birds that fly
directly overhead, "Come, gather for the great
supper of God, 18 to eat the flesh of kings, the flesh of
captains, the flesh of mighty men, the flesh of horses
and their riders, and the flesh of all men, both free
and slave,[c] both small and great." 19 And I saw the
beast and the kings of the earth with their armies
gathered to make war against him who was sitting
on the horse and against his army. 20 And the beast
was captured, and with it the false prophet who in
its presence[d] had done the signs by which he
deceived those who had received the mark of the
beast and those who worshiped its image. These two
were thrown alive into the lake of fire that burns
with sulfur. 21 And the rest were slain by the sword
that came from the mouth of him who was sitting
on the horse, and all the birds were gorged with
their flesh.*

a Some manuscripts *sprinkled with* **b** Greek *shepherd* **c** For the contextual rendering of the Greek word *doulos*, see Preface **d** Or *on its behalf*

Overview: After the rejoicing at the wedding feast of the Lamb and his bride, the text becomes filled with the thrall of battle. Mary Cary, a follower of Thomas Brightman and Henry Archer, believed in the impending return of Christ to establish God's kingdom on earth in 1701. With the exception of Thomas Müntzer, for these commentators the characters and imagery seem to be wholly derivatives of Reformed inheritance.

The rider of the white horse is described, called Faithful and True, as Cary writes in her vision of the general. Furthermore, his eyes are sharp, piercing all things, and on his head are many crowns. On his thigh are the words "King of kings and Lord of lords," which John Bale says is an expression of the fury of the wrath of God Almighty. While some commentators argue that the riders here and at the start of Revelation 6 both depict Jesus, the differences between the riders would seem to indicate otherwise. Bullinger writes of this rider on the white horse as Christ in his coming in glory.

A great multitude celebrates the defeat and destruction of the beast and his followers while looking to the future, to a perfected union of Christ and his bride, the church. From Revelation 19:11–20:15 come in rapid succession seven visions preparatory to the end. Each begins with "I saw." All souls are called to the slaughter and feast.

19:11-16 *The Mounted General: The Rider on the White Horse and Judgment*

Faithful and True. Thomas Brightman: We may not suppose that Christ shall come forth in any visible shape. These things are far from his last coming, as those things that follow will manifest, but he will show forth openly and evidently such a force in the administration of things, as this image represents.

The whole description consisted of four parts. In every one of them the preparation and name should be considered. In this first part the furnishing is a white horse, the name Faithful and True. The similarity of these things with that in Revelation 6:2 has caused some to think this to be the same vision, by which error they confound all things. They differ much in time and in argument. That white horse belongs to the first lists, but this to the last goal. That former went forth a while later after John, when Trajan flourished and his next successors. This last is not seen except after the destruction of Rome. There the confused multitude of all the believers was in view. Here the conversion of the nation of the Jews only is spoken of. Yet in this they agree, that the white horse in both places signifies Christ triumphing by his truth, but then the Gentiles being subdued, now at length a stubborn people being reconciled unto him.

To this thing he carried a suitable name, by which he showed that he will now at last manifest to the whole world how faithful and true he is in performing his promises, and that nothing even the least shall be prevented that he once foreshowed by the prophets concerning the restoring of this nation in the last times. Such a one therefore shall Christ be, notable by these marks, when he shall begin the conversion of this people. His promise shall seem to have been forgotten through long delay, and at length he shall perform them with most plentiful increase of new joy. Revelation of St. John.[1]

Eyes Piercing All Things. Thomas Brightman: The second part of the description: where his eyes are, as it were, a flame of fire, and on his head are many crowns, but a name unknown to all except to himself alone. As touching his eyes, they are most sharp, piercing all things, which as flames of fire consume whatever they see, make light the darkness itself, and set most hidden things in the light. What can hide itself from such eyes? Such a one shall Christ show himself to be in drawing out his people into the light of truth from the hidden dens and darkness wherever they lurked, so that this sharpness of sight shall be very admirable to the world. "I will say to the north," says the Lord, "give, and to the south, do not keep back, bring my sons from afar, and my daughters from the ends of the earth." . . .

The crowns are many because of the many singular victories the Jews shall get when first they shall give their name to Christ from those sundry nations among which they live dispersed, striving as much as they can against their conversion. But why is his name unknown? That here we may know that great mystery where Paul cried out, "O the deepness of the riches both of the wisdom and knowledge of God! How unsearchable are his judgments, and his ways past finding out." . . . There he speaks of this same thing, of the hardening of the Jews for a time, and calling at length in their time. This whole matter he concludes with an admiration of God's wisdom, affirming that no cleverness of any creature can comprehend the infiniteness of the mystery. So, this vision foreshowing the calling of the Jews, a certain choice and separation of an elect people from others who after the fullness of the Gentiles shall come in, presented Christ likewise with an unknown name, because no creature can by any reasoning conceive the exceeding greatness of this judgment and mercy.

Let us therefore reverence this name, which because of the its highnesses must be hidden from every creature. Only let us observe the congruency of things, that the conversion of the Jews comes from the unsearchable wisdom of God as likewise the rejection of them and receiving of the Gentiles. Revelation of St. John.[2]

The Mounted General. Heinrich Bullinger: Our judge comes on horseback, and that on a white horse—not that he needed the help of corruptible horses in heaven, but thus he speaks after the manner of humanity, that we might

[1]Brightman, *Revelation**, 634.

[2]Brightman, *Revelation**, 635-36; citing Is 43:6; Rom 11:33.

imagine greater things. Conquerors ride on white horses. Here is meant therefore that our judge shall be a conqueror and a triumpher. Others suppose the white horse to represent his most pure humanity. I understand the white cloud, for the same took him up from the eyes of his disciples, at which time he ascended into heaven from Mount Olivet. In the same he shall come again to judge. And as kings are carried on horses and chariots, so the psalmist ascribes to God clouds as horses and chariot.

To the judge is added an army, not of angels only, with whom he often repeated in the Gospel that he would come to judgment, but of all the faithful, or saints, which at no time, including here, are sequestered from their head. For at the first sound of the trumpet blow of the archangel, the saints arise, and the living also with the dead are changed and are taken up to meet Christ in the air. Here, here, in the clouds and bright air, the happy and blessed victorious appear with Christ. By and by the ungodly rise also, and those who lived at that day are changed with those who rise again, to pain and confusion. But they see the saints with Christ in heaven and in glory, and feel unlimited, unspeakable torments. The things described in . . . the Wisdom of Solomon doubtless come to pass and are fulfilled.

Saint John therefore says that this army is in heaven, not on earth. He says how they follow Christ. For the same said the apostle also. . . . Moreover, he added that they were clothed and appeared not naked, and he described the kind of garment. They were clothed (he says) in silk, white and clean. For saints in Christ obtain righteousness and glory, are made clean, and are glorified. And this sense Saint John himself has a little before explained to us, saying that silk is the justification of saints.

Out of the judge's mouth proceeds a two-edged and sharp sword, which cuts on either side. It is not sharp on one side and blunt on another; it cuts on both sides indifferently. This represents a just sentence pronounced of God's mouth against the wicked. For against them the sentence of God is a sword, piercing even to their hearts. Therefore it is also called sharp. The judgment of our judge is straight and severe but just and righteous. It is declared in the Gospel what that sword is: truly, that heavy and immutable sentence you get from there into fire everlasting. . . . By this it followed in the words of the Evangelist, that with the same he may strike the heathen, namely, that he may damn and put to perpetual torments all unbelievers.

And he shall rule them with a rod of iron. By the same kind of figure of speech he says the same that he said before. For those who would not receive or acknowledge with repentance the staff of instruction and pastoral discipline shall find in judgment and feel the iron scepter, by which he shall break them all to shards, like potter's vessel. No power shall resist or prevail against him. And this manner of speaking is taken out of the psalm. For Saint John uses gladly the words of Scripture to the end to make his book more commendable or more pleasant and acceptable.

"He treaded the winepress of the wine of wrath," and so on. Again he says the same that he did before but by another parable now uttered and taken out of the Scriptures. . . . The effect is that he will pour out his wrath on the ungodly and punish them most extremely with his almighty hand, to which all things give place, giving their heads a blow. . . .

Again is showed the name of this judge, and in the name is majesty and power, the greatest of all. He has the name written on his garment and on his thigh. By these is declared the true humanity of Christ, after which he is exalted, as the apostle said. . . . And to him is given a name that is above all names. Here he is called King of kings, and Lord of lords, very God, Lord, monarch, and judge of all people. For so do the other apostles speak also. . . . And there might seem in this name of the Judge, as it were, a cause to be showed why he is here appointed judge over all—because he is King and Lord of all. To him be glory forever. Amen. Hundred Sermons on the Apocalypse.[3]

[3]Bullinger, *Hundred Sermons** (1561), 577-81; citing Wis 3; 5; 1 Thess 4; Mt 25; Ps 110; Is 63; Rev 14; Phil 2; Acts 2; 17.

His Name Includes the Elect. John Bale: The eyes of this horseman were as the pure flame of fire, effectual, mighty, and clear. And these are not only his godly understanding and knowledge, by which he perceives, discerns, and judges clearly all things, but also the universal graces of the Holy Spirit. "Upon one sure stone," says Zechariah (whom Paul calls Christ), "shall be seven eyes, which are the seven spirits of God." With these eyes he lightens the hearts of godly people and kindles their minds to the true love of God. His words are a lantern to their feet and a light to their paths. Pure is his commandment, giving all worlds, regions, and ages. For he is the Lord of hosts and the eternal king of glory; he was constituted a principal governor of Zion, the holy hill of the Lord. He gives prosperity to kings and has their victory in his hands. In him as in their head all his elect members have their crowns. He shall crown them with both mercy and loving-kindnesses. For Peter, he has laid up a crown of incorruptible glory; for John, a crown of life; for Paul, a crown of righteousness; and so forth. For the whole conflict, victory, and triumph of the saints is his alone.

He had a special name written or eternally appointed by God his Father, whose excellent majesty no creature who understands was able of their own industry to comprehend. Omnipotent was this name, marvelous, honorable, holy, and terrible, Adonai, Immanuel, a name of salvation, and a name above all names. Indeed, the Lord was his name, or the Lord our Righteous Maker.

No one knows this name but he alone and those to whom he has showed it. Neither flesh nor blood, Gentile nor Jew, hypocrite nor false Christian, has rightly known it. No, though they have said, "Lord, Lord." For none can say that Jesus is the Lord but in the Holy Spirit, who opened all godly truth. In this name is registered the elect number of God's adopted children, whom the world does not know for his and never will. The Image of Both Churches.[4]

Righteous Are You, O Lord. Mary Cary: The first general is described by his name, by his frame, and by his aim.

First, by his name. And he is called Faithful and True, and his name is called the Word of God, and he has a name written, "King of kings, and Lord of lords." And this is the name and title of the Lord Jesus Christ alone.

But second, he is described also by his frame and the posture he is in. Thus he sat upon a white horse, which manifests his purity. And his eyes were as a flame of fire, which shows the piercing, discerning nature of them, being the searcher of hearts and trier of the reins. And on his head are many crowns, which shows that all the crowns of all kingdoms must be put on his head, he who is King of kings and Lord of lords. And this is the frame and posture in which he is.

But third, he is described also by his aim, that in righteousness he judges and makes war. He aims at doing justice, making war against the beast and judging that other army according to righteousness. And that he may so do, his aim is to give them blood to drink, and that in righteousness, for they are worthy, and therefore he is said to be clothed in apparel dipped in blood, and out of his mouth goes a sharp sword, that with it he should smite the nations. Out of his mouth it goes, that is, he commanded with the word of his mouth a sharp sword to smite the nations, and this justly. And his aim is to rule the nations with a rod of iron, and this in righteousness, and to tread the winepress of the fierceness of the wrath of Almighty God. And in all this may it be said to him, "Righteous are you, O Lord, who has judged thus." The Little Horn's Doom and Downfall.[5]

Providential, Spiritual, and Monarchical Kingdom. John (Henry) Archer: The Scripture reveals to us a threefold state of Christ's kingdom. One providential, which is that universal influence and sovereign power by which Jesus Christ manages the affairs of all the world, in

[4]Bale, *Image** (1570), ch. 19.

[5]Cary, *Doom**, 179-80.

heaven, on earth, and under the earth. . . . The field that is the world is called by Christ his kingdom, from which it is that he enlightened every one who comes into the world. . . . For ever since the fall of humankind, the immediate dispensation and government of all things is delegated to him from the Father, so that he is deputed as viceroy or immediate administrator of all things. . . .

A second state of Christ's kingdom is spiritual, which is that sovereignty that by his Word and Spirit he exercises over the consciences of some people, and especially the elect of God the Father, whom by his Word and Spirit he subdues in conscience to an universal obedience to him. . . . But this is not general over all the world, and respecting this, Christ says his kingdom is not of this world and that the kingdom of God is not by observation, that is, after a worldly pomp and honor. . . . And this state of his kingdom was more narrow and obscure till Christ's coming in the flesh and the preaching of the gospel to every creature. . . . And many worthy ones have thought, and many do to this day think, that this is the only state of Christ's kingdom, and therefore appropriate and apply all that is said of his kingdom in Scripture to this state of it. . . .

But they have a further sense, as there is (besides this) a third state of Christ's kingdom, which I may call monarchical. . . . I call this last state of his monarchical because in this, when he has entered into it, he will govern as earthly monarchs have done, that is, universally over the world (in those days known and esteemed) and in a worldly, visible, earthly glory; not by tyranny, oppression, and sensually, but with honor, peace, riches, and whatever in and of the world is not sinful, having all nations and kingdoms doing homage to him, as the great monarchies of the world had. . . .

Of this God gave us a type in the government of the nation of Israel from the time he called them out of Egypt until they desired a king and cast off their judges. . . . [Christ] was an immediate and particular king to them, and was visibly present among them in signs and indications of presence, such as the pillar of the cloud and fire, and after that in the tabernacle, ark, mercy seat, and so on. And he manifestly gave them laws, appearing as a consuming fire, . . . and appointed officers to administer the kingdom, both ordinary and extraordinary, . . . and appointed their generals for wars . . . so that in every way Christ was a monarch and king to Israel.

Therefore indeed when they refused judges and wanted a king like other nations, they cast off him; yet notwithstanding, after he had punished them by one king, namely, Saul, he gave them a king also for a type and shadow of that which he himself did before. For as the nation of Israel in their Mosaic discipline and liturgy was but a type of the nations of the world, whom in a moral way God will bring to be a people to Christ (among whom the Israelites as a firstborn shall be chief), so Christ's government of that nation . . . was a shadow or type of his state of monarchical government, which in due time he will have immediately and visibly over all nations on the earth. Therefore the Israelite kings could not be deposed by people because they were not set up by people, and ruled so absolutely because they ruled by commission immediately from Christ and as types of that his monarchical rule, which in the latter days he means to take up over all the world. THE PERSONAL REIGN OF CHRIST ON EARTH.[6]

JESUS CHRIST WILL REIGN PERSONALLY ON EARTH. MARY CARY: In the first place I shall speak of the personal appearance of Jesus Christ and the resurrection of his saints to reign on earth with him. That Christ shall personally appear is a point that is, I know, much debated and is very much doubted by many saints who are eminently godly and whom I do very much honor and reverence, who yet are confident that he will very gloriously appear in the treading down of his enemies, in the ruining of the beast, and the settling

[6]Archer, *Personal Reign** (1642), 1-4; citing Mt 18:18; 13; Jn 1:9; Acts 2:36; 2 Cor 10:4-5; Rev 21:2, 4-5; 2 Cor 5:17; Ps 33:10-11; Rom 9:15; Phil 2:13; Deut 33:5; Ex 24:17.

of his people in peace, and filling of them with his Spirit; but they question whether our Lord Jesus shall otherwise appear than to their spiritual eyes, and then as now, for now they spiritually discern him in his present footsteps in the world. And it being thus dubious to many, I was inclining to be silent in it, but the light shining so clearly to me in the following Scriptures that I shall mention has such power and force with me that I cannot but hold it forth, leaving it to the more serious consideration of intelligent Christians.

And the position that I shall lay down is this: that our Lord Jesus Christ, having subdued his enemies, shall personally appear on earth and shall raise up the saints who before departed out of this world to come and reign with him on earth. To prove this, we have several Scriptures, and I shall begin first with that known clear place . . . : the description of the total overthrow of the beast and all the armies that were gathered together with him to make war against Jesus Christ and his saints, being laid down in the preceding chapter. In this chapter follows a declaration of what things will succeed it. . . . In these verses is laid down that the saints of God who had been martyrs and sufferers under the beast should be raised from the dead and be advanced to sit on thrones, and judgment should be given unto them, and they shall live and reign with Christ a thousand years.

But though the saints will be thus raised, yet this is not the general resurrection, in which all the just and unjust shall be raised. No, for the text expressly says that the rest of the dead were not raised until this thousand years were finished, and therefore this resurrection that shall be when Christ and his saints must reign on earth is called the first resurrection. And it is said that no wicked one shall have a part in it, but only those who are holy and blessed and who shall never die the second death but shall be priests of God and of Christ, and shall reign with him a thousand years, and others are not to be raised until the end of the thousand years. The Little Horn's Doom and Downfall.[7]

[7]Cary, *Doom**, 212-15.

19:17-21 *The Grim Invitation and Its Outcome*

Last Judgment. Heinrich Bullinger:

> This is the last judgment.
> Apostolic certainty of such.
> That day is known to no one.
> The heavens are opened.
> He comes on a white horse.
> He is faithful and true.
> His eyes are aflame.
> He has a name that no one knows.
> His garment is sprinkled with blood.
> The name of the judge is the Word.

Hundred Sermons on the Apocalypse.[8]

The Stony-Hearted Will Face the Lake of Fire. Thomas Müntzer: There is no surer testimony to authenticate the Bible than the living speech of God when the Father addresses the Son in the heart of man. This Scripture can be read by all elect men, who seek interest in their talents. But the damned will surely fail to do that; their heart is harder than a pebble, from which the master's chisel always slides off. That is why they are called stony by our dear Lord; the seed that falls there bears no fruit, although they welcome the dead word with joy, with great joy and praise. There are, by my soul, others, apart from students and priests and monks, who welcome bookish truth with warm flattery and pomp, but when God wants to write something in their hearts there is no people under the sun which is more opposed to the living Word of God than they are. Nor do they suffer any trials of faith in the spirit of the fear of God; for they are dispatched into the lake where the false prophets will be tormented with antichrist from generation to generation, amen. A Protestation Concerning the Situation in Bohemia.[9]

A Triumph, Not a Battle. Thomas Brightman: The army seemed to be outfitted not so

[8]Bullinger, *Hundred Sermons** (1561), 581.
[9]Müntzer, *Collected Works*, 365-66.

much for battle as for triumph. For what are white horses to war? What fine white and pure linen? A helmet and armor would be more suitable. . . . A triumph is set forth, not a battle, for the enemies in the west and east being at length destroyed in that recent aforementioned war, a glorious peace shall be restored to the church, which no tumultuous noise of troubles shall ever after interrupt. Then all the children of God shall keep a perpetual triumph, all things being removed forever that might procure any trouble, as shall be made more clear from the things following.

"Who are in heaven": The citizens of the holy church on earth, all of them making one sheepfold, shall follow one shepherd, Christ. They are clothed with white and pure fine linen. . . .

"And out of his mouth went": The victory once gotten shall be preserved forever. Neither shall there be any fear of war beginning again, our Captain being so furnished that he will restrain the subdued enemies at his pleasure, for the sword coming out of his mouth shall punish them forthwith, as before he threatened to those of Pergamum that he would fight against them with the Spirit of his mouth. . . . By this is signified that either the enemies shall be destroyed according to the judgment of the sacred Word, the punishment being taken by them that the Word has appointed against them; or at the least they shall be brought to that case that they will—no, they shall—obey those laws the Word will prescribe. This latter seemed to agree better to this place, when all nations shall be obedient to the church, seeking and receiving from it laws and ordinances by which they may be governed. These therefore shall be smitten after this manner.

But if any yet, being stubborn, shall refuse to obey, they shall be subdued with a rod of iron and shall be bridled by a rigorous government; but if they continue in his obstinacy, they will not suffer themselves to be overcome and bowed by an ordinary way, although many together shall conspire to the same wickedness of rebellion. They shall be cast as clusters of grapes into the winepress of the fierceness of God. . . . Therefore the enemies shall have no power ever to rise up again; now of necessity the yoke must be borne by them forever. REVELATION OF ST. JOHN.[10]

HOW CHRIST EXERCISES JUDGMENT. HEINRICH BULLINGER: Immediately after the description of the Judge and a certain lively picture, a description no less clear follows of the judgment, that is to say, how Christ, having vanquished his enemies, committed them to perpetual torments. And the apostle uses prophetic phrases and eloquence. For by figurative speech all souls are called to the slaughter and feast that they might be filled with the flesh of the slain. . . . Again, an allusion is made to the murder and slaughter of enemies, by which wild beasts and ravening birds are filled. There is nothing hereby signified but that Christ shall overthrow all the ungodly and punish them. Before was set forth a supper for the godly, by which they are refreshed and fulfilled. Now is prepared a feast of the solemn slaughter, whereby the ungodly receive no commodity, and neither are they satisfied, but rather are slain and devoured, that is to say, perish.

For no one will imagine that the wicked shall be overthrown at once, and after, wearied of wild beasts and gnawing of birds, so all punishment makes an end. For so should their pain seem to be none at all. But by temporal parables, eternal things are figured. These are taken out of the prophets . . . where it is written in a manner that wars, destructions, and other torments, as it were, killed them, . . . when at the last judgment he commits them to pains everlasting. HUNDRED SERMONS ON THE APOCALYPSE.[11]

ARMAGEDDON. THOMAS BRIGHTMAN: "But the beast was taken": Up to this point has been the declaration of the sixth vial; that of the last followed, which first teaches the destruction of the enemies and in the first place of the beast and his armies. The beast is taken, entrapped, as it were,

[10]Brightman, *Revelation**, 637-38; citing Rev 2:16; Is 63; Lam 1:15.
[11]Bullinger, *Hundred Sermons** (1561), 582-83; citing Is 66; Ezek 39.

with sudden snares, as wild beasts that unawares fall into the nets. For so the word *epistle* seemed to note. And we know that the Lord does rain down snares on the wicked, . . . by which their feet are taken there. . . .

The false prophet is taken together with him, and the two joined together show that the pope of Rome (for he shall retain this name perhaps after the city is destroyed) shall at length utterly perish, both in respect to the civil power by which he is the beast and to the spiritual by which he is the false prophet. The Spirit speaks as of two distinct persons because of that twofold wickedness by which that man of sin is famous, but when I say the pope of Rome, I do not only mean that particular man who then will sit in the chair but also the very state and order of popes, which now wholly shall come to naught, such that no remainders of it shall be left. Only a certain hated memory shall continue, that his impiety has been the cause of the ruin of so many.

"Who wrought miracles": Before there was mention of the false prophet . . . but because there was only a bare name, that it might be unknown to no one whom he speaks of by this name, he describes the same here by certain descriptors that all doubt may be taken away. Who, says he, wrought miracles, by which he deceived those who receive the beast's mark and worshiped his image. By these things he showed most plainly that this false prophet is that second beast. . . . Therefore, let the papists—who will have antichrist to reign three and a half years before Christ shall come to the last judgment, and him to be a singular person—now see whether they proclaim open war against the truth.

All grant that either this second beast or that first is antichrist. Both of them flourished long before the dignity and majesty of Rome the whore began to be diminished. And also both shall remain for some few years after the overthrow of it, as appeared manifestly from this place. Should we limit all this time either with the space of three years or with the bounds of one mortal man? But concerning the time of antichrist, the things that have been spoken in Revelation 17 are so certain and evident that no one can now be in doubt. REVELATION OF ST. JOHN.[12]

[12]Brightman, *Revelation**, 641-44; citing Ps 11:6; Rev 16:13; 13:13.

20:1-10 The Millennium

20 *Then I saw an angel coming down from heaven, holding in his hand the key to the bottomless pit*[a] *and a great chain.* [2]*And he seized the dragon, that ancient serpent, who is the devil and Satan, and bound him for a thousand years,* [3]*and threw him into the pit, and shut it and sealed it over him, so that he might not deceive the nations any longer, until the thousand years were ended. After that he must be released for a little while.*

[4]*Then I saw thrones, and seated on them were those to whom the authority to judge was committed. Also I saw the souls of those who had been beheaded for the testimony of Jesus and for the word of God, and those who had not worshiped the beast or its image and had not received its mark on their foreheads or their hands. They came to life and reigned with Christ for a thousand years.* [5]*The rest of the dead did not come to life until the thousand years were ended. This is the first resurrection.* [6]*Blessed and holy is the one who shares in the first resurrection! Over such the second death has no power, but they will be priests of God and of Christ, and they will reign with him for a thousand years.*

[7]*And when the thousand years are ended, Satan will be released from his prison* [8]*and will come out to deceive the nations that are at the four corners of the earth, Gog and Magog, to gather them for battle; their number is like the sand of the sea.* [9]*And they marched up over the broad plain of the earth and surrounded the camp of the saints and the beloved city, but fire came down from heaven*[b] *and consumed them,* [10]*and the devil who had deceived them was thrown into the lake of fire and sulfur where the beast and the false prophet were, and they will be tormented day and night forever and ever.*

a Greek *the abyss*; also verse 3 b Some manuscripts *from God, out of heaven,* or *out of heaven from God*

Overview: Three images dominate this section. First is the imprisonment of the dragon by an angel who comes down from heaven with the key to the bottomless pit, in which Satan is held for a thousand years. Second, John sees thrones on which sit those given authority to judge. Souls of those beheaded for the sake of their testimony to Jesus come to life and reign with Christ a thousand years. This is the first resurrection. The rest of the dead do not come to life until after a thousand years. Third, when the thousand years are over, Satan is released from his prison and will deceive the nations.

The commentators see the history of the Crusades as depicted in Gog and Magog, marching across the breadth of the earth and surrounding the camp of God's people. Devoured by fire from heaven, they will forever be tormented. Then John sees a great white throne. The living and the dead are judged.

Satan on the Loose Again. Martin Luther: There comes in chapter 20 the stirrup cup: Satan, having been captured a thousand years before, is on the loose again after a thousand years and brings up Gog and Magog, the Turk, the . . . Jew. But they shall soon go with him into the lake of fire. For it is our opinion that this image, which is separate from those which preceded, has been put in because of the Turks, and that the thousand years are to begin about the time this book was written, and that at that time the devil was bound—although the reckoning need not be exactly to the minute. After the Turks, the last judgment follows quickly, at the end of this chapter. Preface to the Revelation of Saint John.[1]

[1]LW 35:409; citing Dan 7.

All Have Had the Gospel Given to Them in These Years. Heinrich Bullinger: St. John answers: "And the remnant were slain with the sword of him who sat on the horse," and so on. Again, where a godly man might marvel how they should be condemned, who born among the Turks, heretics, Jews, and Gentiles never heard the Christian truth? St. John prevents this imagination and by the beginning of Revelation 20 shows with what a majesty, perspicuity, and evidence the verity of Christ's gospel was told to the world, how also all force and power was taken away from the devil, and that by the space of a thousand years, in which the preaching of the gospel thundered continually, so that those who have not received the gospel of Christ are utterly inexcusable. For the preaching of the gospel was not obscure but most clear and manifest, nor short and contracted but published by the space of a thousand years; it was not received by a few little ones but by all people and nations under the sun.

Therefore is it a gross ignorance of the Turks, heretics, Jews, and Gentiles. For although in times past the truth seemed to have been widely known, now it is not so; yet it is certain that the majesty of the gospel has been so great in the world that now all people have heard of it, and by their own malice they hide their eyes, which understand nothing of Christ. Therefore is that saying of the apostle even now of force also: "If our gospel is hidden, it is hidden in those who perish, to whom the God of this world has blinded the minds of those who do not believe, that the light of the gospel should not shine unto them." . . . As a result of this we now gather, that none of those who are damned in the world are damned without deserving. This also the apostle St. Paul has touched on. . . . Here therefore is a profitable and necessary place where the famous preaching of the gospel throughout the world is treated, the course of it enduring a thousand years.

And this treatise proceeds in this order. First is the angel described, after his work or effect is declared, and last is the sealing of the time. Concerning the description of the angel, first indeed he is named an angel, and coming forth abroad; nevertheless, the whole apostolic state is hereby understood. . . . Neither is it a marvel that the order of apostles is signified by an angel. For an angel signifies a messenger, ambassador, or an apostle. And therefore, the prophet . . . called John the Baptist, the forerunner of our Lord, an angel: "Behold, I send my angel before you," and so on. And ministers of the church are more often than ones in this book called angels. But in case the worthiness and nobility of the name pleases the ministers, let the angelical purity and excellent faith please them also. An ambassador does and says nothing except what he has received in commission, of him who sent him; so also let the ministers set forth nothing except what they have received of the Lord in the Scriptures.

Second, this excellent angel is said to come down from heaven, not that the bodies of apostles came from heaven but to the degree that their vocation and office was given them from heaven. For the Son of God, who came down from heaven, chose the apostles and sent them forth into the world. . . . And St. Paul says to the Galatians . . . that he was called and ordained an apostle neither by people nor of people but of God through Christ. As a result of this it appeared how great the authority of apostles is. For they are not what they speak but the Spirit of Christ and of the Father, who speaks in them. Therefore, one who despises their doctrine despises God the Father and the Son. Moreover, those who say the gospel is a new doctrine forged by clever people lie. Hundred Sermons on the Apocalypse.[2]

20:1-3 *The Imprisonment of the Dragon, or Satan*

The Millennium Began in 300. John Napier: The thousand years that Satan was bound . . . began in 300 or thereabout. For proof of

[2]Bullinger, *Hundred Sermons** (1561), 588-90; citing 2 Cor 4:1-6; Rom 1–2; Mal 4:5; Mt 10:1-10; Jn 20:21-23; Mk 16:9-19; Lk 24:50; Gal 1:11.

this, it is evident by histories that after the continual and successive tyranny of ethnic emperors, and last of Diocletian (who in one month made seventeen thousand martyrs), there arose about this three hundredth year of Christ Constantine the Great, a Christian and baptized emperor. He and his successors (except a few of short reign) maintained Christianity and true religion, to the abolishing of Satan's public kingdom, and therefore we say this year Satan is bound.

Second, shortly after this time was the first public and general godly council held by the Christians at Nicaea, in which the apostolic belief was published, the authentic Scriptures authorized, and finally the true Christian religion so received that all Satan's outward opposition was banished, and his public tyranny and kingdom overcome. Yet his lieutenant the antichrist even then began his dissimulate and hypocritical kingdom. Third, we see by the former proposition that Gog and Magog are the armies of the sixth trumpet and vial, and these (by the fourth proposition) were loosed about 1296 to make war. Therefore, about 1296, or rather (as histories precisely report) about 1300,[†] were the armies of Gog and Magog loosed, and so Satan was then loosed to stir them up to battle. From this thirteen hundred years think of the thousand years that Satan lay bound, and it will consequently follow that Satan was first bound in 300.

Fourth, and for confirmation of the former, the text says that as soon as the devil is loosed, he passes forth to stir up and seduce these papistical and Islamic armies of Gog and Magog to strife and warfare. But in that year 1300 began (by Satan's instigation) that proud strife between them for supremacy, both of them assigning to themselves the empire of the whole earth. A Plain Discovery of the Whole Revelation of Saint John.[3]

Satan Was Cast Down in Those Thousand Years. Heinrich Bullinger: And thus was Satan bound and shut up for a thousand years, he who did not possess the faithful of Christ throughout the world, nor ruled them at his pleasure and after his malice, although he has tempted and vexed them. So was the Holy Spirit prevented being given, not that he was not in the world and in the prophets but because he was never so plentifully poured out on all flesh as after the glorifying of our Lord Christ.

In the same sense we say that death and sin are taken away from the faithful and trodden underfoot. As St. Paul therefore . . . said, we are translated out of the kingdom of darkness into the kingdom of light, and he says to the Corinthians that the god of this world has blinded the minds of the unfaithful, so St. John at the present says how the devil is bound and sealed by the space of a thousand years, and he says afterward that the rest of the dead did not revive until the thousand years were fulfilled, that is to say, in all those thousand years those who accorded more to the beast than they did to Christ did not believe.

And they truly through their own fault and instigation of the devil did not believe and perished. Therefore did Satan exercise his force in them. He indeed is bound and tied fast to the faithful, but to the unfaithful free and overfamiliar. Likewise hell is shut to the godly but to the wicked open. Therefore also we confess in the creed life everlasting and not death or damnation everlasting. For the faithful have no hell, or there is no hell prepared for them, but for the ungodly. For Christ has broken hell, but only for his faithful; to the unfaithful all things of hell are yet most strong, and these have hell.

Again the devil is said to be bound, shut up, and sealed, for since the redemption of Christ his power has not been so great in the world as it was before. Therefore St. John expounds himself and says that he should deceive the people no more. What is this more? That he shall not so seduce them from this point as he has done up to this point. Therefore, although in the meanwhile he

[3]Napier, *Plain Discovery**, 62-64. †In 1300, Boniface published the papal bull *Antiquorum fida relatio*, which decreed that 1300 would be a jubilee year and that any Christian could get remission from all sins if they made their confession and went on a pilgrimage to Rome before the end of the year.

shall deceive some, yet in those thousand years he has not reigned so fully, safely, and at large as he did before and as it is permitted him after those thousand years to rage.

Therefore, these things are spoken by a comparison and not absolutely. And the thing itself or experience teaches that they are not to be understood absolutely and after the bare letter. Although therefore Satan has in these thousand years also blown his poison on many and has troubled the world, yet this is nothing in comparison to those things that have followed the thousand years even until this day and shall follow hereafter to the world's end. In old time also he reigned fully among the Gentiles through idolatry. But a thousand years fell down their temples and idols, with all other instruments of ungodliness. Hundred Sermons on the Apocalypse.[4]

20:4-6 *The Reign of the Martyrs*

The First Resurrection. John Bale: This is the first resurrection to life, to rise from sin to repentance, from ignorance to godly knowledge, and from darkness to faith. Through the offense of one man sin entered into the world, and through sin, death. It is therefore necessary to die to sin and to live to righteousness, and so to rise together with Christ, seeking the things that are above and not on earth. For never will those who will not rise by repentance to a new life in him—which is both resurrection and life—come to the second resurrection, which is to the life everlasting. The Image of Both Churches.[5]

A Second Millennial Age. Francis Junius: So this history has two parts: one of the state of the church conflicting with temptations, up to Revelation 16; the other of the state of the same church obtaining victory, up to Revelation 20. The first part has two members most conveniently distributed into their times, of which the first contains a history of the Christian church for 1,260 years, at which time the gospel of Christ was, as it were, taken up from among men into heaven. The second contains a history of the same church until the victory is perfected. And these two members are briefly though distinctly propounded in this chapter, but are both of them more at large discoursed after in due order. A Brief and Learned Commentary.[6]

One Thousand Literal Years. Henry (John) Archer: Now to find out its time of expiring and show how long it is to last, it will be considered that there is of Christ's monarchy a double estate. One is the evening or first part, and the other is the morning or latter part. Now, it is the first part or evening that is usually taken for Christ's kingdom, and that is what we are now speaking of, and the duration of it is expressly determined by the Scripture, which says it shall be a thousand years, or ten generations. . . . It is observable that in all other prophecies, times were obscured by speaking generally (as "a time, times," and so on) or at least putting days for years, . . . but here is plainly said a thousand years so that it is not to be questioned or interpreted as a dark saying. . . .

I know that taking this as a thousand years literally in Revelation has for a long time and to this day been condemned by worthy men as a heresy. But God left the next ages to the first after the apostles to fall into various mistakes for the bringing of error and darkness, out of which antichristianism was to arise for many generations, among which was that they abused this sweet and refreshing prophecy of Christ's kingdom lasting a thousand years and perverted their opinion of it to a kind of Muslim paradise of sensual and sinful pleasures. Therefore holy men taking up that opinion . . . never examined it to find the gold and separate it from the dross, as it was done also elsewhere (and is to this day done with various other opinions abused by popery), and so they found out a spiritual sense of every Scripture that

[4]Bullinger, *Hundred Sermons** (1561), 596-97; citing Col 1:9-14.
[5]Bale, *Image** (1570), ch. 20.
[6]Junius, *Apocalypsis**, 115r.

contained anything about this kingdom of Christ's, and they rejected all literal sense in it, carrying it spiritually.

And they were not wholly mistaken, for there is a spiritual sense in most of those Scriptures, besides a literal (as was showed before). That which is literally applied to this time of Christ's kingdom . . . is also spiritually applied. . . . But their error was that (though truly they expounded these places spiritually, yet) they rejected all literal sense of them, whereas besides their spiritual sense they had a literal sense respecting this time of Christ's kingdom. . . . It was the joint opinion of all believers that Christ should have a kingdom on earth, which should (after it was come to perfection) endure a thousand years. And this is the time I call the evening or first part of Christ's day. . . .

Now, when these thousand years are expired, there shall be a little interruption for a while, . . . by the letting loose of Satan, and his stirring up Gog and Magog to disturb this kingdom, . . . but it shall be but a little while. . . . And when this interruption of cloud is blown away, there shall arise the morning, or latter part, and most glorious time of Christ's day (that which we call the last judgment), which shall last a great while. Indeed, the Scripture does not set down how long this time shall last, but it is evident it must last a long while.

First, . . . it may last a thousand years . . . because this is the time in which God's mercy, justice, truth, power, and so on is to be gloriously revealed before all . . . so that every sinner is to be silenced in his reasonings or convinced that he said and thought amiss. . . . Now this must require a lot of time.

Second, this is the time in which Jesus Christ is to triumph and lord it over all reasonable creatures, to be worshiped and acknowledged by everyone in heaven, on earth, and under the earth. . . . For during the other part of Christ's kingly reign in the thousand years, he is not always visible. . . . But at this time shall Christ sit on the throne of his glory, and every knee shall bow to him, and every tongue shall confess him Lord; therefore surely it shall be no short time. The Personal Reign of Christ on Earth.[7]

The Kingdom of Christ. Thomas Brightman: This kingdom of Christ that began from this time to be great and manifest should never be obscured again as the former kingdoms were, which came to an utter ruin in process of time. For so it is said, "And he shall reign for evermore." Revelation of St. John.[8]

Characterization of the Thousand Years. Heinrich Bullinger: By these St. John declares himself, expounding what those thousand years shall be. Without doubt very many (among whom are counted also the millenarians or chiliasts) do imagine . . . there should be tranquility on earth, and in these years the saints here on earth shall reign corporally with Christ in most exquisite pleasures and joys. For St. John himself refutes this opinion while he showed how the saints should be beheaded by the beast and by his image, and that the others who remain in death should not live again or receive the gospel of Christ. It is therefore manifest that the beast and his image shall be in those thousand years. It is evident that the gospel of Christ shall so shine by those thousand years that Satan should be so straight tied in chains, that nevertheless all should not receive the gospel. Neither should there be quiet tranquility, but the saints for Christ's truth should suffer persecution of the beast, and many should not believe the gospel but rather withstand the same and perish.

Yet the devil in the meantime shall not have so great power as he has obtained since the thousand years were finished. The gospel will not in those thousand years be so darkened as it was corrupted and depraved after. And he speaks with all certain opinions notable and necessary . . . what should be the state of those who either are killed for Christ or reject antichrist: truly that their souls do not sleep

[7]Archer, *Personal Reign** (1642), 37-40; Rev 10:4; Dan 12:11-12; 4, 8; Rev 5–7; 9; 21:4; 2 Cor 5:17; Rev 20:3, 7-9; Rom 2:5; Jude 14-15; Phil 2:10-11; Rom 14:10-11; Ps 110:1; Heb 10:12-13; Phil 2:11.
[8]Brightman, *Revelation* *, 123.

until the judgment but live with Christ in heaven. He treated moreover the first resurrection and second death. Thus, to those who question where the souls of the dead shall go and what they shall do immediately after the corporal death, he answered, and he declares so much as is necessary to know.

Therefore St. John sees seats and those who sit on them. And who are those who sit? He adds by an exposition and says, "And the souls of those who are beheaded." . . . Souls are not beheaded but bodies; the souls remain in their state and life. Therefore he says the souls of those whose bodies were beheaded or slain. And here let us note that St. John speaks not of the bodies reassumed, changed, or raised again at the last judgment but of the souls delivered from the bodies of the martyrs. For he speaks of souls loosed from the bodies before the judgment, according as everyone in his time lived here in this world and is called from there by death. For Aretas† also, bishop of Caesarea, expounded this of the souls of martyrs, yet he does not nevertheless think that no one should be saved unless they die by the tyrant's sword. . . . And we also have showed before that first and chiefly the holy martyrs are rewarded with eternal life, second of all they have honored God truly and have done penance and crucified their flesh with all its desire.

And he says expressly that the saints were beheaded not for theft, murder, and mischief, as also Saint Peter teaches . . . but for the Word of God and testimony of Jesus Christ. The Word of God is the very Son of God our Savior, and the testimony is that wholesome gospel and the very preaching and prophesying of the same, as by many Scriptures we have declared before. They are reckoned moreover among the saints, who have not worshiped the beast and so on. And such are the martyrs beheaded or slain, for they have worshiped God, but the beast and his image they would not worship. Why all who reject antichrist are not slain, and therefore particularly as a peculiar member, he rehearsed also. But what it is to worship the beast and his image and to receive his mark and so on, I have declared before at large. Hundred Sermons on the Apocalypse.[9]

First and Second Resurrection. Heinrich Bullinger: Now is added to this the remnant of the dead, who are neither regenerated through faith nor would give their life for Christ but would rather worship the beast and his image. These, I say, because of their unbelief did not live. For without faith there is no true life in this world. We say nothing here of vital or natural life. And we say that life is double or of two sorts, namely, the one spiritual, which is of faith and of the spirit of God and of Christ, which is by faith received and lived in the hearts of those who are his, and his life in him. For the Lord himself says, "He who eats me, he shall live also for me." The other life is everlasting, that is, of another world, in which we shall see God as he is and shall be as he is, living in God and with God for evermore.

In the reverse way, death is of two sorts, spiritual, by which we live in sin, lacking Christ and his Spirit and void of faith. The apostle, speaking of this death, says that a widow living wantonly, though she is alive, is dead. And the Lord also to the disciple who would return home and bury his parents says, "Let the dead bury their dead." There is also a death everlasting, that is, everlasting wretchedness and misery, which follows the spiritual. Yet see what we have said of double death in Revelation 3, in expounding the epistle to those of Sardis. Therefore St. John here indicates that there shall be many in these thousand years who should not receive the gospel with a lively faith, and therefore should remain in death, as the Lord says. . . .

Therefore, those who suppose that all nations in the whole universal world shall come once to a unity of faith and most assured peace in this life, they err shamefully. Hundred Sermons on the Apocalypse.[10]

---

[9]Bullinger, *Hundred Sermons** (1561), 601-2; citing 1 Pet 4:12-19.
†Arethas, archbishop of Caesarea (c. 850–d. c. 944), was possibly a pupil of the patriarch of Constantinople, Photius.
[10]Bullinger, *Hundred Sermons** (1561), 605-6; Rev 3:1-6; Jn 8:41-45.

The Order of the Visions. David Pareus: "Then I saw": this must be understood of the order of the visions (for he saw this after the former), not of the order of the events, as if this taking of the dragon and these thousand years should in time follow the damnation of the beast. For seeing as the beast is antichrist, certainly his destruction and casting into hell shall be only by the brightness of Christ's coming and in the last judgment, as was shown in the foregoing vision. But after the last judgment, there shall not be a thousand years in which Satan shall be bound and these things be done, which John now sees. And therefore the events of this vision shall not follow but in time go before the events of the foregoing vision.

Therefore, after all other apparitions, this last vision (as it were, in place of a conclusion) is given to John. In it under new types the wonderful binding, loosing, and condemnation of the dragon, and the description of the heavenly Jerusalem, is set forth to John the entire face of the church, prefiguring the history from the first gathering of it among the Gentiles until its last glorification in heaven, not indeed by a vain repetition of the same things but a most profitable revealing of various things from the former mysteries. . . . Now, it was very much for John's (and our) instruction and consolation that none of these things should be hidden from him. Therefore there were weighty reasons why after the other visions this also at last should be exhibited. . . .

"An angel come down from heaven": This angel represents Christ, as the attributes and effects do prove. For he has the key of the bottomless pit, that is, the power of hell and death, which Christ before attributes to himself, . . . and he binds Satan, which is proper to Christ. . . .

John therefore saw Christ in the form of an angel, not falling but descending from heaven, namely, his incarnation. He who descended is the same also who ascended. And no one ascended up to heaven but the one who came down from heaven, even the Son of Man, who is in heaven.

This end of the angel's descending and this cause of the dragon's binding is plainly declared in Revelation 20:3. For if Satan should have been permitted to hold sway any longer among the Gentiles, in vain the apostles had preached the gospel to them. Therefore Satan was to be bound, that is, restrained by the singular power of God, that he should no longer bewitch the nations, who by the preaching of the gospel were to be gathered into the church of Christ.

The key of the bottomless pit is the power of hell. This Christ has one way, antichrist another way, as was there shown. The pope has the same by prevarication; Christ by the power given him from the Father. The pope has it to open the pit of hell and from there to draw out the pestilent smoke of his doctrine and the hellish locusts. Christ has it to shut up the dragon in the bottomless pit.

"A great chain": Long and strong enough to bind the most cruel adversary, in the form of a dragon. . . . This chain does metaphorically denote the omnipotence of Christ and all other means by which he has bound Satan, such as his passion, cross, death, burial, resurrection, ascension, the sending of the Holy Spirit, and chiefly the doctrine of the gospel, by the preaching of it. . . .

"And he laid hold of the dragon": What is this but the casting out of the dragon and his angels into the earth by Michael . . . ? This angel therefore and Michael there spoken of is one, namely, Christ, whose victory over Satan was there depicted generally, that he should no more accuse the elect in the sight of God, but here specially, that he should no more seduce the nations, as it is in Revelation 20:3.

And that we may certainly know that this dragon is the same whom Michael there did vanquish, he is here set forth by the same titles: the old serpent, the devil, Satan, the reason for which we there expounded. Now this so exact a description does altogether constrain us to understand here by the dragon none other save the devil and Satan. A Commentary upon the Divine Revelation.[11]

[11]Pareus, *Revelation**, 501-2; citing Rev 7:2; 8:3; 10:1; 12:13, 9.

CALCULATIONS OF TIME. JOHN (HENRY) ARCHER: So then to 360 or 366 in which this was done, let us add the 1,290 days, which is how long from this it should be before the Jews should be delivered; and it makes 1,650 or 1,656 years of the Lord in which the Israelites are to be delivered by being called to Christianity, both the Jews (who are two tribes that were in Christ's day) and the ten tribes that are Israel. From this time of the conversion of the Israelites for forty-five years after are the twelve tribes to suffer great troubles. Therefore . . . after 1,290 days, he says, "He who comes and waits 1,335 days more is blessed," that is, forty-five years after, for at that time the troubles will be such as never were, . . . namely, to the converted Israelites but not to the Gentile Christians, for these have been troubled by the heathen Roman emperors a long while and after that by the beast that succeeded them, namely, the papacy, . . . but the twelve tribes, who till 656 lived without religion, being converted to Christ, shall have sore trouble for forty-five years after. . . .

By the latter days of this time, the remains of papacy (after Rome's ruin) will have spread and got some head again and join with the enemies of the twelve tribes in the East, and so generally Muslims, heathens, and papists will combine together to ruin the Jews and all other Gentiles who are true Christians. To save them from ruin, Christ will come from heaven. . . .

And in the seventh vial or woe of the seventh trumpet. . . . The nations being angry, Christ's wrath came and destroyed them; and then Christ will set up his kingdom and begin the thousand years and raise the dead saints. . . . Therefore forty-five years after 656, Christ speaks to Daniel, . . . "He shall then stand in the lot," that is, he with the rest of the dead prophets and saints shall be raised up from the dead. So it is likely that Christ's coming from heaven and raising the dead and beginning his kingdom and the thousand years will be about 1700, for it is to be about forty-five years after 1650 or 1656.

Yet I conceive that there may be some conception or more remote beginning of Christ's kingdom sooner, even presently at the end of the sixth trumpet, which brings in the resurrection of the witnesses and the fall of the tenth part of the city, and that by the beginning of the seventh trumpet, which followed presently upon it, about 1666. For it is said that upon the blast of the seventh trumpet, the temple was opened. . . .

Now, the opening of the temple is the revelation of God's truth and worship more clearly then was before . . . which seems necessary to follow after the resurrection of their witnesses and their ascension or taking up to God, and yet this is made the work of the seventh trumpet. Therefore I think that the seventh trumpet may begin presently after the ruin of Rome, 1666, and bring in a pure state of churches, and yet Christ is not to come and begin the thousand years until 1700, for surely in the thousand years there shall be no temple, as was shown before. . . .

And whereas it is said the mystery should be furnished so soon as the seventh trumpet sounded, . . . I suppose it may be truly said, since so great a reformation shall be presently thereafter, and within so few years after, namely, some thirty-four years, the full setting up of the kingdom.

Now, having found out when Christ's kingdom or the thousand years shall begin, it is easy to guess when the last general judgment and the world's end shall be. . . . But after Christ's sufferings and ascension, all the Father's secrets were opened to John, for he was worthy of it, and he reveals them to the churches by John. He opens the meaning of Daniel's time, times, and half a time (which no creature could expound) to be forty-two months or 1,260 days. He says expressly that his kingdom should last a thousand years after it was fully titled, and then should be a little season of disturbance but no hurt to his people, and then comes the last judgment and the end of the world. THE PERSONAL REIGN OF CHRIST ON EARTH.[12]

[12]Archer, *Personal Reign** (1642), 48-51; citing Dan 12:11, 1; Rev 16:13-17; 11:14-15; 2 Pet 3:10; Rev 11:15, 19; 1:5; 3:11-12; 10:7; Mt 24:3; Rev 20:3, 7.

20:7-10 *The Release of Satan*

Satan's Desire to Deceive the Gentiles. Heinrich Bullinger: Therefore he says that when the thousand years are expired, the devil shall be loosed out of that his prison into which he had been shut through the power and might of Christ or preaching of the apostles. For the chain once broken, namely, the sincere doctrine and preaching of the gospel corrupted and depraved, he came out.

And to this end he came out, that he might deceive the Gentiles, that is to say, all people and nations who are dwelling in the four quarters or parts of the earth, I mean in the whole universal world; and to the end he might allure Gog and Magog, namely, fierce men, barbarous, worldly, mocking and contemning the true religion, addicted to robberies, given to evil things, and regarding only corruption and naughtiness—that he might draw, I say, such men to unrighteousness and keep them still in errors. For such does Ezekiel signify Gog and Magog to be.

But those who through the divine grace are not such people, they shall not be deceived of Satan but grounded on Christ, shall persevere in the doctrine of prophets and apostles, shall rightly worship Christ, and shall abhor antichrist and all evil in the world. Hundred Sermons on the Apocalypse.[13]

Gog and Magog Are the Pope and Muhammad. John Bale: Thus under the simulation of religion or pretense of God's law and service, these two tyrants, Gog and Magog, the Romish pope and Muhammad with their whole generations of like spirit with them, have gathered themselves together into one wicked consent against God and his Christ. For under Gog and Magog are comprehended all those whom Satan deceived after he was set at large; though these two have not accorded in other things, they have both agreed in this one point by the devil's enticement, to battle against the Lamb. To withstand the veracity and impugn the truth of the gospel, they have been ready everywhere, in every land, in every city, and in every town. Of one cruel purpose and study to do evil have these two enemies been in all places of the world to persecute Christ's poor congregation. The daily practices of them both so manifestly declare that all the world will see it well enough.

These Isaiah calls that strong multitude, whose spoil Christ shall divide, the smith who blows the coals in the hot fire, and the waster who destroyed; Ezekiel compares them to a raging tempest, Daniel to the king of the north, and Zechariah to the princes of the earth. Their exceeding number (says Saint John) is as the dry sand that has been blasted with the sea, which can in no way be numbered. In this full well may it be considered what a small thing Christ's flock was in comparison to these soldiers of Gog and Magog after Satan's going forth and for the time of their battle. Innumerable were the sects of the pope with those they brought to that false faith and obedience. And so were the prophets of Muhammad with the perverted multitude. Their power was great for the time, and their malice avengeable, yet they were as sand dry and unfruitful. The Image of Both Churches.[14]

Gog and Magog. Heinrich Bullinger: To this is added another thing, that when the thousand years expired Satan should gather Gog and Magog to battle. By this word doubtless St. John has alluded to the prophecy of Ezekiel. . . . Ezekiel seems to have prophesied of the wars of Macedonia and of Antiochus, speaking of it by a prophetic phrase and a hyperbolic amplification. The prophet says that Gog is the land of Magog. And evident it is that Magog was Japheth's son, who dwelt at Mount Elbrus† and extended his empire to Ethiopia and Egypt. And afterward out of the east parts of Asia, Antiochus Epiphanes made war on the people of God. He was a figure of antichrist, as all expositors do confess.

Therefore it is apparent that St. John brings forth these things by way of comparison, as though he should say as in times past the people of Gog and

[13]Bullinger, *Hundred Sermons** (1561), 608-9; citing Ezek 38:1-23.

[14]Bale, *Image** (1570), ch. 20.

Magog did sorely molest and afflict the people of God, so in the times of antichrist most gruesome wars shall arise, by which the church of God shall be shaken and laid waste. And he says truly that the host of these destroyers shall be innumerable. He adds after the manner of the Scripture a parable for perspicuity: as the sand of the sea. And also by another figure of speech he indicates that the enemies of God's people shall be bold and ready to overrun the whole world and send all things into turmoil with wars. For he says,"And they went upon the plains of the land." This is as much as to say that they, being swift and bold, shall ruin all the world. Everywhere and throughout the wide world shall be cruel wars.

For most purposely he adds,"And they gathered around the tents of saints and beloved city." This means that the church of God shall be most grievously plagued with those geographical and barbarous wars. For in times past Jerusalem was called the chosen and beloved city, but after she rejected the word of the Lord, she was no more beloved of God but rather rejected and hated. Therefore, Saint John speaks of the Catholic Church, which Saint Paul also in another place out of Isaiah named "Jerusalem that is above." The same is also called the tents of saints. For the faithful are in the church, as it were, in tents, fighting against Satan, the world, sin, and the flesh. And where he says they gather around the tents of saints, he says somewhat more than if he had written that they assailed or besieged or assaulted the tents of saints. For they gather around them, assaulting them all around and vexing them most grievously as though they were already taken, that no hope can appear to anyone, no refuge or way to escape.

Undoubtedly if we confer these things with histories, we shall find that the church has been many times assailed with cruel wars, but never yet with crueler than after those thousand fatal years, I mean the holy war as they call it. Hundred Sermons on the Apocalypse.[15]

[15]Bullinger, *Hundred Sermons** (1561), 610-11; citing Ezek 38:1-23; 39:1-29; Gal 4:26; Is 2:2-3. †The Caucasus Mountains are a mountain range at the intersection of Asia and Europe.

First Holy War of the Crusades. Heinrich Bullinger: Historiographers report many things of the battle of Troy. Others suppose that those of Assyria and Babylon were greater. Many extol the wars of the Persians and Macedonians, as indeed they were horrible. The Romans have also their Punic, Mithridatic, civil, Cimbrian, and Germanic wars; but I suppose truly that the war they call holy was more cruel than all these, bloodier and sorer, and of longer continuation. In this war have joined together maligned battles, with multitudes of men innumerable—in a manner, all nations and people of the whole world inhabited. Terrible and monstrous slaughters have been made. There have died more hundreds of thousands of men than can be credited. It has continued moreover many years, indeed, more than the former or any wars that ever were in the world. Furthermore, it was done with the most hostile minds.

And what is most relevant for this purpose, in this war were angered the Oriental Saracens, Turks, Egyptians, Babylonians, and other barbarous nations, that they burned with an unquenchable hatred against the Christian religion and went about to pluck it up by the roots, and a great part of it they have plucked up and do not cease to do at this day. That same war, therefore most gruesome of all others, was cause of the persecution of the faithful in the East and West. And . . . for those that who are ignorant in stories, I may note that it is plain that under that child of perdition Pope Gregory VII, there were many and most famous churches in the East and patriarchal churches yet safe, but this pope above all others dealt wickedly against Christ the Son of God and his holy church, as we read in the time of Solomon, after he had revolted many enemies arose against him, and that most cruel.

So in the wicked and tyrannical reign of Gregory VII, Suleiman the Turk invaded Antioch, at the which time the emperors of Greece are said to have been dispatched from the East country. And the Turks, marching forward, are said to have invaded and attacked first the straits or ports of the

Caspian hills, and the country of Armenia, about 764. Of this there is now no time to speak. Suleiman was succeeded by Belchiaroke the Turkish prince, whom others call Belzet, who also invaded Greece itself; the emperors of Constantinople loathed him. Alexius, who then was emperor, is said to have demanded aid of the Western men against the Turks. And also one Peter the Hermit[†] (whom certain historiographers blame most grievously, not without cause), coming out of the East and running throughout the West, cried alarm.

Urbane II . . . called a great council at Clermont in France, wherein he put forth the question of the recovering of the holy land and delivering the Lord's sepulcher out of the hands of the infidels. That council leads me to recall what is described . . . under Ahab and Josaphat for the recovering of Ramoth Gilead[‡] out of the hands of the Syrians. For there was then also a deceiving spirit, there were Arabs, there were Josaphats, and many other things like. And so that I might not write too many words, a journey was decreed against the barbarous infidels of the East. This was done in 1095.

In the meantime Peter the Hermit roused a part and gathered certain thousands, whom he lead through Hungary into Asia. And immediately after followed the unlucky captains the priests Folkemar and Gottschalke, who destroying all with fire and sword were slain. At the last were Godfrey and Baldwyne, most noble princes, with certain excellent captains and noble warriors, with an innumerable multitude of men transported into Asia, which they say was done in 1096. And within four years' time at the most, or three, they had taken by assault or surrender the cities of Nicaea, Heraclea, Tarsus, Antioch, and Jerusalem.

Sugar the abbot of St. Denis reported that there was so much blood shed in the city of Jerusalem that in the very temple itself the horses stood up to the knees in the blood of the slain there.[§] The same man tells of a notable battle fought at Ashkelon, in the which about fifteen thousand footmen and five thousand horsemen of Christians overthrew and discomfited Suleiman of Babylon, furnished with one hundred thousand horsemen and four hundred thousand footmen, and that there were slain in that battle more than one hundred thousand men. And this journey of Godfrey was the first among the worthy voyages of Syria or Asia. Hundred Sermons on the Apocalypse.[16]

What Becomes of Those Who Cleave to Neither Christ nor Antichrist? Heinrich Bullinger: St. John had begun to speak of the universal and last judgment about the end of Revelation 11 and resumed the same to be finished in Revelation 19. There we heard that antichrist should be thrown down out of his seat and glory into hell. There happened a question to arise from them: Those who do not cleave to antichrist yet are not joined with Christ, what shall become of them at the last judgment? When he had solved and showed the equity of God's judgments, he returned to that question, as it were, with a postlude to the description of the general and last judgment, and compendiously describes the same, more generally now than before in Revelation 19. There he seems chiefly to have treated of the destruction of antichrist, yet he showed after a sort also what should happen to the other ungodly. Now he handles more generally the same judgment, showing that all shall be judged in this, and sets forth wholly the same as if it were painted to be seen by our eyes. Hundred Sermons on the Apocalypse.[17]

[16]Bullinger, *Hundred Sermons** (1561), 612-14; citing 2 Kings 22. †Peter the Hermit (1050–1115/31), also Peter of Amiens, was a Roman Catholic priest of Amiens and a key figure during the military expedition from France to Jerusalem, known as the People's Crusade. In the spring of 1096, a number of small bands of knights and peasants, inspired by the preaching of the Crusade, set off from various parts of France (Cologne) and Germany (Worms). The Crusade of the priest Folkmar, beginning in Saxony, persecuted Jews in Magdeburg and later in Prague in Bohemia. Godfrey of Bouillon (1060–1100) was a preeminent leader of the First Crusade and the first ruler of the Kingdom of Jerusalem in 1099–1100. ‡Ramoth-Gilead ("heights of Gilead") was a Levitical city and city of refuge east of the Jordan River in the Hebrew Bible. §Suger (1081–1151) was a French abbot, statesman, and historian. He wrote on abbey construction and was one of the earliest patrons of Gothic architecture. He is widely credited with popularizing the style.
[17]Bullinger, *Hundred Sermons** (1561), 620-21.

The Redeemed Will Not Face the Second Death. Martin Luther: "I shall not be moved." . . . In Adam we were once moved from grace to damnation, but the person redeemed by Christ is no longer moved, that is, in the second sense, into the second death. For through Adam we were moved into the death of nature and of grace. And this is death and the first moving. Indeed, the death of nature is more like a sleep. Therefore, the first moving is into sin, while the second is into damnation and hell. Those who do not believe in Christ, like the Jews, moved into this. He, however, will no longer be moved. He indicates more by saying less, as if he were saying: "Not only will I not be moved in the second sense, but I will also be saved from the first move into sin." But because they remain in the first move voluntarily, they will also be moved again in the second sense . . . : "This is the second death." Psalm 62.[18]

Restoration of the Church. Francis Junius: Now the Lord is entered into his kingdom and has restored his church, in which, most mightily recovered from the profanation of the Gentiles, he may glorify himself—namely, that which the Lord ordained when first he ordained his church, which the faith of the saints now behold accomplished. The Geneva Bible.[19]

[18]LW 10:298; citing Ps 62:2.
[19]Geneva Bible, 115v.

20:11-21:8 From the Old Creation to the New

[11]Then I saw a great white throne and him who was seated on it. From his presence earth and sky fled away, and no place was found for them. [12]And I saw the dead, great and small, standing before the throne, and books were opened. Then another book was opened, which is the book of life. And the dead were judged by what was written in the books, according to what they had done. [13]And the sea gave up the dead who were in it, Death and Hades gave up the dead who were in them, and they were judged, each one of them, according to what they had done. [14]Then Death and Hades were thrown into the lake of fire. This is the second death, the lake of fire. [15]And if anyone's name was not found written in the book of life, he was thrown into the lake of fire.

21 *Then I saw a new heaven and a new earth, for the first heaven and the first earth had passed away, and the sea was no more. [2]And I saw the holy city, new Jerusalem, coming down out of heaven from God, prepared as a bride adorned for her husband. [3]And I heard a loud voice from the throne saying, "Behold, the dwelling place[a] of God is with man. He will dwell with them, and they will be his people,[b] and God himself will be with them as their God.[c] [4]He will wipe away every tear from their eyes, and death shall be no more, neither shall there be mourning, nor crying, nor pain anymore, for the former things have passed away."*

[5]And he who was seated on the throne said, "Behold, I am making all things new." Also he said, "Write this down, for these words are trustworthy and true." [6]And he said to me, "It is done! I am the Alpha and the Omega, the beginning and the end. To the thirsty I will give from the spring of the water of life without payment. [7]The one who conquers will have this heritage, and I will be his God and he will be my son. [8]But as for the cowardly, the faithless, the detestable, as for murderers, the sexually immoral, sorcerers, idolaters, and all liars, their portion will be in the lake that burns with fire and sulfur, which is the second death."

a Or *tabernacle* **b** Some manuscripts *peoples* **c** Some manuscripts omit *as their God*

Overview: According to the teaching of the Reformers, salvation depicted in the Apocalypse begins and ends with God's gracious initiatives in Christ Jesus, as exemplified in Revelation 20–22. Commentator William Perkins affirms election, by which in God's own free will he ordains certain persons to salvation and others to damnation. Revelation gives attention to God's revelation and execution of this decree. Heinrich Bullinger writes of the coming universal judgment now again in Revelation 20. All will be judged by their deeds in accord with the divine decree of election or reprobation. The sea, Death, and Hades give up the dead who were in them. Having played their role, Death and Hades are then thrown into the lake of fire. This is the second death, for those whose name is not found written in the book of life. Luther writes that the redeemed will not face the second death.

A new heaven and new earth are affirmed in Revelation 21. It is a central doctrine of Christian eschatology and depicts the final state of redeemed humanity. Central to the new heaven and a new earth is the holy city, the new Jerusalem. It is God who prepares the church to be the bride of Christ.

20:11-15 *Judgment Before the Great White Throne*

The Last Judgment. Heinrich Bullinger: For after his desired manner he expounded all this matter by a heavenly vision, that he might not seem only to tell the thing to our ears but also to show it forth to be seen by our eyes, with the intent it might be more deeply printed in our minds. And all these things are most certainly and undoubtedly (as I also admonished you before) revealed of the judge Christ himself. But the judge and Lord himself can be ignorant in nothing of this matter. Neither can we perceive that St. John has up to this point been deceived or abused in anything that he has set forth to us but has hit rightly all and singular points, as we see, that can testify his prophecies to be fulfilled. Why then should there be so much as doubt of such things as are spoken of the judgment?

Therefore let us credit these things and not be among the mockers, whom the apostle St. Peter prophesied should come and say, "Where is the promise of his coming?" Doubtless this matter is of greatest importance, the foundation and root of our faith. Here are to us expounded not a few articles of our sincere and catholic faith, chiefly these: "I believe that Christ shall come to judge the quick and the dead; I believe the communion of saints, the resurrection of the flesh, and life everlasting." Let us therefore be diligent in hearing and marking these things, lest we be accounted of the number of those who hear the mysteries of the kingdoms of God without any fruit. But let us rather prepare ourselves to go meet the judge, to the end that we may, with the wise virgins, enter with the bridegroom to the marriage and joys everlasting.

And the description or demonstration of this vision has these things chiefly: who the judge shall be, who shall be judged, how they shall be judged, of what sort shall be the resurrection of the dead; and of everlasting damnation, finally, who shall be properly damned. These things I shall declare as plainly as I can in order according to the grace that God has given me. Hundred Sermons on the Apocalypse.[1]

The Two Books and the Decree of God. John Downame: The reason of the sentence [of judgment], justifying this great Judge before God and the world and to the consciences of all people: in it is opened first the eternal and most righteous decree of God, electing one and reprobating the other. Then the sequels of this election and reprobation: in the elect, love to Christ and to his members, and undoubted fruits and testimonies of their faith; in the reprobate, hardness of heart, without compassion or love for the saints, and a declaration before people and to their own souls of their righteous and just perdition.

John in the Revelation does elegantly describe it by two books, in which those reasons are both written. The first is the book of both their consciences, in which are written the one's wicked works, to convince their damnation to be most just, and the other's holinesses of conversation. The other book is the book of life, which is the eternal election of the latter, to show that they, being many times guilty of foul offenses and the best of all their works weak and imperfect and utterly of no desert, their salvation is altogether free and of God's mere grace and favor in and through Christ. Sum of Sacred Divinity.[2]

Election Is God's Decree. William Perkins: Election is God's decree, by which of his own free will he has ordained certain people to salvation, to the praise of the glory of his grace. . . . This decree is that book of life, in which are written the names of the elect. . . . The execution of this decree is an action by which God, even as he purposed with himself, works all those things he decreed for the salvation of the elect. For those whom God elected to the end that they should inherit eternal life were also elected to those subordinate means, by which, as by steps, they might attain this end, and without which it would be impossible to obtain it. A Golden Chain.[3]

No More Death for God's Elect. Giovanni Diodati: "Him who": namely, Jesus Christ,

[1]Bullinger, *Hundred Sermons** (1561), 621.

[2]Downame, *Sacred Divinity**, 537-38.

[3]Perkins, *Golden Chain**, ch. 15; Eph 1:4-6; 2 Tim 2:19; Rom 8:29-30.

everlasting King of his church and supreme judge of the world. "From his presence": that is to say, at the appearance of his new kingdom, all this form and state of the world was changed in an instant, and vanished away. . . . "The books": terms taken from the public judgments here among people, in which are produced all the writings of the process, information, depositions of witnesses, and so on to show that all actions, even the most secret ones, shall then be rehearsed and made manifest. . . . "Another book": which represents the everlasting election to life and glory in Christ. . . . "Death": that is to say, there was no more either death or sepulcher for God's elect, the command of death over them was quite annihilated; but it remained on the damned, in whom death and the grave were changed into everlasting imprisonment and torments of hell. Pious Annotations upon the Holy Bible.[4]

What Was Hidden Will Be Manifest. John Bale: The books of reckoning . . . were open before the judge. That which before was hidden will then be manifest, and what was secret will then come to light and be disclosed. To him it will be evident who has fulfilled the commanded works of mercy and who has left them undone, their own constancies bearing witness to the same. For what can be hid from him who sees both the inward reins and the secret thoughts of the heart? In this general reckoning shall praise with the eternal reward from the merciful Lord overflow to those whose walking here has been according unto faith. There shall they be reported to have been pitiful to the poor, hungry, thirsty, needy, naked, sick, and in prison.

After this another book was opened of a far different nature from the other books, for it was the sweet book of life, in which is registered all who were predestined to be saved from the world's beginning. And this book is the eternal predestination of God. Before the world's foundation (says St. Paul) the Lord predestinated us into the adoption of his children through Jesus Christ. This book Moses mentioned when he said, "Either pardon this people or else erase me out of your book that you have written." And Christ also to his seventy disciples: "Be glad," he says, "that your names are written in heaven." Moreover, Joshua called this the book of the righteous, and John here the book with seven clasps.

This showed the Holy Spirit here to us, much like the custom daily used among us. For of the most notable men and women our manner is both to long remember the names and to speak of them as occasion gives. So equal is this eternal judge that no personage did he respect in judgment, neither of emperor nor pope, king nor bishop, lord nor priest. But as he is righteous of himself, so judges he righteously. The Image of Both Churches.[5]

Every Person Must Be Judged. William Perkins: I will reward partly in this life and partly at the day of judgment. . . . Hence the papists gather that people must be saved not only by faith but by works, seeing God will reward good works. . . . Their reason stands thus: by what we are judged, by the very same thing we are saved; but we are judged by works, therefore saved by works. The flat major is false, for we must distinguish between judgment and justification. To judge is to declare one just by one's signs as one's works. To justify is to make one just, in which we consider nothing but Christ and our faith applying him to us. So then, we are judged by works, but not justified or saved by works. . . . Christ says not, "I will give for their works," but "I will give them according to their works," as their works are not for them. There he makes works an outward sign and rule, according to which he will frame his judgment to declare people just.

Seeing everyone must be judged, that is, saved or condemned by one's works, then good works are necessary to salvation, for we must be judged by our works and saved according to our works. Therefore they are necessary, not as causes either efficient or helping any way but as fruits, effects,

[4]Diodati, *Pious Annotations**, 110; citing 1 Cor 4:5.

[5]Bale, *Image** (1570), ch. 20.

and signs of our faith, and marks on the way to heaven, which must direct us to eternal life. Lectures upon the Three First Chapters of the Revelation.[6]

Two Resurrections. Mary Cary: In these verses is declared that immediately upon the ruining of all the wicked of the nations, the last and general day of judgment is to follow, when the resurrection of all comes, both just and unjust. I say the last and general day of judgment and resurrection of all because in this Revelation 20 it is clear that here is a mention made of two resurrections, the one to be a thousand years before the other. The first is treated in Revelation 20:4-6 and is there called the first resurrection, and the second is laid down where it is said that the heavens and the earth are then to be annihilated, to fly away at the presence of the Lord, who after these thousand years are finished is to appear on his white throne of righteousness and to judge all the dead, small and great.

They are to stand before him, being all raised out of the graves and out of the sea and all places where the dead have been laid, to be judged righteously, according to the gospel and according to their works. And they being so judged, it will follow that whoever is not found written in the book of life shall be cast into a lake of fire. And this general day of judgment here treated is also treated in several other Scriptures. . . . There our Savior thus describes it and says that in that day he shall sit on the throne of his glory, and before him shall be gathered all nations, and he shall separate them one from another, as a shepherd divides his sheep from the goats, and he shall set the sheep on his right hand but the goats on the left. The Little Horn's Doom and Downfall.[7]

The Final Comfort. Martin Luther: Finally, in chapter 21, the final comfort is depicted. The holy city, fully prepared, shall be led as a bride to the eternal marriage feast. Christ alone is Lord, and all the godless are condemned and go with the devil into hell. Preface to the Revelation of Saint John.[8]

We Must Believe the Promises of the Gospel. William Perkins: We see the damnable practice of most people nowadays, for they hear the word continually preached and read the same, yet the prophet cries out, "Who has believed our sayings?" None fear the threatening of the law, none believe the promises of the gospel. What a heavy and horrible thing is this, that we should not believe the promises of salvation, nor fear the threats of the law for our sins, seeing as it is the doctrine preached and confirmed by the testimony of Christ Jesus, the true and faithful witness of the Father's will to humanity. This is to make Christ a liar, to make him a false prophet and give him the lie.

By the consideration of this, that Christ Jesus is the faithful witness, that the doctrine delivered out of his Word is confirmed by his testimony, we must take heed that we fear and tremble at the threats of the law, that we believe assuredly the promises of the gospel, for those who will not believe have their portion in the lake of fire and brimstone. Lectures upon the Three First Chapters of the Revelation.[9]

Regeneration Finally Accomplished. John Bale: The first heaven, defiled through the pride of the angel, and the first earth, also corrupted by the sinful usage of people, shall vanish clean away and no more be seen. Not that the substance of them shall utterly perish but that their nature, shape, and figure shall change into a much more pure and perfect similitude. It was a custom among the prophets to announce to the afflicted Israelites prosperity, peace, or renovation of the glory of God coming to promise all things new.

"Behold," says the Lord in Isaiah, "I make you new heavens and a new earth, for the old shall

[6]Perkins, *Lectures**, 241-42; citing Rom 2:1-6; Rev 20:11-15.
[7]Cary, *Doom**, 321-23; citing Mt 25:31-46.
[8]LW 35:409.
[9]Perkins, *Lectures**, 34.

never more be thought upon." New is the true church of Christ; so are the people pertaining to the same. In no point are they similar to the pope's holy orders, nor yet to Muhammad's religion. Clear are their hearts, which have received the truth, from all superstitions, and their outward lives from idol observations; perfect are their consciences, and their conversations godly. And this in the regeneration shall be fully accomplished. Not only shall that which is now mortal become immortal, and what is now corruptible then uncorrupted and as the very angels of the Lord, but also the universal heaven shall be then renewed, and so shall the whole face of the earth, and appear more beautiful than now. The Image of Both Churches.[10]

An End to All Miseries. John Napier: The divine prophet Saint John, up to this point prophesying the mutability of this world from the first to the last coming of Christ, in which the Christian church has never had earthly rest, now in this chapter and beginning of the next concludes and ends all these their definite and temporal miseries by assuring them of infinite and eternal joy and rest in that new world and heavenly habitation. He describes it here not as it is, for no eye has seen, nor ear has heard, nor heart can consider the joys of it. . . . But after a certain metaphorical comparison most proper for our senses and capacity that heavenly habitation is described. A Plain Discovery of the Whole Revelation of Saint John.[11]

A Mutual Exchange of Love. Mary Cary: The Spirit being thus abundantly poured out on the saints, they will be filled with love by this, and that in a most eminent manner, so that, as David being filled with the Spirit says, "I will love you, O Lord my strength," so shall they also most truly and cordially say it, with wonderfully raised and inflamed affections. For where much of the Spirit is, there must be much love, for the Spirit of God is the Spirit of love itself. And because of the great love that saints shall have for God, it is said . . . that the children of Zion shall be joyful in their King. He alone indeed shall be the joy of their hearts; in him and in nothing else will they be satisfied: It is not their corn, wine, and oil; it is not all the outward enjoyments they shall then abundantly have; but it is the Lord alone who will be their greatest joy and pleasure.

Therefore . . . it is said, "The Lord, whom you seek, shall suddenly come to his temple; even the messenger of the covenant, in whom you delight." There Jesus Christ is set forth as the object of the saints' love and delight. It is true, he is so now, but in that day he will most eminently be so. . . . The saints are solemnly taken to become the bride, the Lamb's wife, which argues that ardent and entire affection shall then be in the saints to Christ. But then, O what mutual exchanges of love will there be between Christ and his saints! And therefore the Lord thus highly and wonderfully expresses himself, . . . (which I can never read but with great admiration), "In that day shall it be said, fear you not, Zion: for the Lord your God in the midst of you is mighty; he will save you, he will rejoice over you with joy; he will rest in his love; he will joy over you with singing."

What high and marvelous expressions are these, that the most high and holy one should thus express his love to poor, empty, unworthy, nothing creatures! What, that he will rejoice over them! That they shall be a joy to him! Even more, that he will not only love them but rest in his love, as being that in which he can acquiesce, rest, be satisfied. And what? Be so well satisfied in this as to joy over his Zion with singing. O wonderful! What more can be said! Who can sufficiently admire at the height, depth, breadth, and length of this love of God, which surpasses knowledge! And how great must the love of saints be when they come more fully to apprehend this! For this love begets their love: his love to them is the spring of their love to him. The Little Horn's Doom and Downfall.[12]

[10]Bale, *Image** (1570), ch. 21.
[11]Napier, *Plain Discovery**, 244; citing 1 Cor 2:9.
[12]Cary, *Doom**, 248-51; citing Ps 149:3; Mal 3:1; Rev 19:7-8; 21:2-3; Zeph 3:16-17.

THE BRIDE OF CHRIST LIVES IN HOPE. ULRICH ZWINGLI: Though I have spoken amply of the church and how it is the bride of Christ, I shall quote the words of Revelation 21:2 at this point, so that they may not be overlooked. "I John, saw the new Jerusalem come down from heaven, prepared by God as a bride decked out for the bridegroom." Here John wants to show that the church of which we spoke in the first instance does not become bride of Christ on its own, but that it is called from heaven, prepared and decked out for this by God. The very same partner and bride of Christ is called "ekklesia catholica" in Greek; in German it is known as the "universal gathering" which we call by another name in the Confession of Faith, not altogether falsely but not properly either. We say, "I believe in the holy, Christian church." There the two Greek terms "ekklesia catholica" are found which should actually be translated by the term "universal gathering." Since, however, it is none other than the church of Christ, i.e. all Christians united in one faith by the Spirit of God, the two words have been translated into the German by "holy, Christian church." Not bad, indeed, though neither the Latins nor the Greeks say it that way in their own language. . . .

For the meaning is nothing which those people erroneously give who claim that "communion of saints" must be understood as the blessedness of those who out of this time have come to God. For soon thereafter we confess that after this life, eternal life will follow, which is known as blessedness. It is not conceivable to express one opinion by two different articles. Thus the meaning of the article in the Confession is as follows: I believe that the holy universal or Christian church is the one spouse of God. But this universal church is the communion of all godly, believing Christians. It follows then that the gathering of special persons or bishops—even though the just mentioned bishops may all be in one place—is not the church in which and of which we believe. For in it are all godly Christians who will essentially be gathered by God only after this age; but as long as it is here on earth, it lives in hope alone and does not ever come together visibly; however, in the light of the divine Spirit and faith it is always together, even here; only, not visibly. Therefore, all those who are not gathered in one pure divine faith and who are not gathered and joined together in the head of Christ, are not the Christian Church. For there is one faith only, as there is one God and one baptism. DEFENSE OF THE REFORMED FAITH.[13]

WHAT IS EXCOMMUNICATION? MENNO SIMONS: What is meant by separation or excommunication? . . . In the first place, well observe what excommunication of the church of Christ is in power, which was left and taught us in the Word by the Lord's holy apostles, so that you despise none ignorantly, nor say with scorners, "Let them freely excommunicate; their excommunication is not dangerous," and similar unguarded expressions. I tell the truth in Christ and do not lie that I would sooner suffer myself to be cut into pieces until the day of judgment, if it were possible, than to suffer myself to be excommunicated, according to the Scriptures, by the servants of the Lord, from his church. O brethren, beware! EXPLANATION OF THE TRUE APOSTOLIC SEPARATION OR EXCOMMUNICATION.[14]

THE SECOND DEATH. WILLIAM PERKINS: The first death is when the body and soul are separated in this life; the second, when both body and soul are separated from God forever. In which separation . . . consisted the destruction of a person, even the suffering of the fire of the eternal lake. It is then as if he said, "Though one shall suffer the first death, yet one shall not be hurt by the second, one shall escape that fire and lake forever." This is a most comfortable and happy promise to escape the lake of hell. Here note first to whom this promise is made, to those who overcome, to those who renounce themselves, put their trust and faith only in Christ, and labor to keep faith and a good conscience to the end.

[13]Zwingli, *Defense of the Reformed Faith*, 1:44-45; citing Eph 4:5.
[14]Simons, *Complete Writings**, 455-86.

Further, we see by these words that of the two deaths, the second is the worse, and most properly death, for the first is but a preparation to the second. The second is the cruel death and destruction of body and soul. This is yet the madness of people, that they fear the pangs of the first and not of the second, never think of the burning lake—like children who fear shadows and never fear fire or water but suffer themselves to be drowned or burned. LECTURES UPON THE THREE FIRST CHAPTERS OF THE REVELATION.[15]

JOSIAH TURNED AWAY FROM IDOLATRY. MENNO SIMONS: Josiah turned to the Lord with his whole heart, soul, and might, but you dare proudly disregard the God who has created you, deny the Lord who has purchased you, and turn yourselves to dumb idols, to wood, stone, gold, and silver images, to water, bread, and wine, to the unprofitable doctrines and commandments of people, indeed, to open abominations and idolatry, not observing that it stands written, "Idolaters shall have their part in the lake that burns with fire and brimstone." THE TRUE CHRISTIAN FAITH.[16]

21:1-8 *The New Heaven and the New Earth*

THE FATHER SITS ON THE THRONE. JOHN NAPIER: Here the text says, "He who sat on the throne spoke," namely, that same deity and divine essence. But for as much as both the person of the Father and of the Son are meant to sit in this throne, in the next chapter . . . it is to be reasoned whether this is the person of the Father or of the Son who here speaks to St. John. Concerning this we say that although it was the person of Christ who is sitting in this throne lately, at the end of the previous chapter, and judges the world, as both our belief and Revelation 14:14 testify, yet here is there a translation made of persons and it is the Father who now speaks. For not only now has that judgment seat (attributed in the Scriptures to Christ) taken full effect, but also Christ, earlier having perfected his functions of incarnation, teaching, redemption, mediation, and damning and throwing down the wicked, now delivers up the kingdom to God the Father that he may be all in all, as testifies Paul. . . . And again on the other part, now are here introduced the offices and functions of God the Father and Creator anew creating and renewing the world. Because here the functions of the Son are ending and the functions of the Father newly again beginning, this must be the Father who here showed that he is to renew the world, seeing that is his function and office. A PLAIN DISCOVERY OF THE WHOLE REVELATION OF SAINT JOHN.[17]

A PLACE AS WELL AS ITS CITIZENS. HEINRICH BULLINGER: Jerusalem. And a city signifies the place and habitation as well as those who dwell in the place, I mean the citizens themselves. This city therefore is not only the place of the blessed but also the very communion of saints, in old time prefigured in the city of Jerusalem. But he puts a great difference between this our new and that visible and corporal Jerusalem. For he calls ours holy; that other in the land of Palestine was profane, polluted with the blood of Christ, prophets, and apostles, and for the same cause destroyed utterly. Ours is also called new. For the communion of saints shall be renewed on the same day.

And therefore by interpretation followed "coming down from heaven," not that the habitation of saints after judgment will again be in earth but that the glory and renewing shall be granted from heaven by the divine majesty and power. As also St. James is read to have said, "Every good gift and every perfect gift is from above, coming down from the father of lights." And St. Paul also . . . said that the free church is the heavenly Jerusalem. . . . The first man, he says, of the earth was earthly; the second man, the Lord himself from heaven. Such as that earthly one was, such are those also who are

[15]Perkins, *Lectures**, 180-82.
[16]Simons, *Complete Writings**, 324-405.
[17]Napier, *Plain Discovery**, 251-52; citing 1 Cor 15:24-28.

earthly; and such as that heavenly one was, such are those also who are heavenly. And as we have born the image of the earthly man, so shall we bear also the image of the heavenly.

Therefore said St. John most rightly that the church of saints comes down from heaven, namely, from heaven receiving her glory. For again by a demonstration: "Prepared of God, he says, as a bride garnished for her husband." . . . We know, [Paul] says, that if our earthly mansion of this tabernacle is destroyed, we have the building of God, a mansion not made with hands, everlasting in heaven. And he who has prepared us for the same is God. He removes from his saints all corruption but gives and teaches to be purified with all gifts of the body, that so they may be garnished worthily and may dwell in the everlasting bride chamber with their bridegroom, Christ.

Therefore this garnishing consisted in the abolishing of all corruption and mortality, and in the gift of incorruption, immortality, and glory. Of the purifying and decking of the bride speaks the apostle St. Paul also. . . . And in this world begins the purging and trimming, and finally at the end is finished most fitly. For then shall the church have neither spot nor wrinkle, all corruption truly wiped away, and all glory received. Hundred Sermons on the Apocalypse.[18]

All Things Are Purified in the Eternal Country. Heinrich Bullinger: First, the walls are of jasper. Let no one here join to himself carnal things. The jasper is green. The celestial city always flourished; God's protection never failed.

The city itself, that is to say, the buildings in the city, the palaces and houses, are pure gold. For all things are purified in the eternal country. There is no uncleanness, no evil affections; there shall be no trouble or pain. As the Lord said also . . . disputing against the Sadducees. Therefore as gold is most tried and pure, so shall the celestial habitation be most clean. Therefore also must the bodies who shall dwell in heaven be clarified or glorified. He added that this gold most pure is not glass but in brightness represents most pure and shiny glass. For in heaven all things are clear.

And first he says generally that the foundations of the city are beautified with all manner of precious stones, and after he recited by name the stones that are most excellent. Doubtless nothing is more precious, nothing more excellent, than Christ the foundation of our salvation, than the apostolic doctrine, by which we are induced to the knowledge of Christ and of our salvation. And he sets in order twelve stones, with the intent we should understand that there is not one precious stone alone placed for the foundation but a row of one sort in such a length, as the side is square, and so consequently likewise in all parts of the square. For the first order therefore is placed a jasper stone, that is to say, in the first place of the foundation jasper stones are set in their rank; again in the next row on the jaspers are laid sapphires throughout the whole space in such length as the foundation was, and so consequently the other stones were couched and laid in order.

By all of this is signified that the foundation of our salvation is both most excellent and sure. We ought rightly to value this more than the price of all the jewels in the earth. And there are found people godly and beneficial, bestowing or selling these earthly jewels, according to the apostles' doctrine . . . who prepare for themselves a good foundation in another world. There are found fools, who are overmuch in love with jewels, and many times, instead of precious stones that cost very much being polished, they buy glass. . . . Truly precious stones have their use and virtues, and they were not made by God in vain. But we must always remember that saying of the wise man: all things are not right for all people.

There we shall be seen face to face. There we shall most perfectly know all things.

By the register of precious stones he seems to have alluded to the precious stones that were set in the attire of the high bishop. . . . Neither do I doubt that St. John took the arranging partly out of

[18]Bullinger, *Hundred Sermons** (1561), 632-33; Gal 4; 1 Cor 15; 2 Cor 5; Eph 5.

Isaiah. . . . Expounding this place, St. Jerome sends those who desire to know more of stones to Epiphanius† and to *Natural History* 37 of Pliny. Aretas‡ in his commentaries applied the twelve precious stones to the twelve apostles of Christ. There remain, moreover, the writings of Bede on this place, who took out of Thomas Aquinas such things as he has in his commentaries on the Apocalypse. . . .

Moreover, in the fourth place is declared the matter of the gates. They were of one whole pearl every one of them, of which the price is exceedingly great. The gate of heaven is Christ, and the porters of heaven are apostles, as is declared before. Therefore are the gates most precious and strongest. . . . Christ himself and the salvation that is of him are compared to a pearl, which the merchant, selling all he has, buys for himself, thinking himself rich enough if he may have this pearl.

In the fifth place is also described the street, what it is. In the cities here on earth, the streets are many times muddy, though otherwise the cities were never so famous and noble. Where they are notable, they are paved with stone or brick, but the street of our city is paved with gold both clean and bright. For in heaven is found no offense, no obscure darkness. All these things doubtless are spoken most beautifully, but far greater things must be yet understood and imagined. We must endeavor with all our might that the thing the tongue of humankind cannot utter, nor our mind here conceive the greatness and excellence of, we may at the length behold the same in heaven presently and may experience the same in those our glorified bodies, through Jesus Christ our Lord. Hundred Sermons on the Apocalypse.[19]

I Did Not See a Temple. Heinrich Bullinger: The apostle proceeded in the description of the divine or celestial city to comfort and keep the faithful in all temptations and afflictions. Therefore in the seventh place he spoke about the temple. For in famous cities there is no small consideration and praise of churches. This is manifest by all writers of stories, places, and times. What temple is then in heaven? None at all. For St. John says, "And I saw in the city of God no temple." This place is not repugnant with those things that are in Revelation 11 and 15 of the temple in heaven. For the temple is there exhibited in a figure and vision, not that there is indeed any temple in heaven, but that thus might be signified God's justice and certain salvation promised in the Scriptures, as we have in those places declared.

And what is the reason that there appeared no temple in heaven? The divine revelation answered, "For the Lord God Almighty and the Lamb is the temple in that our heavenly country." The use of temples is this: The Lord, first instituting the tabernacle, after that the temple, would have it testified that he will be present in the middle of his people, a father, Lord, and defender. And therefore they are said in the Scriptures to come to the Lord, those who came to either the tabernacle or temple of the Lord. The temple, moreover, was erected for preaching and prayer and the external service of God, for receiving of the sacraments, or offering up of sacrifices. But the saints in the heavenly country have no need of all these things. Therefore they need no temple.

Therefore there is no temple seen in heaven. For the Lord God now showed himself to them to be enjoyed of the same, and the saints are now with him; therefore they need no token of his presence. We are taught by doctrine what God is, what is his will, and that we are saved by the Lamb, but now that we see God himself face to face and that salvation is come by the Lamb of God, what need is there of a temple in heaven? By prayer we ask for life and joys everlasting; now since these are happened to the elect, what need for any house of prayer? Hundred Sermons on the Apocalypse.[20]

[19]Bullinger, *Hundred Sermons** (1561), 659; citing Mt 19; 1 Tim 6; Ex 28; Is 54; Mt 13. †Epiphanius of Salamis (310–403) was the bishop of Salamis, Cyprus, at the end of the 4th century. He is considered a saint and a church father by both the Eastern Orthodox and Roman Catholic Churches. He gained a reputation as a strong defender of orthodoxy. ‡Arethas, archbishop of Caesarea (c. 850–c. 944), was possibly a pupil of the patriarch of Constantinople, Photius.

[20]Bullinger, *Hundred Sermons** (1561), 660.

Citizens of the New Jerusalem. Heinrich Bullinger: He showed in more than one place who are partakers of that light, or who are citizens of this celestial city, and what is the state of the citizens. All nations and saved people are citizens of the eternal country. Here are two things to be noted. First, the Gentiles are made inheritors of glory, and that without any choice. For here excelled not the Jew, nor the Greek, neither Roman nor barbarian. Again, not all without respect do obtain everlasting light, but the saved only, that is to say, those whom Christ has saved and redeemed from sin, the devil, antichrist, and from the curse and the world. And Christ saves the elect and faithful. They therefore shall indeed be partakers of the light: These are the citizens of the country everlasting.

But what is their state and inheritance? They shall walk in the light of God the Father and the Lamb; that is to say, they shall have the fruition of the light and of God himself to their joyful sweetness and fill. For it is a figure of speech, "to walk in the light," for that which is to enjoy light. Truly in Psalm 88 we read with a similar figure of speech, "Lord, they shall walk in the light of your countenance." And again, "You shall make known to me the path of life, the fulfilling of joys is in your sight, and gladness in your right hand for evermore."

But especially the places in heaven and in that palace divine are for kings. Kings are governors and captains of the people . . . who are called kings, princes, governors, magistrates, rulers of the political as well as of ecclesiastical government, doctors, masters, teachers, artificers, and parents. For their duty is to virtuously govern their subjects, scholars, or children, to keep them under awe or discipline, to chastise and direct them to the duties of life and all godliness. If they do this, they shall have a worthy place prepared in heaven. For Daniel says also . . . , "But the teachers shall shine as the brightness of the firmament; and those who bring many to righteousness, as the stars everlastingly." O therefore, O happy are you, if you bring many to execute the office of righteousness. But woe be to you, princes, teachers, masters, and parents, if you are negligent in this. There is prepared for you in hell a place most horrible and miserable, as also Ezekiel has testified. But if kings have their place—a right honorable one—in heaven, therefore do the Anabaptists. Hundred Sermons on the Apocalypse.[21]

Nothing Offensive in Heaven. Heinrich Bullinger: Now therefore in the eleventh place he showed that there shall be nothing in heaven that may offend, that is to say, that shall not be pleasant and delectable, most clean and neat, absolute and complete. The same also must be referred to the persons. For it followed, "except those who are written in the Lamb's book of life." We understand, therefore, how into the kingdom of heaven shall not enter wordmongers, idolaters, liars, deceivers, and whatever is unclean and not purged with the blood of the son of God through faith. This same the apostle affirmed. . . . David also demanded, "Lord, who shall dwell in your tabernacle, or who shall rest in your holy hill?" And answered incontinently, "Those who walk without spot and work righteousness." . . .

Finally, here shall be fulfilled such things as are written . . . concerning those who are prohibited to enter into the church. Therefore this place has a secret doctrine and private admonishment, instructing us that if we want or covet to be heirs of the everlasting country, we should all apply ourselves to righteousness and innocence while we live here on earth. For it shall follow in Revelation 22. For outside are dogs and enchanters and whoremongers and so on. The Lord bring us by the way of righteousness to life everlasting. Hundred Sermons on the Apocalypse.[22]

[21]Bullinger, *Hundred Sermons** (1561), 661-62; citing Dan 12:1-8.
[22]Bullinger, *Hundred Sermons** (1561), 664-65; citing 1 Cor 5:12; 6:1-20; Eph 5:3-12; Ps 15; Deut 23.

21:9-22:15 JERUSALEM AND HER DESTINY

9 Then came one of the seven angels who had the seven bowls full of the seven last plagues and spoke to me, saying, "Come, I will show you the Bride, the wife of the Lamb." 10 And he carried me away in the Spirit to a great, high mountain, and showed me the holy city Jerusalem coming down out of heaven from God, 11 having the glory of God, its radiance like a most rare jewel, like a jasper, clear as crystal. 12 It had a great, high wall, with twelve gates, and at the gates twelve angels, and on the gates the names of the twelve tribes of the sons of Israel were inscribed— 13 on the east three gates, on the north three gates, on the south three gates, and on the west three gates. 14 And the wall of the city had twelve foundations, and on them were the twelve names of the twelve apostles of the Lamb.

15 And the one who spoke with me had a measuring rod of gold to measure the city and its gates and walls. 16 The city lies foursquare, its length the same as its width. And he measured the city with his rod, 12,000 stadia.[a] Its length and width and height are equal. 17 He also measured its wall, 144 cubits[b] by human measurement, which is also an angel's measurement. 18 The wall was built of jasper, while the city was pure gold, like clear glass. 19 The foundations of the wall of the city were adorned with every kind of jewel. The first was jasper, the second sapphire, the third agate, the fourth emerald, 20 the fifth onyx, the sixth carnelian, the seventh chrysolite, the eighth beryl, the ninth topaz, the tenth chrysoprase, the eleventh jacinth, the twelfth amethyst. 21 And the twelve gates were twelve pearls, each of the gates made of a single pearl, and the street of the city was pure gold, like transparent glass.

22 And I saw no temple in the city, for its temple is the Lord God the Almighty and the Lamb. 23 And the city has no need of sun or moon to shine on it, for the glory of God gives it light, and its lamp is the Lamb. 24 By its light will the nations walk, and the kings of the earth will bring their glory into it, 25 and its gates will never be shut by day—and there will be no night there. 26 They will bring into it the glory and the honor of the nations. 27 But nothing unclean will ever enter it, nor anyone who does what is detestable or false, but only those who are written in the Lamb's book of life.

22 Then the angel[c] showed me the river of the water of life, bright as crystal, flowing from the throne of God and of the Lamb 2 through the middle of the street of the city; also, on either side of the river, the tree of life[d] with its twelve kinds of fruit, yielding its fruit each month. The leaves of the tree were for the healing of the nations. 3 No longer will there be anything accursed, but the throne of God and of the Lamb will be in it, and his servants will worship him. 4 They will see his face, and his name will be on their foreheads. 5 And night will be no more. They will need no light of lamp or sun, for the Lord God will be their light, and they will reign forever and ever.

6 And he said to me, "These words are trustworthy and true. And the Lord, the God of the spirits of the prophets, has sent his angel to show his servants what must soon take place."

7 "And behold, I am coming soon. Blessed is the one who keeps the words of the prophecy of this book."

8 I, John, am the one who heard and saw these things. And when I heard and saw them, I fell down to worship at the feet of the angel who showed them to me, 9 but he said to me, "You must not do that! I am a fellow servant with you and your brothers the prophets, and with those who keep the words of this book. Worship God."

10 And he said to me, "Do not seal up the words of the prophecy of this book, for the time is near. 11 Let the evildoer still do evil, and the filthy still be filthy, and the righteous still do right, and the holy still be holy."

12 "Behold, I am coming soon, bringing my recompense with me, to repay each one for what he has done. 13 I am the Alpha and the Omega, the first and the last, the beginning and the end."

[14]Blessed are those who wash their robes,[e] so that they may have the right to the tree of life and that they may enter the city by the gates. [15]Outside are the dogs and sorcerers and the sexually immoral and murderers and idolaters, and everyone who loves and practices falsehood.

a About 1,380 miles; a *stadion* was about 607 feet or 185 meters b A *cubit* was about 18 inches or 45 centimeters c Greek *he* d Or *the Lamb. In the midst of the street of the city, and on either side of the river, was the tree of life* e Some manuscripts *do his commandments*

Overview: The vision of the new Jerusalem opens with one of the seven angels who had the seven bowls full of the seven last plagues speaking to John. John is carried away in the Spirit to a high mountain and shown the holy city Jerusalem coming down out of heaven. Through things earthly and corporal are shown the spiritual and celestial. David Pareus joins Heinrich Bullinger and other commentators in focusing on the physical description of the city, comparing it by analogy to the glory and beauty of an earthly city in its various aspects.

Reformation commentators make note of the fact that no temple is in the city, distinguishing this heavenly city from the earthly Jerusalem. The reason given is that there is no need for such a place for church gatherings, preaching of the Word, and administration of sacraments because the temple is the Lord God the Almighty and the Lamb. For Giovanni Diodati, there is no need for the eternal signs of God's presence that were in the temple because God manifests himself face to face to his elect in Christ.

The river of life flows through the city. The two sides of the river, according to John Bale, are the two Testaments of the Lord, and the tree of life is Jesus Christ. The tree yields its twelve kinds of fruit each month, and the leaves of the tree are for the healing of the nations.

21:9-21 *The Vision of the City*

Ascending to Eternal Things. Heinrich Bullinger: St. John returned to the description of the celestial city, which in the beginning of this chapter he had started. . . . For the Spirit of God will have us by occasion of temporal things ascend with our minds to eternal things, and by temporal things more excellent. Therefore are all things figured with amplifications, hyperbole, and other figures. We shall therefore imagine in these far greater things, as we desire to do whenever we read or hear such things as our Lord has taught under the parables of weddings and feasts. Hundred Sermons on the Apocalypse.[1]

The City as an Allegory. David Pareus: After the capital adversaries with the rest of the ungodly were judged and cast into the lake of fire, here is shown to John the renovation of the world that shall be, as also the heavenly glory of the godly under a twofold type, namely, of a bride gloriously attired and of a most magnificent city. This whole chapter sets forth the illustration of this type, as the wit, art, hand, or tongue of people is able to express nothing more beautiful, more magnificent, more glorious, and sumptuous than this structure. For whatever may seem to conduce to the glory and comeliness of an earthly city with respect to walls, gates, foundation, figure, streets, temples, air, and, last, the wealth of its citizens, ornament, and pleasantness of life—all this John sees here to be most eminent and glorious in this heavenly Jerusalem. By these allegories the Holy Spirit would in some measure foreshadow that unspeakable glory and felicity that the church now militant on earth shall receive in the heavens after the end of her wearisome labors in this warfare, which eye has not seen, ear has not heard, nor has entered into the heart of humanity. A Commentary upon the Divine Revelation.[2]

[1]Bullinger, *Hundred Sermons** (1561), 647-48.
[2]Pareus, *Revelation**, 546-47.

21:22-27 *John's Interpretation of the Vision*

Everlasting Good Promised to Us. Heinrich Bullinger: He proceeds in describing the blessed seats and that life of the world to come under the image of a most goodly and excellent city. We shall understand all things not after the letter but after the spirit. All things are said for our comfort and to the end that we should stoutly contemn this world, the pleasures thereof, and the furies of prosecutors, and should always desire so great and the same everlasting good things promised us that we have heard in the description. Indeed, there are even seen four singular things of this heavenly city as if it were a lively picture, what a light it has, what walls, what gates also, and foundations. Now in the fifth place follows what is the wideness or largeness of this city. For by this are cities commended. And it is necessary that the greatest number of citizens should have the largest or greatest city.

Therefore comes forth one to measure this city, an angel sent to John from heaven, holding in his hand a reed, that is, a long pole or measuring rod, not of wood or lead but of gold. And by the measuring he does, we should esteem the quantity of the blessed state. In the meter therefore and in the measure, we shall not need to seek any great mysteries. For the eternal wisdom and providence of God has prepared seats for his chosen, and that in a golden order, that is, most purified, which is signified by the golden reed or measure. For the judge in St. Matthew provoked the sheep to take the inheritance prepared from the beginning of the world. He alone knows also who are his.

The situation of the city is declared to be planted in a square, by which is signified the strength and stability of the blessed in heaven. For the place is no ball, bowl, or globe, rolling and easy to turn. We do not need to doubt the certainty of it. For hope shames no one, and the one who believes in Christ shall never be confounded. Hundred Sermons on the Apocalypse.[3]

The Court and Temple in the City. David Pareus: Two things are the principal ornaments of a city: the court and temple. In the former judgment is administered. In the temple religious worship is performed. The first, he says, is of pure gold, for in the new heaven and in the new earth shall dwell righteousness, not in civil contracts or distribution of civil goods, which then shall cease, but because in the sweetest conversation of the saints, unrighteousness shall have no place. He does not say that he saw a temple of gold in the city, for had he so said, it would have been no great matter, seeing as Solomon's temple did glitter with pure gold within, by which splendor the magnificence of Christ's spiritual kingdom was conveyed.

Therefore, he says, "I saw no temple in it," by which he distinguishes this heavenly city from the earthly Jerusalem, in which there was a glorious temple dedicated to God's worship. But in the celestial Jerusalem John saw no temple, for there is no need of a place for church gatherings, preaching of the Word, administration of sacraments, rites, and outward exercises of religion, because the ecclesiastical ministries shall be no more, and neither shall God be served with external worship, which in this life he requires of us to the end he may be honored by us, and our weakness and piety sustained by these outward aids. For then all rule, authority, and power (both ecclesiastical and political) shall be abolished. A Commentary upon the Divine Revelation.[4]

Loving God with a Pure Heart Is the Willingness to Be Damned. Martin Luther: You ask whether God has ever willed or may ever will that a man should resign himself to hell and damnation or give himself to the anathema from Christ for the sake of his will. I reply that it happens in many cases and especially in those who are imperfect in charity or pure love for God. For in their case the love of concupiscence which is so deeply rooted in them must necessarily be torn out. But it is not torn out except

[3]Bullinger, *Hundred Sermons** (1561), 650-59.

[4]Pareus, *Revelation**, 567.

through a superabundant infusion of grace or through this very harsh resignation. For "nothing unclean shall enter into the kingdom of God." But now no one knows whether he loves God with a pure heart unless he has experienced in himself that if it should please God he would not desire even to be saved nor would he refuse to be damned. For the damned suffer so severely because they are unwilling to be damned and do not resign themselves to this will of God, which they cannot do without the grace of God. LECTURES ON ROMANS.[5]

THE LAMB IS ITS LIGHT. HEINRICH BULLINGER: And I saw no temple in it. For the Lord God Almighty and the Lamb is the temple of it, and the city has no need of the sun, and neither of the moon, to light it. For the brightness of God lights it, and the Lamb is its light. And the people who are saved shall walk in the light of it, and the kings of the earth shall bring their glory and honor to it. And the its gates shall not be shut by day, for there shall be no night there. And they shall bring the glory and honor of the Gentiles to it. And there shall enter into it no unclean thing, neither whatever works abomination or makes lies, but those who are written in the Lamb's book of life. HUNDRED SERMONS ON THE APOCALYPSE.[6]

THE SAINTS ARE THE TEMPLE. MARY CARY: The word *temple* in the Old Testament is used only for that house that Solomon built in Jerusalem to the Lord, which was called the temple of the Lord, it being the place where God was in a special manner present and where he would in a special manner be worshiped. But in the New Testament it is used first for the church, the saints of God, of which that temple was a figure. For as God was in a special manner present in that temple, so he is in a special manner present in his people. And so we have it, "For you are the temple of the living God, as God has said, I will dwell in them and walk in them, and I will be their God, and they shall be my people." . . . "Do you not know that your bodies are the temple of the Holy Ghost, which is in you," and so on, and thus the word *temple* in the New Testament is used for the saints, as the temple was a figure of them, as they have a special presence of God in them. . . . So he who is of a poor and contrite spirit and trembles at the word of God shall be the house, the temple of God.

But second, the word *temple* in the New Testament, as it is used for those in whom there is a special presence of God, so it is used to signify that means by which knowledge and instruction is given out, as the temple of old was the place where people were to receive instruction and knowledge. And in this sense it is used. . . . "And I saw no temple therein, for the Lord God Almighty and the Lamb are the temple of it." This is spoken of the new Jerusalem, of that glorious state the church shall be in when they shall be all taught of God, from the greatest to the least.

Now, the word *temple* here in the text signifies these.

First, it signifies the saints of God, as they are those in whom God in a special manner dwells. And second, it signifies the ordinances and means whereby knowledge is dispensed and instruction is received, for it is the saints who are as lights in the world, and they both instruct the ignorant and edify one another, especially when they are congregated, assembled together to worship God, according to his own will and to prophesy to edify one another. THE RESURRECTION OF THE WITNESSES.[7]

FACE TO FACE WITH GOD. GIOVANNI DIODATI: "No temple": the meaning is that instead of eternal signs of God's presence that were anciently in the temple, God shall manifest himself face to face, to his elect in Christ, and they shall be all gathered in him to serve him forever. . . . "The Lamb": thus it is shown that in the heavenly glory also Christ shall be the only means of all the communication

[5] LW 25:381.

[6] Bullinger, *Hundred Sermons** (1561), 660.

[7] Cary, *Doom**, 34-37; citing 2 Cor 6:16; 1 Cor 6:19; Is 66:1-2; 57:15.

that the elect shall have in the glory and light of God. . . .

"Shall walk": figurative terms taken from the prophets speaking of the church here in the world to signify the perfect glory, happiness, and fullness that shall be in the heavenly life. Or the everlasting glory is represented not only in regard to the whole body of the church, when it shall be gathered into it, but also in regard to believers in this world who aspire to it as to the end of their race and harbor of their sea voyage, where all spiritual virtues with which they are endowed as true kings in spirit are carried to be there made perfect and to beautify that temple of God. Pious Annotations upon the Holy Bible.[8]

Purgatory Is Not Proved. Martin Chemnitz: From Revelation 21:27 they construct purgatory thus: Into the heavenly city "nothing unclean shall enter." But many souls depart from this world which are not so clean that they merit to be received into heaven, neither so unclear that they should be cast into hell. Therefore, there must of necessity be an intermediate place where they are purged by fire, so that they can at some time enter paradise.

This argument proceeds simply from ignorance of the righteousness of the gospel and from a judgment of reason about justification, which they locate in our own or our inherent righteousness, purity, and perfection. But Scripture loudly proclaims that no one among all the saints in this life can say . . . : "I have made my heart clean; I am pure from my sin." Therefore God has given us an undefiled high priest, the anointed Most Holy, who through himself has made purification of our sins and cleanses from sins. . . . Thus believers possess cleanness in the sight of God by which they can enter paradise, but this does not consist in their own inherent cleanness. . . . Therefore the saints shine in the other world, because "they have washed their robes . . . in the blood of the Lamb."

Truly therefore nothing unclean enters into that heavenly city; but the believers, even though they confess with Isaiah that they are unclean, nevertheless have in Christ the most perfect cleanness. . . . By that saying of John, therefore, papalist purgatory is not in the least proved. For that same John, when in his Apocalypse he saw both the glory of the blest and the punishment of the damned, neither saw nor heard nor dreamed anything about a third place or condition of purgatory. And the very language in Revelation 21:27 shows that it is not venial sins, which the papalists say are cleansed by fire, that are spoke of. For he says that whatever pollutes shall not enter it. Now what things are which defile a man Christ explains. . . . And John himself adds the explanation: "Anyone who practices abomination or falsehood." Therefore he is speaking of sins which exclude from the kingdom of God. Indeed, where does Scripture teach that those who desire to enter paradise must be purged through torrents of fire? Examination of the Council of Trent.[9]

22:1-5 *The Vision of the River of Life and Its Interpretation*

A Most Pure and Commodious River. John Bale: And the angel (St. John says) or gracious purpose of the Lord, who communed with me all this time to bring me yet to a further knowledge of his mysteries, showed to me a most pure and commodious river, which was the wholesome water of life. Nothing other can I suppose this to be by searching the Scriptures except the flowing truth, the word of salvation, or the effectual doctrine of Christ's Holy Spirit. The Image of Both Churches.[10]

Perpetual Application of Christ's Righteousness. Giovanni Diodati: "In the midst": This is spoken as by a relation to the earthly paradise, in the midst of which stood the tree of life. . . . "The tree": All these things are spoken by

[8]Diodati, *Pious Annotations**, 110.

[9]Chemnitz, *Examination*, 3:336-37; citing Prov 20:9; Heb 7:26-27; Dan 9:24; Heb 9:14; 1 Jn 1:7; Rev 7:14; 22:14; Mt 15:18-19.

[10]Bale, *Image** (1570), ch. 22.

figure, for as people live by the fruits of the earth, the fruits are brought forth by the plants, the plants subsist by the watering. So in heaven the church shall enjoy everlasting life by the perfect communion and conjunction it shall have with Christ, represented by the tree of life, in whom all the Father's love is spread forth as a lively spring. "Which bear": this is also said only to show the eternal lastingness and the abundance of this fruit of life.

"The leaves": this is taken out of Ezekiel 47:12 and may be referred to the perpetual application of Christ's righteousness and innocence, which is, as it were, his fair and always fresh flourishing, by which the wound and disease of the soul, which is sin, is healed by remission and absolution. . . . Finally, by this means is expressed that in Christ we have all things necessary for salvation, comprehended in two parts, which are the furnishing with all good things and the freeing from all evil. Pious Annotations upon the Holy Bible.[11]

What Will Pass Away Versus What Is Eternal. Pilgram Marpeck: The difference between the creatures which pass away and end with time and the creatures which are and remain eternally.

Time will cease to be. Sun, moon, stars, and everything that exists in time and for the sake of man (not created to remain eternally) must cease to be for the sake of that which and must remain eternally (such as men and angels which are taken up into God and God into them). For there will no longer be any need for time nor the creatures of time such as animals, birds, fish, light, nor day. For in eternity time ceases, and God himself is day and light. Darkness and night will [depart] from the light, the incarnate Word and Spirit, and go to its eternal place where no grace or creaturely light will ever again be seen. Only the hellish and eternally deadly fire is the revelation and illumination of everlasting torment. Concerning the Love of God in Christ.[12]

The Most Delectable Tree of Life. John Bale: And on either side of the sweet river, which are the two Testaments of the Lord, was standing the most delectable tree of life, Jesus Christ, that Mediator and Father who gives life to the world. Out of the stock of Abraham and David sprang this tree . . . conceived of the Holy Spirit, born of the Virgin Mary, which was also a golden stone of this street. "Blessed are you" (says Elizabeth) "for your believers' sake. For in you is performed the full promise of the Lord." This is that tree that was planted by the riverside and gave forth fruit at his time appointed. As the tree of life was set in the middle of paradise at the beginning, so is he now spiritually grounded in the midst of his church, which is his garden of pleasure. "Behold" (says Christ), "I am with you every day unto the world's end." . . .

This tree is both in the middle of the street and on either side of the river. For both is Christ known of his faithful multitude and comprehended in the Scriptures. David acknowledged himself to be a pure stone of this golden street when he said, "My humble soul has cleaved or fastened to the pavement, you quickening me, Lord, according to your word." The Image of Both Churches.[13]

Adoration of the Saints Is Not Piety. Martin Chemnitz: Neither is there any difference, that it is idolatry if adoration or invocation is given to the devil, but if it is given to the saints it is piety. For in Revelation 19:10 and 22:8-9 John, who was about to adore the angel, was not so foolish and profane to think that angel was the first, supreme, and eternal Beginning, but by this adoration, he wanted to solicit the favor of the angel in order obtain many other benefits from him. The angel, however, sternly forbids John: "You must not do that! . . . Worship God!" Therefore it is clear that the papalist invocations of the saints, which have been described above, are not mere venerations of the saints, but adorations which belong only to God, that is, they are idolatry. Examination of the Council of Trent.[14]

[11]Diodati, *Pious Annotations**, 110-11; citing Gen 2:9; Mal 4:2.
[12]Marpeck, *Writings*, 536-37.
[13]Bale, *Image** (1570), ch. 22.
[14]Chemnitz, *Examination*, 3:435.

Healing Fruit from the Leaves of the Tree. David Pareus: It does not hence follow that these leaves serve to cure the diseases of the nations or repair their health. For it is manifest that Ezekiel is speaking of the state of the church militant, yet subject to many diseases and troubles. Therefore by the leaves he understands the gospel, under which, as it were, is covered a healing fruit, satiating all nations. But here he describes the state of the church triumphant, in which neither sickness nor medicine has any place.

But neither does the angel make this difference, but he calls the elect saints the nations, because formerly they were Gentiles. . . . The nations of those who were saved shall walk in the light of it. . . . They shall ring the glory and honor of the nations to it. A Commentary upon the Divine Revelation.[15]

Rivers Occasion the Abundance of Food. Heinrich Bullinger: Rivers make cities pleasant and delectable. Without fountains, springs, and wholesome waters, cities decay and are scarcely worthy of the names of cities. But in case they want food, they are wholly lost. Therefore, this our heavenly city excelled and is most noble in all these things. It not only has food but gives it to us with great pleasure and finesse most pleasant. For trees in this city do not only bear fruit but give also a pleasantness unspeakable and inestimable. The river, moreover, runs through the middle of the streets; on the banks of either side are trees most beautiful to behold, bearing the fruit of life. And as I have many times in this description intimated, so I repeat now again that those things are not to be understood after the letter, as the millenarians take them. For the Lord talked with us and even lisped to the end we might with the imbecility of our understanding conceive of these things. Hundred Sermons on the Apocalypse.[16]

22:6-15 *John and the Angel*

Do Not Revere the Creature. William Perkins: In the profession of God we are to consider the parts of it and the time appointed for this profession.

The parts are two: the solemn worshiping of God and the glorifying of him.

The second commandment describes such holy and solemn worship as is due to God. . . . "Thou shalt not make": This is the first part of the commandment, forbidding to make an idol. Now an idol is a certain representation and image not only of some feigned God, but also of the true Jehovah. . . . "Thou shalt neither worship false gods nor the true God with a false worship": Many things are here forbidden . . . [such as] a religious reverence of the creature, as when we attribute more to him than we ought. "When I had heard and seen, I fell down to worship before the feet of the angel who showed me these things. But he said to me, 'Do not do that, for I am your fellow servant.'" A Golden Chain.[17]

Civil Honor and Divine Honor. John Calvin: When John was rebuked by the angel because he fell down on his knees before him . . . , we ought not to suppose John to be so senseless as to wish to transfer to an angel the honor due to God alone. But because any reverential act that has been joined with religion cannot but savor of something divine, he could not have "knelt" to the angel without detracting from God's glory. Indeed, we often read that men were worshiped: but such an act was, so to speak, a civil honor. Religion, however, has another concern; as soon as it has been joined with an act of reverence, it carries the profanation of divine honor along with it. Institutes of the Christian Religion.[18]

The Whole Christian People. Theodore Bibliander: The entire Christian world ought to

[15]Pareus, *Revelation**, 576.
[16]Bullinger, *Hundred Sermons** (1561), 665-71.
[17]Perkins, *Golden Chain**, ch. 21; citing Ex 20:4-6.
[18]Calvin, *Institutes* 1.12.3.

be contained in one kingdom and empire, one political system, one home, temple, and church, yes, in one body, whose head is Christ, and the head of Christ is God. And, they should be governed by the same laws which are found in the canonical Scriptures of the Old and New Testament. And, the entire Christian world should be constrained by the same religion. And, there should be one God over all, one orthodox faith, one baptism for the remission of sins, one gathering and communion of the Lord's body and blood, one mediator between God and men, one Jesus Christ, true God and true man. Although all this is true, nevertheless, the property of the Lord, the holy nation, the royal priesthood, the people of his purchasing who have been redeemed by the blood of the Son of God, this people has been divided, split, torn, and rent into sects and divisions more numerous—and these indeed opposed to one another—than all the peoples and nations that even today wretchedly roam around outside the fold of the Christian church, and know not the blessing of Messiah. They do not know the one who was promised from the very beginning of the world and set forth in various types, and longed for with the greatest desire by all the holy fathers. THE FAITHFUL RELATIONSHIP.[19]

DISTINCTIONS IN JUSTIFICATION AND SANCTIFICATION. MARTIN CHEMNITZ: No matter to what justification by faith is attributed, or what it is that justifies us, it at once follows freely that that is the thing on account of which we are received into grace by God; and that faith must set that thing against the judgment of God, lest a person be condemned; that on account of that thing God is rendered reconciled to us, grants us adoption, and receives us to life eternal. . . . Its forensic meaning, as we commonly say, is so manifest that Andrada[†] does not dare to deny it. However, he anxiously seeks examples to prove that in many places in Scripture the word "justify" does not mean to absolve from sins but to adorn the mind with the quality of inherent righteousness. And with this battering ram he expects to overcome the entire doctrine of imputed righteousness. . . .

He quotes also from the Apocalypse for the confirmation of their opinion: "Let him that is righteous be justified still further: and let him that is holy be sanctified still further." But the answer is easy. Andrada fights for the opinion which contends that justification and sanctification are one and the same thing, and he wants to prove this understanding from this statement of John. However, here John, even as Paul . . . , expressly distinguishes between justification and sanctification. The reader therefore sees of what kind these proofs of Andrada are. Nor is this against it, that the justified are commanded to be justified further, since the remission of sins is not mutilated. For sin dwells in the flesh of the justified and often overcomes them, so that they offend in many things. EXAMINATION OF THE COUNCIL OF TRENT.[20]

CONCLUDING NARRATION. HEINRICH BULLINGER: And in good order this last book of the canonical Scripture finishes the godly narration and doctrine with the judgment and end of all things. For the Holy Scripture begins at the first origin of all things and continues a narration until the end of all things, containing in itself the universality of things and all such things as are requisite to be known of needful and profitable matters. And all those things has our good Lord given us to be known in the Holy Scripture, that is to say, in the canonical books. For those who say that all things that pertain to the true and full godliness and salvation of the faithful are not set forth in holy writings, and therefore we have need of traditions, they are false harlots. They indeed have need of those traditions, which will utter their crafty wares; we who esteem all their wares not worth a halfpenny to be bought by anyone need

[19]Bibliander, *Omnium*, 10.

[20]Chemnitz, *Examination*, 1:469, 471-72; citing 1 Cor 6:11. †A celebrated Portuguese theologian of the sixteenth century, born in Coimbra on July 26, 1528; died December 1, 1575, in Lisbon.

none. For Isaiah has sufficiently dissuaded us from their dissuadable and crafty ugliness. . . .

Immediately after the beginning is set a grave asseveration that the things he has said or written up to this point are true, sure, certain, and undoubted. He has in a manner the same sentence also in Revelation 19. And he calls faithful sayings those that are stable, ratified steadfast and undoubted. And the sentence refers to the things he has spoken of the blessed life to the world to come, lest we should be left in any doubtfulness. Again, this refers to the whole narration of this book. And this sentence seems to be a clause of assertion and confirming the certainty of the matter propounded, as are those also in the prophets, "For the Lord has spoken," and again, "Thus sayeth the Lord of hosts," and that same in the Gospel, "Truly I say to you," and in the apostolic epistles, "God is my witness that I do not lie."

And the goodness of God does assist our infirmity—in accordance with which many times we doubt of the truth of God's words and do waver—and confirmed our hope with these anchors, as it were. Therefore these must be diligently rehearsed in and urged in the ecclesiastical doctrine. Aretas,[†] expounding this passage, says, "As the wanted manner of this holy Evangelist is always, so is it here also." For as in his Gospel in token of loyalty he says, "And we know that his testimony is true," so in this place also setting his seal, he says, "These sayings are faithful and true."

Second, he repeated who is the Author of this work and by whom all these things are revealed to him. And truly there is none other Author but the Lord God himself, and that is the God of the holy prophets. This has a great efficacy, for he showed him not only to be one and the same God of both Testaments, who by his Spirit has inspired the prophets and apostles, but also bid us secretly to esteem the verity and certitude of this book of the prophetic matters. HUNDRED SERMONS ON THE APOCALYPSE.[21]

FROM THE APOSTLES' TIME TO THE WORLD'S END. HEINRICH BULLINGER: Now he gathered the sum of such things as he has treated up to this point. The same are chiefly contained in two points. For he showed up to this point what must be done shortly. For this book contains the destinies of the church from the apostles' time to the world's end. HUNDRED SERMONS ON THE APOCALYPSE.[22]

FELICITY AND BLESSEDNESS. HEINRICH BULLINGER: But what profit shall the servants of God look for in this book? In a short sentence he comprises much and says, "Happy is the one who keeps the words of the prophecy of this book." Felicity and blessedness are the fruit that is taken from this book. In this present world, being linked with Christ, we shall walk in the way of righteousness and eschew the crafts of antichrist, and shall not feel the torments that arise in the conscience of the corruption of religion depraved. And when we depart hence, we shall go straight to those blessed seats. This is the high blessedness and felicity.

And let us mark that it is not enough either to have seen or heard or read this book; it must be kept. For we must beware that it does not go in one ear and out the other, that we not forget the things that are told us but that we rather frame our whole life after the doctrine of this book. And he attributed to it the title of prophecy. All the Scripture is called a prophecy, as much as to say divine, but considering how this book for the greater part of it shows things to come into the church, it is rightly called a prophecy. HUNDRED SERMONS ON THE APOCALYPSE.[23]

THE MYSTERIES GOD HAS COMMUNICATED TO US. THE GENEVA BIBLE: But there will be some who will abuse this occasion for evil and will wrest this Scripture to their own destruction, as Peter says. What then? Says the angel, the mysteries of God must not therefore be concealed that it

[21]Bullinger, *Hundred Sermons** (1561), 673-74; citing Is 55.
†Arethas, archbishop of Caesarea (c. 850–c. 944), was possibly a pupil of the patriarch of Constantinople, Photius.

[22]Bullinger, *Hundred Sermons** (1561), 675.
[23]Bullinger, *Hundred Sermons** (1561), 676-77.

has pleased him to communicate to us. Let them be hurtful to others, let such be more and more vile in themselves, whom this Scripture does not please; yet others shall be further conformed by it to righteousness and true holiness. . . . Also (says God by the angel) though there should be no use of this book for people, yet it shall be of this use to me, that it is a witness of my truth to my glory, who will come shortly to give and execute just judgement. The Geneva Bible.[24]

Behold, I Come Quickly. Heinrich Bullinger: The ninth part of this conclusion is of the coming of the Lord to judgment, and the reward prepared for the good, and appointed torments for the impenitent and wicked. . . .

And in this conclusion of St. John the persons are often changed. For now speaks John himself, and loosely he brings in the Lord speaking. As at this present truly he makes the Lord Christ himself to speak and say, "Behold, I come quickly." For the word pronounced out of Christ's mouth is of more authority and has more credit with all than that the apostle speaking. And in saying that he will come shortly, he wants to stir up all to watch, repent, and pray. For in the Gospel he said, "Watch, for you know neither the day nor the hour." Your Lord will come at an hour when you think least. He therefore feared the slothful and unclean persons who comfort themselves that the Lord shall not come at all, and if he come that yet it shall be a long time away and perhaps never. Against them he pleads, says how he will come quickly. Against the same also reasoned Malachi . . . and St. Peter. . . .

Moreover, in affirming that he will come shortly, he comforted the godly who are tempted and tossed diversely in this world. For the godly sometimes cry also that the Lord deferred his coming overlong, that he is of no danger to his enemies. Therefore he says that he will now come soon enough, that is to say, in due time, that he may both deliver his servants and destroy and root out his enemies and contenders. Hundred Sermons on the Apocalypse.[25]

[24]Geneva Bible* (1602), notes on Rev 22:10-11.

[25]Bullinger, *Hundred Sermons** (1561), 684-85; citing Mal 3–4; 2 Pet 3.

22:16-21 Conclusion

[16]"I, Jesus, have sent my angel to testify to you about these things for the churches. I am the root and the descendant of David, the bright morning star."

[17]The Spirit and the Bride say, "Come." And let the one who hears say, "Come." And let the one who is thirsty come; let the one who desires take the water of life without price.

[18]I warn everyone who hears the words of the prophecy of this book: if anyone adds to them, God will add to him the plagues described in this book, [19]and if anyone takes away from the words of the book of this prophecy, God will take away his share in the tree of life and in the holy city, which are described in this book.

[20]He who testifies to these things says, "Surely I am coming soon." Amen. Come, Lord Jesus!

[21]The grace of the Lord Jesus be with all.[a] Amen.

a Some manuscripts *all the saints*

Overview: As John concludes this Apocalypse, which is also a letter and a prophecy, he makes it clear that it is an invitation for all. It is not for John alone but for public examination. It is also clear, he writes, that further revelation is not coming. The Lord Jesus himself speaks and promises that he will certainly come to judgment, to redeem and glorify the godly and to punish the wicked. Following Jesus' invitation to come to him, John extends a benediction to his listeners. After the apostolic manner, he wishes the grace of the Lord Jesus Christ to all the hearers and readers of this book.

22:16-20 *The Invitation*

Accomplish Your Great Mystery. Thomas Brightman: Accomplish at length your great mystery, and let the world acknowledge your long delay to have been only for your mercy, not because of forgetfulness or neglect of your promise. Destroy the Romish beast and the Constantinopolitan dragon; build up your new Jerusalem, in which Christ shall reign and the saints shall rule together with him to enjoy for a time a blessed reign on earth, and most happy and eternal with you in heaven. Hear, Father, to whom no thought of the mind is unknown. Be present, you who are nowhere absent, but hear the prayers before whom you have gone before, by your decree. Then will we bring forth our harps and sing praises to you, celebrating you, the one-in-three God, the Father, the Son, and Holy Spirit, to whom be all honor, praise, and glory forever and ever. Amen. Revelation of St. John.[1]

Judging the Success of the Prophecy. Thomas Brightman: "Seal not": the publishing of a commandment by which there should be free power to everyone to examine and by its success to judge the prophecy. John might not have it for himself alone but should offer it to the trial of a public examination, as at once from the beginning he was bidden, "What you see, write in a book and send it to the seven churches." . . . And again, "Write these things that you have seen, and that are, and that shall be": that is, do not hide it from others but publish it.

But if the public publishing of it is spoken of, why was Daniel, who also brought into open view his prophecy, commanded to shut up his words and to seal the book? Therefore this prohibition of not sealing includes some other thing, namely that things to come are set down in such a way that

[1]Brightman, *Revelation**, 711.

people might be led as by the hand to fully understand the same prophecy by the events present and near at hand. It happened otherwise to Daniel, who was not manifest to every age, for he, dealing with a few overlapping matters, is chiefly employed in things that should lastly come to pass and therefore should expect the appointed time before which it was not to be unfolded.

This partly is to be understood of those more difficult visions, partly of the people of the Jews, whom that prophecy chiefly concerns. What followed confirmed this interpretation, for the time is at hand, as if he should say, "Do not shut up this prophecy, because the time near at hand shall reveal it." But Daniel's was sealed up, for the event's being far to come caused it to lie hidden for a great time. Therefore these words have the same force as the former, "Behold, I come quickly."

"He who does evil, let him do evil still": a preventing of a secret doubt by which the minds of the weak might be weakened, for they see that the ungodly go forward in their ungodliness, and their punishment for many ages differs. Therefore, they might demand, how would he come quickly who so long forbears the wicked? He then answered and warned that no one is to take this in ill part but mind that the ungodly will continue in their wickedness, and the righteous will follow after righteousness, but that there are certain bounds set beyond which they cannot go.

Neither must they wonder that a certain increase of wickedness is permitted for a determined time, for the greater condemnation of the ungodly, but they are to leave those people and to turn their eyes to the elect, whose constant study of godliness ought to strengthen our wavering minds against all stiffness of the reprobate. Therefore these are not the words of one exhorting but of one comforting and admonishing that by those scandals our expectation not be diminished, seeing that there shall be such a state of things even to the last end. Revelation of St. John.[2]

[2]Brightman, *Revelation**, 708-9; citing Rev 1:11.

This Book Is to Be Openly Read. Heinrich Bullinger: The seventh place that is treated in this conclusion forbade John to seal not the book written. The angel says, "Seal it not." And certainly letters and books are accustomed to be sealed, either for credit and confirmation's sake or else that they should not be openly read by all but only those to whom they are addressed. An angel says to Daniel, . . . "And you, Daniel, close the words and seal the book until the last time." He is commanded to shut his book, that is to say, to make an end, and not to look for any more revelation. Finally, he is commanded to shut it for the ungodly, to whom assuredly this book shall seem dark and closed. For it follows that many shall err and knowledge shall be manifold.

For those who are not ruled by the certain and sure Word of God have nothing at all certainly tried and known, but they wander through manifold or sundry and uncertain opinions, judgments, and traditions of people. For Daniel says that knowledge shall be variable, that is to say, there shall be innumerable opinions and sects of the religion and serving of God where nevertheless there is but one only true opinion, doctrine, faith, or religion. The same, I say, Daniel set forth in his book, which book also he sealed, that is to say, confirmed it, as it were, with godly seals as fully authentic or authorized and worthy to be credited.

Why is it that at the present St. John is not commanded in the same sense and meaning to seal his book, which we know to be altogether fully authentic? But this is what the angel meant: "Do not conceal or cover and do not hide this book. God therefore would have it to be written, that it might be a public doctrine in the whole world by which all people might be instructed in the things that are revealed from heaven, so they are not through the crafts and tyranny of antichrist withdrawn from the kingdom of Christ into the kingdom of antichrist, for God wants all these things to all people to be most common and manifestly known." And this sense has Aretas† opened also, saying, "Do not seal them, says he, that is, keep them not sealed to yourself but publish them to all." The reason is added, "For the time is at hand in which truly these things I have said shall come to pass."

Therefore the faithful had need of warning, confirming, and comfort. Considering therefore that this book is set forth that it might admonish, strengthen, and comfort the faithful, the same ought not to be shut but wide open. For this is the good will of God, that this his Word should be preached in his church to the profit of all faithful. Therefore let them consider what they do, those who would have this book not only shut up but clean taken away. Neither ought it to be understood as obscure and full of dark speaking. But to God be praise and thanksgiving, who has vouchsafed to provide for us faithfully and in time by this most profitable and most necessary book. Hundred Sermons on the Apocalypse.[3]

He Who Is Unrighteous, Let Him Be Unrighteous Still. Heinrich Bullinger: Nevertheless, we must here take heed that we do not think that God commanded that the ungodly should proceed to be more ungodly where the angel says, "He who is unrighteous, let him be unrighteous still," and so on. For it seems in manner to be such a saying as what is in the Gospel: "What you do, do it more speedily." For he commanded him to do that thing he knew he would do. After the same sort here also, what he knew the wicked would do, he says they shall do. He does not want their doings to trouble John and the faithful preacher, seeing as there shall be also many good people who shall apply themselves to righteousness.

We are accustomed also to say with a similar phrase, "If it will not otherwise be, we must be content." Not that we direct he who perishes to perish, but we reproach him his madness and signify that he perishes through his own fault, willingly and wittingly. Aretas:[†] "It is no exhortation he says but rather a rebuking of everyone to which he applies himself." And Thomas Aquinas: "The sense is, says he, 'He who will hurt, let him hurt still.' That is, he will hurt by doing other evils, that the angel is understood to have said these things in prophesying, not in wishing," and so on. And so the meaning is that the wicked, containing the prophecy, shall continue to be wicked; the godly again shall grow in the holy study of righteousness. This sense truly seems most plain of all.

It does not differ much from what is read in Daniel 12: "Go, Daniel," says the angel, "and search not overcuriously the instant of the last time, for the sayings are closed and sealed until the last time. Very many shall be purified and made white and cast new. But the wicked shall do wickedly, and all ungodly shall not understand. But the learned shall teach." From these things swore nothing at all the words of the apostle, speaking and prophesying of the later times: "All who will live godly in Christ Jesus shall suffer persecution for righteousness. Notwithstanding evil men and deceivers grow worse and worse, while they both lead others into error and err themselves."

Therefore, seeing as the later age of this world shall be such, let we who are called to this function proceed constantly to announce, set forth, and impress in the very Word of God and revelation of Jesus Christ to all people, regarding as nothing what the world and worldly people speak against it. Hundred Sermons on the Apocalypse.[4]

The Inhabitants of the Holy City. Menno Simons: Behold, thy wall stands firmly upon twelve foundations, thy gates are of pearls, the city is of pure gold, the river of living waters, proceeding from the throne of God and the Lamb, is in the midst of your way, and the tree of life is on either side, and its leaves serve to heal the nation. Happy and holy is he who has part in this city.

Therefore, so purify yourselves, you who seek the Lord, circumcise the foreskin of your hearts, for

[3]Bullinger, *Hundred Sermons** (1561), 679-80. †Arethas, archbishop of Caesarea (c. 850–c. 944), was possibly a pupil of the patriarch of Constantinople, Photius.

[4]Bullinger, *Hundred Sermons** (1561), 681-82; citing Dan 12. †Arethas, archbishop of Caesarea (c. 850–d. c. 944), was possibly a pupil of the patriarch of Constantinople, Photius.

the holy city may be inhabited by no uncircumcised person, the golden streets are trodden by no unclean feet; the unclean, drink not of the pure waters; the fruit of life shall never be eaten by any of the ungodly, "For without are dogs, and sorcerers, and whoremongers, and murderers, and idolaters, and whosoever loveth and maketh a lie." Be ye all minded like Christ Jesus. Be earnest to hold the union of the Spirit through the covenant of peace; ye are all one temple, house, city, mountain, body and church in Christ Jesus. A Foundation and Plain Instruction.[5]

Christ Is Truth. William Perkins: The second title of Christ is Truth. Christ is called true in three respects: first, because without error and ignorance he knows all things as they are in themselves, so creatures do not except by virtue from him. Second, because what he wills and decrees, he wills and decrees seriously, without fraud, deceit, or any contradiction, as appeared in the whole Scriptures, in which is nothing contrary to itself but all without change and alteration. Third, because he makes good all his promises in his Word, he accomplishes and performed them all, he is the performance of the . . . yes and amen.

Seeing as Christ is true—nay, truth itself—we see a difference between Christ and all false spirits, for they are spirits of errors. The devil is a liar from the beginning; he is the father of lies, nay, his nature is to lie, he can do nothing else; but Christ is true—nay, truth itself—every way true. In his knowledge, in his will, and in his promises, he is true.

Seeing as Christ is absolutely true, we must believe in him and believe his promises in his Word without doubting. For seeing as Christ is true—nay, truth itself—what need do we have to call his promises into question? And this should be the very prop of our faith, that he who promises is true and therefore will perform his promise. So, in persecution, in trouble and affliction, trust in Christ. He has promised to help; he will not fail because he is most true of his promise.

Seeing as he is so true, he put forth himself to be followed by us. Christ he knows things truly, and he wills and decrees things seriously, so we should promise, perform, and make good our lawful promises. . . . "The Lord hates the deceitful person." "Without," that is, in hell, "are all deceitful and lying persons." . . . It is a sign of a member of the church and of Christ to be true and faithful and to speak truth from one's heart, for the devil is the author of lies. Lectures upon the First Three Chapters of the Revelation.[6]

Do Not Add to or Take Away from This Prophecy. John Downame: In every age the whole truth of God was delivered by a lively voice as concerning the substance of the doctrine, although in greater clearness upon the coming of Christ than ever it was before, and last and perfectly (in which we are now to rest, both for their substance and manner of revelation) it is fully and absolutely comprehended in the Scriptures. So we shall not need to fly either to visions and revelations, or to human traditions and intentions, to unwritten truths, sentences of fathers, canons of councils, and so on to help us, but all is to be had in the written Word, for when our Savior says, "You err, not knowing the Scriptures," he manifestly teaches that all truth is to be learned from there. And the apostle commended the Scriptures as being able to make us wise unto salvation: "For the whole Scripture," he says, "is inspired of God and is profitable unto doctrine, unto reproof, unto correction, unto instruction in righteousness, that the man of God may be perfect, perfectly fitted to every good work."

Seeing the Word of God is able to thoroughly furnish a minister with all these four things (comprehending all that can be necessary), the one who is to disclose the whole counsel of God to the people, it must be able to inform a common Christian unto salvation. John also gives this

[5]Simons, *Complete Works**, 103-226.

[6]Perkins, *Lectures**, 270-71; citing Ps 55; 15.

testimony of the Scriptures, that they are written to the end that, believing, we might have everlasting life. And Revelation he concludes with this most earnest protestation, "If anyone add to the words of the prophecy of this book, God will add to that one the seven plagues written in this book; and if anyone take away from the words of the book of this prophecy, God will take away that one's part of the tree of life." This, if it is true in that one book alone, how much more shall it hold in all the books of Scripture set together? Sum of Sacred Divinity.[7]

22:21 *The Benediction*

Here Ends the Prophecy of Saint John. John Napier: Here ends Saint John, this holy prophecy of Apocalypse, imploring the grace of God's Spirit through Jesus Christ to abide with all the faithful. Here we also end that interpretation of it, which God by that selfsame grace has made the faithful of these our latter days to understand, in speaking of God's enemies and revealing of his truth, that his church, being purged from antichristianism, may henceforth abide pure, holy, and ready decked as a comely bride, waiting the sudden coming of her Lord and Bridegroom, Christ Jesus. To this God in Trinity and unity, who here gives these graces to us, we do therefore render eternal praise, honor, and glory, forever and ever. Amen. A Plain Discovery of the Whole Revelation of Saint John.[8]

[7]Downame, *Sacred Divinity**, 375-76.

[8]Napier, *Plain Discovery**, 269.

Map of Europe at the Time of the Reformation

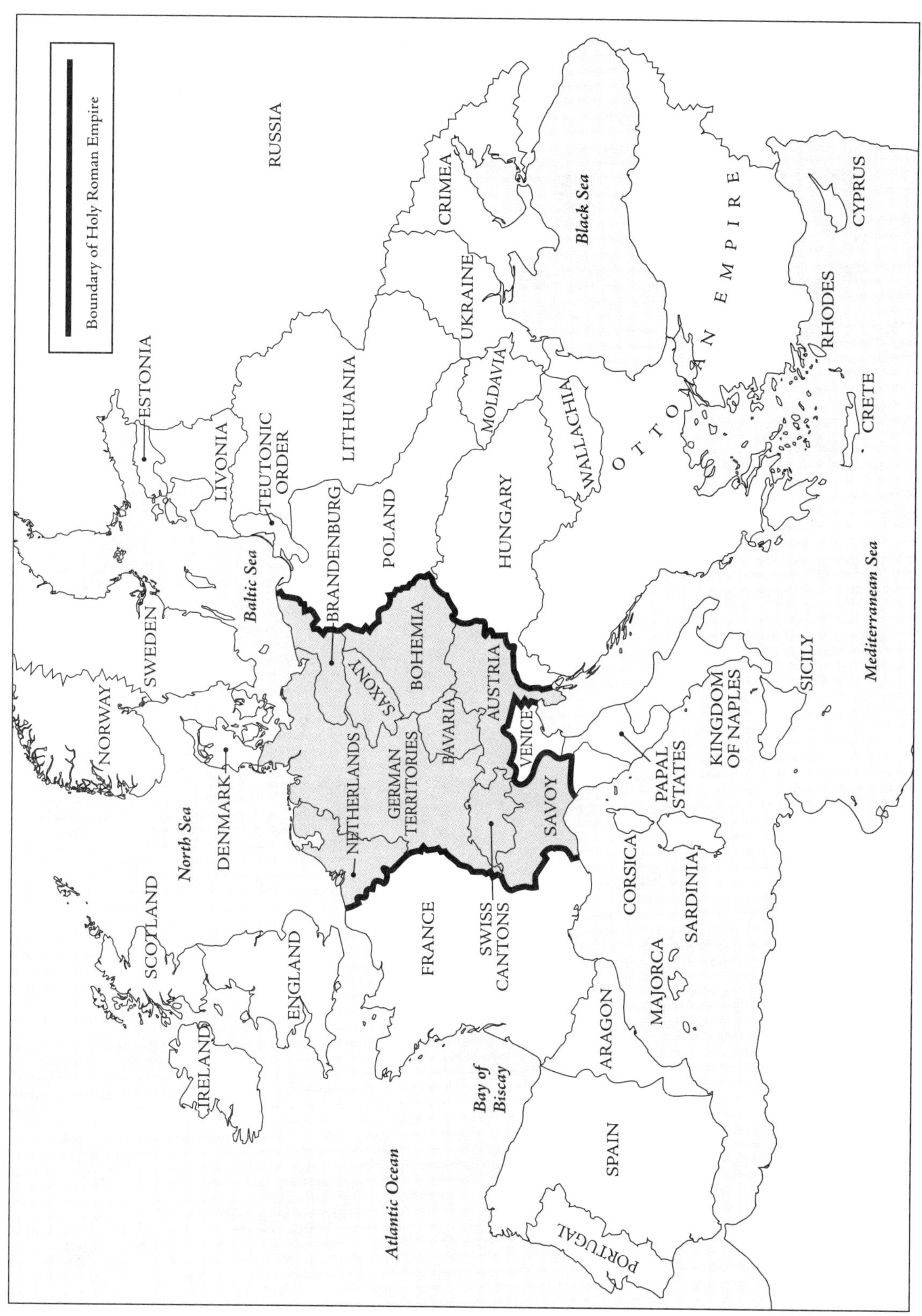

Timeline of the Reformation

	German Territories	France	Spain	Italy	Switzerland	Netherlands	British Isles
1309–1377		Babylonian Captivity of the Papacy					
1337–1453		d. Nicholas of Lyra Hundred Years' War	b. Paul of Burgos (Solomon ha-Levi)(d. 1435) Alonso Tostado (1400–1455)				Hundred Years' War
1378–1415		Western Schism (Avignon Papacy)		Western Schism			
1384							d. John Wycliffe
1414–1418					Council of Basel (1431–1437)		
1415				Council of Constance; d. Jan Hus; Martin V (r. 1417–1431); Council of Florence (1438–1445)			
1450	Invention of printing press						
1452				b. Leonardo da Vinci (d. 1519)			
1453				Fall of Constantinople			
1455–1485	b. Johannes Reuchlin (d. 1522)						War of Roses; rise of House of Tudor
1456	Gutenberg Bible						
1460				Pope Pius II issued *Execrabilis*			
1466		b. Jacques Lefèvre d'Étaples (d. 1536)					
1467						b. Desiderius Erasmus (d. 1536)	b. John Colet (d. 1519)
1469	b. Antoius Broickwy von Königstein (d. 541)						
1470				b. Santes Pagninus (d. 1541)			b. John (Mair) Major (d. 1550)
1475				b. Michelangelo (d. 1564)			
1478	b. Wolfgang Capito (d. 1541)		Ferdinand and Isabella	b. Jacopo Sadoleto (d. 1547)			b. Thomas More (d. 1535)

	German Territories	France	Spain	Italy	Switzerland	Netherlands	British Isles
1480	b. Balthasar Hubmaier (d. 1528); b. Andreas Bodenstein von Karlstadt (d. 1541)						
1481–1530			Spanish Inquisition				
1482					b. Johannes Oecolampadius (d. 1531)		
1483	b. Martin Luther (d. 1546)						
1484	b. Johann Spangenberg (d. 1550)				b. Huldrych Zwingli (d. 1531)		
1485	b. Johannes Bugenhagen (d. 1554)						b. Hugh Latimer (d. 1555)
1486	r. Frederick the Wise, Elector (d. 1525); b. Johann Eck (d. 1543)						
1488	b. Otto Brunfels (d. 1534)						b. Miles Coverdale (d. 1568)
1489	b. Thomas Müntzer (d. 1525); b. Kaspar von Schwenckfeld (d. 1561)						b. Thomas Cranmer (d. 1556)
1491	b. Martin Bucer (d. 1551)		b. Ignatius Loyola (d. 1556)				
1492			Defeat of Moors in Grenada; Columbus discovers America; expulsion of Jews from Spain	Alexander VI (r. 1492–1503)			
1493	b. Justus Jonas (d. 1555)						
1494							b. William Tyndale (d. 1536)
1496	b. Andreas Osiander (d. 1552)					b. Menno Simons (d. 1561)	
1497	b. Philipp Melanchthon (d. 1560); b. Wolfgang Musculus (d. 1563) b. Johannes (Ferus) Wild (d. 1554)						

	German Territories	France	Spain	Italy	Switzerland	Netherlands	British Isles
1498				d. Girolamo Savonarola	b. Conrad Grebel (d. 1526)		
1499	b. Johannes Brenz (d. 1570) b. Justus Menius (d. 1558)			b. Peter Martyr Vermigli (d. 1562)			
1500			b. Charles V (–1558)				
1501	b. Erasmus Sarcerius (d. 1559)						
1502	Founding of University of Wittenberg			Julius II (r. 1503–1513)		b. Frans Titelmans (d. 1537)	
1504					b. Heinrich Bullinger (d. 1575)		
1505	Luther joins Augustinian Order			b. Benedict Aretius (d. 1574)			
1506		b. Augustin Marlorat (d. 1562)		Restoration of St. Peter's begins			
1507				Sale of indulgences approved to fund building			
1508	b. Lucas Lossius (d. 1582)						
1509		b. John Calvin (d. 1564)					r. Henry VIII (–1547)
1510	Luther moves to Rome			b. Immanuel Tremellius (d. 1580)			b. Nicholas Ridley (d. 1555)
1511	Luther moves to Wittenberg						
1512				Sistine Chapel completed			
1512–1517				Fifth Lateran Council; rejection of conciliarism			
1513	Luther lectures on Psalms			r. Pope Leo X (–1521)			b. John Knox (d. 1572)
1515	Luther lectures on Romans	r. Francis I (–1547); b. Peter Ramus (d. 1572)					
1516		Est. French National Church (via Concordat of Bologna)		Concordat of Bologna		Publication of Erasmus's Greek New Testament	
1517	Tetzel sells indulgences in Saxony; Luther's Ninety-five Theses						

	German Territories	France	Spain	Italy	Switzerland	Netherlands	British Isles
1518	Heidelberg Disputation; Luther examined by Cajetan at Diet of Augsburg			Diet of Augsburg			
1519	Leipzig Disputation	b. Theodore Beza (d. 1605)	Cortés conquers Aztecs; Portuguese sailor Magellan circumnavigates the globe		Zwingli appointed pastor of Grossmünster in Zurich; b. Rudolf Gwalther (d. 1586)		
1520	Publication of Luther's "Three Treatises"; burning of papal bull in Wittenberg		Coronation of Charles V	Papal Bull v. Luther: *Exsurge Domine*			
1521	Luther excommunicated; Diet/Edict of Worms—Luther condemned; Luther in hiding; Melanchthon's *Loci communes*	French-Spanish War (–1526)	French-Spanish War; Loyola converts	Papal excommunication of Luther			Henry VIII publishes *Affirmation of the Seven Sacraments* against Luther; awarded title "Defender of the Faith" by Pope
1521–1522	Disorder in Wittenberg; Luther translates New Testament						
1521–1525		First and Second Habsburg–Valois War					
1522	Luther returns to Wittenberg; Luther's NT published; criticizes Zwickau prophets; b. Martin Chemnitz (d. 1586)		Publication of Complutensian Polyglot Bible under Cisneros		Sausage Affair and reform begins in Zurich under Zwingli		b. John Jewel (d. 1571)
1523	Knight's Revolt	Bucer begins ministry in Strasbourg	Loyola writes Spiritual Exercises	r. Pope Clement VII (–1534)	Iconoclasm in Zurich		
1524	Luther criticizes peasants; d. Johann von Staupitz					Erasmus's disputation on free will	
1524–1526	Peasants' War						
1525	Luther marries; execution of Thomas Müntzer; publication of Luther's *Bondage of the Will*				Abolition of mass in Zurich; disputation on baptism; first believers' baptism performed in Zurich		

	German Territories	France	Spain	Italy	Switzerland	Netherlands	British Isles
1526					Zurich council mandates capital punishment of Anabaptists	Publication of Tyndale's English translation of NT	
1527	d. Hans Denck (b. c. 1500) d. Hans Hut (b. 1490) b. Tilemann Hesshus (d. 1588)			Sack of Rome by mutinous troops of Charles V	First Anabaptist executed in Zurich; drafting of Schleitheim Confession		
1528	Execution of Hubmaier						
1529	Second Diet of Speyer; evangelical "protest"; publication of Luther's catechisms; Marburg Colloquy; siege of Vienna by Turkish forces	Abolition of mass in Strasbourg			d. Georg Blaurock (b. 1492)		Thomas More appointed chancellor to Henry VIII
1530	Diet of Augsburg; Confession of Augsburg	d. Francois Lambert (Lambert of Avignon) (b. 1487)	Charles V crowned Holy Roman Emperor				
1531	Formation of Schmalkaldic League				d. H. Zwingli; succeeded by H. Bullinger		
1532		Publication of Calvin's commentary on Seneca; conversion of Calvin	b. Francisco de Toledo (d. 1596)				
1533	b. Valentein Weigel (d. 1588)	Nicholas Cop addresses University of Paris; Cop and Calvin implicated as "Lutheran" sympathizers	b. Juan de Maldonado (d. 1583)				Thomas Cranmer appointed as Archbishop of Canterbury; Henry VIII divorces
1534	First edition of Luther's Bible published	Affair of the Placards; Calvin flees d. Guillame Briçonnet (b. 1470)		Jesuits founded; d. Cardinal Cajetan (Thomas de Vio) (b. 1469)			Act of Supremacy; English church breaks with Rome
1535	Bohemian Confession of 1535; Anabaptist theocracy at Münster collapses after eighteen months				b. Lambert Daneau (d. 1595)		d. Thomas More; d. John Fisher

	German Territories	France	Spain	Italy	Switzerland	Netherlands	British Isles
1536	Wittenberg Concord; b. Kaspar Olevianus (d. 1587)				First edition of Calvin's *Institutes* published; Calvin arrives in Geneva (–1538); First Helvetic Confession	Publication of Tyndale's translation of NT; d. W. Tyndale	d. A. Boleyn; Henry VIII dissolves monasteries (–1541)
1537					Calvin presents ecclesiastical ordinances to Genevan Council		
1538					Calvin exiled from Geneva; arrives in Strasbourg (–1541)		
1539		Calvin publishes second edition of *Institutes* in Strasbourg		d. Felix Pratensis			Statute of Six Articles; publication of Coverdale's Great Bible
1540				Papal approval of Jesuit order			d. Thomas Cromwell
1541	Colloquy of Regensburg	French translation of Calvin's *Institutes* published	d. Juan de Valdés (b. 1500/1510)		d. A. Karlstadt; Calvin returns to Geneva (–1564)		
1542	d. Sebastian Franck (b. 1499)			Institution of Roman Inquisition			War between England and Scotland; James V of Scotland defeated; Ireland declared sovereign kingdom
1543	Copernicus publishes *On the Revolutions of the Heavenly Spheres*; d. Johann Eck (Johann Maier of Eck) (b. 1486)						
1545–1547	Schmalkaldic Wars; d. Martin Luther			First session of Council of Trent			b. Richard Bancroft (d. 1610)
1546	b. Johannes Piscator (d. 1625)						
1547	Defeat of Protestants at Mühlberg	d. Francis I; r. Henri II (–1559)					d. Henry VIII; r. Edward VI (–1553)
1548	Augsburg Interim (–1552) d. Caspar Cruciger (b. 1504) b. David Pareus (d. 1622)						

	German Territories	France	Spain	Italy	Switzerland	Netherlands	British Isles
1549	d. Paul Fagius (b. 1504)	d. Marguerite d'Angoulême (b. 1492)			Consensus Tigurinus between Calvin and Bullinger		First Book of Common Prayer published
1550	b. Aegidius Hunnius (d. 1603)						
1551–1552				Second session of Council of Trent			
1552	d. Sebastian Münster (b. 1488) d. Friedrich Nausea (b. c. 1496)						Book of Common Prayer revised
1553	d. Johannes Aepinus (b. 1449)				Michael Servetus executed in Geneva		Cranmer's Forty-Two Articles; d. Edward VI; r. Mary I (d. 1558)
1554							Richard Hooker (d. 1600)
1555	Diet of Augsburg; Peace of Augsburg establishes legal territorial existence of Lutheranism and Catholicism b. Johann Arndt (d. 1621)	First mission of French pastors trained in Geneva				b. Sibbrandus Lubbertus (d. 1625)	b. Lancelot Andrewes (d. 1626) b. Robert Rollock (d. 1599); d. Hugh Latimer; d. Nicholas Ridley d. John Hooper
1556	d. Pilgram Marpeck (b. 1495) d. Konrad Pellikan (b. 1478) d. Peter Riedemann (b. 1506)		Charles V resigns			d. David Joris (b. c. 1501)	d. Thomas Cranmer
1557							Alliance with Spain in war against France
1558			d. Charles V				b. William Perkins (d. 1602); d. Mary I; r. Elizabeth I (–1603)
1559		d. Henry II; r. Francis II (–1560); first national synod of French reformed churches (1559) in Paris; Gallic Confession		First index of prohibited books issued	Final edition of Calvin's *Institutes*; founding of Genevan Academy	b. Jacobus Arminius (d. 1609)	Elizabethan Settlement

	German Territories	France	Spain	Italy	Switzerland	Netherlands	British Isles
1560	d. P. Melanchthon	d. Francis II; r. Charles IX (1574); Edict of Toleration created peace with Huguenots	d. Domingo de Soto (b. 1494)		Geneva Bible		Kirk of Scotland established; Scottish Confession
1561-1563				Third session of Council of Trent			
1561						Belgic Confession	
1562	d. Katharina Schütz Zell (b. 1497/98)	Massacre of Huguenots begins French Wars of Religion (–1598)					The Articles of Religion—in Elizabethan "final" form (1562/71); publication of Latin edition of Jewel's *Apology*
1563	Heidelberg Catechism						
1564				b. Galileo (d. 1642)	d. J. Calvin		b. William Shakespeare (d. 1616); publication of Lady Ann Bacon's English translation of Jewel's *Apology*
1566	d. Johann Agricola (b. 1494)			Roman Catechism	Second Helvetic Confession		
1567						Spanish occupation	Abdication of Scottish throne by Mary Stuart; r. James VI (1603–1625)
1568						d. Dirk Phillips (b. 1504) Dutch movement for liberation (–1645)	*Bishops' Bible*
1570		d. Johannes Mercerus (Jean Mercier)		Papal Bull *Regnans in Excelsis* excommunicates Elizabeth I			Elizabeth I excommunicated
1571	b. Johannes Kepler (d. 1630)		Spain defeats Ottoman navy at Battle of Lepanto				b. John Downame (d. 1652)
1572		Massacre of Huguenots on St. Bartholomew's Day		r. Pope Gregory XIII (1583–1585)		William of Orange invades	b. John Donne (d. 1631)
1574		d. Charles IX; r. Henri III (d. 1589)					

	German Territories	France	Spain	Italy	Switzerland	Netherlands	British Isles
1575	d. Georg Major (b. 1502); Bohemian Confession of 1575						
1576		Declaration of Toleration; formation of Catholic League		b. Giovanni Diodati (d. 1649)		Sack of Antwerp; Pacification of Ghent	
1577	Lutheran Formula of Concord						England allies with Netherlands against Spain
1578	Swiss Brethren Confession of Hesse d. Peter Walpot		Truce with Ottomans				Sir Francis Drake circumnavigates the globe
1579			Expeditions to Ireland			Division of Dutch provinces	
1580	Lutheran Book of Concord						
1581			d. Teresa of Avila				Anti-Catholic statutes passed
1582				Gregorian Reform of calendar			
1583							b. David Dickson (d. 1663)
1584		Treaty of Joinville with Spain	Treaty of Joinville; Spain inducted into Catholic League; defeats Dutch at Antwerp			Fall of Antwerp; d. William of Orange	
1585	d. Josua Opitz (b. c. 1542)	Henri of Navarre excommunicated		r. Pope Sixtus V (–1590)			
1586							Sir Francis Drake's expedition to West Indies; Sir Walter Raleigh in Roanoke
1587	d. Johann Wigand (b. 1523)	Henri of Navarre defeats royal army					d. Mary Stuart of Scotland
1588		Henri of Navarre drives Henri III from Paris; assassination of Catholic League Leaders	Armada destroyed				English Navy defeats Spanish Armada
1589		d. Henri III; r. Henri (of Navarre) IV (–1610)	Victory over England at Lisbon				Defeated by Spain in Lisbon
1590		Henri IV's siege of Paris		d. Girolamo Zanchi (b. 1516)			Alliance with Henri IV

	German Territories	France	Spain	Italy	Switzerland	Netherlands	British Isles
1592	d. Nikolaus Selnecker (b. 1530)						
1593		Henri IV converts to Catholicism					Books I-IV of Hooker's *Laws of Ecclesiastical Polity* published
1594		Henri grants toleration to Huguenots					
1595		Henri IV declares war on Spain; received into Catholic Church		Pope Sixtus accepts Henri IV into Church			Alliance with France
1596		b. René Descartes (d. 1650) b. Moïse Amyraut (d. 1664)					
1597							Book V of Hooker's *Laws of Ecclesiastical Polity* published
1598		Edict of Nantes; toleration of Huguenots; peace with Spain	Treaty of Vervins; peace with France				
1600	d. David Chytraeus (b. 1531)						
1601							b. John Trapp (d. 1669)
1602					d. Daniel Toussain (b. 1541)		
1603							d. Elizabeth I; r. James I (James VI of Scotland) (–1625)
1604	d. Cyriacus Spangenberg (b. 1528)						d. John Whitgift (b. 1530)
1605						b. Rembrandt (d. 1669)	Guy Fawkes and gunpowder plot
1606							Jamestown Settlement
1607							b. John Milton (d. 1674)
1608							
1610		d. Henri IV; r. Louis XIII (–1643)	d. Benedict Pererius (b. 1535)			The Remonstrance; Short Confession	

	German Territories	France	Spain	Italy	Switzerland	Netherlands	British Isles
1611							Publication of Authorized English Translation of Bible (AV/KJV); George Abbot becomes Archbishop of Canterbury (–1633)
1612							b. Richard Crashaw (d. 1649)
1616							b. John Owen (d. 1683)
1617							b. Ralph Cudworth (d. 1689)
1618–1619						Synod of Dordrecht	
1618–1648	Thirty Years' War						
1620							English Separatists land in Plymouth, Massachusetts
1621							d. Andrew Willet (b. 1562)
1628							Puritans establish Massachusetts Bay colony
1633	d. Christoph Pelargus (b. 1565)						Laud becomes Archbishop of Canterbury
1637	d. Johann Gerhard (b. 1582)					*Statenvertaling*	
1638							d. Joseph Mede (b. 1638)
1640				Diodati's Italian translation of Bible published			
1642–1649							English civil wars; d. Charles I; r. Oliver Cromwell (1660)
1643		d. Louis XIII; r. Louis XIV (–1715)					
1643–1649							Westminster Assembly
1645							d. William Laud (b. 1573)

	German Territories	France	Spain	Italy	Switzerland	Netherlands	British Isles
1648		Treaty of Westphalia ends Thirty Years' War					Books VI and VIII of Hooker's *Laws of Ecclesiastical Polity* posthumously published
1656	d. Georg Calixtus (b. 1586)						
1658							d. Oliver Cromwell
1659							Richard Cromwell resigns
1660							English Restoration; r. Charles II (–1685)
1662							Act of Uniformity; Book VII of Hooker's *Laws of Ecclesiastical Polity* posthumously published
1664						d. Thieleman Jans van Braght (b. 1625)	d. John Mayer (b. 1583)
1671							d. William Greenhill (b. 1591)
1677							d. Thomas Manton (b. 1620)
1678						d. Anna Maria von Schurman (b. 1607)	
1688							Glorious Revolution; r. William and Mary (-1702); d. John Bunyan (b. 1628)
1691							d. Richard Baxter (b. 1615)

BIOGRAPHICAL SKETCHES OF REFORMATION-ERA FIGURES AND WORKS

This list is cumulative, including all the authors cited in the Reformation Commentary on Scripture to date as well as other people relevant to the Reformation and Reformation-era exegesis. For works consulted, see "Sources for Biographical Sketches," p. 251.

Cornelius À Lapide (1567–1637). Flemish Catholic biblical exegete. A Jesuit, Lapide served as professor of Holy Scripture and Hebrew at Louvain for twenty years before taking a similar role in Rome, where he taught until his death. He is best known for his extensive commentaries on the Scriptures. Encompassing all books of the Bible except Job and the Psalms, his work employs a fourfold hermeneutic and draws heavily on the work of patristic and medieval exegetes.

Thomas Adams (1583–1653). Anglican minister and author. He attended the University of Cambridge where he received his BA in 1601 and his MA in 1606. Following his ordination in 1604, Adams served as curate at Northill in Bedfordshire. In 1611, he became vicar of Willmington. Three years later he served the parish of Wingrave, Buckinghamshire, where he remained until 1618. From 1618 to 1623 Adams was preacher at St. Gregory by St. Paul's. He also served as chaplain to Henry Montague, First Earl of Manchester, and Lord Chief Justice of England. Among his most important works are the *Happiness of the Church* (1618) and an extensive commentary on 2 Peter (1638).

Johannes Aepinus (1499–1553). German Lutheran preacher and theologian. Aepinus studied under Martin Luther,* Philipp Melanchthon* and Johannes Bugenhagen* in Wittenberg. Because of his Lutheran beliefs, Aepinus lost his first teaching position in Brandenburg. He fled north to Stralsund and became a preacher and superintendent at Saint Peter's Church in Hamburg. In 1534, he made a diplomatic visit to England but could not convince Henry VIII* to embrace the Augsburg Confession.* His works include sermons and theological writings. Aepinus became best known as leader of the Infernalists, who believed that Christ underwent torment in hell after his crucifixion.

Johann Agricola (c. 1494–1566). German Lutheran pastor and theologian. An early student of Martin Luther,* Agricola eventually began a controversy over the role of the law, first with Melanchthon* and then with Luther himself. Agricola claimed to defend Luther's true position, asserting that only the gospel of the crucified Christ calls Christians to truly good works, not the fear of the law. After this first controversy, Agricola seems to have radicalized his views to the point that he eliminated Luther's *simul iustus et peccator* ("at the same time righteous and sinful") paradox of the Christian life, emphasizing instead that believers have no need for the law once they are united with Christ through faith. Luther responded by writing anonymous pamphlets against antinomianism. Agricola later published a recantation of his views, hoping to assuage relations with Luther, although they were never personally reconciled. He published a commentary on Luke, a series of sermons on Colossians, and a massive collection of German proverbs.

Henry Ainsworth (1571–1622/1623). English Puritan Hebraist. In 1593, under threat of persecution, Ainsworth relocated to Amsterdam, where he served as a teacher in an English congregation. He composed a confession of faith for the community and a number of polemical and exegetical works, including annotations on the Pentateuch, the Psalms and Song of Songs.

Henry Airay (c. 1560–1616). English Puritan professor and pastor. He was especially noted for his preaching, a blend of hostility toward Catholicism and articulate exposition of English Calvinism. He was promoted to provost of Queen's College Oxford (1598) and then to vice chancellor of the university in 1606. He disputed with William Laud* concerning Laud's putative Catholicization of the Church of England, particularly over the practice of genuflection, which Airay vehemently opposed. He also opposed fellow Puritans who wished to separate from the Church of England. His lectures on Philippians were his only work published during his lifetime.

Albert the Great (1201–1280). German theologian, philosopher, scientist, and ecclesiastic. Albert was born in Lauingen, located in the Bavarian-Swabian region. After completing his studies at Padua, Albert joined the Dominicans in 1220s. Upon finishing further theological studies at Cologne, Albert became a conventual lecturer during the 1230s at Hildesheim, Freiberg (Saxony), Regensburg, and Strasbourg. In the early 1240s, Albert was sent to Paris where he became a master of theology, and regent of the university in 1245. He served as regent until 1248. While at Paris, Albert commenced his paraphrases of Aristotle's works. Furthermore, Albert authored a systematic theology, and lectured on the four Gospels and nine books of the Old Testament. Albert is best known for having taught Thomas Aquinas,* who, as his assistant, transcribed his course on the works of Dionysius and Aristotle's *Nicomachean Ethics*.

Alexander (Ales) Alesius (1500–1565). Scottish Lutheran theologian. Following the martyrdom of his theological adversary Patrick Hamilton (c. 1504–1528), Alesius converted to the Reformation and fled to Germany. In 1535 Martin Luther* and Philipp Melanchthon* sent him as an emissary to Henry VIII* and Thomas Cranmer.* He taught briefly at Cambridge, but after the Act of Six Articles reasserted Catholic sacramental theology he returned to Germany, where he lectured at Frankfurt an der Oder and Leipzig. Alesius composed many exegetical, theological and polemical works, including commentaries on John, Romans, 1–2 Timothy, Titus and the Psalms.

Robert Allen (fl. 1596–1612). English Protestant clergyman and writer. Allen is known only by his writings, which reveal few biographical details except that he was a minister and he wrote from London and Suffolk. His works include a theological summary of Proverbs and Ecclesiastes, an exposition of the Gospel, and a catechism.

Andreas Althamer (c. 1500–1539). German Lutheran humanist and pastor. Forced from the chaplaincy at Schwäbisch-Gmünd for teaching evangelical ideas, Althamer studied theology at Wittenberg before serving as a pastor in Eltersdorf, Nuremberg, and Ansbach. A staunch Lutheran, he contended against Reformed theologians at the 1528 disputation at Bern and delivered numerous polemics against Anabaptism. He also composed an early Lutheran catechism, published at Nuremberg in 1528.

William Ames (1576–1633). English Puritan theologian. Heavily influenced by William Perkins* while at Cambridge, Ames was unable to find employment in the English church due to his Puritan commitments. Most of his life was spent in exile in the Netherlands, where he served as chaplain to English forces at The Hague and was the pastor of a small congregation. Best known as a controversialist during his early career, Ames was the theological advisor to the president of the Synod of Dort (1618–1619) and was later installed as chair of theology at the University of Franeker in Friesland. *The Marrow of Theology* (1627) is viewed as a model of seventeenth-century Puritan theology.

Moïse Amyraut (1596–1664). French Reformed pastor and professor. Originally intending to be a lawyer, Amyraut turned to theology after an encounter with several Huguenot pastors and having read Calvin's* *Institutes*. After a brief stint as a parish pastor, Amyraut spent the majority of his career at the Saumur Academy. He was well known for his irenicism and ecumenicism (for example, in advocating intercommunion with Lutherans). Certain aspects of his writings on justification, faith, the covenants and especially predestination proved controversial among the Reformed. His doctrine of election is often called hypothetical universalism or Amyraldianism, stating that Christ's atoning work was intended by God for all human beings indiscriminately, although its effectiveness for salvation depends on faith, which is a free gift of God given only to those whom God has chosen from eternity. Amyraut was charged with grave doctrinal error three times before the National Synod but was acquitted each time. Aside from his theological treatises, Amyraut published paraphrases of almost the entire New Testament and the Psalms, as well as many sermons.

Anabaptists of Trieste (1539). Following a meeting between Swiss Brethren and the Hutterites at Steinabrunn on December 6, 1536, around 140 radicals were arrested and imprisoned in Falkenstein Castle. After six weeks in captivity, the ninety men of the group were forced to march to Trieste to be sold as galley slaves. Twelve days after arrival, all but twelve prisoners managed to escape and return to Moravia, where they published a confession of their beliefs.

Jakob Andreae (1528–1590). German Lutheran theologian. Andreae studied at the University of

Tübingen before being called to the diaconate in Stuttgart in 1546. He was appointed ecclesiastical superintendent of Göppingen in 1553 and supported Johannes Brenz's* proposal to place the church under civil administrative control. An ecclesial diplomat for the duke of Württemberg, Andreae debated eucharistic theology, the use of images, and predestination with Theodore Beza* at the Colloquy of Montbéliard (1586) to determine whether French Reformed exiles would be required to submit to the Formula of Concord.* Andreae coauthored the Formula of Concord. He and his wife had eighteen children.

Lancelot Andrewes (1555–1626). Anglican bishop. A scholar, pastor and preacher, Andrews prominently shaped a distinctly Anglican identity between the poles of Puritanism and Catholicism. He oversaw the translation of Genesis to 2 Kings for the Authorized Version.* His eight-volume collected works—primarily devotional tracts and sermons—are marked by his fluency in Scripture, the Christian tradition and classical literature.

Antoine du Pinet (b. c.1510). French Reformed pastor and translator. Also known as Antoine Pignet, Pinet studied at Orléans at the same time as John Calvin* before pastoring a church at Ville-la-Grand outside Geneva and working as a proofreader and translator for Calvin. Expelled from his pulpit for overly-censorious preaching, Pinet returned to France, where he worked as a tutor. He published numerous works during his life, including a translation of Pliny the Elder's *Natural History* and a commentary on Revelation.

Thomas Aquinas (1225–1274). Dominican medieval theologian. Thomas Aquinas was born into a noble family in Rocasecca, Italy. In 1230 Thomas's father sent him to the abbey at Monte Casino as a child oblate. When, at age fourteen, Thomas was given the choice between taking his final vows and leaving, he chose to go to Naples to study at the school recently founded by the Holy Roman Emperor. While studying at Naples, Thomas came into contact with the Dominicans, and joined this order in 1244. Although his family objected to his decision at first, to the point of actually imprisoning Thomas, they came to accept his decision the following year. Afterwards, Aquinas traveled to Paris where he began his formal studies under Albert the Great (1200–1280). Aquinas followed his teacher to Cologne in 1248 where he was ordained a priest, and completed his course in theology. Four years later, he was appointed a bachelor in the Dominican convent in Paris where he lectured on Peter Lombard's (1096–1160)* *Sentences*. In 1256, Thomas was incepted as a master of the sacred page, and he taught in Paris until 1259. In 1261, he was appointed lecturer at a school in Orvieto. Four years later, Aquinas was transferred to Rome, and in 1268 returned to Paris. In 1272, the Dominican order appointed Aquinas to start a new school in Naples. A mystical experience reportedly caused Aquinas to abruptly cease his writing. Aquinas died at a monastery in Fossanova. In addition to his major works, *Summa Theologia* and *Summa Contra Gentiles*, Aquinas's voluminous corpus includes extensive commentaries on Jeremiah, Lamentations, Isaiah, Job, and an incomplete one on the Psalms. Aquinas also wrote commentaries on the Gospels of Matthew and John as well as the Pauline Epistles. Furthermore, at the request of the pope, Aquinas produced the *Catena Aurea*, a commentary on the four Gospels consisting of exegetical statements by the Latin and Greek fathers. One of the most significant features of Aquinas's biblical commentaries is his emphasis on the literal meaning of a Scriptural text. As a representation of medieval Catholic theology, Aquinas's theology was regularly challenged by the Protestant reformers.

John Archer (d. c.1642). English millenarian preacher. Also known as Henry Archer, he was banned from teaching in London by Archbishop Laud*. He relocated to Hereford and later Arnhem in the Netherlands, where he pastored an English congregation, briefly sharing his pulpit with Thomas Goodwin*.

Benedict Aretius (d. 1574). Swiss Reformed professor. Trained at the universities of Bern, Strasbourg and Marburg, Aretius taught logic and philosophy as well as the biblical languages and theology. He advocated for stronger unity and peace between the Lutheran and Reformed churches. Aretius joined others in denouncing the antitrinitarian Giovanni Valentino Gentile (d. 1566). He published commentaries on the New Testament, as well as various works on astronomy, botany and medicine.

Aristotle (388–322 BC). Ancient Greek philosopher and scientist. Aristotle was born in Stagira, Chalkdice, northern Greece. He is considered the "Father of Western Philosophy" along with his teacher, Plato, because his teaching produced the bases for almost every discipline studied in the Western world. After his father's death while he was still a child, Aristotle was raised by his guardian, Proxenus of Atarneus. At the age of about eighteen, Aristotle joined Plato's Academy in Athens, where he remained until his was thirty-seven. Aristotle's writings cover a wide range of subjects: physics, biology, zoology, metaphysics, logic, ethics, aesthetics, poetry, theater, music, rhetoric, psychology, linguistics, and politics. Shortly after Plato's death, King Philip II of

Macedonia requested his services as a tutor to his son, Alexander the Great. Aristotle began tutoring the young prince in 343 BC. While teaching Alexander, Aristotle was able to acquire hundreds of books for the library of what would become his Lyceum. Aristotle's work profoundly shaped scholarship during the Middle Ages and early modern period as his logic was employed in the exegesis of Scripture and formation of theology. Among the major theologians who incorporated Aristotle's methods into their theological systems was Thomas Aquinas.* Aristotle's methods and categories would also be utilized by many Protestant theologians throughout the sixteenth and seventeenth centuries.

Jacobus Arminius (1559–1609). Dutch Remonstrant pastor and theologian. Arminius was a vocal critic of high Calvinist scholasticism, whose views were repudiated by the Synod of Dordrecht. Arminius was a student of Theodore Beza* at the academy of Geneva. He served as a pastor in Amsterdam and later joined the faculty of theology at the university in Leiden, where his lectures on predestination were popular and controversial. Predestination, as Arminius understood it, was the decree of God determined on the basis of divine foreknowledge of faith or rejection by humans who are the recipients of prevenient, but resistible, grace.

Johann Arndt (1555–1621). German Lutheran pastor and theologian. After a brief time teaching, Arndt pastored in Badeborn (Anhalt) until 1590, when Prince Johann Georg von Anhalt (1567–1618) began introducing Reformed ecclesial policies. Arndt ministered in Quedlinberg, Brunswick, Eisleben and Celle. Heavily influenced by medieval mysticism, Arndt centered his theology on Christ's mystical union with the believer, out of which flows love of God and neighbor. He is best known for his *True Christianity* (1605–1609), which greatly influenced Philipp Jakob Spener (1635–1705) and later Pietists.

John Arrowsmith (1602–1659). English Puritan theologian. Arrowsmith participated in the Westminster Assembly, and later taught at Cambridge. His works, all published posthumously, include three sermons preached to Parliament and an unfinished catechism.

Articles of Religion (1562; revised 1571). The Articles underwent a long editorial process that drew from the influence of Continental confessions in England, resulting in a uniquely Anglican blend of Protestantism and Catholicism. In their final form, they were reduced from Thomas Cranmer's* Forty-two Articles (1539) to the Elizabethan Thirty-Nine Articles (1571), excising polemical articles against the Anabaptists and Millenarians as well as adding articles on the Holy Spirit, good works and Communion. Originating in a 1535 meeting with Lutherans, the Articles retained a minor influence from the Augsburg Confession* and Württemberg Confession (1552), but showed significant revision in accordance with Genevan theology, as well as the Second Helvetic Confession.*

Anne Askew (1521–1546). English Protestant martyr. Askew was forced to marry her deceased sister's intended husband, who later expelled Askew from his house—after the birth of two children—on account of her religious views. After unsuccessfully seeking a divorce in Lincoln, Askew moved to London, where she met other Protestants and began to preach. In 1546, she was arrested, imprisoned and convicted of heresy for denying the doctrine of transubstantiation. Under torture in the Tower of London she refused to name any other Protestants. On July 16, 1546, she was burned at the stake. Askew is best known through her accounts of her arrests and examinations. John Bale (1495–1563), a bishop, historian and playwright, published these manuscripts. Later John Foxe (1516–1587) included them in his *Acts and Monuments*, presenting her as a role model for other pious Protestant women.

Mary Astell (1666–1731). English writer and philosopher. Astell received an informal education from her uncle, a clergyman. Left almost penniless after the death of her parents, she settled in London, where she made her career as a writer. She is best known for her proto-feminist works, including *A Serious Proposal to the Ladies* (1694, 1697), *Some Reflections on Marriage* (1700), and *The Christian Religion, as Professed by a Daughter of the Church of England* (1705). In these works she argues for the moral and intellectual equality of the sexes and the need for women to receive a similar education to men so that they can navigate the world by themselves. Retiring from writing, Astell spent her final decades organizing a charity school for girls in Chelsea backed by the Society for the Propagation of Christian Knowledge.

Augsburg Confession (1530). In the wake of Luther's* stand against ecclesial authorities at the Diet of Worms (1521), the Holy Roman Empire splintered along theological lines. Emperor Charles V sought to ameliorate this—while also hoping to secure a united European front against Turkish invasion—by calling together another imperial diet in Augsburg in 1530. The Evangelical party was cast in a strongly heretical light at the diet by Johann Eck.* For this reason, Philipp Melanchthon* and Justus Jonas* thought it best to strike a conciliatory tone (Luther, as an official outlaw, did not attend), submitting a confession rather than a defense. The resulting Augsburg

Confession was approved by many of the rulers of the northeastern Empire; however, due to differences in eucharistic theology, Martin Bucer* and the representatives of Strasbourg, Constance, Lindau and Memmingen drafted a separate confession (the Tetrapolitan Confession). Charles V accepted neither confession, demanding that the Evangelicals accept the Catholic rebuttal instead. In 1531, along with the publication of the Augsburg Confession itself, Melanchthon released a defense of the confession that responded to the Catholic confutation and expanded on the original articles. Most subsequent Protestant confessions followed the general structure of the Augsburg Confession.

Augustine of Hippo (354–430 AD). North African bishop and theologian. Augustine was born in Thagaste (Ahras, Algeria), a small town in the Roman province to Numidia, the son of a Christian mother, Monica, and a non-Christian father, Patricius, a local official of modest means. Enabled by local patronage, Augustine received a classical education, which afforded him the opportunity to pursue advanced training in rhetoric at Carthage. Upon completing his education at Carthage, Augustine taught rhetoric there as well as in Rome and Milan, where he was appointed official rhetorician of that city. Inspired by his reading of Cicero's *Hortensius*, Augustine embarked upon a quest for wisdom. While in Carthage, Augustine was repulsed by the seemingly simplistic Christianity he encountered, and therefore joined the Manicheans. Having become disillusioned by the Manichaeans' failure to lead him to the wisdom they promised, Augustine was eventually drawn to orthodox Christianity by the preaching of Ambrose (340–397) and his reading of the Neo-Platonist philosopher Plotinus (204–270). As a result of his conversion in 386, Augustine abandoned his secular ambitions in favor of a celibate life fully committed to intellectual and spiritual devotion to God. Towards this end, Augustine returned to north Africa to establish a semi-monastic community. However, in 391, while visiting Hippo Regius, he was forcibly ordained into the priesthood, and made bishop of that church in 396. In addition to his many duties as a bishop, Augustine engaged in controversies against the Manicheans, Donatists, and Pelagians, which took up the remainder of his life and career. He died in 430 while the Vandals besieged Hippo. Among his many works, Augustine devoted several to exegesis. He outlines exegetical principles in his *De Doctrina Christiana* ("On Christian Doctrine"), and he authored extensive series of homilies on most of the books of the New Testament as well as the Old Testament books of Psalms and Genesis (incomplete). During the Reformation era, both Catholic and Protestant theologians appealed to and engaged with Augustine's theology, especially his emphases upon original sin and humanity's need for God's grace.

Authorized Version (1611). In 1604 King James I* commissioned this new translation—popularly remembered as the King James Version—for uniform use in the public worship of the Church of England. The Bible and the Apocrypha was divided into six portions and assigned to six companies of nine scholars—both Anglicans and Puritans—centered at Cambridge, Oxford and Westminster. Richard Bancroft, the general editor of the Authorized Version, composed fifteen rules to guide the translators and to guard against overly partisan decisions. Rather than offer an entirely fresh English translation, the companies were to follow the Bishops' Bible* as closely as possible. "Truly (good Christian Reader)," the preface states, "we neuer thought from the beginning that we should need to make a new Translation, nor yet to make of a bad one a good one . . . but make a good one better, or out of many good ones, one principall good one, not iustly to be excepted against: that hath bene our endeauour, that our mark." Other rules standardized spelling, dictated traditional ecclesial terms (e.g., *church*, *baptize* and *bishop*), and allowed only for linguistic marginal notes and cross-references. Each book of the Bible went through a rigorous revision process: first, each person in a company made an initial draft, then the company put together a composite draft, then a supercommittee composed of representatives from each company reviewed these drafts, and finally two bishops and Bancroft scrutinized the final edits. The text and translation process of the Authorized Version have widely influenced biblical translations ever since.

Elizabeth Avery (fl. 1614-1653). English millenarian prophet. The daughter of an Anglican minister, Avery's religious experiences following the deaths of her children led her to pen a series of prophetic letters to friends which she published in 1647.

Gervase Babington (1549/1550–1610). English Anglican bishop. Born into an influential family, Babington studied at Cambridge and spent time as a preacher at the university and as prebendary of Hereford Cathedral before serving, in turn, as bishop of Llandaff, Exeter, and Worcester. He published a number of sermons, expositions of the Ten Commandments and Lord's Prayer, and notes on Genesis, Exodus, and Leviticus.

Robert Bagnall (b. 1559 or 1560). English Protestant minister. Bagnall authored *The Steward's Last Account* (1622), a collection of five sermons on Luke 16.

Friedrich Balduin (1575–1627). German Lutheran theologian. After spending time in the pastorate at Freiberg and Oelsnitz, Balduin was appointed professor of theology at Wittenberg in 1604, where he remained until the end of his life. He also served as head of the theology faculty, superintendent of churches, and assessor of the consistory. Known for his commitment to Lutheran orthodoxy, Balduin's major works include a commentary on the Pauline letters and writings on exegesis, homiletics, and casuistry.

John Bale (1495-1563) English protestant controversialist, writer, and playwright. Upon embracing the Reformation, Bale left the Carmelite order, and his anti-Catholic plays brought him into the service of Thomas Cromwell*. Exiled to Antwerp during Henry VIII's* rule, he was made Bishop of Ossory in Ireland under Edward VI*, resided on the continent under Mary I*, and returned after the accession of Elizabeth I*. Alongside his prodigious output of polemic plays and writings, Bale also published a historical catalog of British authors and an influential interpretation of Revelation.

John Ball (1585–1640). English Puritan theologian. Ball was a respected educator. He briefly held a church office until he was removed on account of his Puritanism. He composed popular catechisms and tracts on faith, the church and the covenant of grace.

John Barlow (1580/1581?–1629/1630). English Protestant minister. Educated at Oxford, Barlow ministered in Plymouth, Halifax, and Chester. A number of his sermons have been preserved, including his teachings on 2 Timothy 1 and 1 Thessalonians 4:18.

Thomas Bastard (c. 1565–1618). English Protestant minister and poet. Educated at Winchester and New College, Oxford, Bastard published numerous works, including collections of poems and sermons; his most famous title is *Chrestoleros* (1598), a collection of epigrams. Bastard was alleged to be the author of an anonymous work, *An Admonition to the City of Oxford*, which revealed the carnal vices of many clergy and scholars in Oxford; despite denying authorship, he was dismissed from Oxford in 1591. Bastard was recognized as a skilled classical scholar and preacher. He died impoverished in a debtor's prison in Dorchester.

Jeremias Bastingius (1551–1595). Dutch Reformed theologian. Educated in Heidelberg and Geneva, Bastingius pastored the Reformed church in Antwerp for nearly a decade until the Spanish overran the city in 1585; he later settled in Dordrecht. He spent the last few years of his life in Leiden on the university's board of regents. He wrote an influential commentary on the Heidelberg Catechism that was translated into English, Dutch, German and Flemish.

Johann (Pomarius) Baumgart (1514–1578). Lutheran pastor and amateur playwright. Baumgart studied under Georg Major,* Martin Luther* and Philipp Melanchthon* at the University of Wittenberg. Before becoming pastor of the Church of the Holy Spirit in 1540, Baumgart taught secondary school. He authored catechetical and polemical works, a postil for the Gospel readings throughout the church year, numerous hymns and a didactic play (*Juditium Salomonis*).

Richard Baxter (1615–1691). English Puritan minister. Baxter was a leading Puritan pastor, evangelist and theologian, known throughout England for his landmark ministry in Kidderminster and a prodigious literary output, producing 135 books in just over forty years. Baxter came to faith through reading William Perkins,* Richard Sibbes* and other early Puritan writers and was the first cleric to decline the terms of ministry in the national English church imposed by the 1662 Act of Uniformity; Baxter wrote on behalf of the more than 1700 who shared ejection from the national church. He hoped for restoration to national church ministry, or toleration, that would allow lawful preaching and pastoring. Baxter sought unity in theological, ecclesiastical, sociopolitical and personal terms and is regarded as a forerunner of Nonconformist ecumenicity, though he was defeated in his efforts at the 1661 Savoy Conference to take seriously Puritan objections to the revision of the 1604 Prayer Book. Baxter's views on church ministry were considerably hybrid: he was a paedo-baptist, Nonconformist minister who approved of synodical Episcopal government and fixed liturgy. He is most known for his classic writings on the Christian life, such as *The Saints' Everlasting Rest* and *A Christian Directory*, and pastoral ministry, such as *The Reformed Pastor*. He also produced *Catholick Theology*, a large volume squaring current Reformed, Lutheran, Arminian and Roman Catholic systems with each other.

Thomas Becon (1511/1512–1567). English Puritan preacher. Becon was a friend of Hugh Latimer,* and for several years chaplain to Archbishop Thomas Cranmer.* Becon was sent to the Tower of London by Mary I and then exiled for his controversial preaching at the English royal court. He returned to England upon Elizabeth I's* accession. Becon was one of the most widely read popular preachers in England during the Reformation. He published many of his sermons, including a postil, or collection of sermon helps for undertrained or inexperienced preachers.

Belgic Confession (1561). Written by Guy de Brès (1523–1567), this statement of Dutch Reformed faith was heavily reliant on the Gallic Confession,* although more detailed, especially in how strongly it distances the Reformed from Roman Catholics and Anabaptists. The Confession first appeared in French in 1561 and was translated to Dutch in 1562. It was presented to Philip II (1527–1598) in the hope that he would grant toleration to the Reformed, to no avail. At the Synod of Dordrecht* the Confession was revised, clarifying and strengthening the article on election as well as sharpening the distinctives of Reformed theology against the Anabaptists, thus situating the Dutch Reformed more closely to the international Calvinist movement. The Belgic Confession in conjunction with the Heidelberg Catechism* and the Canons of Dordrecht were granted official status as the confessional standards (the Three Forms of Unity) of the Dutch Reformed Church.

Robert Bellarmine (1542–1621). Italian Catholic cardinal. A Jesuit, Bellarmine first taught at Louvain before being appointed chair of polemical theology at the Roman College. Much of Bellarmine's career was devoted to the refutation of Protestant teachings, and his three volume work, the *Controversies* (1586–93), was widely disseminated in the post-Tridentine era as the foremost refutation of the evangelical message. He was influential in the official revision of the Vulgate* text during the reign of Pope Clement VIII (1536–1605), with the resulting version, the Sixto-Clementine Vulgate, providing the basic biblical text for Catholics until Vatican II. Bellarmine is also a controversial figure in the history of science. Appointed to the Holy Office, also known as the Inquisition, by Pope Paul V (1550–1621), it was he who examined Galileo Galilei (1564–1642) and ordered him to treat heliocentrism as a hypothesis rather than a reality, believing the evidentiary threshold had not yet been met. Later in his career, Bellarmine's attention turned to works on devotion and piety, and include his extensive commentary on the Psalms (1611).

Bernard of Clairvaux (1090–1153). French abbot and theologian. Born the son of a Bugundian knight, Bernard became interested in the new reforming movement at Citeaux, and thus abandoned his preparation for a secular career in favor of monastic life there. Towards this end, Bernard persuaded thirty-one of his friends and relatives to follow him to Citeaux, and join the Cistercian order. Among this group were four of Bernard's brothers. In 1115, Bernard went with others of his order to found a Cistercian monastery at Clairvaux. Bernard's austere approach to the monastic life attracted many followers to the point that by the time of his death there were sixty-eight Cistercian houses. Throughout his career, Bernard preached, mediated theological disputes, and advised. Bernard is best known for having preached the Second Crusade (1147–1150) as well as advising his former student, Pope Eugenius III (r. 1145–1153), and engaging in theological controversies with Peter Abelard (1079–1142) and Gilbert of Poitiers (1085–1154). One of the distinguishing characteristics of Bernard's theology is his Christocentric mysticism. Among Bernard's most important works are his treatises *On Consideration* and *On Loving God* along with his *Sermons on the Song of Songs* as well as many other sermons on the liturgical year and other subject. Many of the reformers in the sixteenth century cited Bernard extensively, especially Martin Luther* and John Calvin*.

Richard Bernard (1568–1641). English Puritan minister. A moderate Puritan, Bernard eschewed separation from the Church of England, spending the majority of his career in parish ministry at Batcombe, Somerset. Many of his works, including a handbook for pastors and a household catechism, were well received and printed numerous times during his lifetime.

Theodore Beza (1519–1605). French Reformed pastor and professor. Beza was compatriot and successor to John Calvin* as moderator of the Company of Pastors in Geneva during the second half of the sixteenth century. He was a noteworthy New Testament scholar whose *Codex Bezae* formed the basis of the New Testament section of later English translations. A leader in the academy and the church, Beza served as professor of Greek at the Lausanne Academy until 1558, at which time he moved to Geneva to become the rector of the newly founded Genevan Academy. He enjoyed an international reputation through his correspondence with key European leaders. Beza developed and extended Calvin's doctrinal thought on several important themes such as the nature of predestination and the real spiritual presence of Christ in the Eucharist.

Theodor Bibliander (1504?–1564). Swiss Reformed Hebraist and theologian. Professor of Old Testament at the Zurich Academy from 1531, Bibliander published two Hebrew grammars, a collection of letters by Zwingli* and Oecolampadius*, commentaries on Isaiah, Ezekiel, and Nahum, a Latin translation of the Qur'an, and a tract warning Christians against the threat of Islam. He taught a universalist view of predestination, arguing that God saved all people unless they rejected divine grace. Following a dispute with double-predestinarian Peter Martyr Vermigli*, he was forced into retirement in 1560.

Thomas Bilson (1546/1547?–1616). English Anglican Bishop and theologian. A celebrated preacher and theologian, Bilson served as canon of Winchester Cathedral and warden of Winchester College before becoming bishop of Worcester. He held this position for only one year, however, before his appointment to the wealthier see of Winchester. As an advisor to King James I,* he preached at his coronation, and he was involved with the publication of the 1611 Authorized Version,* being part of the Cambridge company responsible for translating the Apocrypha, the author of part of the front matter, and one of the text's final editors. His extant writings defend the episcopacy against Erastianism, condemn rebellion, and argue for a literal understanding of Christ's descent into hell.

Hugh Binning (1627–1653). Scottish Presbyterian theologian. At the age of eighteen, Binning became a professor of philosophy at the University of Glasgow. In his early twenties he left this post for parish ministry, and died of consumption a few years later. His commentary on the Westminster Confession and a selection of his sermons were published after his death.

Samuel Bird (d. 1604). Anglican minister and author. A native of Essex, Bird matriculated at Queen's College, Cambridge, where he received his BA in 1570 and his MA in 1573, at which time he was also elected a fellow of Corpus Christi College, Cambridge. For reasons unknown, Bird resigned his fellowship sometime in 1576. He spent nearly the entirety of his post-university career as rector of St. Peter's in Ipswich until his death in 1604. Among Bird's major works are *A Friendlie Communication or Dialogue Betweene Paule and Demas, wherein is Disputed How We are to Use the Pleasures of This Life* (1580), *Lectures upon the 11. Chapter of Hebrews and upon the 38. Psalme* (1598), and *Lectures upon the 8 and 9 Chapters of the Second Epistle to the Corinthians* (1598).

Bishops' Bible (1568). Anglicans were polarized by the two most recent English translations of the Bible: the Great Bible (1539) relied too heavily on the Vulgate* and was thus perceived as too Catholic, while the Geneva Bible's* marginal notes were too Calvinist for many Anglicans. So Archbishop Matthew Parker (1504–1575) commissioned a new translation of Scripture from the original languages with marginal annotations (many of which, ironically, were from the Geneva Bible). Published under royal warrant, the Bishops' Bible became the official translation for the Church of England. The 1602 edition provided the basis for the King James Bible (1611).

Christopher Blackwood (1607/1608–1670). English Baptist pastor. Initially an Anglican priest, Blackwood served at the parishes of Stockbury and Rye until Puritan sympathies led him to migrate to New England. Returning to England, he pastored briefly at Cranbrook until Baptist preaching caused him to leave the established church, be rebaptized, and serve as a pastor of a General Baptist congregation in Staplehurst. Joining the Parliamentary Army in their goal to evangelize Ireland, he helped plant a number of Baptist churches and pastored at Wexford, Kilkenny, and Dublin. His numerous writings include treatises on baptism and repentance, a catechism, and a commentary on the first ten chapters of Matthew.

Georg Blaurock (1492–1529). Swiss Anabaptist. Blaurock (a nickname meaning "blue coat," because of his preference for this garment) was one of the first leaders of Switzerland's radical reform movement. In the first public disputations on baptism in Zurich, he argued for believer's baptism and was the first person to receive adult believers' baptism there, having been baptized by Conrad Grebel* in 1525. Blaurock was arrested several times for performing mass adult baptisms and engaging in social disobedience by disrupting worship services. He was eventually expelled from Zurich but continued preaching and baptizing in various Swiss cantons until his execution.

Mary Cary (b. 1620/21) English millenarian interpreter. A popular writer, Cary commented extensively on the prophetic books of the Bible, relating the symbols in the texts to her context and finding signs of the imminent millennial age.

The Chronicle of the Hutterian Brethren. The Hutterites were an anabaptist group established by preacher Jacob Hutter (d. 1536) in Moravia distinguished by the commitment to communal life. Important leaders in the movement included Hans Denck*, Hans Hut*, Leonhard Schiemer* and Hans Schlaffer*. *The Chronicle of the Hutterian Brethren* traces the history of this group and the development of their faith from foundation until 1763. The collection of materials and memories began in the latter half of the sixteenth century by Kapsar Braitmichel (d. 1573) and continued by others until 1665. The task was later picked up by Johannes Waldner (1749-1825), a Hutterite bishop, who documented the history of the group from 1665 to 1763.

Bohemian Confession (1535). Bohemian Christianity was subdivided between traditional Catholics, Utraquists (who demanded Communion in both kinds) and the *Unitas Fratrum*, who were not Protestants but whose theology bore strong affinities to the Waldensians and the Reformed. The 1535 Latin edition of this confession—an earlier Czech edition had already been drafted—was an attempt to clarify and redefine the beliefs of the *Unitas*

Fratrum. This confession purged all earlier openness to rebaptism and inched toward Luther's* eucharistic theology. Jan Augusta (c. 1500–1572) and Jan Roh (also Johannes Horn; c. 1490–1547) presented the confession to King Ferdinand I (1503–1564) in Vienna, but the king would not print it. The *Unitas Fratrum* sought, and with slight amendments eventually obtained, Luther's advocacy of the confession. It generally follows the structure of the Augsburg Confession.*

Bohemian Confession (1575). This confession was an attempt to shield Bohemian Christian minorities—the Utraquists and the *Unitas Fratrum*—from the Counter-Reformation and Habsburg insistence on uniformity. The hope was that this umbrella consensus would ensure peace in the midst of Christian diversity; anyone who affirmed the 1575 Confession, passed by the Bohemian legislature, would be tolerated. This confession was, like the Bohemian Confession of 1535, patterned after the Augsburg Confession.* It emphasizes both justification by faith alone and good works as the fruit of salvation. Baptism and the Eucharist are the focus of the sacramental section, although the five traditional Catholic sacraments are also listed for the Utraquists. Though it was eventually accepted in 1609 by Rudolf II (1552–1612), the Thirty Years' War (1618–1648) rendered the confession moot.

Samuel Bolton (1606–1654). English Anglican minister. Bolton served a number of parishes in London before being elected to the Westminster Assembly. He spent the remainder of his career as master of Christ's College, Cambridge. A number of his writings were published, including works on sin, the sacraments, and Christian freedom.

Book of Common Prayer (1549; 1552). After the Church of England's break with Rome, it needed a liturgical manual to distinguish its theology and practice from that of Catholicism. Thomas Cranmer* drafted the Book of Common Prayer based on the medieval Roman Missal, under the dual influence of the revised Lutheran Mass and the reforms of the Spanish Cardinal Quiñones. This manual details the eucharistic service, as well as services for rites such as baptism, confirmation, marriage and funerals. It includes a matrix of the epistle and Gospel readings and the appropriate collect for each Sunday and feast day of the church year. The 1548 Act of Uniformity established the Book of Common Prayer as *the* authoritative liturgical manual for the Church of England, to be implemented everywhere by Pentecost 1549. After its 1552 revision, Queen Mary I banned it; Elizabeth I* reestablished it in 1559, although it was rejected by Puritans and Catholics alike.

The Book of Homilies (1547; 1563; 1570). This collection of approved sermons, published in three parts during the reigns of Edward VI and Elizabeth I,* was intended to inculcate Anglican theological distinctives and mitigate the problems raised by the lack of educated preachers. Addressing doctrinal and practical topics, Thomas Cranmer* likely wrote the majority of the first twelve sermons, published in 1547; John Jewel* added another twenty sermons in 1563. A final sermon, *A Homily Against Disobedience*, was appended to the canon in 1570. Reprinted regularly, the *Book of Homilies* was an important resource in Anglican preaching until at least the end of the seventeenth century.

Martin (Cellarius) Borrhaus (1499–1564). German Reformed theologian. After a dispute with his mentor Johann Eck,* Borrhaus settled in Wittenberg, where he was influenced by the radical Zwickau Prophets. He travelled extensively, and finally settled in Basel to teach philosophy and Old Testament. Despite his objections, many accused Borrhaus of Anabaptism; he argued that baptism was a matter of conscience. On account of his association with Sebastian Castellio (1515–1563) and Michael Servetus (1511–1553), some scholars posit that Borrhaus was an antitrinitarian. His writings include a treatise on the Trinity and commentaries on the Torah, historical books, Ecclesiastes and Isaiah.

Sigmund Bosch (unknown). German Anabaptist hymn writer. An elder in the Swiss and South German Anabaptist churches, Bosch collaborated with Pilgram Marpeck* in his ministry. He is known to have composed three hymns and a letter on the end times, which he addressed to the congregation in Austerlitz.

John Bourchier (d. 1660). English Puritan parliamentarian. Bourchier served as a justice of the peace in Yorkshire until imprisoned at the outbreak of the English Civil War. After his release, he was elected as the member of parliament for Ripon, and in this capacity he served as a judge at the trial of Charles I and signed the king's death warrant. Deemed too ill for trial with the other regicides, he died soon after the Restoration of the monarchy under Charles II.

John Bowle (d. 1637). Anglican pastor. After matriculating from Cambridge, Bowle was household pastor to Sir Robert Cecil (1563–1612) and held a pastorate at Tilehurst in Berkshire. He was appointed dean of Salisbury in 1620 and bishop of Rochester in 1629.

John Boys (1571–1625). Anglican priest and theologian. Before doctoral work at Cambridge, Boys pastored several parishes in Kent; after completing his studies he was appointed to more prominent positions, culminating in his 1619 appointment as the Dean of Canterbury by James I.* Boys published a popular four-volume postil of the Gospel and epistle readings for the church year, as well as a companion volume for the Psalms.

John Bradford (1510–1555). English Reformer, prebendary of St. Paul's, and martyr. Bradford was born in Blackley, Manchester, to an affluent family. After grammar school, Bradford at first began legal studies at the Inner Temple in London. However, while there, he heard the preaching of a fellow student, and thus converted to an evangelical faith. This conversion caused Bradford to abandon his study of law and enroll at St. Catherine's Hall, Cambridge, to study theology. He completed his MA in 1549, and in the same year, received an appointment of fellow at Pembroke Hall, Cambridge. In August, 1550, Bishop Nicholas Ridley ordained Bradford a deacon, and appointed him his personal chaplain. Bradford's exceptional preaching moved King Edward VI to select him as his chaplain and prebendary at St. Paul's Cathedral. After Mary Tudor succeeded her half-brother to throne, Bradford was tried and convicted of heresy on January 31, 1555. He was executed at the stake on July 1 of the same year.

Anne Bradstreet (1612–1672). English-American Puritan poet. Born in Northampton, Bradstreet married at sixteen and emigrated to the Massachusetts Bay Colony, of which both her father and husband would serve as governors. Mother to eight children, Bradstreet also wrote poetry. Much of her verse reflects on marriage, children, and her Puritan faith. While her writing received a mixed reception from contemporaries, many of whom viewed poetry as outside a woman's purview, she is today celebrated as the most significant early English poet in North America.

Thieleman Jans van Braght (1625–1664). Dutch Radical preacher. After demonstrating great ability with languages, this cloth merchant was made preacher in his hometown of Dordrecht in 1648. He served in this office for the next sixteen years, until his death. This celebrated preacher had a reputation for engaging in debate wherever an opportunity presented itself, particularly concerning infant baptism. The publication of his book of martyrs, *Het Bloedigh Tooneel of Martelaersspiegel* (1660; *Martyrs' Mirror*), proved to be his lasting contribution to the Mennonite tradition. *Martyrs' Mirror* is heavily indebted to the earlier martyr book *Offer des Heeren* (1562), to which Braght added many early church martyrs who rejected infant baptism, as well as over 800 contemporary martyrs.

David Bramley (unknown). English lay preacher. Two works by Bramley survive, an exposition of Matthew 11:25 and a treatise arguing for the acceptance of lay preachers without university training like himself. On both tracts, he is identified simply as a "Preacher of the Gospel."

Johannes Brenz (1499–1570). German Lutheran theologian and pastor. Brenz was converted to the reformation cause after hearing Martin Luther* speak; later, Brenz became a student of Johannes Oecolampadius.* His central achievement lay in his talent for organization. As city preacher in Schwäbisch-Hall and afterward in Württemberg and Tübingen, he oversaw the introduction of reform measures and doctrines and new governing structures for ecclesial and educational communities. Brenz also helped establish Lutheran orthodoxy through treatises, commentaries and catechisms. He defended Luther's position on eucharistic presence against Huldrych Zwingli* and opposed the death penalty for religious dissenters.

Guillaume Briçonnet (1470–1534). French Catholic abbot and bishop. Briçonnet created a short-lived circle of reformist-minded humanists in his diocese under the sponsorship of Marguerite d'Angoulême. His desire for ecclesial reform developed throughout his prestigious career (including positions as royal chaplain to the queen, abbot at Saint-Germain-des-Prés and bishop of Meaux), influenced by Jacques Lefèvre d'Étaples.* Briçonnet encouraged reform through ministerial visitation, Scripture and preaching in the vernacular and active study of the Bible. When this triggered the ire of the theology faculty at the Sorbonne in Paris, Briçonnet quelled the activity and departed, envisioning an ecclesial reform that proceeded hierarchically.

William Bridge (1600?–1670). English Puritan minister. Bridge ministered in Norfolk and Essex until excommunicated as a Nonconformist and exiled, leading him to Rotterdam, where he copastored a church with Jeremiah Burroughs.* Returning to England, he was a member of the Westminster Assembly and pastored at Great Yarmouth until ejected from the ministry by the Act of Uniformity (1662). Many of Bridge's sermons were published during his life, and he also composed a number of works designed to encourage struggling believers.

Walter Bridges (unknown). English Anglican minister. Three works are attributed to Bridges. Two were published anonymously, a sermon on Joab before the House of Commons and a catechism for those taking the Eucharist, while a third, a sermon on unity given before the Lord Mayor and Aldermen of London, names him and his position as preacher at St. Dunstans-in-the-East, London.

Thomas Brightman (1562–1607). English Puritan pastor and exegete. Under alleged divine inspiration, Brightman wrote a well known commentary on Revelation, influenced by Joachim of Fiore (d. 1202). In contrast to the putatively true churches of Geneva and Scotland, he depicted the Church of England as a type of the lukewarm Laodicean church. He believed that the Reformation would result in the defeat of the Vatican and the Ottoman Empire and that all humanity would be regenerated through the spread of the gospel before Christ's final return and judgment.

Hugh Broughton (1549–1612). English Puritan Hebraist and theologian. Following his time as a student and fellow at Cambridge, Broughton established himself as a scholar and preacher in London. His first work, *A Concent of Scripture* (1588), an attempt to harmonize the chronology of Scripture, caused significant controversy and led him to spend much of the next two decades traveling throughout Europe. On the Continent, he built a reputation in disputes with numerous Jewish, Catholic, and Protestant scholars and helped to plant an English Reformed church in Amsterdam, a congregation he may also have pastored for a time. Broughton's extensive writings include comments on numerous aspects of the Old Testament and New Testaments, a genealogy of Christ, and an explication of Christ's descent into hell.

Robert Browne (c. 1550–1633). English Nonconformist minister. While drawn to Puritan teachings, Browne began his career within the Church of England, ministering in London and Cambridge. Convinced that more radical reformation was needed outside the constraints of the state, Browne is recognized as the first to found a separatist church, establishing a congregation in Norwich, with those who followed him becoming known as Brownists. After a brief imprisonment, he left for Middelburg in the Netherlands, gathering a church based on the principles he espoused in his two most important works, *A Treatise of Reformation Without Tarrying* (1582) and *The Life and Manners of All True Christians* (1582), which set forth the foundations of congregationalist church government. Browne did not remain a separatist, however, and after a few years returned to England and reentered the Church of England, serving as a school headmaster and pastoring in Northamptonshire.

Antonio Brucioli (c. 1498–1566). Italian Protestant humanist and translator. Born in Florence, Brucioli and other humanists fled to Lyon after implication in a conspiracy to assassinate Guilio de' Medici (1478–1534, later Pope Clement VII r. 1523–1534). After publishing a series of philosophical dialogues, he returned to Florence, only to be expelled for involvement in further political intrigues, anticlerical writings, and suspected Lutheranism. Settling in Venice, Brucioli established a publishing house and began a prodigious printing program. Best known for rendering the first translation of the Scriptures into Italian directly from Hebrew and Greek, he also composed introductions and commentaries on the books of the Bible and published translations of philosophers such as Cicero, Pliny, and Aristotle. His writings on Scripture were scrutinized for their Protestant teachings, particularly with regard to the sacraments, and he was called before the Inquisition three times. The first time, Brucioli was fined and exiled from Venice; the second, his writings were banned and burned; and the third, he was imprisoned and left to die penniless upon release.

Otto Brunfels (c. 1488–1534). German Lutheran botanist, teacher and physician. Brunfels joined the Carthusian order, where he developed interests in the natural sciences and became involved with a humanist circle associated with Ulrich von Hutten and Wolfgang Capito.* In 1521, after coming into contact with Luther's* teaching, Brunfels abandoned the monastic life, traveling and spending time in botanical research and pastoral care. He received a medical degree in Basel and was appointed city physician of Bern in 1534. Brunfels penned defenses of Luther and Hutten, devotional biographies of biblical figures, a prayer book, and annotations on the Gospels and the Acts of the Apostles. His most influential contribution, however, is as a Renaissance botanist.

Martin Bucer (1491–1551). German Reformed theologian and pastor. A Dominican friar, Bucer was influenced by Desiderius Erasmus* during his doctoral studies at the University of Heidelberg, where he began corresponding with Martin Luther.* After advocating reform in Alsace, Bucer was excommunicated and fled to Strasbourg, where he became a leader in the city's Reformed ecclesial and educational communities. Bucer sought concord between Lutherans and Zwinglians and Protestants and Catholics. He emigrated to England, becoming a professor at Cambridge. Bucer's greatest theological concern was the centrality of Christ's sacrificial death, which achieved justification and sanctification and orients Christian community.

Johannes Bugenhagen (1485–1558). German Lutheran pastor and professor. Bugenhagen, a priest and lecturer at a Premonstratensian monastery, became a city preacher in Wittenberg during the reform efforts of Martin Luther* and Philipp Melanchthon.* Initially influenced by his reading of Desiderius Erasmus,* Bugenhagen grew in evangelical orientation through Luther's works; later, he studied under Melanchthon at the University of Wittenberg, eventually serving as rector and faculty member there. Bugenhagen was a versatile commentator, exegete and lecturer on Scripture. Through these roles and his development of lectionary and devotional material, Bugenhagen facilitated rapid establishment of church order throughout many German provinces.

Henry Bull (d. 1575?). English Protestant theologian and martyrologist. Little is known about Bull's circumstances after he was expelled from Magdalen College, Oxford, for snatching the censer from the hand of a priest officiating Mass. A committed reformer, he edited, translated, compiled, and published a number of Protestant works, including a book of prayers and meditations and writings by John Hooper* and Martin Luther.* He also worked alongside John Foxe* in the compilation of *Acts and Monuments*, while Miles Coverdale's* *The Letters of the Martyrs* is largely Bull's work.

Heinrich Bullinger (1504–1575). Swiss Reformed pastor and theologian. Bullinger succeeded Huldrych Zwingli* as minister and leader in Zurich. The primary author of the First and Second Helvetic Confessions,* Bullinger was drawn toward reform through the works of Martin Luther* and Philipp Melanchthon.* After Zwingli died, Bullinger was vital in maintaining adherence to the cause of reform; he oversaw the expansion of the Zurich synodal system while preaching, teaching and writing extensively. One of Bullinger's lasting legacies was the development of a federal view of the divine covenant with humanity, making baptism and the Eucharist covenantal signs.

Heinrich Bünting (1545–1606). Lutheran theologian and pastor. Bünting was born in Hanover, Germany, and studied theology at the University of Wittenberg, where he graduated in 1569. Upon finishing his studies at Wittenberg, Bünting became a pastor at Lemgo, where he was dismissed in 1575. Afterward he moved to Gronau an der Leine, where he served until his appointment as superintendent in Goslar. However, due to controversy over some of his teachings, Bünting was relieved of his position in 1600, retiring thereafter to Hanover, where he lived the remainder of his life. Bünting's most notable work is his *Itinerarium Sacrae Scripturae* (1581), a summary of biblical geography. Throughout this treatise, Bünting follows the travels of various major biblical figures, highlighting their theological as well as exegetical importance. When published, the *Itinerarium Sacrae Scripturae* was the most complete summary of biblical geography. Among the work's distinctive features is its collection of maps.

John Bunyan (1628–1688). English Puritan preacher and writer. His *Pilgrim's Progress* is one of the best-selling English-language titles in history. Born to a working-class family, Bunyan was largely unschooled, gaining literacy (and entering the faith) through reading the Bible and such early Puritan devotional works as *The Plain Man's Pathway to Heaven* and *The Practice of Piety*. Following a short stint in Oliver Cromwell's parliamentary army, in which Bunyan narrowly escaped death in combat, he turned to a preaching ministry, succeeding John Gifford as pastor at the Congregational church in Bedford. A noted preacher, Bunyan drew large crowds in itinerant appearances and it was in the sermonic form that Bunyan developed his theological outlook, which was an Augustinian-inflected Calvinism. Bunyan's opposition to the Book of Common Prayer and refusal of official ecclesiastical licensure led to multiple imprisonments, where he wrote many of his famous allegorical works, including *Pilgrim's Progress*, *The Holy City*, *Prison Meditations* and *Holy War*.

Michelangelo Buonarroti (1475–1564). Italian Catholic artist and poet. Michelangelo was born in Florence but spent the majority of his career in Rome, completing artworks commissioned by the popes of the early sixteenth century. One of the most recognized artists of all time, his artworks include the *Pietà* (1499), *David* (1501–1504), the ceiling of the Sistine Chapel (1508–1512), *Moses* (1515), and the *Last Judgment* (1536–1541), which remain famous and have done much to shape Western aesthetics. Toward the end of his life, his interests shifted toward architecture, culminating with his contributions to the designs of St. Peter's Basilica in Rome. Michelangelo is thought to have been devoutly Catholic throughout his life, but recent scholarship has considered the complexity of his relationship with the Catholic Reformation and the Protestant movement.

Jeremiah Burroughs (c. 1600–1646). English Puritan pastor and delegate to the Westminster Assembly. Burroughs left Cambridge, as well as a rectorate in Norfolk, because of his nonconformity. After returning to England from pastoring an English congregation in Rotterdam for several years (1637–1641), he became one of only a few dissenters from the official presbyterianism of the Assembly in favor of a congregationalist polity. Nevertheless, he was well known and respected by presbyterian colleagues such as Richard Baxter* for his irenic tone and conciliatory manner. The vast majority of Burroughs's corpus was published posthumously, although during his lifetime he published annotations on Hosea and several polemical works.

William Burton (d. 1616). English Puritan minister. Burton first ministered in Norwich, where he was present for the burning of Francis Kett (d. 1589) for Arianism. He later pastored in Bristol, Reading, and London. Throughout his life, he published a number of his sermons and treatises as well as a brief catechism.

Anthony Cade (d. 1641). Anglican pastor. Cade served as tutor and chaplain to George Villiers, First Duke of Buckingham (1592–1628), a close confidante of King James I* before holding a number of pastoral positions in Leicestershire and Northamptonshire.

Cardinal Cajetan (Thomas de Vio) (1469–1534). Italian Catholic cardinal, professor, theologian and biblical exegete. This Dominican monk was the leading Thomist theologian and one of the most important Catholic exegetes of the sixteenth century. Cajetan is best-known for his interview with Martin Luther* at the Diet of Augsburg (1518). Among his many works are polemical treatises, extensive biblical commentaries and most importantly a four-volume commentary (1508–1523) on the *Summa Theologiae* of Thomas Aquinas.*

Georg Calixtus (1586–1656). German Lutheran theologian. Calixtus studied at the University of Helmstedt where he developed regard for Philipp Melanchthon.* Between his time as a student and later as a professor at Helmstedt, Calixtus traveled through Europe seeking a way to unite and reconcile Lutherans, Calvinists and Catholics. He attempted to fuse these denominations through use of the Scriptures, the Apostles' Creed, and the first five centuries, interpreted by the Vincentian canon. Calixtus's position was stamped as syncretist and yielded further debate even after his death.

John Calvin (1509–1564). French Reformed pastor and theologian. John Calvin was born in Noyon, France. After receiving his primary education in the aristocratic family of Charles de Hangest, he attended the University of Paris to prepare for further study of theology. However, after completing his BA degree, as per his father's instructions, Calvin proceeded to the study of the law at Orleans of Bourges. While at Orleans, Calvin's interests in Greek and Latin literature were reawakened. Upon his father's death, Calvin resumed his study of classical literature at the newly founded College of Royal Readers in Paris under the direction of Guillaume Bude. The product of these studies was his commentary on Seneca's *De Clementia* (1532). Sometime between 1533 and 1534 Calvin experienced a "sudden conversion" due largely to the influence to Martin Luther's 1520 treatises. Calvin's embracing of an evangelical faith forced him to flee France. From there he went to Basel, where he wrote the first edition of his *Institutes of the Christian Religion* in 1536. The *Institutes* became a theological dogmatics for the Reformed churches. Calvin spent most of his career in Geneva (excepting a three-year ministry in Strasbourg with Martin Bucer*). In Geneva, Calvin reorganized the structure and governance of the church and established an academy that became an international center for theological education. He was a tireless writer, revising his *Institutes* several times, and authoring theological treatises as well as biblical commentaries. Calvin is also known for his debates with his contemporaries, including Michael Servetus, whose anti-Trinitarian views led to his execution in Geneva in 1553. Calvin also maintained friendly correspondence with many reformers, including Melanchthon* and Bullinger*, the latter of whom he was able to come to an agreement with regarding the presence of Christ in the Lord's Supper with the signing of the *Consensus Tigurinus* in 1551, which brought a degree of unity between Geneva and Zurich and to the Reformed tradition. One of the foremost figures during the Reformation period, Calvin has an extensive exegetical and theological legacy.

Wolfgang Capito (1478?–1541). German Reformed humanist and theologian. Capito, a Hebrew scholar, produced a Hebrew grammar and published several Latin commentaries on books of the Hebrew Scriptures. He corresponded with Desiderius Erasmus* and fellow humanists. Capito translated Martin Luther's* early works into Latin for the printer Johann Froben. On meeting Luther, Capito was converted to Luther's vision, left Mainz and settled in Strasbourg, where he lectured on Luther's theology to the city clergy. With Martin Bucer,* Capito reformed liturgy, ecclesial life and teachings, education, welfare, and government. Capito worked for the theological unification of the Swiss cantons with Strasbourg.

Pietro Carnesecchi (1508–1567). Italian humanist. Carnesecchi rose in the papal bureaucracy under Medici patronage, but after the death of Clement VII* he began to deviate from Catholic orthodoxy, aligning himself with Juan de Valdés.* While he retained relations with the established church, he also read Protestant works by theologians such as Luther,* Calvin,* and Bucer,* and his only extant doctrinal writing defends Bucer's view of the Eucharist over that of Zwingli.* Carnesecchi was able to avoid arrest by the Inquisition for a time, and his condemnation to death in absentia was pardoned under Pope Pius IV (1499–1565). However, Pius V (1504–1572) was a longtime opponent of Carnesecchi, and upon his election to the papal office, reopened the case and those of a number of others suspected of Protestant leanings. While seeking refuge in Florence, Carnesecchi was betrayed to the Inquisition by Cosimo I de' Medici, and following trial he was beheaded.

François Carrière (d. 1665). French Catholic theologian. A Franciscan doctor of theology, Carrière composed a commentary on the whole Bible, a summary of Catholic doctrine, and a history of the papacy.

John Carter (1554–1635). English Puritan minister. After graduating from Cambridge, Carter served as vicar at Bramford, Suffolk, until disputes over his Puritanism within the congregation led him to be moved to the nearby parish of Belstead.

Denis the Carthusian (1402/1403–1471). Belgian Catholic theologian and mystic. Denis studied philosophy and theology at the University of Cologne before entering the Carthusian monastery at Roermond, where he spent most of his career in strict seclusion. A prodigious writer, his work spanned diverse genres, including popular devotional works, scholastic summaries of Lombard* and Aquinas,* and dogmatic works on numerous topics, including Mary, ecclesiology, and morality. Denis also produced commentaries on every book of the Bible.

Thomas Cartwright (1535–1606). English Puritan preacher and professor. Cartwright was educated at St. John's College, Cambridge, although as an influential leader of the Presbyterian party in the Church of England he was continually at odds with the Anglican party, especially John Whitgift.* Cartwright spent some time as an exile in Geneva and Heidelberg as well as in Antwerp, where he pastored an English church. In 1585, Cartwright was arrested and eventually jailed for trying to return to England despite Elizabeth I's* refusal of his request. Many acknowledged him to be learned but also quite cantankerous. His publications include commentaries on Colossians, Ecclesiastes, Proverbs and the Gospels, as well as a dispute against Whitgift on church discipline.

Sébastien Castellion (1515-1563) French Reformed humanist, pastor, and theologian. Born a peasant, Castellion converted to the evangelical faith while studying at Lyon. He initially aligned himself with John Calvin*, studying with him in Strasbourg and serving with him in Geneva as principal of the Latin school. Theological differences and financial concerns brought Castellion and Calvin into conflict, however, leading to Castellion's dismissal from Geneva. Impoverished and with a large family, he eventually resettled in Basel, where he worked as an editor and published translations of the Bible into Latin (1551) and French (1555). Appointed professor of Greek at the University of Basel, Castellion became a leading advocate for religious toleration, and after condemning the Genevans for executing Michael Servetus in *Concerning Heretics and Whether They Are to be Persecuted* (1554), he built a network of supporters calling for religious toleration, voluntary piety, and an end to religiously-motivated violence.

Mathew Caylie (unknown). English Protestant minister. Caylie authored *The Cleansing of the Ten Lepers* (1623), an exposition of Luke 17:14-18.

Jan Cents (Unknown). Dutch Anabaptist. Believed to be a leader of the Anabaptist congregation in Amsterdam, Cents was the first signer and possibly author of a confession intended to unite Frisian and High German Mennonites.

John Chardon (d. 1601). Irish Anglican bishop. Chardon was educated at Oxford. He advocated Reformed doctrine in his preaching, yet opposed those Puritans who rejected Anglican church order. He published several sermons.

Christian Chemnitz (1615–1666). German Lutheran theologian. Grandnephew of Martin Chemnitz,* Christian Chemnitz was principal at the high school in Jena before serving the church as a deacon and archdeacon in Weimer and Braunschweig then as superintendent in Eisenach. Returning to Jena, he received his doctorate and replaced John Major as professor of theology, also serving as dean of the theology faculty and rector of the university. He wrote on numerous biblical, pastoral, and controversial topics, with his works including a defense of Lutheranism, instructions for young ministers, and a series of sermons on judgement.

Martin Chemnitz (1522–1586). German Lutheran theologian. A leading figure in establishing Lutheran orthodoxy, Chemnitz studied theology and patristics at the University of Wittenburg, later becoming a defender of Philipp Melanchthon's* interpretation of the doctrine of justification. Chemnitz drafted a compendium of doctrine and reorganized the structure of the church in Wolfenbüttel; later, he led efforts to reconcile divisions within Lutheranism, culminating in the Formula of Concord*. One of his chief theological accomplishments was a modification of the christological doctrine of the *communicatio idiomatium*, which provided a Lutheran platform for understanding the sacramental presence of Christ's humanity in the Eucharist.

David Chytraeus (1531–1600). German Lutheran professor, theologian and biblical exegete. At the age of eight Chytraeus was admitted to the University of Tübingen. There he studied law, philology, philosophy, and theology, finally receiving his master's degree in 1546. Chytraeus befriended Philipp Melanchthon* while sojourning in Wittenberg, where he taught the *Loci communes*. While teaching exegesis at the University of Rostock Chytraeus became acquainted with Tilemann Heshusius,* who strongly influenced Chytraeus away from Philippist theology. As a defender of Gnesio-Lutheran theology Chytraeus helped organize churches throughout Austria in accordance with the Augsburg Confession.* Chytraeus coauthored the Formula of Concord* with Martin Chemnitz,* Andreas Musculus (1514–1581), Nikolaus Selnecker* and Jakob Andreae.* He wrote commentaries on most of the Bible, as well as a devotional work titled *Regula vitae* (1555) that described the Christian virtues.

Isidorus Clarius (1495–1555). Italian Catholic humanist, biblical scholar, and bishop. As a leading Benedictine monk, Clarius sought reform the Roman Catholic Church from within. He participated in the commission that composed the *Consilium de Emendanda Ecclesia* (1536), and as bishop of Foligno, he sought to put many of its recommendations into action, demanding moral reform and consistent preaching from the clergy while reorganizing the charitable work of his diocese. Clarius was also open to rapprochement with Protestants. In 1540, he published *Adhortatio ad Concordiam* seeking compromise with the Lutherans, and his annotated revision of the Vulgate text (1542) interacted with Lutheran and Reformed scholars. This confessional openness was scrutinized after Clarius's death, and his edition of the Vulgate was included in the *Index Librorum Prohibitorum* (1557). For his work on the text of Scripture, however, he is recognized by name in the introduction to the 1611 King James Bible.

David Clarkson (1622–1686). English Puritan theologian. After his dismissal from the pastorate on account of the Act of Uniformity (1662), little is known about Clarkson. At the end of his life he ministered with John Owen* in London.

Robert Cleaver (1571–1613). English Puritan pastor. Cleaver served as rector at Drayton in Oxfordshire until silenced by Archbishop Richard Bancroft for advocating Nonconformity. Despite opposition from ecclesiastical authorities, Cleaver enjoyed a reputation as an excellent preacher. His published works include sermons on Hebrews 4 and Song of Songs 2 as well as one on the last chapter of Proverbs. Cleaver also authored *The Parsimony of Christian Children*, which contained a defense of infant baptism against Baptist criticisms.

George Close (unknown). English Protestant preacher. A series of Close's sermons on Matthew 16 were copied and published while he served as a reader at St. Antholin, London.

Michael Cobabus (d. 1686). German Lutheran theologian and mathematician. Trained in philosophy, mathematics, and theology at the University of Rostock, Cobabus remained in the city, serving as rector of the city school until appointed professor of mathematics at the university. He later received a doctorate in theology from the University of Griefswald and exchanged his position in the Rostock mathematics faculty for a professorship in theology.

Johannes Cocceius (1603–1669). German Reformed theologian. Cocceius first served as professor of biblical philology in his hometown of Bremen before moving to Franeker, where he taught Hebrew and theology, and finally to Leiden, where he spent the majority of his career as professor of theology. Cocceius is perhaps best remembered for his exposition of Reformed federal theology, defining the relationship between humanity and God in terms of progressive covenants. His critics, chief among them Gisbertus Voetius (1589–1676), argued that Cocceius's view of salvation history ignored the unity of the Scriptures and spiritualized the Old Testament. His other writings are extensive, including commentaries on all the books of the Bible, an influential Hebrew and Aramaic lexicon, and numerous works on theology, ethics, and philology.

John Colet (1467–1519). English Catholic priest, preacher and educator. Colet, appointed dean of Saint Paul's Cathedral by Henry VII, was a friend of Desiderius Erasmus,* on whose classical ideals Colet reconstructed the curriculum of Saint Paul's school. Colet was convinced that the foundation of moral reform lay in the education of children. Though an ardent advocate of reform, Colet, like Erasmus, remained loyal to the Catholic Church throughout his life. Colet's agenda of reform was oriented around spiritual and ethical themes, demonstrated in his commentaries on select books of the New Testament and the writings of Pseudo-Dionysius the Areopagite.

Vittoria Colonna (1490–1547). Italian Renaissance poet. Born into a noble family, Colonna was betrothed at three years of age to Fernando d'Ávalos (1489–1525), and they married in 1509. D'Ávalos was largely absent on military campaigns during their marriage, while she exercised his governorship of Benvenuto and became involved in the literary circles of Rome and Naples. One of the most important writers of her age, her friends included Pietro Bembo (1470–1547), Marguerite de Navarre,* and Michelangelo Buonarroti.* Writing primarily in the Petrarchan style, Colonna's reputation as a poet grew after the death of her husband, and much of her poetry was dedicated to his memory. Spiritual concerns form a major element of Colonna's writings, promoting contemplation and the ascetic life. While denied her desire to take holy orders in widowhood, Colonna spent much of her life residing in religious communities, and she was actively involved in movements seeking their improvement, collaborating with reformers such as Reginald Pole,* Juan de Valdés,* and Bernardo Ochino.*

Gasparo Contarini (1483–1542). Italian statesman, theologian and reform-minded cardinal. Contarini was an able negotiator and graceful compromiser. Charles V requested Contarini as the papal legate for the Colloquy of Regensburg (1541), where Contarini reached agreement with Melanchthon* on the doctrine of justification (although neither the pope nor Luther* ratified the agreement). He had come to a similar belief in the priority of faith in the work of Christ rather than works as the basis for Christian life in 1511, though unlike Luther, he never left the papal church over the issue; instead he remained within it to try to seek gentle reform, and he adhered to papal sacramental teaching. Contarini was an important voice for reform within the Catholic Church, always seeking reconciliation rather than confrontation with Protestant reformers. He wrote many works, including a treatise detailing the ideal bishop, a manual for lay church leaders, a political text on right governance and brief commentaries on the Pauline letters.

Thomas Cooper (1517?-1594) English Anglican Bishop and scholar. Prior to ordination, Cooper taught at Magdalen College School and worked as a physician. Entering the service of the church in about 1559, he served as dean of Christ Church and Gloucester until becoming Bishop of Lincoln and later Bishop of Winchester. A defender of the Elizabethan church order against Catholics and Puritans, Cooper is best remembered as a lexicographer, with his *Thesaurus Linguae Romanae et Britannicae* (1565) published in multiple editions.

Michel Cop (c. 1501–1566). Swiss Protestant pastor. Son of the physician to Francis I* and childhood friend of John Calvin,* Cop was a cathedral canon until fleeing France after his brother Nicholas's (c. 1501–1566) inaugural sermon as rector of the University of Paris was declared heretical for its Lutheran themes. Cop spent some time in Basel before settling in Geneva, where he served as a pastor, taught Calvin Hebrew, and published a sermon series on Proverbs and Ecclesiastes.

Christoph Corner (1518–1594). German Lutheran theologian. Professor of philosophy, rhetoric, and theology at the University of Frankfurt, Corner participated in the drafting of the Formula of Concord.* He also served as superintendent of churches in Mark Brandenberg.

Antonio del Corro (1527–1591). Spanish Reformed pastor and theologian. After encountering the ideas of Martin Luther* and other reformers, Corro abandoned the Hieronymite order. Leaving Spain to avoid charges of heresy, he traveled through Europe, spending time in Geneva and Lausanne before pastoring churches in France and the Low Countries. The arrival of Spanish armies in the Netherlands saw Corro and his family relocate to England, where he pastored a church of Spanish exiles in London and taught at Temple Church and Oxford. Corro courted controversy throughout his career, entering into debates with a wide array of Protestant theologians. In England, he was suspended from his pastorate for slander and examined a number of times for heresy, with some finding suggestions of Arianism in his Christology. Although these charges were never upheld, they clouded his later career and legacy.

Antonius Corvinus (1501–1553). German Lutheran theologian and administrator. After meeting Luther* and Melanchthon,* Corvinus left the humanist circle of Erasmus* to serve as a pastor in cities including Goslar, Witzenhausen, and Pattensen. A signatory of the Schmalkald Articles,* much of his career was devoted to constructing the organizational apparatus of the Lutheran church, and he established disciplinary procedures and church orders for numerous cities in northern Germany. His expository postils on the Gospels, Epistles, Psalms, and Genesis were also distributed widely in order to aid preachers of the region.

John Cosin (1594–1672). Anglican preacher and bishop. Early in his career Cosin was the vice chancellor of Cambridge and canon at the Durham cathedral. But as a friend of William Laud* and an advocate for "Laudian" changes, he was suspected of being a crypto-Catholic. In 1640 during the Long Parliament a Puritan lodged a complaint with the House of Commons concerning Cosin's "popish innovations." Cosin was promptly removed from office. During the turmoil of the English Civil Wars, Cosin sojourned in Paris among English nobility but struggled financially. Cosin returned to England after the Restoration in 1660 to be consecrated as the bishop of Durham. He published annotations on the Book of Common Prayer* and a history of the canon.

John Cotton (1584–1652). New England Puritan minister. Cotton was born to Puritan parents in Derby, England. He entered Trinity College, Cambridge, graduating with his bachelor's degree in 1603. Afterward, Cotton became a fellow at Emmanuel College, Cambridge, which at the time was heavily influenced by Puritanism. There, Cotton finished his master's degree in 1606. Cotton then served as head lecturer, dean, and catechist for the college. It was in this period that he heard the preaching of Richard Sibbes,* which proved instrumental in Cotton's personal conversion. Cotton received a bachelor of divinity in 1610 from Cambridge and was shortly thereafter ordained into the priesthood of the Church of England. However, Cotton's increasing nonconformity brought him into conflict with episcopal authorities, which prompted him to move to the colony of Massachusetts in July 1633. Upon his arrival, he immediately assumed a position of leadership as the teacher of the First Church of Boston. Throughout his tenure, Cotton exerted significant influence in the civic and ecclesiastical affairs of the colony. He continued in his ministry at First Church until his death on December 23, 1652. Over the course of his ministry, Cotton wrote nearly forty works. Among these were the *Keys of the Kingdom of Heaven, and the Power Thereof* (1644) and *Exposition upon the Thirteenth Chapter of Revelation* (1655).

Council of Constance (1414–1418). Convened to resolve the Western Schism, root out heresy and reform the church in head and members, the council asserted in *Sacrosancta* (1415) the immediate authority of ecumenical councils assembled in the Holy Spirit under Christ—even over the pope. Martin V was elected pope in 1417 after the three papal claimants were deposed; thus, the council ended the schism. The council condemned Jan Hus,* Jerome of Prague (c. 1365–1416) and, posthumously, John Wycliffe. Hus and Jerome, despite letters of safe conduct, were burned at the stake. Their deaths ignited the Hussite Wars, which ended as a result of the Council of Basel's concessions to the Bohemian church. The council fathers sought to reform the church through the regular convocation of councils (*Frequens*; 1417). Martin V begrudgingly complied by calling the required councils, then immediately disbanding them. Pius II (r. 1458–1464) reasserted papal dominance through *Execrabilis* (1460), which condemned any appeal to a future council apart from the pope's authority.

Council of Trent (1545–1563) Convoked by Pope Paul III (r. 1534–1549) with the support of Charles V*, the nineteenth ecumenical council was convened in the northern Italian city of Trent. Attended primarily by Italian clerics, it met in three distinct phases. Beginning in December 1545, during its first eight sessions, the council issued doctrinal decrees, asserting the authority of tradition alongside Scripture, the authenticity of the Vulgate, the prerogative of the church in interpretation, and the necessity of human cooperation in the work of salvation. Ecclesial abuses were also addressed, as attempts were made to eliminate absenteeism and pluralism and devolve power from Rome to bishoprics and parishes. The council was suspended following the outbreak of the plague in Trent in March 1547. A number of Protestant delegates were present during the second phase of the council, which met between May 1551 and April 1552 under the supervision of Pope Julius III (r. 1550–1555). The primary achievement of this period of the council was the clarification of teachings on the seven sacraments, with transubstantiation, the objective efficacy of the Eucharist, and the necessity of auricular confession confirmed as dogma. Reconvened by Pope Pius IV (r. 1559–1565) in 1561, the third phase of the council addressed the relationship between bishops and Rome, resulting in affirmations of the divine appointment of the church hierarchy and the obligation of bishops to reside in their dioceses. Clerical education, the regulation of marriage, and teachings on purgatory, indulgences, the use of images, and the saints were also addressed.

Miles Coverdale (1488–1568). Anglican bishop. Coverdale is known for his translations of the Bible into English, completing William Tyndale's* efforts and later producing the Great Bible commissioned by Henry VIII* (1539). A former friar, Coverdale was among the Cambridge scholars who met at the White Horse Tavern to discuss Martin Luther's* ideas. During Coverdale's three terms of exile in Europe, he undertook various translations, including the Geneva Bible*. He was appointed bishop of Exeter by Thomas Cranmer* and served as chaplain to Edward VI. Coverdale contributed to Cranmer's first edition of the Book of Common Prayer.*

William Cowper (Couper) (1568–1619). Scottish Puritan bishop. After graduating from the University of St. Andrews, Cowper worked in parish ministry for twenty-five years before becoming bishop. As a zealous Puritan and advocate of regular preaching and rigorous discipline, Cowper championed Presbyterian polity and lay participation in church government. Cowper published devotional works, sermon collections and a commentary on Revelation.

Benjamin Coxe (fl. 1646). English Baptist minister. Coxe began his career in the Church of England, ministering at parishes in Devonshire, Bedford, and Coventry. After preaching against infant baptism, he was challenged to a public debate by Richard Baxter.* Coxe lost and was briefly arrested after refusing to leave the city. Following his release, he joined a congregation of Anabaptists in London.

Walter Cradock (1606–1659). Welsh Anglican minister. Cradock was born in Llangwm, Monmouthshire, Wales. After completing his education at the University of Oxford, Cradock assumed his first position as curate at Peterson-super-Ely, Glamorgan. In 1633, Cradock, along with some other Welsh ministers, was reported to Archbishop William Laud* and the Court of High Commission for preaching nonconformity and for refusing the *Book of Sports*. In 1634 Cradock traveled throughout Wexham and Herefordshire encouraging the establishment of Welsh Nonconformist congregations. Cradock later became pastor of an Independent congregation at Llanfair Waterdine in 1639. When the English Civil War began, Cradock and his conventicle moved to Bristol, but when Royalist forces came to occupy the city, he and some of his group departed for All-Hallows-the-Great, where he preached regularly with Henry Jessey (1603–1663). In 1641, Cradock was among the group of preachers for Wales commissioned by the Long Parliament. Later, he served as regular preacher for the Barebones Parliament. Throughout this period, Cradock was an ardent supporter of Oliver Cromwell. Cradock lived the remainder of his life quietly while ministering to a congregation at Llangwm. Throughout his career, Cradock authored a number of devotional works, among which were *Gospel Liberty* (1648) and *Gospel Holiness* (1655).

Thomas Cranmer (1489–1556). Anglican archbishop and theologian. Cranmer supervised church reform and produced the first two editions of the Book of Common Prayer.* As a doctoral student at Cambridge, he was involved in the discussions at the White Horse Tavern. Cranmer contributed to a religious defense of Henry VIII's* divorce; Henry then appointed him Archbishop of Canterbury. Cranmer cautiously steered the course of reform, accelerating under Edward VI. After supporting the attempted coup to prevent Mary's assuming the throne, Cranmer was convicted of treason and burned at the stake. Cranmer's legacy is the splendid English of his liturgy and prayer books.

Richard Crashaw (1612–1649). English Catholic poet. Educated at Cambridge, Crashaw was fluent in Hebrew, Greek and Latin. His first volume of poetry was *Epigrammatum sacrorum liber* (1634). Despite being born into a Puritan family, Crashaw was attracted to Catholicism, finally converting in 1644 after he was forced to resign his fellowship for not signing the Solemn League and Covenant (1643). In 1649, he was made a subcanon of Our Lady of Loretto by Cardinal Palotta.

Herbert Croft (1603–1691). Anglican bishop. As a boy Croft converted to Catholicism; he returned to the Church of England during his studies at Oxford. Before the English Civil Wars, he served as chaplain to Charles I. After the Restoration, Charles II appointed him as bishop. Croft ardently opposed Catholicism in his later years.

John Crompe (d. 1661). Anglican priest. Educated at Cambridge, Crompe published a commentary on the Apostles' Creed, a sermon on Psalm 21:3 and an exposition of Christ's passion.

Oliver Cromwell (1599–1658). Commander of the Parliamentary forces during the English Civil War. Lord Protector of the Commonwealth of England, Scotland, and Ireland. Cromwell was born in Huntingdon, East Anglia, the only surviving son of Robert Cromwell. In 1616, he enrolled at the University of Cambridge as a fellow commoner. However, he withdrew from the university the following year due to his father's death. He represented Huntingdon in Parliament in 1628, and later Cambridge in the Short and Long Parliaments. During the Civil War, he commanded the Parliamentary forces, which he led to victory at the Battles of Marston Moor (1644) and Naseby (1645). After the execution of King Charles I in 1649, he became a member of the Council of State. It was at this time that the monarchy was abolished. In 1653, he was elevated to the position of Lord Protector of the Commonwealth. He declined the crown, though it was offered him in 1657. As Lord Protector, he endeavored to lead the postwar recovery, suppress military resistance, and advance British influence throughout Europe and the world. Moreover, he promoted a limited religious toleration in the kingdoms of England, Scotland, and Ireland. After his death in 1658, his son Richard (1626–1712) succeeded him as Lord Protector. However, due to incompetence, Richard was forced to resign, which paved the way for the Restoration of the monarchy in 1660 with the ascension of Charles II (1630–1685) to the throne. One year after the Restoration, Oliver Cromwell's body was disinterred from Westminster Abbey, hung on the gallows at Tyburn, and cast into an unmarked grave.

Caspar Cruciger (1504–1548). German Lutheran theologian. Recognized for his alignment with the theological views of Philipp Melanchthon,* Cruciger was a scholar respected among both Protestants and Catholics. In 1521, Cruciger came Wittenberg to study Hebrew and remained there most of his life. He became a valuable partner for Martin Luther* in translating the Old Testament and served as teacher, delegate to major theological colloquies and rector. Cruciger was an agent of reform in his birthplace of Leipzig, where at the age of fifteen he had observed the disputation between Luther and Johann Eck.*

Elisabeth Cruciger (c. 1500–1535). German Lutheran hymnist. Following her conversion to Lutheranism, Cruciger left the Praemonstratensian order and relocated to Wittenberg, where she married Caspar Cruciger.* While her authorship has been contested, recent scholarship has assigned Cruciger the place of the first female Lutheran hymnist for her composition of "Lord Christ is the Only Son of God" (Herr Christ der einig Gotts Sohn) (1524).

Ralph Cudworth (d. 1624) English Protestant minister. Father of noted Cambridge Platonist Ralph Cudworth (1617–1688), the elder Cudworth was a fellow of Emanuel College, Cambridge and rector of Aller in Somersetshire.

Marguerite d'Angoulême (1492–1549). French Catholic noblewoman. The elder sister of King Francis I of France, Marguerite was the Queen of Navarre and Duchess of Alençon and Berry. She was a poet and author of the French Renaissance. She composed *The Mirror of a Sinful Soul* (1531)—condemned by the theologians of the Sorbonne for containing Lutheran ideas—and an unfinished collection of short stories, the Heptaméron (1558). A leading figure in the French Reformation, Marguerite was at the center of a network of reform-minded individuals that included Guillame Briçonnet,* Jacques Lefèvre d'Etaples,* Gérard Roussel (1500–1550) and Guillame Farel (1489–1565).

Jakob Dachser (1486–1567). German Anabaptist theologian and hymnist. Dachser served as a Catholic priest in Vienna until he was imprisoned and then exiled for defending the Lutheran understanding of the Mass and fasting. Hans Hut* rebaptized him in Augsburg, where Dachser was appointed as a leader of the Anabaptist congregation. Lutheran authorities imprisoned him for nearly four years. In 1531 he recanted his Radical beliefs and began to catechize children with the permission of the city council. Dachser was expelled from Augsburg as a possible insurrectionist in 1552 and relocated to Pfalz-Neuberg. He published a number of poems, hymns and mystical works, and he versified several psalms.

Jean Daillé (1594–1670). French Reformed pastor. Born into a devout Reformed family, Daillé studied theology and philosophy at Saumur under the most influential contemporary lay leader in French Protestantism, Philippe Duplessis-Mornay (1549–1623). Daillé held to Amyraldianism—the belief that Christ died for all humanity inclusively, not particularly for the elect who would inherit salvation (though only the elect are in fact saved). He wrote a controversial treatise on the church fathers that aggravated many Catholic and Anglican scholars because of Daillé's apparent demotion of patristic authority in matters of faith.

Lambert Daneau (1530?–1595). French Reformed pastor and theologian. After a decade of pastoring in France, following the St. Bartholomew's Day Massacre, Daneau fled to Geneva to teach theology at the Academy. He later taught in the Low Countries, finishing his career in southern France. Daneau's diverse works include tracts on science, ethics and morality as well as numerous theological and exegetical works.

John Davenant (1576–1641). Anglican bishop and professor. Davenant attended Queen's College, Cambridge, where he received his doctorate and was appointed professor of divinity. During the Remonstrant controversy, James I* sent Davenant as one of the four representatives for the Church of England to the Synod of Dordrecht.* Following James's instructions, Davenant advocated a *via media* between the Calvinists and the Remonstrants, although in later years he defended against the rise of Arminianism in England. In 1621, Davenant was promoted to the bishopric of Salisbury, where he was generally receptive to Laudian reforms. Davenant's lectures on Colossians are his best-known work.

William Day (1605–1684). Anglican theologian. Born and raised in Windsor, Berkshire, Day received his early education from Eton College. Afterward, he matriculated at King's College, Cambridge, where he was elected a fellow in 1624. Day received his BA in 1629, and MA in 1632. In 1635, Day was incorporated MA at Oxford and in 1637 became vicar of Mapledurham, Oxfordshire. Throughout his long career, Day conformed to all the ecclesiastical changes dictated by the government through the Restoration, during which he retained his vicarage. Finally, Day was made divinity reader at the King's Chapel, Windsor Chapel. He published two commentaries, *An Exposition of the Book of the Prophet Isaiah* (1654) and *A Paraphrase and Commentary upon the Epistle of St. Paul to the Romans* (1666).

Defense of the Augsburg Confession (1531). See *Augsburg Confession.*

Hans Denck (c. 1500–1527). German Radical theologian. Denck, a crucial early figure of the German Anabaptist movement, combined medieval German mysticism with the radical sacramental theology of Andreas Bodenstein von Karlstadt* and Thomas Müntzer.* Denck argued that the exterior forms of Scripture and sacrament are symbolic witnesses secondary to the internally revealed truth of the

Sprit in the human soul. This view led to his expulsion from Nuremberg in 1525; he spent the next two years in various centers of reform in the German territories. At the time of his death, violent persecution against Anabaptists was on the rise throughout northern Europe.

Stephen Denison (unknown). English Puritan pastor. Denison received the post of curate at St. Katherine Cree in London sometime in the 1610s, where he ministered until his ejection from office in 1635. During his career at St. Katherine Cree, Denison waded into controversy with both Puritans (over the doctrine of predestination) and Anglicans (over concerns about liturgical ceremonies). He approached both altercations with rancor and rigidity, although he seems to have been quite popular and beloved by most of his congregation. In 1631, William Laud* consecrated the newly renovated St. Katherine Cree, and as part of the festivities Denison offered a sermon on Luke 19:27 in which he publicly rebuked Laud for fashioning the Lord's house into a "den of robbers." Aside from the record of his quarrels, very little is known about Denison. In addition to *The White Wolf* (a 1627 sermon against another opponent), he published a catechism for children (1621), a treatise on the sacraments (1621) and a commentary on 2 Peter 1 (1622).

Arthur Dent (d. 1607). English Puritan preacher. Ordained in the Church of England, Dent ministered in Essex, where he made his Puritan sympathies clear and was disciplined for refusing to wear a surplice and make the sign of the cross. He published a number of works, including an exposition of the Articles of Faith and an exposition of Revelation targeted against the Roman Catholic Church.

Marie Dentière (1495–1561). Belgian Reformed theologian. Dentière relinquished her monastic vows and married Simon Robert (d.1533), a former priest, in Strasbourg. After Robert died, she married Antoine Froment (1508–1581), a reformer in Geneva, and became involved in the reform of that city. Her best-known writings are a tract addressed to Marguerite d'Angoulême,* the *Very Useful Epistle* (1539), in which she espoused the evangelical faith and the right of women to interpret and teach scripture, and a preface to Calvin's sermon on 1 Timothy 2:8-12. Dentière is the only woman to have her name inscribed on the International Monument to the Reformation in Geneva.

Edward Dering (c. 1540–1576). English Puritan preacher. An early Puritan, Dering's prospects of advancement in the Elizabethan church were effectively ended after a sermon in front of the Queen in which he described her as an "untamed and unruly heifer" while criticizing the state of the church and clergy. While continuing with intemperate and critical attacks throughout his career, Dering established himself as a preacher at St. Paul's Cathedral in London, where he became known for his pastoral concern and desire to teach the assurance of salvation.

Jean D'Espagne (1591–1659). French Independent pastor. After leading churches at Orange and the Hague, D'Espagne departed under accusations of immorality and settled in London, where he pastored a French congregation. A fractious figure, he led a group that separated from the established French congregation and entered into numerous controversies. Many of his extant writings are targeted toward errors he perceived in the theology and practice of others.

David Dickson (1583?–1663). Scottish Reformed pastor, preacher, professor and theologian. Dickson defended the Presbyterian form of ecclesial reformation in Scotland and was recognized for his iteration of Calvinist federal theology and expository biblical commentaries. Dickson served for over twenty years as professor of philosophy at the University of Glasgow before being appointed professor of divinity. He opposed the imposition of Episcopalian measures on the church in Scotland and was active in political and ecclesial venues to protest and prohibit such influences. Dickson was removed from his academic post following his refusal of the oath of supremacy during the Restoration era.

Veit Dietrich (1506–1549). German Lutheran preacher and theologian. Dietrich intended to study medicine at the University of Wittenberg, but Martin Luther* and Philipp Melanchthon* convinced him to study theology instead. Dietrich developed a strong relationship with Luther, accompanying him to the Marburg Colloquy (1529) and to Coburg Castle during the Diet of Augsburg (1530). After graduating, Dietrich taught on the arts faculty, eventually becoming dean. In 1535 he returned to his hometown, Nuremberg, to pastor. Later in life, Dietrich worked with Melanchthon to reform the church in Regensburg. In 1547, when Charles V arrived in Nuremberg, Dietrich was suspended from the pastorate; he resisted the imposition of the Augsburg Interim to no avail. In addition to transcribing some of Luther's lectures, portions of the Table Talk and the very popular *Hauspostille* (1544), Dietrich published his own sermons for children, a manual for pastors and a summary of the Bible.

Louis de Dieu (1590–1642). Dutch Reformed pastor and linguist. Committed to his pastoral and teaching ministry in Leiden, Dieu turned down the opportunity to teach theology and Old Testament at the University of Utrecht. He published grammars of Hebrew (1626) and Persian (1639); a comparative grammar of Hebrew, Aramaic, and

Syriac (1628); and a collection of writings on the New Testament text.

Giovanni Diodati (1576–1649). Italian Reformed theologian. Diodati was from an Italian banking family who fled for religious reasons to Geneva. There he trained under Theodore Beza;* on completion of his doctoral degree, Diodati became professor of Hebrew at the academy. He was an ecclesiastical representative of the church in Geneva (for whom he was a delegate at the Synod of Dordrecht*) and an advocate for reform in Venice. Diodati's chief contribution to the Italian reform movement was a translation of the Bible into Italian (1640–1641), which remains the standard translation in Italian Protestantism.

John Dod (c. 1549–1645). English Puritan pastor. Over the course of his lengthy pastoral career (spanning roughly sixty years), Dod was twice suspended for nonconformity and twice reinstated. A popular preacher, he published many sermons as well as commentaries on the Ten Commandments and the Lord's Prayer; collections of his sayings and anecdotes were compiled after his death.

John Donne (1572–1631). Anglican poet and preacher. Donne was born into a strong Catholic family. However, sometime between his brother's death from the plague while in prison in 1593 and the publication of his *Pseudo-Martyr* in 1610, Donne joined the Church of England. Ordained to the Anglican priesthood in 1615 and already widely recognized for his verse, Donne quickly rose to prominence as a preacher—some have deemed him the best of his era. His textual corpus is an amalgam of erotic *and* divine poetry (e.g., "Batter My Heart"), as well as a great number of sermons.

Dordrecht Confession (1632). Dutch Mennonite confession. Adriaan Cornelisz (1581–1632) wrote the Dordrecht Confession to unify Dutch Mennonites. This basic statement of Mennonite belief and practice affirms distinctive doctrines such as nonresistance, shunning, footwashing, and the refusal to swear oaths. Most continental Mennonites subscribed to this confession during the second half of the seventeenth century.

Johann George Dorsche (1597–1659). German Lutheran theologian. Dorsche pastored briefly at Entzheim before being called to Strasbourg, where he earned his doctorate, was appointed professor of theology, and served as a preacher at the cathedral. He spent the last five years of his life as professor of theology at the University of Rostock. Dorsche published a number of theological works as well as commentaries on the Gospels and Hebrews.

John Downame (c. 1571–1652). English Puritan pastor and theologian. See *English Annotations*.

Charles Drelincourt (1595–1669). French Reformed pastor, theologian and controversialist. After studying at Saumur Academy, Drelincourt pastored the Reformed Church in Paris for nearly fifty years. He was well known for his ministry to the sick. In addition to polemical works against Catholicism, he published numerous pastoral resources: catechisms, three volumes of sermons and a five-volume series on consolation for the suffering.

The Dutch Annotations (1657). See *Statenvertaling*.

Daniel Dyke (d. 1614). English Puritan preacher. Born of nonconformist stock, Dyke championed a more thorough reformation of church practice in England. After the promulgation of John Whitgift's* articles in 1583, Dyke refused to accept what he saw as remnants of Catholicism, bringing him into conflict with the bishop of London. Despite the petitions of his congregation and some politicians, the bishop of London suspended Dyke from his ministry for refusing priestly ordination and conformity to the Book of Common Prayer.* All of his work was published posthumously; it is mostly focused on biblical interpretation.

John Eachard (unknown). English Anglican minister. After graduating with his master of arts from Trinity College, Cambridge, Eachard was the vicar at Darsham in Suffolk. At least two of his sermons, one on Matthew 3:10 and another on Revelation 12:11, were published in his lifetime.

Johann Eck (Johann Maier of Eck) (1486–1543). German Catholic theologian. Though Eck was not an antagonist of Martin Luther* until the dispute over indulgences, Luther's Ninety-five Theses (1517) sealed the two as adversaries. After their debate at the Leipzig Disputation (1519), Eck participated in the writing of the papal bull that led to Luther's excommunication. Much of Eck's work was written to oppose Protestantism or to defend Catholic doctrine and the papacy; his *Enchiridion* was a manual written to counter Protestant doctrine. However, Eck was also deeply invested in the status of parish preaching, publishing a five-volume set of postils. He participated in the assemblies at Regensburg and Augsburg and led the Catholics in their rejection of the Augsburg Confession.

Edward VI of England (1537–1553). English monarch. Son of Henry VIII* and Jane Seymour (1508–1537), Edward ascended to the throne as a minor, leaving the practical power of the monarchy in the hands of those appointed by the Regency council as Lord Protector of the Realm, first, his uncle, Edward Seymour, duke of

Somerset (1500–1552), and afterwards, John Dudley, duke of Northumberland (1504–1553). Under Somerset and Northumberland, and with Thomas Cranmer* installed as Archbishop of Canterbury, the eclectic reforms made during the reign of Henry VIII were drawn into the service of a thoroughly Protestant transformation. During the reign of Edward, communion in two kinds was instituted, all services were held in the vernacular, and a series of ecclesiastical visitations oversaw the suppression of Catholic religion. Alongside the flood of Protestant refugees from the continent that sheltered in the kingdom, the publication of the revised Book of Common Prayer*, the Book of Homilies* and the Forty–Two Articles (1553) helped establish the future direction of Anglicanism.

Elizabeth I of England (1533–1603) English monarch. The daughter of Henry VIII* (r. 1509–1547) and Anne Boleyn (c. 1501–1536), Elizabeth outwardly conformed to Catholicism during the reign of her sister Mary I (r. 1553–1558), but her Protestant upbringing encouraged the hopes of many reformers upon her accession in 1558. With the 1559 Elizabethan Settlement, Elizabeth redefined England as a Protestant country, with the Act of Supremacy asserting the monarch as the head of the English church, and the Act of Uniformity establishing the 1559 *Book of Common Prayer** as the valid order of service within the realm. However, Elizabeth resisted the aggressive persecution of Catholics for political reasons, while also allowing some traditional vestments, furniture and ceremonies to be retained. Her moderate and pragmatic reforms frustrated many who wished for more thorough change and led to the emergence of the Puritan movement. Elizabeth faced numerous threats during her reign, including the machinations of Scottish Catholics and claims to the throne of Mary Stuart (1542–1547), leading to her rival's imprisonment and execution in 1587; the attempted invasion of England by Spain, which culminated in the celebrated defeat of the Spanish Armada in 1588; and a Catholic rebellion in Ireland that was suppressed during the Nine Years War (1594–1603). Elizabeth never married, and was succeeded on the throne by James I* following her death in 1603.

Edward Elton (1569–1624). Puritan minister. Elton served as pastor of St. Mary Magdalen's Church in Bermondsey, Surrey. Richard Baxter* praised him for his exegetical works, among which were *Three Excellent Pious Treatises in Sundry Sermons upon the Whole Seventh, Eighth, and Ninth Chapters of the Epistle to the Romans* and *An Exposition of the Epistle of St. Paul to the Colossians*.

English Annotations (1645; 1651; 1657). Under a commission from the Westminster Assembly, the editors of the English Annotations—John Downame* along with unnamed colleagues—translated, collated and digested in a compact and accessible format several significant Continental biblical resources, including Calvin's* commentaries, Beza's* *Annotationes majores* and Diodati's* *Annotations*.

Desiderius Erasmus (1466–1536). Dutch Catholic humanist and pedagogue. Erasmus, a celebrated humanist scholar, was recognized for translations of ancient texts, reform of education according to classical studies, moral and spiritual writings and the first printed edition of the Greek New Testament. A former Augustinian who never left the Catholic Church, Erasmus addressed deficiencies he saw in the church and society, challenging numerous prevailing doctrines but advocating reform. He envisioned a simple, spiritual Christian life shaped by the teachings of Jesus and ancient wisdom. He was often accused of collusion with Martin Luther* on account of some resonance of their ideas but hotly debated Luther on human will.

George Estey (c. 1560–1601). English Anglican priest. After graduating from Cambridge, Estey was ordained in the Church of England and served as vicar of St. Mary in Bury St. Edmunds, Suffolk.

Paul Fagius (1504–1549). German Reformed Hebraist and pastor. After studying at the University of Heidelberg, Fagius went to Strasbourg where he perfected his Hebrew under Wolfgang Capito.* In Isny im Allgäu (Baden-Württemberg) he met the great Jewish grammarian Elias Levita (1469–1549), with whom he established a Hebrew printing press. In 1544 Fagius returned to Strasbourg, succeeding Capito as preacher and Old Testament lecturer. During the Augsburg Interim, Fagius (with Martin Bucer*) accepted Thomas Cranmer's* invitation to translate and interpret the Bible at Cambridge. However, Fagius died before he could begin any of the work. Fagius wrote commentaries on the first four chapters of Genesis and the deutero-canonical books of Sirach and Tobit.

Guillaume Farel (1489–1565) French Reformed preacher and theologian. At the vanguard of the French Reformation, Farel was a student of Jacques Lefèvre d'Étaples* and member of Archbishop Briçonnet's* circle in Meaux until his desire for more rapid change saw him depart in 1523 to preach the Protestant message in Basel, Montbéliard, Strasbourg, Bern, and Aigle. During this period of his ministry, he composed the first French Protestant book, an evangelical commentary on the Lord's Prayer and the Apostle's Creed, as well as the first French Confession of Faith. A catalyst in Geneva's acceptance of the Reformation in 1536, it was Farel who persuaded Calvin* to settle in the city. After he and Calvin were banished from Geneva in 1538, Farel accepted the pastorate in Neuchâtel, a position he held until his death while continuing to travel and support the Reformation in the French-speaking lands.

John Fary (unknown). English Puritan pastor. Fary authored *God's Severity on Man's Sterility* (1645), a sermon on the fruitless fig tree in Luke 13:6-9.

Margaret Fell (1614–1702). English Quaker. Known as the "Mother of Quakerism," Fell was born at Dalton-in-Furness in northern England. The daughter of a local judge, she married Thomas Fell, who was a judge as well as a member of Parliament, representing Lancashire. In 1652, under the preaching of George Fox (1624–1691), Fell and her daughters became members of the Society of Friends (the Quakers). From that time onward, she became a pivotal figure in the subsequent development of the Quaker movement. Throughout her extensive correspondence to powerful members of the nobility, including King Charles II (r. 1660–1685), she pleaded for the release of imprisoned Quakers. Fell was arrested in 1664 for leading Quaker meetings and for her refusal to swear the Oath of Obedience, and she was sentenced to four and a half years imprisonment. After her release, she married George Fox in 1669, her first husband having died eleven years earlier. In addition to her advocacy for incarcerated Quakers, Fell enhanced the work of the Quaker Women's Meeting, which consisted of caring for the sick and elderly as well as orphans and prisoners. Her exegetical works include *For Mannaseth Ben Israel* and *A Loving Salutation to the Seed of Abraham*, both published in 1656, and translated into Hebrew (the latter believed to have been translated by the Jewish philosopher Benedict Spinoza). Moreover during her imprisonment, she authored her most famous treatise, *Women's Speaking Justified, Proved and Allowed of by the Scriptures.*

Dudley Fenner (1558?–1587). English Puritan minister. Fenner ministered briefly in Kent before following his mentor Thomas Cartwright* to Antwerp, where he was ordained in the Reformed church. After pastoring the English congregation alongside Cartwright, Fenner returned to his previous congregation in Kent, but he was soon suspended and arrested for refusing to conform to the Book of Common Prayer* and Thirty-Nine Articles.* Once released, he returned to the Low Countries, spending the remainder of his career leading an English congregation in Middelburg. He composed devotional and polemical writings as well as commentaries on Song of Songs and Philemon.

William Fenner (1600–1640). English Puritan pastor. After studying at Cambridge and Oxford, Fenner ministered at Sedgley and Rochford. Fenner's extant writings, which primarily deal with practical and devotional topics, demonstrate a zealous Puritan piety and a keen interest in Scripture and theology.

Charles Ferme (1566–1617). Scottish Reformed pastor and educator. After studying and teaching at the University of Edinburgh, Ferme pastored in Philorth, where he later served as the principal of a newly chartered university. The reconstitution of the episcopacy brought challenges for Ferme, and his resistance saw him imprisoned a number of times, including a three-year incarceration on the Isle of Bute. His only extant writing is a logical analysis of Romans.

Henry Ferne (1602–1662). English Protestant minister. Ferne ministered at a number of parishes in the north of England before serving as an extraordinary chaplain to Charles I* after earning his doctorate of divinity. A committed Royalist, he left official ministry during the Civil War (1642–1651), though he often preached, wrote a number of theological treatises against the Roman Catholics, and accompanied the king on a number of occasions. After the Restoration, Ferne served as master at Trinity College, Cambridge, and dean of Ely Cathedral before becoming bishop of Chester.

Richard Ferrers (Unknown). English poet. Ferrers is remembered for his poem *The Worth of Woman* (1622), defending the equality and value of women.

First Helvetic Confession (1536). Anticipating the planned church council at Mantua (1537, but delayed until 1545 at Trent), Reformed theologians of the Swiss cantons drafted a confession to distinguish themselves from both Catholics and the churches of the Augsburg Confession.* Heinrich Bullinger* led the discussion and wrote the confession itself; Leo Jud, Oswald Myconius, Simon Grynaeus and others were part of the assembly. Martin Bucer* and Wolfgang Capito* had desired to draw the Lutheran and Reformed communions closer together through this document, but Luther* proved unwilling after Bullinger refused to accept the Wittenberg Concord (1536). This confession was largely eclipsed by Bullinger's Second Helvetic Confession.*

John Fisher (1469–1535). English Catholic bishop and theologian. This reputed preacher defended Catholic orthodoxy and strove to reform abuses in the church. In

1521 Henry VIII* honored Fisher with the title *Fidei Defensor* ("defender of the faith"). Nevertheless, Fisher opposed the king's divorce of Catherine of Aragon (1485–1536) and the independent establishment of the Church of England; he was convicted for treason and executed. Most of Fisher's works are polemical and occasional (e.g., on transubstantiation, against Martin Luther*); however, he also published a series of sermons on the seven penitential psalms. In addition to his episcopal duties, Fisher was the chancellor of Cambridge from 1504 until his death.

Matthias Flacius (1520–1575). Lutheran theologian. A native of Croatia, Matthias Flacius commenced his studies at the University of Tubingen, and completed them at Wittenberg, where through Luther's influence, he embraced the university's evangelical theology. Flacius began his career as instructor of Hebrew at the University of Wittenberg in 1544, and remained in this post until 1549. As a devoted follower of Luther's teachings, Flacius sought to defend them in their purity which drove him and Nikolaus von Amsdorf as leaders of the Gnesio-Lutherans to oppose the more moderate positions of Philipp Melanchthon and his sympathizers, the Philippists, in several controversies concerning the role of free will and good works in justification as well as relations with Calvinism. After serving as a professor at the University of Jena (1557–1561), Flacius spent the remainder of his life as an independent scholar, frequently moving from one city to another to escape persecution. Flacius died in Frankfurt am Main in 1575. His important exegetical works are *De vocabula Dei* (1549), *Clavis Scripturae Sacrae* (1567), and *Glossa Novi Testamenti* (1570). Flacius also published two historical works, *Catalogus Testium Veritatis* (1556) and the *Magdeburg Centuries*.

Marcantonio Flaminio (1498–1550). Italian humanist and poet. Flaminio was dependent on patronage, and he spent much of his life in the houses of noble benefactors in Bologna, Genoa, and Verona. While he never left the Roman church, he was drawn to intellectual currents that sought reform. In Naples, he participated in an intellectual circle that included Juan de Valdés* and Pietro Carnesecchi* before joining the house of Cardinal Pole* in Viterbo. Alongside his poetry and humanistic writings, Flaminio also edited one of the most significant Italian texts of the Reformation, Benedetto de Mantova's* *The Benefit of Christ* (1543).

John Flavel (c. 1630–1691). English Puritan pastor. Trained at Oxford, Flavel ministered in southwest England from 1650 until the Act of Uniformity in 1662, which reaffirmed the compulsory use of the Book of Common Prayer. Flavel preached unofficially for many years, until his congregation was eventually allowed to build a meeting place in 1687. His works were numerous, varied and popular.

Giovanni Battista Folengo (1490–1559). Italian Catholic exegete. In 1528 Folengo left the Benedictine order, questioning the validity of monastic vows; he returned to the monastic life in 1534. During this hiatus Folengo came into contact with the Neapolitan reform-minded circle founded by Juan de Valdés.* Folengo published commentaries on the Psalms, John, 1–2 Peter and James. Augustin Marlorat* included Folengo's comment in his anthology of exegesis on the Psalms. In 1580 Folengo's Psalms commentary was added to the Index of Prohibited Books.

John Forbes (1568?–1634). Scottish Reformed pastor. While minister at Alford in Aberdeenshire, Forbes was appointed moderator of the Presbyterian Aberdeen Assembly, which met against the orders of King James I.* Refusing to accept the monarch's jurisdiction, he was exiled to the Continent and settled in the Netherlands, where he pastored English congregations at Middleburg and Delft until forced out under the reforms of Archbishop Laud.*

Francisco Forerius (1523-1581) Portuguese Catholic theologian. A Dominican monk, Forerius was a preacher to the Portuguese court. He represented the king to the Council of Trent*, where he worked on the *Index Librorum Phohibitorum*, helped revise the missal and breviary, and contributed to the composition of the catechism. After returning to Portugal, Forerius served as prior of the Dominican convent in Lisbon.

Formula of Concord (1577). After Luther's* death, intra-Lutheran controversies between the Gnesio-Lutherans (partisans of Luther) and the Philippists (partisans of Melanchthon*) threatened to cause a split among those who had subscribed to the Augsburg Confession.* In 1576, Jakob Andreae,* Martin Chemnitz,* Nikolaus Selnecker,* David Chytraeus* and Andreas Musculus (1514–1581) met with the intent of resolving the controversies, which mainly regarded the relationship between good works and salvation, the third use of the law, and the role of the human will in accepting God's grace. In 1580, celebrating the fiftieth anniversary of the presentation of the Augsburg Confession to Charles V (1500–1558), the *Book of Concord* was printed as the authoritative interpretation of the Augsburg Confession; it included the three ancient creeds, the Augsburg Confession, its Apology (1531), the Schmalkald Articles,* Luther's *Treatise on the Power and Primacy* *of the Pope* (1537) and both his Small and Large Catechisms (1529).

John Foxe (1516–1587). English Protestant martyrologist, historian. John Foxe was born in Boston, Lincolnshire. After completing his early education, Foxe became a fellow at Magdalen College, Oxford, where he completed his BA degree in 1537, and MA in 1543. Also he was lecturer in logic from 1539 to 1540. However, in 1545, Foxe was forced to resign from Magdalen because he had adopted Protestant beliefs. After leaving Oxford, Foxe became tutor to the children of the Earl of Surrey. During this time Foxe made the acquaintance of John Bale (1495–1562) who fostered his interest in history. When Mary Tudor ascended the throne of England in 1553, Foxe fled to the continent. While there, Foxe traveled to Frankfurt, where in 1555 he met Edmund Grindal (1519–1583), who had been composing accounts of Protestant martyrs. Foxe later joined Grindal in Basel, where he translated his narratives into Latin. Foxe published the book resulting from his labors in Basel in 1559. After Elizabeth I* succeeded to the throne in the same year, Foxe returned to England. Upon his return he began working with the printer, John Day, who published the first English edition of Foxe's work. This voluminous work, *The Acts and Monuments*, underwent four editions during the remainder of the author's lifetime. *The Acts and Monuments* contributed significantly to the development of the national identity and piety of Elizabethan England. Shorter versions of this work are known simply as *Foxe's Book of Martyrs*.

Francis I of France (1494–1547). French monarch. Francis ascended to the French throne following the death of Louis XII (1462–1515), who was both his cousin and father-in-law. Much of Francis's reign was dominated by warfare. In Italy, victory over the Swiss allowed him to assert his dynastic claim to the Duchy of Milan, and extract liberties for the French church from Pope Leo X* through the Concordat of Bologna. His campaign against Charles V* was less successful, however, as Milan was lost and following defeat at the Battle of Pavia, Francis was taken prisoner. His release was negotiated by his sister, Marguerite d'Angouleme*, though he reneged in its terms once reaching safety, ensuring continued conflict with the Holy Roman Emperor throughout his reign. Francis fostered humanistic learning within his kingdom, and while he resisted Lutheran and other evangelical thought, he gave some space for its expression, giving protection to scholars such as those gathered around his sister and Bishop Guillaume Briçonnet* at Meaux. His desire for social order saw him take increasingly strident steps against the Reformation, however, particularly after his bedchamber was pamphleted during the Affair of the Placards, and the final years of his reign saw a significant increase in attempts to reassert Catholic doctrine and stamp out Protestantism with persecution.

Sebastian Franck (1499–1542). German Radical theologian. Franck became a Lutheran in 1525, but by 1529 he began to develop ideas that distanced him from Protestants and Catholics. Expelled from Strasbourg and later Ulm due to his controversial writings, Franck spent the end of his life in Basel. Franck emphasized God's word as a divine internal spark that cannot be adequately expressed in outward forms. Thus he criticized religious institutions and dogmas. His work consists mostly of commentaries, compilations and translations. In his sweeping historical *Chronica* (1531), Franck supported numerous heretics condemned by the Catholic Church and criticized political and church authorities.

Leonhard Frick (d. 1528). Austrian Radical martyr. See *Kunstbuch*.

John Frith (1503–1533). English reformer, author, and martyr. Frith was born in Westerham, Kent. He was the son of Richard Frith, the innkeeper of the White Horse Inn. After receiving his earlier education at Sevenoaks Grammar School and Eton College, Frith matriculated at Queen's College, Cambridge, where Stephen Gardiner (1497–1555), future bishop of Winchester, and opponent of the English Reformation, was his tutor. Frith graduated with his BA degree in 1525, having obtained proficiency in Latin and mathematics. While still a student, Frith met Thomas Bilney (1495–1531), who most likely introduced him to evangelical faith. After graduating, Frith became a junior canon at Christ Church, Oxford. However, while at Oxford, Frith along with nine others was imprisoned in a fish cellar for possessing what ecclesiastical authorities considered "heretical books." Upon his release, Frith traveled to the Continent, where he assisted William Tyndale* with his translation work. Also while on the Continent, Frith translated some antipapal polemical works, and authored *A Disputation of Purgatory*. Upon Frith's return to England in 1532, he was arrested and imprisoned several times for publicly preaching against transubstantiation and purgatory. Eventually, Frith was imprisoned in the Tower of London, and later transferred to Newgate Prison. He was burned at the stake on July 4, 1533.

Libert Froidmont (1587–1653). Belgian philosopher, scientist, and theologian. A childhood friend of Cornelius Jansen (1585–1638), Froidmont entered the Society of Jesus and his early career was focused on philosophy and the sciences, teaching at Antwerp, Saint-Michel, and Louvain. Drawn to the rigorous but controversial Augustinianism of Jansen, Froidmont earned his doctorate in theology in 1628 and succeeded Jansen as chair of theology at Louvain. While publishing a number of theological and exegetical works, including a commentary on Paul's letters, Froidmont was also active in the scientific and philosophical debates of his era. He published against Nicolas Copernicus (1473–1543) and Galileo Galilei (1564–1642), whom he argued were wrong but not heretical, and was one of the first to engage with the thought of René Descartes (1596–1650).

William Fulke (1538–1589). English Protestant theologian. Responsible for preaching and lecturing on Old Testament and other subjects, William Fulke courted controversy during his tenure as fellow at Cambridge. He was briefly expelled for his advocacy of Vestarians and later resigned until acquitted of being in an incestuous marriage. He left Cambridge to serve as chaplain to Robert Dudley, Earl of Leicester (1532–1588), returning almost a decade later as master of Pembroke College. He is best remembered as a controversialist and was the author of numerous anti-Catholic tracts.

Thomas Fuller (1608–1661). English Protestant minister. Fuller, the son of a minister, graduated from Cambridge, and his early career was overseen by his uncle John Davenant,* who secured his nephew a number of pastoral positions. Known for his wit and moderation, Fuller was a chaplain in the Royal army during the Civil War (1642–1651), and he served as an extraordinary chaplain to King Charles II (1630–1685) after the Restoration. He composed a number of exegetical and pastoral works, but he is primarily remembered for his historical writings. These include histories of the Crusades and the church in England as well as a biographical dictionary, the *History of the Worthies of England* (1622).

Gallic Confession (1559). This confession was accepted at the first National Synod of the Reformed Churches of France (1559). It was intended to be a touchstone of Reformed faith but also to show to the people of France that the Huguenots—who faced persecution—were not seditious. The French Reformed Church presented this confession to Francis II (1544–1560) in 1560, and to his successor, Charles IX (1550–1574), in 1561. The later Genevan draft, likely written by Calvin,* Beza* and Pierre Viret (1511–1571), was received as the true Reformed confession at the seventh National Synod in La Rochelle (1571).

Geneva Bible (originally printed 1560). During Mary I's reign many English Protestants sought safety abroad in Reformed territories of the Empire and the Swiss Cantons, especially in Calvin's* Geneva. A team of English exiles in Geneva led by William Whittingham (c. 1524–1579) brought this complete translation to press in the course of two years. Notable for several innovations—Roman type, verse numbers, italics indicating English idiom and not literal phrasing of the original languages, even variant readings in the Gospels and Acts—this translation is most well known for its marginal notes, which reflect a strongly Calvinist theology. The notes explained Scripture in an accessible way for the laity, also giving unlearned clergy a new sermon resource. Although controversial because of its implicit critique of royal power, this translation was wildly popular; even after the publication of the Authorized Version (1611) and James I's* 1616 ban on its printing, the Geneva Bible continued to be the most popular English translation until after the English Civil Wars.

Johann Gerhard (1582–1637). German Lutheran theologian, professor and superintendent. Gerhard is considered one of the most eminent Lutheran theologians, after Martin Luther* and Martin Chemnitz.* After studying patristics and Hebrew at Wittenberg, Jena and Marburg, Gerhard was appointed superintendent at the age of twenty-four. In 1616 he was appointed to a post at the University of Jena, where he reintroduced Aristotelian metaphysics to theology and gained widespread fame. His most important work was the nine-volume *Loci Theologici* (1610–1625). He also expanded Chemnitz's harmony of the Gospels *(Harmonia Evangelicae)*, which was finally published by Polykarp Leyser (1552–1610) in 1593. Gerhard was well-known for an irenic spirit and an ability to communicate clearly.

George Gifford (c. 1548–1600). English Puritan pastor. Gifford was suspended for nonconformity in 1584. With private support, however, he was able to continue his ministry. Through his published works he wanted to help develop lay piety and biblical literacy.

George Gifford (d. 1620). English Puritan minister. A celebrated preacher in Maldon, Essex, Gifford was removed from the pulpit when he refused to subscribe to Articles of Conformity drawn up by Archbishop John Whitgift.* Allowed to continue ministry in the office of lecturer, he also served as a representative for Essex at Puritan synods. He published numerous works, including a primer for common Christians, a dialogue between a Catholic and a Protestant, and two works on witchcraft.

Anthony Gilby (c. 1510–1585). English Puritan translator. During Mary I's reign, Gilby fled to Geneva, where he assisted William Whittingham (c. 1524–1579) with the Geneva Bible.* He returned to England to pastor after Elizabeth I's* accession. In addition to translating numerous continental Reformed works into English—especially those of John Calvin* and Theodore Beza*—Gilby also wrote commentaries on Micah and Malachi.

Bernard Gilpin (1517–1583). Anglican theologian and priest. In public disputations, Gilpin defended Roman Catholic theology against John Hooper (c. 1495–1555) and Peter Martyr Vermigli.* These debates caused Gilpin to reexamine his faith. Upon Mary I's accession, Gilpin resigned his benefice. He sojourned in Belgium and France, returning to pastoral ministry in England in 1556. Gilpin dedicated himself to a preaching circuit in northern England, thus earning the moniker "the Apostle to the North." His zealous preaching and almsgiving roused royal opposition and a warrant for his arrest. On his way to the queen's commission, Gilpin fractured his leg, delaying his arrival in London until after Mary's death and thus likely saving his life. His only extant writing is a sermon on Luke 2 confronting clerical abuses.

Paul Glock (c. 1530–1585). German Radical preacher. A teenage convert to Hutterite Anabaptism, Glock spent nineteen years imprisoned at Hohenwittlingen, unwilling to recant. While incarcerated, he wrote hymns, a confession and defense of his beliefs, and numerous letters that proved influential in the development of Anabaptist thought. After helping extinguish a fire at the prison in 1576, Glock was freed and settled with the Brethren in Moravia.

Glossa ordinaria. This standard collection of biblical commentaries consists of interlinear and marginal notes drawn from patristic and Carolingian exegesis appended to the Vulgate*; later editions also include Nicholas of Lyra's* *Postilla*. The *Glossa ordinaria* and the *Sentences* of Peter Lombard (c. 1100–1160) were essential resources for all late medieval and early modern commentators.

Franciscus Gomarus (1563–1641). Dutch Reformed theologian and pastor. A religious refugee at an early age, Gomarus's family was forced to leave Bruges for the Palatinate, with Gomarus receiving a Reformed education at Strasbourg, Neustadt, Oxford, Cambridge, and Heidelberg. He pastored at Frankfurt am Main until becoming professor of theology at the University of Leiden, where he came into extended conflict with colleague Jacobus Arminius* over predestination. Gomarus left Leiden in protest when Conradus Vorstius,* a follower of Arminius with Socinian tendencies, was appointed over his objections. Gomarus then pastored briefly at Middelburg before teaching at the Reformed academy at Saumur and the University of Groningen. Representing the university at the Synod of Dordrecht,* Gomarus was a leading opponent of Remonstrant theology and a key figure in ensuring their censure.

Robert Gomersall (1602–1646?). English Protestant minister and dramatist. Little is known of Gomersall's life beyond his graduation from Oxford and entrance into the ministry. He published a number of poetic and dramatic works, including a tragedy on the life of Italian prince Ludovicio Sforza (1452–1508) and a poetic meditation on Judges 19–20.

Thomas Goodwin (1600–1679). Puritan minister. Goodwin was born October 5, 1600, in Norfolk. After receiving his early education from local schools, Goodwin matriculated at Christ College, Cambridge, which was a prime center of Puritan influence. He graduated with the BA degree in 1616 and MA in 1620. Upon receiving his MA, Goodwin became a fellow and lecturer at the university. In October 1620, Goodwin experienced a profound conversion on his twentieth birthday. After his conversion, Goodwin joined the Puritan party at Cambridge. He was licensed to preach in the Church of England in 1625. Three years later, Goodwin became lecturer at Trinity Church. He served as vicar of this church from 1632 to 1634. Unwilling to comply with Archbishop William Laud's* directives for conformity, Goodwin was forced to resign all of his ecclesiastical and academic positions, and leave Cambridge. During the remainder of the 1630s, due to John Cotton's* influence, Goodwin came to adopt the principles of Independency. In 1639, in order to escape the increasing restrictions of unauthorized preachers, Goodwin fled to the Netherlands, where he worked with other English Independent exiles. In 1641, Goodwin returned to England per Parliament's request, and preached before it on April 27, 1642. Goodwin was later appointed a delegate to the Westminster Assembly. In the Assembly, Goodwin proved himself to be one of the foremost advocates of Independency. After the Westminster Assembly adjourned, Goodwin was appointed a lecturer at Oxford, and a year later became president of Magdalen College. Furthermore, Goodwin served as an advisor to Oliver Cromwell (1599–1658) and as the Lord Protector's Oxford commissioner. Goodwin also tended to Cromwell on his deathbed. In addition to his university and advisory duties, Goodwin pastored an Independent church at Oxford. Notably, Goodwin was one of the primary authors of the Savoy Declaration of Faith (1658), which served as the confession of faith for the Independent/

Congregational churches. When Charles II ascended to the throne of England in 1660, Goodwin withdrew from Oxford to London, where he pastored an Independent congregation until his death at the age of eighty. Throughout his career, Goodwin produced an enormous literary corpus, which includes many exegetical works. Best known among these are his expositions of Ephesians and Revelation.

Marie le Jars de Gournay (1565–1645). French Catholic writer and editor. Born into the minor nobility, the early death of Gournay's father led her family to relocate to their estate in Picardy, where she taught herself Latin and Greek. After reading the *Essais* (1580) of Michel de Montaigne (1533–1592), she committed herself to a life of literature and became active in the intellectual circles of Paris. While she translated many classical writings, she is best known for her editorial work on Montaigne's essays and her advocacy for the rights of women, laid out in a number of writings including *The Equality of Men and Women* (1622) and *The Ladies' Grievance* (1626).

Simon Goulart (1543–1628) French Reformed pastor, translator, and theologian. Goulart spent most of his career as a pastor in Geneva and its surrounds, particularly at the city parish of St. Gervais, and was the leader of the Company of Pastors during the last decades of his life. A prolific translator, he published numerous French editions of classical, patristic, and contemporary works from diverse authors including Plutarch, Seneca, Chrysostom, Cyprian, Tertullian, Beza*, Perkins* and Vermigli*. He also composed numerous devotional writings, important histories of early French Protestantism, and polemical treatises supporting the Huguenot cause.

Thomas Granger (1578–1627). English Protestant pastor. After completing his studies at Cambridge, Granger ministered to congregations at Butterwick and Horbling in Lincolnshire.

Conrad Grebel (c. 1498–1526). Swiss Radical theologian. Grebel, considered the father of the Anabaptist movement, was one of the first defenders and performers of believers' baptism, for which he was eventually imprisoned in Zurich. One of Huldrych Zwingli's* early compatriots, Grebel advocated rapid, radical reform, clashing publicly with the civil authorities and Zwingli. Grebel's views, particularly on baptism, were influenced by Andreas Bodenstein von Karlstadt* and Thomas Müntzer.* Grebel advocated elimination of magisterial involvement in governing the church; instead, he envisioned the church as lay Christians determining their own affairs with strict adherence to the biblical text, and unified in volitional baptism.

William Greenhill (1591–1671). English Puritan pastor. Greenhill attended and worked at Magdalen College. He ministered in the diocese of Norwich but soon left for London, where he preached at Stepney. Greenhill was a member of the Westminster Assembly of Divines and was appointed the parliament chaplain by the children of Charles I. Oliver Cromwell included him among the preachers who helped draw up the Savoy Declaration. Greenhill was evicted from his post following the Restoration, after which he pastored independently. Among Greenhill's most significant contributions to church history was his *Exposition of the Prophet of Ezekiel.*

Catharina Regina von Greiffenberg (1633–1694). Austrian Lutheran poet. Upon her adulthood her guardian (and half uncle) sought to marry her; despite her protests of their consanguinity and her desire to remain celibate, she relented in 1664. After the deaths of her mother and husband, Greiffenberg abandoned her home to debtors and joined her friends Susanne Popp (d. 1683) and Sigmund von Birken (1626–1681) in Nuremberg. During her final years she dedicated herself to studying the biblical languages and to writing meditations on Jesus' death and resurrection, which she never completed. One of the most important and learned Austrian poets of the Baroque period, Greiffenberg published a collection of sonnets, songs and poems (1662) as well as three sets of mystical meditations on Jesus' life, suffering and death (1672; 1683; 1693). She participated in a society of poets called the Ister Gesellschaft.

Lady Jane Grey (1537–1554). English Protestant monarch, sometimes known as "the Nine Days Queen." The eldest daughter of Henry Grey and Frances Brandon, the daughter of Henry VIII's* younger sister Mary, Jane received an extensive Protestant and humanist education. She married Lord Guildford Dudley (c. 1535–1554), son of Edward VI's* chief minister John Dudley, Duke of Northumberland (1504–1553). Seeking to avoid succession by Edward's Catholic half-sister Mary I, Edward and Northumberland conspired to alter the order of succession, naming Jane as heir in the king's will. Following Edward's death, Jane reluctantly took the crown on July 9, 1553, but Northumberland and other Protestants were unable to raise adequate support for her claim and the Privy Council proclaimed Mary queen on July 19. Upon Mary's accession, Jane was imprisoned in the Tower of London and after trial was executed alongside her husband for treason. A handful of her writings exist demonstrating her religious affections, while the story of her martyrdom is prominent in John Foxe's *Acts and Monuments.*

Edmund Grindal (c. 1519–1583). English Anglican archbishop. Grindal began his career in the church as chaplain to Nicholas Ridley* and King Edward VI* until forced to exile in Strasbourg during the reign of Mary I.* Returning to England upon the accession of Elizabeth I,* Grindal helped set the direction for the Church of England, participating in the 1559 Westminster Conference and serving as a member of the committee revising the liturgy. A moderate reformer, he reluctantly became bishop of London despite concerns over continuing Roman practices such as the wearing of vestments and the use of wafer bread for communion. His tenure as archbishop of York was marked by disputes with Presbyterians who wished to abolish the episcopacy and prayer book. Grindal was appointed Archbishop of Canterbury in 1575, but a conflict with Queen Elizabeth I hampered his ability to make change. He refused her request to suppress the "prophesyings" of Puritan clergy and meetings for theological discussion and sermon preparation. After addressing a remonstrance to the queen, he refused to resign, and he was stripped of the administrative power of his position until his death.
Hugo Grotius (1583–1645). Dutch lawyer, statesman, and humanist. Grotius began practicing law at The Hague in 1599, was appointed Advocate-General of the Fisc for the provinces of Holland, Zeeland, and West Friesland in 1607 and in 1613 became pensionary of Rotterdam. As debates between Calvinists and Arminians came to national significance, Grotius sided with the Remonstrants, especially in his rejection of Reformed arguments for the independence of the church, defending the right of the state to appoint ministers and adjudicate over matters of doctrine. Following the victory of Maurice of Orange (1567–1635) over Grotius's patron Johan van Oldenbarnevelt (1547–1619) and the condemnation of Arminianism at the Synod of Dordrecht* (1618–1619), Grotius was imprisoned, though only briefly, as he escaped in a book chest and fled to Paris. Unable to secure return from exile, Grotius became a Swedish ambassador to France while seeking religious toleration and the establishment of a Christian republic. A number of his works from this period, in particular *De Jure Belli ac Pacis* (On the law of war and peace, 1625) made a significant contribution to the establishment of international law.
Argula von Grumbach (c. 1490–c. 1564) German Lutheran noblewoman. Grumbach, an attendant of Queen Kunigunde of Austria (1465–1520), was one of the first women to publish in support of the Reformation. She is best known for letters from 1523 and 1524 written in defense of Arsacius Seehofer (1503–1545), a lecturer at the university of Ingolstadt accused of Lutheranism. For unknown reasons, Grumberg ceased to publish after 1524, although her private correspondence after this time demonstrates a continued effort to support evangelical reform.
Johann Jacob Grynaeus (1540–1617). Swiss Reformed theologian. Raised Lutheran, Grynaeus replaced his father as pastor at Rotelen. After becoming professor of Old Testament at Basel, however, Grynaeus caused conflict by embracing Reformed theology. He avoided controversy by spending two years at the University of Heidelberg. Upon his return to Basel, his opponents had largely died, and he was made superintendent of the church in the city and professor of New Testament. Grynaeus aligned the Basel church with his Reformed convictions and reorganized the city's educational system while preaching regularly and composing numerous theological, exegetical, and practical works.
William Guild (1586–1657). Scottish Reformed minister and theologian. Guild was born in Aberdeen and educated at Marischal College. He was licensed to preach in 1605 and ordained to serve as minister of the parish of King Edward in 1608. In 1617, Guild joined the protest for the liberties of the Scottish national church. While in Edinburgh, Guild met the acquaintance of Bishop Lancelot Andrewes,* who was accompanying King James VI/I* on his royal visit to the city. Moreover, Guild dedicated his best-known work, *Moses Unveiled* (1620), to both Andrewes and the king. He was later appointed chaplain to Charles I, and shortly thereafter received the degree of doctor of divinity. In 1631, Guild was given his second charge in Aberdeen. When he assumed this charge, Guild expressed his support for episcopacy. He signed the National Covenant in 1638 with some conditions. However, when in 1640 an army came to Aberdeen to enforce full subscription to the Covenant, Guild fled to the Netherlands. After returning to Scotland later that year, he was appointed Guild Principal for King's College Aberdeen, but was deprived of this post by Oliver Cromwell's (1599–1658) military commissioners in 1651. Following his deprivation, Guild lived in retirement until his death in Aberdeen.
Rudolf Gwalther (1519–1586). Swiss Reformed preacher. Gwalther was a consummate servant of the Reformed church in Zurich, its chief religious officer and preacher, a responsibility fulfilled previously by Huldrych Zwingli* and Heinrich Bullinger.* Gwalther provided sermons and commentaries and translated the works of Zwingli into Latin. He worked for many years alongside Bullinger in structuring and governing the

church in Zurich. Gwalther also strove to strengthen the connections to the Reformed churches on the Continent and England: he was a participant in the Colloquy of Regensburg (1541) and an opponent of the Formula of Concord.*

Matthias Hafenreffer (1561–1619). German Lutheran theologian. After holding pastoral positions in Herenberg, Ehingen, and Stuttgart, Hafenreffer was appointed professor of theology at Tübingen, a position he held for more than twenty-five years. He composed exegetical works on Nahum, Habakkuk, and Ezekiel, a number of polemical works, and a theological *loci communes* that served as a common textbook within the Lutheran churches for much of the seventeenth century.

Henry Hall (unknown). English Protestant preacher. A fellow of Trinity College, Cambridge, Hall preached and published a sermon given before the House of Commons in 1644 on Matthew 11:12.

Joseph Hall (1574–1656). English Anglican bishop and controversialist. After studying at Cambridge, Hall courted controversy with a series of satires before entering the ministry of the Church of England. As a pastor, Hall served parishes in Suffolk and Essex and was chosen by James I* as an English delegate at the Synod of Dordrecht.* Upon his return, Hall was appointed bishop of Exeter and later transferred to the see of Norwich, where, despite his low-church preferences, his defense of the episcopacy saw him convicted of praemunire by the Puritan parliament and imprisoned in the Tower of London for a short time with a number of other bishops. Hall's literary output was extensive and included controversial tracts against the Brownists and Arminians, treatises on virtue and union with Christ, and numerous devotional works.

Hans Has von Hallstatt (d. 1527). Austrian Reformed pastor. See *Kunstbuch*.

Henry Hammond (1605–1660). Anglican priest. After completing his studies at Oxford, Hammond was ordained in 1629. A Royalist, Hammond helped recruit soldiers for the king; he was chaplain to Charles I. During the king's captivity, Hammond was imprisoned for not submitting to Parliament. Later he was allowed to pastor again, until his death. Hammond published a catechism, numerous polemical sermons and treatises as well as his *Paraphrase and Annotations on the New Testament* (1653).

Jörg Haug (Unknown) German Anabaptist leader. Haug was a radical preacher during the 1525 Peasant's Revolt and composed a tract entitled *A Christian Order of a True Christian* (1524) enumerating seven degrees of faith reached by Christians.

Peter Hausted (d. 1645). Anglican priest and playwright. Educated at Cambridge and Oxford, Hausted ministered in a number of parishes and preached adamantly and vehemently against Puritanism. He is best known for his play *The Rival Friends*, which is filled with invective against the Puritans; during a performance before the king and queen, a riot nearly broke out. Haustead died during the siege of Banbury Castle.

Erhart Hegenwald (Unknown). Swiss Protestant teacher and doctor. A teacher at the Pfäffen Monastery in St. Gallen and at the Schola Carolina in Zurich, Hegenwald recorded the minutes of Zwingli's* First Zurich Disputation in 1523. Correspondence demonstrates he remained in contact with the Zurich reformers while he studied medicine at Wittenberg, and after graduating in 1526, he may have practiced as a physician in Frankfurt.

Heidelberg Catechism (1563). This German Reformed catechism was commissioned by the elector of the Palatinate, Frederick III (1515–1576) for pastors and teachers in his territories to use in instructing children and new believers in the faith. It was written by theologian Zacharias Ursinus (1534–1583) in consultation with Frederick's court preacher Kaspar Olevianus* and the entire theology faculty at the University of Heidelberg. The Heidelberg Catechism was accepted as one of the Dutch Reformed Church's Three Forms of Unity—along with the Belgic Confession* and the Canons of Dordrecht—at the Synod of Dordrecht,* and became widely popular among other Reformed confessional traditions throughout Europe.

Philipp Heilbrunner (1546-1616) German Lutheran pastor and theologian. Heilbrunner pastored churches at Lustnau, Bernhausen, and Lauingen, where he also taught theology. He was involved in establishing the Formula of Concord* and was a disputant at the Regensburg Colloquy (1601).

Ursula Hellrigel (b. c. 1521). Austrian Anabaptist. Imprisoned for her heterodox beliefs at 17, authorities sought Hellrigel's recantation, but she refused to acquiesce. After five years she was released from prison and exiled from the Tyrol. The thirty-sixth hymn in the first known Anabaptist hymnal, the *Ausbund* (1654), is commonly attributed to her.

Niels Hemmingsen (1513–1600). Danish Lutheran theologian. Hemmingsen studied at the University of Wittenberg, where he befriended Philipp Melanchthon.* In 1542, Hemmingsen returned to Denmark to pastor and to teach Greek, dialectics and theology at the University of Copenhagen. Foremost of the Danish theologians, Hemmingsen oversaw the preparation and publication of the first Danish Bible (1550). Later in his career he became embroiled in controversies because of his Philippist theology, especially regarding the Eucharist. Due to rising tensions with Lutheran nobles outside of Denmark, King Frederick II (1534–1588) dismissed Hemmingsen from his university post in 1579, transferring him to a prominent but less internationally visible Cathedral outside of Copenhagen. Hemmingsen was a prolific author, writing commentaries on the New Testament and Psalms, sermon collections and several methodological, theological and pastoral handbooks.

Henry IV of France (1553–1610). French monarch. Son of Jeanne of Navarre* and Antoine de Bourbon (1518–1562), Henry's religious loyalties wavered throughout his life. Raised Protestant at the behest of his mother, he practiced Catholicism while attending the Valois court. After his mother's death in 1572, Henry succeeded her as King of Navarre and soon afterwards married Margaret of Valois (1553–1615), the daughter of Henry II of France (1519–1559) and Catherine de' Medici (1519–1589). Their wedding provided the occasion for the St. Bartholomew's Day Massacre, when Catholic forces seized the opportunity to decimate the Huguenot leadership gathered to celebrate the nuptials in Paris, leading to an outbreak of mob violence that devastated the Huguenot movement. A great proportion of the Protestants in France were killed in the weeks that followed the wedding, while many others, including Henry, reconverted to Catholicism. In 1576, Henry escaped the influence of the Valois court, returned his allegiance to Protestantism and took a leadership role amongst the Huguenots. Following the assassination of Henry III of France (1551–1589), Henry was the presumptive heir, but French Catholics were unwilling to accept his rule and Henry was unable to assert his prerogative outside Huguenot strongholds. In 1593, therefore, Henry converted again to Catholicism, with legend claiming he justified his decision with the phrase "Paris is worth a mass." Over the following years, Henry established his authority throughout his kingdom, and while remaining Catholic, provided some relief to Protestants, particularly through the Edict of Nantes (1598), essentially ending the Religious Wars. Henry's pragmatic reign ended with his assassination by a Radical Catholic in 1610.

King Henry VIII of England (1491–1547). English monarch. The second son of Henry VII (r. 1485–1509) and Elizabeth of York (1466–1503), Henry VIII succeeded his father to the English throne, his elder brother Edward having died in 1502. Soon after accession, he married his brother's widow, Catherine of Aragon (1485–1536). Following several stillbirths and the birth of a daughter, Mary, Henry, who was desperate for a male heir to head off dynastic challenges, wished separation from Catherine in order to marry Anne Boleyn (c. 1501–1536). Believing his marriage cursed as it transgressed the commands in Leviticus against marrying a brother's widow, Henry sought dispensation from the church for his annulment and remarriage. While the case was first heard by a papal legate in England, it was transferred to Rome upon the order of Pope Clement VII*, who wished to placate Charles V, Catherine's nephew, whose troops had recently sacked Rome and held the pope under house arrest. Henry asserted praemunire, arguing that as king, he was supreme in his own kingdom. With the formation of the Reformation Parliament in 1529, the legislative process to disentangle the English Church from the Roman was begun. The issue of Henry's divorce was finalized in 1533, after Thomas Cranmer* became Archbishop of Canterbury and declared his marriage to Catherine invalid. While Henry's divorce, assertion of royal supremacy, and subversion of Catholic institutions gave impetus to English Protestantism, Henry's beliefs remained essentially Catholic, and these continued to be enforced by law. He ultimately married six times, and was succeeded by Edward VI*, his son by his third wife, Jane Seymour (1508–1537). Elizabeth I*, Henry's daughter by Anne Boleyn, later became Queen and with the Elizabethan Settlement in 1559, redefined England as a Protestant country.

George Herbert (1593–1633). Anglican minister, theologian, and poet. Herbert was born in Montgomery Powys, Wales, on April 3, 1593, to a noble family. After completing his early education at Westminster School, Herbert matriculated at Trinity College, Cambridge, in 1609. He graduated with both his bachelor's and master's degrees. Shortly thereafter Herbert was elected a fellow of the college, and then became Reader of Rhetoric. From 1620 to 1627, Herbert was Public Orator for the University of Cambridge. In 1624, Herbert was elected to Parliament. However, after the death of King James I,* and of his other major patrons, Herbert withdrew from politics to pursue a career in the church. Toward this end, Herbert was ordained to the priesthood of the Church of England in 1630, and appointed rector of Fugglestone St. Peter and later Bemerton St. Andrews in Wiltshire near Salisbury. While at St. Andrews, Herbert composed his collection of poems titled *The Temple* and his guide for rural ministers, *A Priest to the*

Temple, or The Country Parson: His Character and Rule of Holy Life. Twice a week Herbert traveled to Salisbury, where he attended services at Salisbury Cathedral. Following the services, Herbert would compose music with the cathedral musicians. Herbert died of consumption in 1633.

Tilemann Hesshus (1527–1588). German Lutheran theologian and pastor. Hesshus studied under Philipp Melanchthon* but was a staunch Gnesio-Lutheran. With great hesitation—and later regret—he affirmed the Formula of Concord.* Heshuss ardently advocated for church discipline, considering obedience a mark of the church. Unwilling to compromise his strong convictions, especially regarding matters of discipline, Hesshus was regularly embroiled in controversy. He was expelled or pressed to leave Goslar, Rostock, Heidelberg, Bremen, Magdeburg, Wesel, Königsberg and Samland before settling in Helmstedt, where he remained until his death. He wrote numerous polemical tracts concerning ecclesiology, justification, the sacraments and original sin, as well as commentaries on Psalms, Romans, 1–2 Corinthians, Galatians, Colossians and 1–2 Timothy, and a postil collection.

Edo Hilderich (1533–1599). German Lutheran historian and theologian. Hilderich (also named Hildericus) was born to a noble family in Frisia. After attending a local school, Hilderich went on to the University of Wittenberg, where he received the degree of master of philosophy in 1556. Among his teachers was Philipp Melanchthon.* In 1559, Hilderich was appointed to the Faculty of Arts at Wittenberg. He also served as professor of mathematics at the University of Jena from 1564 until 1567, when he resigned the post in order to return to the arts faculty at Wittenberg, of which he became dean in 1570. Three years later he became rector of the academy in Magdeburg, and went from there to the University of Frankfurt in 1575. In 1577, Hilderich became professor of history and Hebrew at Frankfurt. Following the expulsion of the Reformed theologians from the University of Heidelberg in 1578, he went there to be the second professor of theology and Hebrew language. He received his doctorate at Heidelberg a year later. However, Hilderich's refusal to sign the Formula of Concord resulted in removal from his post. On June 3, 1581, he accepted the professorship of theology at the University of Altdorf, where he later became rector in 1582, and professor of Hebrew in 1584. Hilderich's most important exegetical work is his *Oratio de politia et hierarchia populi Iudaici*, published in 1570, in which he traces the history of ancient Israel's government.

Samuel Hieron (1576?–1617). English Puritan minister. After graduating from Cambridge, Hieron became a minister in the Church of England and gained a reputation as a popular preacher in London before becoming the vicar at Modbury in Devonshire. Many of his sermons were published during his lifetime, and he also composed treatises on prayer and the value of Scripture.

Cornelis Hoen (c. 1460–1524). Dutch humanist, jurist, and theologian. A lawyer at the Court of Holland at the Hague, Hoen was prosecuted in 1523 over his sympathy for the evangelical message. He proposed a symbolic interpretation of Christ's presence in the Eucharist justified with reference to Matthew 24:23 in an influential, posthumously-published treatise.

Melchior Hoffman (1495?–1543). German Anabaptist preacher. First appearing as a Lutheran lay preacher in Livonia in 1523, Hoffman's claim to direct revelation, his perfectionist teachings and his announcements that the end of the world would occur in 1533 saw him alienated from both Lutheran and Reformed circles. After converting to Anabaptism in Strasbourg in 1530, a city he claimed would rise as the spiritual Jerusalem, Hoffman escaped brief arrest and fled to the Netherlands, where his preaching made him the first to bring the radical faith to the Low Countries. Believing himself to be Elijah, Hoffman gathered numerous followers, including future Anabaptist leaders Obbe Philips* and Jan Mathijs (d. 1534), until his arrest in Strasbourg in 1533, whereupon he was imprisoned for the final decade of his life. A tendency toward mystical allegory and apocalyptic exegesis supported by direct revelation is found in his writings, which include commentaries on Romans, Revelation, and Daniel 12 alongside numerous tracts, pamphlets, and letters.

Nathaniel Holmes (1599–1678). English Puritan theologian. Educated at Oxford, Holmes was a preacher in the Anglican Church until his millenarian views led him to establish an independent congregation. His publications include defenses of infant baptism and exclusive psalmody; treatises against witchcraft, usury, and astrology; and a commentary on the Song of Solomon.

Christopher Hooke (unknown). English Puritan physician and pastor. Hooke published a treatise promoting the joys and blessings of childbirth (1590) and a sermon on Hebrews 12:11-12. To support the poor, Hooke proposed a bank funded by voluntary investment of wealthy households.

Richard Hooker (c. 1553–1600). Anglican priest. Shortly after graduating from Corpus Christi College Oxford, Hooker took holy orders as a priest in 1581. After his

marriage, he struggled to find work and temporarily tended sheep until Archbishop John Whitgift* appointed him to the Temple Church in London. Hooker's primary work is *The Laws of Ecclesiastical Polity* (1593), in which he sought to establish a philosophical and logical foundation for the highly controversial Elizabethan Religious Settlement (1559). The Elizabethan Settlement, through the Act of Supremacy, reasserted the Church of England's independence from the Church of Rome, and, through the Act of Uniformity, constructed a common church structure based on the reinstitution of the Book of Common Prayer.* Hooker's argumentation strongly emphasizes natural law and
anticipates the social contract theory of John Locke (1632–1704).

Thomas Hooker (1586–1647). English-American Puritan Preacher. Hooker ministered at churches in Surrey and Essex and established a school to teach pastors until threatened with arrest as Archbishop Laud* worked to suppress Puritanism. Fleeing to Holland and then New England, he pastored a church in New Town (later Cambridge), Massachusetts before playing an important role in the foundation of Hartford, Connecticut and assisting with the composition of the state constitution.

John Hooper (d. 1555). English Protestant bishop and martyr. Impressed by the works of Huldrych Zwingli* and Heinrich Bullinger,* Hooper joined the Protestant movement in England. However, after the Act of Six Articles was passed, he fled to Zurich, where he spent ten years. He returned to England in 1549 and was appointed as a bishop. He stoutly advocated a Zwinglian reform agenda, arguing against the use of vestments and for a less "popish" Book of Common Prayer.* Condemned as a heretic for denying transubstantiation, Hooper was burned at the stake during Mary I's reign.

John Hoskin (unknown). English Protestant preacher. Hoskin published a sermon on Matthew 18:23 in 1610 in which he is identified as a minister of God's Word and student of divinity.

Rudolf Hospinian (Wirth) (1547–1626). Swiss Reformed theologian and minister. After studying theology at Marburg and Heidelberg, Hospinian pastored in rural parishes around Zurich and taught secondary school. In 1588, he transferred to Zurich, ministering at Grossmünster and Fraumünster. A keen student of church history, Hospinian wanted to show the differences between early church doctrine and contemporary Catholic teaching, particularly with regard to sacramental theology. He also criticized Lutheran dogma and the Formula of Concord*. Most of Hospinian's corpus consists of polemical treatises; he also published a series of sermons on the Magnificat.

Hans Hotz (dates unknown). Swiss Anabaptist leader. Born in Grüningen, near Zurich, Hotz was an associate of Georg Blaurock.* He defended Anabaptism as spokesman for the Swiss Brethren at disputations in Zofingen (1532) and Bern (1538).

John Howson (1557?–1632). English Anglican bishop. Howson held a number of pastoral positions in Oxfordshire before becoming vice chancellor of Oxford University. An opponent of Puritanism, he was appointed bishop of Oxford in 1619, and then to the bishopric of Durham in 1628, where he was an advocate for the reform program of Archbishop Laud.*

Caspar Huberinus (1500–1553). German Lutheran theologian and pastor. After studying theology at Wittenberg, Huberinus moved to Augsburg to serve as Urbanus Rhegius's* assistant. Huberinus represented Augsburg at the Bern Disputation (1528) on the Eucharist and images. In 1551, along with the nobility, Huberinus supported the Augsburg Interim, so long as communion of both kinds and regular preaching were allowed. Nevertheless the people viewed him as a traitor because of his official participation in the Interim, nicknaming him "Buberinus" (i.e., scoundrel). He wrote a number of popular devotional works as well as tracts defending Lutheran eucharistic theology against Zwinglian and Anabaptist detractions.

Balthasar Hubmaier (1480/5–1528). German Radical theologian. Hubmaier, a former priest who studied under Johann Eck,* is identified with his leadership in the peasants' uprising at Waldshut. Hubmaier served as the cathedral preacher in Regensberg, where he became involved in a series of anti-Semitic attacks. He was drawn to reform through the early works of Martin Luther*; his contact with Huldrych Zwingli* made Hubmaier a defender of more radical reform, including believers' baptism and a memorialist account of the Eucharist. His involvement in the Peasants' War led to his extradition and execution by the Austrians.

Aegidius Hunnius (1550–1603). German Lutheran theologian and preacher. Educated at Tübingen by Jakob Andreae (1528–1590) and Johannes Brenz,* Hunnius bolstered and advanced early Lutheran orthodoxy. After his crusade to root out all "crypto-Calvinism" divided Hesse into Lutheran and Reformed regions, Hunnius joined the Wittenberg theological faculty, where with Polykarp Leyser (1552–1610) he helped shape the university into an orthodox stronghold. Passionately confessional, Hunnius developed and nuanced the orthodox doctrines of predestination, Scripture, the church and Christology (more explicitly Chalcedonian), reflecting their codification in the Formula of Concord.* He was unafraid to engage in confessional polemics from the pulpit. In addition to his many treatises (most notably *De persona Christi*, in which he defended Christ's ubiquity), Hunnius published commentaries on Matthew, John, Ephesians and Colossians; his notes on Galatians, Philemon and 1 Corinthians were published posthumously.

Jan Hus (d. 1415). Bohemian reformer and martyr. This popular preacher strove for reform in the church, moral improvement in society, and an end to clerical abuses and popular religious superstition. He was branded a heretic for his alleged affinity for John Wycliffe's writings; however, while he agreed that a priest in mortal sin rendered the sacraments inefficacious, he affirmed the doctrine of transubstantiation. The Council of Constance* convicted Hus of heresy, banned his books and teaching, and, despite a letter of safe conduct, burned him at the stake.

Hans Hut (1490–1527). German Radical leader. Hut was an early leader of a mystical, apocalyptic strand of Anabaptist radical reform. His theological views were shaped by Andreas Bodenstein von Karlstadt,* Thomas Müntzer* and Hans Denck,* by whom Hut had been baptized. Hut rejected society and the established church and heralded the imminent end of days, which he perceived in the Peasants' War. Eventually arrested for practicing believers' baptism and participating in the Peasants' War, Hut was tortured and died accidentally in a fire in the Augsburg prison. The next day, the authorities sentenced his corpse to death and burned him.

George Hutcheson (1615–1674). Scottish Puritan pastor. Hutcheson, a pastor in Edinburgh, published commentaries on Job, John and the Minor Prophets, as well as sermons on Psalm 130.

Roger Hutchinson (d. 1555). English reformer. Little is known about Hutchinson except for his controversies. He disputed against the Mass while at Cambridge and debated with Joan Bocher (d. 1550), who affirmed the doctrine of the celestial flesh. During the Marian Restoration he was deprived of his fellowship at Eton because he was married.

Andreas Hyperius (1511–1564). Dutch Protestant theologian. After a peripatetic humanist education that encompassed studies in theology, canon law, and medicine, Hyperius became professor of theology at Marburg in 1541 and held this position until his death. Often viewed as mediating between Lutheran and Reformed thought, Hyperius was particularly concerned with the practical application of theology, demonstrated in his composition of the first Protestant text on homiletic method.

Abraham Ibn Ezra (1089–c. 1167). Spanish Jewish rabbi, exegete and poet. In 1140 Ibn Ezra fled his native Spain to escape persecution by the Almohad Caliphate. He spent the rest of his life as an exile, traveling through Europe, North Africa and the Middle East. His corpus consists of works on poetry, exegesis, grammar, philosophy, mathematics and astrology. In his commentaries on the Old Testament, Ibn Ezra restricts himself to *peshat* (see *quadriga*).

Valentin Ickelshamer (c. 1500–1547). German Radical teacher. After time at Erfurt, he studied under Luther,* Melanchthon,* Bugenhagen* and Karlstadt* in Wittenberg. He sided with Karlstadt against Luther, writing a treatise in Karlstadt's defense. Ickelshamer also represented the Wittenberg guilds in opposition to the city council. This guild committee allied with the peasants in 1525, leading to Ickelshamer's eventual exile. His poem in the Marpeck Circle's *Kunstbuch** is an expansion of a similar poem by Sebastian Franck.*

Arthur Jackson (1593?–1666). English Presbyterian minister. Known for his pastoral concern, Jackson served at a number of parishes in London. Imprisoned briefly for his support of the Royalist cause, after the Restoration, he was ejected from ministry following the 1662 Act of Uniformity. Jackson's primary works are a series of annotations of many books of the Old Testament.

Thomas Jackson (1579–1640). Anglican theologian and priest. Before serving as the president of Corpus Christi College at Oxford for the final decade of his life, Jackson was a parish priest and chaplain to the king. His best known work is a twelve-volume commentary on the Apostles' Creed.

King James I of England (VI of Scotland) (1566–1625). English monarch. The son of Mary, Queen of Scots, James ascended to the Scottish throne in 1567 following his mother's abdication. In the Union of the Crowns (1603), he took the English and Irish thrones after the death of his cousin, Elizabeth I.* James's reign was tumultuous and tense: Parliament and the nobility often opposed him, church factions squabbled over worship forms and ecclesiology, climaxing in the Gunpowder Plot. James wrote treatises on the divine right of kings, law, the evils of smoking tobacco and demonology. His religious writings include a versification of the Psalms, a paraphrase of Revelation and meditations on the Lord's Prayer and passages from Chronicles, Matthew and Revelation. He also sponsored the translation of the

Authorized Version*—popularly remembered as the King James Version.

Cornelius Jansen (1585–1638). Dutch Catholic bishop and theologian. Jansen studied and taught in France and Holland, joining the theological faculty of the University of Leuven after receiving his doctorate. He later became bishop of Ypres. An ardent Augustinian, his posthumously published work *Augustinus* (1640) caused great controversy by advocating for the utterly gratuitous character of God's grace in opposition to the teachings of Jesuit Luis de Molina (1536–1609), which put greater emphasis on human choice. Due to its perceived Protestant leanings, *Augustinus* was judged heretical, and Jansen's followers, known as Jansenists, took up his cause in a series of conflicts that carried on into the eighteenth century.

Anna Jansz (d. 1539) Dutch Anabaptist martyr. A wealthy heiress, Jansz was initially drawn into the apocalyptic anabaptism surrounding the Münster rebellion, penning her "Trumpet Song," replete with apocalyptic imagery. After some time in England, she became a close follower of pacifist Anabaptist preacher David Joris*, with this association leading to her execution by drowning for heresy. After her death, hagiographers depicted her as a model martyr.

Jeanne of Navarre (1528–1572) French Reformed noblewoman. Daughter of Henry II, King of Navarre (1503–1555) and Marguerite d'Angoulême*, Jeanne was forced into a strategic marriage at age 12 by her uncle, Francis I* to William, Duke of Cleves (1516–1592). Shifting political alignments allowed her an annulment after four years and in 1548 she wed the first Prince of the Blood, Antoine de Bourbon (1518–1562). Jeanne took the throne of her father, and after making a public announcement of her conversion to the evangelical faith, established a Reformed community at Béarn. A regular correspondent of reformers such as Calvin* and Beza* and an advocate for the reformation of her lands, Jeanne nevertheless remained largely neutral and advocated tolerance during the first years of religious war. At the outbreak of the Third War of Religion (1569–1570), however, she recognized her moderate position was untenable, and from the Protestant stronghold of La Rochelle served as political head for the Huguenot cause alongside Gaspard de Coligny (1519–1572), commander of the Huguenot armed forces.

Michael Jermin (1591–1659). English Protestant pastor. Jermin's early career was spent on the Continent, where he served as chaplain for Elizabeth Stuart, queen of Bohemia (1596–1662) and earned a doctorate of divinity from the University of Leiden. Returning to England, he earned a second doctorate at Oxford before becoming chaplain to Charles I* and serving as rector of St. Martin, Ludgate. A Royalist, he was deprived of his living during the English Civil War (1642–1651), and while he continued to preach occasionally, he was forced to survive on charity.

John Jewel (1522–1571). Anglican theologian and bishop. Jewel studied at Oxford where he met Peter Martyr Vermigli.* After graduating in 1552, Jewel was appointed to his first vicarage and became the orator for the university. Upon Mary I's accession, Jewel lost his post as orator because of his Protestant views. After the trials of Thomas Cranmer* and Nicholas Ridley,* Jewel affirmed Catholic teaching to avoid their fate. Still he had to flee to the continent. Confronted by John Knox,* Jewel publicly repented of his cowardice before the English congregation in Frankfurt, then reunited with Vermigli in Strasbourg. After Mary I's death, Jewel returned to England and was consecrated bishop in 1560. He advocated low-church ecclesiology, but supported the Elizabethan Settlement against Catholics and Puritans. In response to the Council of Trent, he published the *Apoligia ecclesiae Anglicanae* (1562), which established him as the apostle for Anglicanism and incited numerous controversies.

St. John of the Cross (Juan de Yepes y Álvarez) (1542–1591). Spanish Catholic mystic. Born into poverty, Álvarez entered the Carmelite order in Medina del Campo, where, after studying theology at Salamanca, he met the famed mystic Teresa of Ávila (1515–1582). Drawn to her vision of the contemplative life, with two others, he established the first house of Discalced (barefoot) Carmelite Friars and became a leader in the Catholic reform movement. An exceptional administrator and spiritual leader, for more than twenty years, John of the Cross sought to return his order to its original vision of asceticism and prayer while establishing many new reformed Carmelite houses. He encountered significant resistance in his work for renewal, however, and spent nine months imprisoned and tortured by his Carmelite superiors. Considered among the foremost poets in Spanish literary history, his poems, including *The Spiritual Canticle*, *Ascent of Mount Carmel*, and *The Dark Night of the Soul* demonstrate his overriding desire for spiritual growth and closeness to God.

Francis Johnson (1562–1618). English Brownist pastor. A popular Puritan preacher at Cambridge, Johnson was arrested for slander and factitiousness after a sermon criticizing the ecclesiastical hierarchy and the comfortable lives of the ministers at the school. Retracting some of his

statements, he was released and expelled from Cambridge. While pastoring an English church in the Netherlands, he came across writings from followers of Robert Browne* and became convinced of the need to separate from the established church and commit to congregational church polity, but his attempts to institute these changes in the church led to his firing. Returning to England, Johnson became pastor of the Brownist church in London, for which he was arrested numerous times until he convinced the Privy Council to allow him to found a Brownist church in Newfoundland. The expedition was canceled, however, and he returned to the Netherlands, where he pastored separatist churches, some alongside
Henry Ainsworth* and John Smyth,* until his death.

Justus Jonas (1493–1555). German Lutheran theologian, pastor and administrator. Jonas studied law at Erfurt, where he befriended the poet Eobanus Hessus (1488–1540), whom Luther* dubbed "king of the poets"; later, under the influence of the humanist Konrad Muth, Jonas focused on theology. In 1516 he was ordained as a priest, and in 1518 he became a doctor of theology and law. After witnessing the Leipzig Disputation, Jonas was converted to Luther's* cause. While traveling with Luther to the Diet of Worms, Jonas was appointed professor of canon law at Wittenberg. Later he became its dean of theology, lecturing on Romans, Acts and the Psalms. Jonas was also instrumental for reform in Halle. He preached Luther's funeral sermon but had a falling-out with Melanchthon* over the Leipzig Interim. Jonas's most influential contribution was translating Luther's *The Bondage of the Will* and Melanchthon's *Loci communes* into German.

Robert Jones. A pseudonym; see Thomas Lushington.

William Jones (1561–1636). Anglican minister and theologian. After teaching at Cambridge, Jones ministered at East Bergholt in Suffolk for forty-four years, publishing a commentary on Philemon and Hebrews and tracts on suffering, the nativity, and arrangements to be made before one's death.

David Joris (c. 1501–1556). Dutch Radical pastor and hymnist. This former glass painter was one of the leading Dutch Anabaptist leaders after the fall of Münster (1535), although due to his increasingly radical ideas his influence waned in the early 1540s. Joris came to see himself as a "third David," a Spirit-anointed prophet ordained to proclaim the coming third kingdom of God, which would be established in the Netherlands with Dutch as its *lingua franca*. Joris's interpretation of Scripture, with his heavy emphasis on personal mystical experience, led to a very public dispute with Menno Simons* whom Joris considered a teacher of the "dead letter." In 1544 Joris and about one hundred followers moved to Basel, conforming outwardly to the teaching of the Reformed church there. Today 240 of Joris's books are extant, the most important of which is his *Twonder Boek* (1542/43).

Ursula Jost (d. 1532/39) German anabaptist prophet. Residing near Strasbourg, Jost and her husband Leonhard (16th Century), a butcher, experienced visions which were recorded and published with the assistance of Melchior Hoffman*. Her prophesies were significant among Melchiorites, aligning their present context, especially the Peasant's War, with apocalyptic imagery and the end of the world.

Jörg Haugk von Jūchsen (unknown). German Radical preacher. Nothing is known of Haugk's life except that during the 1524–1525 Peasants' War in Thuringia, he was elected as a preacher by the insurrectionists in his district. He composed one extant tract, titled *A Christian Order of a True Christian: Giving an Account of the Origin of His Faith*, published in 1526 but likely written before the Peasants' War. While lacking reference to most distinctive Anabaptist doctrines, this pamphlet became popular among radicals as it set out the stages of Christian growth toward perfection.

Franciscus Junius (1545-1602) French Reformed pastor, translator, and theologian. Educated in Bourges and Geneva, Junius pastored in Antwerp until religious violence forced him to flee to Germany, where he oversaw a refugee church in Schonau. He also served as a chaplain to Protestant armies and worked with Immanuel Tremellius* to provide a translation of the Hebrew scriptures before being appointed Professor of Theology at Neustadt, a position he also held at the universities of Heidelberg and Leiden.

Andreas Bodenstein von Karlstadt (Carlstadt) (1486–1541). German Radical theologian. Karlstadt, an early associate of Martin Luther* and Philipp Melanchthon* at the University of Wittenberg, participated alongside Luther in the dispute at Leipzig with Johann Eck.* He also influenced the configuration of the Old Testament canon in Protestantism. During Luther's captivity in Wartburg Castle in Eisenach, Karlstadt oversaw reform in Wittenberg. His acceleration of the pace of reform brought conflict with Luther, so Karlstadt left Wittenberg, eventually settling at the University of Basel as professor of Old Testament (after a sojourn in Zurich with Huldrych Zwingli*). During his time in Switzerland, Karlstadt opposed infant baptism and repudiated Luther's doctrine of Christ's real presence in the Eucharist.

Edward Kellett (d. 1641). Anglican theologian and priest. Kellett published a sermon concerning the reconversion of an Englishman from Islam, a tract on the soul, and a discourse on the Lord's Supper in connection with Passover.

David Kimchi (Radak) (1160–1235). French Jewish rabbi, exegete and philosopher. Kimchi wrote an important Hebrew grammar and dictionary, as well as commentaries on Genesis, 1–2 Chronicles, the Psalms and the Prophets. He focused on *peshat* (see *quadriga*). In his Psalms commentary he attacks Christian interpretation as forced, irrational and inadmissible. While Sebastian Münster* censors and condemns these arguments in his *Miqdaš YHWH* (1534–1535), he and many other Christian commentators valued Kimchi's work as a grammatical resource.

Moses Kimchi (Remak) (1127–1190). French Jewish rabbi and exegete. He was David Kimchi's* brother. He wrote commentaries on Proverbs and Ezra-Nehemiah. Sebastian Münster* translated Kimchi's concise Hebrew grammar into Latin; many sixteenth-century Christian exegetes used this resource.

Andreas Knöpken (c. 1468–1539). German Lutheran pastor. Knöpken worked in Pomerania as assistant to Johannes Bugenhagen* before relocating to Riga. Here he served as pastor of St. Peter's, and after a brief setback that saw him return to his previous position, he returned and won a disputation before the authorities, which allowed him to undertake the evangelical reform of the city. Knöpken oversaw the reorganization of the churches and schools, composed the church order, wrote a commentary on Romans, and arranged a number of hymns based on the Psalms.

John Knox (1513–1572). Scottish Reformed preacher. Knox, a fiery preacher to monarchs and zealous defender of high Calvinism, was a leading figure of reform in Scotland. Following imprisonment in the French galleys, Knox went to England, where he became a royal chaplain to Edward VI. At the accession of Mary, Knox fled to Geneva, studying under John Calvin* and serving as a pastor. Knox returned to Scotland after Mary's death and became a chief architect of the reform of the Scottish church (Presbyterian), serving as one of the authors of the Book of Discipline and writing many pamphlets and sermons.

Antonius Broickwy von Königstein (1470–1541). German Catholic preacher. Very little is known about this important cathedral preacher in Cologne. Strongly opposed to evangelicals, he sought to develop robust resources for Catholic homilies. His postils were bestsellers, and his biblical concordance helped Catholic preachers to construct doctrinal loci from Scripture itself.

Kunstbuch. In 1956, two German students rediscovered this unique collection of Anabaptist works. Four hundred years earlier, a friend of the recently deceased Pilgram Marpeck*—the painter Jörg Probst—had entrusted this collection of letters, tracts and poetry to a Zurich bindery; today only half of it remains. Probst's redaction arranges various compositions from the Marpeck Circle into a devotional anthology focused on the theme of the church as Christ incarnate (cf. Gal 2:20).

Osmund Lake (c. 1543–1621). English Pastor who ministered at Ringwood in Hampshire.

Thomas Lamb (d. 1686). English Nonconformist minister. Lamb earned a living as a soap boiler while serving as a teaching elder and occasional preacher at a congregational church in London. Convicted of the necessity of adult baptism and the invalidity of infant baptism, he formed a Particular Baptist congregation and led this church for four years before rejoining the Church of England as a layman, retracting his former teachings and becoming a vocal opponent of separatism. Toward the end of his life, he turned to philanthropy, seeking to improve the lives of the poor and prisoners and to further the religious education of children.

François Lambert (Lambert of Avignon) (1487–1530). French Reformed theologian. In 1522, after becoming drawn to the writings of Martin Luther* and meeting Huldrych Zwingli,* Lambert left the Franciscan order. He spent time in Wittenberg, Strasbourg, and Hesse, where Lambert took a leading role at the Homberg Synod (1526) and in creating a biblically based plan for church reform. He served as professor of theology at Marburg University from 1527 to his death. After the Marburg Colloquy (1529), Lambert accepted Zwingli's symbolic view of the Eucharist. Lambert produced nineteen books, mostly biblical commentaries that favored spiritual interpretations; his unfinished work of comprehensive theology was published posthumously.

Eitelhans Langenmantel (d. 1528). German Radical writer. The son of the mayor of Augsburg, Langenmantel was converted to Anabaptism and was rebaptized by Hans Hut* in 1527. Arrested for his heterodox views later that year, he was freed after accepting the validity of infant baptism during a debate, but after renouncing his recantation in 1528, he was rearrested and beheaded. Seven tracts he composed during 1526 and 1527 survive, focusing on the Lord's Supper and the moral life.

Emilia Lanier (1569–1645). English poet. The daughter of a musician at the court of Elizabeth I,* she received a humanist education at the home of Susan Bertie, Countess of Kent (b. 1554). Following a long affair with Henry Carey (1526–1596), Lord Chamberlain to the queen, and after conceiving a child, she married a distant cousin, Alfonso Lanier (unknown). She is best known for a book of poetry written in the hope of securing a patron, *Salve Deus Rex Judaeorum* (1611), which contains a number of protofeminist themes. Modern scholars have also suggested she may be the "Dark Lady" who appears in a number of William Shakespeare's (1564–1616) sonnets.

Hugh Latimer (c. 1485–1555). Anglican bishop and preacher. Latimer was celebrated for his sermons critiquing the idolatrous nature of Catholic practices and the social injustices visited on the underclass by the aristocracy and the individualism of Protestant government. After his support for Henry's petition of divorce he served as a court preacher under Henry VIII* and Edward VI. Latimer became a proponent of reform following his education at Cambridge University and received license as a preacher. Following Edward's death, Latimer was tried for heresy, perishing at the stake with Nicholas Ridley* and Thomas Cranmer.*

William Laud (1573–1645). Anglican archbishop, one of the most pivotal and controversial figures in Anglican church history. Early in his career, Laud offended many with his highly traditional, anti-Puritan approach to ecclesial policies. After his election as Archbishop of Canterbury in 1633, Laud continued to strive against the Puritans, demanding the eastward placement of the Communion altar (affirming the religious centrality of the Eucharist), the use of clerical garments, the reintroduction of stained-glass windows, and the uniform use of the Book of Common Prayer.* Laud was accused of being a crypto-Catholic—an ominous accusation during the protracted threat of invasion by the Spanish Armada. In 1640 the Long Parliament met, quickly impeached Laud on charges of treason, and placed him in jail for several years before his execution.

Ludwig Lavater (1527–1586). Swiss Reformed pastor and theologian. Under his father-in-law Heinrich Bullinger,* Lavater became an archdeacon in Zurich. In 1585 he succeeded Rudolf Gwalther* as the city's Antistes. He authored a widely disseminated book on demonology, commentaries on Chronicles, Proverbs, Ecclesiastes, Nehemiah and Ezekiel, theological works, and biographies of Bullinger and Konrad Pellikan.*

Laws and Liberties of the Inhabitants of Massachusetts (1647). North American colonial constitution. The first printed set of laws in the American colonies, the 1647 *Laws and Liberties of the Inhabitants of Massachusetts* was a revision of the *Massachusetts Body of Liberties* (1641), a legal code collected by Puritan minister Nathaniel Ward (1578–1652). The *Laws and Liberties* codified Puritan expectations of doctrine and morality, and included provision for the punishment for heresy, stipulating banishment for Anabaptism. The majority of the document consists of practical clauses addressing general and specific aspects of communal and commercial life.

John Lawson (unknown). Seventeenth-century English Puritan. Lawson wrote *Gleanings and Expositions of Some of Scripture* (1646) and a treatise on the sabbath in the New Testament.

Jacques Lefèvre d'Étaples (Faber Stapulensis) (1460?–1536). French Catholic humanist, publisher and translator. Lefèvre d'Étaples studied classical literature and philosophy, as well as patristic and medieval mysticism. He advocated the principle of *ad fontes*, issuing a full-scale annotation on the corpus of Aristotle, publishing the writings of key Christian mystics, and contributing to efforts at biblical translation and commentary. Although he never broke with the Catholic Church, his views prefigured those of Martin Luther,* for which he was condemned by the University of Sorbonne in Paris. He then found refuge in the court of Marguerite d'Angoulême, where he met John Calvin* and Martin Bucer.*

Edward Leigh (1602–1671). English Puritan biblical critic, historian and politician. Educated at Oxford, Leigh's public career included appointments as a Justice of the Peace, an officer in the parliamentary army during the English Civil Wars and a member of Parliament. Although never ordained, Leigh devoted himself to the study of theology and Scripture; he participated in the Westminster Assembly. Leigh published a diverse corpus, including lexicons of Greek, Hebrew and juristic terms, and histories of Roman, Greek and English rulers. His most important theological work is *A Systeme or Body of Divinity* (1662).

John Lightfoot (1602–1675). Anglican priest and biblical scholar. After graduating from Cambridge, Lightfoot was ordained and pastored at several small parishes. He continued to study classics under the support of the politician Rowland Cotton (1581–1634). Siding with the Parliamentarians during the English Civil Wars, Lightfoot relocated to London in 1643. He was one of the original members of the Westminster Assembly, where he defended a moderate Presbyterianism. His best-known work is the six-volume *Horae Hebraicae et Talmudicae* (1658–1677), a verse-by-verse commentary illumined by Hebrew customs, language and the Jewish interpretive tradition.

Wenceslaus Linck (1482–1547). German Lutheran theologian and preacher. As dean of the theology faculty at the University of Wittenberg and successor to Johannes von Staupitz* as the prior of the Augustinian Monastery, Linck worked closely with Martin Luther* and attended the Heidelberg Disputation with him. He replaced Staupitz as vicar-general of the Augustinian order in 1520 in Germany, a capacity in which he pronounced all members free from their vows before renouncing the order himself. After periods of ministry in Munich and Altenburg, Linck settled in Nuremberg, where he became known as an exemplary preacher and an advisor to cities undertaking Protestant reform. He published a significant number of sermons and practical tracts as well as a paraphrase and annotations on the Old Testament.

Henry Lok (1553?–1608?). English Puritan poet. Patronized by Sir Robert Cecil (1563–1612), Lok served the secretary of state as a foreign agent, working to gather intelligence in Scotland, southern France, and Spain. After falling out of favor, Lok served at least two sentences in debtors' prison and died penniless. He published two works: a collection of devotional sonnets and a paraphrase of Ecclesiastes.

Peter Lombard (1095–1160). Scholastic theologian, bishop of Paris. Though little is known about his life, some records indicate that Lombard came from the region of Novara in Lombardy. Bernard of Clairvaux* patronized his studies at Reims, and later recommended him for further study at St. Victor in Paris. In 1144, Lombard participated in an examination of the writings of Gilbert of Poitiers for heresy. Lombard became a canon at Notre Dame in 1145, and an archdeacon there in 1156. Meanwhile he spent a year and a half in Rome as an assistant to Theobald, bishop of Paris. Lombard was elected bishop of Paris in 1159. He died less than a year later. Lombard's most important work was the *Four Books of the Sentences*, which served as the standard textbook for theology throughout the remainder of the Middle Ages, and at the beginning of the early modern period. Additionally, Lombard produced commentaries on the Psalms and Pauline epistles.

Johannes Lonicer (1499–1569). German Lutheran theologian and linguist. After studying in Erfurt and Wittenberg, Lonicer renounced his Augustinian vows. He briefly taught Hebrew at the University of Freiburg, but controversy saw him flee to Strasburg, where he worked with a printer, translating some early Lutheran vernacular works into Latin. At the opening of the University of Marburg, Lonicer was appointed to teach Greek and Hebrew, and he later also served as professor of theology.

Lucas Lossius (1508–1582). German Lutheran teacher and musician. While a student at Leipzig and Wittenberg, Lossius was deeply influenced by Melanchthon* and Luther,* who found work for him as Urbanus Rhegius's* secretary. Soon after going to work for Rhegius, Lossius began teaching at a local gymnasium (or secondary school), *Das Johanneum*, eventually becoming its headmaster. Lossius remained at *Das Johanneum* until his death, even turning down appointments to university professorships. A man of varied interests, he wrote on dialectics, music and church history, as well as publishing a postil and a five-volume set of annotations on the New Testament.

Sibrandus Lubbertus (c. 1555–1625). Dutch Reformed theologian. Lubbertis, a key figure in the establishment of orthodox Calvinism in Frisia, studied theology at Wittenburg and Geneva (under Theodore Beza*) before his appointment as professor of theology at the University of Franeker. Throughout his career, Lubbertis advocated for high Calvinist theology, defending it in disputes with representatives of Socinianism, Arminianism and Roman Catholicism. Lubbertis criticized the Catholic theologian Robert Bellarmine and fellow Dutch reformer Jacobus Arminius*; the views of the latter he opposed as a prominent participant in the Synod of Dordrecht.*

Thomas Lushington (1590–1661). English Anglican minister. Best known as the tutor of polymath Sir Thomas Browne (1605–1682), Lushington also served as a chaplain to Richard Corbet, bishop of Oxford. Committed to the program of Archbishop Laud,* he lost his position during the English Civil Wars and retired to write. Most of his works were published anonymously or pseudonymously, including a translation of a commentary on Hebrews by Polish theologian Johannes Crellius (1590–1633) as G. W. and a series of sermons given at Oxford as Robert Jones.

Martin Luther (1483–1546). German Lutheran priest, professor, and theologian. Martin Luther was born in Eisleben, Saxony, to an entrepreneurial minor. Upon completing his earlier education at Eisenach, Luther matriculated at the University of Erfurt where he completed his BA in 1502, and MA in 1505. While at Erfurt, Luther studied the philosophy of William of Ockham (1285–1347), and his disciple, Gabriel Biel

(1420–1495). After receiving his MA, Luther proceeded to the study of law. However, a number of events culminating in his promise to St. Anne (the patron saint of minors) to become a monk compelled Luther to withdraw from law school and join the Augustinian monastery at Erfurt in 1505. At this monastery, Luther was ordained a priest. Later, the Augustinians sent Luther to the University of Wittenberg to study theology. In 1512, Luther received his doctorate, and took up the post of lecturer in Bible at Wittenberg, a position he would hold the rest of his life. While a professor at this university, Luther reinterpreted the doctrine of justification. Convinced that righteousness comes only from God's grace, he disputed the sale of indulgences with his *Ninety-Five Theses*, which he reportedly posted to the door of All Saints' Church in Wittenberg on October 31, 1517. Luther's positions brought conflict with Rome. He challenged the Mass, transubstantiation, and communion in one kind, and his denial of papal authority led to excommunication. Though Luther was condemned by the Diet of Worms, Frederick III, the Elector of Saxony, provided him safe haven. Luther later returned to Wittenberg with public order collapsing under Andreas Bodenstein von Karlstadt* and steered a more cautious path of reform. Among his most influential works are three treatises published in 1520: *To the Christian Nobility of the German Nation, On the Babylonian Captivity of the Church*, and *On the Freedom of a Christian*. His rendering of the Bible and liturgy in the vernacular, as well as his hymns and sermons, proved extensively influential.

Georg Major (1502–1574). German Lutheran theologian. Major was on the theological faculty of the University of Wittenberg, succeeding as dean Johannes Bugenhagen* and Philipp Melanchthon.* One of the chief editors on the Wittenberg edition of Luther's works, Major is most identified with the controversy bearing his name, in which he stated that good works are necessary to salvation. Major qualified his statement, which was in reference to the totality of the Christian life. The Formula of Concord* rejected the statement, ending the controversy. As a theologian, Major further refined Lutheran views of the inspiration of Scripture and the doctrine of the Trinity.

John (Mair) Major (1467–1550). Scottish Catholic philosopher. Major taught logic and theology at the universities of Paris (his alma mater), Glasgow and St Andrews. His broad interests and impressive work drew students from all over Europe. While disapproving of evangelicals (though he did teach John Knox*), Major advocated reform programs for Rome. He supported collegial episcopacy and even challenged the curia's teaching on sexuality. Still he was a nominalist who was critical of humanist approaches to biblical exegesis. His best-known publication is *A History of Greater Britain, Both England and Scotland* (1521), which promoted the union of the kingdoms. He also published a commentary on Peter Lombard's *Sentences* and the Gospel of John.

Juan de Maldonado (1533–1583). Spanish Catholic biblical scholar. A student of Francisco de Toledo,* Maldonado taught philosophy and theology at the universities of Paris and Salamanca. Ordained to the priesthood in Rome, he revised the Septuagint under papal appointment. While Maldonado vehemently criticized Protestants, he asserted that Reformed baptism was valid and that mixed confessional marriages were acceptable. His views on Mary's immaculate conception proved controversial among many Catholics who conflated his statement that it was not an article of faith with its denial. He was intrigued by demonology (blaming demonic influence for the Reformation). All his work was published posthumously; his Gospel commentaries were highly valued and important.

Thomas Manton (1620–1677). English Puritan minister. Manton, educated at Oxford, served for a time as lecturer at Westminster Abbey and rector of St. Paul's, Covent Garden, and was a strong advocate of Presbyterianism. He was known as a rigorous evangelical Calvinist who preached long expository sermons. At different times in his ecclesial career he worked side-by-side with Richard Baxter* and John Owen.* In his later life, Manton's Nonconformist position led to his ejection as a clergyman from the Church of England (1662) and eventual imprisonment (1670). Although a voluminous writer, Manton was best known for his preaching. At his funeral in 1677, he was dubbed "the king of preachers."

Benedetto da Mantova (c. 1495–c. 1556). Italian Catholic monk. Benedetto entered the Benedictine order in Mantua and served as dean at San Giorgio Maggiore in Venice. At San Nicolò l'Arena on Mt. Etna, he became acquainted with Waldensian and Protestant thought, which influenced his composition of *The Benefit of Christ*, one of the most significant Italian writings of the Reformation. Marcantonio Flaminio* was asked to rewrite the text in more elegant prose before its anonymous publication in 1543, and although the work drew the ire of the Inquisition, Benedetto's authorship was not uncovered during his lifetime. His increasingly radical spiritualism saw him arrested in Padua, though nothing of his later life is known.

Felix Mantz (d. 1527). Swiss Anabaptist Leader. An early supporter of Zwingli* in Zurich, Mantz's frustration with the pace of the magisterial Reformation led him to found an independent congregation, the Swiss Brethren, with Conrad Grebel,* Georg Blaurock,* and others. Mantz and Grebel represented the Brethren in two disputations with Zwingli over infant baptism in 1525. Defeated, the Brethren refused to cease meeting and rebaptizing adults, which they considered a first baptism, leading to suppression by the Zurich authorities. Mantz was able to spread his message for a time, traveling through a number of Swiss regions despite several arrests. Imprisoned by the Zurich authorities in March 1526 with Grebel and Blaurock, he briefly escaped, but having returned to his practice of believers' baptism, he was executed by drowning, the punishment for Anabaptism, in January 1527.

Lucrezia Marinella (1571–1653). Venetian poet and writer. While famous for her writings, very little is known of Marinella's personal life. As was expected of a women of her class, she spent most of her life in seclusion, and she did not participate in public life. She married a physician, but the fact that she had two children is only known from her will. Marinella's writings spanned a number of subjects, including, philosophy, religious poetry, and proto-feminist texts on the abilities of women and their place in society. Perhaps her best-known work is *The Nobility and Excellence of Women and the Defects and Vices of Men* (1600), in which she argues for the moral and intellectual superiority of women.

Augustin Marlorat (c. 1506–1562). French Reformed pastor. Committed by his family to a monastery at the age of eight, Marlorat was also ordained into the priesthood at an early age in 1524. He fled to Geneva in 1535, where he pastored until the Genevan Company of Pastors sent him to France to shepherd the nascent evangelical congregations. His petition to the young Charles IX (1550–1574) for the right to public evangelical worship was denied. In response to a massacre of evangelicals in Vassy (over sixty dead, many more wounded), Marlorat's congregation planned to overtake Rouen. After the crown captured Rouen, Marlorat was arrested and executed three days later for treason. His principle published work was an anthology of New Testament comment modeled after Thomas Aquinas's* *Catena aurea in quatuor Evangelia*. Marlorat harmonized Reformed and Lutheran comment with the church fathers, interspersed with his own brief comments. He also wrote such anthologies for Genesis, Job, the Psalms, Song of Songs and Isaiah.

Pilgram Marpeck (c. 1495–1556). Austrian Radical elder and theologian. During a brief sojourn in Strasbourg, Marpeck debated with Martin Bucer* before the city council; Bucer was declared the winner, and Marpeck was asked to leave Strasbourg for his views concerning paedobaptism (which he compared to a sacrifice to Moloch). After his time in Strasbourg, Marpeck traveled throughout southern Germany and western Austria, planting Anabaptist congregations. Marpeck criticized the strict use of the ban, however, particularly among the Swiss brethren. He also engaged in a christological controversy with Kaspar von Schwenckfeld.*

Stephen Marshall (c. 1594–1655). English Presbyterian minister. Known for his Nonconformist preaching, Marshall pastored in Essex before appearing on the national stage prior to the Civil War (1642–1651). An advocate of armed rebellion against a lawful sovereign over religious matters, he preached before Parliament a number of times, was a member of the Westminster Assembly, and served as lecturer at St. Margaret's, Westminster. He also ministered to Archbishop Laud* and Charles I* before their executions.

Gregory Martin (1542?–1582). English Catholic priest and translator. After studying at Oxford, Martin tutored the sons of the Duke of Norfolk until leaving for the college of Douai, where he received his doctorate. He taught for two years at the English college in Rome before returning to the college of Douai, which was temporarily based at Rheims. While he composed a number of polemical writings, he is best known as the primary translator of the Douai-Rheims Bible, an English translation of the Vulgate with commentary and notes intended to provide a Catholic alternative to the influx of Protestant annotated English Bibles. The New Testament was published at Douai in 1582 and the Old Testament at Rheims in 1609–1610.

Mary I of England (1516–1558). English monarch. Daughter of Henry VIII* and his first wife Catherine of Aragon (1509–1553), Mary was raised in the strict Catholicism of her mother. Her succession of Edward VI, her half-brother, was briefly contested by Lady Jane Grey*, daughter of Henry VIII's younger sister, in whom Protestants placed their hopes, but unable to raise adequate support, this challenge was quickly dismissed. Upon her ascent, Mary set about the task of restoring the Catholic religion, a reversal of royal policy that was positively received by much of the populace. While able to reestablish relations with the Pope and reassert the mass and other aspects of Catholicism, the impoverishment of the church following the dissolution of the monasteries and the closure of the chantries was difficult to overcome. Other aspects of popular piety, including the cult of the saints, pilgrimages, and the doctrine of purgatory, were not restored during her reign. Mary looms large in the Protestant imagination, and her persecution of evangelicals led to the moniker "Bloody Mary." The accounts of martyrs such as Thomas Cranmer*, Hugh Latimer*, and Nicholas Ridley* were immortalized in John Foxe's (1516–1587) *Acts and Monuments** and became a mainstay of Protestant propaganda.

Johannes Mathesius (1504–1565). German Lutheran theologian and pastor. After reading Martin Luther's* *On Good Works*, Mathesius left his teaching post in Ingolstadt and traveled to Wittenberg to study theology. Mathesius was an important agent of reform in the Bohemian town of Jáchymov, where he pastored, preached and taught. Over one thousand of Mathesius's sermons are extant, including numerous wedding and funeral sermons as well as a series on Luther's life. Mathesius also transcribed portions of Luther's Table Talk.

Chiara Matraini Contarini (1514–1604). Italian Catholic poet. Widowed at twenty-seven, Matraini became active in the literary circles of Lucca and Pescia. Her early published works were composed on secular topics, and include love poetry, songs, a reflection on warfare, and a translation of Isocrates's (436–338 BC) *Ad Demonicum*. Later in her life, she wrote on spiritual topics, publishing a series of spiritual meditations, reflections on the penitential psalms, and a treatise on Mary.

Anthony Maxey (d. 1618). Anglican minister. Maxey was born in Essex and educated at Westminster School. After completing his early education at Westminster, Maxey matriculated at Trinity College, Cambridge, in 1578. Maxey graduated Cambridge with the BA (1581), MA (1585), BD (1594), and DD (1608) degrees. However, he was unable to obtain a fellowship at Trinity. King James I* appointed Maxey as his chaplain and dean of Windsor on June 21, 1612. Maxey was also inducted into the Order of the Garter. He died on May 3, 1618. Maxey's published works consist of three sermons: *The Churches Sleep*; *The Golden Chain of Man's Salvation*; and *The Fearful Point of Hardening*.

John Mayer (1583–1664). Anglican priest and biblical exegete. Mayer dedicated much of his life to biblical exegesis, writing a seven-volume commentary on the entire Bible (1627–1653). Styled after Philipp Melanchthon's* *locus* method, Mayer's work avoided running commentary, focusing instead on textual and theological problems. He was a parish priest for fifty-five years. In the office of priest Mayer also wrote a popular catechism, *The English Catechisme, or a Commentarie on the Short Catechisme* (1621), which went through twelve editions in his lifetime.

Joseph Mede (1586–1638). Anglican biblical scholar, Hebraist and Greek lecturer. A man of encyclopedic knowledge, Mede was interested in numerous fields, varying from philology and history to mathematics and physics, although millennial thought and apocalyptic prophesy were clearly his chief interests. Mede's most important work was his *Clavis Apocalyptica* (1627, later translated into English as *The Key of the Revelation*). This work examined the structure of Revelation as the key to its interpretation. Mede saw the visions as a connected and chronological sequence hinging around Revelation 17:18. He is remembered as an important figure in the history of millenarian theology. He was respected as a mild-mannered and generous scholar who avoided controversy and debate, but who had many original thoughts.

Philipp Melanchthon (1497–1560). German Lutheran educator, reformer, and theologian. Philipp Melanchthon was born in the Palatinate, the son of an armorer. He attended the Latin school in Pforzheim, where he lived with the sister of Johannes Reuchlin* to whom he was related by marriage. Having completed his early education, Melanchthon went on to attend the University of Heidelberg, where he received his BA in 1511. Afterwards, he earned his MA from the University of Tubingen in 1514. In 1518, Reuchlin recommended Melanchthon for the new professorship of Greek at the University of Wittenberg, where he remained for the rest of his life. There, Melanchthon taught Greek, rhetoric, and logic. Melanchthon is known as the partner and successor to Martin Luther* in reform in Germany and for his pioneering *Loci Communes*, which served as a theological textbook. Melanchthon participated with Luther in the Leipzig disputation, helped implement reform in Wittenberg, and was a chief architect of the Augsburg Confession.* Later, Melanchthon and Martin Bucer* worked for union between reformed and Catholic churches. On account of Melanchthon's ecumenical disposition and his modification of several of Luther's doctrines, he was held in suspicion by some.

Andrew Melville (1545–1622). Scottish Reformed theologian. Melville was born at Baldovie on August 1, 1545, to an evangelical family. After finishing his early education at Montrose Grammar School, he matriculated at St. Mary's College, St. Andrews, in 1559. Melville graduated St. Andrews in 1564, after which he traveled to Paris, where he studied Greek, Hebrew, mathematics, and other languages. While in Paris, Melville came under the influence of Petrus Ramus,* whose pedagogical methods he would later utilize in Scotland. From there, he proceeded to Poitiers to study law. There, he became regent of the College of St. Marceon. However, when Poitiers came under siege, Melville departed the city for Geneva, where Theodore Beza* warmly received him. Shortly after Melville's arrival in Geneva, he assumed the chair of humanities at the academy. Melville remained in this position at the academy until 1573, when he returned to Scotland. In 1574, Melville was appointed principal of the College of Glasgow. While in this post, Melville led in the reform of the college's curriculum, and engaged in ecclesiastical controversy. He served on the committee that drafted the Second Book of Discipline, and was elected moderator of the General Assembly in 1578. In 1580, Melville became principal of St. Mary's College, St. Andrews, where he initiated the same types of reform as he did at Glasgow. Throughout his career, Melville denounced royal ecclesiastical supremacy, arguing strongly for the autonomy of the national church. For this he was summoned to the Privy Council in Edinburgh in 1584 on the possible charge of treason for his resistance to royal ecclesiastical authority. Though they could not charge Melville with sedition, the Privy Council still determined to consign him to trial, but Melville managed to escape to England. While in England, he visited Puritan leaders at Oxford and Cambridge. He also lectured on Genesis in London. Melville returned to Scotland in 1585, and became rector of the University of St. Andrews in 1590. He was eventually deprived of this rectorship in 1587 for his opposition to episcopacy. In 1606, along with several ministers, he was summoned to appear before Hampton Court, where he gave some uncompromising speeches. These speeches resulted in Melville's imprisonment in several places, including the Tower of London. Melville was released from the Tower on April 19, 1611, and from there traveled to France. Having arrived in France, Melville proceeded through Paris and Rouen to Sedan, where he assumed the chair of theology. He remained in Sedan until his death in 1622. Melville authored an extensive literary corpus, which includes a commentary on Romans.

Justus Menius (1499–1558). German Lutheran pastor and theologian. Menius was a prominent reformer in Thuringia. He participated in the Marburg Colloquy and, with others, helped Martin Luther* compose the Schmalkald Articles.* Throughout his career Menius entered into numerous controversies with Anabaptists and even fellow Lutherans. He rejected Andreas Osiander's (d. 1552) doctrine of justification—that the indwelling of Christ's divine nature justifies, rather than the imputed alien righteousness of Christ's person, declared through God's mercy. Against Nikolaus von Amsdorf (1483–1565) and Matthias Flacius (1520–1575), Menius agreed with Georg Major* that good works are necessary to salvation. Osiander's view of justification was censored in Article 3 of the Formula of Concord*; Menius's understanding of the relationship between good works and salvation was rejected in Article 4. Menius translated many of Luther's Latin works into German. He also composed a handbook for Christian households and an influential commentary on 1 Samuel.

Johannes Mercerus (Jean Mercier) (d. 1570). French Hebraist. Mercerus studied under the first Hebrew chair at the Collège Royal de Paris, François Vatable (d. 1547), whom he succeeded in 1546. John Calvin* tried to recruit Mercerus to the Genevan Academy as professor of Hebrew, once in 1558 and again in 1563; he refused both times. During his lifetime Mercerus published grammatical helps for Hebrew and Chaldean, an aid to the Masoretic symbols in the Hebrew text, and translated the commentaries and grammars of several medieval rabbis. He himself wrote commentaries on Genesis, the wisdom books, and most of the Minor Prophets. These commentaries—most of them only published after his death—were philologically focused and interacted with the work of Jerome, Nicholas of Lyra,* notable rabbis and Johannes Oecolampadius.*

Sebastian Meyer (1465-1545) German Reformed theologian. Born in Neunenberg am Rhein, Meyer studied at the University of Basel before entering the Franciscan order. Convinced by Luther's teachings, Meyer was the primary voice in Bern's acceptance of the Reformation and participated in the debates that led to the conversion of Zurich. Later in his career, he taught in Basel, Strasbourg, and Augsburg, fought against growing Anabaptist influence in the Swiss cantons, and composed commentaries on Revelation and Paul's letters to the Corinthians.

Thomas Mocket (1602–1670?). British Puritan minister. Mocket ministered in Wales and England, publishing numerous works, including a catechism, a tract on the duties of Christians, and an excursus on the celebration of Christmas.

Peter Moffett (d. 1617). English Protestant clergyman. Rector at Fobbing, Essex, Moffett published a commentary on the Song of Solomon and a sermon on 1 Timothy 1:16.

Ambrose Moibanus (1494–1554). German Lutheran bishop and theologian. Moibanus helped reform the church of Breslau (modern Wroclaw, Poland). He revised the Mass, bolstered pastoral care and welfare for the poor, and wrote a new evangelical catechism.

Olympia Morata (1526/27–1555). Italian Protestant humanist and theologian. Daughter of a humanist scholar, her father taught in the court of Ferrara, and she was raised alongside Anna d'Este (1531–1607), daughter of Protestant Renée of France (1510–1574) and later wife of Francis, Duke of Guise (1519–1563), a central antagonist in the St. Bartholomew's Day Massacre. A precocious scholar, Morata's classical, humanist, and biblical studies drew her toward the evangelical currents of the court, but these Protestant leanings also raised the constant suspicion of the Inquisition. In 1550, Morata married Andreas Grundler (unknown), a German Protestant doctor, and moved to his native Schweinfurt, where, facing limited opportunities due to her gender, she continued her studies and privately tutored in Greek and the classics. She developed an extensive correspondence with friends, especially noblewomen she had met at court, and Protestant leaders including Luther*, Melanchthon* and Matthias Flacius (1520–1575), whom she asked to translate some of Luther's work into Italian. Most of Morata's writings were destroyed during the siege of Schweinfurt in 1553–1554, and while she was able to resettle in Frankfurt, she died of tuberculosis soon afterwards. In her writings that survived the siege, her scholarly erudition is clear, and her letters demonstrate a ministerial care for her correspondents and desire for the spread of the Reformation message.

Thomas More (1478–1535). English Catholic lawyer, politician, humanist and martyr. More briefly studied at Oxford, but completed his legal studies in London. After contemplating the priesthood for four years, he opted for politics and was elected a member of Parliament in 1504. A devout Catholic, More worked with church leaders in England to root out heresy while he also confronted Lutheran teachings in writing. After four years as Lord Chancellor, More resigned due to heightened tensions with Henry VIII* over papal supremacy (which More supported and Henry did not). Tensions did not abate. More's steadfast refusal to accept the Act of Supremacy (1534)—which declared the King of England to be the supreme ecclesial primate not the pope—resulted in his arrest and trial for high treason. He was found guilty and beheaded with John Fisher (1469–1535). Friends with John Colet* and Desiderius Erasmus,* More was a widely respected humanist in England as well as on the continent. Well-known for his novel *Utopia* (1516), More also penned several religious treatises on Christ's passion and suffering during his imprisonment in the Tower of London, which were published posthumously.

Henry Morley (d. 1616). English Protestant preacher. Morley published a sermon of the cleansing of the leper given at St. Paul's Cathedral in London during an outbreak of the plague in 1603.

Sebastian Münster (1488–1552). German Reformed Hebraist, exegete, printer, and geographer. After converting to the Reformation in 1524, Münster taught Hebrew at the universities of Heidelberg and Basel. During his lengthy tenure in Basel he published more than seventy books, including Hebrew dictionaries and rabbinic commentaries. He also produced an evangelistic work for Jews titled *Vikuach* (1539). Münster's *Torat ha-Maschiach* (1537), the Gospel of Matthew, was the first published Hebrew translation of any portion of the New Testament. Despite his massive contribution to contemporary understanding of the Hebrew language, Münster was criticized by many of the reformers as a Judaizer.

Thomas Müntzer (c. 1489–1525). German Radical preacher. As a preacher in the town of Zwickau, Müntzer was influenced by German mysticism and, growing convinced that Martin Luther* had not carried through reform properly, sought to restore the pure apostolic church of the New Testament. Müntzer's radical ideas led to expulsions from various cities; he developed a highly apocalyptic theology, in which he heralded the last days that would establish the pure community out of suffering, prompting Müntzer's proactive role in the Peasants' War, which he perceived as a crucial apocalyptic event. Six thousand of Müntzer's followers were annihilated by magisterial troops; Müntzer was executed.

John Murcot (1625–1654). English Puritan pastor. After completing his bachelor's at Oxford in 1647, Murcot was ordained as a pastor, transferring to several parishes until in 1651 he moved to Dublin. All his works were published posthumously.

Simon Musaeus (1521–1582). German Lutheran theologian. After studying at the universities of Frankfurt an der Oder and Wittenberg, Musaeus began teaching Greek at the Cathedral school in Nuremberg and was ordained. Having returned to Wittenberg to complete a doctoral degree, Musaeus spent the rest of his career in numerous ecclesial and academic administrative posts. He opposed Matthias Flacius's (1505–1575) view of original sin—that the formal essence of human beings is marred by original sin—even calling the pro-Flacian faculty at Wittenberg "the devil's latrine." Musaeus published a disputation on original sin and a postil.

Wolfgang Musculus (1497–1563). German Reformed pastor and theologian. Musculus produced translations, biblical commentaries and an influential theological text, *Loci communes Sacrae Theologiae* (*Commonplaces of Sacred Theology*), outlining a Zwinglian theology. Musculus began to study theology while at a Benedictine monastery; he departed in 1527 and became secretary to Martin Bucer* in Strasbourg. He was later installed as a pastor in Augsburg, eventually performing the first evangelical liturgy in the city's cathedral. Displaced by the Augsburg Interim, Musculus ended his career as professor of theology at Bern. Though Musculus was active in the pursuit of the reform agenda, he was also concerned for ecumenism, participating in the Wittenberg Concord (1536) and discussions between Lutherans and Catholics.

Georg Mylius (1548–1607). German Lutheran pastor and theologian. Mylius began his career as a preacher in Augsburg, rising to superintendent of the churches in the city after receiving his doctorate in theology. He was arrested and ejected from the city by the Catholic-dominated council for his opposition to the Gregorian calendar, returning briefly to learn of the death of his pregnant wife and child. After grieving in Ulm, Mylius spend the remainder of his career as a preacher and professor of theology at Wittenberg, with a brief hiatus teaching at Jena.

Hans Nadler (unknown). German Radical layperson. An uneducated and illiterate needle salesman, after receiving baptism from Hans Hut* in 1527, Nadler sought to share the faith with those he met during his extensive travels. He is remembered through the records of his arrest and examination, recorded by a court reporter, which give insight into his beliefs and activities as a committed Anabaptist layperson, whereby he affirmed believer's baptism, the spiritual reception of the Eucharist, and nonresistance.

John Napier (1550-1617) Scottish Protestant mathematician and theologian. A nobleman, Napier spent most of his life at Merchiston Castle in Edinburgh, where he entertained a number of scholarly pursuits. In mathematics, he is celebrated as the inventor of logarithms and other tools to simplify calculations. He used his knowledge of physics to invent weapons for the defense of Scotland and also investigated aspects of the occult. A convinced protestant, he was a member of the commission appointed to investigate the Catholic Spanish Blanks plot (1592) and composed a commentary on Revelation, with a dedication to King James I* calling for further reform of the church.

Friedrich Nausea (c. 1496–1552). German Catholic bishop and preacher. After completing his studies at Leipzig, this famed preacher was appointed priest in Frankfurt but was run out of town by his congregants during his first sermon. He transferred to Mainz as cathedral preacher. Nausea was well connected through the German papal hierarchy and traveled widely to preach to influential ecclesial and secular courts. Court preacher for Ferdinand I (1503–1564), his reform tendencies fit well with royal Austrian theological leanings, and he was enthroned as the bishop of Vienna. Nausea thought that rather than endless colloquies only a council could settle reform. Unfortunately he could not participate in the first session of Trent due to insufficient funding, but he arrived for the second session. Nausea defended the laity's reception of the cup and stressed the importance of promulgating official Catholic teaching in the vernacular.

Melchior Neukirch (1540–1597). German Lutheran pastor and playwright. Neukirch's pastoral career spanned more than thirty years in several northern German parishes. Neukirch published a history of the Braunschweig church since the Reformation and a dramatization of Acts 4–7. He died of the plague.

Nicholas of Lyra (1270–1349). French Catholic biblical exegete. Very little is known about this influential medieval theologian of the Sorbonne aside from the works he published, particularly the *Postilla litteralis super totam Bibliam* (1322–1333). With the advent of the printing press this work was regularly published alongside the Latin Vulgate and the *Glossa ordinaria*. In this running commentary on the Bible Nicholas promoted literal interpretation as the basis for theology. Despite his preference for literal interpretation, Nicholas also published a companion volume, the *Postilla moralis super totam Bibliam* (1339), a commentary on the spiritual meaning of the biblical text. Nicholas was a major conversation partner for many reformers though many of them rejected his exegesis as too literal and too "Jewish" (not concerned enough with the Bible's fulfillment in Jesus Christ).

John Norden (1547–1625). English devotional writer. Norden was born at Somerset, and in 1564 entered Hart Hall, Oxford where he graduated with his BA in 1568, and MA in 1573. Norden spent most of his life Middlesex, moving later to St. Giles in the Fields in 1619, where he remained until his death in 1625. Throughout his life, Norden distinguished himself also as a cartographer, chorographer, and antiquarian. His best known devotional work was his Progress of Piety (1596).

Alexander Nowell (1517–1602). Anglican theologian. Born in Lancashire, Nowell was educated at Brasenose College, Oxford where he shared a room with the future martyrologist John Foxe. Nowell was elected a fellow at the same college, where he spent thirteen years. In 1543, he was appointed master of Westminster School, and in December, 1551, a prebendary of Westminster Abbey. Though elected to the House of Commons in 1553, Nowell was permitted to assume his seat because as a prebendary, he had a seat in Convocation. Because of his evangelical convictions, Nowell lost prebendary in 1554, after which he fled to the Continent, traveling first to Strasbourg, and then to Frankfurt. When Elizabeth I ascended the throne, Nowell returned to England where he afterwards served as chaplain to Edmund Grindal. In 1561 Nowell became Dean of St. Paul's Cathedral, a post which he held until his death. Nowell's best known work was his Catechism originally written in Latin (1563), and translated into English by Thomas Norton in 1570.

Bernardino Ochino (1487–1564). Italian Reformed theologian. After serving as vicar general of the Franciscan order, Ochino left the foundation of the Capuchins, where he assisted in the composition of their constitution and served as vicar general. A famed preacher, his teaching came to the attention of the Inquisition as it began to reflect the thought of Juan de Valdés. Summoned to Rome in 1542, he fled to Geneva with Peter Martyr Vermigli* where his Reformed orthodoxy, tinged with Franciscan mysticism, was brought into the open. Following his flight, Ochino led an unstable life, with brief stays in Basel, Strasbourg, and Augsburg before moving to England with Vermigli in 1548 where he was able to compose a significant treatise against the Roman church. His doctrinal orthodoxy was questioned by the pastor of the Italian congregation in London, but his case left unresolved when he departed for Geneva, then Basel and Zurich, at the accession of Mary*. As pastor of a congregation of Italian refugees in Zurich, Ochino courted considerable controversy. He refused to have his works approved by the city magistrates before publication, and his opponents alleged that his Dialogi XXX (1563) included questionable teachings on the Trinity and divorce while seeming to advocate polygamy. Expelled from Zurich in 1563, he died in Moravia the following year.

Charles Odingsells (d. 1637). English Protestant preacher. Odingsells published two sermons on prophesying and miracles from Matthew 7 given at Langar in Nottinghamshire.

Johannes Oecolampadius (Johannes Huszgen) (1482–1531). Swiss-German Reformed humanist, reformer and theologian. Oecolampadius (an assumed name meaning "house light") assisted with Desiderius Erasmus's* Greek New Testament, lectured on biblical languages and exegesis and completed an influential Greek grammar. After joining the evangelical cause through studying patristics and the work of Martin Luther,* Oecolampadius went to Basel, where he lectured on biblical exegesis and participated in ecclesial reform. On account of Oecolampadius's effort, the city council passed legislation restricting preaching to the gospel and releasing the city from compulsory Mass. Oecolampadius was a chief ally of Huldrych Zwingli,* whom he supported at the Marburg Colloquy (1529).

Kaspar Olevianus (1536–1587). German Reformed theologian. Olevianus is celebrated for composing the Heidelberg Catechism and producing a critical edition of Calvin's *Institutes* in German. Olevianus studied theology with many, including John Calvin,* Theodore Beza,* Heinrich Bullinger* and Peter Martyr Vermigli.* As an advocate of Reformed doctrine, Olevianus oversaw the shift from Lutheranism to Calvinism throughout Heidelberg, organizing the city's churches after Calvin's Geneva. The Calvinist ecclesial vision of Olevianus entangled him in a dispute with another Heidelberg reformer over the rights of ecclesiastical discipline, which Olevianus felt belonged to the council of clergy and elders rather than civil magistrates.

Josua Opitz (c. 1542–1585). German Lutheran pastor. After a brief stint as superintendent in Regensburg, Opitz, a longtime preacher, was dismissed for his support of Matthias Flacius's (1520–1575) view of original sin. (Using Aristotelian categories, Flacius argued that the formal essence of human beings is marred by original sin, forming sinners into the image of Satan; his views were officially rejected in Article 1 of the Formula of Concord.*) Hans Wilhelm Roggendorf (1533–1591) invited Opitz to lower Austria as part of his Lutheranizing program. Unfortunately Roggendorf and Opitz never succeed in getting Lutheranism legal recognition, perhaps in large part due to Opitz's staunch criticism of Catholics, which resulted in his exile. He died of plague.

Lucas Osiander (1534–1604). German Lutheran pastor. For three decades, Osiander—son of the controversial Nuremberg reformer Andreas Osiander (d. 1552)—served as pastor and court preacher in Stuttgart, until he fell out of favor with the duke in 1598. Osiander produced numerous theological and exegetical works, as well as an influential hymnal.

John Owen (1616–1683). English Puritan theologian. Owen trained at Oxford University, where he was later appointed dean of Christ Church and vice chancellor of the university, following his service as chaplain to Oliver Cromwell. Although Owen began his career as a Presbyterian minister, he eventually departed to the party of Independents. Owen composed many sermons, biblical commentaries (including seven volumes on the book of Hebrews), theological treatises and controversial monographs (including disputations with Arminians, Anglicans, Catholics and Socinians).

Ephraim Pagitt (1575–1647). English Protestant minister. Pagitt ministered at St. Edmunds in London until forced into retirement for his Royalist tendencies during the Civil War (1642–1646). Some of his later writings demonstrate sympathy for Presbyterian theology, and he became an opponent of Baptists and other sectarians. His most popular writing was *Heresiography* (1662), in which he set out to catalog the heretics he identified within the church.

Santes Pagninus (c. 1470–1541). Italian Catholic biblical scholar. Pagninus studied under Girolamo Savonarola* and later taught in Rome, Avignon and Lyons. He translated the Old Testament into Latin according to a tight, almost wooden, adherence to the Hebrew. This translation and his Hebrew lexicon *Thesaurus linguae sanctae* (1529) were important resources for translators and commentators.

Johann Pappus (1549–1610). German Lutheran theologian. After a decade as a teacher of Hebrew and professor of theology at the Strasbourg academy, Pappus was appointed president of the city's company of pastors. Despite resistance from the Reformed theologian Johann Sturm (1507–1589), he led the city away from its Swiss Reformed alliances and toward subscription to the Lutheran Formula of Concord. A talented humanist, Pappus published more than thirty works on controversial, theological, historical, and exegetical subjects.

David (Wängler) Pareus (1548–1622). German Reformed pastor and theologian. Born at Frankenstein in Lower Silesia, Pareus studied theology at Heidelberg under Zacharias Ursinus (1534–1583), the principal author of the Heidelberg Catechism.* After reforming several churches, Pareus returned to Heidelberg to teach at the Reformed seminary. He then joined the theological faculty at the University of Heidelberg, first as a professor of Old Testament and later as a professor of New Testament. Pareus edited the *Neustadter Bibel* (1587), a publication of Martin Luther's* German translation with Reformed annotations—which was strongly denounced by Lutherans, especially Jakob Andreae* and Johann Georg Sigwart (1554–1618). In an extended debate, Pareus defended the orthodoxy of Calvin's exegesis against Aegidius Hunnius,* who accused Calvin of "judaizing" by rejecting many traditional Christological interpretations of Old Testament passages. Towards the end of his career, Pareus wrote commentaries on Genesis, Hosea, Matthew, Romans, 1 Corinthians, Galatians, Hebrews and Revelation.

Catherine Parr (1512–1548). The last of King Henry VIII's* six wives, Catherine Parr was Queen Consort to Henry from 1543 until his death in 1547. She enjoyed a close relationship with two of her step children, Elizabeth and Edward (the future Queen Elizabeth I* and King Edward VI), involving herself extensively in their education. Having married three more times after the death of Henry VIII, Catherine died in 1548. Her published works are *Psalms or Prayers* (1543) and a *Lamentation of a Sinner* (1548).

Paul of Burgos (Solomon ha-Levi) (c. 1351–1435). Spanish Catholic archbishop. In 1391 Solomon ha-Levi, a rabbi and Talmudic scholar, converted to Christianity, receiving baptism with his entire family (except for his wife). He changed his name to Paul de Santa Maria. Some have suggested that he converted to avoid persecution; he himself stated that Thomas Aquinas's* work persuaded him of the truth of Christian faith. After studying theology in Paris, he was ordained bishop in 1403. He actively and ardently persecuted Jews, trying to compel them to convert. In order to convince Jews that Christians correctly interpret the Hebrew Scriptures, Paul wrote *Dialogus Pauli et Sauli contra Judaeos, sive Scrutinium Scripturarum* (1434), a book filled with vile language toward the Jews. He also wrote a series of controversial marginal notes and comments on Nicholas of Lyra's* *Postilla*, many of which criticized Nicholas's use of Jewish scholarship.

Christoph Pelargus (1565–1633). German Lutheran pastor, theologian, professor and superintendent. Pelargus studied philosophy and theology at the University of Frankfurt an der Oder, in Brandenburg. This irenic Philippist was appointed as the superintendent of Brandenburg and later became a pastor in Frankfurt, although the local authorities first required him to condemn Calvinist theology, because several years earlier he had been called before the consistory in Berlin under suspicion of being a crypto-Calvinist. Among his most important works were a four-volume commentary on *De orthodoxa fide* by John of Damascus (d. 749), a treatise defending the breaking of the bread during communion, and a volume of funeral sermons. He also published commentaries on the Pentateuch, the Psalms, Matthew, John and Acts.

Konrad Pellikan (1478–1556). German Reformed Hebraist and theologian. Pellikan attended the University of Heidelberg, where he mastered Hebrew under Johannes Reuchlin. In 1504 Pellikan published one of the first Hebrew grammars that was not merely a translation of the work of medieval rabbis. While living in Basel, Pellikan assisted the printer Johannes Amerbach, with whom he published some of Luther's* early writings. He also worked with Sebastian Münster* and Wolfgang Capito* on a Hebrew Psalter (1516). In 1526, after teaching theology for three years at the University of Basel, Huldrych Zwingli* brought Pellikan to Zurich to chair the faculty of Old Testament. Pellikan's magnum opus is a seven-volume commentary on the entire Bible (except Revelation) and the Apocrypha; it is often heavily dependent upon the work of others (esp. Desiderius Erasmus* and Johannes Oecolampadius*).

William Pemble (1591–1623). Puritan theologian and author. Pemble was born in Egerton, Kent. He was educated at Magdalen College, Oxford, where he graduated with his BA degree in 1614. Afterward he moved to Magdalen Hall, where he became a reader and tutor in divinity. He received his MA in 1618. Primarily a Hebrew scholar, Pemble authored commentaries on Ecclesiastes (1629), the first nine chapters of Zechariah (1629), and portions of Ezra, Nehemiah, and Daniel. Pemble also wrote *An Introduction to the Worthy Receiving the Sacrament* (1628), as well as treatises on predestination and justification. He died of a fever on April 14, 1623.

Benedict Pererius (1535–1610). Spanish Catholic theologian, philosopher and exegete. Pererius entered the Society of Jesus in 1552. He taught philosophy, theology, and exegesis at the Roman College of the Jesuits. Early in his career he warned against neo-Platonism and astrology in his *De principiis* (1576). Pererius wrote a lengthy commentary on Daniel, and five volumes of exegetical theses on Exodus, Romans, Revelation and part of the Gospel of John (chs. 1–14). His four-volume commentary on Genesis (1591–1599) was lauded by Protestants and Catholics alike.

William Perkins (1558–1602). English Puritan preacher and theologian. Perkins was a highly regarded Puritan Presbyterian preacher and biblical commentator in the Elizabethan era. He studied at Cambridge University and later became a fellow of Christ's Church college as a preacher and professor, receiving acclaim for his sermons and lectures. Even more, Perkins gained an esteemed reputation for his ardent exposition of Calvinist reformed doctrine in the style of Petrus Ramus,* becoming one of the first English reformed theologians to achieve international recognition. Perkins influenced the federal Calvinist shape of Puritan theology and the vision of logical, practical expository preaching.

François Perrault (1577–1657). French Reformed pastor for over fifty years. His book on demonology was prominent, perhaps because of the intrigue at his home in 1612. According to his account, a poltergeist made a commotion and argued points of theology; a few months later Perrault's parishioners slew a large snake slithering out of his house.

Dirk Philips (1504–1568). Dutch Radical elder and theologian. This former Franciscan monk, known for being severe and obstinate, was a leading theologian of the sixteenth-century Anabaptist movement. Despite the fame of Menno Simons* and his own older brother Obbe, Philips wielded great influence over Anabaptists in the Netherlands and northern Germany where he ministered. As a result of Philips's understanding of the apostolic church as radically separated from the children of the world, he advocated a very strict interpretation of the ban, including formal shunning. His writings were collected and published near the end of his life as *Enchiridion oft Hantboecxken van de Christelijcke Leere* (1564).

Obbe Philips (1500–1568). Dutch radical leader. Trained as a physician, Philips was drawn to mystical Anabaptism, as taught by Melchior Hoffman (1495–1543) in his hometown of Leewarden. After adult rebaptism and ordination, he preached in Amsterdam, Delft, Appingedam, and Grongen, and he ordained other leaders including his brother Dirk Philips*, David Joris*, and Menno Simmons*. Disillusioned with the growth of revolutionary, enthusiastic, and apocalyptic elements within Anabaptism and unable to reconcile any visible church with the church of God, Philips withdrew from the radical movement in 1540, after which nothing is known of his life. His only extant writing, entitled *The Confession of Obbe Philips*, was published after his death and recounts elements of the history of the Anabaptist movement and defends his departure from the movement.

James Pilkington (1520-1576). Protestant bishop of Durham and Elizabethan author. Born in Lancashire, Pilkington received his early education at Manchester Grammar School. Afterwards, he entered Pembroke College, Cambridge, and later transferred to St. John's College, Cambridge, from where he graduated with his BA degree in 1539, and MA in 1542. Pilkington was appointed vicar of Kendal in 1545, but resigned this position shortly thereafter in order to return to Cambridge. While there, Pilkington was granted a license to preach, and was awarded the degree of Bachelor of Theology in 1551. In this same year, Pilkington became president of the college. When Mary Tudor succeeded her half-brother, Edward VI, in 1553, Pilkington fled to the Continent where he traveled to Zurich, Geneva, Frankfurt, and Strasbourg. He returned to England in 1559 when Elizabeth I ascended the throne of England. After returning to England, Pilkington became Regius Professor of Divinity at Cambridge and after, bishop of Durham in 1560. Pilkington's major work was his voluminous commentary on the Prophet Haggai.

Charles Pinner (Unknown). English Protestant pastor. Pinner studied at New College, Oxford, and served as rector at Wootton Bassett in Wiltshire. His extant writings include two sermons on 1 Timothy and two on 1 Peter.

Hector Pinto (c. 1528–1584). Portuguese Catholic theologian and exegete. A member of the order of Saint Jerome, Pinto taught theology and Scripture at the Universities of Sigüenza and Coimbra. A respected theologian and exegete, he published commentaries on Daniel, Nahum, Jeremiah, and Isaiah and an influential devotional work, *The Image of the Christian Life.*

Caritas Pirckheimer (1466–1532). German Catholic nun. Sister of famed humanist Wilibald Pirckheimer (1470–1530), Caritas received a humanistic education before entering the Franciscan convent at Nuremberg. Extolled by Erasmus* as one of the most learned women in Europe, Pirckheimer served as abbess at the advent of the Reformation, and her experiences are recorded in a journal covering the pivotal years of 1524–1528. While Nuremberg accepted Lutheran theology under the leadership of the city council and preachers such as Andreas Osiander (1498–1552), Pirckheimer defended the right of her order to continue in their vocation. She ultimately won a concession after a visit from Philipp Melanchthon* in 1525, who recommended that the council allow those who wished to remain in the cloister to live out their vows in peace.

Johannes Piscator (1546–1625). German Reformed theologian. Educated at Tübingen (though he wanted to study at Wittenberg), Piscator taught at the universities of Strasbourg and Heidelberg, as well as academies in Neustadt and Herborn. His commentaries on both the Old and New Testaments involve a tripartite analysis of a given passage's argument, of scholia on the text and of doctrinal loci. Some consider Piscator's method to be a full flowering of Beza's* "logical" scriptural analysis, focused on the text's meaning and its relationship to the pericopes around it.

Amandus Polanus von Polansdorf (1561–1610). German Reformed educator and theologian. Polanus spent his career as an educator, serving as a tutor for noble families and a teacher at the Bohemian Brethren school in Moravia before earning his doctorate and becoming professor of Old Testament and later dean of the theological faculty at the University of Basel. His best-known work is the *Syntagma theologiae christianae* (1609), a compendium of Reformed dogmatics.

Constantino Ponce de la Fuente (1502–1559). Spanish Protestant theologian and preacher. A priest in Seville, Ponce de la Fuente was a critic of the established church and associated with the evangelical circle in the city. A popular preacher, he authored a catechism and a number of books on doctrine and the Christian life that focused on the work of Christ. Charged with heresy by the Inquisition, he admitted to the authorship of a number of heretical writings and died in prison awaiting trial while his works were added to the Index of Prohibited Books.

Matthew Poole (1624–1679). English Nonconformist minister. Having made known his preference for simplicity in worship, Matthew Poole was rector of St Michael-le-Querne until the passing of the 1662 Act of Uniformity led him to resign. Living off his inheritance, he preached occasionally and composed some brief tracts but devoted much of his effort to the compilation of Latin biblical commentary in the *Synopsis criticorum* (1669) and the composition of his own annotations on Scripture. He died in Amsterdam, having fled London during the Popish Plot (1678–1681). He believed his life was in danger for his anti-Catholic writings as part of a Catholic conspiracy to kill Charles II, which was ultimately revealed as a fiction concocted by Titus Oates (1649–1705).

Thomas Porter (d. 1667). English Anglican minister. A graduate of Christ's College, Cambridge, Porter ministered in Flintshire in Cheshire and at Whitchurch in Shropshire. Among his published works are a sermon on Matthew 5:13 and a response to antitrinitarian John Knowles (fl. 1646–1668).

Gabriel Powell (1575–1611). Puritan minister. Powell was born at Ruabon in Denbighshire in 1575. Having completed his studies at Jesus College, Oxford, Powell became master of the free-school in Ruthen. During his tenure at Ruthen, Powell closely studied the writings of the church fathers as well as philosophy, and afterward endeavored to publish several works based on this research. Finding his present location to be a hinderance to his literary objectives, Powell relocated to Oxford, entering St. Mary's Hall, where he finished his anticipated projects. Powell is chiefly known for his literary debate with Thomas Bilson (1547–1619) concerning Christ's descent into hell. Later, Richard Vaughan (1550–1607), bishop of London, appointed Powell his domestic chaplain. Powell died on December 31, 1611. In addition to many controversial and polemical works, Powell wrote a commentary on Romans 1.

Vavasor Powell (1617–1670). Welsh Puritan minister and author. Powell was born at Knucklas, Radnorshire, Wales. After completing his education at Jesus College, Oxford, Powell returned to Wales to assume the position of a local schoolmaster. During this time, Powell came under the influence of Walter Cradock's* preaching as well as the writings of Richard Sibbes* and William Perkins,* resulting in his conversion to Puritanism. Soon thereafter he became an itinerant preacher, traveling throughout Wales. He was arrested twice for nonconformity. During the Civil War, Powell first preached in London, and shortly thereafter pastored an Independent congregation in Wales. On December 26, 1641, Royalist forces arrested and imprisoned Powell. In 1646, as victory for the Puritans appeared inevitable, Powell was released, and allowed to return to Wales, having received a letter of endorsement from the Westminster Assembly. Back in Wales, Powell played a prominent role in the Westminster Assembly's 1650 commission for the better propagation of the gospel throughout Wales. In 1653, Powell returned to London, where he preached at St. Ann Blackfriars. It was at this time that Powell denounced Oliver Cromwell (1599–1658) for assuming the position of Lord Protector. For this reason, he was arrested and imprisoned. At the Restoration in 1660, Powell was again arrested and imprisoned for unauthorized preaching for seven years. Though released in 1667, Powell was once more arrested and incarcerated. He remained in custody until his death on October 27, 1660. Powell authored many poems and a concordance to the Bible.

Felix Pratensis (d. 1539). Italian Catholic Hebraist. Pratensis, the son of a rabbi, converted to Christianity and entered the Augustinian Hermits around the turn of the sixteenth century. In 1515, with papal permission, Pratensis published a new translation of the Psalms based on the Hebrew text. His *Biblia Rabbinica* (1517–1518), printed in Jewish and Christian editions, included text-critical notes in the margins as well as the Targum and rabbinic commentaries on each book (e.g., Rashi* on the Pentateuch and David Kimchi* on the Prophets). Many of the reformers consulted this valuable resource as they labored on their own translations and expositions of the Old Testament.

John Preston (1587–1628). Puritan minister and author. Preston was born at Upper Heyford, Northamptonshire, on October 27, 1587. He studied philosophy at King's College and Queen's College, Cambridge, earning his bachelor's degree in 1607. He became a fellow at Queen's in 1609, and a prebendary at Lincoln Cathedral a year later. During this period, Preston studied medicine and astronomy. In 1611, he received the MA degree. Sometime afterward, he experienced a conversion under the preaching of John Cotton.* After his conversion, Preston went on to study theology, concentrating mainly on Thomas Aquinas,* Duns Scotus, and William of Ockham. From there, he proceeded to the reformers, especially John Calvin.* Preston was appointed court chaplain in 1615. In this position he was influential in the promotion of Puritans to high civil office. Preston later assumed the positions of dean and catechist at Queen's College, Cambridge, where he distinguished himself by preaching a series of sermons that formed the basis of his body of divinity. In 1622, he received the degree of bachelor of divinity, becoming thereafter master of Emmanuel College, Cambridge. While at Emmanuel, Preston participated in the conflict between Calvinism and Arminianism. Moreover, in the same year, Preston succeeded John Donne* as preacher at Lincoln's Inn. Two years later, Preston accepted the lectureship at Trinity Church. He died at the age of forty in 1628. Throughout his prodigious career, Preston authored a sizable corpus, which includes published sermons on Romans.

Quadriga. The *quadriga*, or four senses of Scripture, grew out of the exegetical legacy of Paul's dichotomy of letter and spirit (2 Cor 3:6), as well as church fathers like Origen (c. 185–254), Jerome (c. 347–420) and Augustine* (354–430). Advocates for this method—the primary framework for biblical exegesis during the medieval era—assumed the necessity of the gift of faith under the guidance of the Holy Spirit. The literal-historical meaning of the text served as the foundation for the fuller perception of Scripture's meaning in the three spiritual senses, accessible only through faith: the allegorical sense taught what should be believed, the tropological or moral sense taught what should be done, and the anagogical or eschatological sense taught what should be hoped for. Medieval Jewish exegesis also had a fourfold interpretive method—not necessarily related to the *quadriga*—called *pardes* ("grove"): *peshat*, the simple, literal sense of the text according to grammar; *remez*, the allegorical sense; *derash*, the moral sense; and *sod*, the mystic sense related to Kabbalah. Scholars hotly dispute the precise use and meaning of these terms.

Edward Rainbow[e] (1608–1684). Anglican minister, scholar, and bishop. Rainbow was born at Lincolnshire on April 20, 1608. After completing his education, Rainbow matriculated at Corpus Christi College, and later transferred to Magdalene College, Cambridge, where he graduated with the BA (1627), MA (1630), BD (1637), and DD (1643). He was elected a fellow at Magdalene in 1633 and a master there in 1642. In 1630, Rainbow accepted the mastership of the Kirton-in-Lindsey but shortly afterward moved to London. In 1632, Rainbow took holy orders and preached his first sermon in April of that year. His first appointment was that of curate of Savoy Hospital. Rainbow was recalled to Cambridge in 1633 and elected a fellow. Four years later he became dean of Magdalene and master of the same college in 1642. Though dismissed from his mastership by Parliament in 1650, Rainbow was restored to it in the year of the Restoration (1660). At the same time, he was appointed chaplain to the king. In 1661, Rainbow became dean of Peterborough, and appointed vice chancellor of Cambridge a year later. Rainbow was elected bishop of Carlisle in 1664. As bishop, Rainbow led in the systemic reform of his diocese. Rainbow died March 26, 1684. His published works consist of three published sermons and an incomplete treatise, *Verba Christi*.

Petrus Ramus (1515–1572). French Reformed humanist philosopher. Ramus was an influential professor of philosophy and logic at the French royal college in Paris; he converted to Protestantism and left France for Germany, where he came under the influence of Calvinist thought. Ramus was a trenchant critic of Aristotle and noted for his method of classification based on a deductive movement from universals to particulars, the latter becoming branching divisions that provided a visual chart of the parts to the whole. His system profoundly influenced Puritan theology and preaching. After returning to Paris, Ramus died in the Saint Bartholomew's Day Massacre.

Rashi (Shlomo Yitzchaki) (1040–1105). French Jewish rabbi and exegete. After completing his studies, Rashi founded a yeshiva in Troyes. He composed the first comprehensive commentary on the Talmud, as well as commentaries on the entire Old Testament except for 1–2 Chronicles. These works remain influential within orthodox Judaism. Late medieval and early modern Christian scholars valued his exegesis, characterized by his preference for peshat (see quadriga).

Reformatio Legum Ecclesiasticarum (1552). Under the leadership of Archbishop of Canterbury Thomas Cranmer,* Edward VI* established a committee of thirty-two bishops, theologians, and lawyers including Nicholas Ridley,* John Hooper,* Peter Martyr Vermigli,* Matthew Parker (1504–1575), and William Cecil (1520–1598) to align the laws of the English church with Reformed theology and English civil law. Completed in 1552, it touched on diverse topics, including church organization, doctrine and heresy, qualifications for ministry, and marriage and divorce. It was brought before Parliament in 1553, where it was blocked by John Dudley, Duke of Northumberland (1504–1553), who wished to decrease church powers, and then dropped upon the accession of Mary I. A manuscript of the proposal revised by John Foxe (1516/1517–1587) was published in 1671, and while some elements of the Reformatio Legum Ecclesiasticarum were adopted under Elizabeth I, thoroughgoing reform of ecclesiastical law was not brought about until the *Book of Canons* (1604).

Remonstrance (1610). See *Synod of Dordrecht*.

Johannes Reuchlin (1455–1522). German Catholic lawyer, humanist and Hebraist. Reuchlin held judicial appointments for the dukes of Württemberg, the Supreme Court in Speyer and the imperial court of the Swabian League. He pioneered the study of Hebrew among Christians in Germany, standing against those who, like Johannes Pfefferkorn (1469–1523), wanted to destroy Jewish literature. Among his many works he published a Latin dictionary, an introductory Greek grammar, the most important early modern Hebrew grammar and dictionary (*De rudimentis hebraicis*; 1506), and a commentary on the penitential psalms.

Edward Reynolds (1599–1676). Anglican bishop. Reynolds succeeded John Donne* as the preacher at Lincoln's Inn before entering parish ministry in Northamptonshire. During the English Civil Wars, he supported the Puritans because of his sympathy toward their simplicity and piety—despite believing that Scripture demanded no particular form of government; later he refused to support the abolition of the monarchy. Until the Restoration he ministered in London; afterward he became the bishop of Norwich. He wrote the general thanksgiving prayer which is part of the morning office in the *Book of Common Prayer*.*

Urbanus Rhegius (1489–1541). German Lutheran pastor. Rhegius, who was likely the son of a priest, studied under the humanists at Freiburg and Ingolstadt. After a brief stint as a foot soldier, he received ordination in 1519 and was made cathedral preacher in Augsburg. During his time in Augsburg he closely read Luther's* works, becoming an enthusiastic follower. Despite his close friendship with Zwingli* and Oecolampadius,* Rhegius supported Luther in the eucharistic debates, later playing a major role in the Wittenberg Concord (1536). He advocated for peace during the Peasants' War and had extended interactions with the Anabaptists in Augsburg. Later in his career he concerned himself with the training of pastors, writing a pastoral guide and two catechisms. About one hundred of his writings were published posthumously.

Lancelot Ridley (d. 1576). Anglican preacher. Ridley was the first cousin of Nicholas Ridley,* the bishop of London who was martyred during the Marian persecutions. By Cranmer's* recommendation, Ridley became one of the six Canterbury Cathedral preachers. Upon Mary I's accession in 1553, Ridley was defrocked (as a married priest). Ridley returned to Canterbury Cathedral after Mary's death. He wrote commentaries on Jude, Ephesians, Philippians and Colossians.

Nicholas Ridley (c. 1502–1555). Anglican bishop. Ridley was a student and fellow at Cambridge University who was appointed chaplain to Archbishop Thomas Cranmer* and is thought to be partially responsible for Cranmer's shift to a symbolic view of the Eucharist. Cranmer promoted Ridley twice: as bishop of Rochester, where he openly advocated Reformed theological views, and, later, as bishop of London. Ridley assisted Cranmer in the revisions of the Book of Common Prayer.* Ridley's support of Lady Jane Grey against the claims of Mary to the throne led to his arrest; he was tried for heresy and burned at the stake with Hugh Latimer.*

Peter Riedemann (1506–1556). German Radical elder, theologian and hymnist. While traveling as a Silesian cobbler, Riedemann came into contact with Anabaptist teachings and joined a congregation in Linz. In 1529 he was called to be a minister, only to be imprisoned soon after as part of Archduke Ferdinand's efforts to suppress heterodoxy in his realm. Once he was released, he moved to Moravia in 1532 where he was elected as a minister and missionary of the Hutterite community there. His *Account of Our Religion, Doctrine and Faith* (1542), with its more than two thousand biblical references, is Riedemann's most important work and is still used by Hutterites today.

John Robinson (1576–1625). English Puritan pastor. After his suspension for nonconformity, Robinson fled to the Netherlands with his congregation, eventually settling in Leiden in 1609. Robinson entered into controversies over Arminianism, separation and congregationalism. Most of his healthy congregants immigrated to Plymouth in 1620; Robinson remained in Leiden with those unable to travel.

John Rogers (1505–1555). English Protestant Bible translator. Rogers was born in Deritend, Birmingham. After receiving his early education at the Guild School of St. John the Baptist, Rogers matriculated at Pembroke Hall, Cambridge, where he graduated with the BA degree in 1526. He served as rector of Holy Trinity the Less in London from 1532 to 1534, when he left for the Continent to serve as chaplain to the English merchants of the Company of the Merchant Adventurers. It was at this time that he met William Tyndale,* under whose influence he came to embrace an evangelical faith. After Tyndale's death, Rogers completed his late colleague's translation of the Old Testament, which had ended with 2 Chronicles, by adding Miles Coverdale's translation of the remainder, including the Apocrypha. The resulting work, known as the "Matthew Bible" (Rogers published it under the pseudonym "Thomas Matthew") was published in 1537. It has the distinction of being the first complete English Bible translated essentially from the original languages to be printed. "Matthew's Bible" served as the basis for the Great Bible (1540), which in turn was used by those who prepared the Bishops' Bible (1568), on which later the King James Version (1611) was produced. In 1540, Rogers enrolled at the University of Wittenberg, where he became close friends with Philipp Melanchthon.* During his three years at Wittenberg, Rogers was a superintendent of the Lutheran Church in northern Germany. When Rogers returned to England in 1548, he published a translation of Melanchthon's *Considerations of the Augsburg Interim*, and later served in a variety of ecclesiastical roles. Rogers was burned at the stake for heresy during the reign of Mary Tudor on February 4, 1555.

Nehemiah Rogers (1593–1660). Anglican priest. After studying at Cambridge, Rogers ministered at numerous parishes during his more than forty-year career. In 1643, he seems to have been forced out of a parish on account of being a Royalist and friend of William Laud.* Rogers published a number of sermons and tracts, including a series of expositions on Jesus' parables in the Gospels.

Richard Rogers (1550?–1618). English Presbyterian minister. Rogers spent much of his career as lecturer at Wethersfield, Essex, where he was well-known as a Nonconformist. His writings, which include an introduction to the Christian life and a commentary on the book of Judges, demonstrate his Puritan leanings.

Thomas Rogers (d. 1616). Anglican theologian and translator. Rogers attended Christ Church, Oxford, where he completed his BA degree in 1573 and MA in 1576. Later he served as rector of Horrigner in Suffolk, and chaplain to Archbishop of Canterbury, Richard Bancroft. He died at Horringer and was buried in his church. Among his many works were an exposition of the Thirty-Nine Articles as well as a paraphrase of the Psalms and a translation of Niels Hemmingsen's commentary on Psalm 84.

Robert Rollock (c. 1555–1599). Scottish Reformed pastor, educator and theologian. Rollock was deeply influenced by Petrus Ramus's* system of logic, which he implemented as a tutor and (later) principal of Edinburgh University and in his expositions of the Bible. Rollock, as a divinity professor and theologian, was instrumental in diffusing a federalist Calvinism in the Scottish church; he lectured on theology using the texts of Theodore Beza* and articulated a highly covenantal interpretation of the biblical narratives. He was a prolific writer of sermons, expositions, commentaries, lectures and occasional treatises.

David Runge (1564–1604). German Lutheran theologian. First appointed professor of Hebrew at the University of Greifswald, Runge supported and later replaced his father in teaching philosophy and theology. After receiving his doctorate, he was named to the theological faculty at Wittenberg, where he also served as dean and rector of the university.

Johann Rurer (1480–1542). German Lutheran pastor. Rurer was court chaplain to Margrave Casimir of Brandenberg–Kulmbach (1481–1527), and the first Protestant pastor in Ansbach. Conflict over church order and his desire for reform led to his expulsion, but he was recalled after Casimir's death by his successor, George (1484–1543), who sought a throughgoing Lutheran reformation of the town and appointed Rurer preacher at the collegiate church.

Samuel Rutherford (1600–1661). Scottish Reformed theologian. Rutherford was born in Nisbet, Roxburghshire. After completing his early education at Jedborough, Rutherford enrolled at the University of Edinburgh, where he received his MA degree in 1621. In 1623, Rutherford was appointed professor of humanities at Edinburgh. Two years later, he was dismissed from his position on account of misbehavior with the woman who would later be his wife. Sometime after this incident, he underwent a spiritual conversion. In 1625, Rutherford commenced the study of theology at Edinburgh. Upon finishing his studies, Rutherford was called to pastor a church in Antwoth by Solway in Kirkcudbrightshire. Throughout his ministry, Rutherford proved to be an ardent opponent to episcopacy. For this, he was summoned to appear before the Court of High Commission in 1630. Despite the court's warnings to cease and desist, Rutherford continued his nonconformity. Rutherford also participated extensively in the Arminian controversy, writing treatises against Arminius as well as the Jesuits. Since Rutherford's virulent opposition to Arminianism placed him in direct opposition with the English episcopacy, he was once again summoned by the Court of High Commission in 1636. After a three-day trial, Rutherford was deprived of his ministerial office and ordered not to preach anywhere in Scotland. Meanwhile he was confined to Aberdeen. In 1638, when the National Covenant was signed and Presbyterianism restored in Scotland, Rutherford left Aberdeen and assumed the post of professor of theology at St. Mary's College, St. Andrews. Later, Rutherford served as a commissioner to the Westminster Assembly, where he contributed to the discussions related to the Shorter Catechism. In 1647, Rutherford returned to Scotland, where he was appointed principal of St. Mary's College, and rector of the university in 1651. After the monarchy was restored, Rutherford was charged with treason, and deprived of all his ecclesiastical and university positions. He died on March 30, 1661. Throughout his career, Rutherford published many sermons and theological works, most famous of which is *Lex Rex* (The law is king), a treatise arguing against the divine right of kings.

Jacopo Sadoleto (1477–1547). Italian Catholic Cardinal. Sadoleto, attaché to Leo X's court, was appointed bishop in 1517, cardinal in 1536. He participated in the reform commission led by Gasparo Contarini.* However, he tried to reconcile with Protestants apart from the commission, sending several letters to Protestant leaders in addition to his famous letter to the city of Geneva, which John Calvin* pointedly answered. Sadoleto published a commentary on Romans that was censored as semi-Pelagian. His insufficient treatment of prevenient grace left him vulnerable to this charge. Sadoleto emphasized grammar as the rule and norm of exegesis.

Alfonso Salmerón (1515–1585). Spanish Catholic exegete and theologian. While studying at the Sorbonne, Salmerón met Ignatius Loyola (1491–1556) and, with five others, took a vow of poverty and service to church and pope. After ministering in France, the group traveled to Rome, where they were given papal approval to form the Society of Jesus. Salmerón helped write the constitutions of the order, and following the priorities of the Jesuits, spent much of his career focused on education. He lectured throughout Italy, served briefly on the faculty of the University of Ingolstadt, and, in Naples, founded one of the first Jesuit colleges. He also undertook a number of missions as a papal emissary and served as a papal theologian at all three meetings of the

Council of Trent. His primary works are his commentaries on the New Testament, which cover the Gospels, Acts, and Paul's letters.

Heinrich Salmuth (1522–1576). German Lutheran theologian. After earning his doctorate from the University of Leipzig, Salmuth served in several coterminous pastoral and academic positions. He was integral to the reorganization of the University of Jena. Except for a few disputations, all of Salmuth's works—mostly sermons—were published posthumously by his son.

Robert Sanderson (1587–1663). Anglican bishop and philosopher. Before his appointment as professor of divinity at Oxford in 1642, Sanderson pastored in several parishes. Because of his loyalty to the Crown during the English Civil Wars, the Parliamentarians stripped Sanderson of his post at Oxford. After the Restoration he was reinstated at Oxford and consecrated bishop. He wrote an influential textbook on logic.

Edwin Sandys (1519–1588). Anglican bishop. During his doctoral studies at Cambridge, Sandys befriended Martin Bucer.* Having supported the Protestant Lady Jane Grey's claim to the throne, Sandys resigned his post at Cambridge upon Mary I's accession. He was then arrested and imprisoned in the Tower of London. Released in 1554, he sojourned on the continent until Mary's death. On his return to England he was appointed to revise the liturgy and was consecrated bishop. Many of his sermons were published, but his most significant literary legacy is his work as a translator of the Bishop's Bible (1568), which served as the foundational English text for the translators of the King James Bible (1611).

Erasmus Sarcerius (1501–1559). German Lutheran superintendent, educator and pastor. Sarcerius served as educational superintendent, court preacher and pastor in Nassau and, later, in Leipzig. The hallmark of Sarcerius's reputation was his ethical emphasis as exercised through ecclesial oversight and family structure; he also drafted disciplinary codes for regional churches in Germany. Sarcerius served with Philipp Melanchthon* as Protestant delegates at the Council of Trent, though both withdrew prior to the dismissal of the session; he eventually became an opponent of Melanchthon, contesting the latter's understanding of the Eucharist at a colloquy in Worms in 1557.

Adam Sasbout (1516-1553) Dutch Catholic monk. A lector at the Franciscan monastery in Louvain, Sasbout authored exegetical works on Leviticus and Isaiah and many of his sermons were published posthumously.

Michael Sattler (c. 1490–1527). Swiss Radical leader. Sattler was a Benedictine monk who abandoned the monastic life during the upheavals of the Peasants' War. He took up the trade of weaving under the guidance of an outspoken Anabaptist. It seems that Sattler did not openly join the Anabaptist movement until after the suppression of the Peasants' War in 1526. Sattler interceded with Martin Bucer* and Wolfgang Capito* for imprisoned Anabaptists in Strasbourg. Shortly before he was convicted of heresy and executed, he wrote the definitive expression of Anabaptist theology, the Schleitheim Articles.*

Girolamo Savonarola (1452–1498). Italian Catholic preacher and martyr. Outraged by clerical corruption and the neglect of the poor, Savonarola traveled to preach against these abuses and to prophesy impending judgment—a mighty king would scourge and reform the church. Savonarola thought that the French invasion of Italy in 1494 confirmed his apocalyptic visions. Thus he pressed to purge Florence of vice and institute public welfare, in order to usher in a new age of Christianity. Florence's refusal to join papal resistance against the French enraged Alexander VI (r. 1492–1503). He blamed Savonarola, promptly excommunicating him and threatening Florence with an interdict. After an ordeal by fire turned into a riot, Savonarola was arrested. Under torture he admitted to charges of conspiracy and false prophecy; he was hanged and burned. In addition to numerous sermons and letters, he wrote meditations on Psalms 31 and 51 as well as *The Triumph of the Cross* (1497).

Leupold Scharnschlager (d. 1563). Austrian Radical elder. See *Kunstbuch.*

Leonhard Schiemer (d. 1528) Austrian radical martyr. Troubled by the hypocrisies he experienced, Schiemer left the Franciscan order and spent a period of time wandering. Attracted to the teachings of Hans Hut* after hearing him debate Balthasar Hubmaier* in Moravia, he was rebaptized and traveled widely throughout Austria and Southern Germany, spreading the Anabaptist message until he was arrested in Rattenberg, where he was condemned to death and beheaded. A number of his essays and hymns survive, dispersed among the *Kunstbuch** and other collections of radical writings.

Hans Schlaffer (c. 1490–1528). Austrian Radical martyr. Drawn by Luther's theology, Schlaffer resigned his priesthood in 1526 only to turn to Anabaptism soon afterward. While contemporaries recognized his ability as a preacher, he never settled in a ministry position. He spent time among Radical congregations in Freistadt, Nicholsburg, Augsburg, Nuremberg, and Regensburg before his arrest in Schatz, where he was executed. Nine writings by Schlaffer remain, most of which were composed during his imprisonment. They include confessions of his beliefs and devotional works, which have been preserved among Hutterite churches.

Schleitheim Articles (1527). After the death of Conrad Grebel* in 1526 and the execution of Felix Manz (born c. 1498) in early 1527, the young Swiss Anabaptist movement was in need of unity and direction. A synod convened at Schleitheim under the chairmanship of Michael Sattler,* which passed seven articles of Anabaptist distinctives—likely defined against both magisterial reformers and other Anabaptists with less orthodox and more militant views (e.g., Balthasar Hubmaier*). Unlike most confessions, these articles do not explicitly address traditional creedal interests; they explicate instead the Anabaptist view of the sacraments, church discipline, separatism, the role of ministers, pacifism and oaths. Throughout the document there is a resolute focus on Christ's example. Also referred to as the Schleitheim Confession and the Schleitheim Brotherly Union, the Schleitheim Articles are considered the definitive statement of Anabaptist theology, particularly regarding separatism.

Schmalkald Articles (1537). In response to Pope Paul III's (1468–1549) 1536 decree ordering a general church council to solve the Protestant crisis, Elector John Frederick (1503–1554) commissioned Martin Luther* to draft the sum of his teaching. Intended by Luther as a last will and testament—and composed with advice from well-known colleagues Justus Jonas,* Johann Bugenhagen,* Caspar Cruciger,* Nikolaus von Amsdorf (1483–1565), Georg Spalatin (1484–1545), Philipp Melanchthon* and Johann Agricola*—these articles provide perhaps the briefest and most systematic summary of Luther's teaching. The document was not adopted formally by the Lutheran Schmalkald League, as was hoped, and the general church council was postponed for several years (until convening at Trent in 1545). Only in 1580 were the articles officially received, by being incorporated into the *Book of Concord* defining orthodox Lutheranism.

Sebastian Schmidt (1617–1696). German Lutheran theologian. After serving as pastor in Entzheim and rector of the high school in Lindau, Schmidt became professor of theology at Strasbourg. His body of writings is extensive and includes commentaries on many of the Pauline letters, Hebrews, John, and Jeremiah.

Dietrich Schnepff (1525–1586). German Lutheran pastor and theologian. Schnepff taught briefly at the city school in Tübingen while working toward his theological doctorate before taking pastorates in Derendingen and Nürtingen. Returning to Tübingen as professor of theology, Schnepff also took on additional roles as rector of the university and pastor of the Collegiate Church.

Anna Maria van Schurman (1607–1678). Dutch Reformed polymath. Van Schurman cultivated talents in art, poetry, botany, linguistics and theology. She mastered most contemporary European languages, in addition to Latin, Greek, Hebrew, Arabic, Farsi and Ethiopian. With the encouragement of leading Reformed theologian Gisbertus Voetius (1589–1676), van Schurman attended lectures at the University of Utrecht—although she was required to sit behind a wooden screen so that the male students could not see her. In 1638 van Schurman published her famous treatise advocating female scholarship, *Amica dissertatio . . . de capacitate ingenii muliebris ad scientias*. In addition to these more polemical works, van Schurman also wrote hymns and poems, including a paraphrase of Genesis 1–3. Later in life she became a devotee of Jean de Labadie (1610–1674), a former Jesuit who was also expelled from the Reformed church for his separatist leanings. Her *Eucleria* (1673) is the most well known defense of Labadie's theology.

Kaspar von Schwenckfeld (1489–1561). German Radical reformer. Schwenckfeld was a Silesian nobleman who encountered Luther's* works in 1521. He traveled to Wittenberg twice: first to meet Luther and Karlstadt,* and a second time to convince Luther of his doctrine of the "internal word"—emphasizing inner revelation so strongly that he did not see church meetings or the sacraments as necessary—after which Luther considered him heterodox. Schwenckfeld won his native territory to the Reformation in 1524 and later lived in Strasbourg for five years until Bucer* sought to purify the city of less traditional theologies. Schwenckfeld wrote numerous polemical and exegetical tracts.

Scots Confession (1560). In 1560, the Scottish Parliament undertook to reform the Church of Scotland and to commission a Reformed confession of faith. In the course of four days, a committee—which included John Knox*—wrote this confession, largely based on Calvin's* work, the Confession of the English Congregation in Geneva (1556) and the Gallic Confession.* The articles were not ratified until 1567 and were displaced by the Westminster Confession (1646), adopted by the Scottish in 1647.

Abraham Scultetus (1566–1625). Silesian Reformed theologian. Scultetus spent the majority of his career in service of the Palatinate, holding a number of pastoral roles before becoming court preacher to Elector Frederic V (1596–1632). Appointed professor of theology at

Heidelberg in 1618, he represented the Palatinate at the Synod of Dordrecht* (1618–1619), where he opposed the theology of the Remonstrants. Scultetus is often vilified for encouraging Reformed Frederic V to take the crown of Lutheran Bohemia, an act that led to war and the defeat of Frederic V, but his exegetical, historical, and pastoral teachings nevertheless garnered significant respect from his contemporaries.

Second Helvetic Confession (1566). Believing he would soon die, Heinrich Bullinger* penned a personal statement of his Reformed faith in 1561 as a theological will. In 1563, Bullinger sent a copy of this confession, which blended Zwingli's and Calvin's theology, to the elector of the Palatinate, Frederick III (1515–1576), who had asked for a complete explication of the Reformed faith in order to defend himself against aggressive Lutheran attacks after printing the Heidelberg Confession.* Although not published until 1566, the Second Helvetic Confession became the definitive sixteenth-century Reformed statement of faith. Theodore Beza* used it as the organizing confession for his *Harmonia Confessionum* (1581), which sought to emphasize the unity of the Reformed churches. Bullinger's personal confession was adopted by the Reformed churches of Scotland (1566), Hungary (1567), France (1571) and Poland (1571).

Obadiah Sedgwick (c. 1600–1658). English Puritan minister. Educated at Oxford, Sedgwick pastored in London and participated in the Westminster Assembly. An ardent Puritan, Sedgwick was appointed by Oliver Cromwell (1599–1658) to examine clerical candidates. Sedgwick published a catechism, several sermons and a treatise on how to deal with doubt.

Nikolaus Selnecker (1530–1592). German Lutheran theologian, preacher, pastor and hymnist. Selnecker taught in Wittenberg, Jena and Leipzig, preached in Dresden and Wolfenbüttel, and pastored in Leipzig. He was forced out of his post at Jena because of suspicions that he was a crypto-Calvinist. He sought refuge in Wolfenbüttel, where he met Martin Chemnitz* and Jakob Andreae.* Under their influence Selnecker was drawn away from Philippist theology. Selnecker's shift in theology can be seen in his *Institutio religionis christianae* (1573). Selnecker coauthored the Formula of Concord* with Chemnitz, Andreae, Andreas Musculus (1514–1581), and David Chytraeus.* Selnecker also published lectures on Genesis, the Psalms, and the New Testament epistles, as well as composing over a hundred hymn tunes and texts.

Jean de Serres (1540–1598). French Reformed pastor and historian. Serres fled France under persecution and studied at Lausanne and Geneva before being called to the Genevan parish of Jussy. After publishing a commentary on the French civil wars, he was disciplined and deposed for abandoning his ministry. Relocating to Lausanne, Serres became principal of the college and published a three-volume translation of Plato's works then moved to reform the College of Nimes. He became an advisor to King Henry IV* and was given the title "Historian of France." In this role, he sought resolution of the civil wars and composed a short history of France.

Short Confession (1610). In response to some of William Laud's* reforms in the Church of England—particularly a law stating that ministers who refused to comply with the Book of Common Prayer* would lose their ordination—a group of English Puritans immigrated to the Netherlands in protest, where they eventually embraced the practice of believer's baptism. The resulting Short Confession was an attempt at union between these Puritans and local Dutch Anabaptists ("Waterlanders"). The document highlights the importance of love in the church and reflects optimism regarding the freedom of the will while explicitly rejecting double predestination.

Richard Sibbes (1577–1635). English Puritan preacher. Sibbes was educated at St. John's College, Cambridge, where he was converted to reforming views and became a popular preacher. As a moderate Puritan emphasizing interior piety and brotherly love, Sibbes always remained within the established Church of England, though opposed to some of its liturgical ceremonies. His collected sermons constitute his main literary legacy.

Menno Simons (c. 1496–1561). Dutch Radical leader. Simons led a separatist Anabaptist group in the Netherlands that would later be called Mennonites, known for nonviolence and renunciation of the world. A former priest, Simons rejected Catholicism through the influence of Anabaptist disciples of Melchior Hoffmann and based on his study of Scripture, in which he found no support for transubstantiation or infant baptism. Following the sack of Anabaptists at Münster, Simons committed to a nonviolent way of life. Simons proclaimed a message of radical discipleship of obedience and inner purity, marked by voluntary adult baptism and communal discipline.

Henry Smith (c. 1550–1591). English Puritan minister. Smith stridently opposed the Book of Common Prayer* and refused to subscribe to the Articles of Religion,* thus limiting his pastoral opportunities. Nevertheless he gained a reputation as an eloquent preacher in London. He published sermon collections as well as several treatises.

John Smyth (d. 1612). English Baptist minister. Ordained as an Anglican clergyman, Smyth served as a lecturer in Lincoln, but left the established church for a separatist congregation in Gainsborough. Moving to Amsterdam, he began to follow the teachings of Jacobus Arminius* and led a group to break away from the English Reformed congregation, undertake rebaptism, and form their own church. He soon decided he did not have the authority to establish a church and baptize, but trying to lead his congregation on another course saw him excommunicated with a number of his close followers. This smaller group was rejected when they attempted to join a Mennonite congregation, and so were forced to form another congregation, which dissolved after Smyth's death. Smyth wrote a number of the earliest English treatises expressing Baptist principles including *The Differences of the Churches of the Separation* (1608) and *The Character of the Beast* (1609). He also wrote a reflection on the Lord's Prayer, *A Paterne of True Prayer* (1605).

Domingo de Soto (1494–1560). Spanish Catholic theologian. Soto taught philosophy for four years at the University in Alcalá before entering the Dominican order. In 1532 he became chair of theology at the University of Salamanca; Soto sought to reintroduce Aristotle in the curriculum. He served as confessor and spiritual advisor to Charles V, who enlisted Soto as imperial theologian for the Council of Trent. Alongside commentaries on the works of Aristotle and Peter Lombard (c. 1100–1160), Soto commented on Romans and wrote an influential treatise on nature and grace.

Fausto Sozzini (1539–1604). Italian theologian. Without a formal education, Sozzini used his inherited wealth to travel widely throughout Europe after his family came under the suspicion of the Inquisition for Lutheranism. Spending time in Lyons, Zurich, and Geneva, he published his first work, an explanation of the prologue to John's Gospel, claiming Christ was not divine, but a human worthy of respect due his divinely appointed office. Returning to Italy, Sozzini served at the Florentine court of Isabella de Medici (1542–1576) for more than a decade, departing for Basel, then Transylvania and Poland after her death. His thoroughgoing rationalism saw him elevate human reason over divine revelation and traditional doctrine. He rejected the doctrine of the Trinity and Nicene orthodoxy, instead arguing that Christ was not divine and did not make atonement for humanity, but rather served as a model of victory over death for all people.

Cyriacus Spangenberg (1528–1604). German Lutheran pastor, preacher and theologian. Spangenberg was a staunch, often acerbic, Gnesio-Lutheran. He rejected the Formula of Concord* because of concerns about the princely control of the church, as well as its rejection of Flacian language of original sin (as constituting the "substance" of human nature after the fall). He published many commentaries and sermons, most famously seventy wedding sermons (*Ehespiegel* [1561]), his sermons on Luther* (*Theander Luther* [1562–1571]) and Luther's hymns (*Cithara Lutheri* [1569–1570]). He also published an analysis of the Old Testament (though he only got as far as Job), based on a methodology that anticipated the logical bifurcations of Peter Ramus.*

Johann Spangenberg (1484–1550). German Lutheran pastor and catechist. Spangenberg studied at the University of Erfurt, where he was welcomed into a group of humanists associated with Konrad Muth (1470–1526). There he met the reformer Justus Jonas,* and Eobanus Hessius (1488–1540), whom Luther* dubbed "king of the poets." Spangenberg served at parishes in Stolberg (1520–1524), Nordhausen (1524–1546) and, by Luther's recommendation, Eisleben (1546–1550). Spangenberg published one of the best-selling postils of the sixteenth century, the *Postilla Teütsch*, a six-volume work meant to prepare children to understand the lectionary readings. It borrowed the question-answer form of Luther's *Small Catechism* and was so popular that a monk, Johannes Craendonch, purged overt anti-Catholic statements from it and republished it under his own name. Among Spangenberg's other pastoral works are *ars moriendi* ("the art of dying") booklets, a postil for the Acts of the Apostles and a question-answer version of Luther's *Large Catechism*. In addition to preaching and pastoring, Spangenberg wrote pamphlets on controversial topics such as purgatory, as well as textbooks on music, mathematics and grammar.

John Spilsbury (1593–1668). English Baptist pastor. A cobbler by trade, Spilsbury left congregationalism to found the first Particular Baptist church in London, teaching a theology that attempted to fuse Reformed teachings on the covenant and particular atonement with the Anabaptist demand for adult baptism upon confession of faith. He composed a number of works on baptism and may have been an author of the 1644 London Baptist Confession of Faith.

Georg Spindler (1525–1605). German Reformed theologian and pastor. After studying theology under Caspar Cruciger* and Philipp Melanchthon,* Spindler accepted a pastorate in Bohemia. A well-respected preacher, Spindler published postils in 1576 which some of his peers viewed as crypto-Calvinist. To investigate this allegation Spindler read John Calvin's* *Institutes*, and subsequently converted to the Reformed faith. After years of travel, he settled in the Palatinate and pastored there until his death. In addition to his Lutheran postils,

Spindler also published Reformed postils in 1594 as well as several treatises on the Lord's Supper and predestination.
Statenvertaling (1637). The Synod of Dordrecht* commissioned this new Dutch translation of the Bible ("State's Translation"). The six theologians who undertook this translation also wrote prefaces for each biblical book, annotated obscure words and difficult passages, and provided cross-references; they even explained certain significant translation decisions. At the request of the Westminster Assembly, Theodore Haak (1605–1690) translated the *Statenvertaling* into English as *The Dutch Annotations Upon the Whole Bible* (1657).
John Stalham (d. 1681). English Puritan minister. Stalham likely ministered in Edinburgh before becoming vicar of Terling in Essex. An opponent of Quakerism who sought to remove disreputable ministers from their pulpits, Stalham himself lost his position with the 1662 Act of Uniformity, leading him to found a congregational church in the same village.
Johann von Staupitz (d. 1524). German Catholic theologian, professor and preacher. Frederick the Wise summoned this Augustinian monk to serve as professor of Bible and first dean of the theology faculty at the University of Wittenberg. As Vicar-General of the Reformed Augustinian Hermits in Germany, Staupitz sought to reform the order and attempted unsuccessfully to reunite with the conventional Augustinians. While in Wittenberg, Staupitz was Martin Luther's* teacher, confessor and spiritual father. He supported Luther in the early controversies over indulgences, but after releasing Luther from his monastic vows (to protect him), he distanced himself from the conflict. He relocated to Salzburg, where he was court preacher to Cardinal Matthäus Lang von Wellenburg (d. 1540) and abbot of the Benedictine monastery. Staupitz wrote treatises on predestination, faith and the love of God. Many of his sermons were collected and published during his lifetime.
Peter Sterry (d. 1672). English Puritan theologian. Associated with the Cambridge Platonists, Sterry was closely aligned with the Parliamentarians during the English Civil War, serving as chaplain to Robert Greville (1607–1643) and Oliver Cromwell.* After the execution of Charles I, he was appointed preacher to the Council of State and asked to examine its ministers. Cast out from influence after Cromwell's death, Sperry spent the last years of his career writing and tutoring private students.
Petrus Stevartius (1549–1624). German Catholic theologian. A Jesuit, Stevartius spent most of his career as professor of exegesis at the University of Ingolstadt, also serving as rector and procurator. He also established a library for the school and an orphanage in the city. His writings include commentaries on most Pauline letters and James and a defense of the Jesuits.
Michael Stifel (1486–1567). German Lutheran mathematician, theologian and pastor. An Augustinian monk, Stifel's interest in mysticism, apocalypticism and numerology led him to identify Pope Leo X as the antichrist. Stifel soon joined the reform movement, writing a 1522 pamphlet in support of Martin Luther's* theology. After Luther quelled the fallout of Stifel's failed prediction of the Apocalypse—October 19, 1533 at 8 a.m.—Stifel focused more on mathematics and his pastoral duties. He was the first professor of mathematics at the University of Jena. He published several numerological interpretations of texts from the Gospels, Daniel and Revelation. However, Stifel's most important work is his *Arithmetica Integra* (1544), in which he standardized the approach to quadratic equations. He also developed notations for exponents and radicals.
John Stoughton (1593?–1639). English Puritan minister. Stoughton pastored at Aller in Somerset and St. Mary Aldermanbury in the city of London. A Puritan, he was briefly arrested by Archbishop Laud, accused of financially supporting the Puritan cause. A collection of his sermons and other writings was published after his death.
Viktorin Strigel (1524–1569). German Lutheran theologian. Strigel taught at Wittenberg, Erfurt, Jena, Leipzig and Heidelberg. During his time in Jena he disputed with Matthias Flacius (1520–1575) over the human will's autonomy. Following Philipp Melanchthon,* Strigel asserted that in conversion the human will obediently cooperates with the divine will through the Holy Spirit and the Word of God. In the Weimar Disputation (1560), Strigel elicited Flacius's opinion that sin is a substance that mars the formal essence of human beings. Flacius's views were officially rejected in Article 1 of the Formula of Concord*; Strigel's, in Article 2. In 1567 the University of Leipzig suspended Strigel from teaching on account of suspicions that he affirmed Reformed Eucharistic theology; he acknowledged that he did and joined the Reformed confession on the faculty of the University of Heidelberg. In addition to controversial tracts, Strigel published commentaries on the entire Bible (except Lamentations) and the Apocrypha.
William Strode (1602–1645). English Anglican minister, dramatist, and poet. A Royalist and an opponent of Puritanism, Strode spent most of his life around Oxford, where he studied and then served as a public orator and canon of Christ Church. A popular poet, he also preached

a number of times before the king and had a number of his plays performed at court.

William Strong (d. 1654). English Independent minister. Forced to leave his ministry in Dorset by Royalists during the Civil War, Strong built a reputation as a preacher in London, ministering to an independent congregation at St. Dunstan's-in-the-West. Many of his sermons were published, as well as treatises on communion with God and the covenants.

Johann Sutell (1504–1575). German Lutheran pastor. After studying at the University of Wittenberg, Sutell received a call to a pastorate in Göttingen, where he eventually became superintendent. He wrote new church orders for Göttingen (1531) and Schweinfurt (1543), and expanded two sermons for publication, *The Dreadful Destruction of Jerusalem* (1539) and *History of Lazarus* (1543).

Swiss Brethren Confession of Hesse (1578). Anabaptist leader Hans Pauly Kuchenbecker penned this confession after a 1577 interrogation by Lutheran authorities. This confession was unusually amenable to Lutheran views—there is no mention of pacifism or rejection of oath taking.

Synod of Dordrecht (1618–1619). This large Dutch Reformed Church council—also attended by English, German and Swiss delegates—met to settle the theological issues raised by the followers of Jacobus Arminius.* Arminius's theological disagreements with mainstream Reformed teaching erupted into open conflict with the publication of the *Remonstrance* (1610). This "protest" was based on five points: that election is based on foreseen faith or unbelief; that Christ died indiscriminately for all people (although only believers receive salvation); that people are thoroughly sinful by nature apart from the prevenient grace of God that enables their free will to embrace or reject the gospel; that humans are able to resist the working of God's grace; and that it is possible for true believers to fall away from faith completely. The Synod ruled in favor of the Contra-Remonstrants, its Canons often remembered with a TULIP acrostic—total depravity, unconditional election, limited atonement, irresistible grace, perseverance of the saints—each letter countering one of the five Remonstrant articles. The Synod also officially accepted the Belgic Confession,* Heidelberg Catechism* and the Canons of Dordrecht as standards of the Dutch Reformed Church.

Arcangela Tarabotti (1604–1652). Italian Catholic nun. At the age of eleven, Tarabotti entered a Benedictine convent as a student-boarder; three years later her father forced her to take monastic vows. The dignity of women and their treatment in the male-controlled institutions of early modern Venice concerned Tarabotti deeply. She protested forced cloistering, the denial of education to women, the exclusion of women from public life and the double standards by which men and women were judged. Tarbotti authored numerous polemical works and an extensive correspondence.

Johannes Tauler (c. 1300–1361). German mystical theologian. A Dominican friar and disciple of Meister Eckhart (c. 1260–c. 1328), Tauler spent most of his career as a mendicant preacher in Strasburg and Basel. Known through a collection of about eighty German sermons, Tauler taught a practical spirituality, accessible to those outside the cloister and intended to draw his audience to deeper contemplation of the divine nature.

Richard Taverner (1505–1575). English Puritan humanist and translator. After graduating from Oxford, Taverner briefly studied abroad. When he returned to England, he joined Thomas Cromwell's (1485–1540) circle. After Cromwell's beheading, Taverner escaped severe punishment and retired from public life during Mary I's reign. Under Elizabeth I,* Taverner served as justice of the peace, sheriff and a licensed lay preacher. Taverner translated many important continental Reformation works into English, most notably the Augsburg Confession* and several of Desiderius Erasmus's* works. Some of these translations—John Calvin's* 1536 catechism, Wolfgang Capito's* work on the Psalms and probably Erasmus Sarcerius's* postils—he presented as his own work. Underwritten by Cromwell, Taverner also published an edited version of the Matthew Bible (1537).

Francis Taylor (1590–1656). English Presbyterian minister. After graduating from Cambridge, Taylor served as vicar of Yalding in Kent and rector of Clapham in Surrey. He was a member of the Westminster Assembly of Divines and was a member of the College of Six Preachers at Canterbury Cathedral.

Jeremy Taylor (1613–1667). Anglican theologian, preacher, and author. Son of a barber, Taylor studied at Cambridge before the patronage of Archbishop Laud* drew him into the work of the English church. After serving as chaplain to Laud and King Charles I (1600–1649), he entered parish ministry. Following the outbreak of the Civil War (1642–51), his commitment to the Royalist cause saw him imprisoned at least three times. Withdrawing to Wales, he ran a school preparing students for university while serving as chaplain to the earl of Carbery. Known for his skill as a writer, it was here that Taylor composed many of his best known works, including his popular devotional manuals, *The Rules and Exercises of Holy Living* (1650), and *The Rules and*

Exercises of Holy Dying (1651). After the Restoration, Taylor was made Bishop of Down and Connor in Ireland and served as vice-chancellor of the University of Dublin.
Thomas Taylor (1576–1633). English Puritan pastor. Taylor ministered in Watford and Reading before becoming minister at St. Mary Aldermanbury in the city of London. He wrote more than fifty works on diverse topics, including a commentary on Titus, a response to the Gunpowder Plot, and an explanation of the role of the law under the gospel.
Thomas Taylor (1576–1632). Puritan minister and commentator. Taylor was born in Richmond, Yorkshire. He was educated at Christ's College, Cambridge, where he earned the degrees of Bachelor of Arts (1595) and Master of Arts (1598). Prior to entering pastoral ministry, Taylor served as a fellow and lecturer in Hebrew at the university. Throughout his academic career, Taylor was significantly influenced by the writings of William Perkins.* At the age of twenty-five, Taylor preached a virulent sermon against the papacy before Queen Elizabeth I.* As a Puritan, Taylor denounced the ecclesiastical policies of Archbishop Richard Bancroft.* In 1612, Taylor became minister of a church in Watford, Hertfordshire. While serving this charge, Taylor preached regularly in Berkshire and Reading. Moreover, Taylor formed and led a Puritan seminary, where he personally trained Nonconformist preachers. In the early 1620s, Taylor served as a chaplain to Edward Conway (1564–1631), secretary of state under James VI/I* (1566–1625). In 1625, Taylor was called to be curate and lecturer at St. Aldermanbury, London. While there, he organized and ran another Puritan seminary. Two years later, Taylor joined several other Puritans' efforts to send relief to oppressed Reformed ministers on the Continent. Taylor retired from his labors in 1630 due to ill health. He died of pleurisy in 1632. His main works include *Christ Revealed; or The Old Testament Explained* and *An Exposition of Titus*.
Teresa of Ávila (1515–1582). Spanish monastic reformer and mystical theologian. Born into a wealthy merchant family, Teresa entered the Carmelite order at Ávila in 1535. While Teresa initially enjoyed the lax practices of the convent, reading devotional literature caused her to deepen her spirituality, and in 1555 she began to have visions of God and claimed to have mystical union with him. Convinced the monastic life required complete withdrawal, Teresa could no longer tolerate the practices of her Carmelite cloister and founded the Discalced Carmelites with John of the Cross* (1542–1591) in 1562, which was committed to enclosure and strict asceticism. By her death, she had personally founded fourteen houses for her new order despite significant resistance from Carmelite leaders. She also wrote extensively. Her best-known works are *The Way of Perfection* (1577), a method for the contemplative life, and *The Interior Castle* (1577), a manual for spiritual growth.
Thirty-Nine Articles. See *Articles of Religion*.
Thomas Thorowgood (1595–1669). English Puritan pastor. Thorowgood was a Puritan minister in Norfolk and the chief financier of John Eliot (1604–1690), a Puritan missionary among the Native American tribes in Massachusetts. In 1650, under the title *Jews in America, or, Probabilities that Americans be of that Race*, Thorowgood became one of the first to put forward the thesis that Native Americans were actually the ten lost tribes of Israel.
Thirty-Three Articles (1617). Frisian Anabaptist confession. Also known as the "Confession of Faith According to God's Word," the Thirty-Three Articles was composed by members of the Old Frisians, a Dutch Mennonite sect, at a time when they were coming into conflict with other Anabaptist groups.
John Tillinghast (1604–1655). English Puritan minister. Tillinghast began his ministry in the Church of England, pastoring two congregations in Sussex until he moved to London and became an independent, leading him to pastor Puritan congregations in Suffolk and Norfolk. He was a member of the Fifth Monarchists, a millenarian Puritan sect that believed the political upheaval of their time was ushering in the kingdom of Christ.
Frans Titelmans (1502–1537). Belgian Catholic philosopher. Titelmans studied at the University of Leuven, where he was influenced by Petrus Ramus.* After first joining a Franciscan monastery, Titelmans realigned with the stricter Capuchins and moved to Italy. He is best known for his advocacy for the Vulgate and his debates with Desiderius Erasmus* over Pauline theology (1527–1530)—he was deeply suspicious of the fruits of humanism, especially regarding biblical studies. His work was published posthumously by his brother, Pieter Titelmans (1501–1572).
Francisco de Toledo (1532–1596). Spanish Catholic theologian. This important Jesuit taught philosophy at the universities of Salamanca and Rome. He published works on Aristotelian philosophy and a commentary on Thomas Aquinas's* work, as well as biblical commentaries on John, Romans and the first half of Luke. He was also the general editor for the Clementine Vulgate (1598).
John Tombes (1603–1676). English Baptist pastor. After leaving Oxford, Tombes held many pastoral positions in Anglican churches throughout the Midlands until founding a Baptist church in Bewdley, Worcestershire. He left this congregation following a debate with Richard

Baxter,* leading him to take on a number of pastoral positions in Herefordshire while continuing to seek public debates and writing against Quakerism and Roman Catholicism.

Laurence Tomson (1539–1608). English Reformed politician and translator. Tomson was born in Northhamptonshire and educated at Magdalen College, Oxford. He graduated with his BA degree (1559) and MA degree (1564). Tomson was a fellow at Magdalen until he resigned in 1569. Prior to this resignation, Tomson was part of a diplomatic delegation to France. From 1575 to 1587, Tomson served in the House of Commons and attended the royal court at Windsor in 1582. He went on further embassies throughout Europe, where he occasionally lectured on Hebrew. Tomson died on March 29, 1608. Tomson's chief exegetical contribution was his revised text and annotations of the New Testament of the Geneva Bible.

Edward Topsell (d. 1638?). English Protestant minister. Topsell held a number of pastoral posts in Sussex, Dorset, and the Midlands before being appointed perpetual curate of St. Botolph's, Aldersgate, in the city of London. While he composed a number of religious works, including his lectures on Ruth, which were so popular they appeared in three editions, he is primarily remembered for his two illustrated works on natural history, which cataloged four-footed animals and serpents.

Alonso Tostado (1400–1455). Spanish Catholic bishop and exegete. Tostado lectured on theology, law and philosophy at the University of Salamanca, in addition to ministering in a local parish. Tostado entered into disputes over papal supremacy and the date of Christ's birth. Tostado's thirteen-volume collected works include commentaries on the historical books of the Old Testament and the Gospel of Matthew.

Daniel Toussain (1541–1602). Swiss Reformed pastor and professor. Toussain became pastor at Orléans after attending college in Basel. After the third War of Religion, Toussain was exiled, eventually returning to Montbéliard, his birthplace. In 1571, he faced opposition there from the strict Lutheran rulers and was eventually exiled due to his influence over the clergy. He returned to Orléans but fled following the Saint Bartholomew's Day Massacre (1572), eventually becoming pastor in Basel. He relocated to Heidelberg in 1583 as pastor to the new regent, becoming professor of theology at the university, and he remained there until his death.

John Trapp (1601–1669). Anglican biblical exegete. After studying at Oxford, Trapp entered the pastorate in 1636. During the English Civil Wars he sided with Parliament, which later made it difficult for him to collect tithes from a congregation whose royalist pastor had been evicted. Trapp published commentaries on all the books of the Bible from 1646 to 1656.

Immanuel Tremellius (1510–1580). Italian Reformed Hebraist. Around 1540, Tremellius received baptism by Cardinal Reginald Pole (1500–1558) and converted from Judaism to Christianity; he affiliated with evangelicals the next year. On account of the political and religious upheaval, Tremellius relocated often, teaching Hebrew in Lucca; Strasbourg, fleeing the Inquisition; Cambridge, displaced by the Schmalkaldic War; Heidelberg, escaping Mary I's persecutions; and Sedan, expelled by the new Lutheran Elector of the Palatine. Many considered Tremellius's translation of the Old Testament as the most accurate available. He also published a Hebrew grammar and translated John Calvin's* catechism into Hebrew.

Richard Turnbull (d. 1593). English minister. A preacher in London, Richard Turnbull published sermons on James, Jude, and Psalm 15.

William Tyndale (Hychyns) (1494–1536). English reformer, theologian and translator. Tyndale was educated at Oxford University, where he was influenced by the writings of humanist thinkers. Believing that piety is fostered through personal encounter with the Bible, he asked to translate the Bible into English; denied permission, Tyndale left for the Continent to complete the task. His New Testament was the equivalent of a modern-day bestseller in England but was banned and ordered burned. Tyndale's theology was oriented around justification, the authority of Scripture and Christian obedience; Tyndale emphasized the ethical as a concomitant reality of justification. He was martyred in Brussels before completing his English translation of the Old Testament, which Miles Coverdale* finished.

John Udall (1560?–1592). English Puritan pastor. Udall began his pastoral career in the Anglican parish of Kingston-upon-Thames, becoming known for his preaching and Puritan convictions, particularly his rejection of the episcopacy. While facing discipline for his views, he published anonymous and pseudonymous pamphlets critical of the established church alone and with friends, leading to his losing his position in London and relocating to Newcastle, where he continued in ministry and criticism. Udall was arrested under suspicion of complicity in publishing the critical tracts and, unwilling to deny that he wrote them, was convicted and sentenced to death. The death sentence was not carried out, however, and he remained in prison almost two years until pardoned, but died soon after release.

Zacharias Ursinus (1534-1583) German Reformed theologian. Ursinus began his studies at Wittenberg under Melanchthon*, and after teaching briefly in his home city of Breslau, continued his education at many centers of reformation learning, with stops in Strasbourg, Paris, Geneva and Zurich. Called by Elector Frederick III (1515-1576) to teach theology at the *Collegium Sapientiae* in Heidelberg and further reform in the city, Ursinus alongside Kaspar Olevianus*, was a primary author of the *Heidelberg Catechism**. Ejected from his position after the death of the Elector, Ursinus ended his career as chair of theology at the reformed academy in Neustadt.

Guillaume du Vair (1556–1621). French Catholic priest, lawyer, and writer. While du Vair took holy orders in his youth, much of his life was spent serving the state as a counselor of the parliament of Paris, a representative of King Henry IV both in France and abroad, and as Keeper of the Seals, the highest legal office in the country. The last four years of his life were spent as the bishop of Lisieux. His studies on Epictetus and the Stoics, and attempts to relate Stoicism to the Christian faith, were influential in the dissemination of this philosophy during the seventeenth and eighteenth centuries. He also wrote significant works on politics, the moral life, prayer, and the use and abuse of the French language.

Juan de Valdés (1500/10–1541). Spanish Catholic theologian and writer. Although Valdés adopted an evangelical doctrine, had Erasmian affiliations and published works that were listed on the Index of Prohibited Books, Valdés rebuked the reformers for creating disunity and never left the Catholic Church. His writings included translations of the Hebrew Psalter and various biblical books, a work on the Spanish language and several commentaries. Valdés fled to Rome in 1531 to escape the Spanish Inquisition and worked in the court of Clement VII in Bologna until the pope's death in 1534. Valdés subsequently returned to Naples, where he led the reform- and revival-minded Valdesian circle.

Henry Vaughan (1617/1618–1661). English Protestant preacher. Possibly a student at Christ's College, Cambridge, Vaughan published a sermon on Matthew 5:20 given to the House of Commons.

Thomas Venatorius (c. 1490–1551). German Lutheran theologian, mathematician, and humanist. Following a humanistic education, Venatorius spent the majority of his career in Nuremberg, where he advocated for reform as the head of the city's school system and as a preacher and pastor in the city's churches. His theological and pastoral works include one of the first Protestant works on ethics, a short catechism, and a commentary on 1 Timothy. He also edited the first Greek edition of Archimedes's writings and translated Aristophanes's *Plutus*.

Peter Martyr Vermigli (1499–1562). Italian Reformed humanist and theologian. Vermigli was one of the most influential theologians of the era, held in common regard with such figures as Martin Luther* and John Calvin.* In Italy, Vermigli was a distinguished theologian, preacher and advocate for moral reform; however, during the reinstitution of the Roman Inquisition Vermigli fled to Protestant regions in northern Europe. He was eventually appointed professor of divinity at Oxford University, where Vermigli delivered acclaimed disputations on the Eucharist. Vermigli was widely noted for his deeply integrated biblical commentaries and theological treatises.

Matthieu Virel (fl. 1561–1595). French Reformed pastor and theologian. Only two episodes from Virel's life are known: he preached the reformation message at Namur in 1561, and sixteen years later he pastored a French congregation in Basel. He published two known works: an excursus on the calendar and a brief summary of the Christian religion.

Pierre Viret (1511–1571). Swiss Reformed pastor and teacher. Converted to Protestantism at the University of Paris, Viret returned to his hometown, Orbe, where Guillaume Farel* brought him into ministry. Preaching also at Payerne and Neuchâtel, Viret's success in spreading the Reformed faith led to an assassination attempt before he and Farel sought to reform Geneva. Soon after the Genevan Assembly voted to accept the Reformation, Viret relocated to Lausanne, where he established the Reformed faith, served as chief pastor, and founded a Reformed academy. After almost twenty-five years, he was exiled from the city, spending a short time pastoring and teaching in Geneva until establishing himself in southern France, where he brought the evangelical faith to Lyons, pastored, and served as an advisor to Jeanne d'Albret, the queen of Navarre (1528–1572).

Juan Luis Vives (1492?–1540). Spanish Catholic humanist. Born into a Jewish family but baptized Catholic, Vives spent most of his life outside Spain following the persecution of his family by the Inquisition. After studying in Paris, he lived in Bruges, where he became part of the intellectual circle around Erasmus,* and taught at Oxford toward the end of his life. Vives largely avoided entering into religious controversies, and his works received a mixed reception from both Catholics and Protestants. He is best known for his educational and social writings, including an influential Latin primer, works on pedagogy and women's education, and arguments for pacifism and poor relief.

Gisbertus Voetius (1589–1676). Dutch Reformed theologian. Voetius pastored at Vlijmen and Heusden and served as the youngest delegate at the Synod of Dordrecht* before becoming professor of theology and Oriental languages at the University of Utrecht. While Voetius's writings demonstrate concern for missions, practical piety, and personal purity, he also entered into numerous theological controversies during his career. His Reformed commitments led to ongoing conflicts with Arminians and Catholics, and he sought to uphold the importance of the Old Testament against Johannes Cocceius's (1603–1669) formulation of the covenants. He also entered into debate with René Descartes (1596–1650) and his followers, arguing from an Aristotelian perspective that to accept Cartesian skepticism was to reject biblical truth and the Christian tradition.

Conradus Vorstius (1569–1622). Dutch Arminian-Socinian theologian. A student of David Paraeus* and Johannes Piscator,* Vorstius's Socinian tendencies emerged during his tenure as professor of theology at Steinfurt. After an apology and examination, he was allowed to replace Arminius* as professor of theology at Leiden though never permitted to teach, as his questioning of the doctrine of atonement and the eternity, foreknowledge, and omnipresence of God drew wide censure, ultimately from King James I of England.* Exiled to Gouda and deposed at the Synod of Dordrecht,* Vorstius published numerous theological works and a commentary on the Pauline letters.

Vulgate. In 382 Pope Damasus I (c. 300–384) commissioned Jerome (c. 347–420) to translate the four Gospels into Latin based on Old Latin and Greek manuscripts. Jerome completed the translation of the Gospels and the Old Testament around 405. It is widely debated how much of the rest of the New Testament was translated by Jerome. During the Middle Ages, the Vulgate became the Catholic Church's standard Latin translation. The Council of Trent recognized it as the official text of Scripture.

George Walker (1581–1651). Puritan minister. Walker was born at Hawkshead, Lancashire, and educated at St. John's College, Cambridge. After graduating Cambridge, Walker moved to London, where he became rector of St. John the Evangelist on Watling Street in 1614. He served this parish for nearly forty years. Throughout his ministry, Walker showed himself to be an ardent opponent of the papacy and practices within the Church of England that he deemed not sufficiently reformed. Toward this end, Walker engaged numerous disputations and literary debates with both conformists and Catholics. For his sermons that were critical of the Church of England, he was summoned to appear before Archbishop Laud in 1635 and the Star Chamber in 1638, which fined and imprisoned him for twelve weeks. On another occasion, Walker was incarcerated for as long as two years for his nonconformity until released by the Long Parliament. In 1643, Walker was selected to serve in the Westminster Assembly and to participate in the trial of Laud. Walker died in London. Among his many published sermons and polemical works is a treatise on justification.

Thomas Walkington (d. 1621). Anglican minister and author. Born in Lincoln, he was educated at Cambridge, graduating with his BA in 1597 and his MA in 1600. Walkington was elected a fellow at St. John's College, Cambridge, in 1602. Later, he received a BD from Oxford and a DD from Cambridge. He served as rector of parishes in Northamptonshire, Lincolnshire, and Middlesex. A prolific author, Walkington published works on diverse subjects. Among his biblical works are *An Exposition of the First Two Verses of the Sixth Chapter to the Hebrews in form of a Dialogue* (1609) and *Theologicall Rules to Guide Us in the Understanding and Practice of Holy Scripture* (1615).

Peter Walpot (d. 1578). Moravian Radical pastor and bishop. Walpot was a bishop of the Hutterite community after Jakob Hutter, Peter Riedemann* and Leonhard Lanzenstiel. Riedemann's *Confession of Faith* (1545; 1565) became a vital authority for Hutterite exegesis, theology and morals. Walpot added his own *Great Article Book* (1577), which collates primary biblical passages on baptism, communion, the community of goods, the sword and divorce. In keeping with Hutterite theology, Walpot defended the community of goods as a mark of the true church.

Richard Ward (c. 1601–1684). English Anglican pastor. Educated at Cambridge and St. Andrews, Ward pastored in London and Essex. His published writings include a commentary on Matthew and an explanation of the Solemn League and Covenant (1643), which allied Scottish Covenanters and English Parliamentarians during the First English Civil War (1642–1646).

Thomas Watson (d. 1686). English Puritan pastor. After graduating from Cambridge, Watson became pastor of St. Stephen Walbrook in the city of London, a pulpit he served for twenty years, though he was imprisoned for a year for his part in the plot of Christopher Love (1618–1651) to restore Charles II to the throne. A well-respected preacher, Watson was expelled from official ministry by the 1662 Act of Uniformity, though he continued to preach in private until his retirement. While Watson published many sermons and devotional works, he is perhaps best known for *A Body of Divinity* (1692), a series of sermon on the Westminster Catechism.

Valentin Weigel (1533–1588). German Lutheran pastor. Weigel studied at Leipzig and Wittenberg, entering the pastorate in 1567. Despite a strong anti-institutional bias, he was recognized by the church hierarchy as a talented preacher and compassionate minister of mercy to the poor. Although he signed the Formula of Concord,* Weigel's orthodoxy was questioned so openly that he had to publish a defense. He appears to have tried to synthesize several medieval mystics with the ideas of Sebastian Franck,* Thomas Müntzer* and others. His posthumously published works have led some recent scholars to suggest that Weigel's works may have deeply influenced later Pietism.

Hieronymus Weller von Molsdorf (1499–1572). German Lutheran theologian. Originally intending to study law, Weller devoted himself to theology after hearing one of Martin Luther's* sermons on the catechism. He boarded with Luther and tutored Luther's son. In 1539 he moved to Freiburg, where he lectured on the Bible and held theological disputations at the Latin school. In addition to hymns, works of practical theology and a postil set, Weller published commentaries on Genesis, 1–2 Samuel, 1–2 Kings, Job, the Psalms, Christ's passion, Ephesians, Philippians, 1–2 Thessalonians and 1–2 Peter.

Westminster Assembly (1643–1652). English church council. Called by English Parliament to advise on church reform, the Westminster Assembly was made up of more than 120 clergymen, thirty parliamentary observers, and a delegation from the Church of Scotland. Beginning with a review of the Articles of Religion,* the most heated debates were undertaken over ecclesiology, as factions argued for presbyterianism, congregationalism, Erastianism, and episcopalianism, with the council ultimately recommending presbyterianism to the parliament. Much of the legacy of the assembly is held in the major documents it produced, the *Directory for Public Worship* (1644), *The Form of Presbyterial Church Government* (1645), the *Westminster Confession of Faith* (1646), the *Shorter Catechism* (1647), and the *Larger Catechism* (1648), which became foundational for the English and Scottish churches and many of the Reformed denominations.

William Whitaker (1547/1548–1595). English Puritan theologian. Whitaker spent most of his career at Cambridge, where he served as Regius Professor of Divinity and master of St. John's College. While his tenure was occasionally opposed due to his Puritanism, he was nevertheless widely respected, and he published numerous significant works on topics including the Protestant doctrine of Scripture, original sin, grace, and ecclesiastical authority. He also drafted the Lambeth Articles (1595), a proposed addendum to the Thirty-Nine Articles* endorsing double predestination, but the changes were rejected by Elizabeth I*.

John Whitgift (1530–1604). Anglican archbishop. Though Whitgift shared much theological common ground with Puritans, after his election as Archbishop of Canterbury (1583) he moved decisively to squelch the political and ecclesiastical threat they posed during Elizabeth I's* reign. Whitgift enforced strict compliance to the Book of Common Prayer,* the Act of Uniformity (1559) and the Articles of Religion.* Whitgift's policies led to a large migration of Puritans to Holland. The bulk of Whitgift's published corpus is the fruit of a lengthy public disputation with Thomas Cartwright,* in which Whitgift defines Anglican doctrine against Cartwright's staunch Puritanism.

Johann Wigand (1523–1587). German Lutheran theologian. Wigand is most noted as one of the compilers of the *Magdeburg Centuries*, a German ecclesiastical history of the first thirteen centuries of the church. He was a student of Philipp Melanchthon* at the University of Wittenburg and became a significant figure in the controversies dividing Lutheranism. Strongly opposed to Roman Catholicism, Wigand lobbied against innovations in Lutheran theology that appeared sympathetic to Catholic thought. In the later debates, Wigand's support for Gnesio-Lutheranism established his role in the development of confessional Lutheranism. Wigand was appointed bishop of Pomerania after serving academic posts at the universities in Jena and Königsburg.

Thomas Wilcox (c. 1549–1608). English Puritan theologian. In 1572, Wilcox objected to Parliament against the episcopacy and the Book of Common Prayer,* advocating for presbyterian church governance. He was imprisoned for sedition. After his release, he preached itinerantly. He was brought before the courts twice more for his continued protest against the Church of England's episcopal structure. He translated some of Theodore Beza* and John Calvin's* sermons into English, and he wrote polemical and occasional works as well as commentaries on the Psalms and Song of Songs.

Johann (Ferus) Wild (1495–1554). German Catholic pastor. After studying at Heidelberg and teaching at Tübingen, this Franciscan was appointed as lector in the Mainz cathedral, eventually being promoted to cathedral preacher—a post for which he became widely popular but also controversial. Wild strongly identified as Catholic but was not unwilling to criticize the curia. Known for an irenic spirit—criticized in fact as *too* kind—he was troubled by the polemics between all parties of the Reformation. He preached with great lucidity, integrating the liturgy, Scripture and doctrine to exposit Catholic worship and teaching for common people. His sermons on John were pirated for publication without his knowledge; the Sorbonne banned them as heretical. Despite his popularity among clergy, the majority of his works were on the Roman Index until 1900.

Andrew Willet (1562–1621). Anglican priest, professor, and biblical expositor. Willet was a gifted biblical expositor and powerful preacher. He walked away from a promising university career in 1588 when he was ordained a priest in the Church of England. For the next thirty-three years he served as a parish priest. Willet's commentaries summarized the present state of discussion while also offering practical applications for preachers. They have been cited as some of the most technical commentaries of the early seventeenth century. His most important publication was *Synopsis Papismi, or a General View of Papistrie* (1594), in which he responded to many of Robert Bellarmine's critiques. After years of royal favor, Willet was imprisoned in 1618 for a month after presenting to King James I* his opposition to the "Spanish Match" of Prince Charles to the Infanta Maria. While serving as a parish priest, he wrote forty-two works, most of which were either commentaries on books of the Bible or controversial works against Catholics.

Thomas Wilson (d. 1586). English Anglican priest. A fellow of St John's, Cambridge, Wilson fled to Frankfurt to escape the Marian Persecution. After his return to England, he served as a canon and Dean of Worcester.

George Wither (1588–1667). English poet, satirist, and hymn writer. Wither was born in Bentworth, Hampshire. After finishing his early education under the tutelage of a local minister, Wither continued his studies at Magdalen College, Oxford. Afterward, he studied law at the Inns of Chancery. Wither commenced his literary career with the publication of an elegy on the occasion of the death of Henry Frederick, Prince of Wales (1594–1612). Most of Wither's literary works consist of satirical pamphlets for which he was regularly arrested, imprisoned, and released. He fought in the Parliamentary Army during the Civil War. A conforming Anglican, Wither composed numerous hymns as well as translations of the Psalms. Two of Wither's major works are *Preparation to the Psalter* (1619), in which he explores various literary aspects of the Bible, and *Hymns and Songs of the Church* (1622/1623). He died in London.

John Woolton (c. 1535–1594). Anglican bishop. After graduating from Oxford, Woolton lived in Germany until the accession of Elizabeth I.* He was ordained as a priest in 1560 and as a bishop in 1578. Woolton published many theological, devotional and practical works, including a treatise on the immortality of the soul, a discourse on conscience and a manual for Christian living.

John Wycliffe (c. 1330–1384). English theologian, philosopher, and reformer known as "the Morning Star of the Reformation." While holding benefices from a number of parishes, Wycliffe spent the majority of his career at Oxford, where he studied, taught, and served as head of Balliol College. His early work focused on logic and metaphysics, but after entering into the service of John of Gaunt, Duke of Lancaster (1340–1399) and serving as a royal envoy to discuss taxes with papal representatives, Wycliffe turned his attention to more practical concerns. His criticism of papal power and wealth drew initially civil and ecclesiastical approval, but application of his principle that any headship profiting the governor rather than the governed is illegitimate to the English church brought controversy and censure. This criticism increased as he rejected transubstantiation, criticized monasticism, argued along Augustinian lines that only the invisible body of the elect constituted the true church, that Scripture belongs to the body of the elect rather than the institutional church, and that as many leaders of the visible church were likely reprobate, their offices and sacraments were invalid. While dismissed from Oxford in 1381, powerful defenders protected Wycliffe from further consequences during his lifetime, but he was condemned as a heretic at the Council of Constance (1515), whence he was exhumed and his remains burned. While largely condemned by contemporaries, Wycliffe, and his followers, the Lollards, are often viewed as forerunners of the Reformation who prepared the way for the tumult of the sixteenth century.

Girolamo Zanchi (1516–1590). Italian Reformed theologian and pastor. Zanchi joined an Augustinian monastery at the age of fifteen, where he studied Greek and Latin, the church fathers and the works of Aristotle and Thomas Aquinas.* Under the influence of his prior, Peter Martyr Vermigli,* Zanchi also imbibed the writings of the Swiss and German reformers. To avoid the Inquisition, Zanchi fled to Geneva where he was strongly attracted to the preaching and teaching of John Calvin.* Zanchi taught biblical theology and the *locus* method at academies in Strasbourg, Heidelberg, and Neustadt. He also served as pastor of an Italian refugee congregation. Zanchi's theological works, *De tribus Elohim* (1572) and

De natura Dei (1577), have received more attention than his commentaries. His commentaries comprise about a quarter of his literary output, however, and display a strong typological and christological interpretation in conversation with the church fathers, medieval exegetes, and other reformers.

Katharina Schütz Zell (1497/98–1562). German Reformed writer. Zell became infamous in Strasbourg and the Empire when in 1523 she married the priest Matthias Zell, and then published an apology defending her husband against charges of impiety and libertinism. Longing for a united church, she called for toleration of Catholics and Anabaptists, famously writing to Martin Luther* after the failed Marburg Colloquy of 1529 to exhort him to check his hostility and to be ruled instead by Christian charity. Much to the chagrin of her contemporaries, Zell published diverse works, ranging from polemical treatises on marriage to letters of consolation, as well as editing a hymnal and penning an exposition of Psalm 51.

Martha Elizabeth Zitter (Unknown). German Catholic nun. Zitter entered the Ursuline convent in Erfurt during her teenage years. Most of what is known about her is drawn from a letter she composed to her mother, explaining her decision to leave the order and become Lutheran, which focuses on aspects of her vows and Roman Catholic piety she believes to be unbiblical. Despite this public departure from the Roman church, however, Zitter returned toward the end of her life.

Ulrich Zwingli (1484–1531). Swiss Reformed humanist, preacher and theologian. Zwingli studied at the University of Vienna, and afterwards the University of Basel, where he received his BA and MA in 1504 and 1506. Ordained in September 1506, Zwingli became priest of the church in Glarus where he taught himself Greek, and read deeply in the church fathers. During this period, Zwingli was also greatly impacted by the writings of Desiderius Erasmus*. In 1516, Zwingli accepted the position of priest at the Benedictine Abbey at Einsiedeln in Schwyz, where he intently studied the Greek New Testament, and learned Hebrew. When he became a preacher in the city cathedral at Zurich, Zwingli enacted reform through sermons, public disputations, and conciliation with the town council, abolishing the Mass and images in the church. Zwingli broke with the lectionary preaching tradition, instead preaching serial expository biblical sermons. He later was embroiled in controversy with Anabaptists over infant baptism and with Martin Luther* at the Marburg Colloquy (1529) over their differing views of the Eucharist. Zwingli, serving as chaplain to Zurich's military, was killed in the Second Battle of Kappel.

SOURCES FOR BIOGRAPHICAL SKETCHES

General Reference Works

Allgemeine Deutsche Biographie. 56 vols. Leipzig: Duncker & Humblot, 1875–1912; reprint, 1967–1971. Accessible online via deutsche-biographie.de/index.html.

Baskin, Judith R., ed. *The Cambridge Dictionary of Judaism and Jewish Culture*. New York: Cambridge University Press, 2011.

Benedetto, Robert, ed. *The New Westminster Dictionary of Church History*. Vol. 1. Louisville: Westminster John Knox Press, 2008.

Bettenson, Henry and Chris Maunder, eds. *Documents of the Christian Church*. 3rd ed. Oxford: Oxford University Press, 1999.

Betz, Hans Dieter, Don Browning, Bernd Janowski and Eberhard Jüngel, eds. *Religion Past & Present: Encyclopedia of Theology and Relgion*. 13 vols. Leiden: Brill, 2007–2013.

Bremer, Francis J. and Tom Webster, eds. *Puritans and Puritanism in Europe and America: A Comprehensive Encyclopedia*.
2 vols. Santa Barbara, CA: ABC-CLIO, 2006.

Ghisalberti, Alberto Maria, ed. *Dizionario Biografico degli Italiani*. 100 vols. Istituto della Enciclopedia italiana, Roma, 1960–2020. Online edition available at treccani.it.

Gritsch, Eric W. *A History of Lutheranism*. Minneapolis: Fortress Press, 2002.

Haag, Eugene and Émile Haag. *La France protestante ou vies des protestants français*. 2nd ed. 6 vols. Paris: Sandoz & Fischbacher, 1877–1888.

Hillerbrand, Hans J., ed. *Oxford Encyclopedia of the Reformation*. 4 vols. New York: Oxford University Press, 1996.

Kolb, Robert, and Timothy J. Wengert, eds. *The Book of Concord: The Confessions of the Evangelical Lutheran Church*. Translated by Charles Arand et al. Minneapolis: Fortress, 2000.

McKim, Donald K., ed. *Dictionary of Major Biblical Interpreters*. Downers Grove, IL: InterVarsity Press, 2007.

Müller, Gerhard, et al., ed. *Theologische Realenzyklopädie*. Berlin: Walter de Gruyter, 1994.

Neue Deutsche Biographie. 28 vols. projected. Berlin: Duncker & Humblot, 1953–. Accessible online via deutsche-biographie.de/index.html.

New Catholic Encyclopedia. 15 vols. New York: McGraw-Hill, 1967; 2nd ed., Detroit: Thomson-Gale, 2002.

Oxford Dictionary of National Biography. 60 vols. Oxford: Oxford University Press, 2004.

Pelikan, Jaroslav. *The Christian Tradition*. 5 vols. Chicago: University of Chicago Press, 1971–1989.

Stephen, Leslie, and Sidney Lee, eds. *Dictionary of National Biography*. 63 vols. London: Smith, Elder and Co., 1885–1900.

Terry, Michael, ed. *Reader's Guide to Judaism*. New York: Routledge, 2000.

Wordsworth, Christopher, ed. *Lives of Eminent Men connected with the History of Religion in England*. 4 vols. London: J. G. & F. Rivington, 1839.

Additional Works for Individual Sketches

Akin, Daniel L. "An Expositional Analysis of the Schleitheim Confession." *Criswell Theological Review* 2 (1988): 345-70.

Astell, Mary. *The Christian Religion, as Professed by a Daughter of the Church of England*. Edited by Jacqueline Broad. Toronto: Iter Inc and the Center for Reformation and Renaissance Studies, 2013.

Bald, R. C. *John Donne: A Life*. Oxford: Oxford University Press, 1970.

Beeke, Joel, and Randall J. Pederson. *Meet the Puritans*. Grand Rapids: Reformation Heritage Books, 2006.

Bireley, Robert, *The Refashioning of Catholicism, 1450–1700*, Washington, DC: Catholic University of America Press, 1999.

Blok, P. J., and P. C. Molhuysen, eds. *Nieuw Nederlandsch Biografisch Woordenboek*. 10 vols.

Brackney, William H. *A Genetic History of Baptist Thought: With Special Reference to Baptists in Britain and North America*. Atlanta: Mercer University Press, 2004.

———. *Historical Dictionary of the Baptists*. 2nd ed. Lanham, MD: Scarecrow, 2009.

Brook, Benjamin. *The Lives of the Puritans*. 3 vols. London: James Black, 1813. Reprint, Pittsburgh, PA: Soli Deo Gloria, 1994.

Brown, Peter. *Augustine of Hippo: A Biography*. Berkeley & Los Angeles, CA: University of California Press, 1967.

Bruening, Michael W. *Refusing to Kiss the Slipper: Opposition to Calvinism in the Francophone Reformation*. Oxford Studies in Historical theology. New York: Oxford University Press, 2021.

Burke, David G. "The Enduring Significance of the KJV." *Word and World* 31, no. 3 (2011): 229-44.

Campbell, Gordon. *Bible: The Story of the King James Version, 1611–2011*. Oxford: Oxford University Press, 2010.

Cathcart, William. *The Baptist Encyclopaedia*. 3 vols. Philadelphia: Louis H. Everts, 1881.

Charles, Amy. *A Life of George Herbert*. Ithaca, NY: Cornell University Press, 1977.

Christian, Jacob. *The Sovereign Map: Theoretical Approaches to Cartography Throughout History*. Chicago: University of Chicago Press, 2006.

Coffey, John. *Politics, Religion, and the British Revolutions: The Thought of Samuel Rutherford*. Cambridge: Cambridge University Press, 1997.

Colish, Marcia. *Peter Lombard*, 2 vols. Leiden, Netherlands: Brill, 1993.

Culpepper, Scott. *Francis Johnson and the English Separatist Influence: The Bishop of Brownism's Life, Writings, and Controversies*. Macon, GA: Mercer University Press, 2011.

Doornkaat Koolman, J ten. "The First Edition of Peter Riedemann's 'Rechenschaft.'" *Mennonite Quarterly Review* 36, no. 2 (1962): 169-70.

Emerson, Everett H. *John Cotton*. New York: Twayne, 1990.

Fischlin, Daniel and Mark Fortier, eds. *Royal Subjects: Essays on the Writings of James VI and I*. Detroit: Wayne State University Press, 2002.

Fishbane, Michael A. "Teacher and the Hermeneutical Task: A Reinterpretation of Medieval Exegesis." *Journal of the American Academy of Religion 43*, no. 4 (1975): 709-21.

Friedmann, Robert. "Second Generation Anabaptism as Illustrated by the Walpot Era of the Hutterites." *Mennonite Quarterly* 44, no. 4 (1970): 390-93.

Frymire, John M. *The Primacy of the Postils: Catholics, Protestants, and the Dissemination of Ideas in Early Modern Germany*. Leiden: Brill, 2010.

Furcha, Edward J. "Key Concepts in Caspar von Schwenckfeld's Thought, Regeneration and the New Life." *Church History* 37, no. 2 (1968): 160-73.

Gerace, Antionio. *Biblical Scholarship in Louvain in the 'Golden' Sixteenth Century*. Göttingen: Vandenhoeck & Ruprecht, 2019.

Gordon, Bruce, *The Swiss Reformation*. Manchester: Manchester University Press, 2002.

Greaves, Richard L. *Society and Religion in Elizabethan England*. Minneapolis: University of Minnesota, 1981.

Greiffenberg, Catharina Regina von. *Meditations on the Incarnation, Passion, and Death of Jesus Christ*. Edited and translated by Lynne Tatlock. The Other Voice in Early Modern Europe. Chicago: University of Chicago Press, 2009.

Grendler, Paul. "Italian biblical humanism and the papacy, 1515-1535." In *Biblical Humanism and Scholasticism in the Age of Erasmus*. Edited by Erika Rummel, 225-76. Leiden: Brill, 2008.

Guggisberg, Hans R. *Sebastian Castellio 1515-1563: Humanist and Defender of Religious Toleration in a Confessional Age*. Translated and Edited by Bruce Gordon. St Andrews Studies in Reformation History. New York: Routledge, 2017.

Haemig, Mary Jane. "Elisabeth Cruciger (1500?–1535): The Case of the Disappearing Hymn Writer." *Sixteenth Century Journal* 32, no. 1 (2001): 21-44.

Harpley, W., ed. *Report and Transactions of the Devonshire Association for the Advancement of Science, Literature and Art* 24 (July 1882). Plymouth: William Brendon and Son, 1892.

Heiden, Albert van der. "Pardes: Methodological Reflections on the Theory of the Four Senses." *Journal of Jewish Studies* 34, no. 2 (1983): 147-59.

Hendrix, Scott H., ed. and trans. *Early Protestant Spirituality*. New York: Paulist Press, 2009.

Hobbs, R. Gerald. "Is Abbot Isidore Also Among the Prophets?": Protestant Influences upon the Annotated Bible of Isidore Clarius." *Renaissance and Reformation*. New series, 17, No. 1 (Winter 1993): 53-71.

Hvolbek, Russell H. "Being and Knowing: Spiritualist Epistemology and Anthropology from Schwenckfeld to Böhme." *Sixteenth Century Journal* 22, no. 1 (1991): 97-110.

Kahle, Paul. "Felix Pratensis—a Prato, Felix. Der Herausgeber der Ersten Rabbinerbibel, Venedig 1516/7." *Die Welt des Orients* 1, no. 1 (1947): 32-36.

Kelly, Joseph Francis. *The Ecumenical Councils of the Catholic Church: A History*. Collegeville, MN: Liturgical Press, 2009.

Koop, Karl, ed. *Confessions of Faith in the Anabaptist Tradition 1527–1660*. Translated by Cornelius J. Dyck et al. CRR 11. Kitchener, ON: Pandora Press, 2006.

Lake, Peter. *The Boxmaker's Revenge: "Orthodoxy", "Heterodox" and the Politics of the Parish in Early Stuart London*. Stanford, CA: Stanford University Press, 2001.

Lane, Anthony N. S. *Calvin and Bernard of Clairvaux*. Princeton, NJ: Princeton Theological Seminary, 1996.

Lane, Belden C. *Ravished by Beauty: The Surprising Legacy of Reformed Spirituality*. Oxford: Oxford University Press, 2011.

Lee, Jason K. *The Theology of John Smyth* (Macon, GA: Mercer University Press, 2003).

Lockhart, Paul Douglas. *Frederick II and the Protestant Cause: Denmark's Role in the Wars of Religion, 1559–1596*. Leiden: Brill, 2004.

Lubac, Henri de. *Medieval Exegesis: The Four Senses of Scripture*. 3 vols. Translated by Mark Sebanc and E. M. Macierowski. Grand Rapids: Eerdmans, 1998–2009.

Manetsch, Scott, *Calvin's Company of Pastors: Pastoral Care and the Emerging Reformed Church, 1536–1609*. Oxford: Oxford University Press, 2013.

Manschereck, Clyde Leonard. *Melanchthon, the Quiet Reformer*. New York: Abingdon, 1958.

Marinella, Lucrezia. *The Nobility and Excellence of Women and the Defects and Vices of Men*. Edited and translated by Anne Dunhill. Chicago: University of Chicago Press, 1999.

Matheson, Peter, *Argula von Grumbach: A Woman's Voice in the Reformation*. Edinburgh: T&T Clark, 1995.

McGuire, Daniel Patrick. *The Difficult Saint: Bernard of Clairvaux and his Tradition*. Collegeville, MN: Cistercian Publication, 1991.

McKinley, Mary B. "Volume Editor's Introduction." In *Epistle to Marguerite of Navarre and Preface to a Sermon by John Calvin*, edited and translated by Mary B. McKiney. Chicago: University of Chicago Press, 2004.

M'Crie, Thomas. *The Life of Andrew Melville*. 2 vols. Edinburgh: William Blackwood, 1819.

Norton, David. *A Textual History of the King James Bible*. New York: Cambridge University Press, 2005

Nuttall, Geoffrey. *The Welsh Saints, 1640–1660: Walter Cradock, Vavasor Powell, Morgan Llwyd*. Cardiff: University of Wales Press, 1957.

Oberman, Heiko A. *Luther: Man Between God and the Devil*. New York, NY: Doubleday, 1989.

O'Meara, Thomas F. *Albert the Great: Theologian and Scientist*. Chicago: New Priory Press, 2013.

Packull, Werner O. "The Origins of Peter Riedemann's Account of Our Faith." *Sixteenth Century Journal* 30, no. 1 (1999): 61-69.

Papazian, Mary Arshagouni, ed. *John Donne and the Protestant Reformation: New Perspectives*. Detroit: Wayne State University Press, 2003.

Paulicelli, Eugenia. "Sister Arcangela Tarabotti: Hair, Wigs and Other Vices." In *Writing Fashion in Early Modern Italy: From Sprezzatura to Satire*, by idem, 177-204. Farnham, Surrey, UK: Ashgate, 2014.

Pragman, James H. "The Augsburg Confession in the English Reformation: Richard Taverner's Contribution." *Sixteenth Century Journal* 11, no. 3 (1980): 75-85.

Rashi. *Rashi's Commentary on Psalms*. Translated by Mayer I. Gruber. Atlanta: Scholars Press, 1998.

Raynor, Brian. *John Frith: Scholar and Martyr*. Kent, UK: Pond View Books, 2000.

Reid, Jonathan A. *King's Sister—Queen of Dissent: Marguerite of Navarre (1492–1549) and her Evangelical Network*. Leiden: Brill, 2009.

Schmidt, Josef, "Introduction" in Johannes Tauler, *Sermons*. New York: Paulist Press, 1985, 1-34.

Smith, Hannah. "Mary Astell, *A Serious Proposal to the Ladies* (1694), and the Anglican Reformation of Manners in Late-Seventeenth-Century England." In *Mary Astell: Reason, Gender, Faith*, edited by William Kolbrenner and Michal Michelson, 31-48. New York: Routledge, 2007.

Spinka, Matthew. *John Hus: A Biography*. Princeton, NJ: Princeton University Press, 1968.

———. *John Hus at the Council of Constance*. New York: Columbia University Press, 1968.

———. *John Hus and the Czech Reform*. Hamden, CT: Archon Books, 1966.

Steinmetz, David C. *Reformers in the Wings: From Geiler von Kayserberg to Theodore Beza*. Oxford: Oxford University Press, 2000.

———. "The Superiority of Pre-Critical Exegesis." *Theology Today* 37, no. 1 (1980): 27-38.

Stjerna, Kirsi. *Women of the Reformation*. Malden, MA: Blackwell Publishing, 2009.

Synder, C. Arnold. "The Confession of the Swiss Brethren in Hesse, 1578." In *Anabaptism Revisited: Essays on Anabaptist/Mennonite Studies in Honor of C. J. Dyck*. Edited by Walter Klaassen, 29-49. Waterloo, ON; Scottdale, PA: Herald Press, 1992.

———. "The Schleitheim Articles in Light of the Revolution of the Common Man: Continuation or Departure?" *Sixteenth Century Journal* 16, no. 4 (1985): 419-30.

Thornton, Wallace. *John Foxe and His Monument: A Theological-Historical Perspective*. Birmingham, AL: Aldersgate Heritage Press, 2013.

Todd, Margo. "Bishops in the Kirk: William Cowper of Galloway and the Puritan Episcopacy of Scotland." *Scottish Journal of Theology*, 57 (2004): 300-312.

Tschackert, Paul. "Varel, Edo Hilderich of." In *General German Biography* (ADB). Volume 39. Leipzig: Duncker & Humblot, 1895.

Van Liere, Frans. *An Introduction to the Medieval Bible*. New York: Cambridge University Press, 2014.

Voogt, Gerrit. "Remonstrant-Counter-Remonstrant Debates: Crafting a Principled Defense of Toleration after the Synod of Dordrecht (1619–1650)." *Church History and Religious Culture* 89, no. 4 (2009): 489-524.

Wabuda, Susan. "Henry Bull, Miles Coverdale, and the Making of *Foxe's Book of Martyrs*." In *Martyrs and Martyrologies: Papers Read at the 1992 Summer Meeting and the 1993 Winter Meeting of the Ecclesiastical History Society*, edited by Diana Wood, 245-58. Oxford: Blackwell, 1993.

Wallace, Dewey D. Jr. "George Gifford, Puritan Propaganda and Popular Religion in Elizabethan England." *Sixteenth Century Journal* 9, no. 1 (1978): 27-49.

Wawrykow, Joseph P. *The Westminster Handbook to Thomas Aquinas*. Louisville, KY: Westminster John Knox, 2005.

Wendel, Francois. *Calvin: The Origins and Development of His Religious Thought*. New York: Harper & Row, 1963.

Wengert, Timothy J. "'Fear and Love' in the Ten Commandments." *Concordia Journal* 21, no. 1 (1995): 14-27.

Wiesner-Hanks, Merry, ed. *Convents Confront the Reformation: Catholic and Protestant Nuns in Germany*. Translated by Joan Skocir and Merry Wiesner-Hanks. Milwaukee: Marquette University Press, 1996.

———. "Philip Melanchthon and John Calvin against Andreas Osiander: Coming to Terms with Forensic Justification." In *Calvin and Luther: The Continuing Relationship*, edited by R. Ward Holder, 63-87. Göttingen: Vandenhoeck & Ruprecht, 2013.

Wilkinson, Robert J. *Tetragrammaton: Western Christians and the Hebrew Name of God*. Leiden: Brill, 2015.

Yarnell, Malcolm. "Christopher Blackwood: Exemplar of the Seventeenth-Century Particular Baptists." *Southwestern Journal of Theology* 57, no 2 (Spring 2015): 181-205.

BIBLIOGRAPHY

Primary Sources and Translations Used in the Volume

Alcasar, Ludovici ab. *Vestigatio Arcani Sensus in Apocalpsi.* Antwerp: Heredes Martini Nutii, 1614, 1619.

Alsted, Johann Heinrich. *Diatribe de mille annis apocalypticis.* 2nd ed. Frankfurt: Conradi Eifridi, 1630.

Ames, William. *Bellarminus Enervatus.* 4 vols. Oxford, 1629.

———. *The Marrow of Sacred Divinity drawne out of the Holy Scriptures, and the interpreters thereof, and brought into method.* London: Edward Griffin, 1642. Digital copy online at http://name.umdl.umich.edu/A25291.0001.001.

Archer, Henry (John). *The Personal Reigne of Christ upon Earth.* London, 1642.

———. *The personal reign of Christ upon earth in a treatise wherein is fully and largely laid open and proved that Jesus Christ, together with the saints, shall visibly possess a monarchical state and kingdom in this world ...* London, 1661.

Augustine. *On Christian Doctrine.* Translated by D. W. Robertson. Indianapolis: Bobbs-Merrill, 1958.

Avery, Elizabeth. *Scripture-prophecies opened which are to be accomplished in these last times, which do attend the second coming of Christ: in several letters written to Christian friends.* London: Giles Calvert, 1647. Digital copy online at http://name.umdl.umich.edu/A26260.0001.001.

Bale, John. *The Examinations of Anne Askew.* Edited by Debapriya Basu. https://anne-askew.humanities.uva.nl/texts/the-examinations-of-anne-askew/index.htm.

———. *The image of both Churches after the most wonderfull and heauenly Reuelation of sainct Iohn the Euangelist, contayning a very fruitfull exposition or paraphrase vpon the same. Wherin it is conferred with the other scriptures, and most auctorised histories. Compyled by Iohn Bale an exyle also in thys lyfe, for the faithfull testimony of Iesu.* London: Thomas East, 1570. Digital copy online at http://name.umdl.umich.edu/A02872.0001.001.

———. *The Image of Both Churches, Being an Exposition of the Most Wonderful Book of Revelation.* Edited by Henry Christmas. Select Works of John Bale. Parker Society 1. Cambridge: Cambridge University Press, 1849.

Beard, Thomas. *Antichrist the Pope in Rome: or, The Pope of Rome Is Antichrist.* London, 1625.

Bede. *Explanatio Apocalypsis.* PL 93.129-206.

Bellarmine, Robert. *Roberti Bellarmini Politiani Opera Omnia.* Edited by Justinus Fevre. 8 vols. Paris: n.p., 1870–1874.

Beza, Theodore. *A learned treatise of the plague.* London: Thomas Ratcliffe and Edward Thomas, 1665.

Beza, Theodore, and Franciscus Junius. *Commentary on Revelation: Apocalypsis. A Brief and Learned Commentarie upon the Revelation of Saint John the Apostle and Evangelist, applied unto the History of the Catholic and Christian Church. Written in Latine by M Francis Junius Doctor of Divinity, and Professor in the University of Heidelberg: And translated into English for the benefit of those that understand not the Latin.* Imprinted at London by Richard Field for Robert Dexter, 1592.

Bibliander, Theodore. *Ad omnium ordinum reip. Christianae principes uiros, populumque Christianum Relatio fidelis Theodori Bibliandri: Quod a solo Verbo filioque Dei tum exacta cognitio praesentium temporum &*

futurorum, atque ipsius etiam Antichristi, maximae pestis totius orbis, tum recta optimaque moderatio reipublicae et totius vitae Christianae petenda sit. Basel: Operinus, 1545.

Boveland, Karin, Christoph Peter Burger, and Ruth Steffen, eds. *Der Antichrist und die Fünfzehn Zeichen vor dem Jüngsten Gericht*. 2 vols. Hamburg: Friedrich Loittig, 1959.

Brightman, Thomas. *Apocalypsis Apocalypseos....* Frankfurt, 1609.

———. *The Revelation of S. John, Illustrated with Analysis and Scholions*. 1st English ed. Amsterdam: Thomas Stafford, 1644. Digital copy online at https://www.google.com/books/edition/The_Revelation_of_Saint_John_Illustrated/wdfOtRdRaFoC?gbpv=1.

Broughton, Hugh. *A Revelation of the Holy Apocalyps*. London, 1630.

Bucer, Martin. *De Regno Christi*. In *Melanchthon and Bucer*, translated and edited by W. Pauck. 174-394. Library of Christian Classics 19. Philadelphia: Westminster, 1969.

Bullinger, Heinrich. *Ad J. Cochlaei de canonica scriptura et catholice ecclesiae authoritate labellum*. Zürich: Froschouer, 1544.

———. *Commentarius in II Epist. Argumentum posterioris Epistolae ad Thessalonicenses*. Zürich: Froschouer, 1537.

———. *Daniel sapientissimus Dei propheta*. Zürich: Froschouer, 1565.

———. *Das Jüngste Gericht*. Zürich: Froscheuer, 1555.

———. *De fine saeculi et iudicio venturo Domini nostri Jesu Christi: deq[ue] periculis nostri huius seculi corruptissimi grauissimis, & qua ratione fiant innoxia pijs, orationes duae, habitae in coetu cleri*. Basel: Oporinus, 1557.

———. *De origine erroris libri duo. Zürich: Froschouer*, 1539.

———. *De propheta libri duo. Zürich: Froschouer*. 1525.

———. *De prophetae officio. Zürich: Froschouer*, 1532.

———. *De testament seu foedere Dei unico et eterno*. Zürich: Froschouer, 1534.

———. *Der alt gloub*. Zürich: Froschouer, 1539.

———. *Diarium annales vitae der Jahre 1504–1575*. Edited by Emil Egli. Basel: Basler Buch und Antiquariatshandlung, 1904.

———. *Heinrich Bullinger Briefwechsel*. Edited by Ulrich Gäbler and Endre Zsindely. Zürich: Theologischer Verlag, 1973.

———. *A Hundred Sermons upon the Apocalypse of Jesu Christe, revealed by the angel of the Lord: but seen or received and written by the holy Apostle and Evangelist S. John*. Translated by John Day. London: John Day, 1561. Digital copy online at https://archive.org/details/BullingerHenry.

———. *In apocalypsim conciones centum*. Basel: Operinus, 1557.

———. *Jeremias fidelissiimus et laboriosissimus Dei propheta, expositus per Heinrychum Bullingerum, concionibus CLXX*. Zürich: Froschouer, 1575.

Burton, Henry. *The Sounding of the Last Two Trumpets, the sixth and the seventh; or meditations on chapters IX–X of the Revelations*. London, 1641.

Calvin, John. *The Epistle of Paul the Apostle to the Hebrews, and the First and Second Epistles of Peter*. Edited by D. W. Torrance and T. F. Torrance. CCNT 12. Grand Rapids, MI: Eerdmans, 1963.

———. *The Epistles of Paul to the Romans and Thessalonians*. Translated by R. MacKenzie. CCNT 8. Grand Rapids, MI: Eerdmans, 1960.

———. *Institutes of the Christian Religion*. Edited by John T. McNeill. Translated by Ford Lewis Battles. 2 vols. Philadelphia: Westminster, 1975.

———. *Psychopannychia. Vivere apud Christum non dormire animos sanctos, qui in fide Christi decedunt: assertion*. 1st ed. Strassburg, 1542.

———. *Psychopannychia*. CO 5:170-232.

Carion, Johann. *Chronicon Carionis expositum et auctum Multis Et Veteribus Et Recentibus Historiis a P. Melanthone et C. Peucero*. Wittenberg: Haeredes Johannis Cratonis, 1580.

Cartwright, Thomas. *A Confutation of the Rhemist translation, glosses and annotations on the New Testament*. London, 1589.

———. *A Confutation of the Rhemist translation, glosses and annotations on the New Testament*. New York: Leavitt, Lord, 1834.

Cary, Mary. *The little horns doom & dovvnfall or A scripture-prophesie of King James, and King Charles, and of this present Parliament, unfolded*. London, 1651. Digital copy online at http://name.umdl.umich.edu /A81085.0001.001.

———. *The resurrection of the witnesses and Englands fall from (the mystical Babylon) Rome clearly demonstrated to be accomplished, whereby great encouragement is administred to all saints, but especially to the saints in England, in the handling of a part of the eleventh chapter of the Revelation*. London: Giles Calvert, 1648. Digital copy online at http://name.umdl.umich.edu/A35274.0001.001.

Chemnitz, Martin. *Examination of the Council of Trent*. Translated by Fred Kramer. 4 vols. St. Louis: Concordia, 1971–1986.

Chytraeus, David. *Explicatio Apocalypsis Johannis apostoli*. Wittenberg: J. Crato, 1564.

———. *A postil or orderly disposing of certeine epistles vsually red in the Church of God, vppon the Sundayes and holydayes throughout the whole yeere*. Translated by Arthur Golding. London: Henrie Bynneman, 1570. Digital copy online at http://name.umdl.umich.edu/A18772.0001.001.

Cocceius, Johannes. *Cogitationes de apoc. St. Johannis. In Opera Omnia*. 12 vols. Amsterdam, 1701–1706.

Cotton, John. *The Bloody, Tenent, Washed and Made White in the Bloud of the Lamb*. London: Matthew Symmons for Hannah Allen, 1647.

———. *The Churches Resurrection, or the Opening of the Fifth and Sixth Verses of the 20th Chap. of the Revelation*. London, 1642.

———. *An Exposition, upon the Thirteenth Chapter, of the Revelation*. London, 1656.

———. *The Pouring out of the Seven Vials: or an Exposition of the 16 Chapter of the Revelation, with an Application of it to our Times*. London, 1645.

Cranach, Lucas. *Passional Christi und Antichristi*. Edited by Wilhelm Scherer. Deutsche Drucke älterer Zeit in Nachbildungen 3. Berlin: G. Grote'sche Verlagsbuchhandlung, 1885.

Crespin, Jean. *Histoire des vrays Tesmoins de la verit; de l'évangile, a qui de leur sang l'ont signée, depuis Jean Hus usques au temps present*. Geneva: P. Auberr, 1570.

Cressener, Drue. *A Demonstration of the First Principles of the Protestant Applications of the Apocalypse*. London: Criswell, 1689.

Daneau, Lambert. *A treatise, touching Antichrist VVherein, the place, the time, the forme, the workmen, the vpholders, the proceeding, and lastly, the ruine and ouerthrow of the kingdome of Antichrist, is plainly laid open out of the word of God: where also manie darke, and hard places both of Daniell and the Reuelation are made manifest*. London: Thomas Orwin, 1589.

Daubuz, Charles. *A Perpetual Commentary on the Revelation of St. John*. London: B. Tooke, 1720.

Diodati, Giovanni. *Pious annotations, upon the Holy Bible expounding the difficult places thereof learnedly, and plainly: with other things of great importance*. London: Nicholas Fussell, 1643. Digital copy online at http:// name.umdl.umich.edu/A36033.0001.001.

Downame, John. *The Christian warfare wherein is first generally shewed the malice, power and politike stratagems of the spirituall ennemies of our saluation, Sathan and his assistants the world and the flesh, with the meanes also whereby the Christian may withstand and defeate them: and afterwards more speciallie their particvlar temptatiions, against the seuerall causes and meanes of our saluation, whereby on the one side they allure vs to security and presumption, and on the other side, draw vs to doubting and desperation, are expressed and answered: written especially for their sakes who are exercised in the spirituall conflict of temptations, and are afflicted in conscience in the sight and sense of their sinnes.* London: Felix Kyngston, 1604. Digital copy online at http://name.umdl.umich.edu/A20752.0001.001.

———. *A guide to godlynesse or a Treatise of a Christian life shewing the duties wherein it consisteth, the helpes inabling & the reasons parswading vnto it ye impediments hindering ye practise of it, and the best meanes to remoue them whereunto are added diuers prayers and a treatise of carnall securitie by Iohn Douname Batcheler in Diuinitie and minister of Gods Word.* London: Felix Kingstone, 1622. Digital copy online at http://name.umdl.umich.edu/A20762.0001.001.

———. *The summe of sacred diuinitie briefly & methodically propounded: more largly & cleerely handled and explaned.* London: Willi Stansby, 1625. Digital copy online at http://name.umdl.umich.edu/A20766.0001.001.

Du Pinet, Antoine. *Familere et Brieve Exposition*, 1539, 3 (IB149)

Durham, James. *A Commenterie Upon the Book of the Revelation.* Amsterdam: J. F. Stamm, 1660.

Edwards, Jonathan. *Apocalyptic Writings.* Edited by Stephen Stein. New Haven, CT: Yale University Press, 1977.

Eliot, John, and Thomas Mayhew. *Tears of Repentance, or a Further Narrative of the Progress of the Gospel Amongst the Indians in New England.* London: P. Cole, 1653.

Elliott, Edward Bishop. *Horae Apocalypticae, or a Commentary on the Apocalypse Critical and Historical including also an examination of the chief prophecies of Daniel Volume 2—Primary Source Edition.* 3 vols. London: Seeley, Burnside, and Seeley, 1844.

Erasmus, Desiderius. *Erasmus' Annotations on the New Testament. Galatians to the Apocalypse. Facsimile of the final Latin Text with all earlier Variants.* Edited by Anne Reeve. Leiden: Brill, 1993.

Field, John, and Thomas Wilcox. "An Admonition to Parliament." In *The Reformation of the Church: A Collection of Reformed and Puritan Documents on Church Issues*, edited by Iain Murray, 83-94. London: Banner of Truth Trust, 1965.

Flacius, Matthias (Illyricus). *Catalogus testium veritatis.* Basel: I. Operinum, 1556.

———. *Historia Ecclesiae Christi.* Basel: I. Operinum, 1559–1574.

———. *Novum Testamentumex versione Erasmi Glossa compendiaria.* Basel: P. Pernam and T. Dietrich, 1570.

Foxe, John. *Acts and Monuments…* London: John Day, 1563.

———. *The Acts and Monuments of John Foxe.* Edited by Stephen Reed Cattley. 8 vols. London: R. B. Seeley and W. Burnside, 1841.

Fulke, William. *Confutation of the Rhemish Testament.* New York: Leavitt, Lord, 1834.

Funck, Johannes. *Chronologia. Hoc est Omnium temporum et annorum ab initio Mundi usque ad resurrectionem Domini Nostri Iesu Christi, computatio.* Nuremberg, 1545.

Geneva Bible. 1590 facsimile ed. Milwaukee: University of Wisconsin Press, 1969.

Goodwin, Thomas. *A Sermon on the Fifth Monarchy.* London, 1654.

———. *The Works of Thomas Goodwin, D. D. With general preface by John C. Miller.* Edinburgh: James Nichol, 1861.

———. *Zerubbabel's Encouragement to Finish the Temple. A Sermon Preached before the Honourable House of Commons, at their Late Solemne Fast.* London: Printed for R. D., 1642.

Hall, Edmund. *Manus Testium Mouvens, or A presbyterial glosse upon many of those obscure prophetick texts in Canticles, Isay, Jeremiah, Ezekiel, Daniel, Habakkuk, Zachary, Matthew, Romans, and the Revelations: which point at the great day of the vvitnesses rising; Antichrists ruine, and the Jews conversion, neare about this time. VVherein Dr. Homes, with the rest of hte independent antichristian time-servers are clearly confuted, and out of their own writings condemned: and against them proved, that the present usurpers in England are that antichristian party who have slain the witnesses, and shall reign but three yeers and a half, which time is almost at an end. To this book must be joyned Lingua testium, being its proper preface.* London: n.p., 1651.

Hoffman, Melchior. *Ausslegung der heimlichen Offenbarung Johannis*. 1530.

———. *Das XII Capitel des propheten Daniels ausgelegt*. Stockholm: Königliche Druckkerei, 1526.

———. "Daniel XII." *In Anabaptism in Outline: Selected Primary Sources*, edited and translated by Walter Klaasen, 326-28. Scottdale, PA: Herald Press, 1981.

———. *Die Ordonanntie Godts*. 1530.

———. *Prophetische Gesicht und Offenbarung der götlichen werkung zu diser letsten zeit*. 1530.

Hopkins, Samuel. *A Treatise on the Millennium. Boston*, 1793.

Hubmaier, Balthasar. *Balthasar Hubmaier: Theologian of Anabaptism*. Edited and translated by H. Wayne Pipkin and John H. Yoder. Scottdale, PA: Herald Press, 1989.

Hus, Jan. *Historia et Monumenta Joannis Hus atque Hieronymi Pragensis confessorum Christi*. Edited by Matthias Flacius Illyricus. 2 vols. Nuremberg, 1558.

———. *De Anatomia Antichristi, Liber unus*. Argentorati: Joannes Schottus, 1524?–1525?

Hutterian Brethren, trans. *The Chronicle of the Hutterian Brethren*. Rifton, NY: Plough, 1987.

Jewel, John. *An apologie or answere in defence of the Churche of Englande with a briefe and plaine declaration of the true religion professed and vsed in the same*. Translated by Anne Cooke Bacon. London: Reginald Wolfe, 1564. Digital copy online at http://name.umdl.umich.edu/A04459.0001.001

Junius, Francis. *Apocalypsis. A Brief and Learned Commentarie upon the Revelation of Saint John the Apostle and Evangelist, applying unto the history of the Catholicke and Christian Church. Written in Latine by M. Francis Junius, Doctor of Diuinitie, and professor in the Universitie of Heidelberge: And translated into English for the benefit of those that vnderstand not the Latine. Imprinted at London by Richard Field for Robert Dexter, dwelling in Paules Church yard at the signe of the brazen serpent*, 1592.

Jurieu, Pierre. *The accomplishment of the Scripture prophecies, or, The approaching deliverance of the church proving that the papacy is the antichristian kingdom . . . that the present persecution may end in three years and-half, after which the destruction of Antichrist shall begin, which shall be finisht in the beginning of the next age, and then the kingdom of Christ shall come upon earth*. London: n.p., 1687.

Krebs, Manfred, and Hans Georg Rott, eds., *Quellen zur Geschichte der Täufer, Elsass I und II*. Gütersloh, Germany: Mohn, 1959–1960.

Lambert (d'Avignon), Francis. *Exegeseos in sanctam divi Joannis Apocalypsim Libri VII*. Marburg, Germany: Academia Marpurgensi Praelecti, 1528.

Lapide, Cornelius. *Commentarius in Apocalypsim*. Lyon, 1627.

Liechty, Daniel, ed. and trans. *Early Anabaptist Spirituality: Selected Writings*. Classics of Western Spirituality. Mahwah, NJ: Paulist, 1994.

Lilburne, John. *Lilburne tract: Pamphlets or broadsides by or relating to John Lilburne and the Levellers*. London, 1645–1653.

———. *A worke of the Beast or a Relation of a most vnchristian censure, executed vpon Iohn Lilburne, (novv prisoner in the fleet) the 18 of Aprill 1638. With the heavenly speech vttered by him at the time of his fuffering [sic]. Uery vsefull for these times both for the encouragement of the godly to suffer, and for the terrour and shame of the Lords adversaries*. Printed in the year the beast was wounded, 1638.

Lowman. Moses. *A Paraphrase and Notes upon the Revelation of St. John*. London: J. Noon, 1737.

Ludus de Antichristo. Translated by John Wright. Toronto: Pontifical Institute of Medieval Studies, 1967.

Luther, Martin. *Martin Luther's Sämmtliche Werke*. Frankfurt and Erlangen: J. G. Plochman, 1826–1857.

———. *Martin Luthers Werke*. Edited by W. M. L. Dewette. Berlin, 1825–1828.

———. *Supputatio canonrum mundi*. WA 53:1-182.

———. *Three Treatises*. Philadelphia: Fortress, 1960.

Malvenda, Thomas. *De antichristo liibrii undecim*. Rome apud Carolum Vulliettum, 1604.

Marpeck, Pilgram. *The Writings of Pilgram Marpeck*. Edited and translated by William Klassen and Walter Klassen. Scottdale, PA: Herald Press, 1978.

Martyr, Peter. *Loci communes*. Zürich: Froschouer, 1580.

Mede, Joseph. *Clavis Apocalyptica ex innatis et incsitis visionum characterisbus ervta et demonstrate*. Cantabrigiae, 1627.

———. *The Key of the Revelation searched and demonstrate out of the Naturall and Proper Characters of the Visions*. Translated by Richard More. London: Roger Norton, 1677.

———. "Remaines on some Passages in the Apocalypse." In *The works of the pious and profoundly-learned Joseph Mede, B.D., sometime fellow of Christ's Colledge in Cambridge*, ch. 1. London: Printed by Roger Norton for Richard Royston, 1672. Digital copy online at http://name.umdl.umich.edu/A50522.0001.001.

———. *The Works of the Pious and Profoundly-Learned Joseph Mede, B.D., sometime fellow of Christ's Colledge in Cambridge*. Edited by J. Worthington. London: Roger Norton, 1677.

Melanchthon, Philip. *The Augsburg Confession*. 1540.

———. *Die Histori Thome Müntzers*. Hagenaw: Durch J. Secerium Getruck, 1525.

Meyer, Sebastian. *Apocalypsis. D. Sebastiani Meyer Ecclesiastae Bernensis in Apocalypsim Divi Johannis Apostoli, Commentarius*. Zürich: Froschhouer, 1554. Digital copy online at www.digitale-sammlungen.de/en/view/bsb10144021?page=,1.

Milic of Kromeriz. *Libellus de Antichristo. In Regulae veteris et novi testament*. Edited by Vlastoml Kybal. Oeniponte: Libraria Universiitatis Wagnerana, 1911.

Muggleton, Ludowicke. *A true interpretation of the eleventh chapter of the Revelation of St. John, and other texts in that book as also many other places of Scripture whereby is unfolded, and plainly declared the whole councel of God concerning Himself, the Devil, and all mankinde, from the foundation of the world, to all eternity: never before revealed by any of the sons of men, until now*. London, 1662.

Müller, Lydia, ed. *Glaubenszeugnisse Oberdeutscher Taufgesinnter*. Leipziig: M. Heinsius Nachfolger, 1938.

Müntzer, Thomas. *The Collected Works of Thomas Müntzer*. Edited by Peter Matheson. Edinburgh: T&T Clark, 1988.

———. *Schriften und Briefe: Kritische Gesamtausgabe*. Gütersloh, Germany: Mohn, 1968.

Musper, H. T., ed. *Der Antichrist und die Fünfzehn Zeichen*. 2 vols. Munich: Prestel-Verlag, 1970.

Napier, John. *A Plaine Discovery of the Whole Revelation of Saint John set downe in two treatises: the one searching and prouing the true interpretation thereof: the other applying the same paraphrastically and historically to the text. Set foorth by Iohn Napeir L. of Marchistoun younger. Whereunto are annexed certaine oracles of Sibylla, agreeing with the Reuelation and other places of Scripture*. Edinburgh: Robert Walde-graue, 1593. Digital copy online at http://name.umdl.umich.edu/A07988.0001.001.

Nicholas of Lyra. Postlla super Apostolorum, Epistolas canonicales, et Apocalypsim. Mantua: Paulus de Butzbach, 1480.

Oecumenius. *Commentary on the Apocalypse*. Translated by John N. Suggit. Washington, DC: Catholic University of America Press, 2006.

———. *The Complete Commentary of Oecumenius on the Apocalypse*. Edited by H. C. Hoskier. Ann Arbor: University of Michigan Press, 1928.

Osiander, Andreas. *The conjectures of the ende of the worlde*. Translated by George Joye. [Antwerp?]: n.p., 1548.

Pareus, David. *In divinam Ad Romanos S. Pauli Apostoli Epistolam Commentarius*. Heidelberg, 1630.

———. *In Divinam Apocalypsin s. Apostoli et evangelistae Johannis Commentarius*. Heidelbergae: Impensisi Jonae Rosae, Typisi Johannis Lancellotii, 1618.

———. *A Commentary Upon the Divine Revelation of the Apostle and Evangelist John, translated out of the Latin into English by Elias Arnold*. Amsterdam: Printed by C. P., 1644.

Perkins, William. *A golden chaine, or the description of theologie containing the order of the causes of saluation and damnation, according to Gods woord. A view of the order wherof, is to be seene in the table annexed.* London: Edward Alde, 1591. Digital copy online at http://name.umdl.umich.edu/a09353.0001.001.

———. *Lectures vpon the three first chapters of the Reuelation: preached in Cambridge anno Dom. 1595. by Master William Perkins, and now published for the benefite of this Church.* London: Richard Field, 1604. Digital copy online at http://name.umdl.umich.edu/A09442.0001.001.

Primasius. *Comentariorius super Apocalypsim.* PL 68.793-936.

Purvey, John. *Commentarius in Apocalypsin ante centum annos aeditus.* Wittenberg: n.p., 1528.

Ribera, Francisco. *Commentarius in Apocalypsim.* Salamanca, Spain: Excudebat Petrus Lassus, 1585, 1591.

Robinson, Hastings, ed. *Original Letters Relative to the English Reformation: Written During the Reigns of King Henry VIII, King Edward VI and Queen Mary, chiefly from the archives of Zürich.* Published for the Parker Society. Cambridge: Cambridge University Press, 1842-1847.

Rogers, John. *Ohel or Beth-shemesh. A Tabernacle for the Sun.* London: Printed for R.I and G. and H. Everden, 1653.

Roth, Friedrich, ed. "Zur Geschichte der Wiedertäufer in Oberschwaben: Part II, Zur Lebensgeschichte Eitelhans Langenmantels von Augsburg." Zeitschrift des historischen Veriens für Schwaben und Neuber 27 (1900): 1-45.

Sattler, Michael. "Letter to the Church at Horb." In *The Legacy of Michael Sattler*, edited and translated by John H. Yoder, 61. Scottdale, PA: Herald Press, 1973.

Schiemer, Leonhard. "A Letter to the Church at Rattenburg." In *Anabaptism in Outline: Selected Primary Sources*, edited and translated by Walter Klaasen, 324. Scottdale, PA: Herald Press, 1981.

Schornbaum, Karl, ed. *Quellen zur Geschichte der Täufer*, Bayern I. Markgraftum Brandenburg (QgT 2). Güttersloh, Germany: C. Bertelsmann, 1934.

———. *Quellen zur Geschichte der Täufer, Bayern II. Reichsstädte (QgT 5).* Güttersloh, Germany: C. Bertelsmann, 1951.

Severtus, Michael. *Christianismi Restitutio.* Vienna, 1553.

Simons, Menno. *The Complete Writings of Menno Simons.* Translated by John F. Funk. Elkhart, IN: John F. Funk, 1871. Digital copy online at www.mennosimons.net/completewritings.html.

———. *Fundamentum. Ein Fundament und klare Ausweisung von der Seligmachenden Lehre unsers Herren Jesu Christi.* Basel: Horst, 1740.

Sleidanus, Johannes. *A Briefe Chronicle of the Foure Principall Empyres.* Translated by Stephen Wythers. London: Rouland Hall, 1563.

Snyder, C. Arnold, and Linda A. Huebert Hecht, eds. *Profiles of Anabaptist Women: Sixteenth-Century Reforming Pioneers.* Waterloo, ON: Wilfrid Laurier University Press, 1996.

Tillinghast, John. *Knowledge of the Times, or, The Resolution of the Question.* London: R. J. for L. Chapman, 1654.

Tyconius. *Exposition of the Apocalypse.* Translated by Francis X. Gumerlock. Washington, DC: Catholic University of America Press, 2017.

Victorinus of Poetovio. *Sur l'Apocalypse et autres ecrits.* Edited by Martine Dulaey. SC 423. Paris: Cerf, 1997.

Zwingli, Huldrych. *Commentary on True and False Religion.* Edited by Samuel M. Jackson and Clarence N. Heller. Durham, NC: Labyrinth, 1981.

———. *De vera et falsa religione commentarius.* 1525.

———. *The Defense of the Reformed Faith.* Translated by E. J. Furcha. Vol. 1 of *Huldrych Zwingli: Writings.* Allison Park, PA: Pickwick, 1984.

———. *Sämtliche Werke.* Edited by Emil Egli, Georg Finsler, and Walther Köhler. Leipzig: M. Heinsius Nachfolger, 1911.

Other Works Cited in the Volume

Aells, H. *Martin Bucer*. New Haven, CT: Yale University Press, 1931.

Aichele, Klaus. *Das Antichristdram des Mittelalters, der Reformation und Gegenreformation*. The Hague: Martin Nijhoff, 1974.

Albrecht, O., ed. "Luthers Arbeiten an der Ueberstezun und Auslegung des Propheten Daniel in den Jahren 1530 und 1541." *Archiv für Reformationsgeschichtichte* 23 (1926): 47.

Allo, P. E.-B. *L'Apocalypse*. Paris: Librairie Victor Lecoffre, 1921.

Althaus, Paul. *The Theology of Martin Luther*. Translated by R. C. Schultz. Philadelphia: Fortress, 1966.

Arbusow, Leonid. *Die Einführung der Reformation in Liv-, Est- und Kurland*. Leipzig: M. Heiinsius Nachfollger, 1921.

Asendorf, Ulrich. *Eschatologie bei Luther*. Göttingen: Vandenhoeck & Ruprecht, 1967.

Avis, Paul D. L. *The Church in the Theology of the Reformers*. Atlanta: John Knox, 1981.

Bächtold, Hans Ulrich. *Heinrich Bullinger vor dem Rat: Zur Gestaltung und Verwaltung des Zürcher Staatswesens in den Jahren 1531 bis 1575*. Bern: Peter Lang, 1982.

Backus, Irena. *Reformation Readings of the Apocalypse: Geneva, Zurich, and Wittenberg*. New York: Oxford University Press. 2000.

Bailey, Richard. "Melchior Hoffman: Proto Anabaptist and [First] Printed in Kiel, 1527–1529." *Church History* 59, no. 2 (1990): 175-90.

Baker, J. Wayne. *Heinrich Bullinger and the Covenant: The Other Reformed Tradition*. Athens: Ohio University Press, 1980.

Balke, Wilhelm. *Calvin and the Anabaptist Radicals*. Translated by William J. Heynen. Grand Rapids, MI: Eerdmans, 1981.

Ball, Bryan. *A Great Expectation: Eschatological Thought in English Protestantism to 1660*. Leiden: Brill, 1975.

Barnes, Robin. *Prophecy and Gnosis: Apocalypticism in the Wake of the Lutheran Reformation*. Stanford, CA: Stanford University Press, 1988.

———. "Review: Varieties of Apocalyptic Experience in Reformation Europe." *Journal of Interdisciplinary History* 33, no. 2 (Autumn 2002): 261-74.

Bauckham, Richard. "The Martyrdom of Enoch and Elijah: Jewish or Christian?" *Journal of Biblical Literature* 95 (1976): 447-58.

———. *Tudor Apocalypse*. Oxford: Sutton Courtenay, 1978.

Becker, Reinhard P., ed. *German Humanism and the Reformation*. New York: Continuum, 1983.

Beckwith, I. T. *The Apocalypse of John*. New York: Macmillan, 1919.

Bellard, Werner. *Wolfgang Schultheyss. Wege und Wondlungen eines Strassburger Spiritualisten und Zeitgenosen Martin Bucers*. Frankfurt: Erwin von Steinbach-Stiflung, 1976.

Bensing, Manfred. *Thomas Müntzer und der Thüringer Aufstand, 1525*. Berlin: VEB Deutscher Verlag der Wissenschaften, 1966.

Benz, Ernst. "Die Geschichtstheologie der Franziskaner-spiritualen des 13 und 14 Jahrhunderts nach neuen Quellen." *Zeitschrift fur Kirchengeschichte* 52 (1933): 90-121.

———. "Die Kategorian des eschatologischen Zeitbewusstseins." *Deutsche Vierteljahrsschrift für Literaturwissenschaft und Geistesgeschichte* 11 (1933): 203-15.

———. *Ecclesia Spiritualis: Kirchenidee und Geschichtstheologie der Franziskanischen Reformation*. Stuttgart: W. Kolhammer, 1934.

Berchtold-Belart, Jakob. *Das Zwinglibild und die Zürcherischen Reformationschroniken*. Leipzig: Verlag von M. Heinsius, 1929.

Berger, Heinrich. *Calvins Geschichtsauffassung*. Zürich: Zwingli, 1955.

Betts, R. R. "The Regulae Veteris et Novi Testamenti of Matej z Janova." *Journal of Theological Studies* 32 (1931): 344-51.

Blickle, Peter. *The Revolution of 1525: The German Peasants' War from a New Perspective.* Translated by Thomas A. Brady Jr. and H. C. Erik Middelfort. Baltimore: Johns Hopkins University Press, 1981.

Bloomfield, Morton, and Marjorie Reeves. "The Penetration of Joachimism into Northern Europe." *Speculum* 29 (1954): 772-93.

Böhmer, Heinrich. *Studien zu Thomas Müntzer.* Leipzig, 1922.

Bonner, Gerald. *Saint Bede in the Tradition of Western Apocalyptic Commentary.* Newcastle upon Tyne: J. & P. Bealls, 1966.

Bousset, Wilhelm. *The Antichrist Legend.* Translated by A. H. Keanne. London: Hutchinson, 1896.

———. *Die Offenbarung Johannis.* Göttingen: Vandenhoeck & Ruprecht, 1906.

Bouwsma, William J. *Concordiai Mundi: The Career and Thought of Guillaume Postel, 1510–1581.* Cambridge, MA: Harvard University Press, 1957.

Boyer, Paul. *When Time Shall Be No More.* Cambridge, MA: Belknap, 1992.

Brady, David. *The Contribution of British Writers Between 1560 and 1830 to the Interpretation of Revelation 13, 16–18 (The Number of the Beast): A Study in the History of Exegesis.* Tübingen: Mohr, 1983.

Bräuer, Siegfried, and Wolfgang Ullmann. *Theologischen Schriften aus dem Jahr 1523.* Berlin: Evangelische Verlagsanstalt, 1982.

Bray, Gerald. *The Church: A Theological and Historical Account.* Grand Rapids, MI: Baker Academic, 2016.

Brinkmann, Günther. *Die Irenik des David Pareus: Frieden und Einheit ihrer Relevanz zur Warheitfrage.* Hildesheim, Germany: Gerstenberg, 1972.

Brodrick, James. *Robert Bellermine.* London: Burns and Oates, 1961.

Brown, Peter. *Augustine of Hippo: A Biography.* Berkeley: University of California Press, 1969.

Brütsch, Charles. *Die Offenbarung Jesu Christi.* Zürich: Zwingli Verlag, 1970.

Buck, Lawrence P., and Jonathan W. Zophy, eds. *The Social History of the Reformation.* Columbus: Ohio State University Press, 1972.

Burdach, Konrad. *Vom Mittelalter zur Reformation: Forschungen zur Geschichte der Deutschen Bildung.* Berlin: Weidmannsche Buchhandlung, 1913.

Büsser, Fritz, ed. *Heinrich Bullinger Werke.* 4 vols. Zürich: Theologische Verlag, 1972.

———. *Huldrych Zwingli: Reformation als Prophetischer Auftrag.* Göttingen: Musterschmidt, 1973.

Charles, R. H. *Critical and Exegetical Commentary on the Revelation of St. John.* 2 vols. International Critical Commentary. Edinburgh: T&T Clark, 1913.

———. *Studies in the Apocalypse.* Edinburgh: T&T Clark, 1913.

Chrisman, Miriam Usher. *Strasbourg and the Reform: A Study in the Process of Change.* New Haven, CT: Yale University Press, 1967.

Christe, Yves, ed. *L'Apocalypse de Jean.* Geneva: Libraire E. Droz, 1979.

Christianson, Paul. *Reformers and Babylon: English Apocalyptic Visions from the Reformation to the Eve of the Civil War.* Toronto: University of Toronto Press, 1978.

Clasen, Claus-Peter. *Anabaptism: A Social History, 1528–1618.* Ithaca, NY: Cornell University Press, 1972.

Clemen, Otto. *Flugschriften aus den ersten Jahren der Reformation.* 4 vols. Leipzig: Rudolf Haupt, 1909.

Cohn, Norman. *The Pursuit of the Millennium: Revolutionary Millenarians and Mystical Antichrists of the Middle Ages.* Rev. ed. New York: Oxford University Press, 1970.

Collins, Adela Yarbro. *Crisis and Catharsis: The Power of the Apocalypse.* Philadelphia: Westminster, 1984.

Collins, John J., ed. *Apocalypse: The Morphology of a Genre.* Semeia Studies 14. Missoula, MT: Scholars Press, 1979.

———. *The Apocalyptic Imagination: An Introduction to Jewish Apocalyptic Literature*. 3rd ed. Grand Rapids, MI: Eerdmans, 2016.

———, ed. *The Encyclopedia of Apocalypticism*. Vol. 1, *The Origins of Apocalypticism in Judaism and Christianity*. New York: Continuum, 2000.

Collinson, Patrick. *The Birthpangs of Protestant England: Religious and Cultural Change in the Sixteenth and Seventeenth Centuries*. London: Macmillan, 1988.

———. *The Elizabethan Puritan Movement*. Berkeley: University of California Press, 1967.

Cornelius, Carl Adolph. *Geschichte des Münsterischen Aufruhrs*. 2 vols. Leipzig: T. D. Wiegel, 1855–1860.

Court, John M. *Myth and History in ihe Book of Revelation*. Atlanta: John Knox, 1979.

Courvoisier, Jacques. *De la Réforme au Protestantisme: Essai d'ecclesiologie réformée*. Paris: Editions Beauchesne, 1977.

Crome, A. "Appendix: A Comparison of Editions of Brightman's Revelation of the Revelation." In *The Restoration of the Jews: Early Modern Hermeneutics, Eschatology, and National Identity in the Works of Thomas Brightman*, 213. Dordrecht: Springer International, 2014.

Cunningham, Andrew, and Ole Peter Grell. *The Four Horsemen of the Apocalypse: Religion, War, Famine, and Death in Reformation Europe*. New York: Cambridge University Press, 2001.

Daly, Brian E. *The Hope of the Early Church. A Handbook of Patristic Eschatology*. Cambridge: Cambridge University Press, 1991.

Dannenbauer, Heinrich. *Luther als religiöser Volksschrifteller, 1517–1520: Ein Beitrag zu der Frage nach den Ursachen der Reformation*. Tübingen: Mohr, 1930.

Davidson, James West. *The Logic of Millennial Thought: Eighteenth-Century New England*. New Haven, CT: Yale University Press, 1977.

Dawson, Jane. "The Apocalyptic Thinking of the Marian Exiles." In *Prophecy and Eschatology: Studies in Church History*, edited by Michael Wilks, 77. Subsidia 10. Oxford: Blackwell, 1994.

DeJong, J. A. *As the Waters Cover the Sea*. Kampen, The Netherlands: J. H. Kok, 1970.

Deppermann, Klaus. *Melchior Hoffman: Sociale Unruhen und apokalyptische Visionen im Zeitalter der Reformation*. Göttingen: Vandenhoeck & Ruprecht, 1979.

Dulaey, Martine. "Jerome 'editeur' du Commentaire sur l'Apocalypse de Victorinus Poetovio." *Revue des Etudes Augustiniennes* 37 (1991): 199-236.

Dülmen, Richard van, ed. *Das Täuferreich zu Münster 1534–1535. Berichte und Dokmente*. Munich: Deutscher Taschenbuch Verlag, 1974.

Ebeling, Gerhard. *Luther: An Introduction to His Thought*. Translated by R. A. Wilson. Philadelphia: Fortress, 1970.

Edwards, Mark. *Luther's Last Battles: Politics and Polemics*. Ithaca, NY: Cornell University Press, 1983.

Eisenstein, Elizabeth L. *The Printing Press as an Agent of Change: Communication and Cultural Transformations in Early-Modern Europe*. Cambridge: Cambridge University Press, 1979.

Elert, Werner. *The Structure of Lutheranism: The Theology and Philosophy of Life Especially in the Sixteenth and Seventeenth Centuries*. St. Louis: Concordia, 1962.

Elliger, Walter. *Thomas Müntzer: Leben und Werk*. Göttingen: Vandenhoeck & Ruprecht, 1975.

Elton, G. R., ed. *The New Cambridge Modern History: The Reformation, 1520–1559*. Cambridge: Cambridge University Press, 1958.

Emmerson, K., and Bernard McGinn. *The Apocalypse in the Middle Ages*. Ithaca, NY: Cornell University Press, 1993.

Emmerson, Richard K. *Antichrist in the Middle Ages: A Study of Medieval Apocalypticism, Art, and Literature*. Seattle: University of Washington Press, 1981.

Fairfield, Leslie P. *John Bale: Mythmaker for the English Reformation*. West Lafayette, IN: Purdue University Press, 1976.

Farner, Oskar. *Huldrych Zwingli*. 4 vols. Zürich: Zwingli Verlag, 1943–1960.

Fast, Heinold, ed. *Der linke Flügel der Reformation*. Bremen: Schünemann Verlag, 1962.

Fatio, Oliver. *Methode et theologie: Lambert Daneau et les debuts de la schlolastique reformée*. Geneva: Libraire E. Droz, 1976.

Firth, Katherine R. *The Apocalyptic Tradition in Reformation Britain, 1530–1645*. New York: Oxford University Press, 1979.

Ford, J. Massyngberde. *Revelation*. New York: Doubleday, 1975.

Forell, G. W. "Justification and Eschatology in Luther's Thought." *Church History* 38 (1969): 164-74.

Fredriksen, Paula. *When Christians Were Jews: The First Generation*. New Haven, CT: Yale University Press, 2018.

Friesen, Abraham. *Thomas Müntzer, a Destroyer of the Godless: The Making of a Sixteenth Century Religious Revolutionary*. Berkeley: University of California Press, 1990.

Froom, Leroy. *The Prophetic Faith of Our Fathers*. 4 vols. Washington, DC: Review and Herald, 1948.

Fukuyama, Francis. *The End of History and the Last Man*. New York: Free Press, 2006.

Gäbler, Ulrich, and Erland Herkenrath, eds. *Heinrich Bullinger, 1504–1575: Gesammelte Aufätze zum 400. Todestag*. Zürich: Theologischer Verlag, 1973.

Gabriele, Matthew. and John T. Palmer, eds. *Apocalypse and Reform from Late Antiquity to the Middle Ages*. New York: Routledge, 2018.

Gelnas, Y. D. "La critique de Thomas d'Aquin sur l'exegese de Joachim de Fiore." In *Tommaso d'Aquino nel suo settino centenaria*, 1:368-75. Rome, 1974.

Gentry, Kenneth. *Before Jerusalem Fell: Dating the Book of Revelation*. Tyler, TX: Institute for Christian Economics, 1998.

Gerrish, Brian A. *The Old Protestantism and the New*. Chicago: University of Chicago Press, 1982.

Greengrass, Mark. *Christendom Destroyed: Europe 1517–1648*. New York: Viking, 2014.

Gribben, Crawford. "Deconstructing the Geneva Bible: The Search for a Puritan Poetic." *Literature and Theology* 14, no. 1 (March 2000): 1-16.

———. *The Puritan Millennium: Literature and Theology, 1550–1682*. Rev. ed. Eugene, OR: Wipf & Stock, 2008.

Grundmann, Herbert. *Studien uber Joachim*. Leipzig: Teubner, 1927.

Gumerlock, Tyconius. *Exposition of the Apocalypse*. Translated by Francis X. Gumerlock. Washington, DC: Catholic University of America Press, 2017.

Hall, G. F. "Luther's Eschatology." *Augustana Quarterly* 25 (1944): 13-21.

Hanson, Paul. *The Dawn of Apocalyptic: The Historical and Sociological Roots of Jewish Apocalyptic Eschatology*. Minneapolis: Augsburg, 1979.

Habig, Marion A., ed. *St. Francis of Assisi: Writings and Early Biographies: English Omnibus of the Sources for the Life of St. Francis*. Chicago: Franciscan Herald, 1973.

Hausleiter, Johannes. *Commentarius in Apocalypsin*. CSEL 49. Vienna: Hoelder, Pichler, Tempsky, 1916.

Headley, John M. *Luther's View of Church History. New Haven, CT: Yale University Press, 1963.*

Heal, Felicity. *Reformation in Britain and Ireland*. Oxford: Clarendon, 2003.

Heitz, C. "Rententissement de l'Apocalypse dans l'art de l'epoque carolingienne." In *L'Apocalypse*, edited by Yves Christe, 217-43. Geneva: Droz, 1979.

Hendrix, S. *Luther and the Papacy*. Philadelphia: Fortress, 1981.

Hill, Christopher. *Antichrist in Seventeenth-Century England*. London: Oxford University Press, 1971.

———. *The Century of Revolution: 1603–1714. London: Routledge, 1961.*

———. *The World Turned Upside Down: Radical Ideas During the English Revolution.* Reprint, New York: Penguin, 2020.

Hillerbrand, H. J. "The Antichrist in the Early German Reformation: Reflections on Theology and Propaganda." In *Germania Illustrata*, edited by A. C. Fix and S. C. Karant-Nunn, 3-17. Kirksville, MO: Sixteenth Century Journal, 1992.

Hofmann, Hans-Ulrich. *Luther und die Johannes-Apokalypse.* Tübingen: Mohr Siebeck, 1982.

Holder, R. Ward, ed. *Calvin and Luther: The Continuing Relationship.* Göttingen: Vandenhoeck & Ruprecht, 2013.

Holl, K. "Martin Luther on Luther." Translated by H. C. Erick Midelfort. In *Interpreters of Luther: Essays in Honor of Wilhelm Pauck*, edited by Jaroslav Pelikan, 9-34. Philadelphia: Fortress, 1968.

Hollweg, Walter. *Heinrich Bullingers Hausbuch.* Neukirchen: Kreis Moers Neukirchener Verlag, 1956.

Holwerda, D. E. "Eschatology and History: A Look at Calvin's Eschatological Vision." In *Exploring the Heritage of John Calvin: Essays in Honor of John Bratt*, edited by D. E. Holwerda, 110-39. Grand Rapids, MI: Baker Books, 1976.

Horst, Iirvin, ed. *The Dutch Dissenters.* Kirk-historische Bijdragen 13. Leiden: Brill, 1986.

Hotson, Howard. *Paradise Postponed: Johann Heinrich Alsted and the Birth of Calvinist Millenarianism.* Dordrecht: Kluwer Academic, 2000.

Kaminsky, Howard. *A History of the Hussite Revolution.* Berkeley: University of California Press, 1967.

Kamlah, Wilhelm. *Apokalypse und Geschichtstheologie: Die mittelalterliche Auslegung der Apokalypse vor Joachin von Fiore.* Berlin: Verlag Dr. Emil Ebering, 1935.

Kawerau, Peter. *Melchior Hoffman als religiöser Denker.* Haarlem: De Erven F. Bohm, 1954.

Kestenberg-Gladstein, Ruth. "The Third Reich: A Fifteenth Century Polemic Against Joachimism, and Its Background." *Journal of the Warburg and Courtald Institute* 18 (1955): 245-95.

Koch, Ernst. *Die Theologie der Confessio Helvetica Posterior.* Neukirchen: Neukirchener Verlag, 1968.

Köhler, Walter. "Das Taufertum in Calvins *Institutio* von 1536." *Mennonitische Geschichtsblatter* 2 (1936): 1-4.

Kolb, Robert. *Nikolaus von Amsdorf (1483–1565): Popular Polemics in the Preservation of Luther's Legacy.* Nieuwkoop, The Netherlands: De Graaf, 1978.

Kolb, Robert, Irene Dingel, and L'ubomir Batka, eds. *The Oxford Handbook of Martin Luther's Theology.* Oxford: Oxford University Press, 2014.

Korn, Dietrich. *Das thema des Jüngsten Tages in der Deutschen Literatur des 17. Jahrhunderts.* Tübingen: Max Niemeyer, 1957.

Krey, Philip D. W., and Lesley Smith, eds. *Nicholas of Lyra: The Senses of Scripture.* Studies in the History of Christian Thought. Leiden: Brill, 2000.

Kristeller, Paul Oskar. *Renaissance Thought: The Classic, Scholastic, and Humanist Strains.* New York: Harper Torchbooks, 1961.

Krohn, Barthold Nicolaus. *Geschichte der fanatischen und enthusiastischen Wiedertäufer vornehmlich in Niederdeutschland: Melchior Hofmann und die Secte der Hofmannianer.* Lepzig: Bernard Christian Breitkopf, 1758.

Laistner, M. L. W. *Thought and Letters in Western Europe: A.D. 500 to 900.* 2nd ed. Ithaca, NY: Cornell University Press, 1957.

Lamont, William M. *Godly Rule: Politics and Religion, 1603–1660.* London: St. Martin's, 1969.

Larkin, Clarence. *The Book of Revelation.* N.p.: CreateSpace, 2017.

Leff, Gordon. *Heresy in the Later Middle Ages: The Relation of Heterodoxy to Dissent c. 1250–c. 1450. Vol. 1.* New York: Barnes and Noble, 1967.

Lerner, R. E. "Refreshment of the Saints." *Traditio* 32 (1976): 101-5.
Lindberg, Carter. *The European Reformations*. 2nd ed. Malden, MA: Wiley-Blackwell, 2011.
———. *The Reformation Theologians: An Introduction to Theology in the Early Modern Period*. Malden, MA: Wiley-Blackwell, 2017.
List, Günter. *Chiliastische Utopie und Radikale Reformation: Die Erneuerung der Idee vom tausend-jährigen Reich im 16.* Jahrhundert. Munich: Wilhelm Fink, 1973.
Liu, Tai. *Dischord in Zion: The Puritan Divines and the Puritan Revolution, 1640–1660*. The Hague: Nijhoff, 1973.
Locher, Gottfried. *Die Zwinglische Reformation in Rahmen der europäischen Kirchengeschichte*. Göttingen: Vandenhoeck & Ruprecht, 1979.
Lupton, Lewis. *A History of the Geneva Bible*. London: Fauconberg, 1966.
MacCulloch, Diarmaid. *The Reformation: A History*. New York: Viking, 2003.
Madigan, Kevin. *Medieval Christianity: A New History*. New Haven, CT: Yale University Press, 2015.
Massing, Michael. *Fatal Discord: Erasmus, Luther, and the Fight for the Western Mind*. New York: Harper One, 2018.
Matthias, Riedl. *A Companion to Joachim of Fiore*. Leiden: Brill, 2017.
McCoy, Charles S., and J. Wayne Baker. *Fountainhead of Federalism: Heinrich Bullinger and the Covenantal Tradition with a Translation of* De testamento seu foedere Dei uniico et aeterno *(1534)*. Louisville, KY: Westminster John Knox, 1991.
McGinn, Bernard. "The Abbot and the Doctors: Scholastic Reactions to the Radical Eschatology of Joachim of Fiore." *Church History* 40 (1971): 30-47.
———. *Apocalyptic Spirituality*. Classics of Western Spirituality. New York: Paulist, 1979.
———, ed. *The Encyclopedia of Apocalypticism*. Vol. 2, Apocalypticism in Western History and Culture. New York: Continuum, 2000.
———. "The Significance of Bonaventure's Theology of History." *Journal of Religion 58 supplement* (1978): 565-81.
———. *Visions of the End: Apocalyptic Traditions in the Middle Ages*. New York: Columbia University Press, 1979.
McNeill, John T. *The History and Character of Calvinism*. Oxford: Oxford University Press, 1967.
Meinhold, Peter. "Thomas von Aquin und Joachim von Fiore Deutung der Geschichte." *Speculum* 27 (1976): 66-76.
Metzger, Bruce M. *Breaking the Code: Understanding the Book of Revelation*. Rev. and updated by David A. deSilva. Nashville: Abingdon, 2019.
Molnar, Amadeo. "Le movement préhussite et la fin des temps." *Communio Viatorum* 1 (1958): 27-32.
Moreschini, Claudio, and Enrico Norelli. *Early Christian Greek and Latin Literature*. Vol. 1 Grand Rapids, MI: Baker Academic, 2005.
Mozley, J. F. *John Foxe and His Book*. London: SPCK, 1940.
Müller, Gerhard. *Franz Lambert von Avignon und die Reformation in Hessen*. Marburg: N. G. Elwert, 1958.
Müller, Richard A. "The Hermeneutic of Promise and Fulfillment in Calvin's Exegesis of the Old Testament Prophecies of the Kingdom." In *The Bible in the Sixteenth Century*, edited by David Steinmetz, 68-82. Durham, NC: Duke University Press, 1990.
Murphy, Frederick J. *Fallen Is Babylon: The Revelation to John*. Harrisburg, PA: Trinity Press International, 1998.
Murray, George. *Millennial Studies*. Grand Rapids, MI: Baker Book House, 1975.
Murray, Iain. *The Puritan Hope: Revival and Interpretation of Prophecy*. Edinburgh: Banner of Truth Trust, 1971.

Neuser, Wilhelm. *Hans Hut: Leben und Wirken bis zum Nikolsburger Religionsgespräch*. Berlin: H. Blanke, 1913.

Nuttall, Geoffrey. *Visible Saints*. Oxford: Blackwell, 1957.

Oberman, Heiko. A. *Luther, Mensch zwishen Gott und Teufel*. Berlin: Severin und Siedler, 1982.

Olsen, V. Norskov. *John Foxe and the Elizabethan Church*. Berkeley: University of California Press, 1973.

Oyer, John S. *Lutheran Reformers Against Anabaptists*. The Hague: Martinus Nijhoff, 1964.

Ozment, Steven E. *The Age of Reform, 1250–1550: An Intellectual and Religious History of Late Medieval and Reformation Europe*. New Haven, CT: Yale University Press, 1980.

———. *Mysticism and Dissent: Religious Ideology and Social Protest in the Sixteenth Century*. New Haven, CT: Yale University Press, 1973.

Pagels, Elaine. *Revelations: Visions, Prophecy, and Politics in the Book of Revelation*. New York: Penguin Books, 2013.

Parker, T. H. L. *John Calvin: A Biography*. Philadelphia: Westminster, 1975.

Patrides, C. A., and Joseph Wittreich, eds. *The Apocalypse in English Renaissance Thought and Literature*. Ithaca, NY: Cornell University Press, 1984.

Pelikan, Jaroslav. "Luther's Attitude Toward John Hus." *Concordia Theological Monthly* 19 (1948): 747-63.

———. *The Reformation of the Bible: The Bible of the Reformation*. New Haven, CT: Yale University Press, 1996.

———. "Some Uses of Apocalypse in the Magisterial Reformers." In *The Apocalypse in English Renaissance Thought and Literature*, edited by C. A. Patrides and Joseph Wittreich, 74-92. Ithaca, NY: Cornell University Press, 1984.

Pestalozzi, Carl. *Heinrich Bullinger: Leben und ausgewälte Schriften*. Elberfeld: R. L. Friderichs, 1858.

Petersen, Rodney. *Preaching in the Last Days: The Theme of "Two Witnesses" in the Sixteenth and Seventeenth Centuries*. New York: Oxford University Press, 1993.

Peuckert, W.-E. *Die Grosse Wende: Das apokalyptische Saeculum und Luther, Geistesgeschichte und Volskunde*. Vol 2. Hamburg: Classen & Geverts, 1948.

Pitkin, Barbara. "Calvin, Theology, and History." *Seminary Ridge Review* 12, no. 2 (Spring 2010): 1-16.

Polman, P. Pontianus. *L'Elément historique dans la controverse religieuse du XVIs siècle*. Gembloux, Belgium: J. Duculot, 1932.

Potter, G. R. *Zwingli*. Cambridge: Cambridge University Press, 1976.

Preuss, Hans. *Die Vorstellungen vom Antichrist im späteren Mittelalter, bei Luther in der Konfessionellen Polemik*. Leipzig: J. C. Hinrichs, 1906.

———. *Martin Luther, der Prophet*. Gütersloh, Germany: C. Bertelsmann, 1933.

Prévost, Jean-Pierre. *How to Read the Apocalypse*. New York: Crossroad, 1993.

Prigent, Pierre. *Apocalypse 12. Histoire de L'exégèse*. Tübingen: Mohr Siebeck, 1959.

Quistorp, Heinrich. *Die letzten Dinge im Zeugnis Calvins*. Güttersloh: Bertelsmann, 1941.

Reeves, Marjorie. *The Influence of Prophecy in the Later Middle Ages: A Study in Joachimism*. Oxford: Clarendon, 1969.

———. *Joachim of Fiore and the Prophetic Future*. New York: Sutton, 1999.

Rendtorff, Trutz, ed. "Prophetie in der Reformation. Elemente, Argumente und Bewegungen." In *Charisma und Institution*, edited by Trutz Rendtorff, 102-9. Gütersloh: G. Mohn, 1985.

Selderhuis, Herman. "Kirche unter dem Kreuz: die Ekklesiologie Heinrich Bullinger." In *Heinrich Bullinger (1504–1575): Leben, Denken, Wirkung. Internationaler Bullingerkongress 2004*, edited by Emidio Campi and Peter Opitz, 513-36. Zürich: Theologische Verlag Zürich, 2007.

Smith, John Hazel. *Two Latin Comedies by John Foxe the Martyrologist*. Ithaca, NY: Cornell University Press, 1973.

Smolinski, Reiner. "Caveat Emptor: Pre- and Postmillennialism in the Late Reformation Period." In *Millenarianism and Messianism in Early Modern European Culture: The Millenarian Turn*, edited by J. E. Force and R. H. Popkin, 145-69. Dordrecht: Kluwer Academic, 2001.

Southern, R. W. "Presidential Address: Aspects of the European Tradition of Historical Writing. Vol. 2: Hugh of St. Victor and the Idea of Historical Development." *Transactions of the Royal Historical Society* 21 (1971): 159-79.

Spinka, Matthew. *John Hus at the Council of Constance*. New York: Columbia University Press, 1965.

Stein, Stephen J. *The Encyclopedia of Apocalypticism*. Vol. 3, *Apocalypticism in the Modern Period and the Contemporary Age*. New York: Continuum, 2000.

Steinmetz, David C., ed. *The Bible in the Sixteenth Century*. Durham, NC: Duke University Press, 1990.

Tanner, N. ed. Documents of the Ecumenical Councils. Washington, DC: Georgetown University Press, 1990.

Taylor, Marion Ann, ed. *Handbook of Women Biblical Interpreters: A Historical and Biographical Guide*. Grand Rapids: Baker, 2012.

Tillich, Paul. Systematic Theology. Vol. 1. Chicago: University of Chicago Press, 1951.

Toft, Daniel John. "Shadows of Kings: The Political Thought of David Pareus, 1548–1622." PhD diss., University of Wisconsin, 1970.

Toon, Peter, ed. *Puritans, the Millennium and the Future of Israel: Puritan Eschatology, 1600–1660*. London: Clarke, 1970.

Torrance, Thomas F. *Kingdom and Church: A Study in the Theology of the Reformation*. Edinburgh: Oliver and Boyd, 1956.

Wannenmacher, Julia Eva. *Joachim of Fiore and the Influence of Inspiration*. New York: Routledge, 2016.

Way, Peter. "A 'Lutheryan' Copy of St. Augustine." *Humanae Literae* 8 (2003): 69-116; *Lutheran Quarterly* 14, no. 4 (Winter 2000): 373-408.

Weber, Otto. "Calvins Lehre von der Kirche." in *Die Treue Gottes in der Geschichte der Kirche*, vol. 2, *Gesammelte Aufsätze, 19-104*. Neukirchen: Neukirchen Verlag des Erziehungsvereigns, 1968.

Weinrich, William C. Introduction to *Revelation*. ACCS New Testament 12. Downers Grove, IL: InterVarsity Press, 2005.

Williams, George H. *The Radical Reformation*. Kirksville, MO: Truman State University Press, 1993.

Wilson, John. *Pulpit in Parliament*. Princeton, NJ: Princeton University Press, 1969.

Wilson, Peter. *The Thirty Years War: Europe's Tragedy*. Cambridge, MA: Belknap, 2009.

Workman, H. B. *John Wyclif: A Study of the English Medieval Church*. 2 vols. Oxford: Oxford University Press, 1926.

Zakai, Avihu. "From Judgment to Salvation: The Image of the Jews in the English Renaissance." *Westminster Theological Journal* 59 (1997): 213-30.

———. "Thomas Brightman and English Apocalyptic Tradition." In *Menasseh ben Israel and His World, edited by* Yosef Kaplan, Henry Méchoulan, and Richard H. Popkin, 31-44. Leiden: Brill Academic, 1989.

Zimmerli, Walter., ed. *Psychopannychia*. Leipzig, 1932.

Author and Writings Index

Subject Index

Scripture Index